Street by Street

BERKSHIRE

GW00373104

PLUS CAMBERLEY, EGHAM, HEATHROW AIRPORT, HENLEY-ON-THAMES, MARLOW, STAINES, TADLEY, VIRGINIA WATER, YATELEY

Enlarged Areas Bracknell, Maidenhead, Newbury, Reading, Slough, Windsor, Wokingham

1st edition May 2001

© Automobile Association Developments Limited 2001

This product includes map data licensed from Ordnance Survey® with the permission of the Controller of Her Majesty's Stationery Office. © Crown copyright 2000. All rights reserved. Licence No: 399221.

Published by AA Publishing (a trading name of Automobile Association Developments Limited, whose registered office is Norfolk House, Priestley Road, Basingstoke, Hampshire, RG24 9NY. Registered number 1878835).

Mapping produced by the Cartographic Department of The Automobile Association.

A CIP Catalogue record for this book is available from the British Library.

Printed by G. Canale & C. s.p.a., Torino, Italy

The contents of this atlas are believed to be correct at the time of the latest revision. However, the publishers cannot be held responsible for loss occasioned to any person acting or refraining from action as a result of any material in this atlas, nor for any errors, omissions or changes in such material. The publishers would welcome information to correct any errors or omissions and to keep this atlas up to date. Please write to Publishing, The Automobile Association, Fanum House, Basing View, Basingstoke, Hampshire, RG21 4EA.

Ref: MX057

Key to map pages	ii-iii
Key to map symbols	iv-1
Enlarged scale pages	2-15
Street by Street	16-183
Index – towns & villages	184
Index – streets	185-207
Index – featured places	208-211

ii

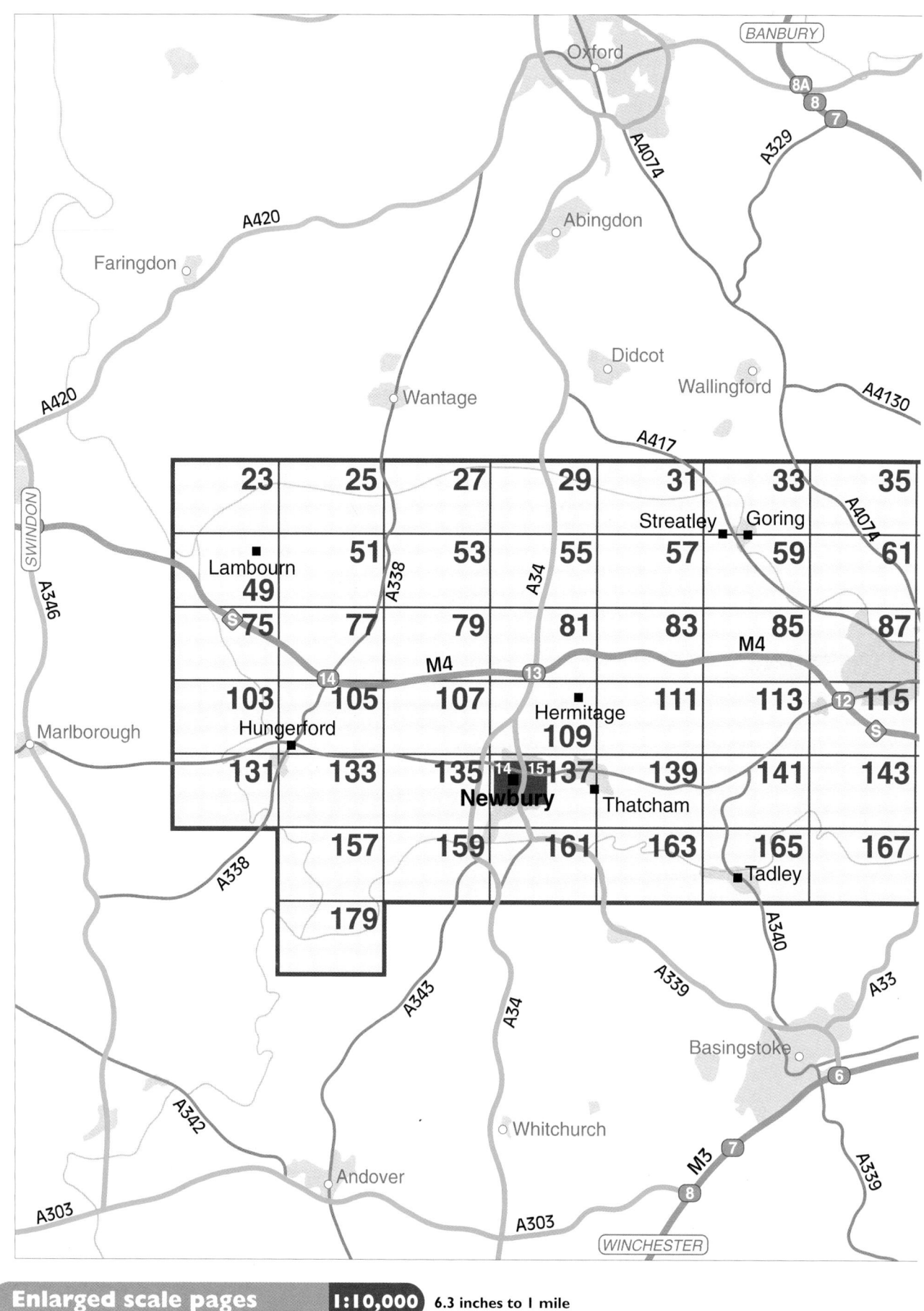

23	25	27	29	31	33	35
49	51	53	55	57	59	61
75	77	79	81	83	85	87
103	105	107	109	111	113	115
131	133	135	137	139	141	143
157	159	161	163	165	167	
179						

Enlarged scale pages   1:10,000   6.3 inches to 1 mile

0   1/4   miles   1/2   3/4

0   1/4   1/2   kilometres   3/4   1   1 1/4

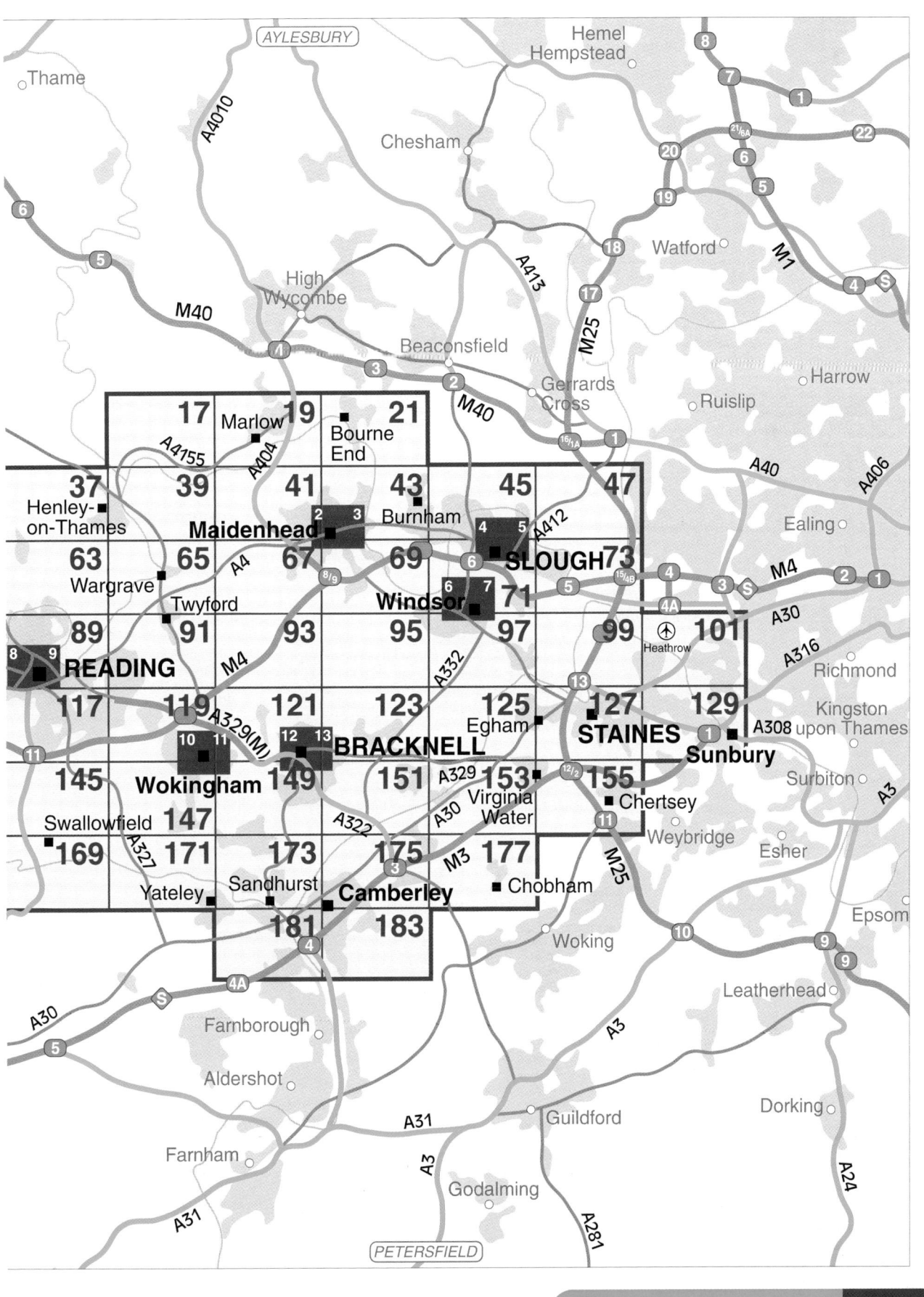

AYLESBURY

Thame

Hemel Hempstead

Chesham

A4010

M40

High Wycombe

Beaconsfield

A413

M25

Watford

M1

8
7
1
22
21/6A
20
6
5
19
18
17

4
S

Gerrards Cross

Ruislip

Harrow

16/1A

1

A40

A406

Ealing

| 17 | Marlow 19 | Bourne End 21 |
| 37 | 39 | 41 Maidenhead | 43 Burnham | 45 | 47 |

A4155

A404

3

2

M40

2
3
4
5

A412

| 63 Wargrave | 65 | A4 67 | 69 | SLOUGH 73 |

Twyford

8/9

6

5

15/4B

M4

2
1

| 89 | 91 | 93 | 95 | 97 | 99 | 101 |

READING

8
9

M4

A332

6
7
Windsor 71

A30

4
4A
3
S

Heathrow

A316

Richmond

| 117 | 119 | 121 | 123 | 125 Egham | 127 STAINES | 129 |

A329(M)

13

Kingston upon Thames

A308

| 145 | Wokingham 149 | 151 | 153 Virginia Water | 155 |

10
11

12
13
BRACKNELL

A329

A30

12/2

11

1

Sunbury

Chertsey

Weybridge

Surbiton

A3

Esher

Epsom

| 169 | 147 171 | 173 | 175 | 177 |

Swallowfield

A327

A322

3

M3

Sandhurst

Camberley

Chobham

M25

Woking

Leatherhead

9
9

| 181 | 183 |

4

4A

S

Farnborough

Aldershot

5

A30

Farnham

A31

A31

A3

Guildford

A3

Dorking

A24

Godalming

A281

PETERSFIELD

3.6 inches to 1 mile

Scale of main map pages **1:17,500**

0   1/2   miles   1

0   1/2   1   kilometres   1 1/2   2

Junction 9	Motorway & junction
Services	Motorway service area
	Primary road single/dual carriageway
Services	Primary road service area
	A road single/dual carriageway
	B road single/dual carriageway
	Other road single/dual carriageway
	Restricted road
	Private road
← ←	One way street
	Pedestrian street
	Track/ footpath
	Road under construction
⟫⟪	Road tunnel
P	Parking

P+🚌	Park & Ride
🚌	Bus/coach station
	Railway & main railway station
	Railway & minor railway station
⊖	Underground station
⊖	Light railway & station
+++++++++++	Preserved private railway
LC	Level crossing
•—•—•—•—•	Tramway
------------	Ferry route
....	Airport runway
– · – · – · –	Boundaries- borough/ district
▾▾▾▾▾▾▾▾▾	Mounds
93	Page continuation 1:17,500
7	Page continuation to enlarged scale 1:10,000

River/canal lake, pier	Toilet with disabled facilities
Aqueduct lock, weir	Petrol station
465 ▲ Winter Hill — Peak (with height in metres)	PH Public house
Beach	PO Post Office
Coniferous woodland	Public library
Broadleaved woodland	i Tourist Information Centre
Mixed woodland	Castle
Park	Historic house/building
Cemetery	Wakehurst Place NT — National Trust property
Built-up area	M Museum/art gallery
Featured building	† Church/chapel
City wall	Country park
A&E Accident & Emergency hospital	Theatre/performing arts
Toilet	Cinema

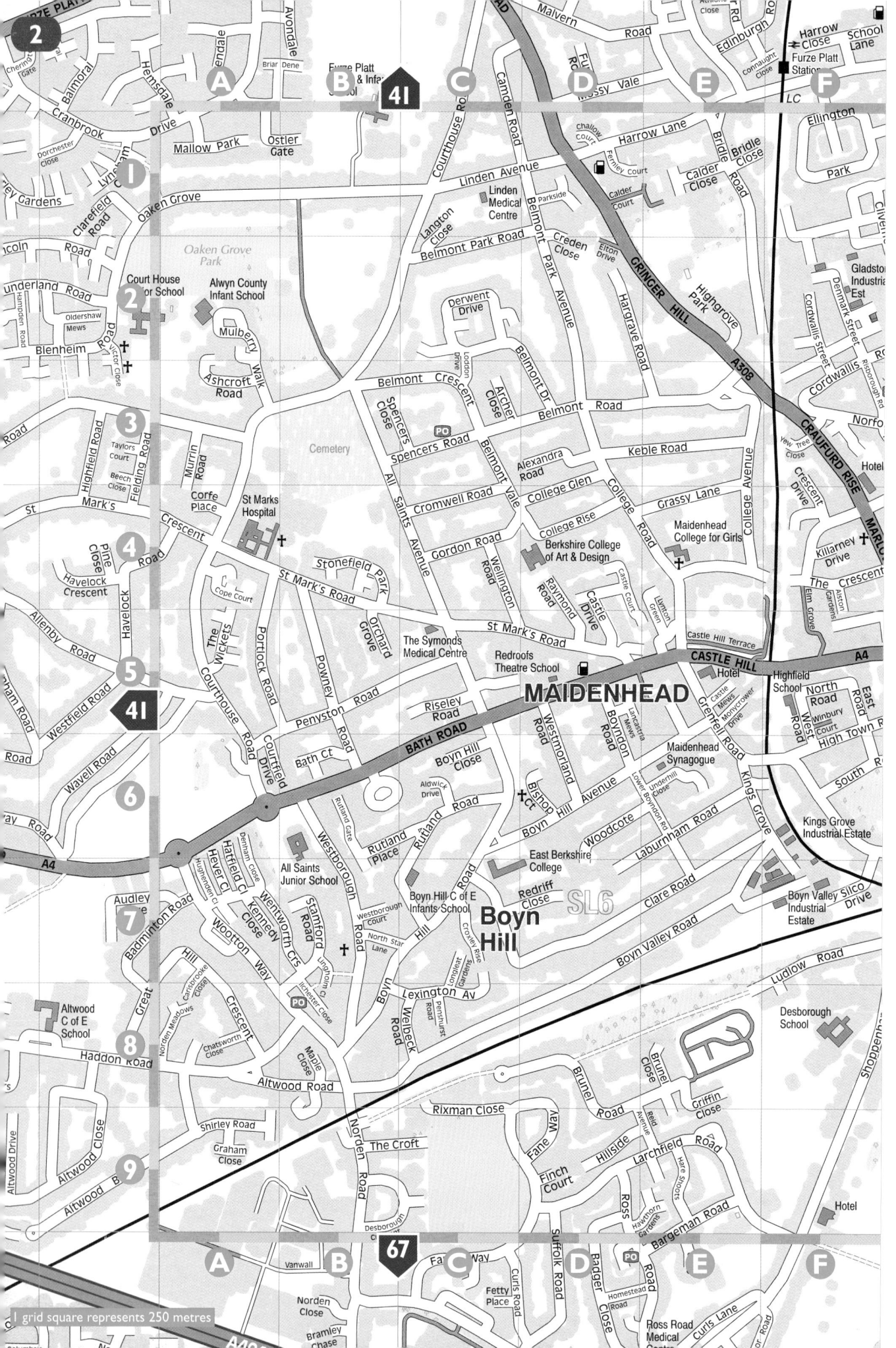

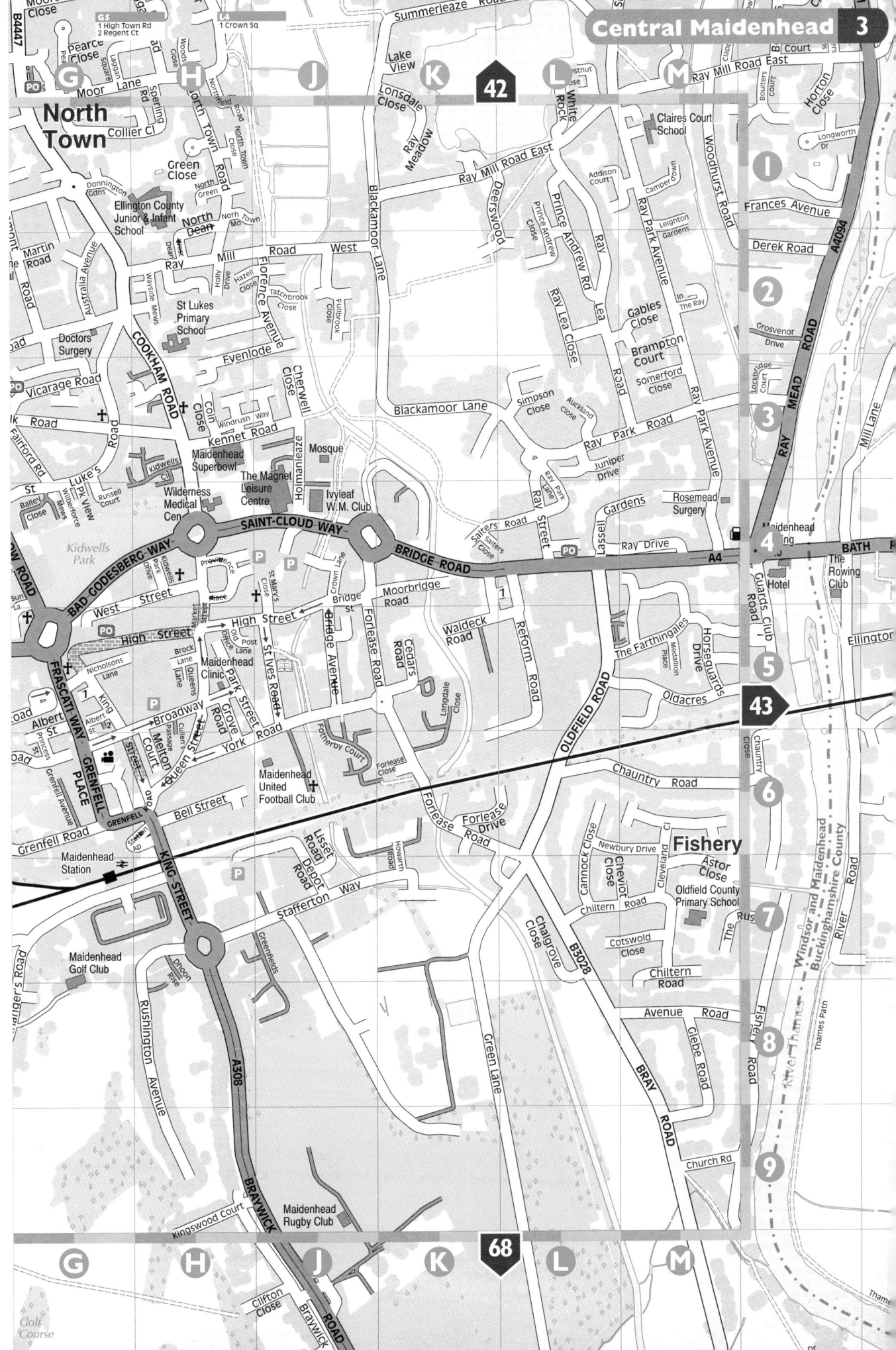

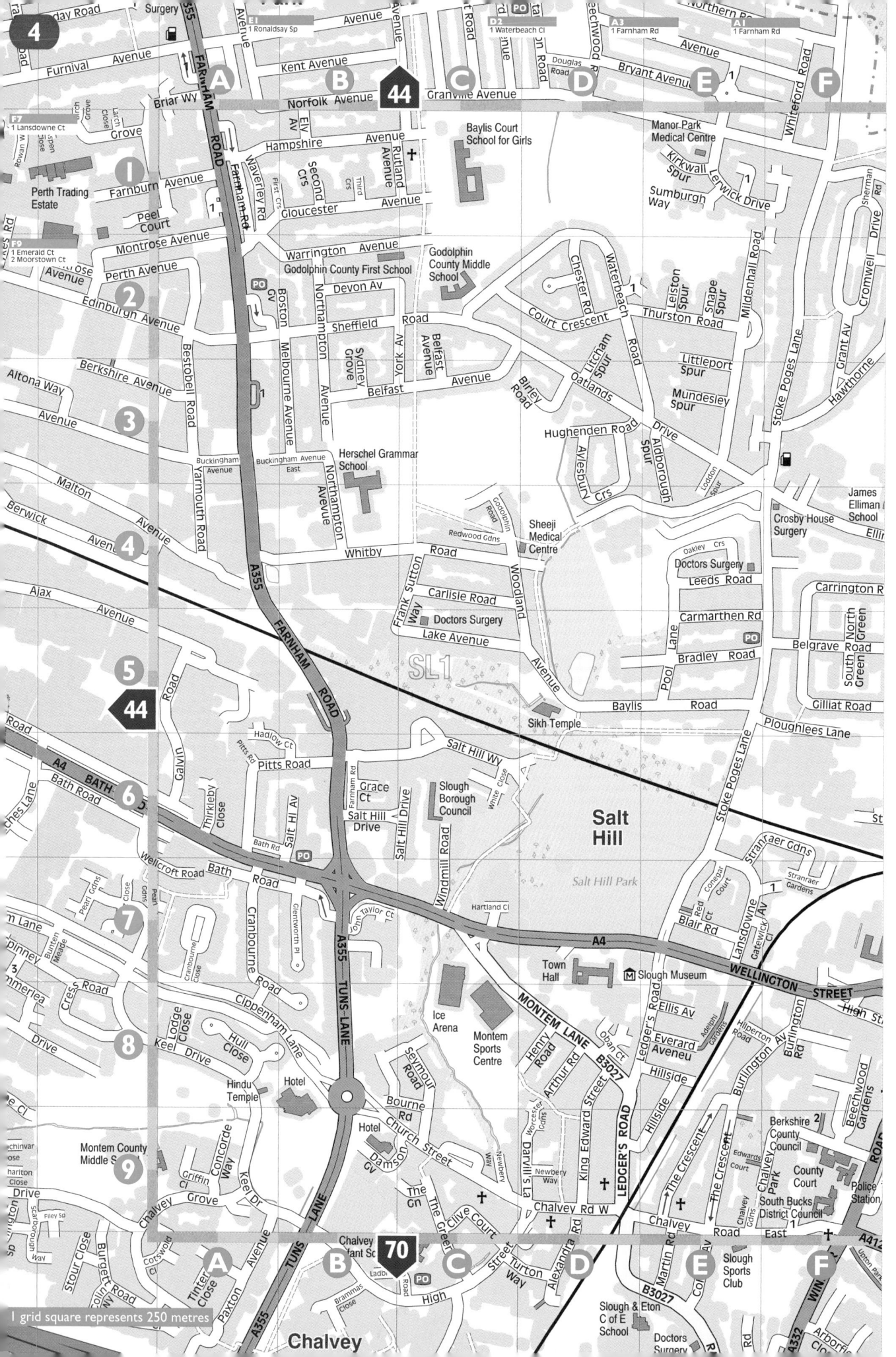

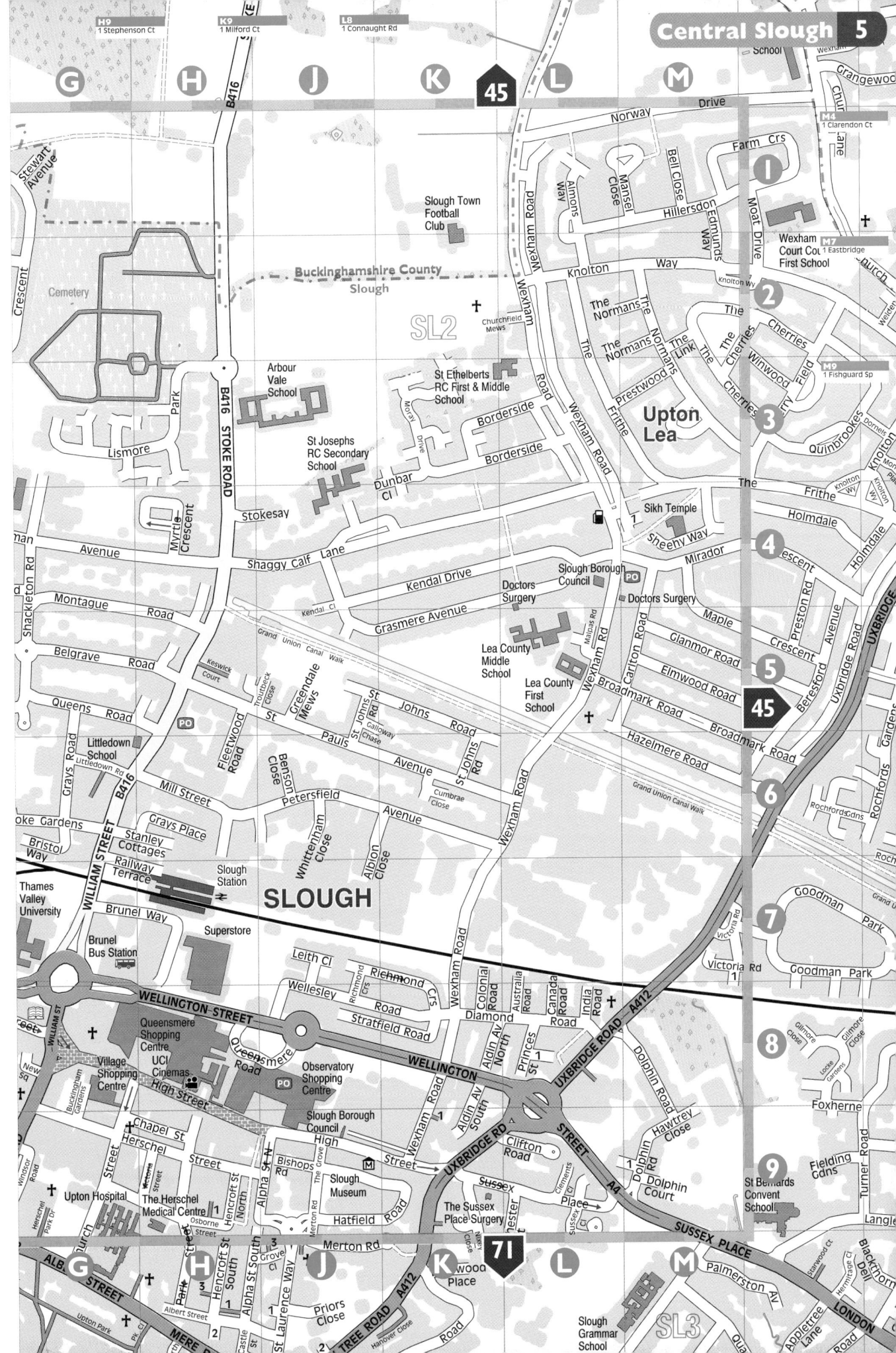

G H J K 45 L M

I
2
3
4
45
6
7
8
9

1 Stephenson Ct
1 Milford Ct
1 Connaught Rd

H9
K9
L8

M4
1 Clarendon Ct

M7
1 Eastbridge

M9
1 Fishguard Sp

Norway
Drive

Slough Town
Football
Club

Buckinghamshire County
Slough

SL2

Churchfield
Mews

Cemetery

Stewart
Avenue

Crescent

Park

Lismore

Stoke Road B416

Myrtle
Crescent

Stokesay

Arbour
Vale
School

St Josephs
RC Secondary
School

Dunbar
Cl

St Ethelberts
RC First & Middle
School

Borderside

Borderside

Moray
Drive

Shaggy Calf Lane

Kendal Drive

Kendal Cl

Grasmere Avenue

Doctors
Surgery

Slough Borough
Council

PO

Doctors Surgery

Sikh Temple

Sheehy Way

Mirador

Lea County
Middle
School

Lea County
First
School

Wexham Road

Maltas Rd

Carlton Road

Broadmark Road

Hazelmere Road

Grand Union Canal Walk

Glanmor Road

Elmwood Road

Broadmark Road

Maple

Crescent

Beresford Avenue

Preston Rd

Holmdale

Holmdale

escent

The Frithe

Knolton Wy

Knolton Wy

The

Knolton
Pla

Dornells

Quinbrookes

The Cherries

Cherries

Fry Field

Winwood

The Cherries

The Link

The Normans

Prestwood

Frithe

The Normans

The Normans

Knolton

Way

Knolton Wy

Wexham
Road

Wexham
Road

Norway
Way

Almons
Way

Mansel
Close

Hillersdon

Bell Close

Edmunds Way

Farm Crs

Moat Drive

Wexham
Court Cou
First School

Upton
Lea

Shackleton Rd

Montague
Road

Belgrave
Road

Queens Road

Grays Road

Littledown
School

Littledown Rd

Avenue

an

Keswick
Court

PO

Greendale Mews

Troutbeck
Close

Fleetwood Road

St
Pauls

Benson
Close

St Johns
Rd

Galloway
Chase

St Johns Road

Avenue

St
Johns
Rd

Grand Union Canal Walk

Cumbrae
Close

Grand Union Canal Walk

B416

Mill Street

Grays Place

Petersfield

Avenue

Whittenham Close

Albion Close

oke Gardens

Bristol
Way

WILLIAM STREET

Stanley
Cottages

Railway
Terrace

Slough
Station

SLOUGH

Thames
Valley
University

Brunel Way

Superstore

Brunel
Bus Station

Wexham Road

Victoria Rd

Uxbridge Road A412

UXBRIDGE

Rochfords Gdns

Rochfords

Roch

Grand U

Goodman
Park

Goodman Park

Gilmore
Close

Gilmore

Lodge
Gardens

Foxherne

Fielding
Gdns

Turner Road

St Bernards
Convent
School

Langle

LONDON

Blackthorn
Dell

Appletree Lane

Hermitage Ct

Starwood Ct

SL3

Quain

Slough
Grammar
School

Palmerston Av

SUSSEX PLACE

St Laurence Way

Chester

Nicola

Clements

Sussex
Place

The Sussex
Place Surgery

Dolphin
Court

Hawtrey
Close

Dolphin
Rd

Dolphin Road

Clifton
Road

UXBRIDGE RD A412

STREET

UXBRIDGE ROAD A412

A4

Wellesley
Road

Richmond
Crs

Richmond
Crs

Stratfield Road

Leith Cl

WELLINGTON STREET

WELLINGTON

Queensmere
Road

Queensmere
Shopping
Centre

UCI
Cinemas

High Street

Village
Shopping
Centre

Buckingham
Gardens

New
Sq

Chapel St

Herschel
Street

Windsor
Rd

Upton Hospital

The Herschel
Medical Centre

Herschel
Park Dr

ALBERT
STREET

Albert Street

Upton Park

MERE R

Priors
Close

Castle St

Hanover Close

REE ROAD A412

Wood
Place

G H J K 71 L M

Observatory
Shopping
Centre

PO

Slough Borough
Council

High
Street

Bishops
Rd

The Grove

Alpha St North

Slough
Museum

Hatfield Road

Merton Rd

Merton Rd

Hencroft St
North

Alpha St South

Hencroft St
South

Osborne
Street

Chapel St

Herschel
Street

Aldin Av
North

Aldin Av
South

Princes
St

Diamond
Road

Colonial
Road

Australia
Road

Canada
Road

India Road

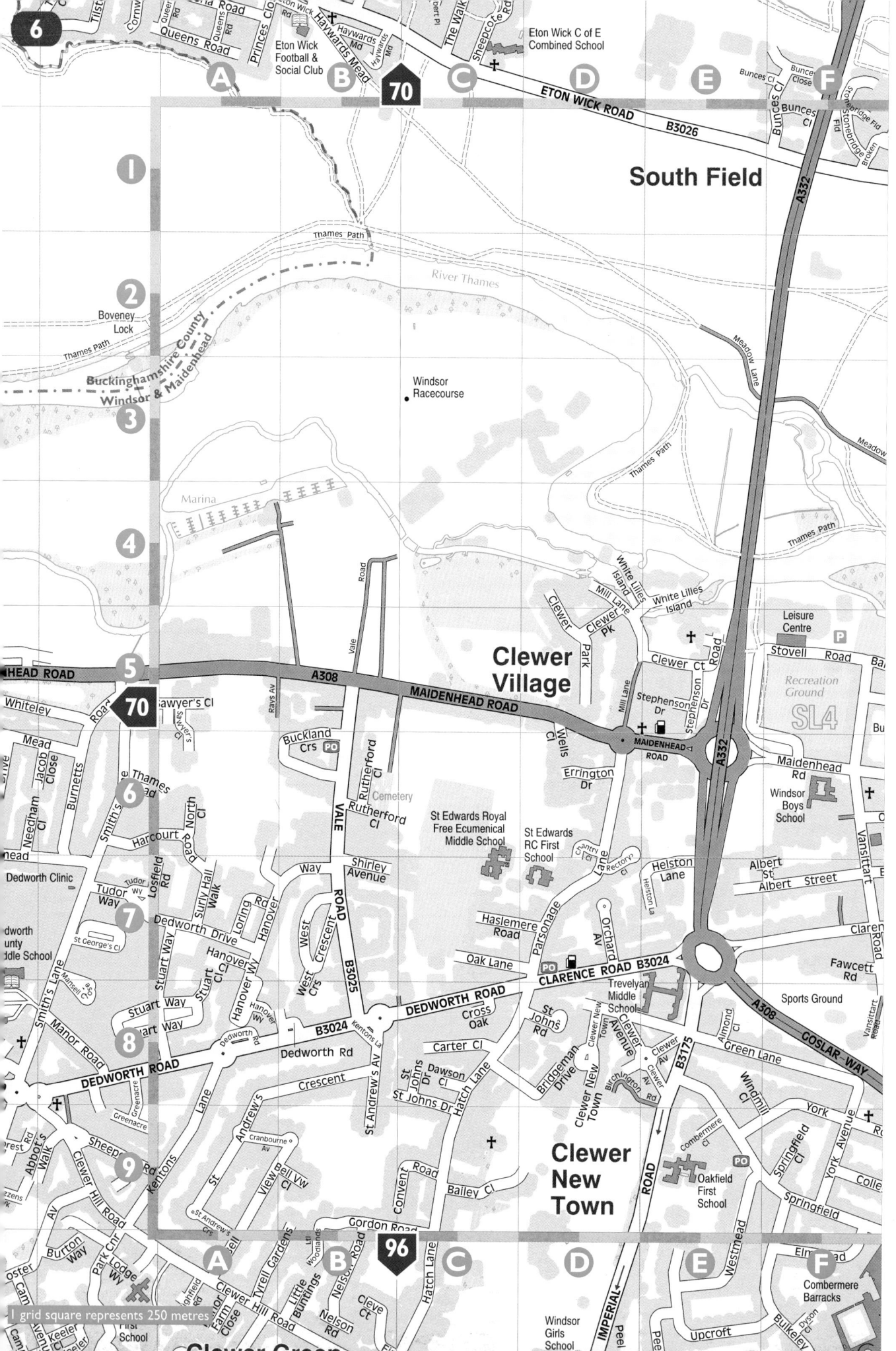

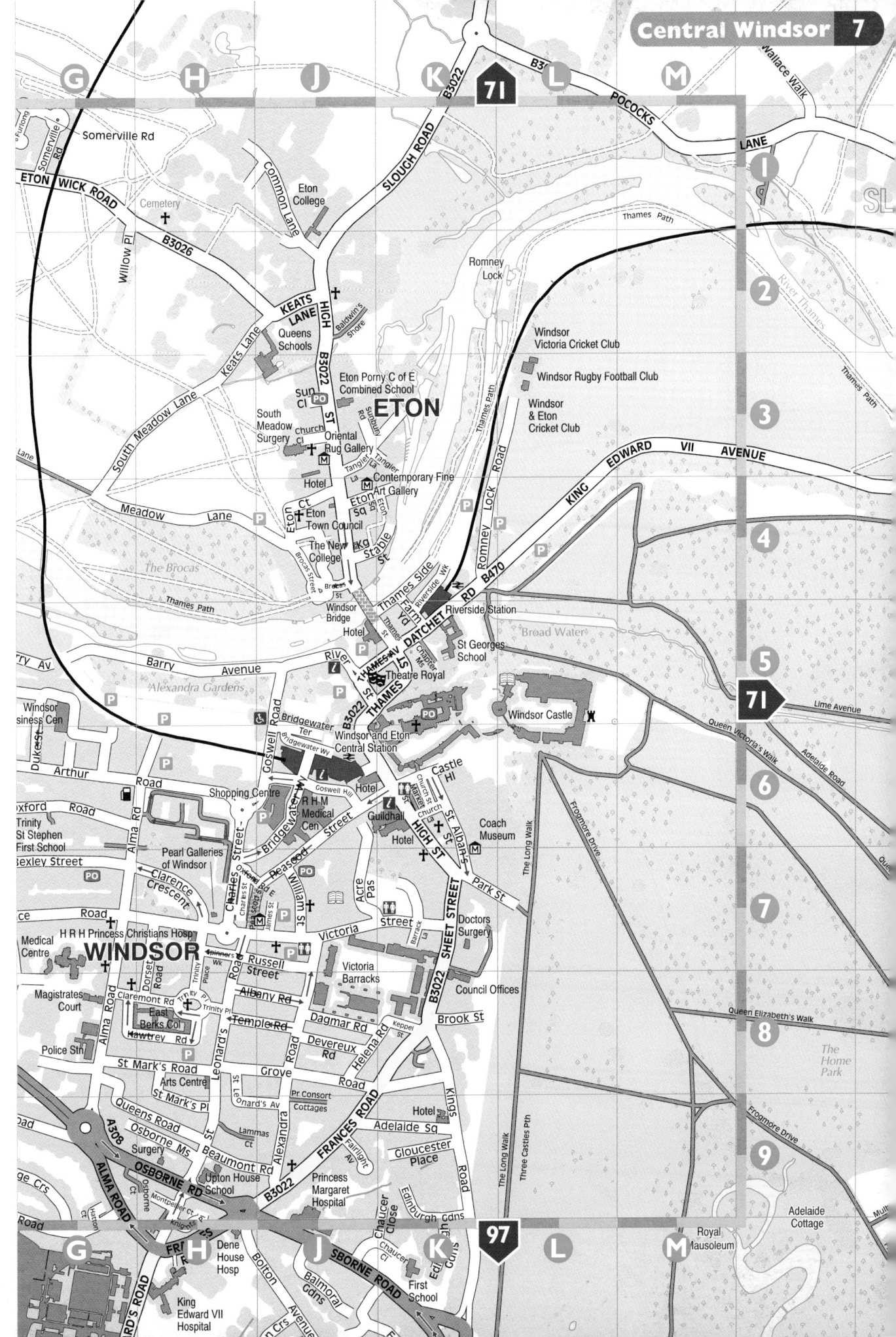

G H J K 71 L M

B3022 B3 POCOCKS

Wallace Walk

LANE

I

Somerville Rd

ETON WICK ROAD

Somerville Rd

Cemetery

B3026

Willow Pl

Eton College

SLOUGH ROAD

Thames Path

SL

River Thames

2

KEATS LANE

HIGH ST

Baldwin's Shore

Romney Lock

Thames Path

Queens Schools

Keats Lane

Windsor Victoria Cricket Club

South Meadow Lane

B3022 ST

sun Cl PO

Eton Porny C of E Combined School

Windsor Rugby Football Club

3

South Meadow Surgery

Church Cl

Oriental Rug Gallery

ETON

Windsor & Eton Cricket Club

Hotel

Tangier La

Contemporary Fine Art Gallery

Tangier

Sunbury Rd

KING EDWARD VII AVENUE

Meadow Lane

Eton Ct

Eton Sq

Eton Town Council

Thames Path

Romney Lock Road

P

4

The Brocas

Eton

Stable St

Brocas Street

The New College

KG

B470

P

Thames Side

RD

5

Thames Path

Brocas St

Windsor Bridge

Thames St

Riverside Wk

DATCHET

Riverside Station

Broad Water

Barry Avenue

River

THAMES AV

St Georges School

71

Lime Avenue

Barry Av

Alexandra Gardens

P

THAMES ST

Theatre Royal

Queen Victoria's Walk

Windsor Business Cen

P

Bridgewater Ter

B3022 THAMES

Chapel

Windsor Castle

Adelaide Road

6

Dukes St

P

Bridgewater Rd

Goswell Road

Bridgewater Wy

Windsor and Eton Central Station

PO

Castle Hl

Oxford Road

Arthur Road

Goswell Hill

Hotel

Church St

Market St

Coach Museum

Oxford Road

Shopping Centre

P

R H M Medical Cen

Guildhall

Church St

St Albans St

The Long Walk

Froomore Drive

Trinity St Stephen First School

Alma Rd

Pearl Galleries of Windsor

Bridgewater St

Peascod St

Hotel

HIGH ST

Park St

7

Bexley Street

PO

Clarence Crescent

Charles Street

Charles St

William St

PO

Acre Pas

Barrack La

Doctors Surgery

Queen Elizabeth's Walk

Medical Centre

H R H Princess Christians Hosp

WINDSOR

Spinners Wk

Russell Street

Victoria Street

Barrack St

B3022 SHEET STREET

Council Offices

8

Road

Dorset Road

Trinity Place

James St

Victoria Barracks

The Home Park

Magistrates Court

Claremont Rd

Trinity Pl

Albany Rd

Dagmar Rd

Helena Rd

Brook St

Queen Elizabeth's Walk

Police Stn

East Berks Col Hawtrey Rd

Temple Rd

Devereux Rd

Keppel St

Kings Road

Froomore Drive

9

A308

Queens Road

St Mark's Road

St Mark's Pl

Leonard's

St Leonard's Av

Grove Road

Pr Consort Cottages

Hotel

Three Castles Pth

The Long Walk

Arts Centre

Lammas Ct

Alexandra

Road

Adelaide Sq

ALMA ROAD

Osborne Ms

Surgery

Beaumont Rd

FRANCES ROAD

Fairlight Av

Gloucester Place

Adelaide Cottage

OSBORNE RD

Montpelier Ct

Osborne

Upton House School

B3022

Princess Margaret Hospital

Edinburgh Gdns

Royal Mausoleum

Hatton

Knights

FR

Dene House Hosp

FRANCES

Bolton Ave

SBORNE ROAD

Chaucer Close

Chaucer Cl

Edi Gdns

G H J 97 K L M

King Edward VII Hospital

King Edward VII Hospital

Balmoral Gdns

First School

RD'S ROAD

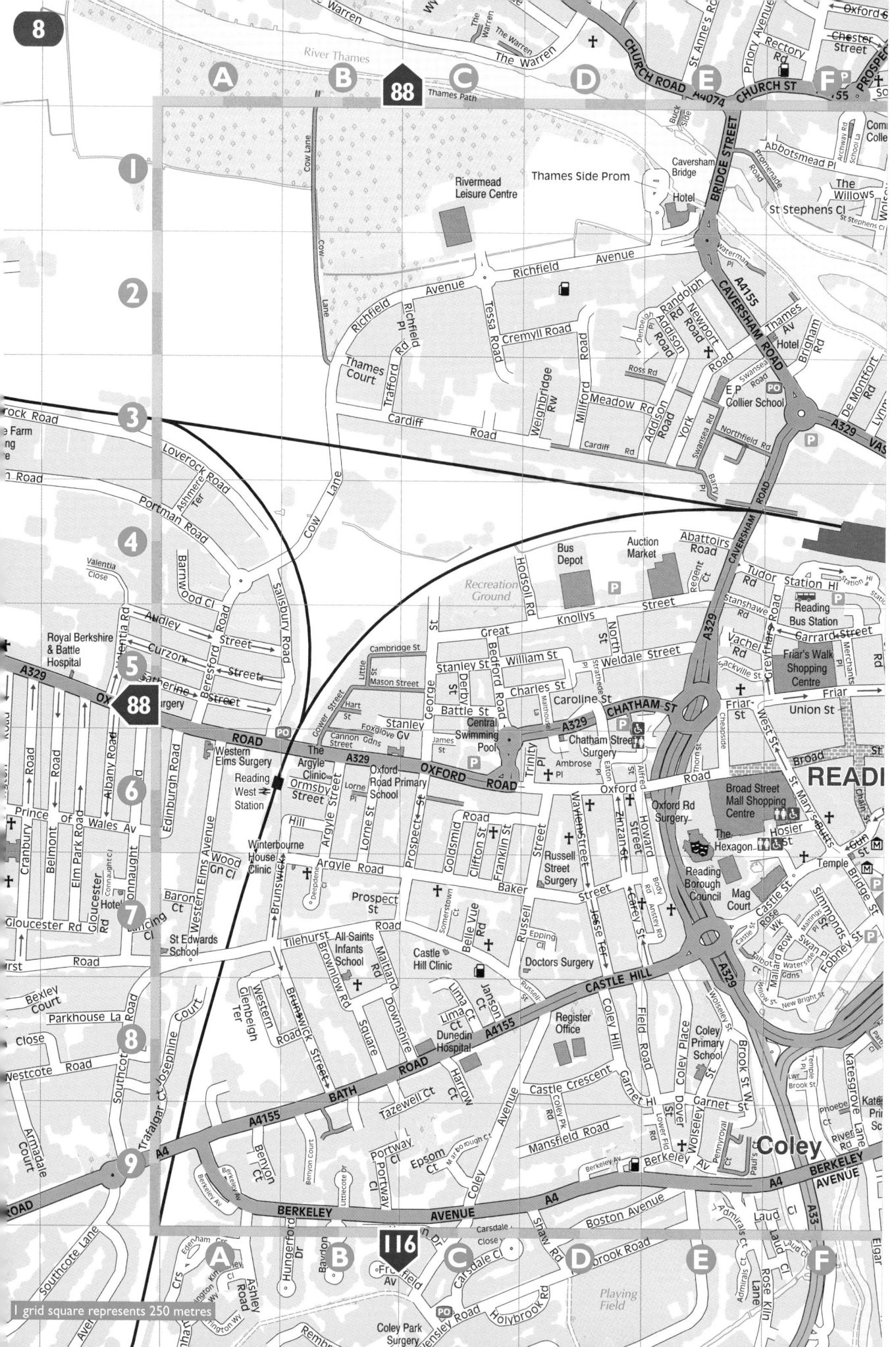

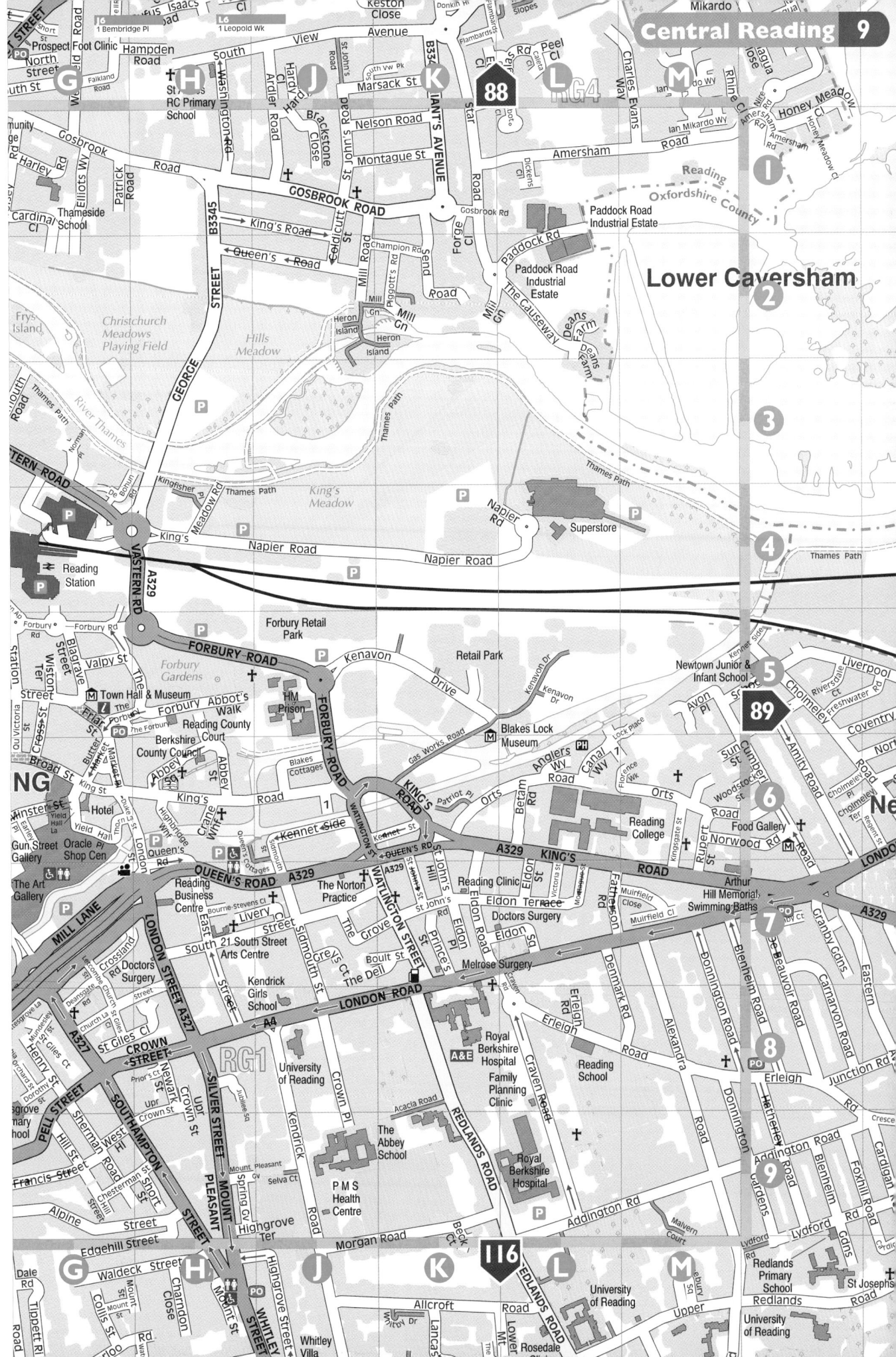

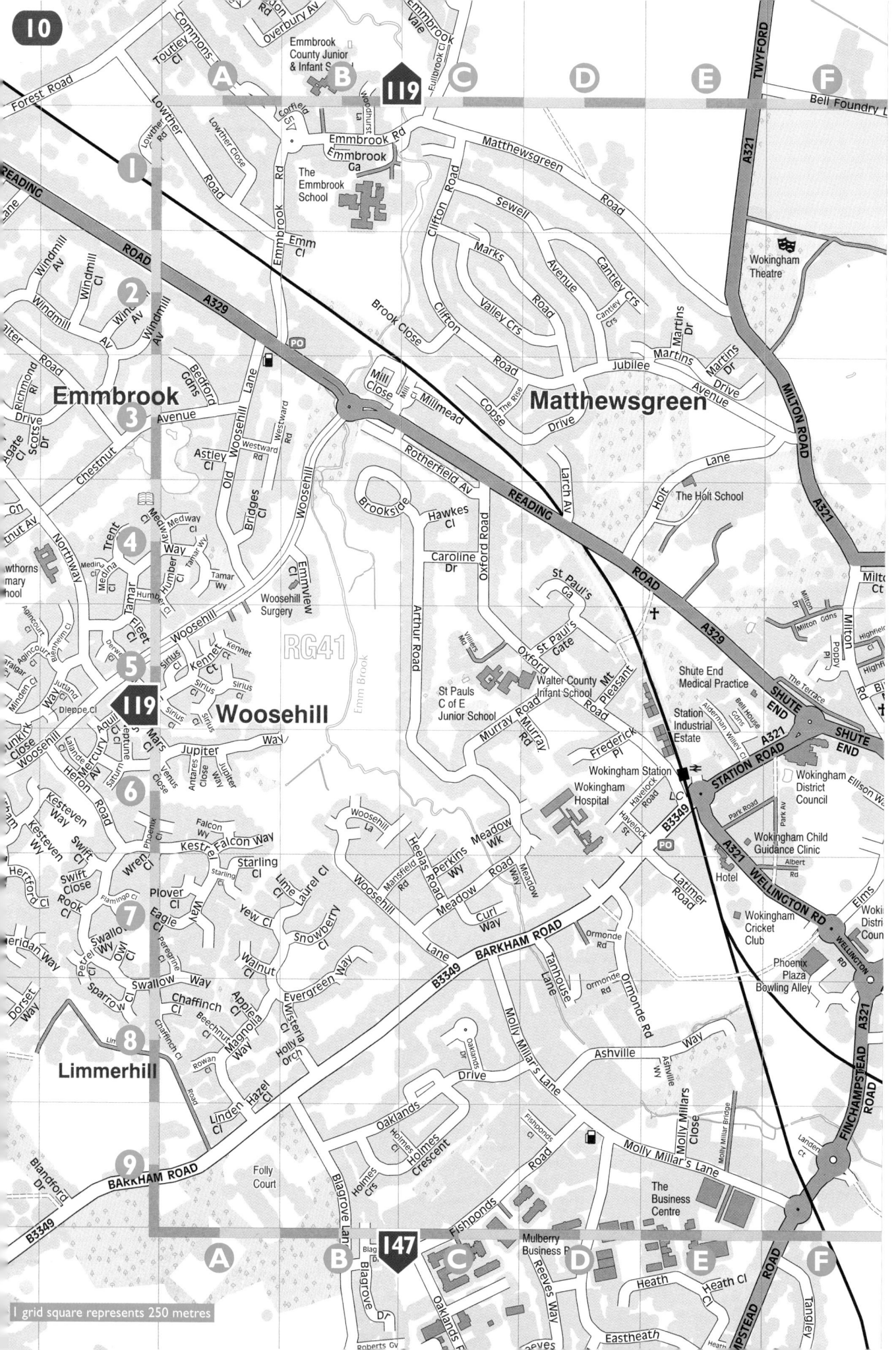

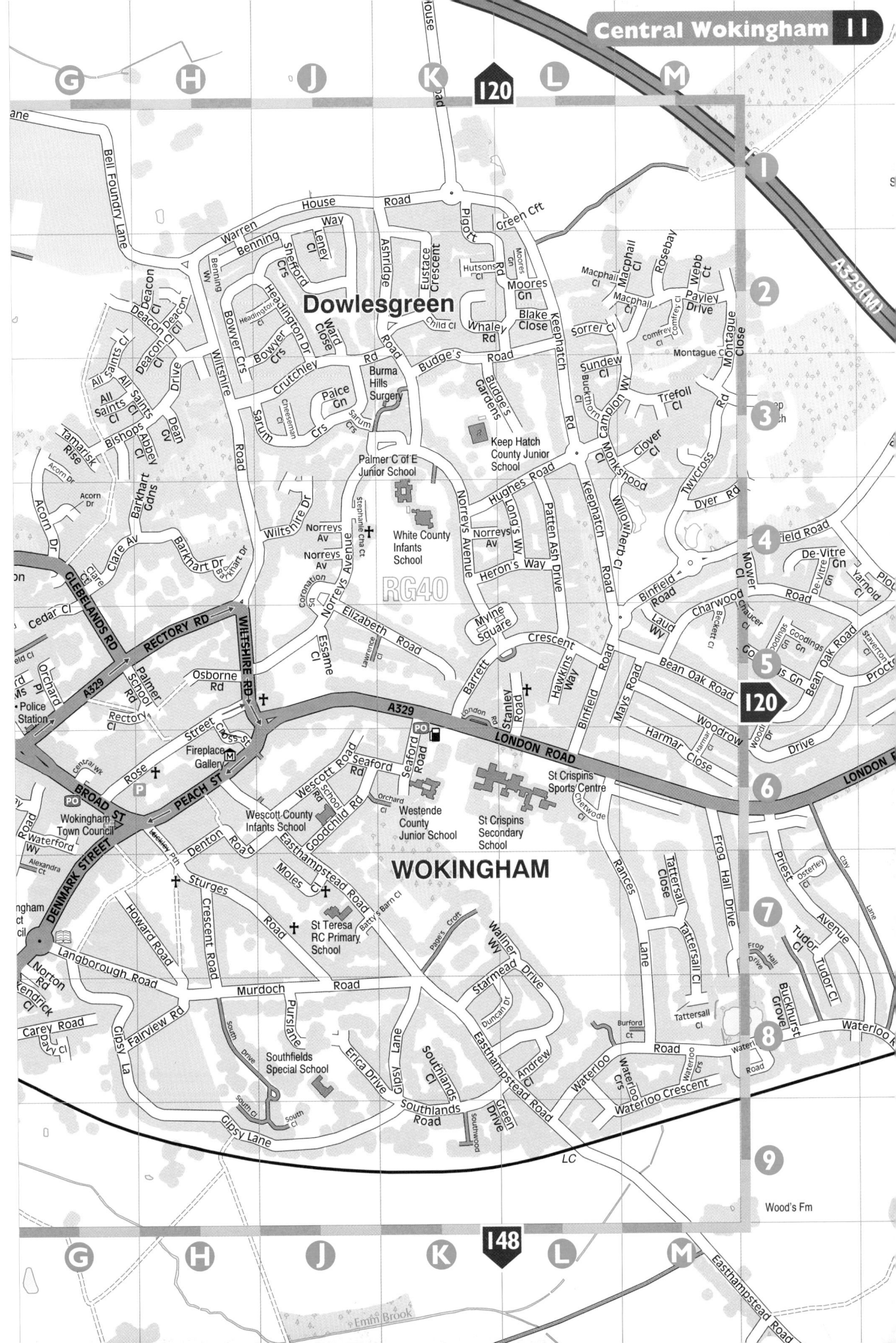

120

G H J K L M

A329(M)

1

2

3

4

5

120

6

7

8

9

Dowlesgreen

Bell Foundry Lane
Warren House Road
Benning Way
Leney Cl
Ashridge Rd
Shefford Crs
Headington Dr
Bowyer Crs
Crutchley Rd
Bowyer Crs
Ward Close
Palce Gn
Cheeseman Crs
Sarum Crs
Sarum Rd
Wiltshire
Wiltshire Dr
Pigott Rd
Green Cft
Hutsons Cl
Moores Gn
Moores Gn
Whaley Rd
Blake Close
Budge's Rd
Child Cl
Budge's Gardens
Keephatch Rd
Macphail Cl
Macphail Cl
Macphail Cl
Rosebay
Webb Ct
Payley Drive
Comfrey Cl
Montague Close
Montague Rd
Sorrel Cl
Sundew Cl
Buckthorn Cl
Campion Wy
Trefoil Cl
Clover Cl
Twycross Rd
Dyer Rd
Monkshood

Deacon Cl
Deacon Cl
Deacon Drive
All Saints Cl
All Saints Cl
All Saints Cl
Bishops Cl
Abbey Cl
Dean Gv
Tamarisk Rise
Acorn Dr
Acorn Dr
Barkhart Gdns
Clare Av
Clare
Cedar Cl

Burma Hills Surgery

Keep Hatch County Junior School

Palmer C of E Junior School

White County Infants School

RG40

Norreys Av
Norreys Av
Norreys Avenue
Stephanie Cha ct
Coronation Sq
Norreys Avenue
Elizabeth Road
Essame Cl
Lawrence
Hughes Road
Long's Wy
Patten Ash Drive
Norreys Av
Heron's Way
Mylne Square
Willowherb Cl
Binfield Road
De-Vitre Gn
Field Road
Yarnold
De-Vitre Rd
Mower Road
Charwood Wy
Beckett Cl
Laud Wy
Chaucer
Goodings Gn
Goodings Gn
Go.. Gn
Proctor
Staverton Rd
Bean Oak Road

GLEBELANDS RD
A329
RECTORY RD
WILTSHIRE RD
Palmer School Rd
Osborne Rd
Rectory Cl
Cross St
Street
Rose Av
Fireplace Gallery
PO
BROAD ST
PEACH ST
Weckley Pth
Wokingham Town Council
Alexandra Cl
Waterford Wy
DENMARK STREET
Norton Rd
Kendrick
Langborough Road
Carey Road
Gipsy La
Fairview Rd
South Drive
South Cl
South Cl
Gipsy Lane

• Police Station

Hawkins Way
Crescent
Barrett
London Rd
Stanley Road
Binfield Road
Mays Road
Woodrow Dr
Harmar Close
Harmar
Woodrow
LONDON ROAD
Bean Oak Road
Wood..
Drive
120
LONDON

A329
LONDON ROAD
PO
St Crispins Sports Centre
Chetwode
St Crispins Secondary School
Seaford Road
Seaford Rd
Wescott Road
School Rd
Goodchild Rd
Orchard Cl
Westende County Junior School
Wescott County Infants School
Denton Road
Easthampstead Road
Moles
St Teresa RC Primary School
Battys Barn Cl
Page's Croft
WOKINGHAM
Sturges Road
Crescent Road
Murdoch Road
Howard Road
Pursiane Lane
Erica Drive
Southfields Special School
Southlands Cl
Southlands Road
Southwood
Green Drive
Walmef Drive
Starmead Drive
Duncan Dr
Andrew Cl
Rances Lane
Waterloo Road
Burford Ct
Tattersall Cl
Tattersall Close
Tattersall Cl
Frog Hall Drive
Priest Avenue
Osterley Cl
City
Frog Hall Drive
Tudor Cl
Tudor Cl
Buckhurst Grove
Waterloo Road
Waterloo Crs
Waterloo Crescent
Waterloo Cres
Waterlo

LC

Wood's Fm

148

G H J K L M
Easthampstead Road
Emm Brook

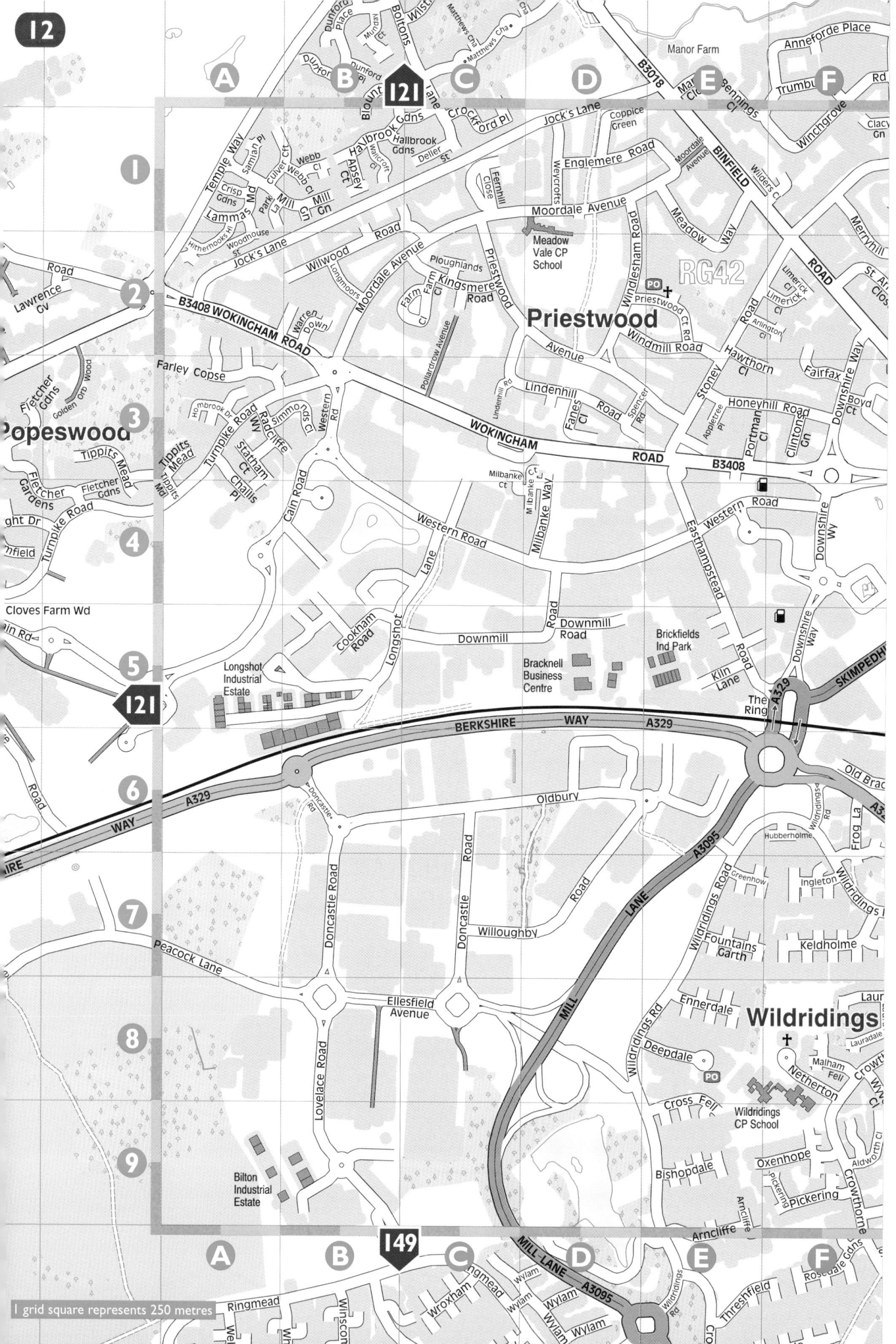

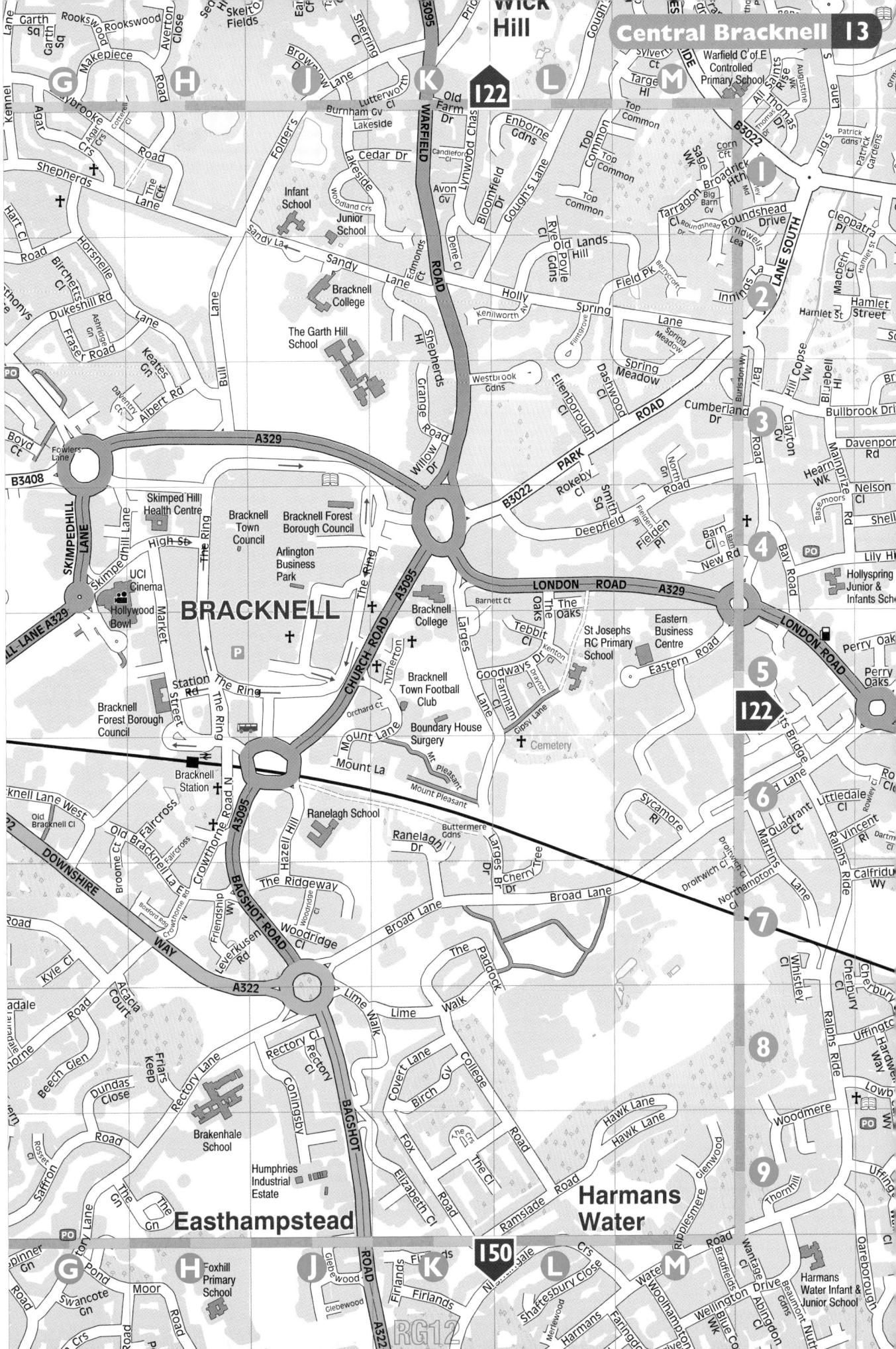

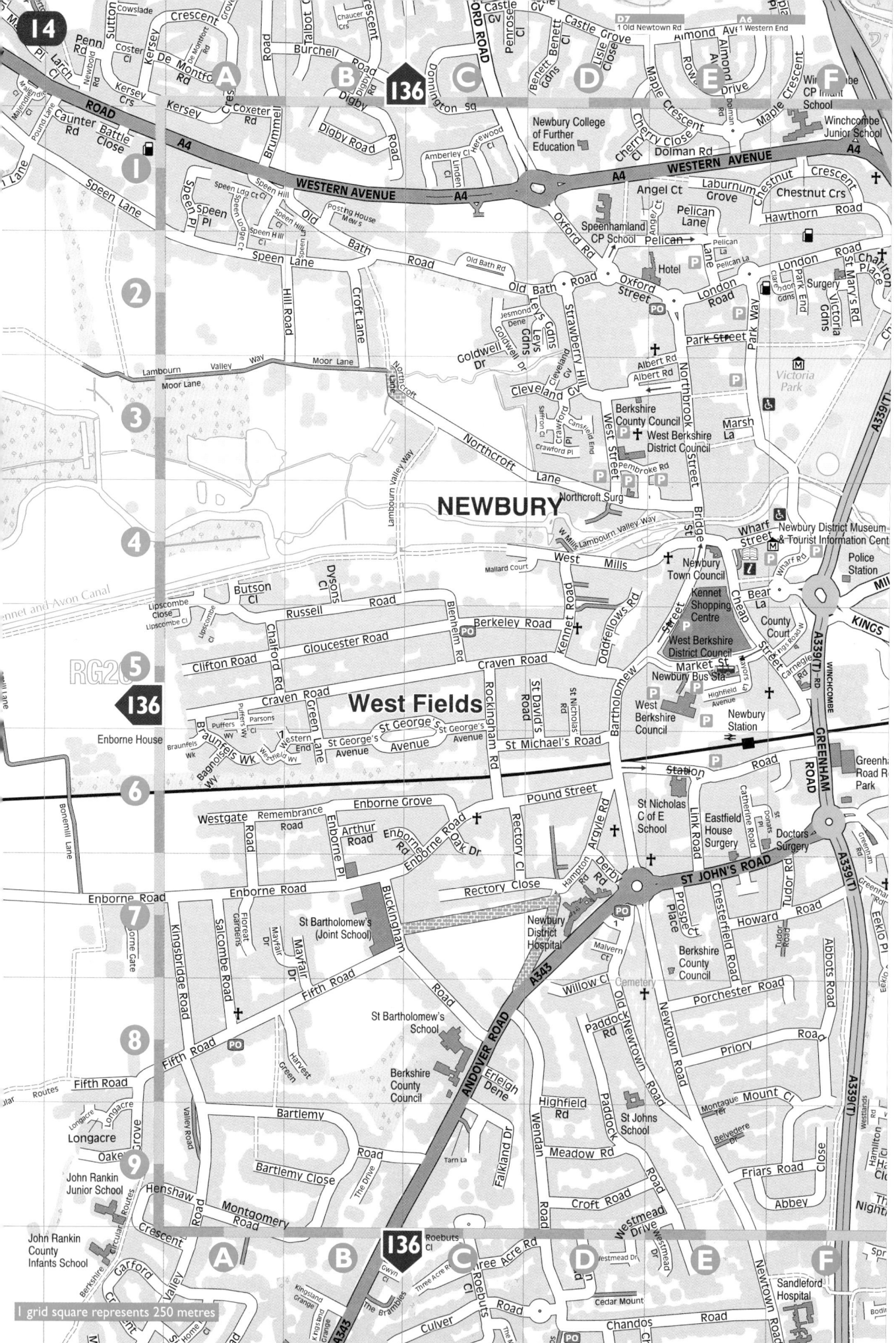

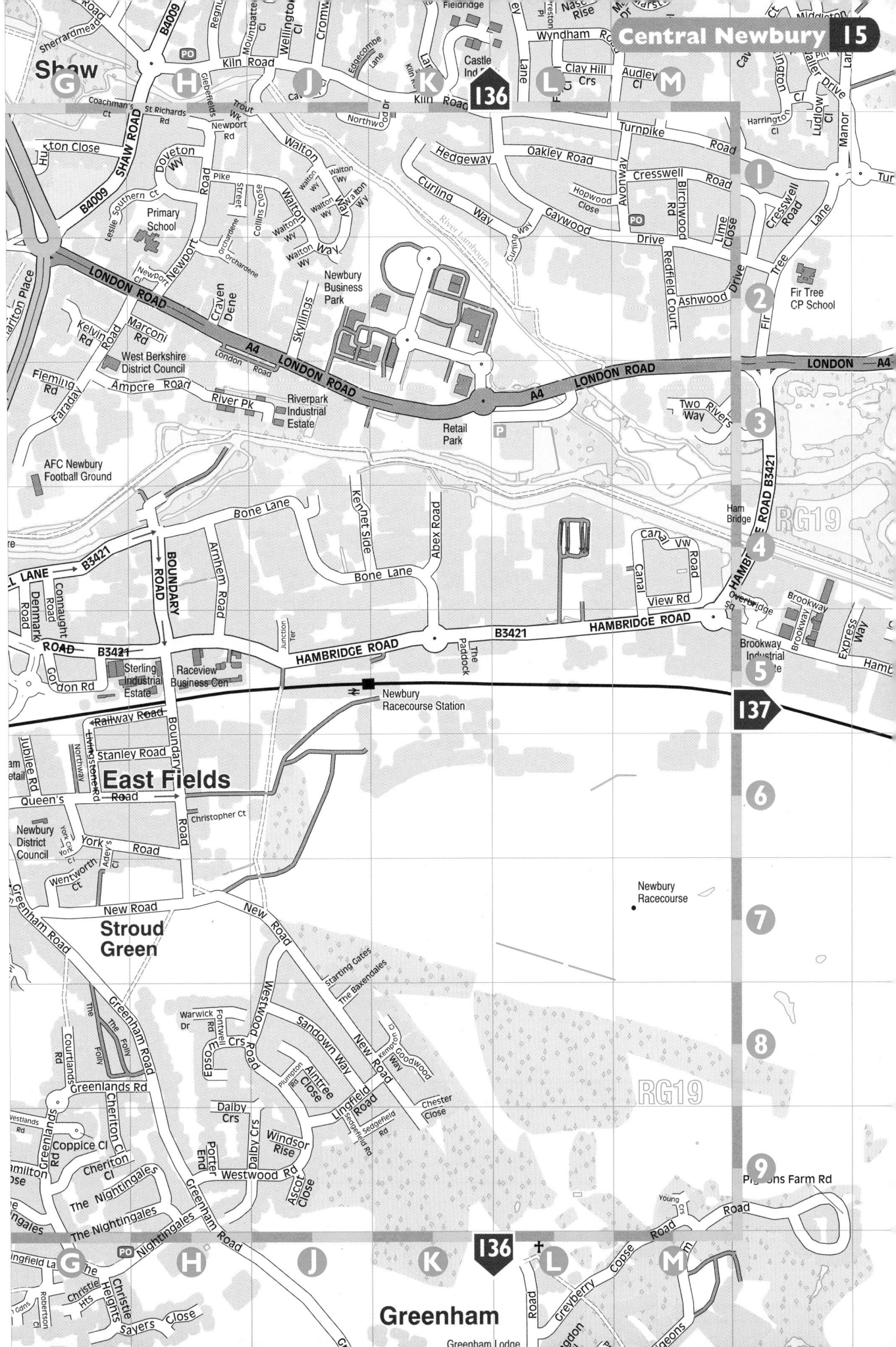

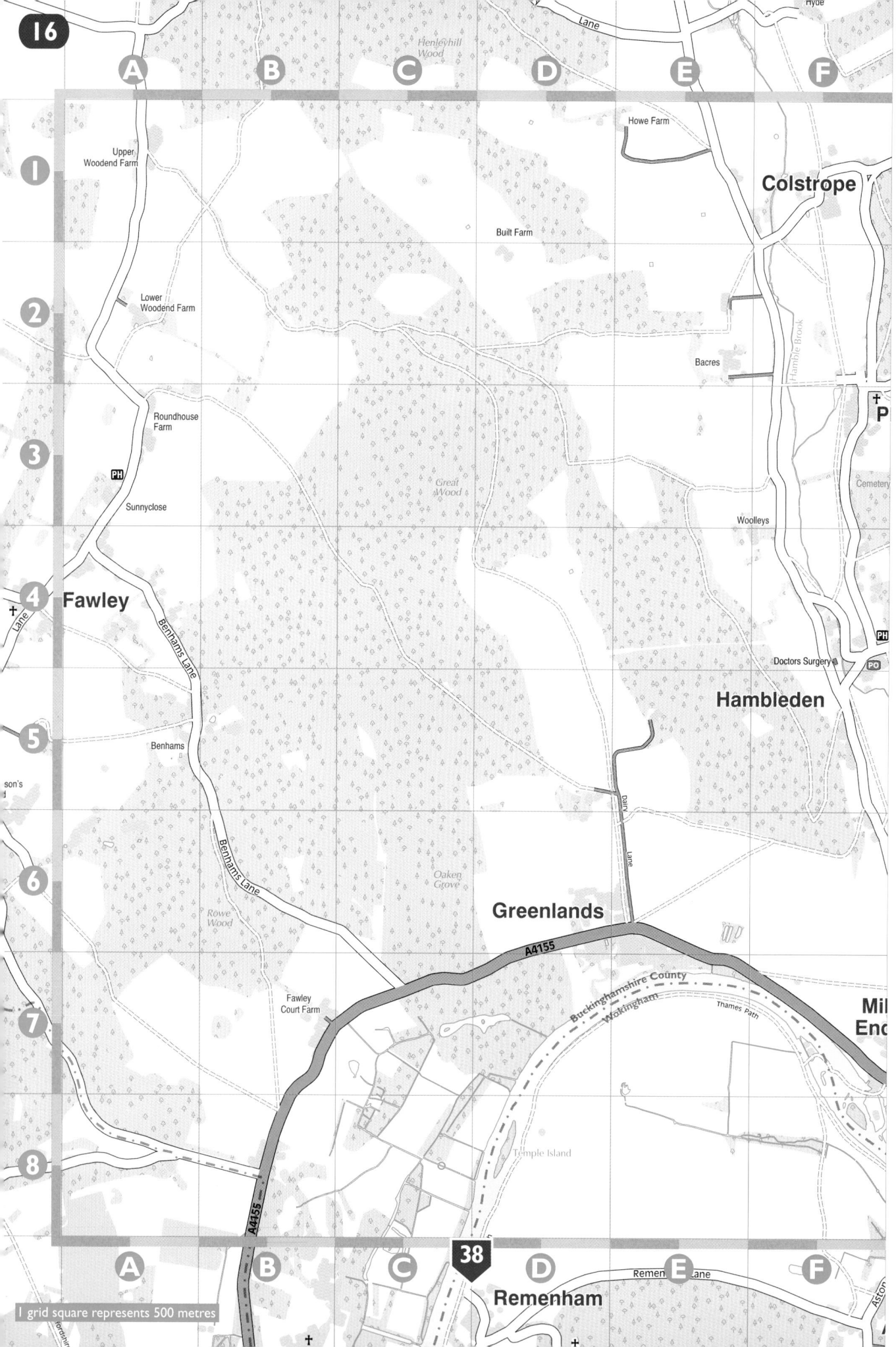

A
B
C
D
E
F

1

2

3

4

5

6

7

8

Upper
Woodend Farm

Lower
Woodend Farm

Roundhouse
Farm

PH

Sunnyclose

Fawley

Benhams Lane

Benhams

Benhams Lane

Rowe
Wood

Fawley Court Farm

Henley-hill
Wood

Built Farm

Great
Wood

Oaken
Grove

A4155

Greenlands

Fawley Court Farm

Temple Island

Howe Farm

Colstrope

Hamble Brook

Bacres

Cemetery

Woolleys

PH

Doctors Surgery

Hambleden

Dairy Lane

Buckinghamshire County

Wokingham

Thames Path

**Mil
End**

Remenham Lane

Lane

Hyde

son's

Lane

A4155

38

Remenham

Aston

ordshire

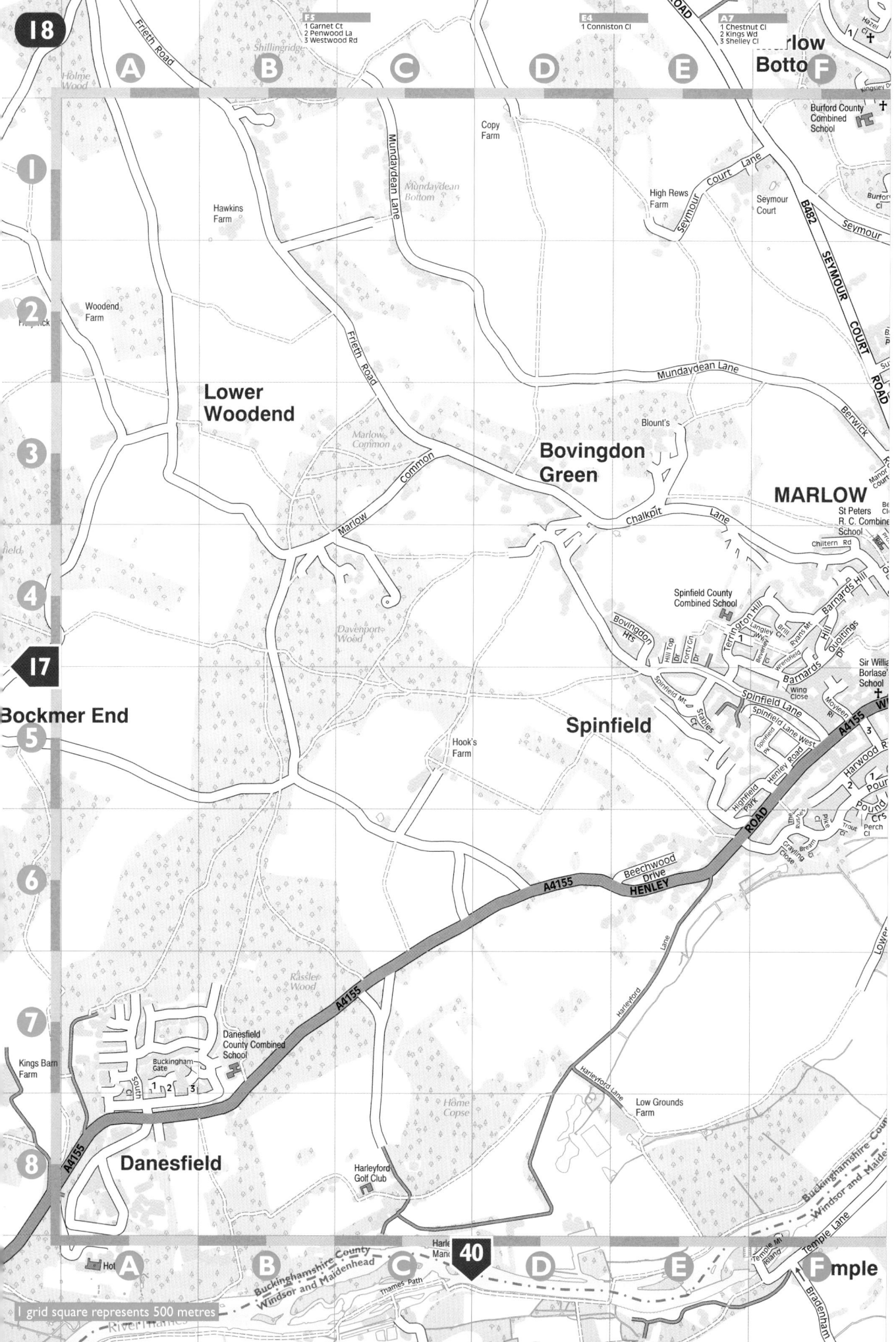

18

F5
1 Garnet Ct
2 Penwood La
3 Westwood Rd

E4
1 Conniston Cl

A7
1 Chestnut Cl
2 Kings Wd
3 Shelley Cl

A **B** **C** **D** **E** **F**

Marlow Botto

Burford County Combined School

1

Holme Wood

Frieth Road

Shillingridge

Hawkins Farm

Mundaydean Lane

Copy Farm

Mundaydean Bottom

High Rews Farm

Seymour Court Lane

Seymour Court

B482

SEYMOUR COURT ROAD

Seymour

2

Fr__nck

Woodend Farm

Frieth Road

Mundaydean Lane

Berwick

3

Lower Woodend

Marlow Common

Blount's

Bovingdon Green

MARLOW

St Peters R. C. Combined School

Chiltern Rd

Marlow Common

Chalkpit Lane

Spinfield County Combined School

Terrington Hill

Langley Wds

Brill

Barnards Hill

Quotings

4

field

Davenport Wood

Bovingdon Hts

Hill Top Dr

Forty Grn

Spinfield Mt

Spinfield Lane

Barnards

Wing Close

Sir William Borlase's School

17

5

Bockmer End

Spinfield

Stables

Spinfield Lane West

Henley Road

Highfield Park

A4155

Harwood Rd

Pound

Pound Crs

Perch Cl

Trout

Pike

6

Hook's Farm

Beechwood Drive

HENLEY

A4155

ROAD

Crawling Close

Bream

Rushes

7

Rassler Wood

A4155

Danesfield County Combined School

Kings Barn Farm

Buckingham Gate

South

1 2 3

Harleyford

Harleyford Lane

Low Grounds Farm

Lane

8

A4155

Danesfield

Home Copse

Harleyford Golf Club

Buckinghamshire County Windsor and Maidenhead

A Hol **B** **C** **40** **D** **E** **F** mple

Buckinghamshire County Windsor and Maidenhead

Thames Path

Harl Man

Temple Lane

Temple Mi

Bradenham

River Thames

1 grid square represents 500 metres

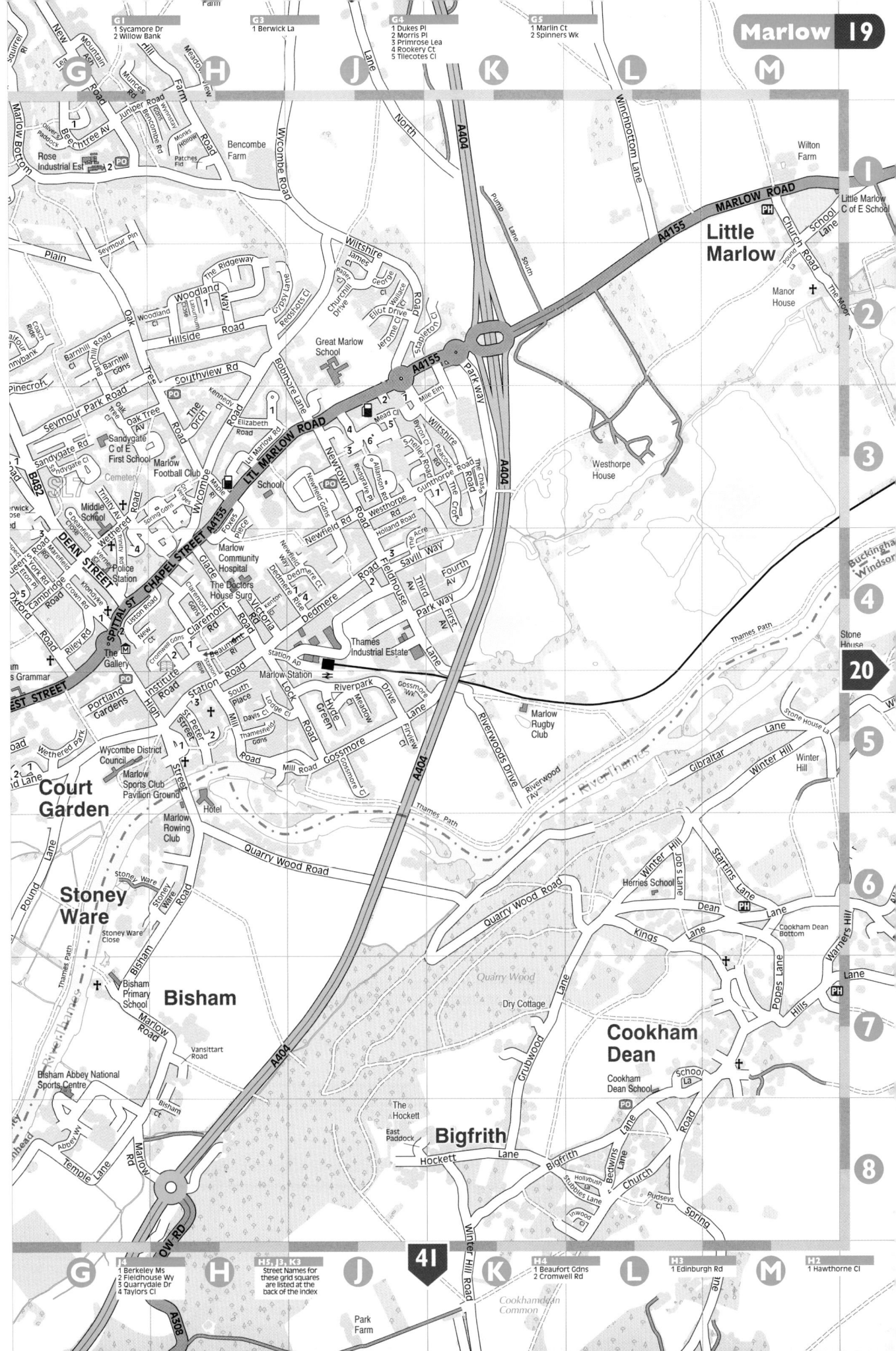

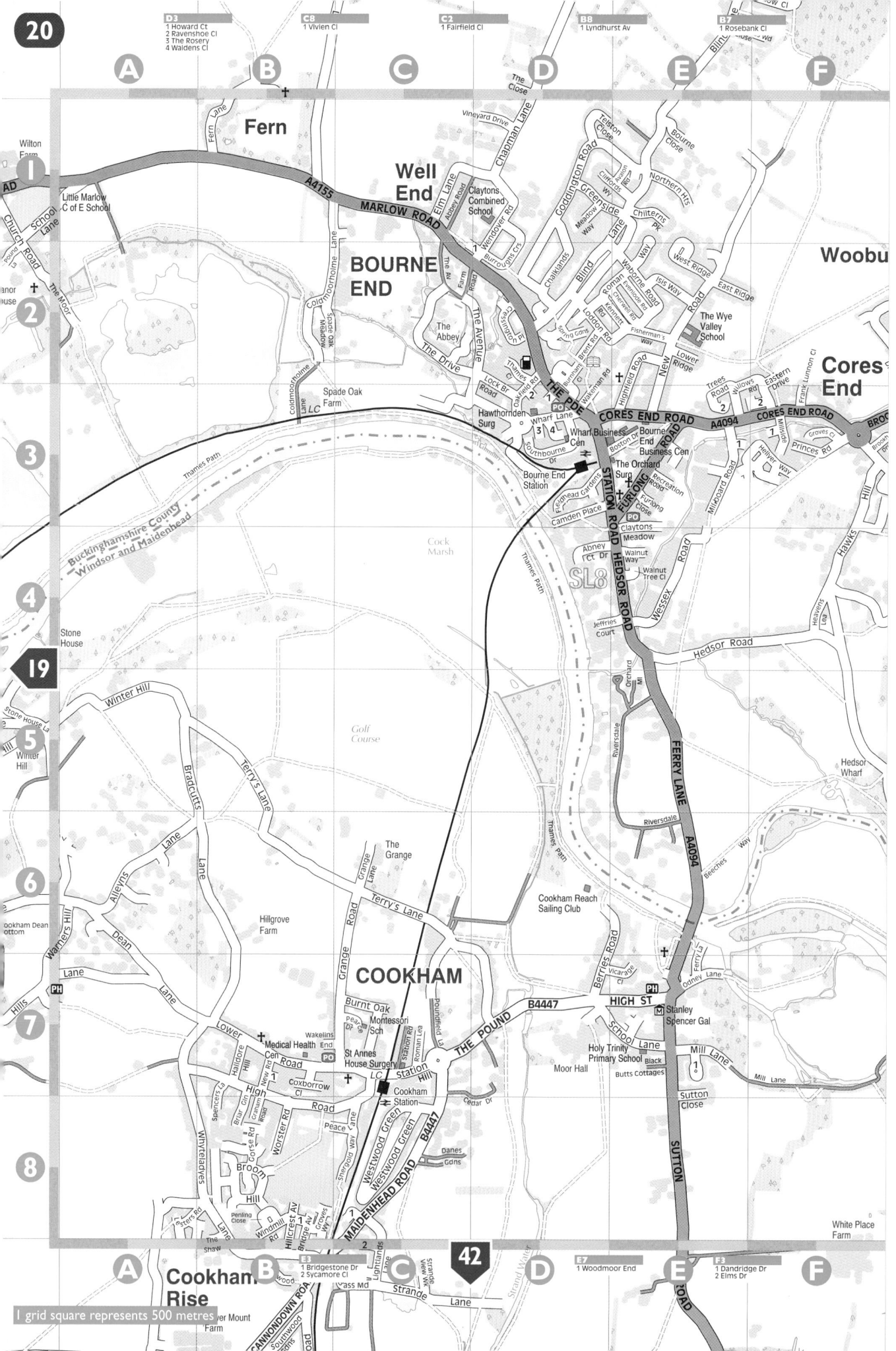

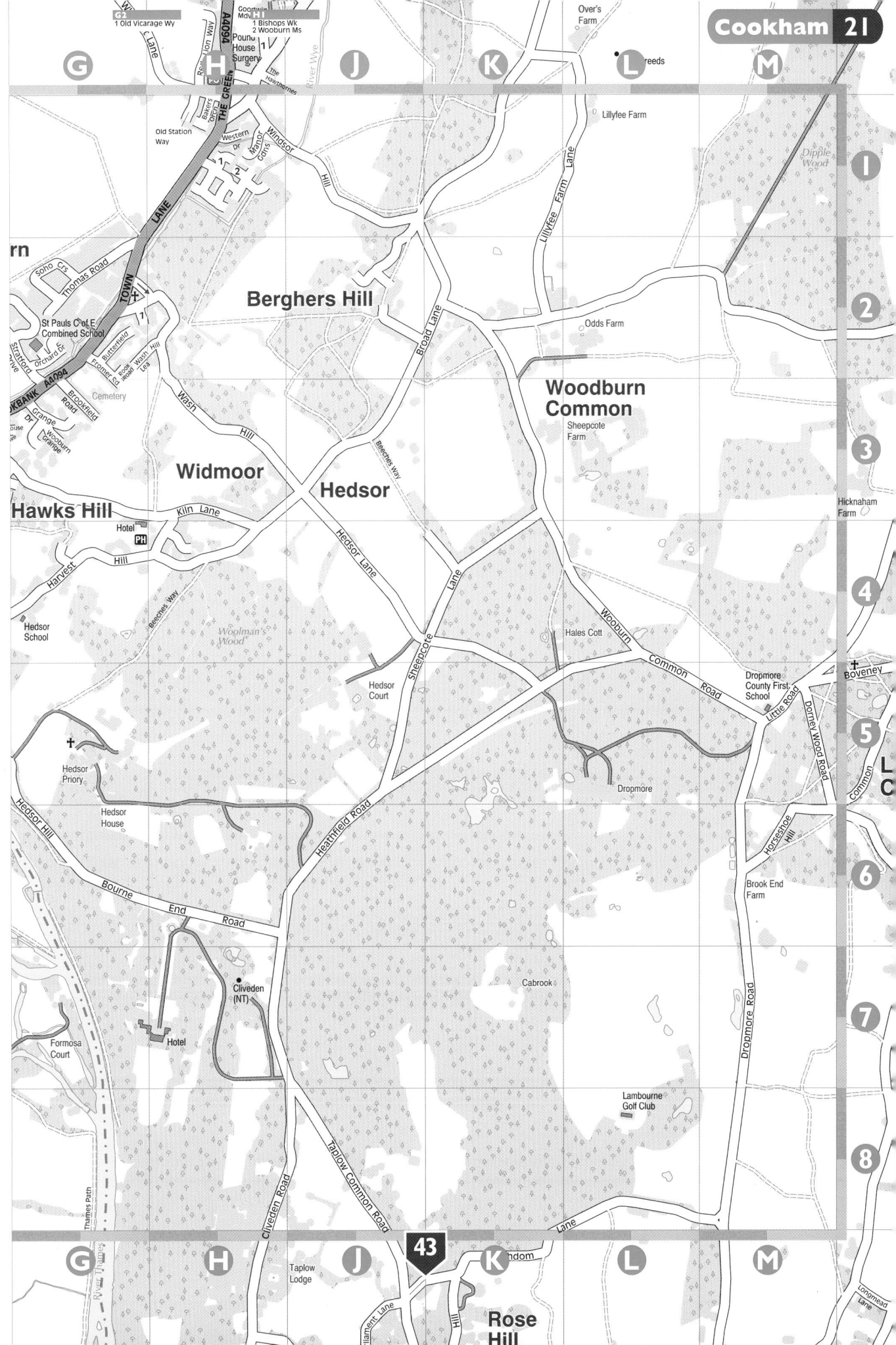

G H J K L M

G2
1 Old Vicarage Wy

1 Bishops Wk
2 Wooburn Ms

Over's
Farm

reeds

Lillyfee Farm

Dipple
Wood

I

Pound
House
Surgery

The
Hawthornes

River Wye

Old Station
Way

Western
Dr

Manor
Courts

Windsor

Hill

Lillyfee Farm Lane

2

Soho Crs

Thomas Road

Berghers Hill

Broad Lane

Odds Farm

St Pauls C of E
Combined School

Butterfield

Wash. Hill

Lea

**Woodburn
Common**

Hicknaham
Farm

3

Cemetery

Wooburn
Grange

Grange

Brookfield

Wash

Hill

Beeches Way

Sheepcote
Farm

Widmoor

Hedsor

Hawks Hill

Kiln Lane

Hotel

PH

Harvest

Hill

Beeches Way

Hedsor Lane

Sheepcote Lane

Wooburn

Common Road

Boveney

4

Hedsor
School

Woolman's
Wood

Hedsor
Court

Hales Cott

Dropmore
County First
School

Little Road

Dorney Wood Road

5

L
C

Hedsor
Priory

Hedsor
House

Dropmore

Horseshoe Hill

6

Common

Hedsor Hill

Bourne

End

Road

Heathfield Road

Brook End
Farm

Cabrook

Dropmore Road

7

Cliveden
(NT)

Hotel

Formosa
Court

Thames Path

Lambourne
Golf Club

8

River Thames

Cliveden Road

Taplow
Lodge

Taplow Common Road

43

Hill

ndom

Lane

Longmead
Lane

G H J K L M

**Rose
Hill**

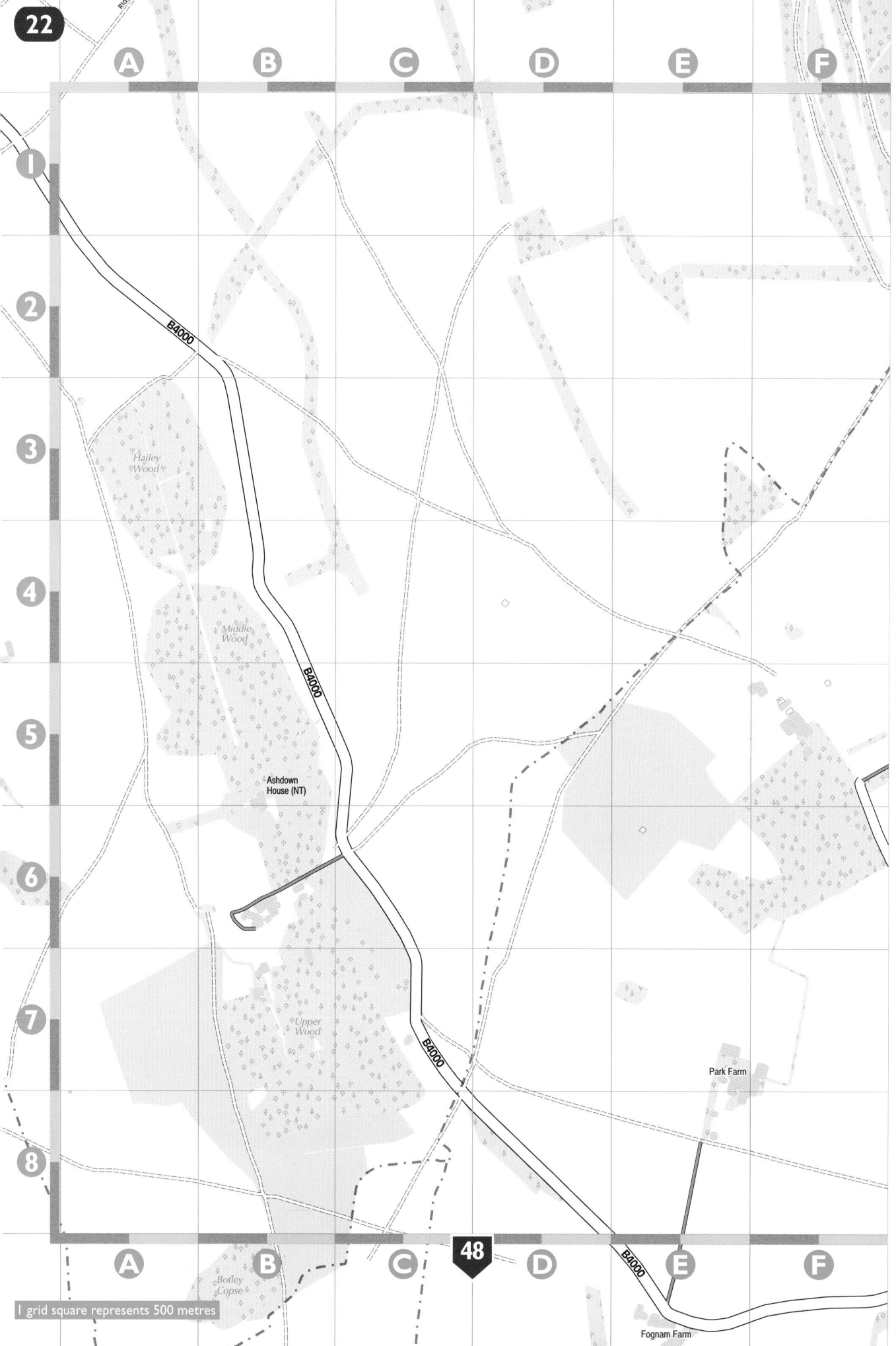

A B C D E F

I

2

3

4

5

6

7

8

A B 48 C D E F

Ridge

B4000

Hailey
Wood

Middle
Wood

Ashdown
House (NT)

B4000

Upper
Wood

B4000

Park Farm

B4000

Botley
Copse

Fognam Farm

1 grid square represents 500 metres

G   H   J   K   L   M

1

2

3

4

24

5

6

Lam

7

8

Oxfordshire County
West Berkshire

Wellbottom Down

Lambourn Valley Way

Sevenbarrows
House

Postdown Farm

Maddle Farm

B4001

B4001

Maddle Road

Lambourn Valley Way

Newbarn Farm

**Wether
Down**

Foxbury Farm

**Upper
Lambourn**

High Street

49

Lambourn Valley Way

WA GE ROAD

G   B4000   H   J   K   L   M

Cemetery

A   B   C   D   E   F

B4001

*Folly
Clump*

Ridgeway

Greendown Farm

Oxfordshire County
West Berkshire

Cockleberry Farm

Sheepdrove Farm

Stancombe Farm

Warren Farm

Lambourn Downs

ether
own

Foxbury Farm

College Farm

Sheepdrove Road

A   B   C   **50**   D   E   F

1 grid square represents 500 metres

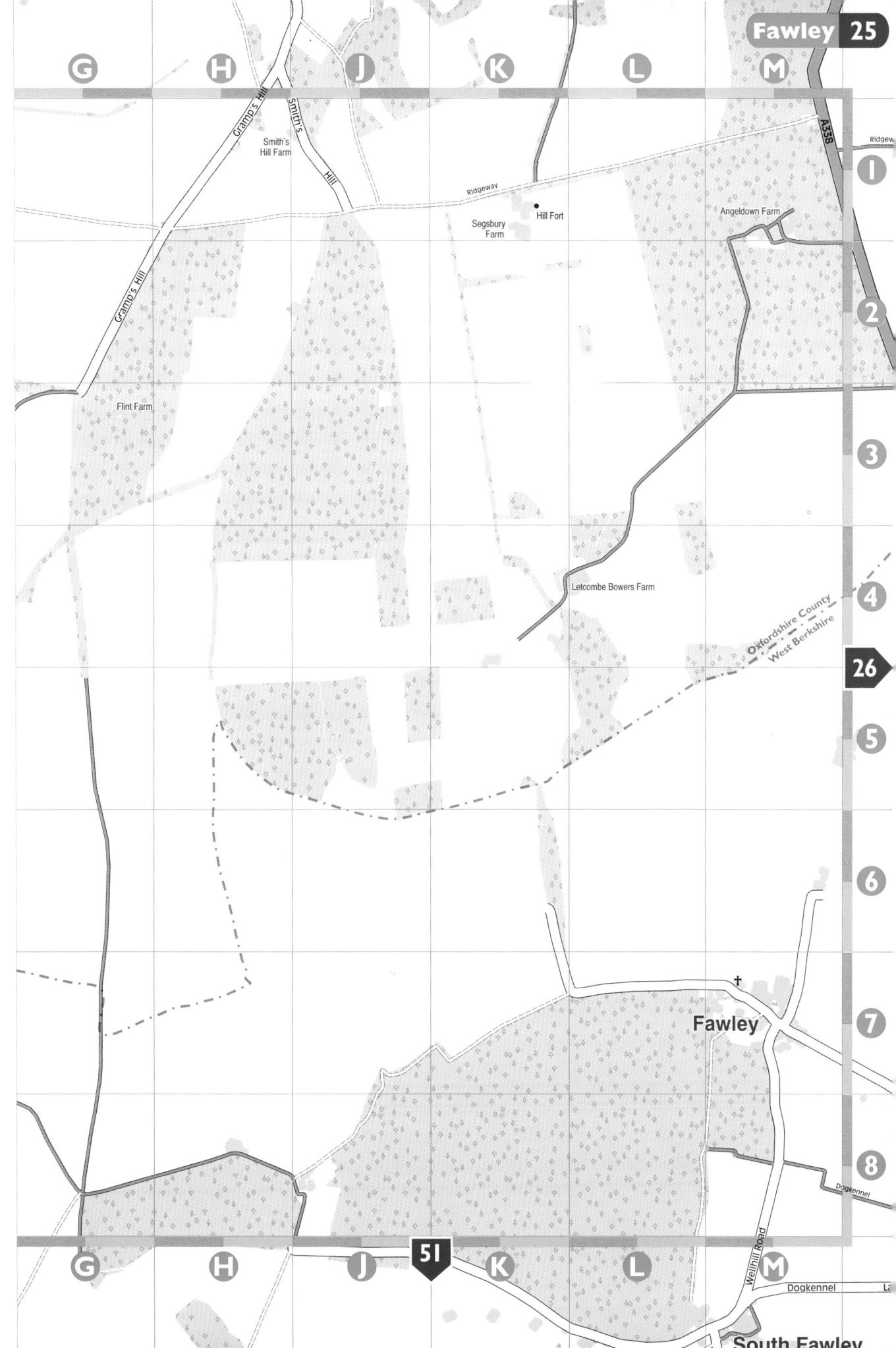

G H J K L M

I

A338

Ridgew

2

Gramp's Hill

Smith's Hill

Smith's Hill Farm

Ridgeway

Segsbury Farm

Hill Fort

Angeldown Farm

Flint Farm

3

Letcombe Bowers Farm

4

Oxfordshire County
West Berkshire

26

5

6

Fawley

7

†

8

Dogkennel

Wellhill Road

G H J K L M

Dogkennel La

South Fawley

A   B   Pewit Farm   C   D   E   F

White House Farm

Ridgeway
The Ridgeway

I

Ridgeway

Ridgeway

Yew
Down

B4494

Lattin
Down
Kiln

2

Lattin Down

Lockinge Kiln

3

Lockinge Down

CHAINHILL ROAD

e C
Berkshire

4

25

Little Coombe
Farm

Coombe
Lodge

5

Farmborough
Down

6

Farnborough Down Farm

7

Woolley
Down

8

Dogkennel   Lane

ogkennel   Lane   A   A338   B   52   C   D   E   F

Woolley House

1 grid square represents 500 metres

G   H   J   K   L   M

Ridgeway

Ridgeway Down

Betterton
Down

Wether
Down

Down Barn

West
Ginge
Down

I

2

The
Warren

Farm

3

Lands End

Oxfordshire County
West Berkshire

Copperage Road

4

Old
Down

28

Moonlight Barn

5

Hernehill
Down

Pond
Close   **Farnborough**

Copperage   Road

6

B4494

Catmore Road

7

California Farm

8

Brightwalton
Common

Lower Barn

Wickslett
Copse

Common Lane

B4494

G   H   J   K   L   M

Catmore

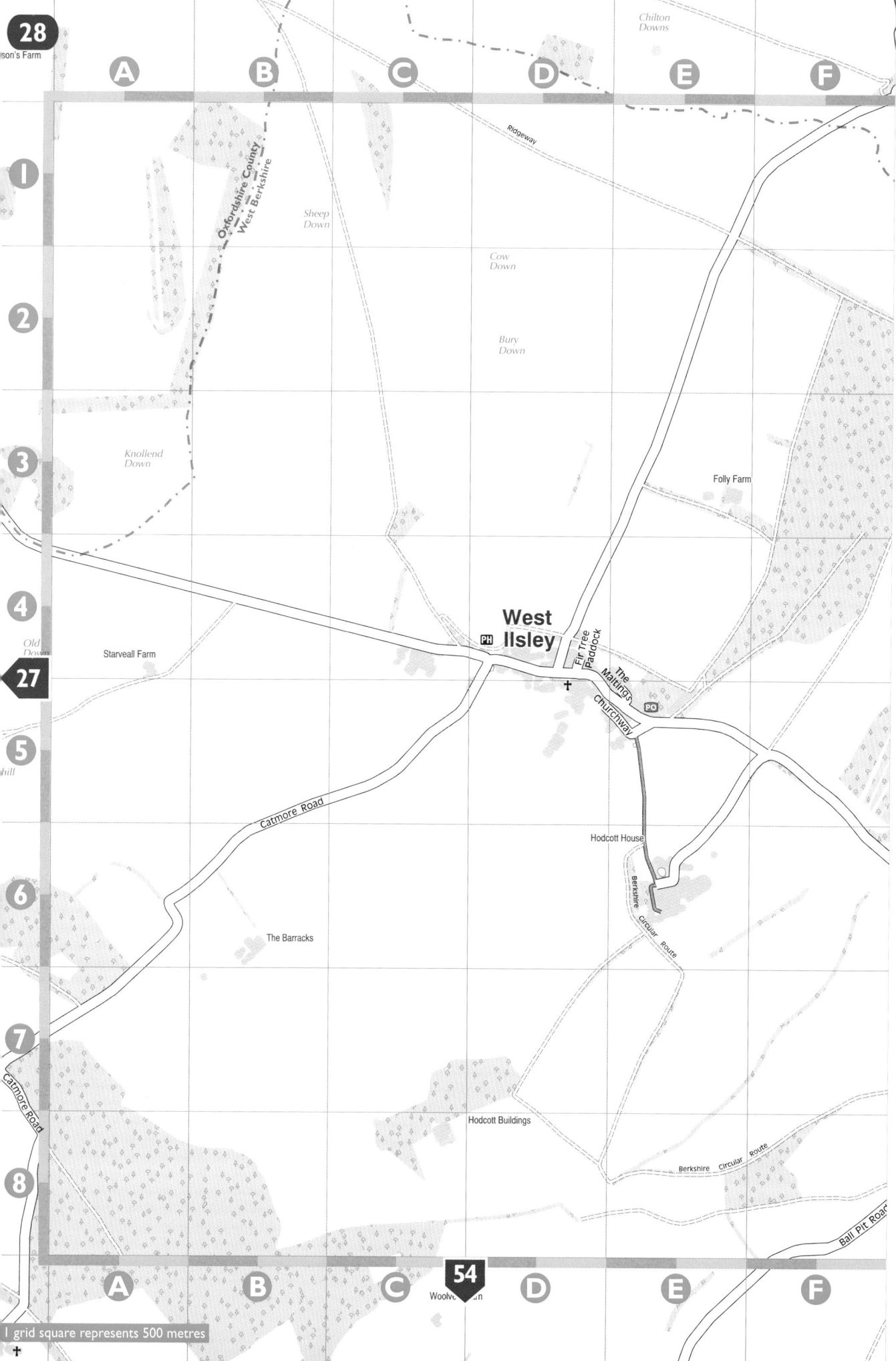

son's Farm

A　**B**　**C**　**D**　**E**　**F**

1

Ridgeway

Chilton
Downs

Oxfordshire County
West Berkshire

Sheep
Down

Cow
Down

2

Bury
Down

Folly Farm

3

Knollend
Down

Old
Down

27

4

Starveall Farm

**West
Ilsley**
PH

Fir Tree
Paddock

The
Maltings

PO

Churchway

5

hill

Catmore Road

Hodcott House

6

The Barracks

Berkshire

Circular　Route

7

Catmore Road

Hodcott Buildings

Berkshire　Circular　Route

8

Ball Pit Road

A　**B**　**C**　**54**　**D**　**E**　**F**

Woolve....n

1 grid square represents 500 metres

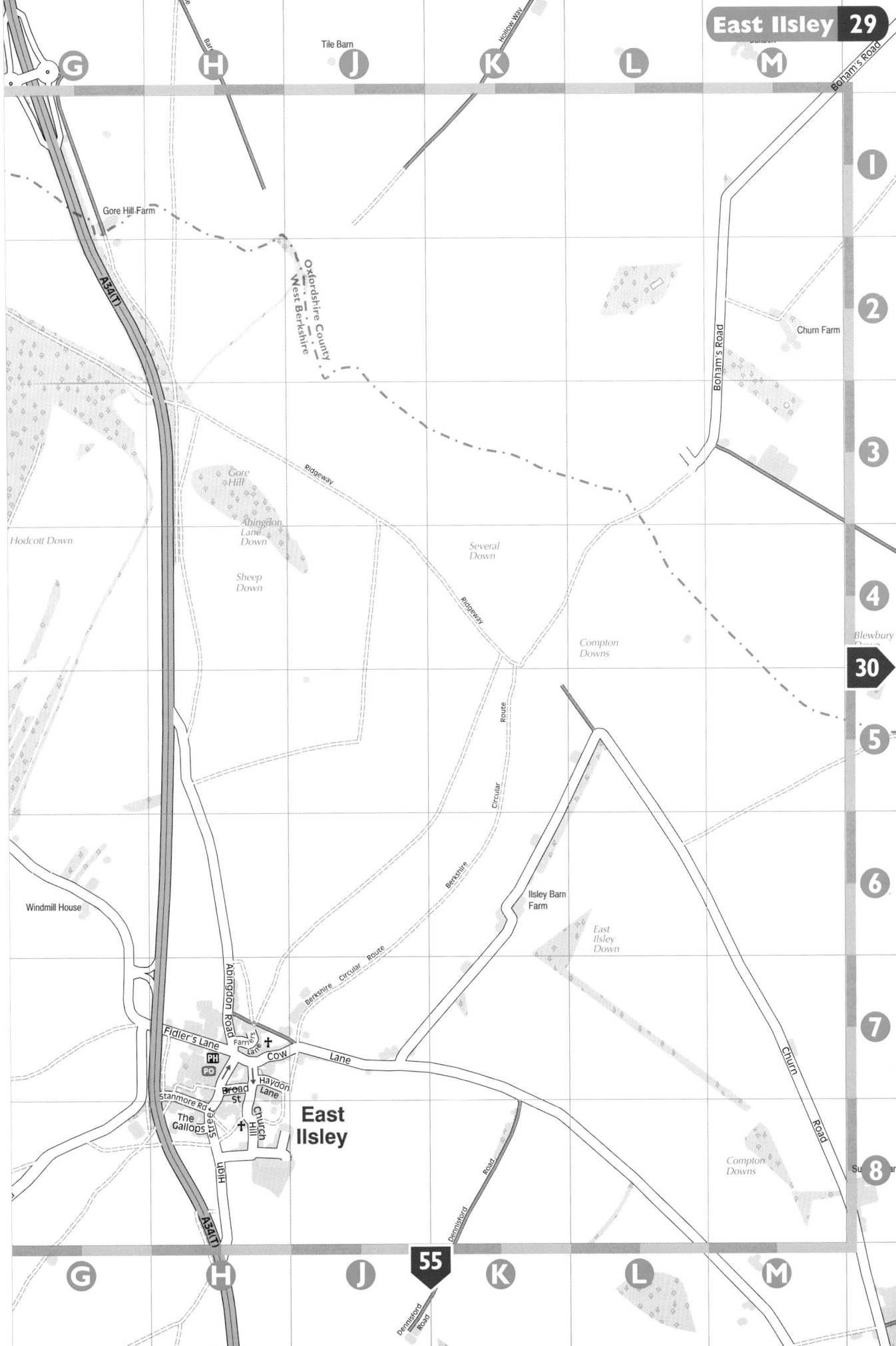

G   H   J   K   L   M

Bonam's Road

I

Tile Barn

Hollow Way

2

Gore Hill Farm

Churn Farm

Oxfordshire County
West Berkshire

3

A34(T)

Gore
Hill

Ridgeway

Hodcott Down

Abingdon
Lane
Down

Several
Down

4

Sheep
Down

Ridgeway

Blewbury
Down

Compton
Downs

30

5

Circular   Route

Berkshire

6

Ilsley Barn
Farm

Windmill House

East
Ilsley
Down

Churn   Road

7

Berkshire   Circular   Route

Abingdon Road

Fidler's Lane

Farm
Lane

PH
PO

Cow   Lane

Broad
St

Haydon
Lane

Stanmore Rd

Street

Dennisford   Road

The
Gallops

Church Hill

Compton
Downs

High

**East
Ilsley**

8

A34(T)

Dennisford   Road

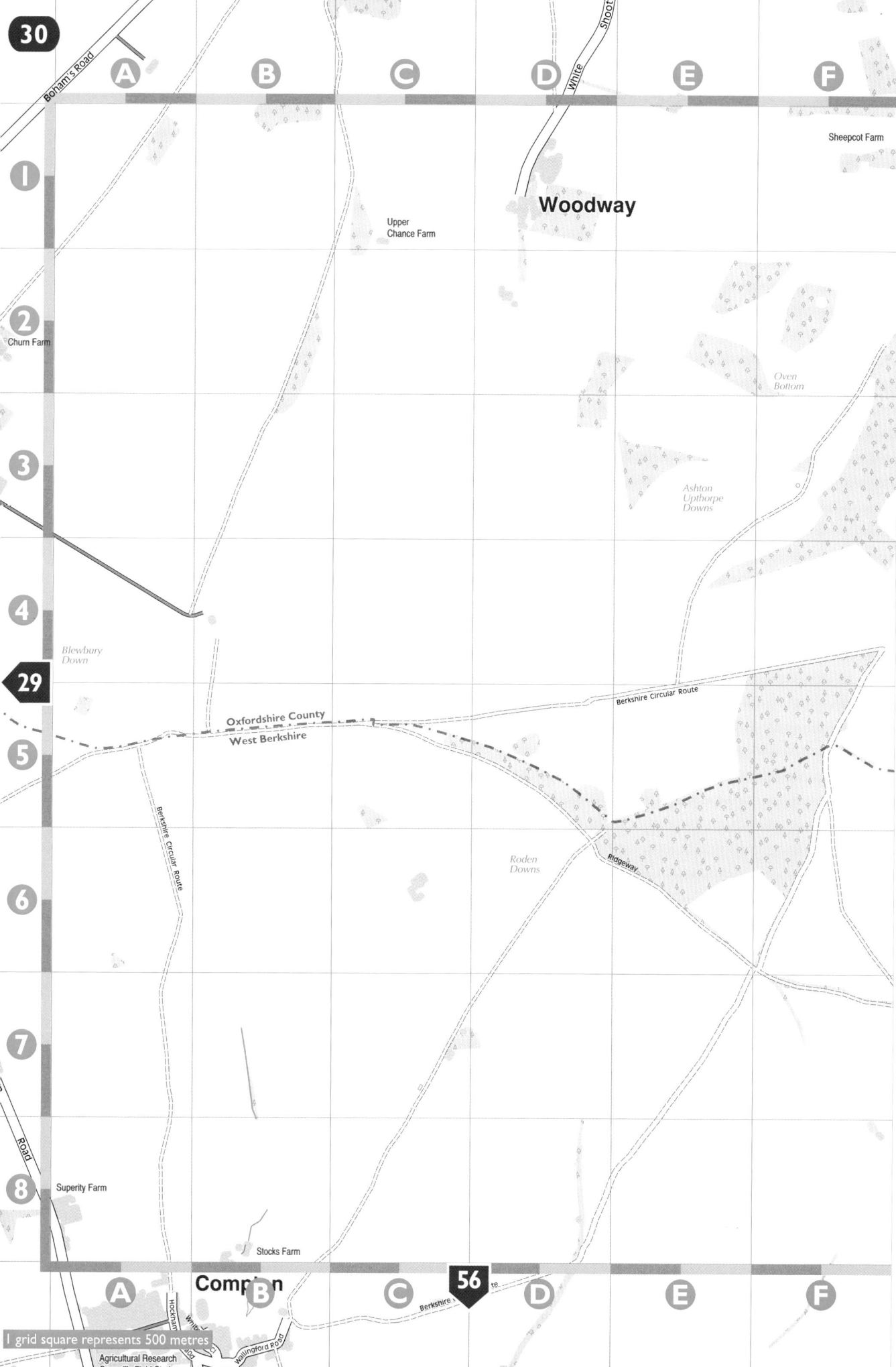

A B C D E F

Sheepcot Farm

1

Woodway

Upper
Chance Farm

2

Churn Farm

Oven
Bottom

3

Ashton
Upthorpe
Downs

4

Blewbury
Down

29

Berkshire Circular Route

Oxfordshire County

West Berkshire

5

Berkshire Circular Route

Roden
Downs

Ridgeway

6

7

8

Superity Farm

Stocks Farm

A B C D E F

Compton

56

Berkshire

Agricultural Research

1 grid square represents 500 metres

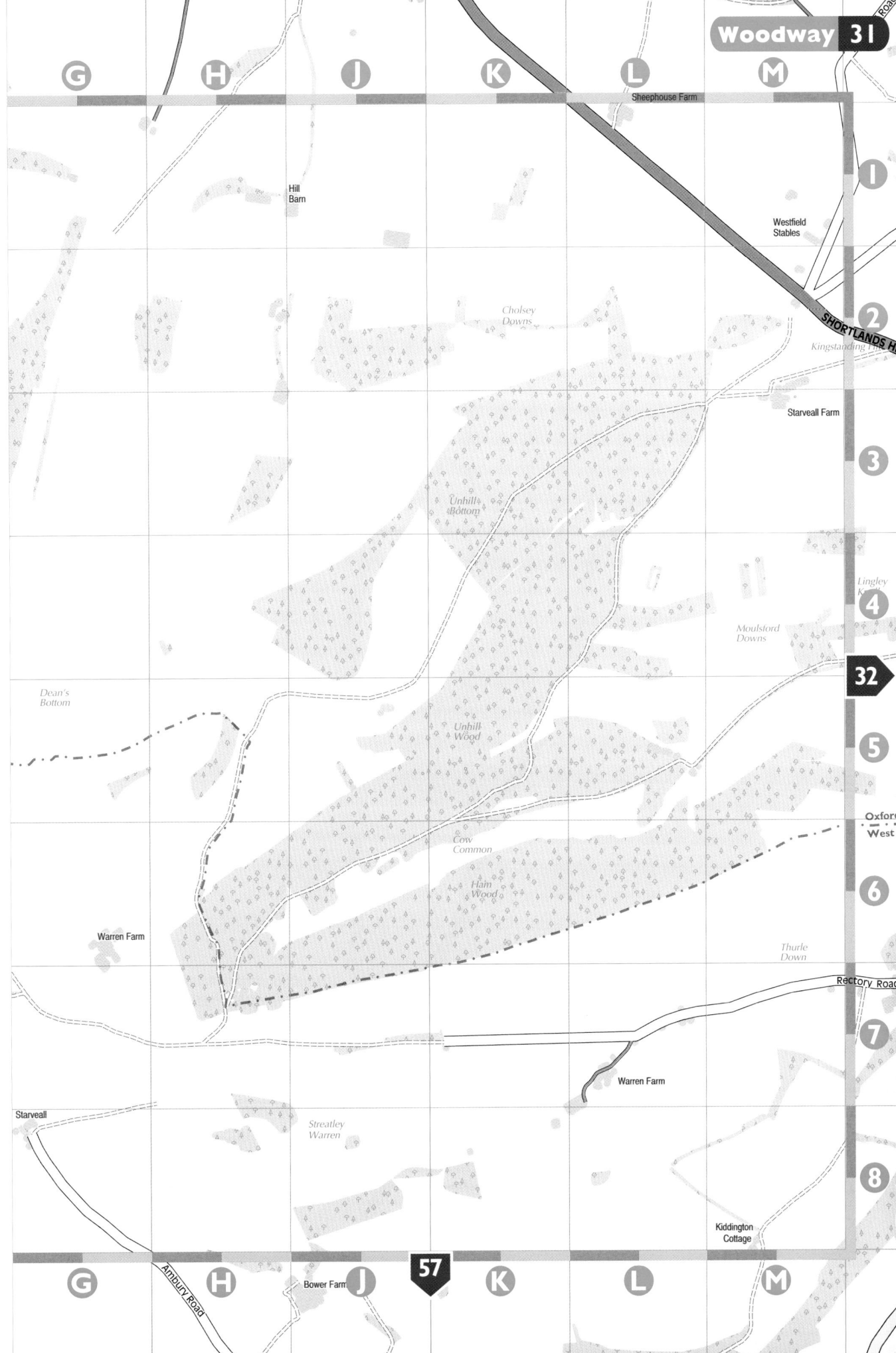

G   H   J   K   L   M

Sheephouse Farm

Hill
Barn

Westfield
Stables

SHORTLANDS HI

Cholsey
Downs

Kingstanding

Starveall Farm

Unhill
Bottom

Lingley
K

Moulsford
Downs

Dean's
Bottom

32

Unhill
Wood

5

Oxford
West

Cow
Common

Ham
Wood

6

Warren Farm

Thurle
Down

Rectory Road

7

Warren Farm

Starveall

Streatley
Warren

8

Kiddington
Cottage

G   H   J   K   L   M

Ambury Road

Bower Farm

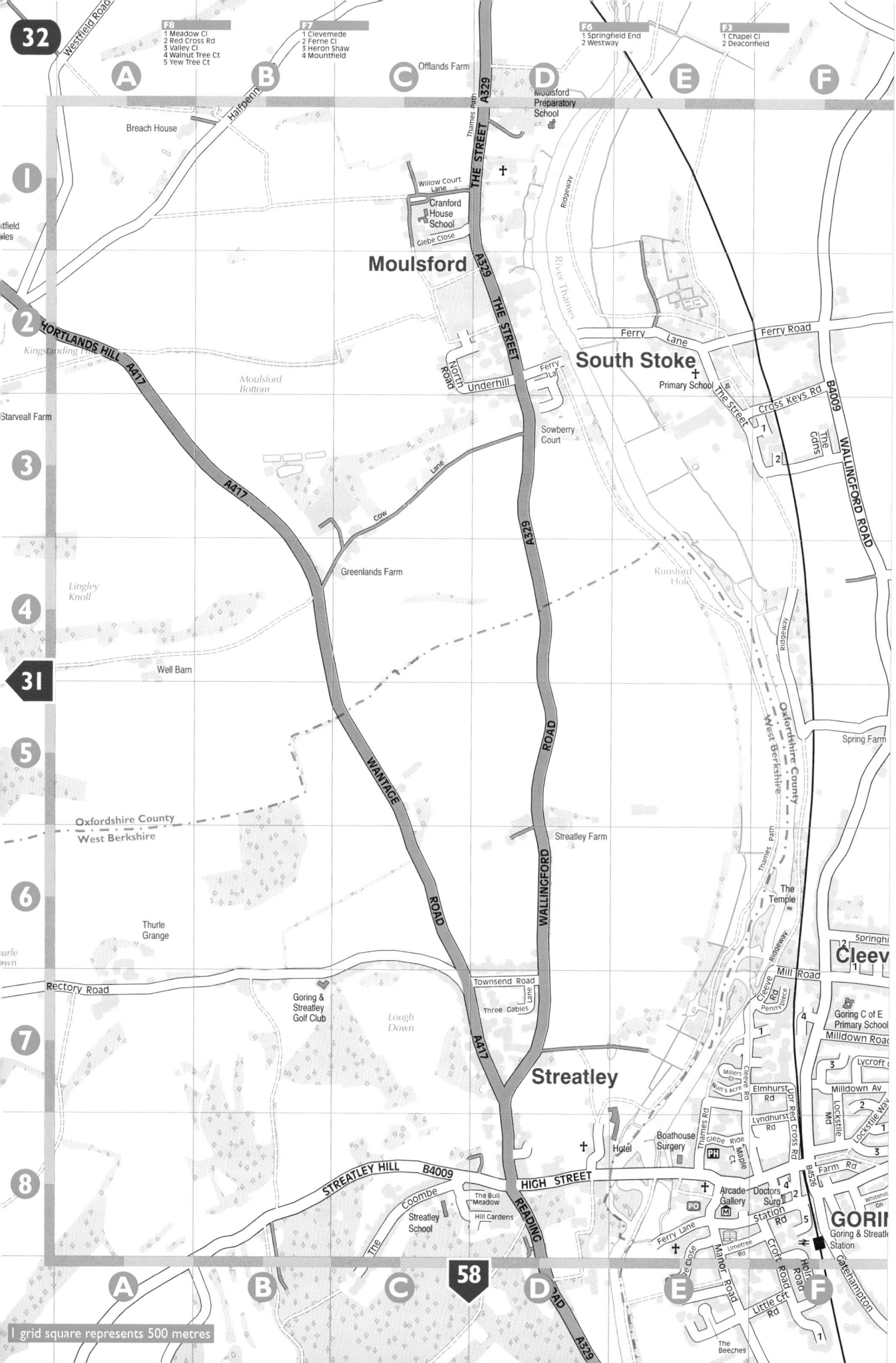

A   B   C   D   E   F

F8
1 Meadow Cl
2 Red Cross Rd
3 Valley Cl
4 Walnut Tree Ct
5 Yew Tree Ct

F7
1 Clevemede
2 Ferne Cl
3 Heron Shaw
4 Mountfield

F6
1 Springfield End
2 Westway

F3
1 Chapel Cl
2 Deaconfield

Westfield Road

Breach House

Halfpenn

Offlands Farm

The Street A329

Moulsford Preparatory School

I

Westfield ables

Willow Court Lane

Cranford House School

Glebe Close

Moulsford

†

Ridgeway

River Thames

2   SHORTLANDS HILL A417

Kingstanding Hill

Moulsford Bottom

North Road

Underhill

Ferry La

Ferry Lane

South Stoke

Ferry Road

Primary School

The Street

Cross Keys Rd

B4009

WALLINGFORD ROAD

Starveall Farm

3   A417

Cow Lane

Sowberry Court

The Gdns

1

2

Lingley Knoll

Greenlands Farm

Runsford Hole

4

Well Barn

A329 ROAD

Oxfordshire County

West Berkshire

Ridgeway

Oxfordshire County / West Berkshire

Spring Farm

31

5   WANTAGE

WALLINGFORD ROAD

Thames path

West Berkshire

Oxfordshire County / West Berkshire

Streatley Farm

The Temple

6   ROAD

Thurle Grange

Ridgeway

Mill Road

Springhi

Cleev

urle own

Rectory Road

Goring & Streatley Golf Club

Lough Down

Townsend Road

Three Gables

Maple Lane

Cleeve Rd

Penny Place

4

Goring C of E Primary School

Milldown Road

1

7   A417

Streatley

Nun's Acre

Millers Cl

Cleeve

Rd

Elmhurst Rd

Lyndhurst Rd

Thames Rd

Glebe Ride

Upr Red Cross Rd

3

Lycroft

Milldown Av

Locksti Rd

2

Lockstile Way

8   STREATLEY HILL B4009

The Coombe

Streatley School

Hill Gardens

The Bull Meadow

†

Hotel

READING ROAD

Boathouse Surgery

PH

†

Arcade Gallery

PO

M

Station Rd

Doctors Surg

Maple Ct

Farm Rd

B526

Whitehill Gn

GORIN

A   B   C   **58**   D   E   F

Ferry Lane

e Close

Manor Road

Limetree Rd

Croft Road

Holt Road

5

Goring & Streatley Station

Little Crt Rd

Catehampton

The Beeches

A329

G H J K L M

Watch Folly

Swan's Way

Swan's Way

Braziers Park

1

Woodcote Road

Icknield Farm

Ivol Barn

Ouseley Barn

2

RED LANE

A4074

3

South Stoke Road

Upper Cadley's

Dea Wood

4

Grove Farm

South Stoke Road

34

Broad Street Farm

5

Beech Lane

Beech Farm

Beech Lane

6

Icknield Road

Wroxhills Wood

Elmorepark Wood

Icknield Pl

PO

Elvendon

Road

Summerfield Rd

Cleeve Down

Battle Road

Elvendon Lan

7

Fairfield Rd

Elvendon Priory

Park Wood

ROAD

B4526

READING

Burntwood

8

NG

ey

59

Flint Ho

G H J K L M

Road

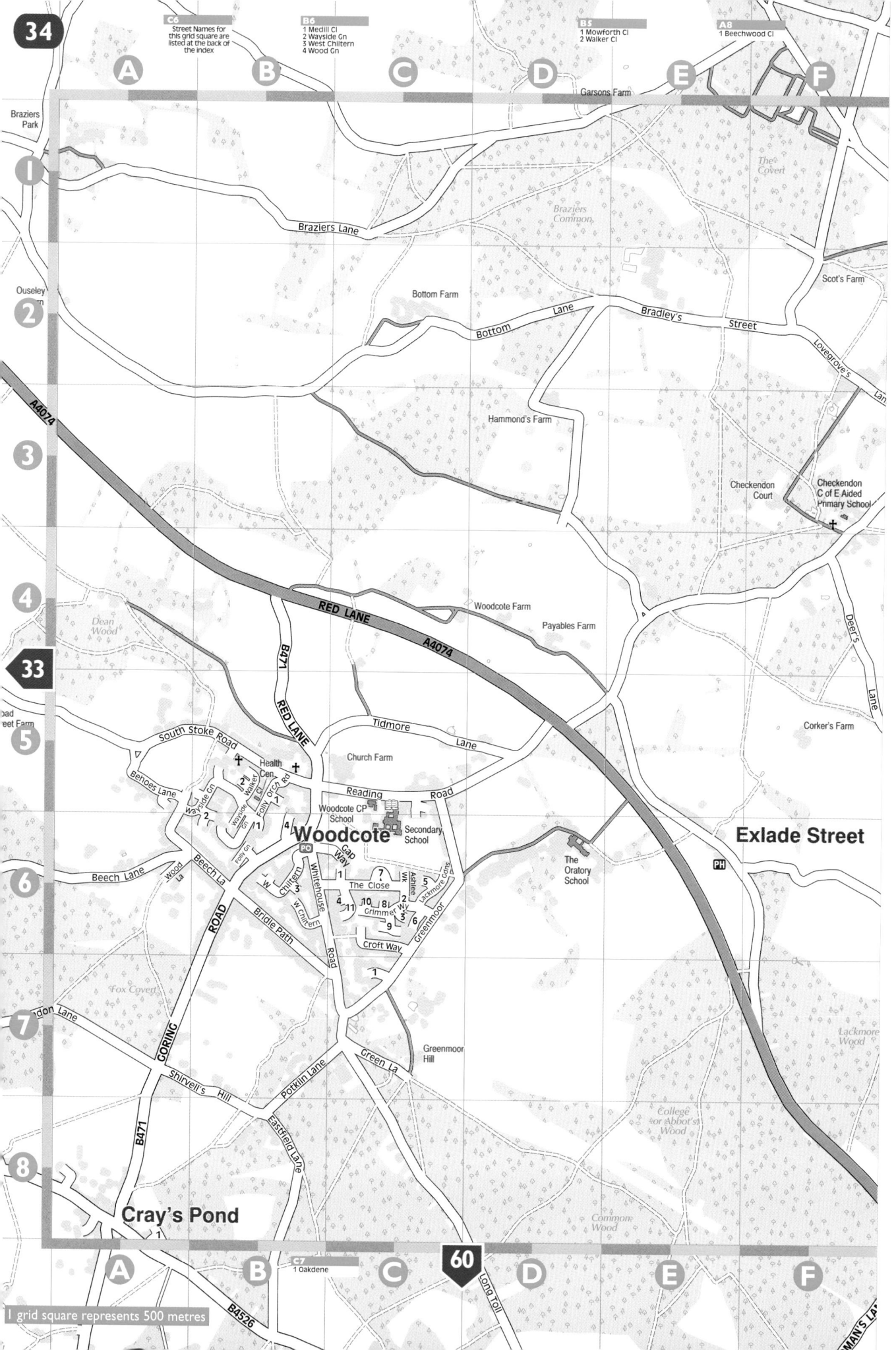

C6
Street Names for
this grid square are
listed at the back of
the index

A   B   C   D   E   F

1

Braziers
Park

The
Covert

Braziers Lane

Braziers
Common

Scot's Farm

2

Ouseley
n

Bottom Farm

Bottom   Lane

Bradley's   Street

Lovegrove's   La

3

A4074

Hammond's Farm

Checkendon
Court

Checkendon
C of E Aided
Primary School

4

Dean
Wood

RED LANE

B471

Woodcote Farm

A4074

Payables Farm

Deer's   Lane

33

5

oad
eet Farm

South Stoke Road

RED LANE

Tidmore   Lane

Church Farm

Corker's Farm

Health
Cen.

Behoes Lane

Wayside Gn

Walker Cl

Folly Orcd Rd

Reading   Road

Woodcote CP
School

Secondary
School

The
Oratory
School

Exlade Street

PH

6

Beech Lane

Wood La

Beech La

Woodcote

PO

Gap Way

Chiltern

Whitehouse

W

The Close

Grimmer

Greenmoor

Ashlee

Lackmore Gdns

Croft Way

W Chiltern

Road

Bridle Path

GORING   ROAD

7

don Lane

Fox Covert

Greenmoor
Hill

Green La

Lackmore
Wood

Shirvell's   Hill

Potklin Lane

College
or Abbot's
Wood

8

B471

Eastfield Lane

Cray's Pond

Common
Wood

A   B   C   D   E   F

B4526

Long Toll

MAN'S LA

1 grid square represents 500 metres

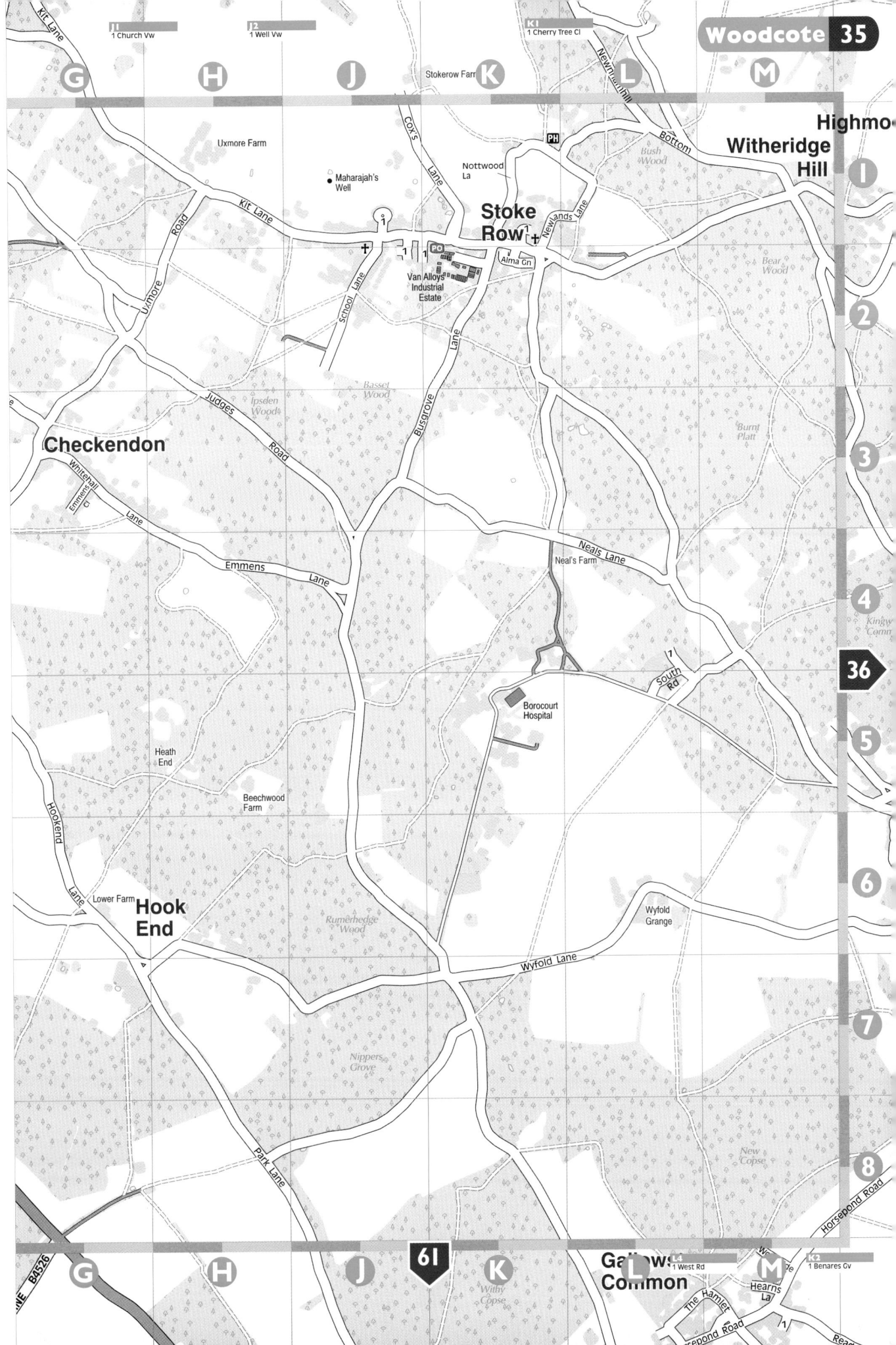

G   H   J   Stokerow Farm   K   New Hill   L   M

Highmo

Witheridge Hill

Uxmore Farm

Bottom

Bush Wood

1

Nottwood La

Maharajah's Well

Cox's Lane

Stoke Row +

Bear Wood

Kit Lane

Newlands Lane

PH

PO

Alma Gn

1

Uxmore Road

School Lane

Van Alloys Industrial Estate

2

Busgrove Lane

Basset Wood

Ipsden Wood

Burnt Platt

Judges Road

3

Checkendon

Neals Lane

Neal's Farm

4

Whitehall Lane

Emmens Cl

Kingw Comn

Emmens Lane

36

South Rd

Borocourt Hospital

5

Heath End

Beechwood Farm

6

Hookend Lane

Lower Farm

Hook End

Wyfold Grange

Rumerhedge Wood

Wyfold Lane

7

Nippers Grove

New Copse

Horsepond Road

8

Park Lane

B4526

61

Gallows Common

The Hamlet

Hearns La

G   H   J   K   L   M

Withy Copse

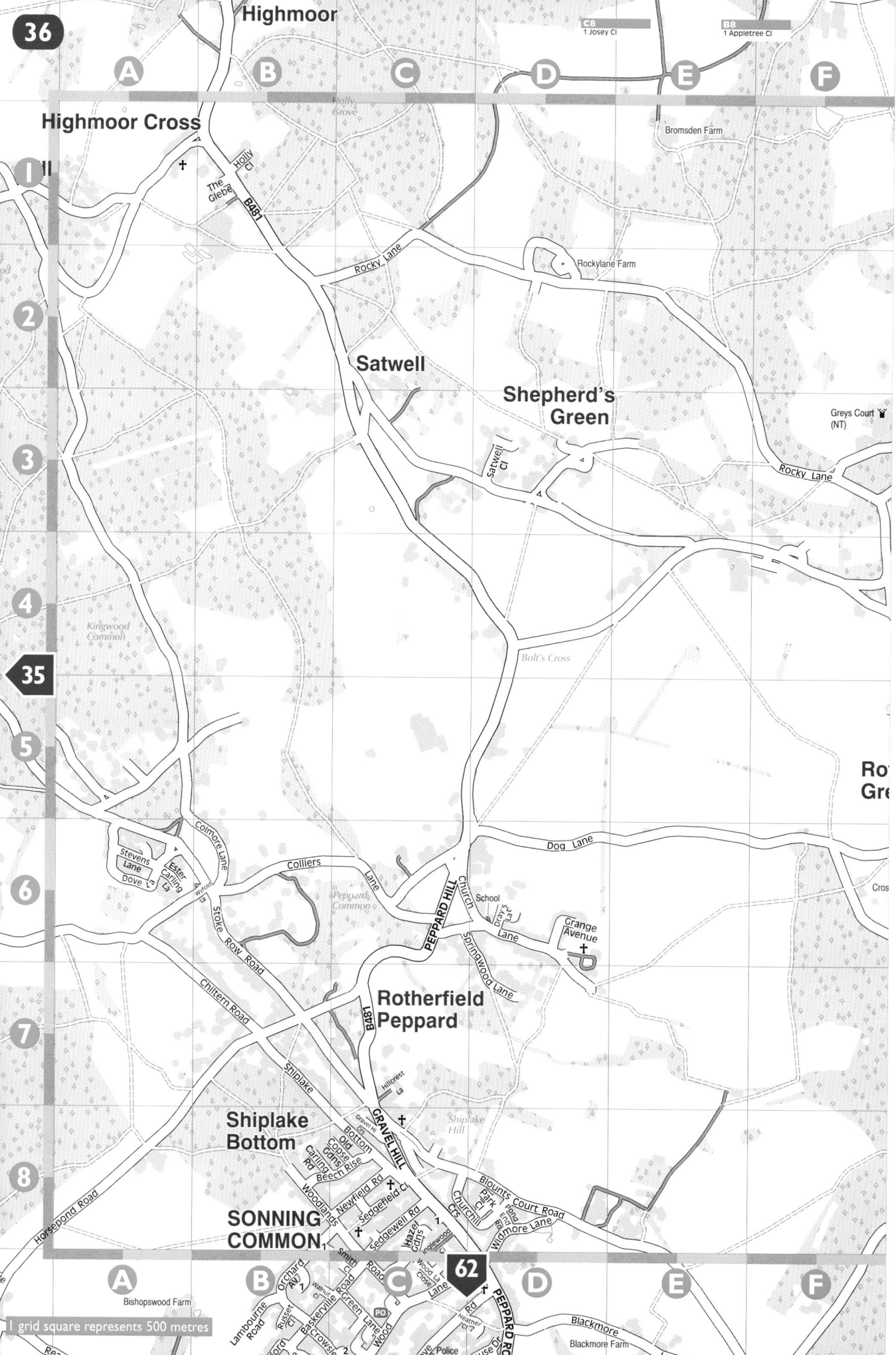

Lower Assendon

Broadplat

Greys Green

etherfield
eys

Harpsden
Bottom

Mays
Green

Labels on map:

Bix
Manor Farm
Brawns House
Lawrence's Farm
Lambridge Wood
New Farm
Lower Hernes
Badgemore House
Lambridge Lane
Lambridge Wood Road
Barn La
Fair Mile
The Grove
Oxfordshire Way
The Mou
Clements
Luker
Bowling Cl
Crisp
Cooper Rd
Simmons Road
Aven
Badgemore CP School
HOP
Townlands Hospital
Be
The
The West
Pra
Park's
Pack And Prime La
Ancastle
Gr
The Henley College
Paradise Road
Leaver Rd
Tilebarn Cl
Deanfield
Harcourt Cl
Haywards Cl
Sacred H
RC Scho
St Anne's Rd
Church Cl
Hernes
Hernes Estate
Elizabeth Close
St Mary's Cl
Elizabeth Cl
Two Tree Ln
Chiltern Cl
Valley Road
Nichola's Road
Gainsborough Crs
Gainsborough Rd
Gainsborough Hl
Greys Rd
Knappe Cl
Gravett Cl
Pendleton
Bassett
Sherwood
Greys Road
Highlands Lane
Chalcraft Cl
Primary School
Coldharbour Cl
Auton Pl
Green La
Cowfields Farm
Makins Road
Lovell Cl
Gillotts Cl
Wootten
St Katherine's Rd
Blandy Rd
slanes
Highlands Farm
Henley District Indoor Sports Centre
Gillotts School
Upper House Farm
Kings Farm Lane
Devil's Hill
Crowsley Park
Old Pla
Gillott's Lane
Chalk Hill
Hunt's Farm
White Hill
Perseverance Hill

PH

A4130
Bix Hill
Great Hill
Henley Park

63
38

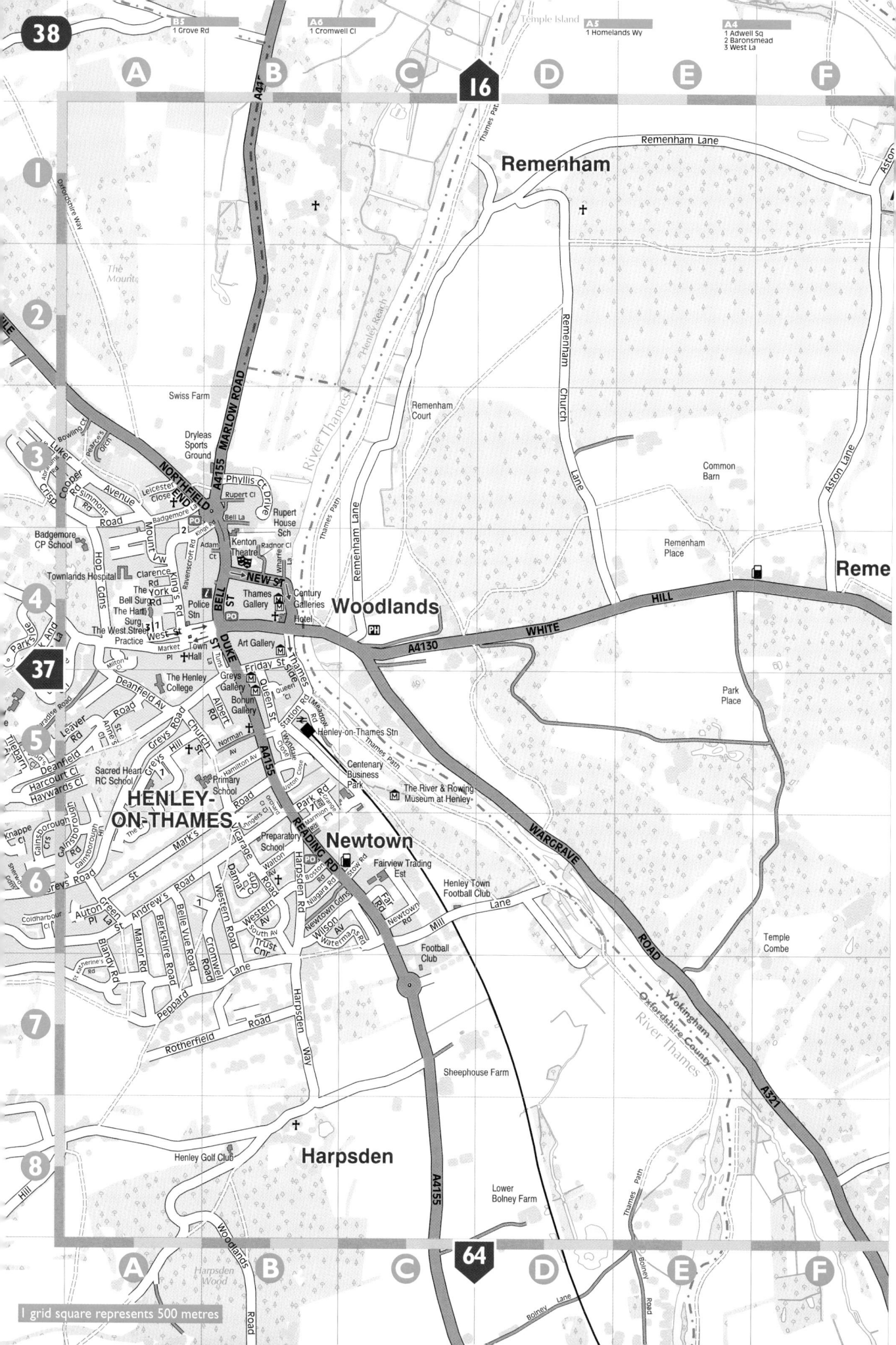

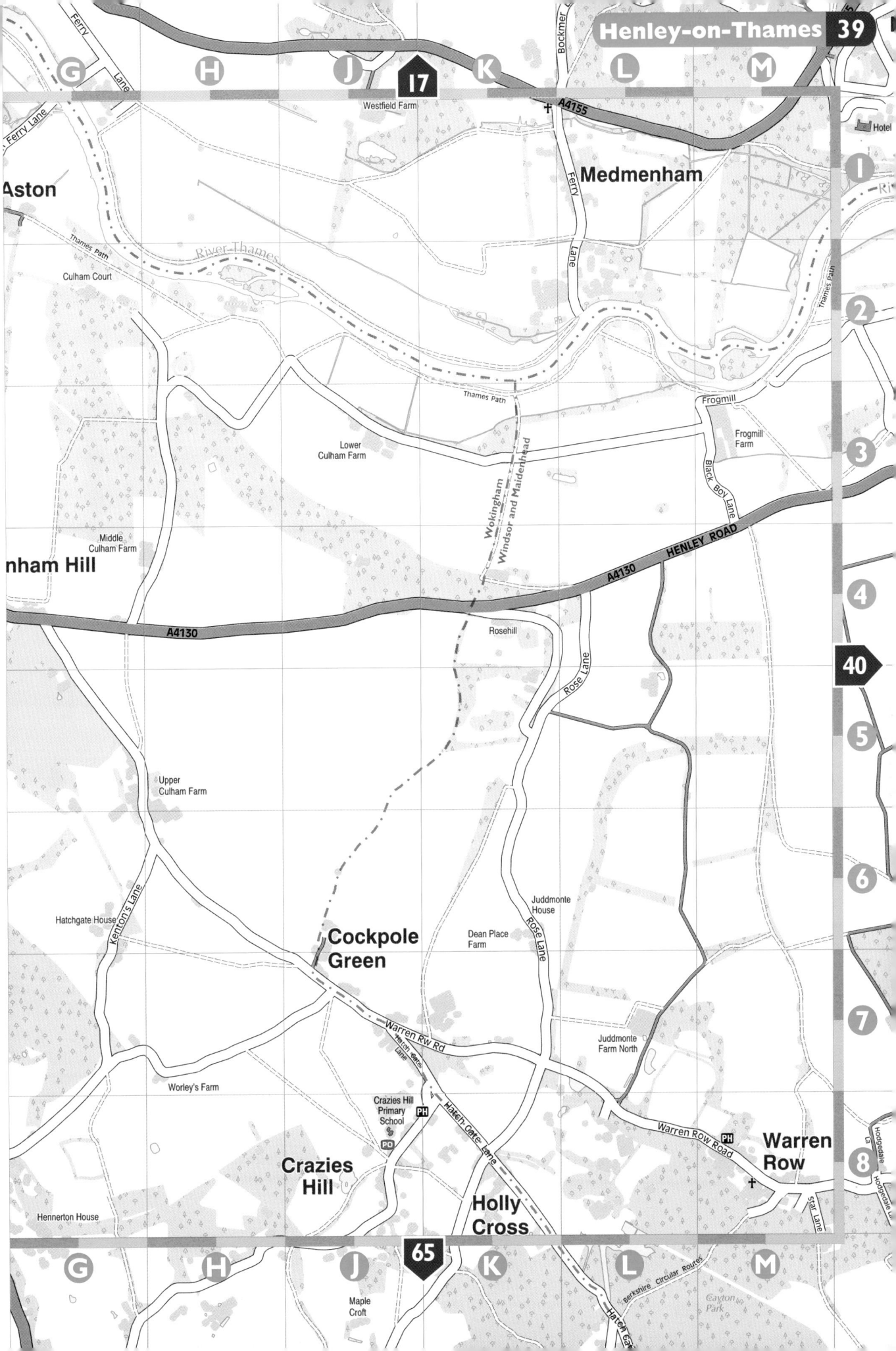

G H J **17** K L M

Westfield Farm

† A4155

Medmenham

Ferry Lane

Bockmer

Hotel

I

Aston

Thames Path

Culham Court

River Thames

2

Thames Path

Frogmill

Frogmill Farm

3

Lower Culham Farm

Black Boy Lane

Wokingham Windsor and Maidenhead

Middle Culham Farm

HENLEY ROAD

nham Hill

A4130

Rosehill

4

A4130

Rose Lane

40

Upper Culham Farm

5

Kenton's Lane

Hatchgate House

6

Juddmonte House

Cockpole Green

Dean Place Farm

Rose Lane

Warren Rw Rd

7

Worley's Farm

Hatch Gate Lane

Juddmonte Farm North

Crazies Hill Primary School PH

Warren Row Road PH

Warren Row

PO

Hatch Gate Lane

†

8

Crazies Hill

Holly Cross

Hennerton House

Maple Croft

Berkshire Circular Routes

Cayton Park

Hoopdale

Star Lane

65

G H J **65** K L M

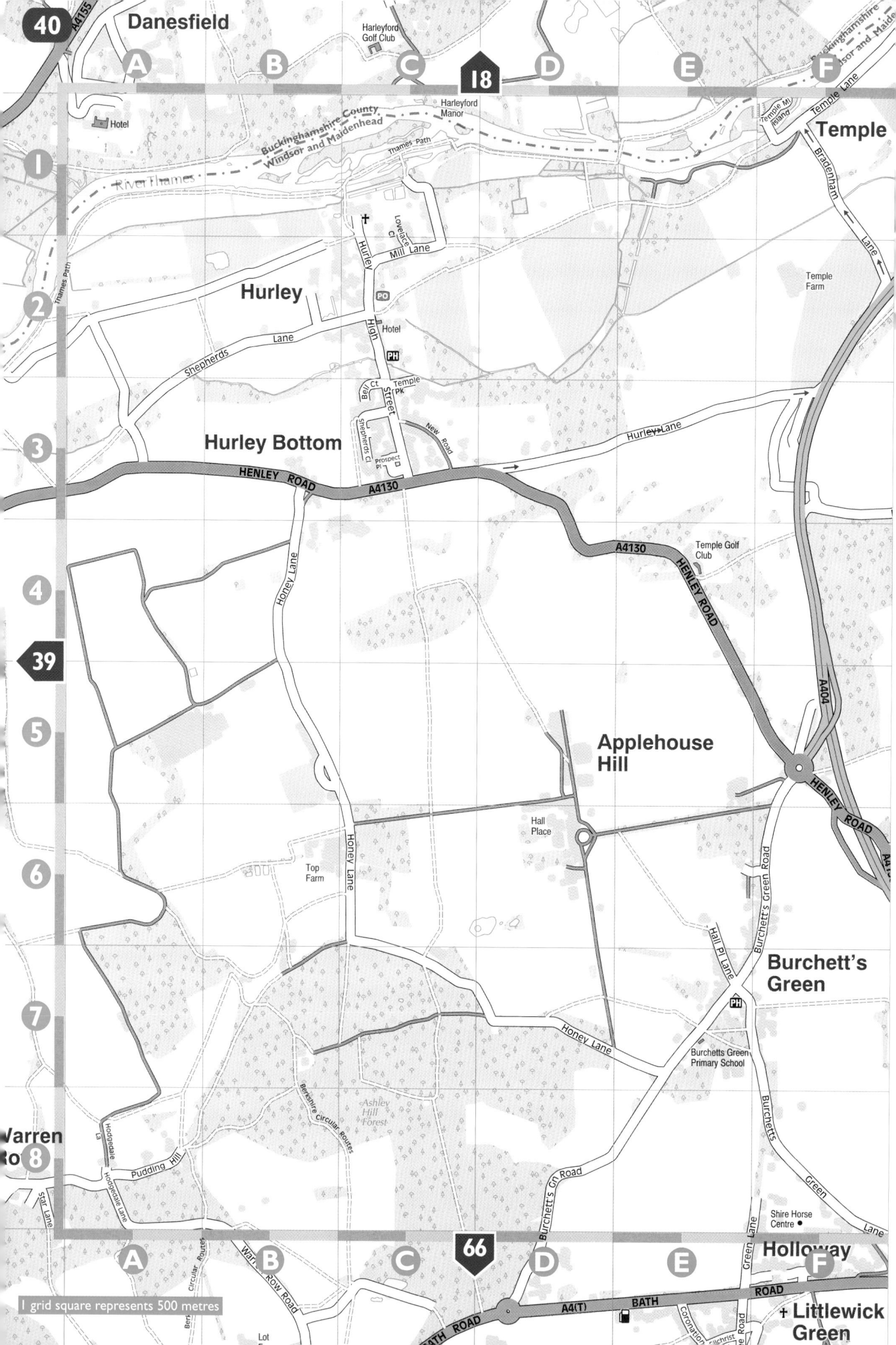

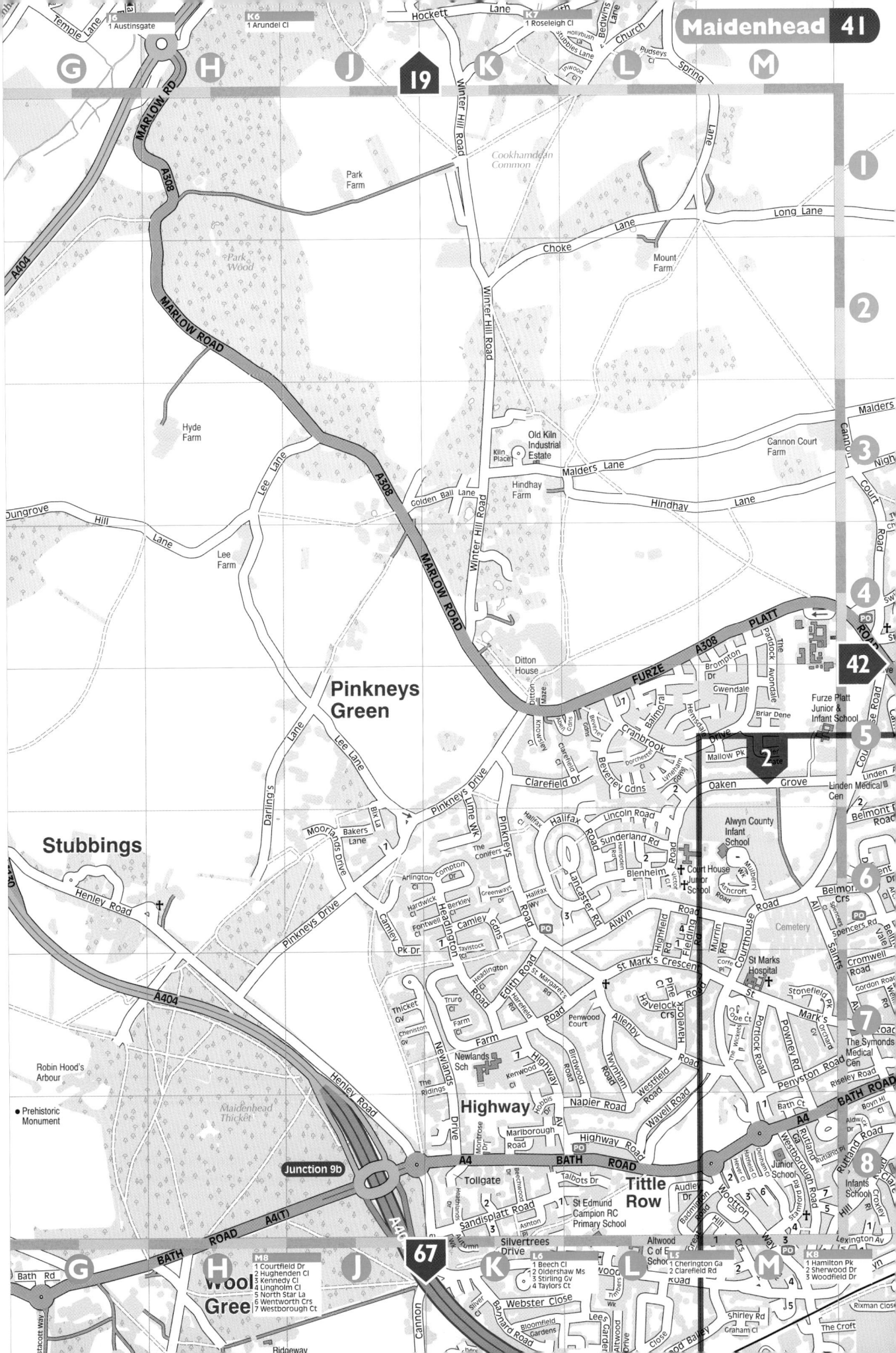

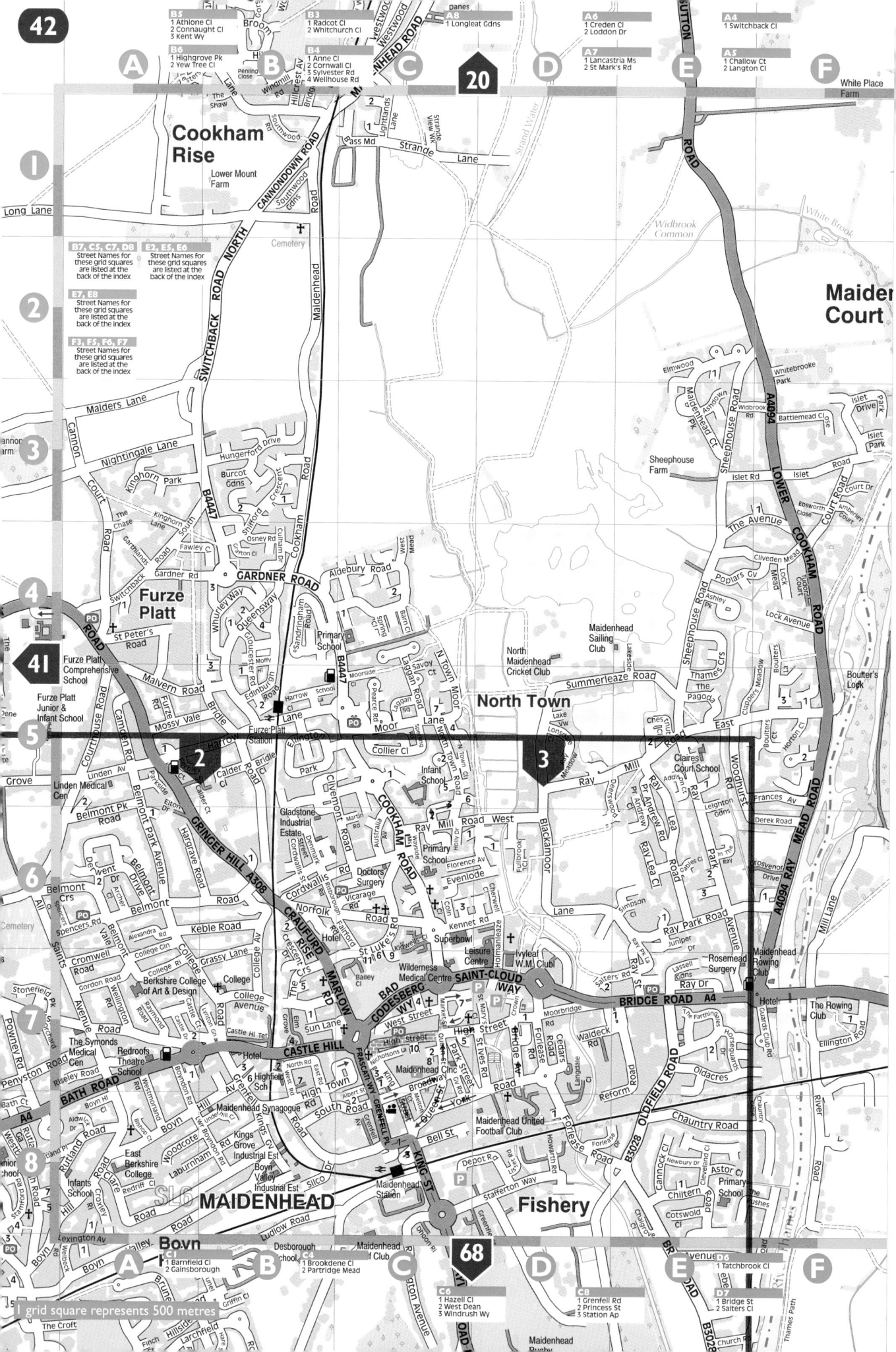

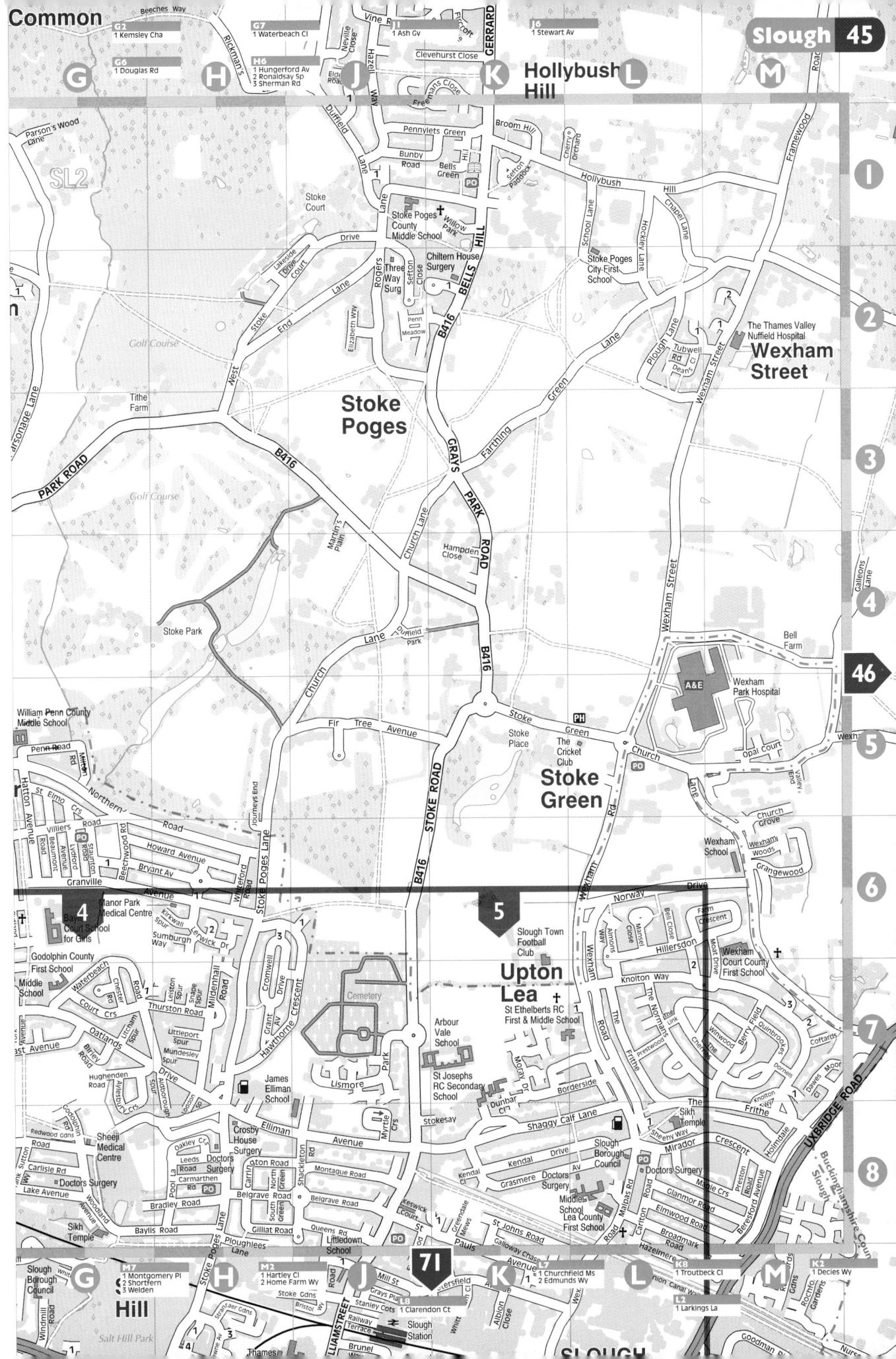

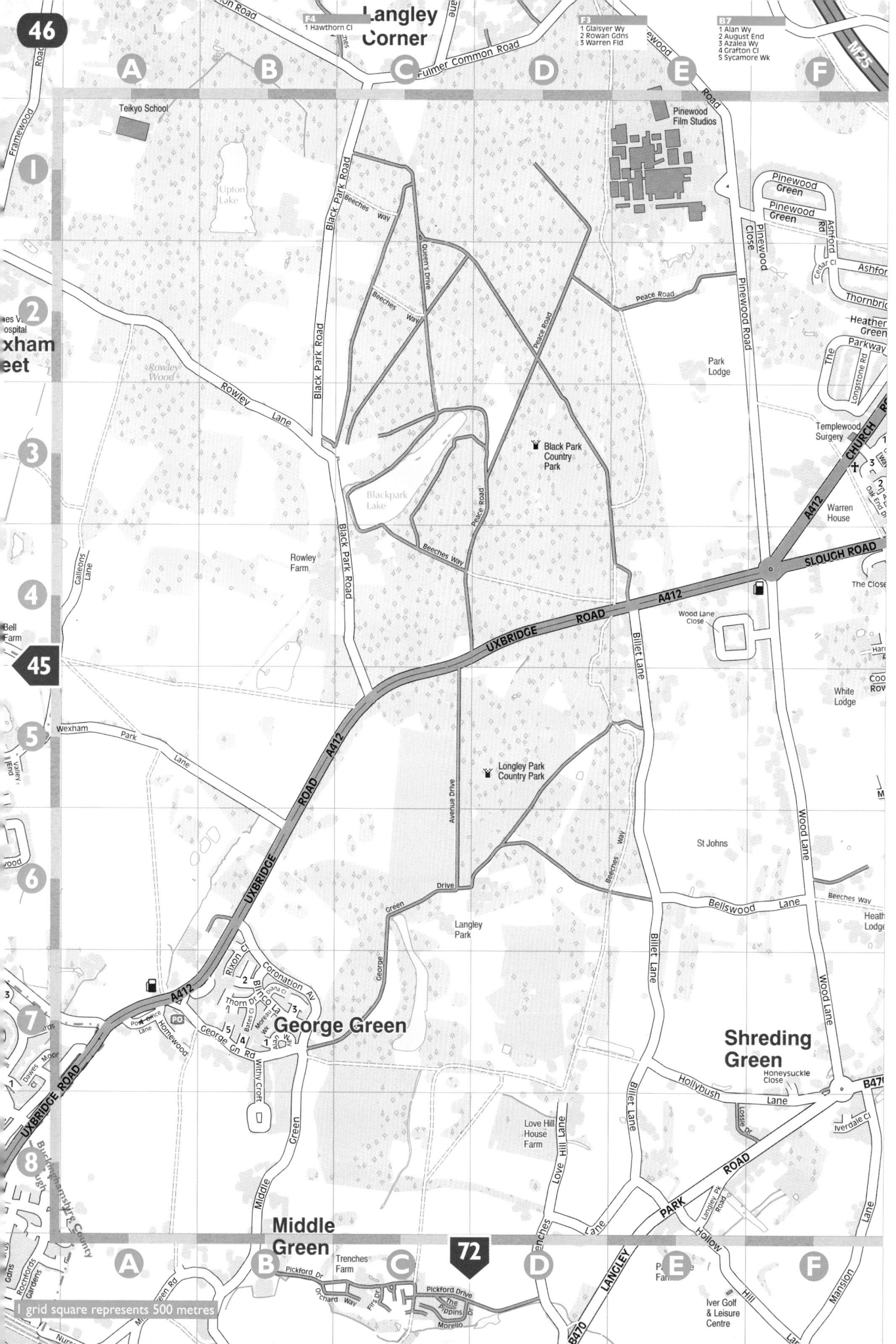

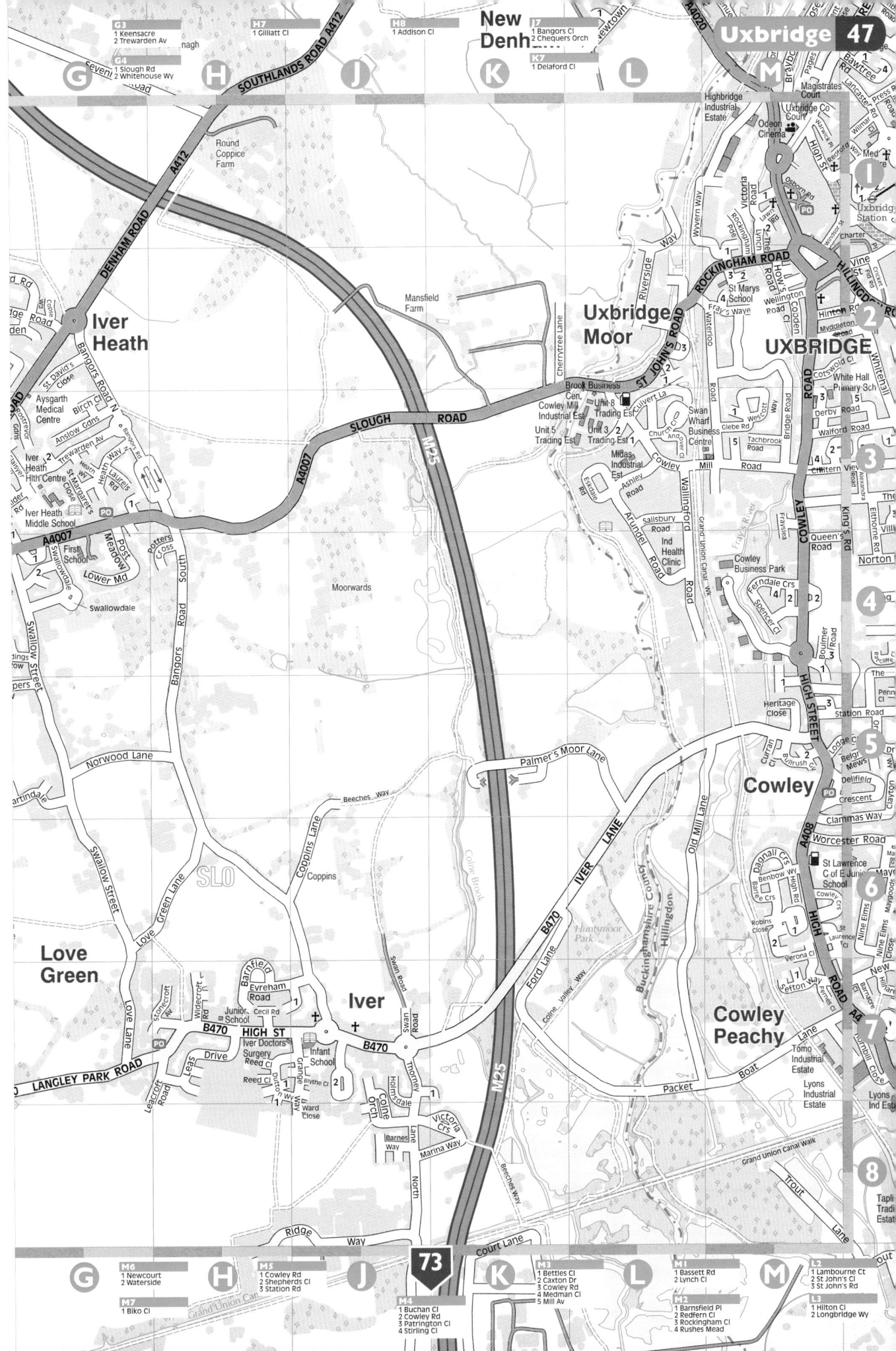

A B C **22** D E F

I

2

3

4

5

6

7

8

A B C **74** D E F

Botley Copse

Fognam Farm

B4000

Row Down

Near Down

West Berkshire
Wiltshire County

Down Farm

Bailey Hill Farm

M4

Baydon Hole

Farncombe Down

Downsmead

St Nicholas C of
Primary School

Finches Lane

Lodge Down

PO

Ermin Close

Manor Lane

Walronds Cl

Baydon

M4

Lodge Farm

Baydon Road

Platt Lane

enhills

M4

ze Farm

K3
1 Parsonage Pl

L3
1 Atherton Pl
2 The Broadway
3 Church Cl
4 The Granthams

L4
1 Beales Farm Rd

Newbarn Farm

Down

G

H

J

Upper Lamb rn

Street

High

B4000

23

K

Lambourn Valley Way

L

M

Sheed

I

1

2

3

4

50

5

6

7

8

Cemetery

Malt Shovel La

B4000

Hill

Drain

UPPER LAMBOURN ROAD

Lambourn Valley Way

The Park

Hill House Stables

Folly Road

Child St

Rockfel Road

Derby Cl

Crowle Rd

HUNGERFORD HILL

B4000

PARSONAGE

St Michael's

St La

PO

B4000 HIGH ST

Edwards Hill

Greenways

Sheep Fair Wy

The Classics

Lynch Wood

Northfields

North Farm

WANTAGE ROAD

B4001 WANTAGE ROAD

Sheepdrove Road

Essex Pl

Lynch La

Honey Hl

Coose Cn

Walker

Gwyns Piece

OXFORD STREET

Big Lane

Lambourn

Chapel La

Foxbury

Tubbs Farm

Newbury St

Mill Lane

Aintree

Station Rd

The Old Station Yd

Bockhampton

Lambourn

Lambourn C of E Primary School

The Lambourn Sports Club

The Lambourn Surg

southbank gdns

Woodbury

Newbury Rd

Francombes Field

Farncombe Farm

Farm Combe

aydon Road

Windmill Farm

Coppington Down

Boldstart Farm

White Shute

Thorn Copse

Kingwood House

Willis Farm

Fox Farm

Baydon Road

B4000

G

H

J

K

75

Lambourn Woodlands

L

M

M3
1 North Farm Cl

Membury Service Area

Foxbury Farm

24

College Farm

Sheepdrove Road

F8
1 Downlands

I

Sheepdrove

2

Drove Farm

Chestnut Lane

Eastbury
Down

Eastbury Grange

3

Poors'
Furze

Fair
View

4

Long

Hedge

Eastbury
Fields

49

Road

5

River Lambourn

6

Thornhill
Copse

Manor Farm

Downs
Cl

Lambourn Valley Way

7

Eastbury

Station Rd

Burford's

Rogers's La

Front

Straight

1

8

Westfield Farm

Back Street

Humphrey's La

Lane

I grid square represents 500 metres

G H J K L M

25

Dogkennel

South Fawley

Dogkennel La

Wellhill Road

Dogkennel Lane

Cranes Farm

Well Copse

Whatcombe

Pound's Farm

East Garston Down

Oakhedge Copse

52

Hasham Copse

Henley Farm

Lodge Copse

Trindledown Farm

Wantage Road

Buckham Hill

School Lane

East Garston

College Way

Trindledown Copse

Northfield Farm Industrial Est

River Lambo

Maidencourt Farm

1

2

3

4

5

6

7

8

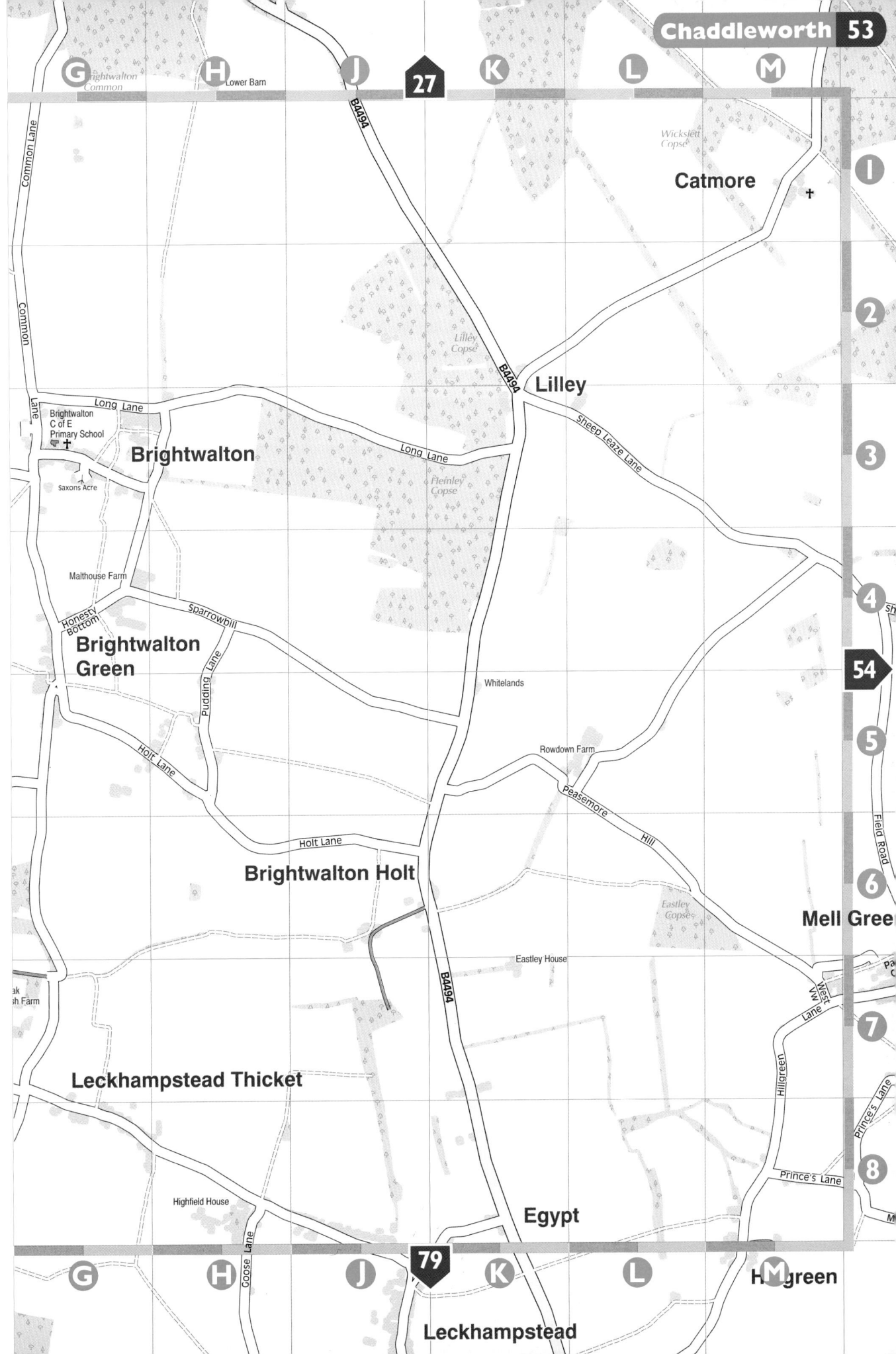

G H J 27 K L M

I

Wicksleet Copse

Catmore

Brightwalton Common

Lower Barn

B4494

2

Lilley Copse

B4494

Lilley

3

Long Lane

Sheep Leaze Lane

Brightwalton C of E Primary School

Brightwalton

Long Lane

Common Lane

Common Lane

Lane

Saxons Acre

Pleinley Copse

Malthouse Farm

4

54

Honesty Bottom

Sparrowbill

Brightwalton Green

Whitelands

5

Pudding Lane

Rowdown Farm

Peasemore Hill

Holt Lane

6

Mell Gree

Field Road

Holt Lane

Brightwalton Holt

Eastley Copse

Eastley House

West Vw Lane

7

B4494

Hillgreen

Leckhampstead Thicket

Prince's Lane

8

Highfield House

Goose Lane

Prince's Lane

Egypt

G H J 79 K L H M green

Leckhampstead

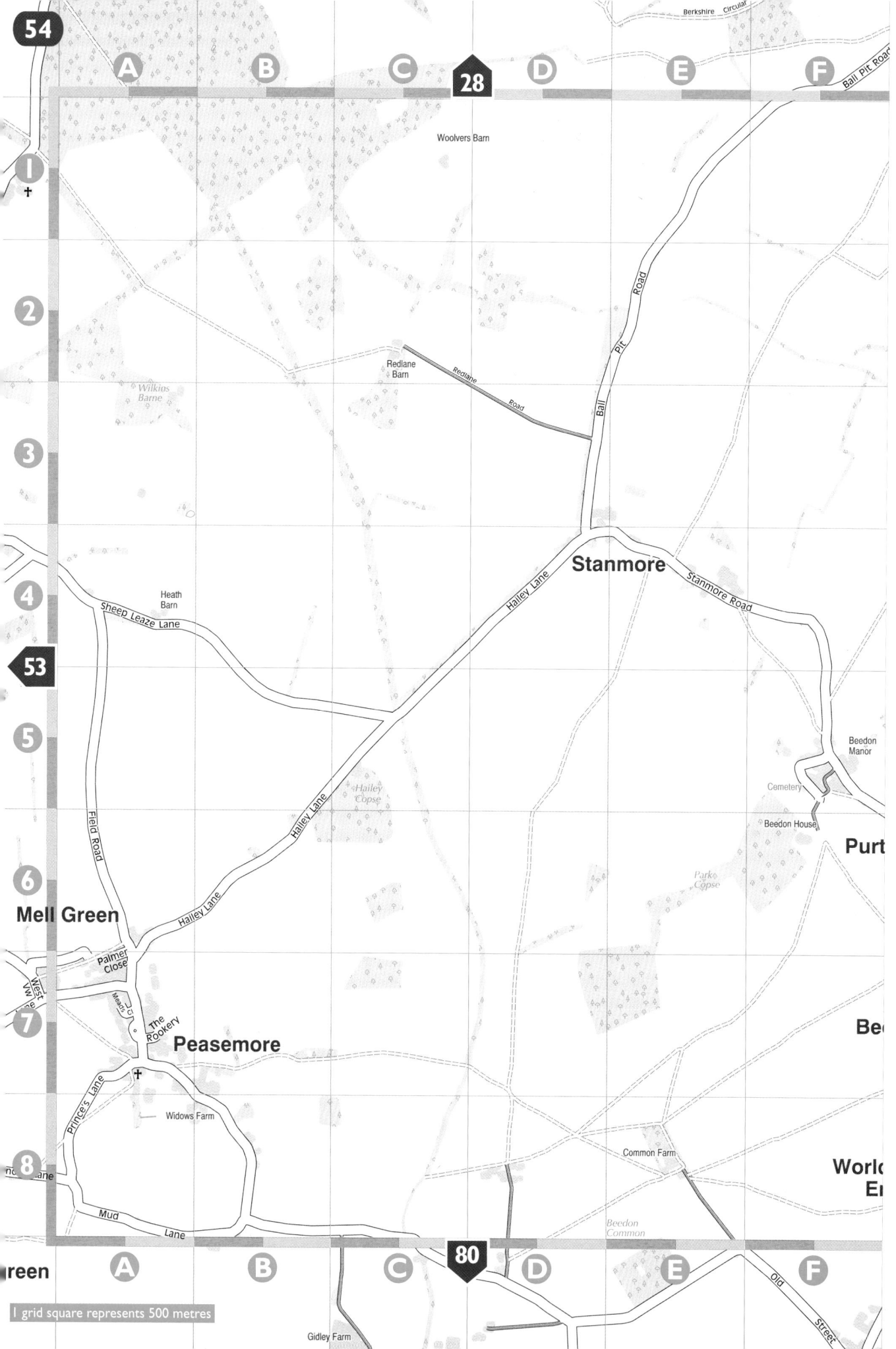

A B C **28** D E F Ball Pit Road

†

2

3

4

53

5

6

7

8

Woolvers Barn

Wilklos Barne

Redlane
Barn

Redlane

Road

Ball Pit Road

Berkshire Circular

Stanmore

Hailey Lane

Stanmore Road

Beedon
Manor

Cemetery

Beedon House

Purt

Heath
Barn

Sheep Leaze Lane

Hailey Lane

*Hailey
Copse*

Field Road

Hailey Lane

*Park
Copse*

Mell Green

Hailey Lane

Palmer
Close

West
Vie

Meals Cl

The
Rookery

Peasemore

Be

Princes Lane

†

Widows Farm

Wor
E

Common Farm

8

ne Lane

Mud

Lane

*Beedon
Common*

80

reen

A B C **80** D E F

Old Street

Gidley Farm

I grid square represents 500 metres

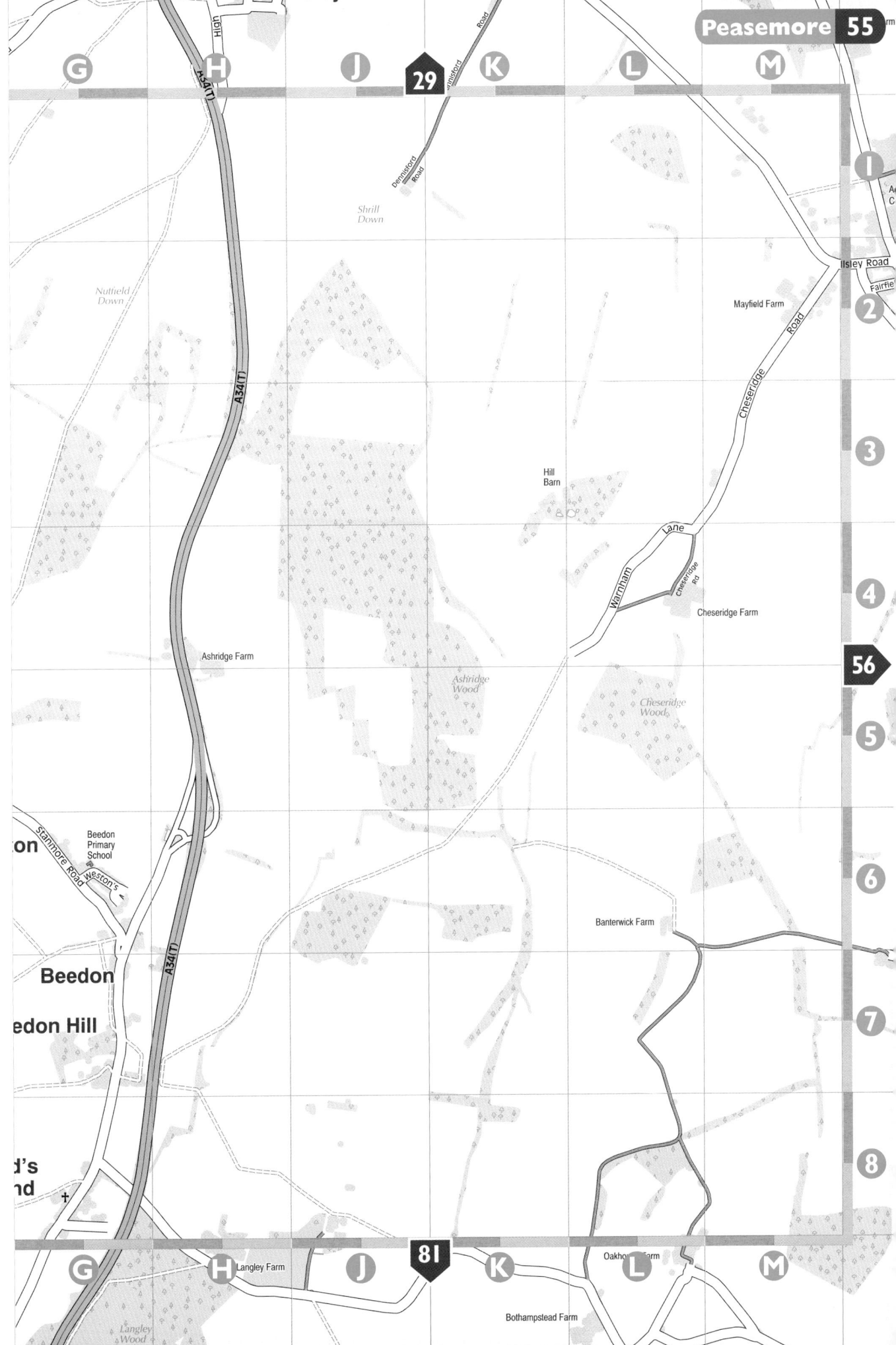

A   Stocks Farm   **B**   **C**   **30**   **D**   **E**   **F**

Berkshire Circular Route

Compton

I

Agricultural Research
Council's Field Station

Whitewalls Ct

Wallingford Road

Hockham Road

Meadow Crs

Horn St

Cheap St

Yew Tree Stables

2

Ilsley Road

High   Street

Fairfield

Westfields

Newbury Lane

Manor Crs

Gordon Crs

Burrell Road

School Road

Wilton Cl

PO

Shepherds Rise

The Downs School

Downlands
Sports Centre

Shepherds

Wt

Compton C of E
Primary School

Aldworth   Road

Downs   Road

Uplands
Stables

3

Shepherds
Hill

Coombe   Road

4

New Farm

Woodrows Farm

55

5

Cow
Down

Woodend Farm

Perborough
Castle

6

7

Milkhill Farm

Beech
Wood

8

Station Hill

**Hampstead
Norreys**

Water St

Scott La

A   **B**   The Cuttings   The   **C**   **82**   **D**   **E**   **F**

Newbury Hl

CHURCH ST

PO

Forge Hill

Beech Close

Hampstead Norreys
Primary School

Wyld Court
Rainforest

WYLD COURT HILL

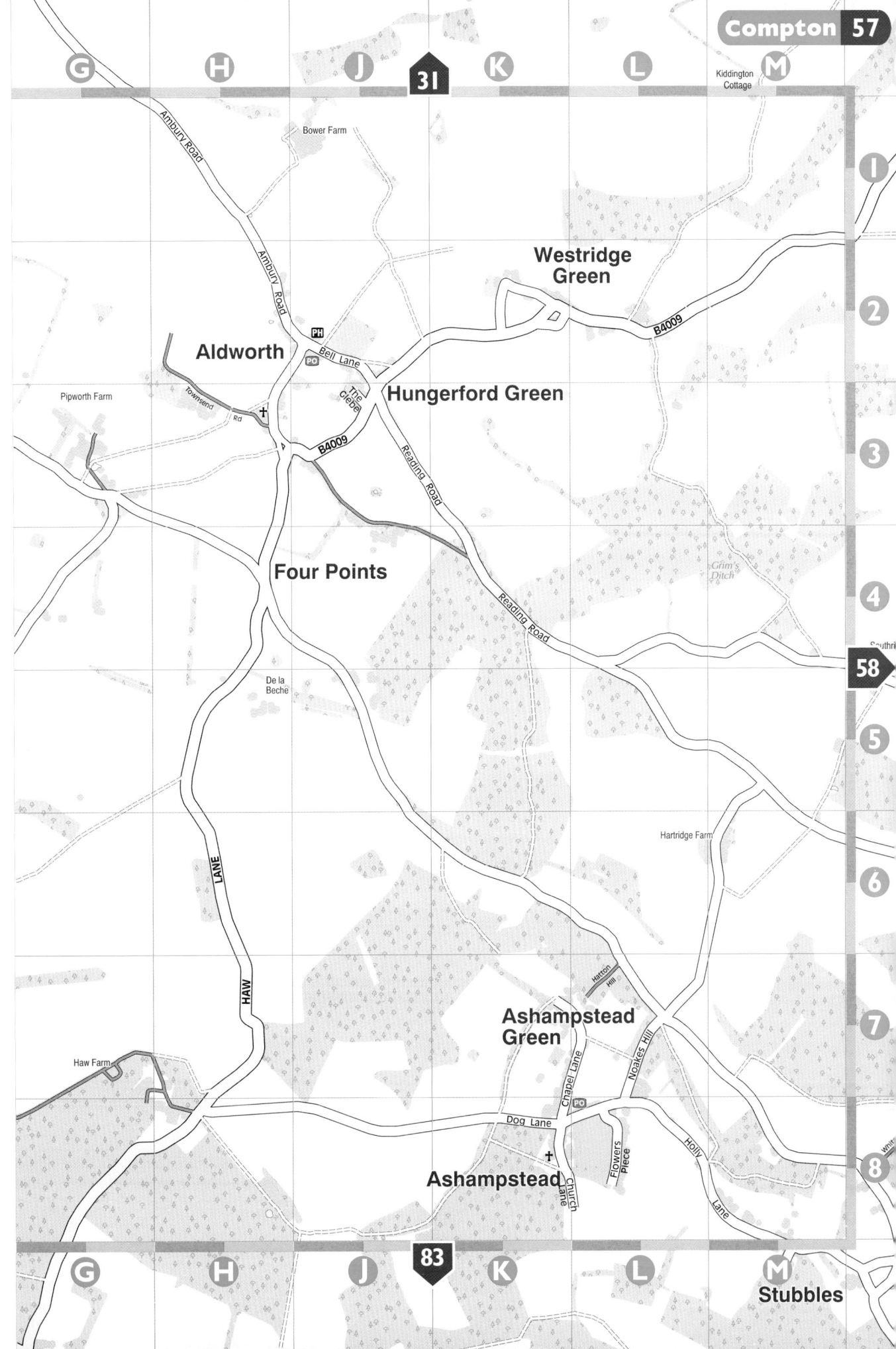

G H J **31** K L M

Kiddington
Cottage

I

Ambury Road

Bower Farm

2

Westridge
Green

B4009

Aldworth

PH

Bell Lane

PO

Pipworth Farm

Townsend

The Glebe

Hungerford Green

Rd

3

B4009

Reading Road

Four Points

Grim's
Ditch

4

Southri...

De la
Beche

58

5

Reading Road

Hartridge Farm

6

HAW LANE

Harton Hill

7

Haw Farm

**Ashampstead
Green**

Chapel Lane

Noakes Hill

PO

Holly Lane

Dog Lane

Flowers Piece

Ashampstead

Church Lane

Whit...

8

Stubbles

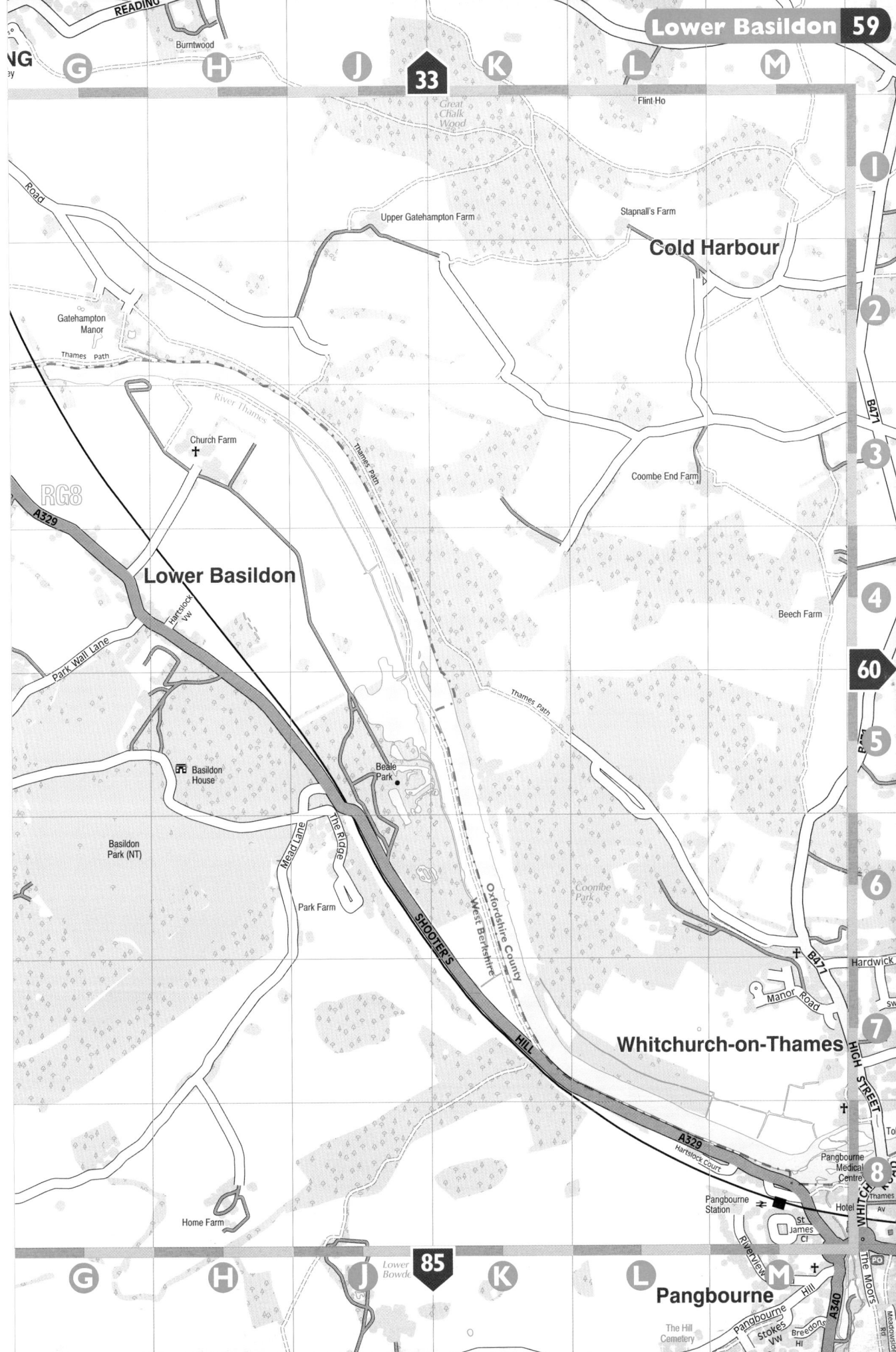

READING

G   H   J   33   K   L   M

I

2

3

4

60

5

6

7

8

Burntwood

Great Chalk Wood

Flint Ho

Upper Gatehampton Farm

Stapnall's Farm

Cold Harbour

Gatehampton Manor

Thames Path

River Thames

Church Farm

Coombe End Farm

RG8

A329

Lower Basildon

Hartslock Vw

Beech Farm

Park Wall Lane

Thames Path

Basildon House

Beale Park

Basildon Park (NT)

Mead Lane

The Ridge

Park Farm

SHOOTER'S

West Berkshire

Oxfordshire County

Coombe Park

B471

Hardwick

Manor Road

SW

Whitchurch-on-Thames

HILL

Home Farm

A329

Hartslock Court

Pangbourne Medical Centre

Thames Av

Hotel

WHITCHURCH

HIGH STREET

Tok

Pangbourne Station

St James Cf

PO

The Moors

Meadowside Rd

G   H   J   Lower Bowde   85   K   L   M   **Pangbourne**

Riverview

The Hill Cemetery

Pangbourne Hill

Stokes Vw

Breedon Hi

A340

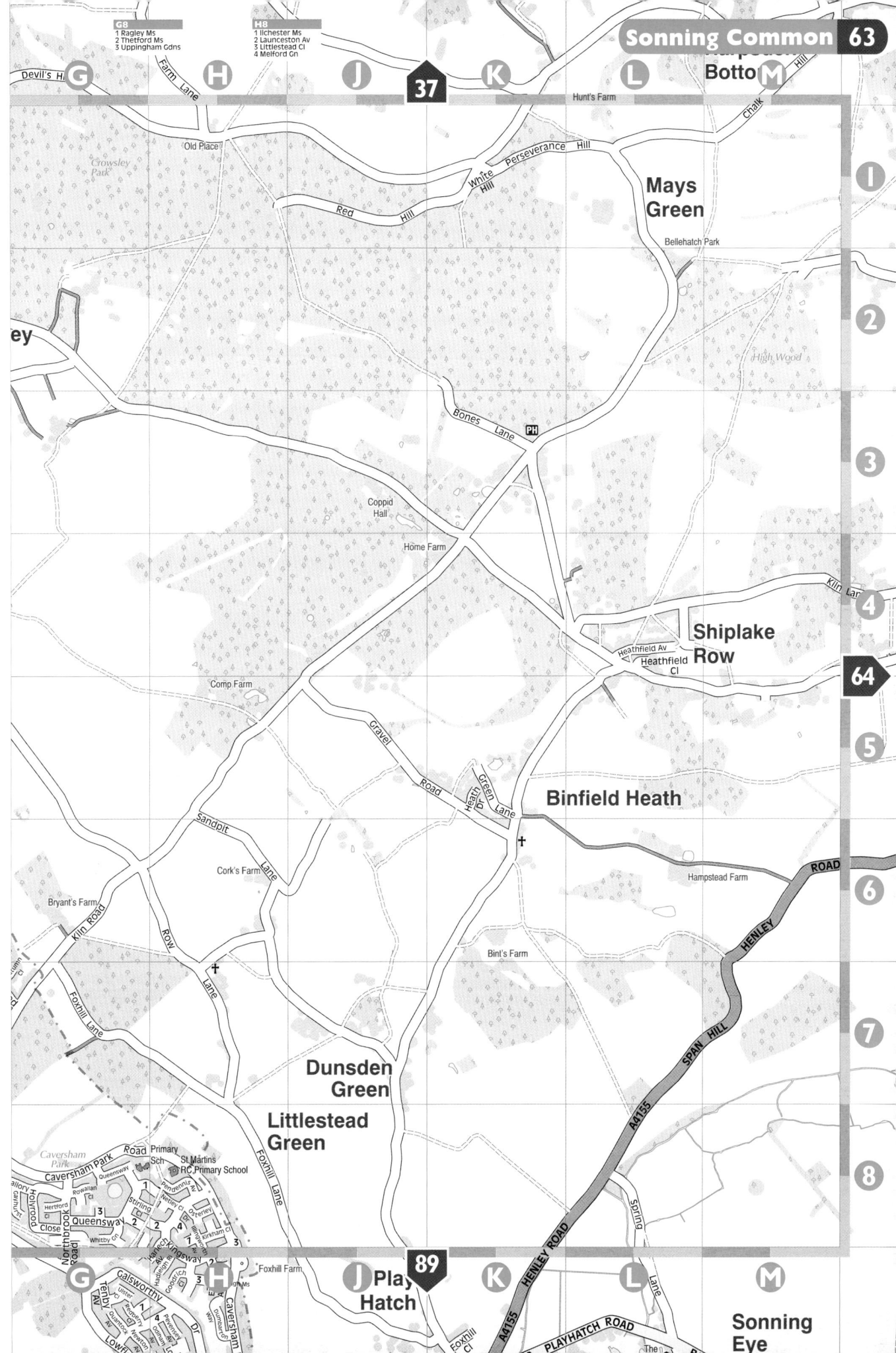

G8
1 Ragley Ms
2 Thetford Ms
3 Uppingham Gdns

H8
1 Ilchester Ms
2 Launceston Av
3 Littlestead Cl
4 Melford Gn

Devil's H.

G

Farm Lane

H

J

37

K

L

Botto

M

Hunt's Farm

Chalk Hill

I

Old Place

Crowsley Park

ey

Red Hill

White Hill

Perseverance Hill

Mays Green

Bellehatch Park

2

High Wood

3

Bones Lane

PH

Coppid Hall

Home Farm

Kiln Lane

4

Heathfield Av

Heathfield Cl

Shiplake Row

64

Comp Farm

Gravel Road

Green Lane

Heath Dr

Binfield Heath

5

Sandpit Lane

Cork's Farm Lane

Hampstead Farm

ROAD

6

Bryant's Farm

Kiln Road

Row Lane

†

†

Bint's Farm

HENLEY

SPAN HILL

7

Foxhill Lane

Dunsden Green

Littlestead Green

Caversham Park

Caversham Park Road

Primary Sch

St Martins RC Primary School

A4155

8

Queensway

Rowallan

Hertford Close

Queensway

Stirling

Pendennis

Trenley

Netley Cl

Kirkham Cl

Foxhill Lane

Foxhill Farm

Spring

G

Holyrood

Northbrook Road

Tenby Av

Galsworthy Dr

Kingsway

Raspberry

Dunmock

Weston

Whitby Gn

H

Dunman

Way

J

89

Play Hatch

K

HENLEY ROAD

L

Lane

M

A4155

PLAYHATCH ROAD

Sonning Eye

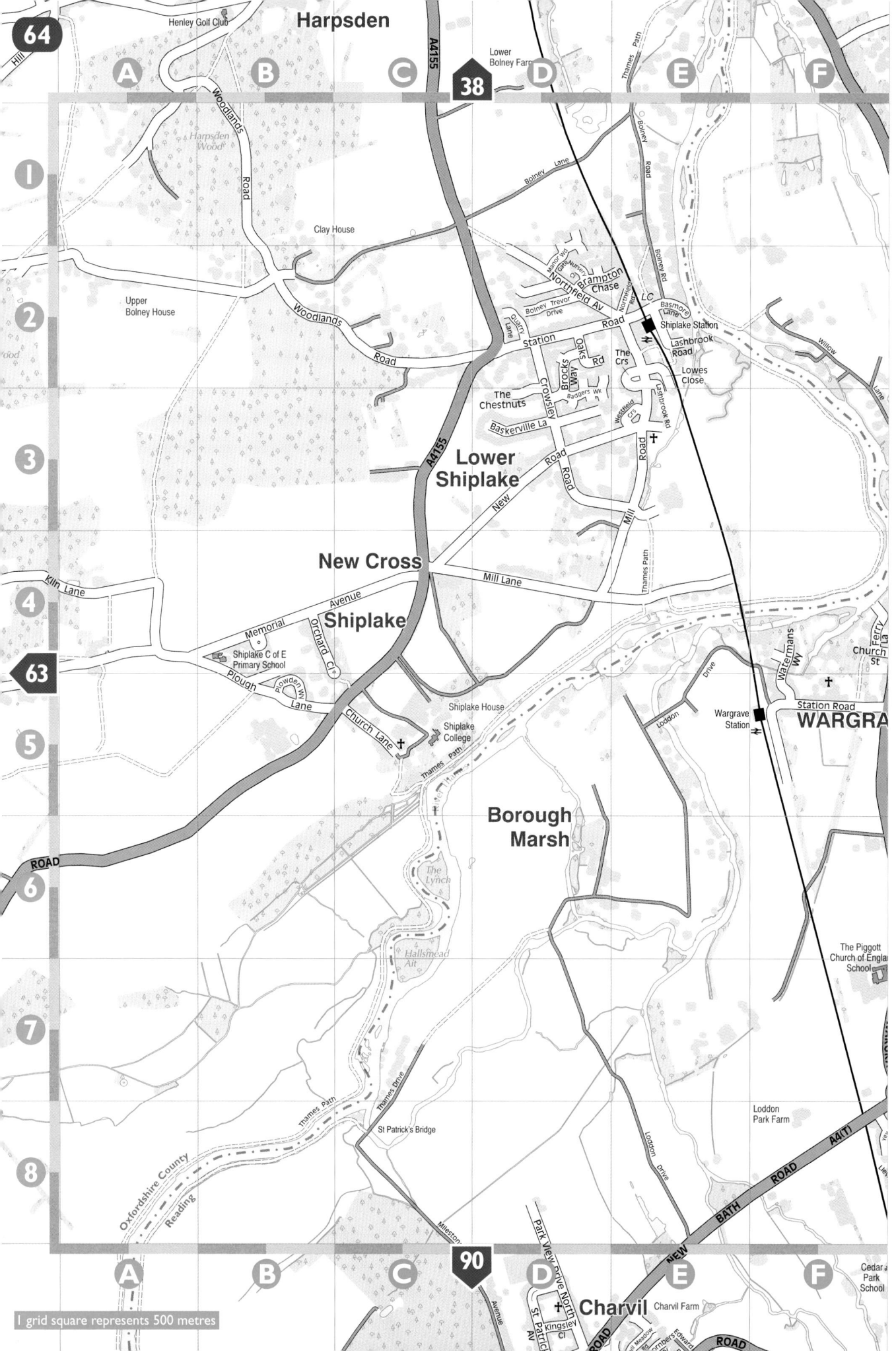

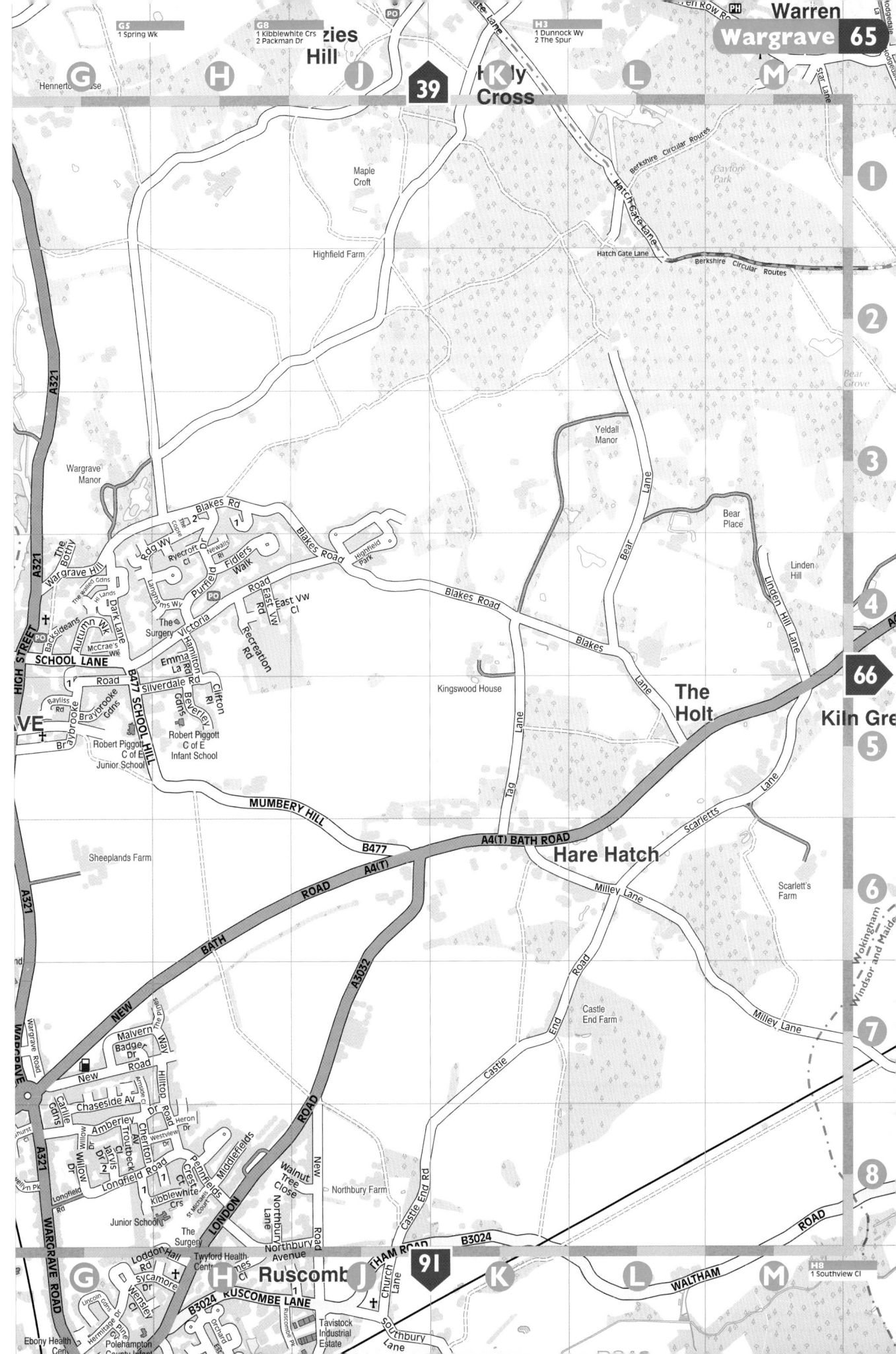

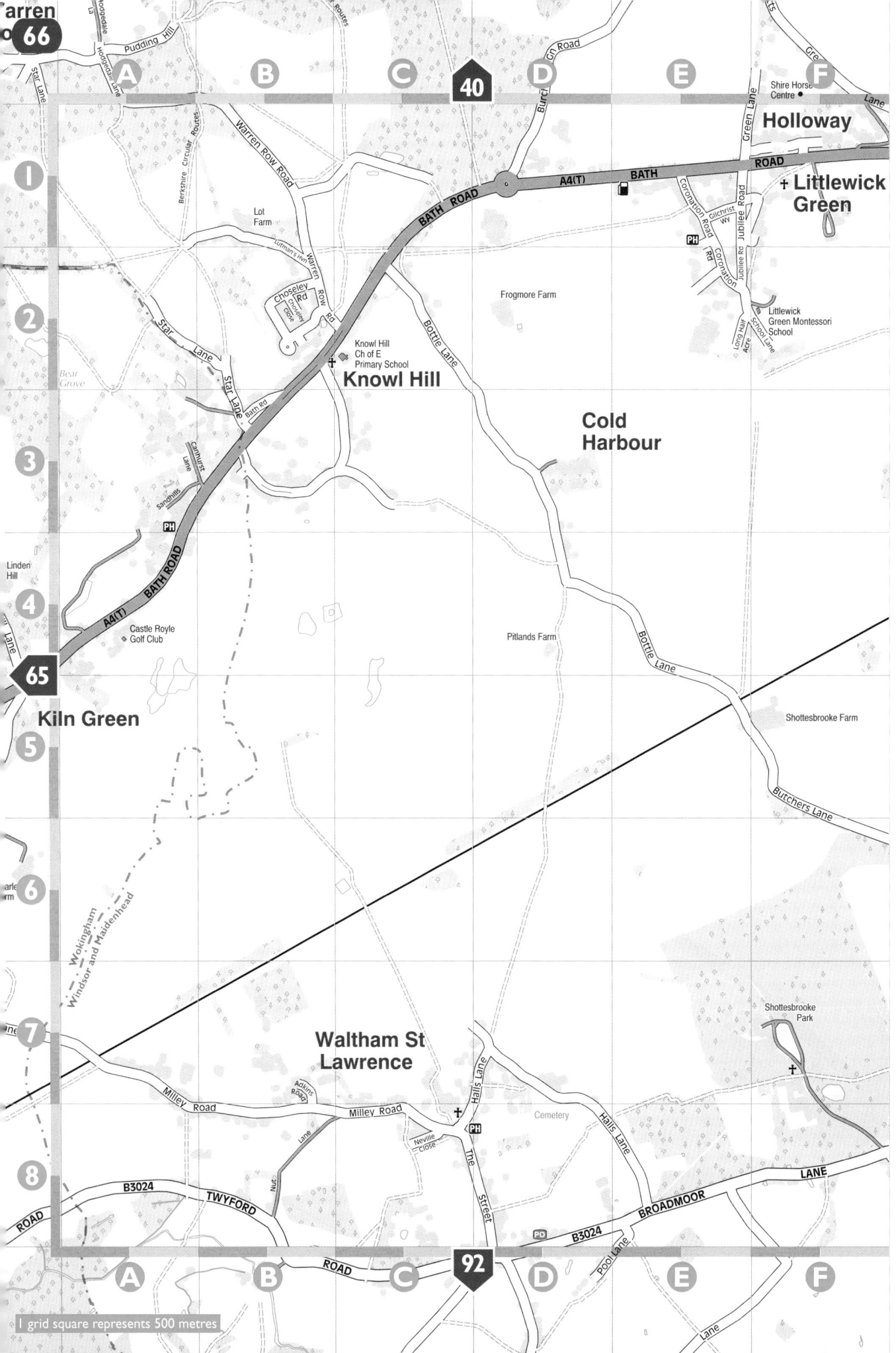

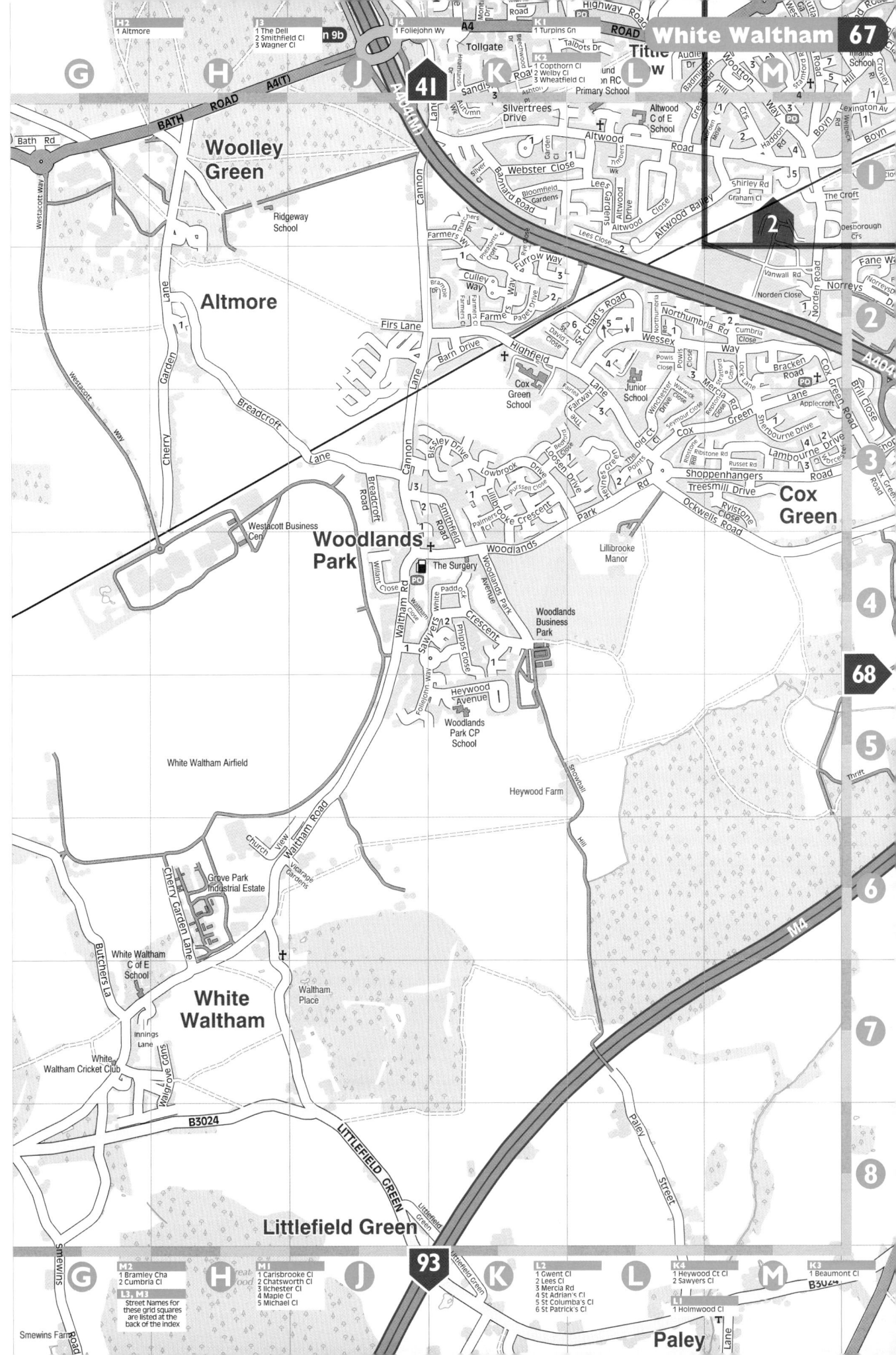

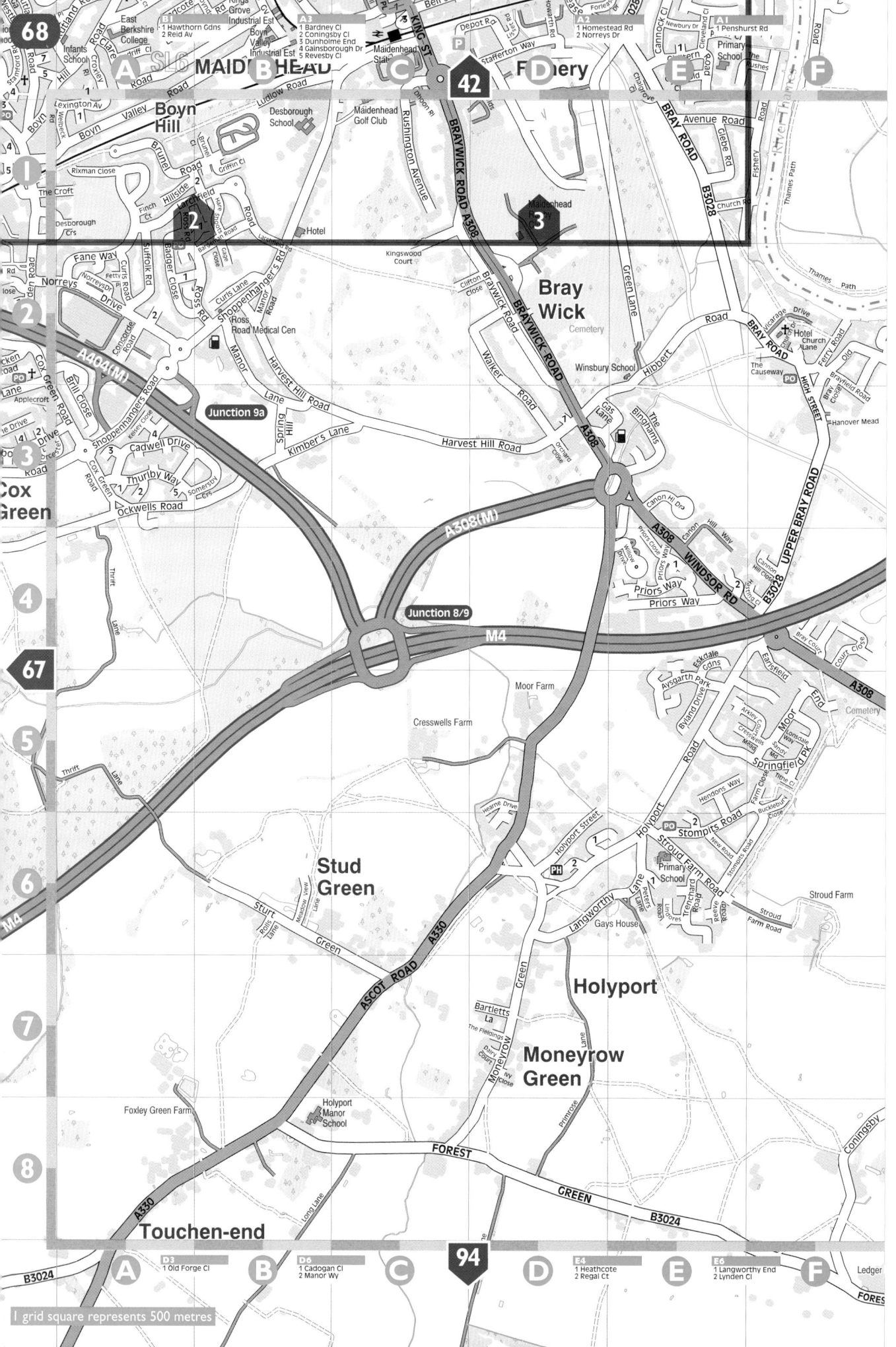

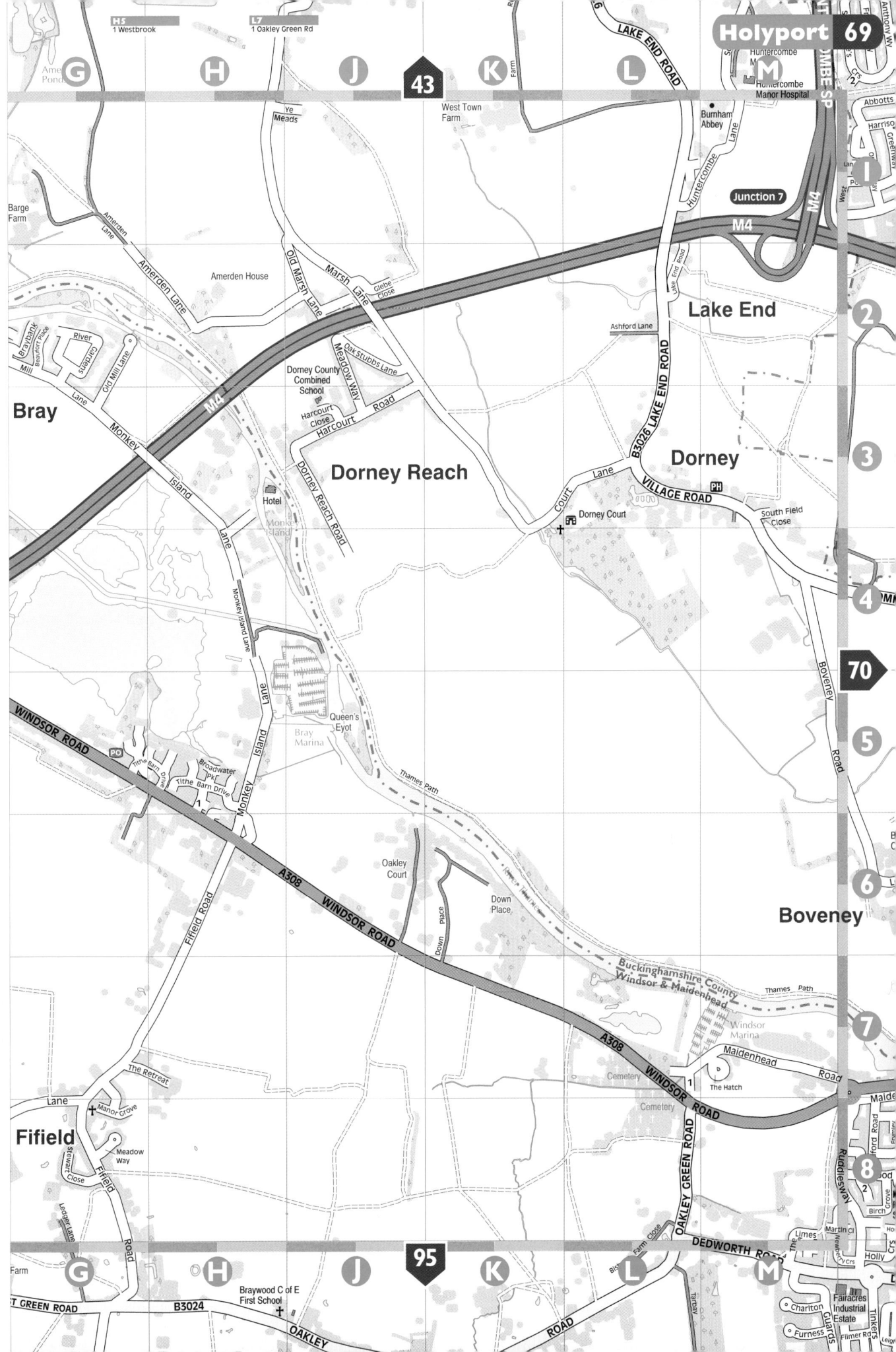

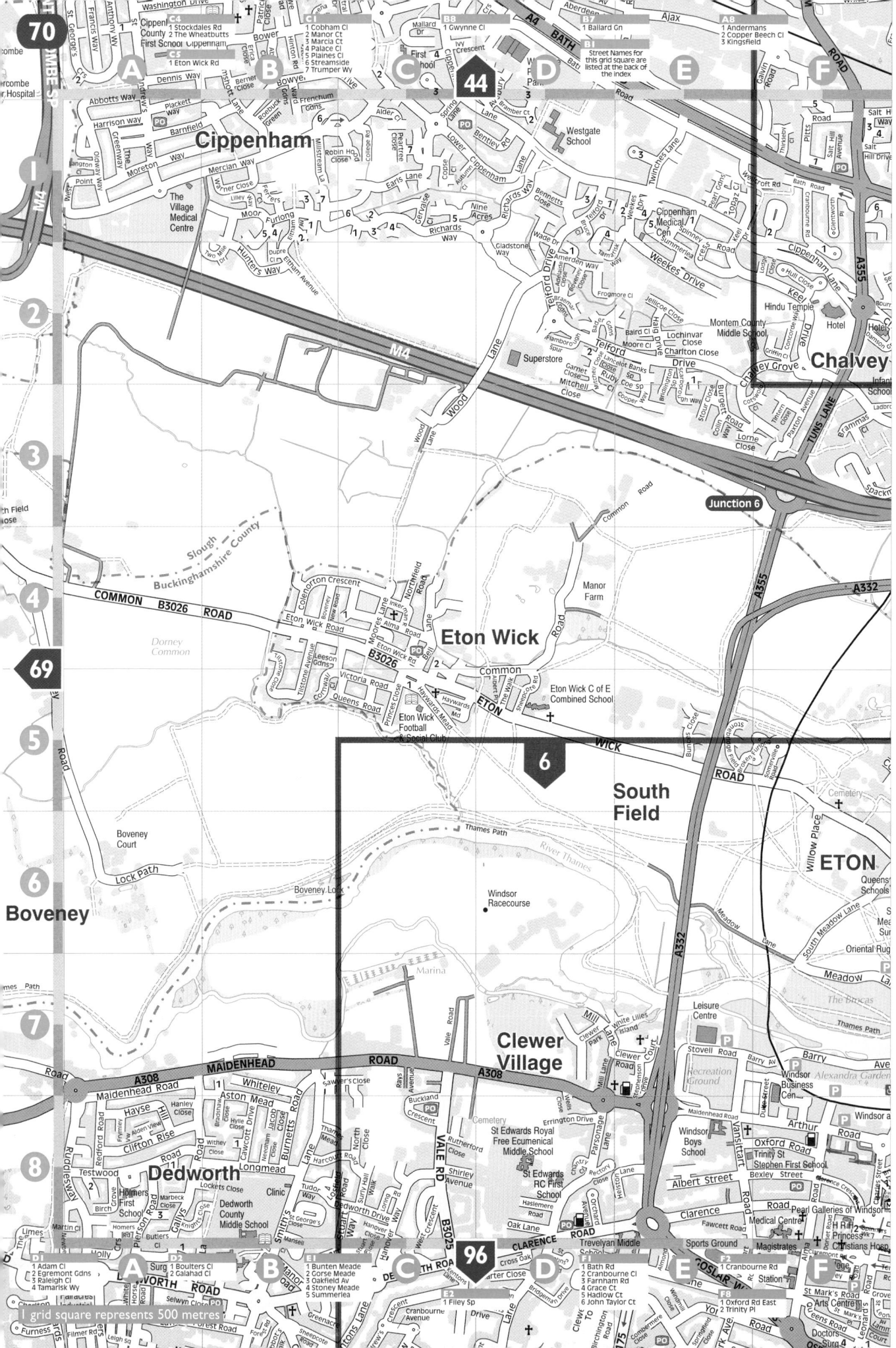

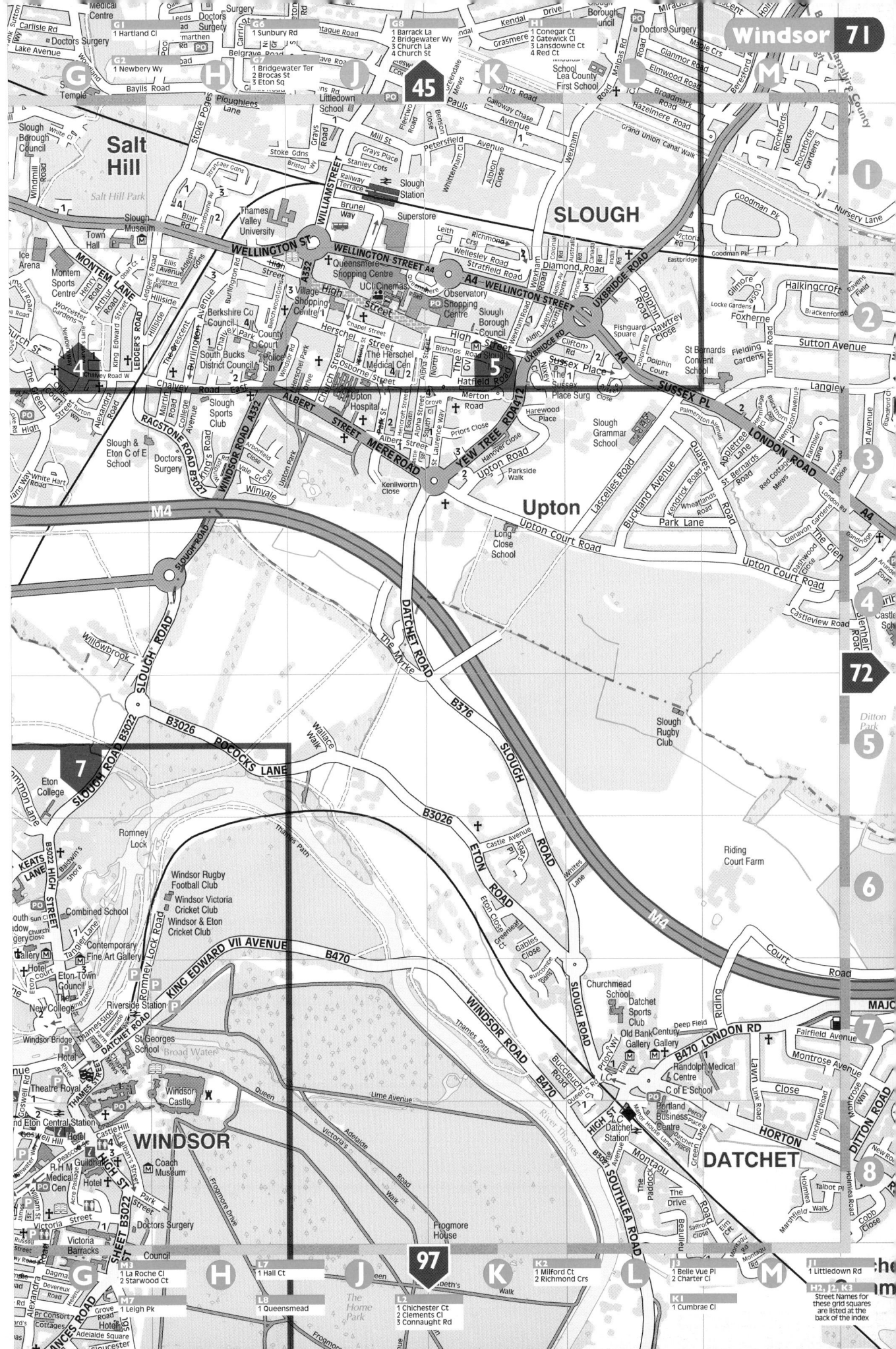

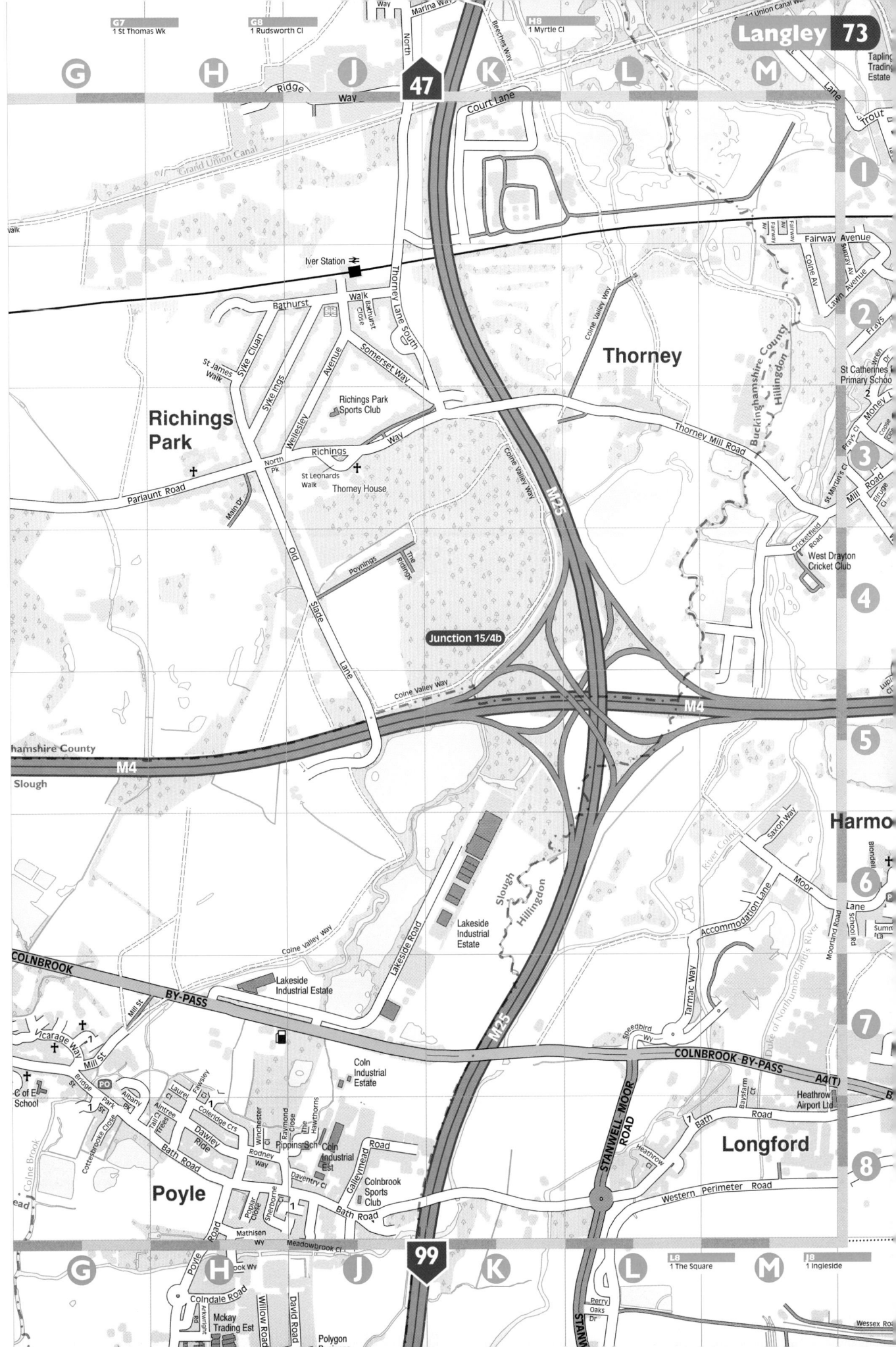

G7
1 St Thomas Wk

G8
1 Rudsworth Cl

H8
1 Myrtle Cl

G   H   J   47   K   L   M

Ridge   Way   Court Lane

Marina Way

North

Beeches Way

Grand Union Canal

Trout   Lane

Tapling Trading Estate

I

Iver Station

Fairway Avenue

Bathurst

Walk

Bathurst Close

Thorney Lane South

Colne Av

Bukzy Av

Lawn

Thorney

Frays

2

St Catherines Primary School

St James Walk

Syke Cluan

Avenue

Wellesley

Somerset Way

Way

Richings

Richings Park Sports Club

Buckinghamshire County Hillingdon

St Martin's Cl

Money Ct

Eruge

Mill   Road

3

Richings Park

North Pk

St Leonards Walk

Thorney House

Thorney Mill Road

Colne Valley Way

Cricketfield Road

West Drayton Cricket Club

Parlaunt Road

Main Dr

Old

The Prabys

Poynings

Slade

Colne Valley Way

M25

4

Junction 15/4b

Lane

Colne Valley Way

M4

5

hamshire County

M4

Slough

Harmo

Saxon Way

Blondel

Lane

Summ 'La

6

Slough Hillingdon

River Colne

Accommodation Lane

Moor

School Rd

Colne Valley Way

Lakeside Road

Lakeside Industrial Estate

Duke of Northumberland's River

Tarmac Way

7

COLNBROOK   BY-PASS

Mill St

Lakeside Industrial Estate

M25

Speedbird Wy

COLNBROOK-BY-PASS   A4(T)

Vicarage Way

Mill St

Coln Industrial Estate

Bysfarm Rd

Heathrow Airport Ltd

Bath

Road

B

C of E School

Bridge St

PO

Albany Pk

Aintree Cl

Laurel Cl

Fawley

Coleridge Crs

Winchester Cl

The Hawthorns

Raymond Close

Heathrow Cl

Bath

Longford

8

Park

Dawley Ride

Rodney Way

Pippins Sch

Road

Galleymead

Colne Brook

Bath Road

Cottersbrooke Close

Poplar Close

Sherborne

Mathisen Wy

Daventry Cl

Coln Industrial Est

Colnbrook Sports Club

Western   Perimeter   Road

STANWELL MOOR ROAD

Poyle

Poyle Road

Meadowbrook Cl

Bath Road

G   H   99   J   K   L   M

L8
1 The Square

J8
1 Ingleside

Coindale Road

Arkwright Rd

Hook Wy

Willow Road

David Road

Mckay Trading Est

Polygon

STANW

Perry Oaks Dr

Wessex Ro

A B C **48** D E **M4** F

M4

1

Baydon Wood

2

3

Baydon Manor

4

Membury
Farm

Balak Farm

5

Preston

6

B4192

Crowood Farm

Witcha Farm

*Love's
Copse*

7

Crowood House

Eastridge House

8

s Farm

*Little
Wood*

A B C **102** D E F

Whittonditch

*Oaken
Coppice*

1 grid square represents 500 metres

ove

G H J K L M

49

Lambourn Woodlands

Fox Farm

Baydon Road

B4000

Membury Service Area

Hotel

Membury Service Area

M4

Dixon's Farm

PH

Rooksnest

Hilldrop Lane

BAYDON ROAD

B4000

Membury Airfield
Industrial Estate

Membury
Business Park

Walls
Copse

Hilldrop Farm

Burgess's Farm

Stony Lane

†

M4

Wood
S

76

Leigh Farm

Holt
Copse

Lyckweed Farm

B4001

STAG

Half Mile Road

Ragnal

HILL

Bearfield

West Berkshire
Wiltshire County

Lane

Raffin
Stud

Whitehill
Wood

**Crooked
Soley**

Foxbury
Wood

**Straight
Soley**

B4001

Briary
Wood

103

G H J K L M

I 2 3 4 5 6 7 8

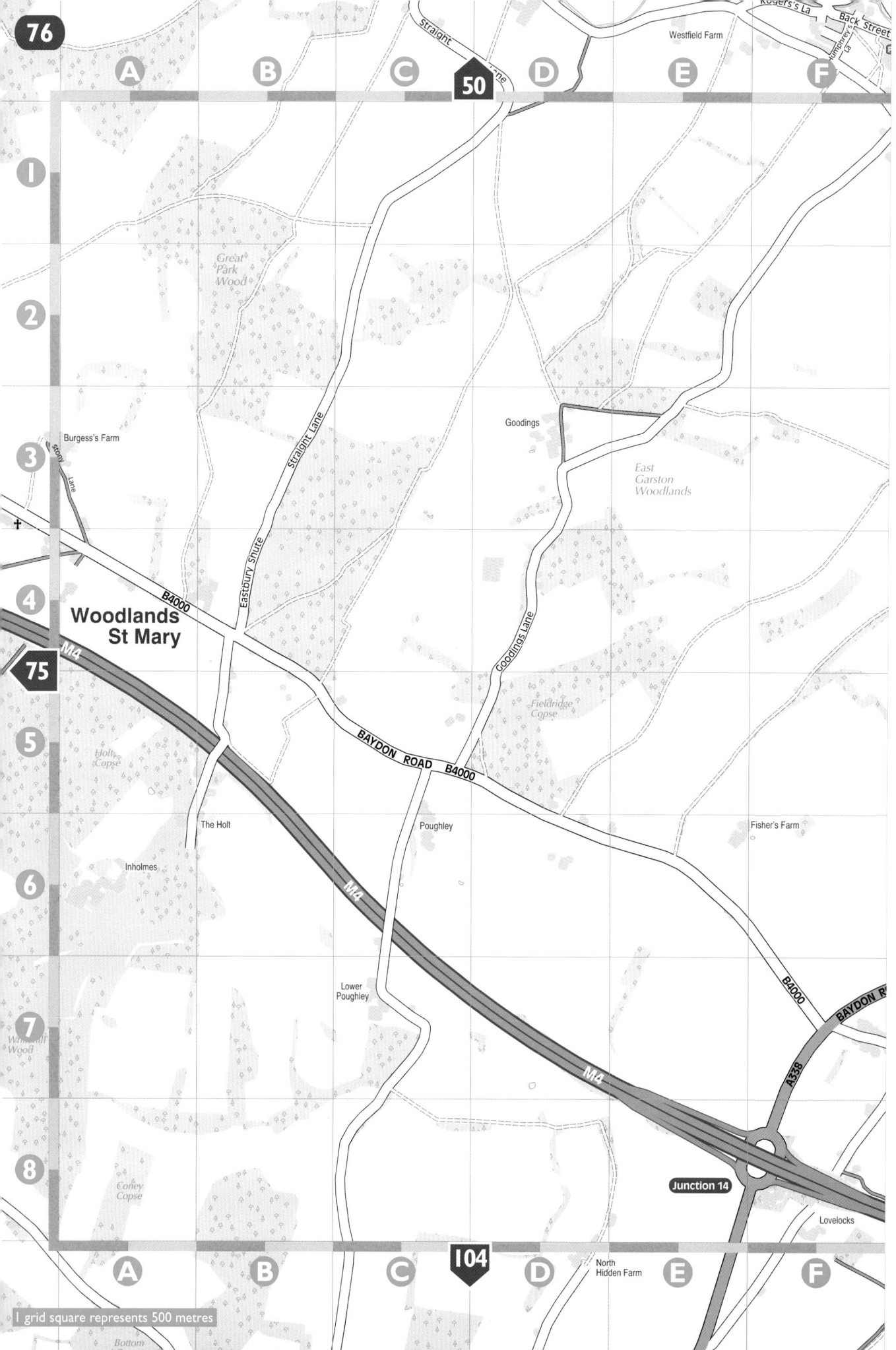

A B C **50** D E F

I

2

3

Burgess's Farm

Great Park Wood

Stony Lane

Eastbury Shute

Straight Lane

Straight Lane

Goodings

East Garston Woodlands

Goodings Lane

4

Woodlands St Mary

B4000

75

M4

5

Holt Copse

Fieldridge Copse

BAYDON ROAD B4000

The Holt

Poughley

Fisher's Farm

6

Inholmes

M4

Windmill Wood

7

Lower Poughley

A338

BAYDON R

B4000

8

Coney Copse

Junction 14

Lovelocks

North Hidden Farm

Bottom

Westfield Farm

Rogers's La

Back Street

Humphrey's La

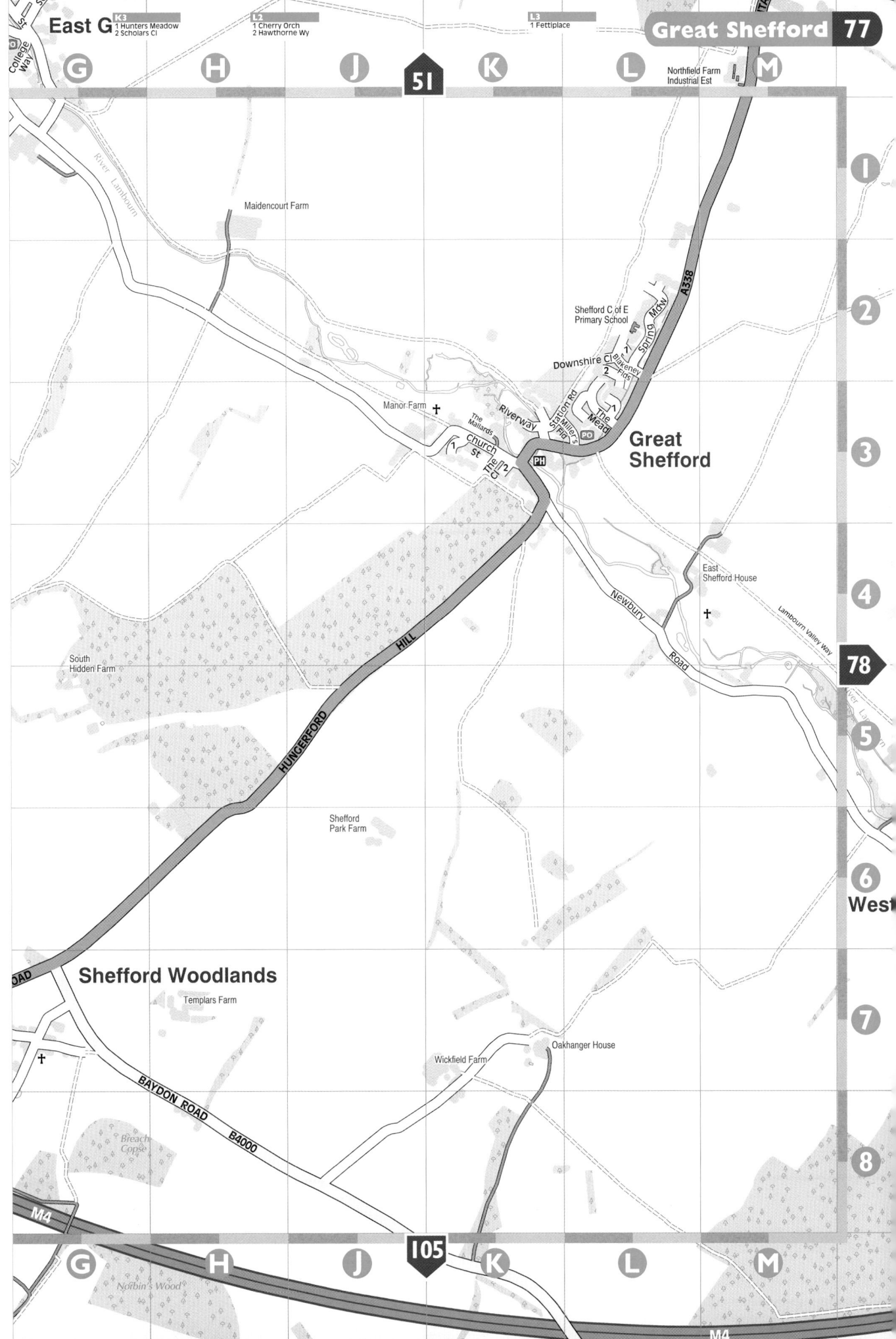

East G
K3 1 Hunters Meadow
2 Scholars Cl
L2 1 Cherry Orch
2 Hawthorne Wy
L3 1 Fettiplace
Great Shefford 77

G H J 51 K L M

Northfield Farm
Industrial Est

I

Maidencourt Farm

2

Shefford C of E
Primary School

Downshire Cl

A338

Spring Mdw

Blakeney
Flds

The Mead

PO

**Great
Shefford**

3

Manor Farm

Riverway

The
Mallards

Church
St

The
FC

PH

Station Rd
Miller's Bdg

East
Shefford House

Newbury

Lambourn Valley Way

4

78

South
Hidden Farm

HUNGERFORD HILL

Road

5

Shefford
Park Farm

6

West

Shefford Woodlands

7

Templars Farm

Oakhanger House

Wickfield Farm

BAYDON ROAD B4000

Breach
Copse

8

M4

G H J 105 K L M

Norbin's Wood

M4

A   B   C   D   E   F

52

Hangman's Stone Lane

Lower
Barn

I

West Berks
Golf Club

Hangman's Stone Lane

Glen Miller Close

Twinwoods

Eisenhower Avenue

Nodmore
Corner

2

Elton
Wood

Down
Copse

Poughley Farm

3

Lambourn Valley

4

77

River Lambourn

5

Elton Farm

6

Weston

Lambourn   Valley   Way

7

†

Welford

Welford
Park

8

Lambourn   Valley   Way

A   B   C   D   E   F

M4 106

Tullock Farm

Hill

River Lambourn

Easton

G   Highfield Ho.   H   J   **53**   K   **Egypt**   L   M   Mu

Hillgreen

1

Leckhampstead

Goose Lane

Manor Lane

Chapel Farm

2

Shop Lane

3

B4494

Rowbury Farm

North Heath Farm

4

Pope's Wood

80

5

Penclose Wood

PH

Bradleywood Farm

Hop Castle

6

Penclose Farm

M4

7

Wyfield Manor Farm

8

Borough Hill

Westbrook Farm

G   H   J   **107**   K   L   Lower Farm   M

PH

Winterbourne

A B 54 C D E F

green

1

E5
1 Hazeldene

E4
1 Pointers Cl

D6
1 Park Sowbury

World
En

Mu Lane

Old Street

2

Gidley Farm

Elmgrove Farm

Northfields

Tudor Av

3

Chapel Wood

Downend

Downs Farm

Bardown

Downend Lane

4

Hazelhanger Farm

North Heath Farm

North Heath

Freshfields Lane

Middle Farm

Chieveley

79

Gidley Lane

5

PH

School Road

Manor Lane

Church La

High Street

East Lane

Road

Oxford

PO 1

6

Chieveley County Primary School

Heathfields

School Road

Graces Lane

Horsemoor

Green Lane

A34(T)

Priors Cou

7

Ogdown House

B4494

Green Lane

Newbury Showground

Radnall Farm

Junction 13

M4

8

Bussock Mayne

Bussock Wood

Chieveley Service Area

A B 108 C D E F

PH

Snelsmore Farm

J8
1 Bomford Cl
2 Clough Dr
3 Roy Cl
4 Thompson Cl

G **H** **J** 55 **K** **L** **M**

I

Langley Farm

Oakhouse Farm

Langley Wood

Bothampstead Farm

2

Trumpletts Fa

Bothampstead

Malthouse

3

Four
Elms

Bradley
Court

4

Oareborough Lane

82

Old Street

5

Oare

Manor Lane

Priors
Court
School

Kiln Farm

Colyer Cl

Hermitage
Primary
School

Orchard
Cl

Little Hung.fo

6

Priorscourt Farm

Old Street

Old
Street

Roebuck
Wood

HAMPSTEAD NORREYS ROAD

Chapel Lane

Deacons Lane

Pond La

Yatten

M4

Dine's Wy

Kiln Cl

Yattendon Road

7

Ridgeway Close

PO

Priors Ct Road

Doctors
Lane

NEWBURY ROAD

Lipscomb
Close

Briants
Piece

Cemetery

Hermitage

Crabtree Lane

Faircross
Quarters

Faircross
Quarters

Charlotte
Close

8

Crabtree Close

White Cl

Collins Drive

7

2

3

4

Woodside Drive

Stanting Hill

G **H** **J** 109 **K** **L** **M** Marlston Road

Woodlands Cl

LONG LANE

Grimsbury Castle

Kiln

PH

Drive

Curridge

A B C **56** D E F

Station Hill

Hampstead Norreys

The Cuttings

NEWBURY HILL

The Cl

Water St

Scotlalls La

Pendals Close

CHURCH ST

PO

FORGE HILL

Beech Close

Hampstead Norreys Primary School

Beechcroft

WYLD COURT HILL B4009

Wyld Court Rainforest

Wyld Court Stud

I

Trumpletts Farm

2

B4009

3

Eling

Manstone Farm

River Pang

4

81

Everington Lane

Common Barn Cotts

Everington House

5

M4

Birch Farm

6

ungerford

Yattendon Road

Pond La

Lane

Manor House

7

Hatchets Lane

Frilsham

8

RG18

Hawkridge House

Hawk W

Wellhouse Lane

Marlston Road

A B **110** C D E F

Wellhouse

G   H   J   **57**   K   L   M

Stubbles

I

Pyt Ho

2

Ch'
Co   n

3

Suck's Lane

Calvesleys Farm

4

84

PH Hotel
† Yattendon C of E
Primary School
PO
Chapel Lane   Church La   Yattendon Court

Yattendon Lane

5

ockendon

Yattendon

†

**Burnt
Hill**

The
Withys
Home Farm

6

Coombe
Wood

Frilsham Park

Scratchf

7

Frilsham
Common

Magpie Farm

PH

Mazelands Farm

8

Berkshire Circular Routes

High Copse

idge
ood

Berkshire

G   H   J   **III**   K   L   M

Hawkridge Farm

A   B   C   58   D   E   F

bbles

1

Quick's †
Green

Upper Basildon

Pyt House

Ashampstead Road

Hill
Corner
Lane

Whitemoor

Tenaplas Dr

Kiln Ride

Car
Go

Emery
Acres

Basildon School

Woodgreen Farm

Mead Lane

Aldworth

Beckfords

Maple
La

Blandy's Lane

Darby La

PH
PO

†
Pangbourne Road

New

2

Ashampstead
Common

Road

Gardeners Lane

3

Child's
Court Farm

Suck's Lane

Herons
Farm

4

Slade Gate

St Andrews
School

5

Strouds

Bottomhouse Farm

6

M4

Greathouse
Wood

7

Scratchface Lane

Hewins
Wood Farm

Dark Lane

Ashampstead Road

8

Bradfield House

Rushall Farm

Bradfield
College

A   B   C   112   D   E   F

Rusha Manor
Farm

Back Lane

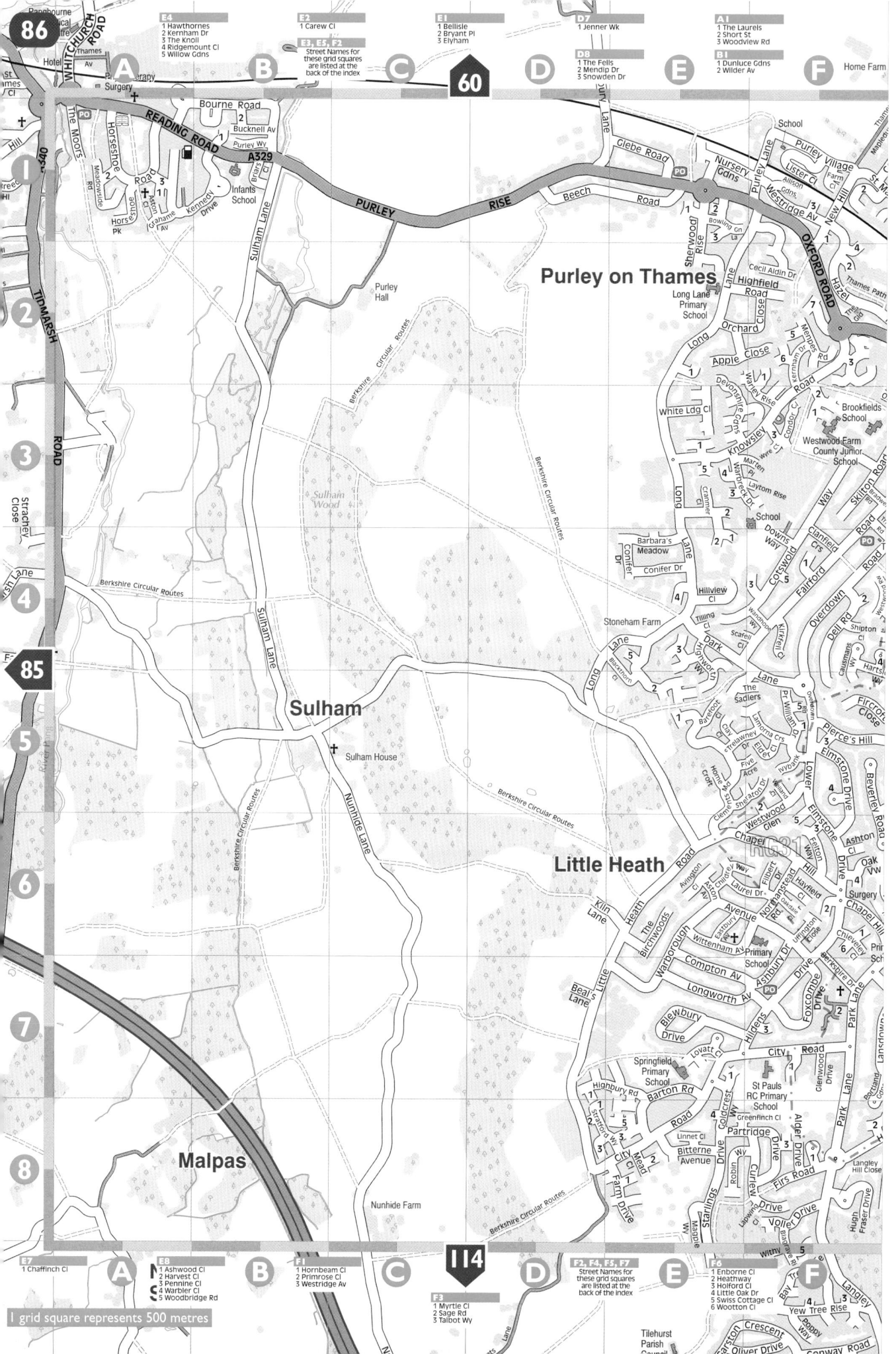

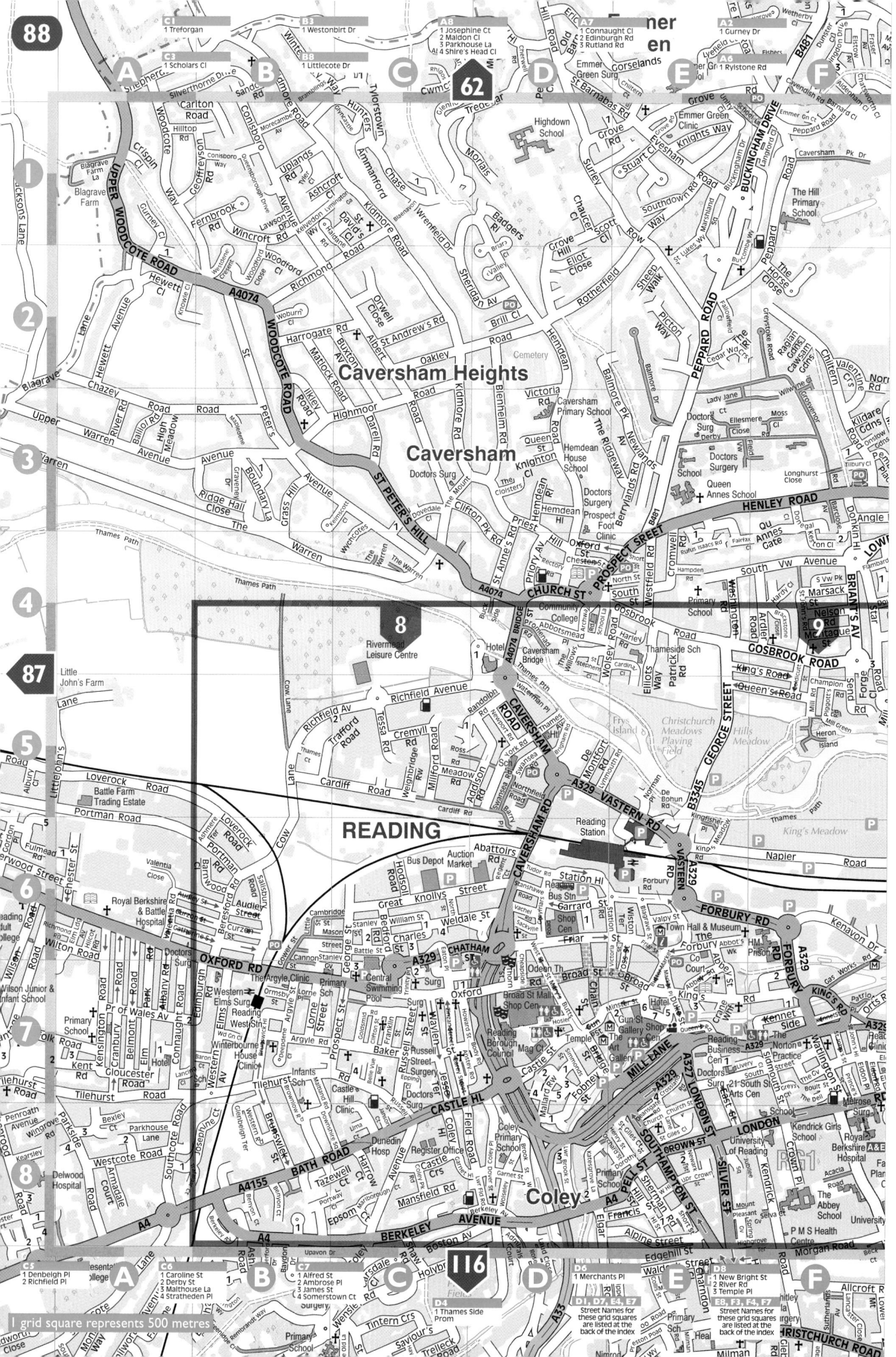

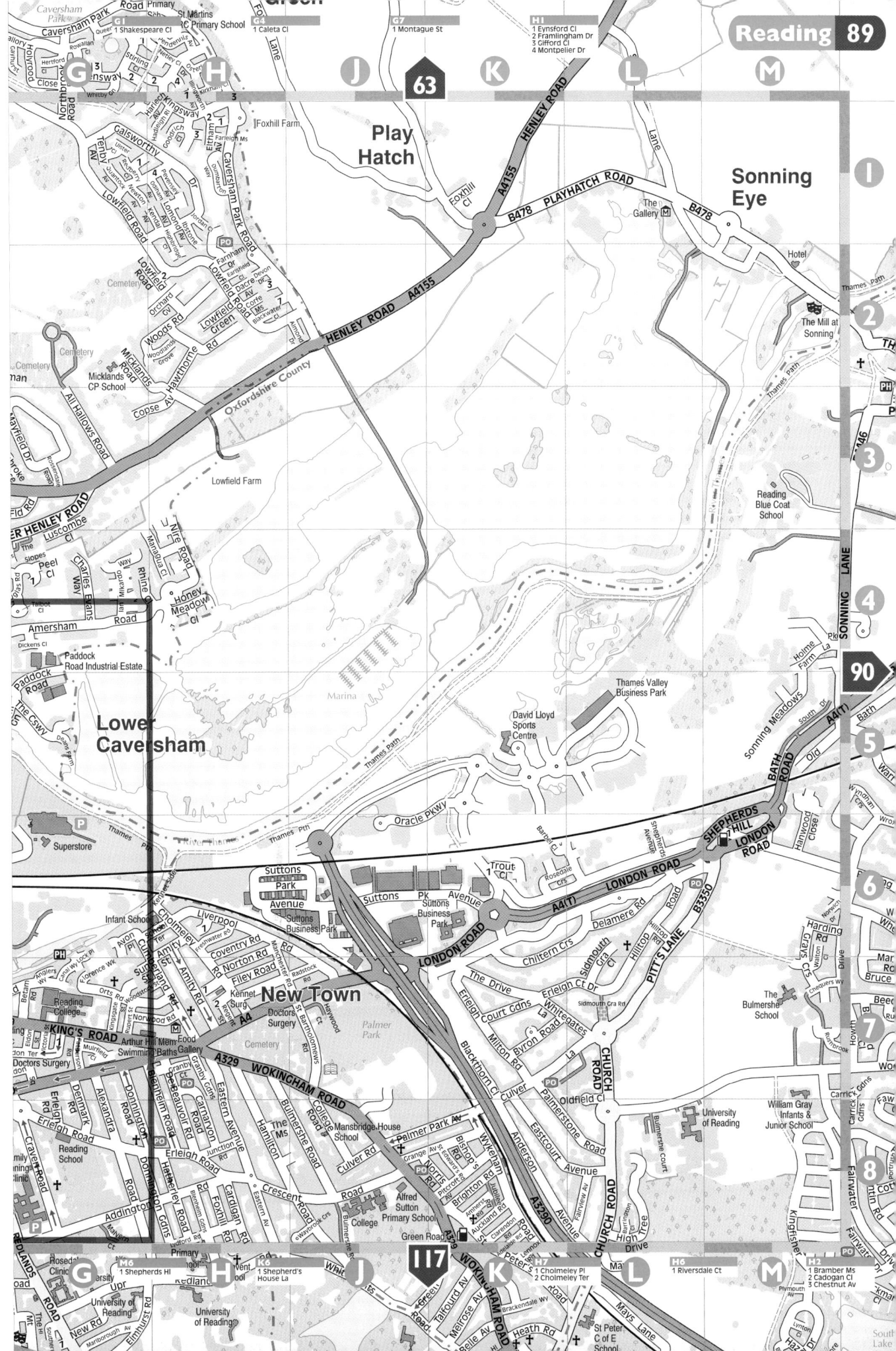

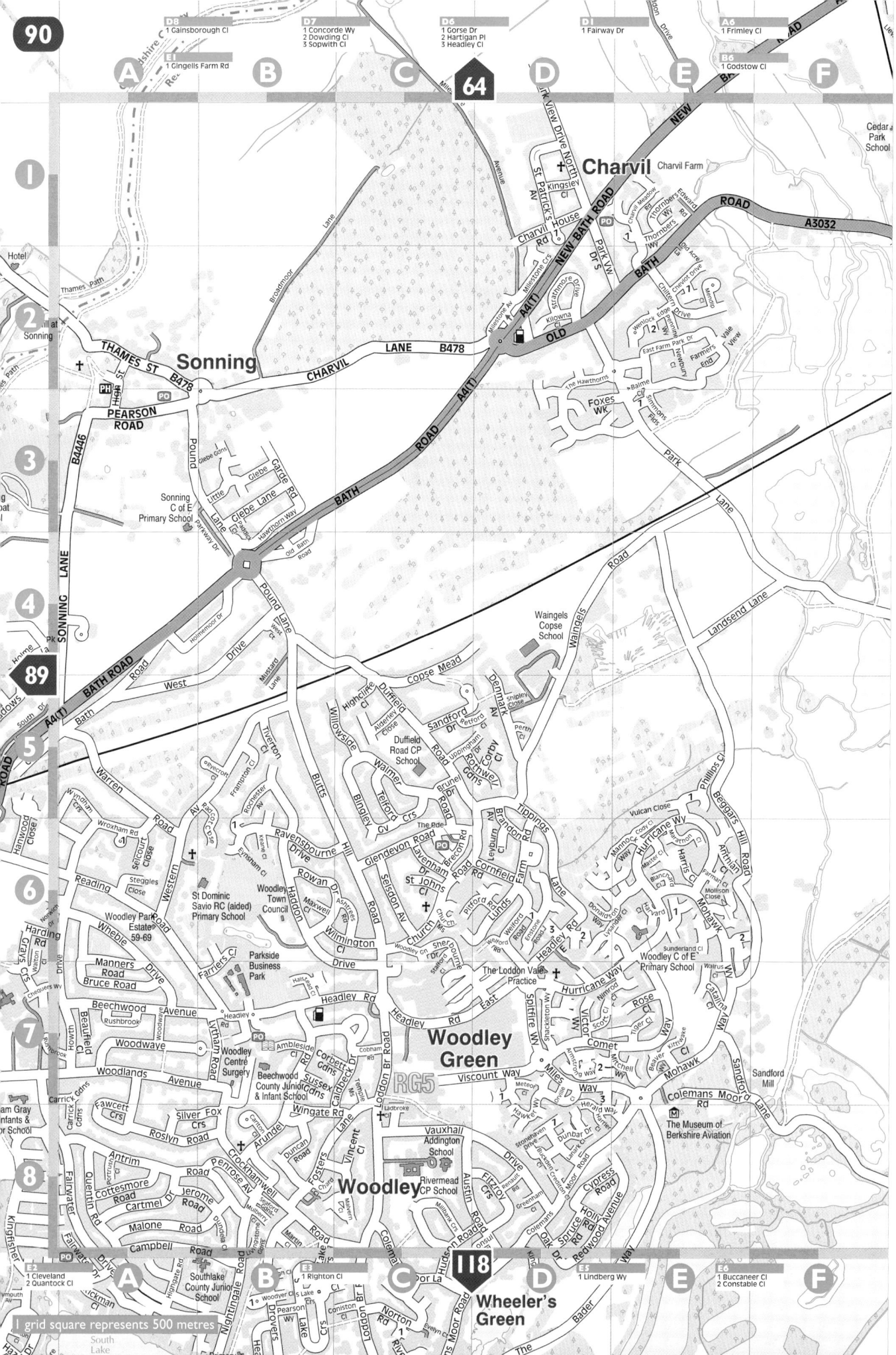

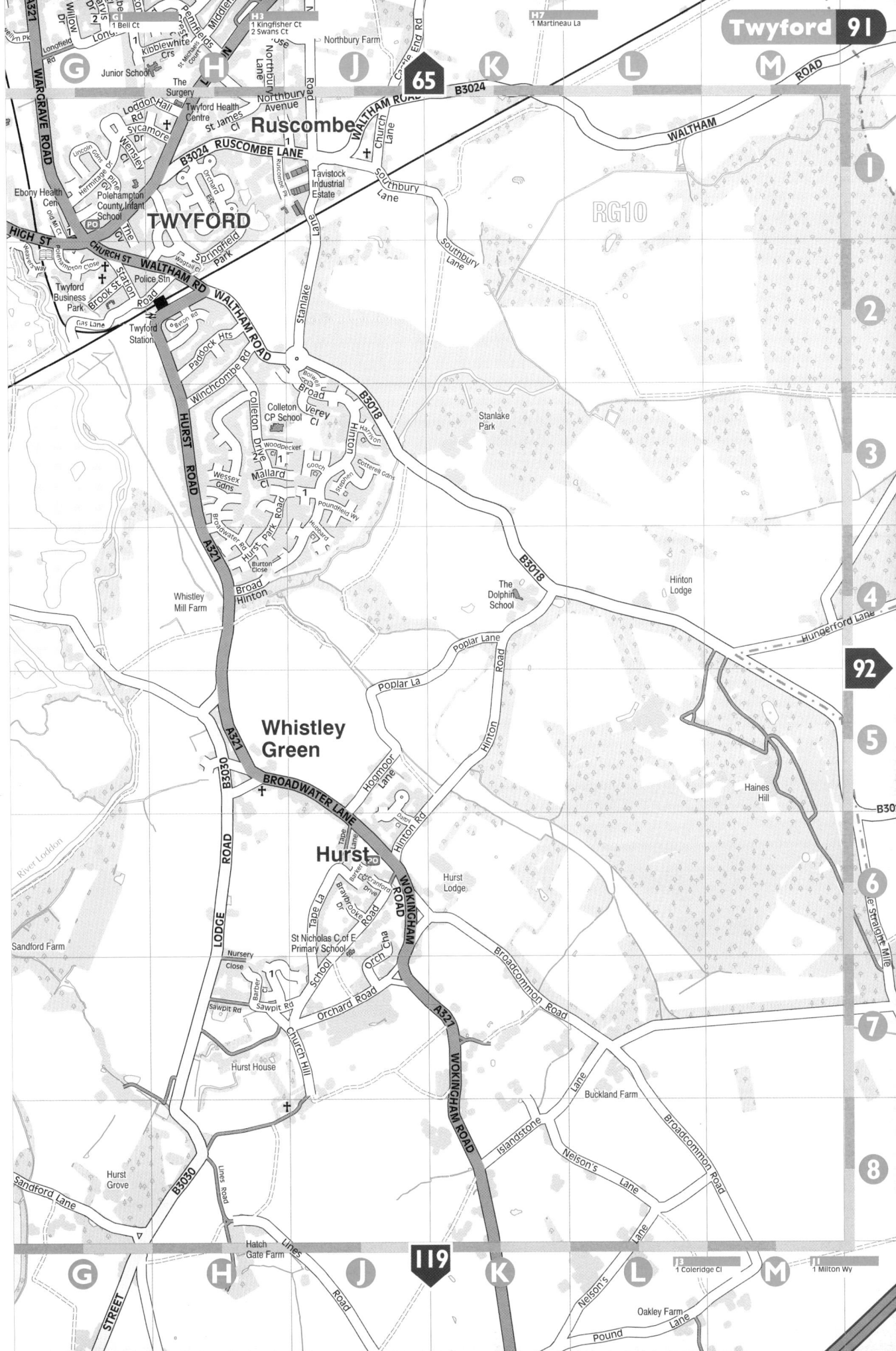

G H J **67** K L M

FIELD GREEN

Littlefield Gree **67**

Littlefield Green

Great
Wood

Smewins Road

Smewins Farm

**Paley
Street**

Sheepcote Lane

B3024

I

Long Lan

2

A330

Braywoo

Pondwood Farm

M4

The Cut

Mare Lane

Drift Road

3

4

Howe Lane

Howe Lane

Buck
Farm House

Windsor and Maidenhead
Bracknell Forest

94

**Hawthorn
Hill**

5

Cruchfi
Manor

Great
Hazes

Spinningwheel Lane

Mill

Westley

Westleymill

Pendry's Lane

Pendry's
Lane

A3095

Felix
Farm

Howe Lane

Gough's Barn

6

**Jealott's
Hill**

Weller's

ROAD

Bottle Lane

Lane

Maidenhead
Road

7

B3018

Allanbay
Park

Hazelwood Lane

Ticklebank Row

MAIDENHEAD

**Moss
End**

**Tickleback
Row**

Bottle Lane

hurst Lane

Buckle Lane

Bowyer's Lane

8

Hill Farm

G H J **121** K L M

A3095

HILL

Weller's Lane

G **H** **J** **K** **L** **M**

Meadow
L7
1 Broadway
2 Hawthorne Dr

Stewart
Close

Level Lane

Fifield Road

ST GREEN ROAD

B3024

OAKLEY

Fifield Lane

Braywood C of E
First School

GREEN

OAKLEY

GREEN

ROAD

Oakley Green

Bishops Farm Close

Tarbay Lane

OAKLEY

DEDWORTH ROAD

The Limes

Martin Cr

Newberts

Birch Grove

Holly

Fairacres
Industrial
Estate

I

Chariton

Furness

Guards Road

Filmer Rd

Lovel Jay Lane

Leigh

Kenneally

Alexander
First
School

Liddell

Nicholls

Wright

Sidney
Road

Pell Road

Bastford Way

Whit

Rowland
Close

Fran

Gilman

Bryer Pl

Wilton Crescent

Snowt

2

Tennis
Lawn
Club

Tarbay Farm

St Leon

3

Braywood House

New
Lodge Farm

Drift Road

Windsor and Maidenhead

Bracknell Forest

New
Lodge

St Leonards
Farm

Leonards Road

St

4

96

Drift Road

Home
Farm

Windsor
Forest

5

Winkfield Lane

**Winkfield
Place**

Winkfield Plain

WINKFIELD

B3022

Cranbou
Chase

6

Old Dairy Farm

Barton
Lodge

Winkfield Lane

Crouch Lane

Ash Farm

Spinney Lane

Park Lane

Central Way

Berkeley Dr

PO

7

2 Elm Drive

Squires

Waverly Way

Wavingbri

Ranelagh Farm

Crouch Lane

B3022

STREET

Cranbourne

B383

MOUNTS

Kingsmead

W
Gre

8

St Marys Lane

G **V** **kfield**

H

J

123

K

L

M

HILL

Fernhill
Park

Forest Farm

A33

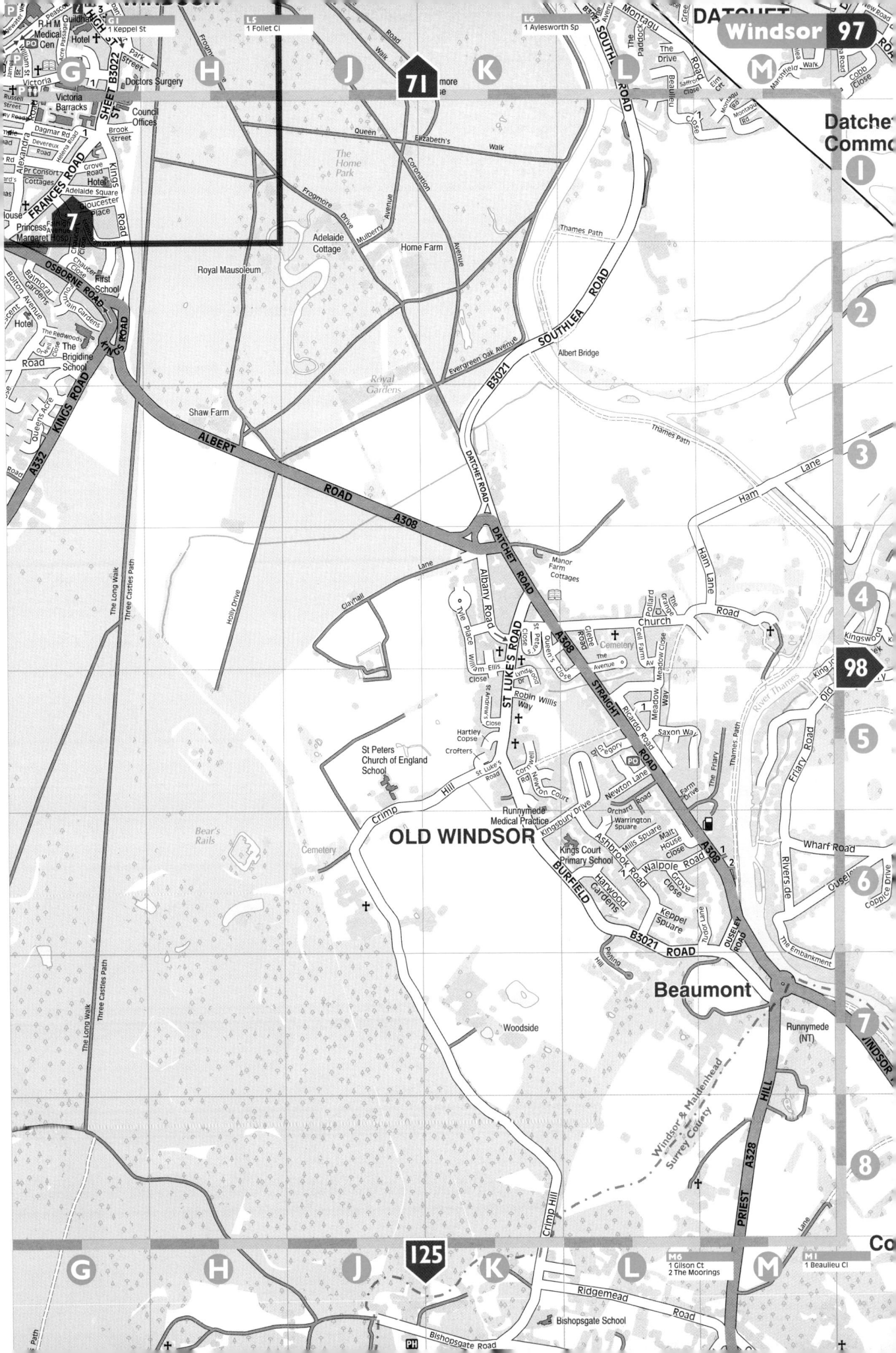

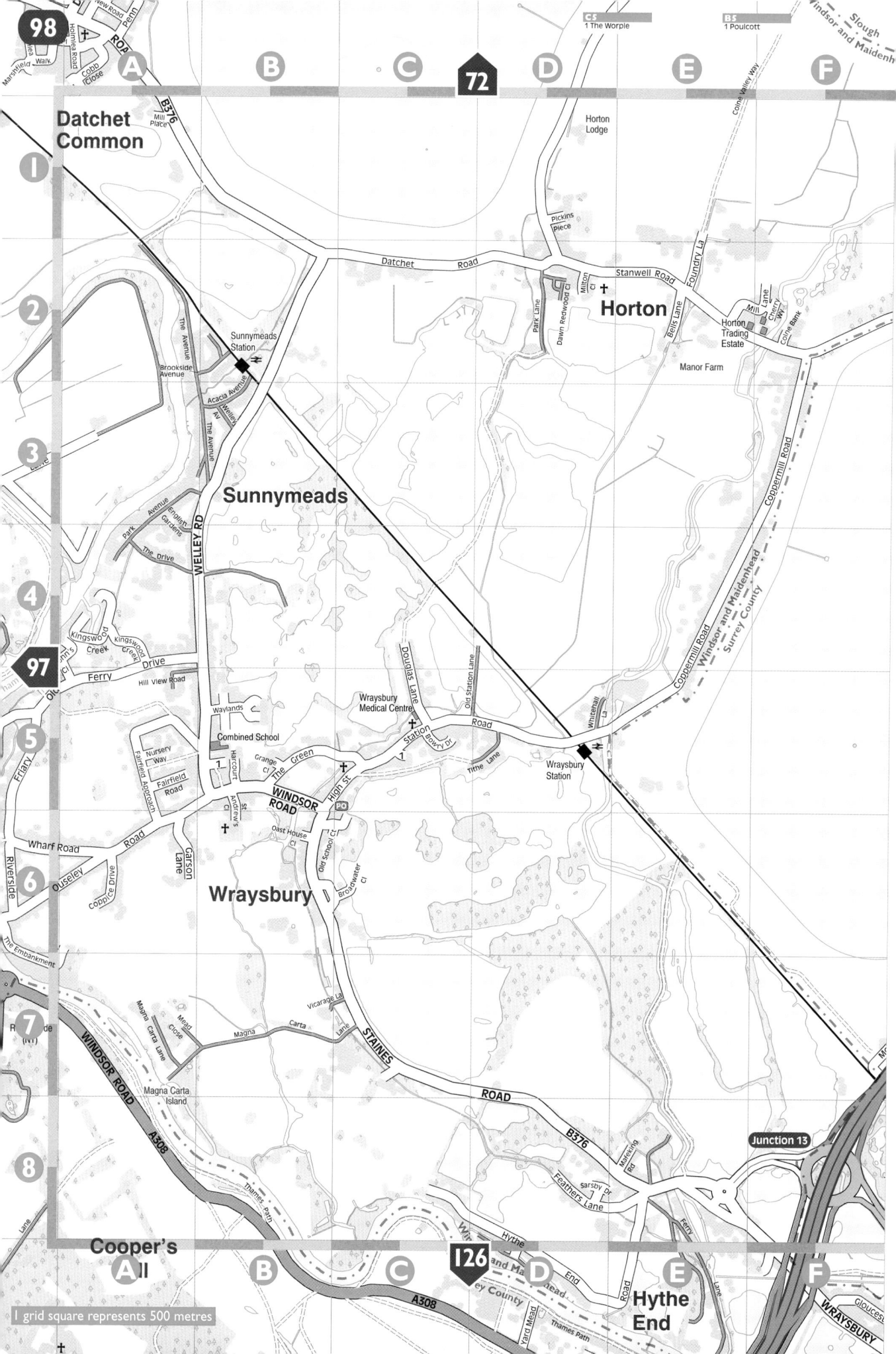

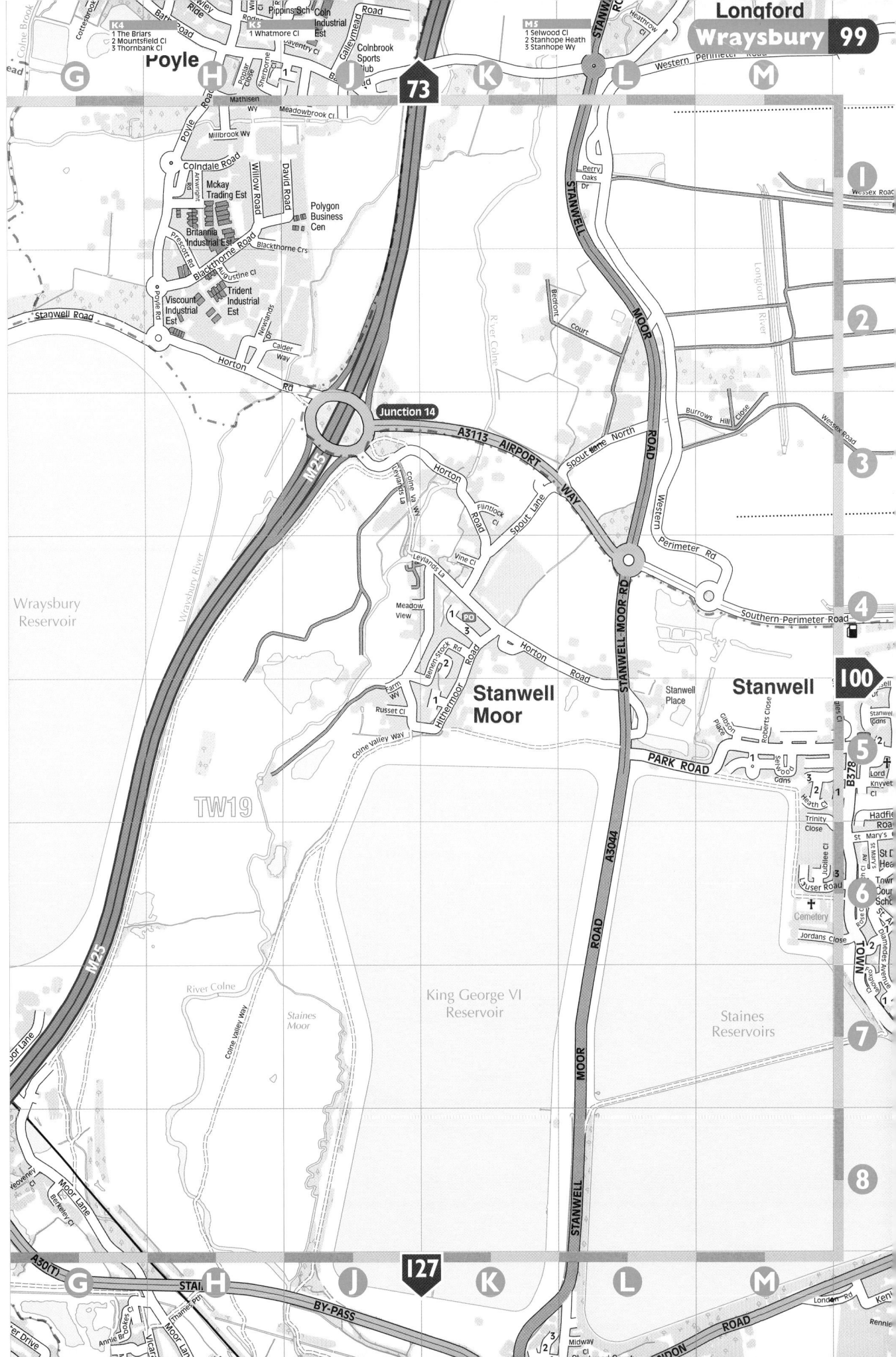

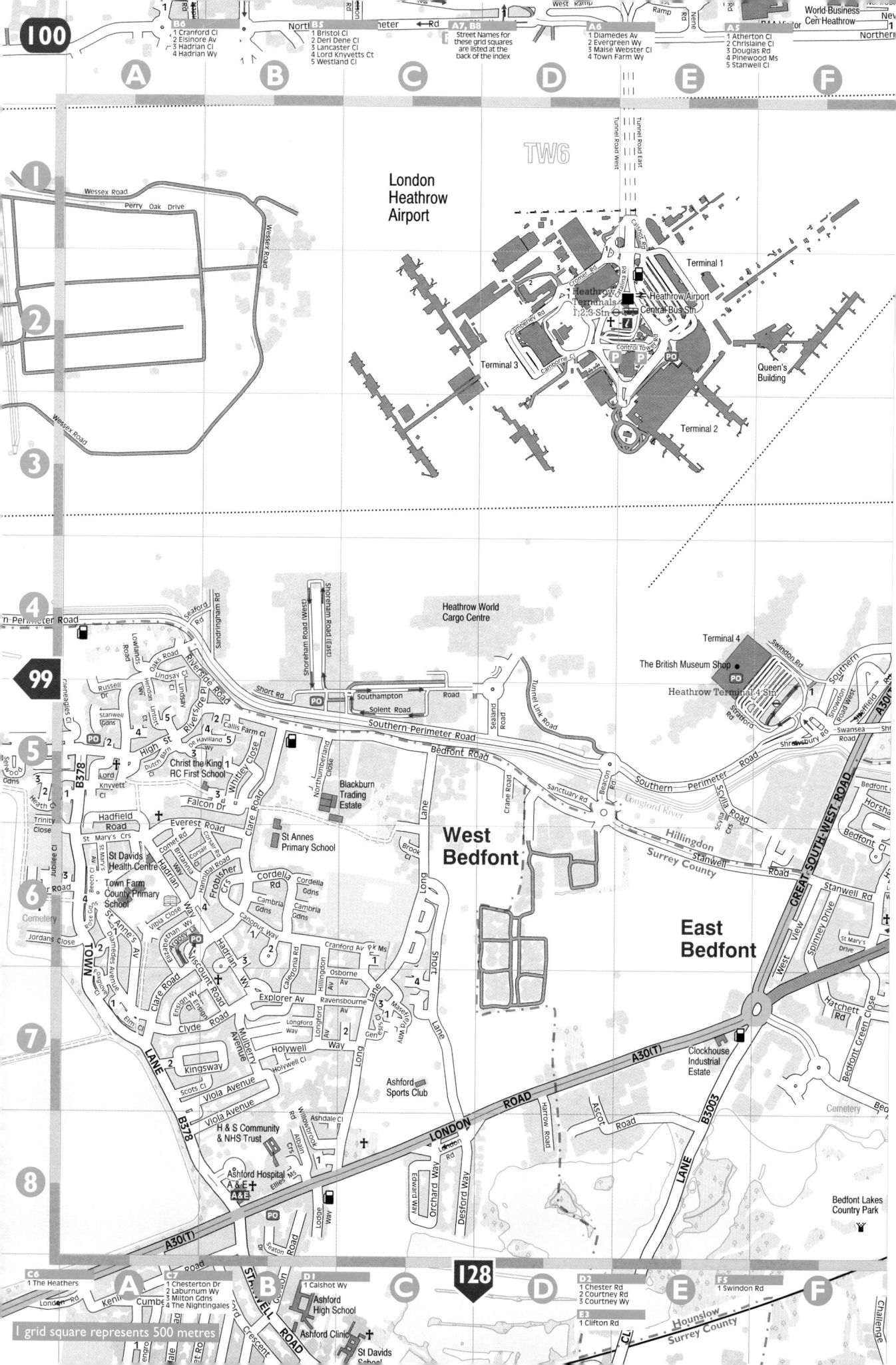

B6
1 Cranford Cl
2 Elsinore Av
3 Hadrian Cl
4 Hadrian Wy

North B5
1 Bristol Cl
2 Deri Dene Cl
3 Lancaster Cl
4 Lord Knyvetts Ct
5 Westland Cl

Street Names for
these grid squares
are listed at the
back of the index

A6
1 Diamedes Av
2 Evergreen Wy
3 Maise Webster Cl
4 Town Farm Wy

A7, B8

A5
1 Atherton Cl
2 Chrislaine Cl
3 Douglas Rd
4 Pinewood Ms
5 Stanwell Cl

World Business
Cen Heathrow

A   B   C   D   E   F

TW6

London
Heathrow
Airport

Terminal 1

Heathrow Airport
Central Bus Stn

Heathrow
Terminals
1,2,3 Stn

Control Tower

Queen's
Building

Terminal 3

Terminal 2

1

Wessex Road

Perry Oak Drive

Wessex Road

Wessex Road

2

3

4

99

Heathrow World
Cargo Centre

Terminal 4

The British Museum Shop

Heathrow Terminal 4 Stn

Swindon Rd

Southern

Shoreham Road (West)

Shoreham Road (East)

Seaford Rd

Sandringham Rd

Riverside Road

Short Rd

Southampton

Solent Road

Road

Southern Perimeter Road

Bedfont Road

Tunnel Link Road

Sealand Road

Crane Road

Sanctuary Rd

Beacon Rd

Southern Perimeter Road

Scylla Rd

Longford River

Hillingdon

Stanwell
Road

Surrey County

Bedfont

5

Russell
Dr

Lowlands
Road

Oaks Road

Lindsay

Lindsay

High St

De Havilland
Wy

Dutch Barn

Callis Farm Cl

Whitley Close

Clare Road

Northumberland
Close

Blackburn
Trading
Estate

Long
Lane

**West
Bedfont**

Brook
Cl

**East
Bedfont**

Stanwell Gdns

Christ the King
RC First School

Falcon Dr

St Annes
Primary School

Hadfield
Road

Everest Road

Cordelia
Rd

Cordelia
Gdns

Cambria
Rd

Cambria
Gdns

Campus Way

Cranford Av

Pk Ms

GREAT SOUTH WEST ROAD

West
View

Spinney Drive

Hatchett
Rd

Bedfont
Cl

Horshar

Bedfont

Stanwell Rd

St Mary's
Drive

6

Trinity
Close

St Mary's Crs

St Davids
Health Centre

Town Farm
County Primary
School

Viola Close

Hadrian

Frobisher
Crs

Comet Rd

Britannia

Corsair

Hannibal Rd

Cemetery

Jordans Close

7

Cemetery

Elm Cl

St Anne's Av

Diamedes Av

Clare Road

Viscount Road

Mulberry Avenue

Clyde Road

Ensign Wy

Holywell

Longford
Way

Explorer Av

Ravensbourne
Av

Osborne
Av

Caledonia Rd

Hillingdon

Longford
Way

Long
Lane

Maxey
Rd

Gen

Kingsway

Scots Cl

Viola Avenue

Viola Avenue

Holywell

Ashford
Sports Club

TOWN
LANE

B378

A30(T)

Clockhouse
Industrial
Estate

Ascot
Road

B3003

Cemetery

8

H & S Community
& NHS Trust

Ashford Hospital
A&E
A&E

Willowbrook

Ashdale Cl

Altain

Crs

PO

Seaton
Road

Kent
Road

Cumbe

London Rd

B378

LANE

A30(T)

LONDON

ROAD

London

Edward
Way

Orchard Way

Desford
Way

Harrow
Road

Bedfont Green Close

Bedfont Lakes
Country Park

Hounslow

Surrey County

Challenge

C6
1 The Heathers

C7
1 Chesterton Dr
2 Laburnum Wy
3 Milton Gdns
4 The Nightingales

D1
1 Calshot Wy

128

D2
1 Chester Rd
2 Courtney Rd
3 Courtney Wy

E3
1 Clifton Rd

F5
1 Swindon Rd

A   B   C   D   E   F

Ashford
High School

Ashford Clinic

St Davids
School

STANWELL
ROAD

Crescent

1 grid square represents 500 metres

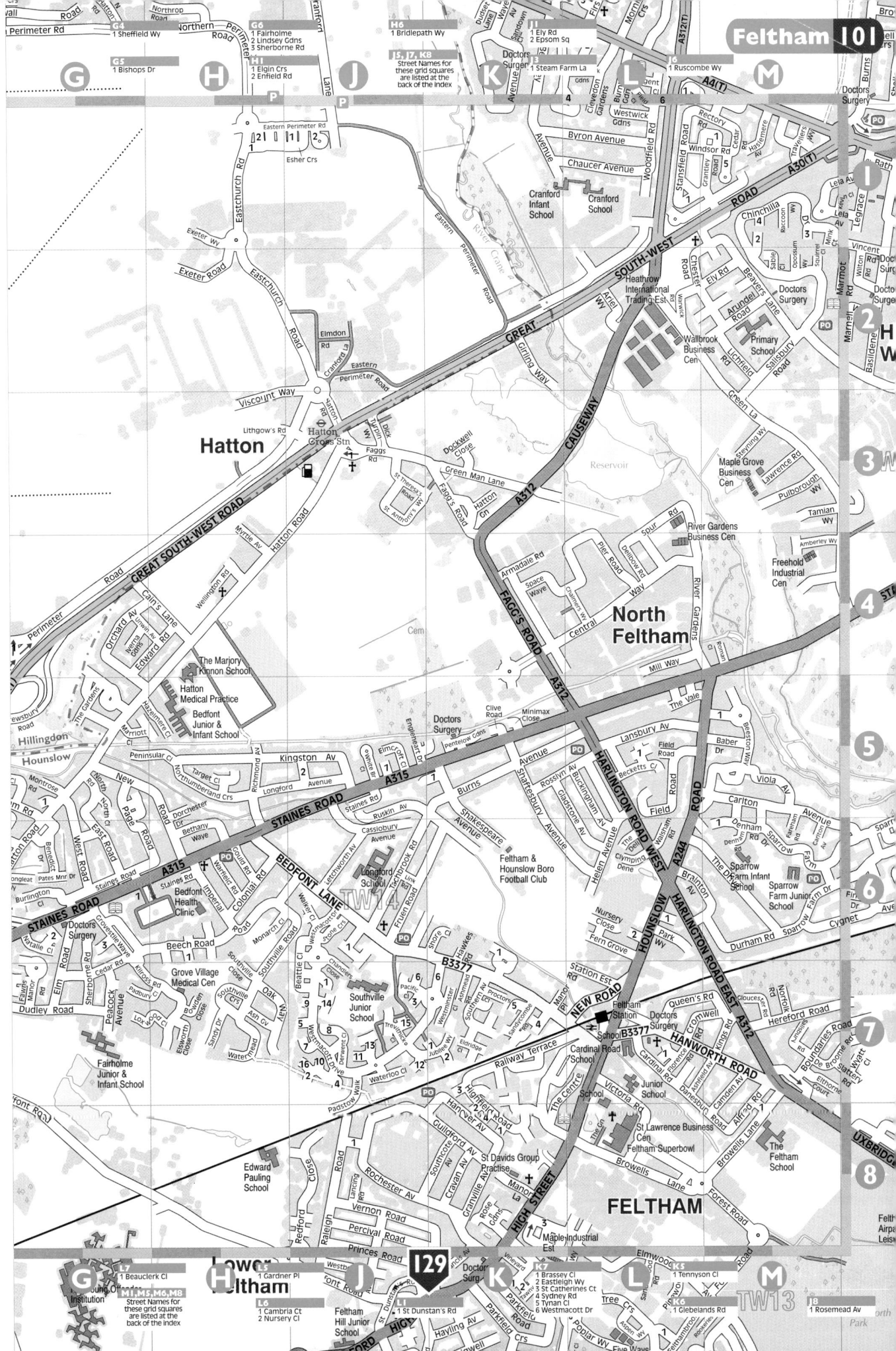

A2
1 Atherton Cl
2 Whitehill Cl

A   B   C   **74**   D   E   F

I

Little
Wood

Whittonditch

Oaken
Coppice

's
Farm

Love's Lane

Ashley
Piece

Ashley Piece

Crowood Lane

Road

Swan's Bottom

Townfield

Chapel La

Orchard Cl

Isles Rd

Oxford St

Whittonditch

2

PO

Scholard's Lane

Stanhard La

Union St

Green Acres

Halfway Lane

**New
Town**

The Paddocks

Street

Newtown

Road

Ramsbury

River Kennet

Knighton

3

Park
Coppice

4

5

ell's Farm

6

Rudge
Coppice

Lawn
Coppice

Littlecote

7

Rudge

Rudge
Farm House

West Berkshire
Wiltshire County

8

Church   **130**   Road

Littlecote Road

A   B   C   **130**   D   E   F

Green Farm

I grid square represents 500 metres

G

H

Crooked Soley J

75

K **Straight Soley**

L

M

Ramsbury 103

I

2

3

104

5

Leverton

6

7

8

Foxbury Wood

Briary Wood

B4001

Wiltshire County
West Berkshire

Old Hayward Rd

B4192

Chilton Foliat

Chilton Foliat College of Education Aided School

Glebe Pl

Chilton Park Farm

Chilton

Manor Farm

B4192

STAG HILL

B4001

Whitelocks Piece

Leverton Lane

B4192

Leverton

Brickkiln Copse

Wiltshire County
West Berkshire

B4192

CHARNHAM ST

Heronqate

A4

BATH ROAD

Hopgrass Farm

River Dun

The Surgery

Hungerford Community
Health Clinic

Parsonage La

Church Rd

Cake Wood

G

H

J 131

Marsh Lane

K **Marsh G**

L

Shalbourne Cl

Smithand

M

Chilton Way

Avon Canal

LC

Regent Cl

Atherton Cs

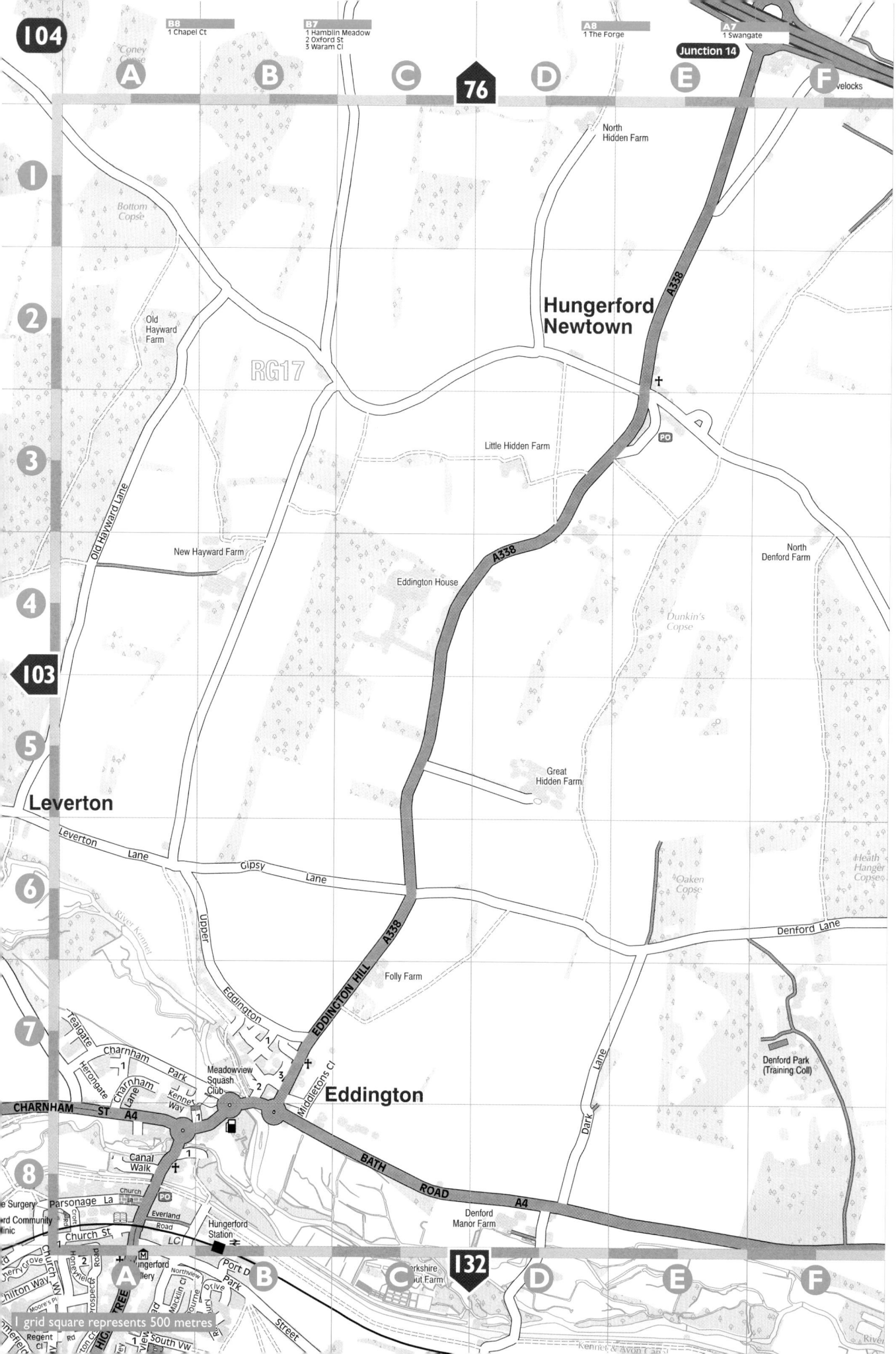

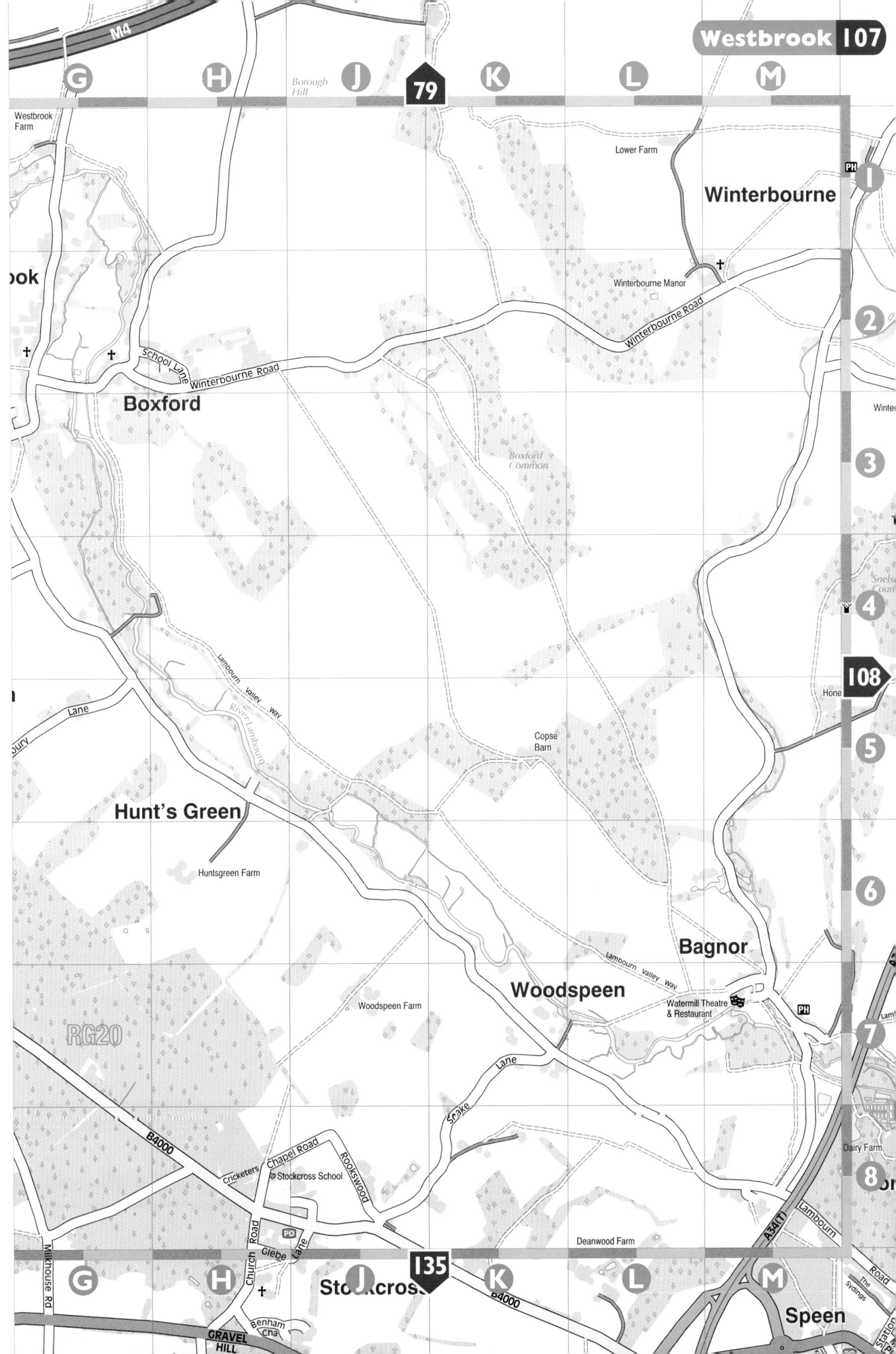

M4

G   H   Borough Hill   J   79   K   L   M   PH   1

Westbrook Farm

Lower Farm

Winterbourne

Winterbourne Manor

Winterbourne Road   2

bok

Winte

School Lane   Winterbourne Road   3

Boxford

Boxford Common

4

Lambourn valley Way   108

River Lambourn   Hone

bury   Copse Barn   5

Lane

Hunt's Green

6

Huntsgreen Farm

Lambourn Valley Way   **Bagnor**

Woodspeen   PH

RG20   Woodspeen Farm   Watermill Theatre & Restaurant   7

Lane   Snake   Lambourn

B4000   Dairy Farm

Chapel Road   8

Cricketers   Stockcross School   Rookswood

Milkhouse Rd   Church Road   PO   Glebe Lane   Deanwood Farm

G   H   J   135   K   L   M   **Speen**

Stockcross   B4000

Benham Cha

GRAVEL HILL

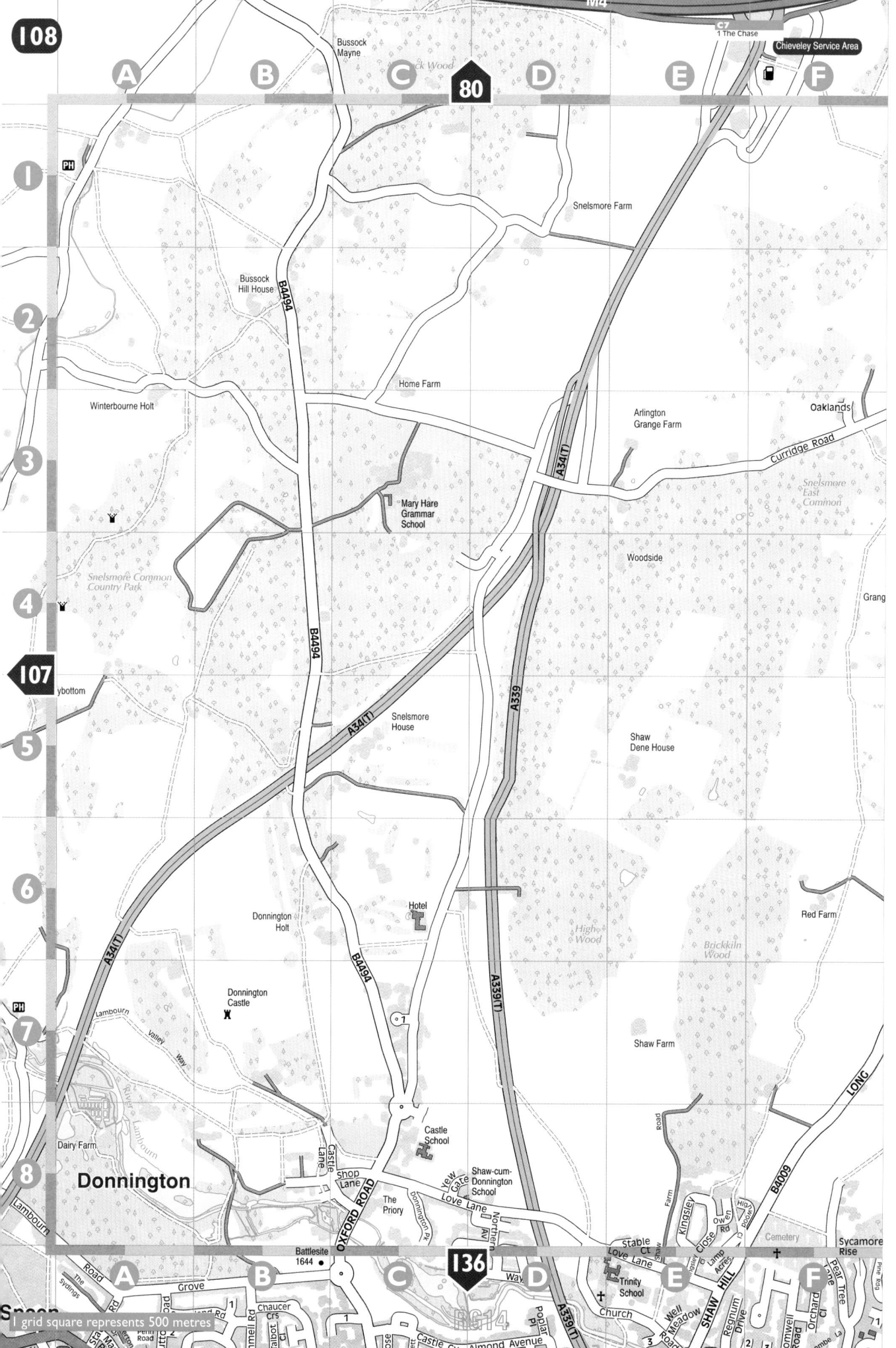

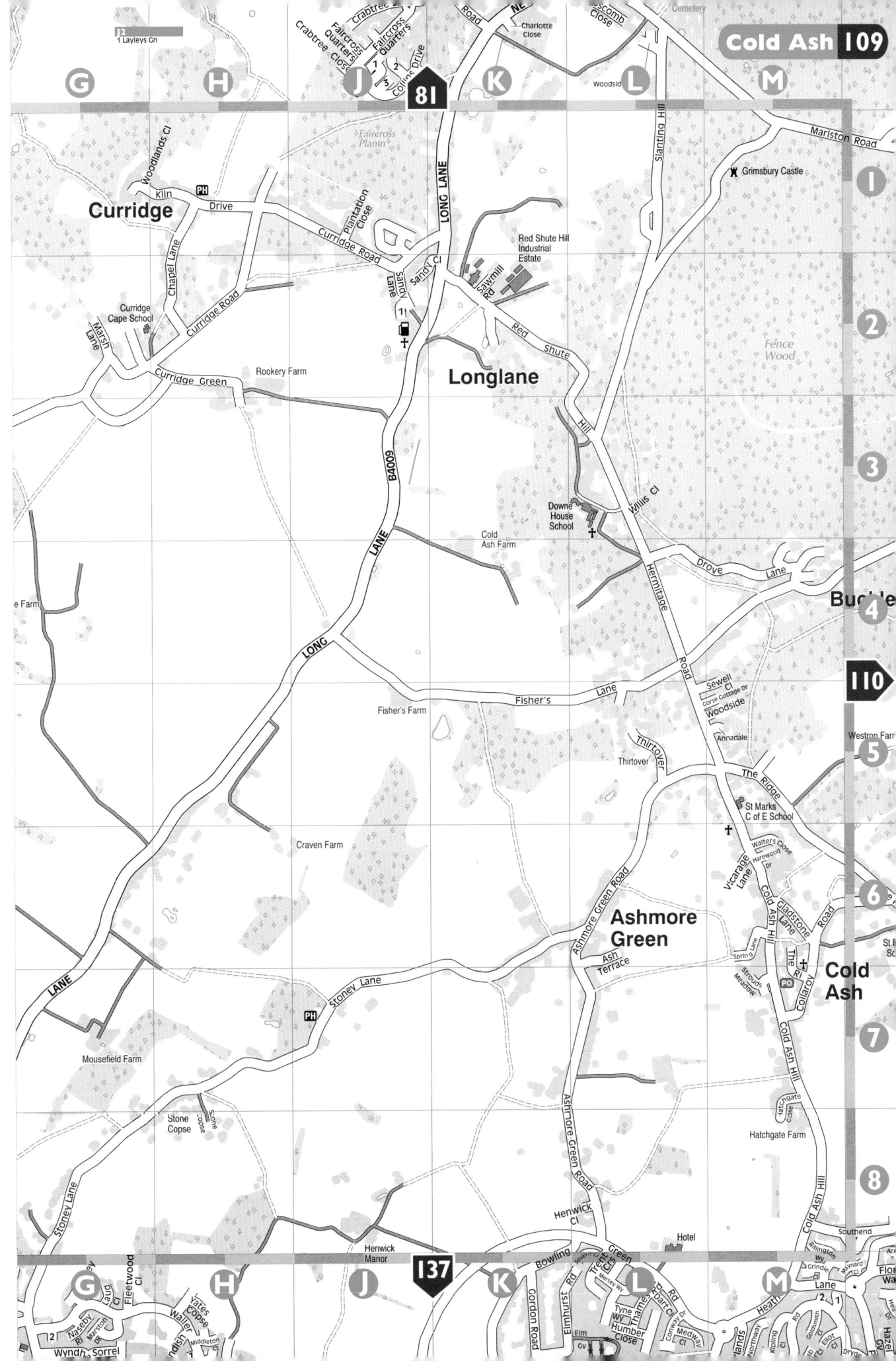

G H J **81** K L M

I

Curridge

Grimsbury Castle

Woodlands Cl

Kiln PH Drive

Chapel Lane

Plantation Close

Crabtree Quarters

Faircross Quarters

Crabtree Close

Charlotte Close

Woodside

NE

Collins Drive

Marlston Road

Curridge Road

Curridge Road

Sandy Cl

Sandy Lane

LONG LANE

Red Shute Hill Industrial Estate

Sawmill Cl

2

Curridge Cape School

Marsh Lane

Curridge Green

Rookery Farm

Red Shute Hill

Fence Wood

Longlane

3

B4009 LANE

Willis Cl

Downe House School

Cold Ash Farm

Hermitage Road

Drove Lane

Bucklet

4

110

LONG

Fisher's Lane

Fisher's Farm

Sewell Cl

Gorse Cottage Dr

Woodside

Annadale

Westron Farr

5

Thirtover

Thirtover

The Ridge

St Marks C of E School

Walters Close

Harewood Dr

Craven Farm

Vicarage Lane

Gladstone Lane

Cold Ash Hill

6

LANE

Ashmore Green Road

Ash Terrace

Spring Lane

The Ri

PO

Strouds Meadow

Collatoy Road

Cold Ash Hill

St M So

Cold Ash

Stoney Lane

PH

7

Mousefield Farm

Stone Copse

Stone Copse

Ashmore Green Road

Hatchgate B4009

Hatchgate Farm

8

Stoney Lane

Fleetwood Cl

Yates Copse

Waller

Henwick Manor

Henwick Cl

Bowling Green

Hotel

Southend

Cold Ash Hill

Heath Rd

G H **137** J K L M

Naseby Maud

Candish Middleton

Wyndh Sorrel

Elmhurst Rd

Gordon Road

Elm Cl Cv

Trenchard Tyne Wy Thames Cl Humber Close Conway Wy Medway Cl Severn Cres Mersey Wy

Northway Eliot

Godsmith

Maynard

Grindle

Brya

Florl Wa

Lane

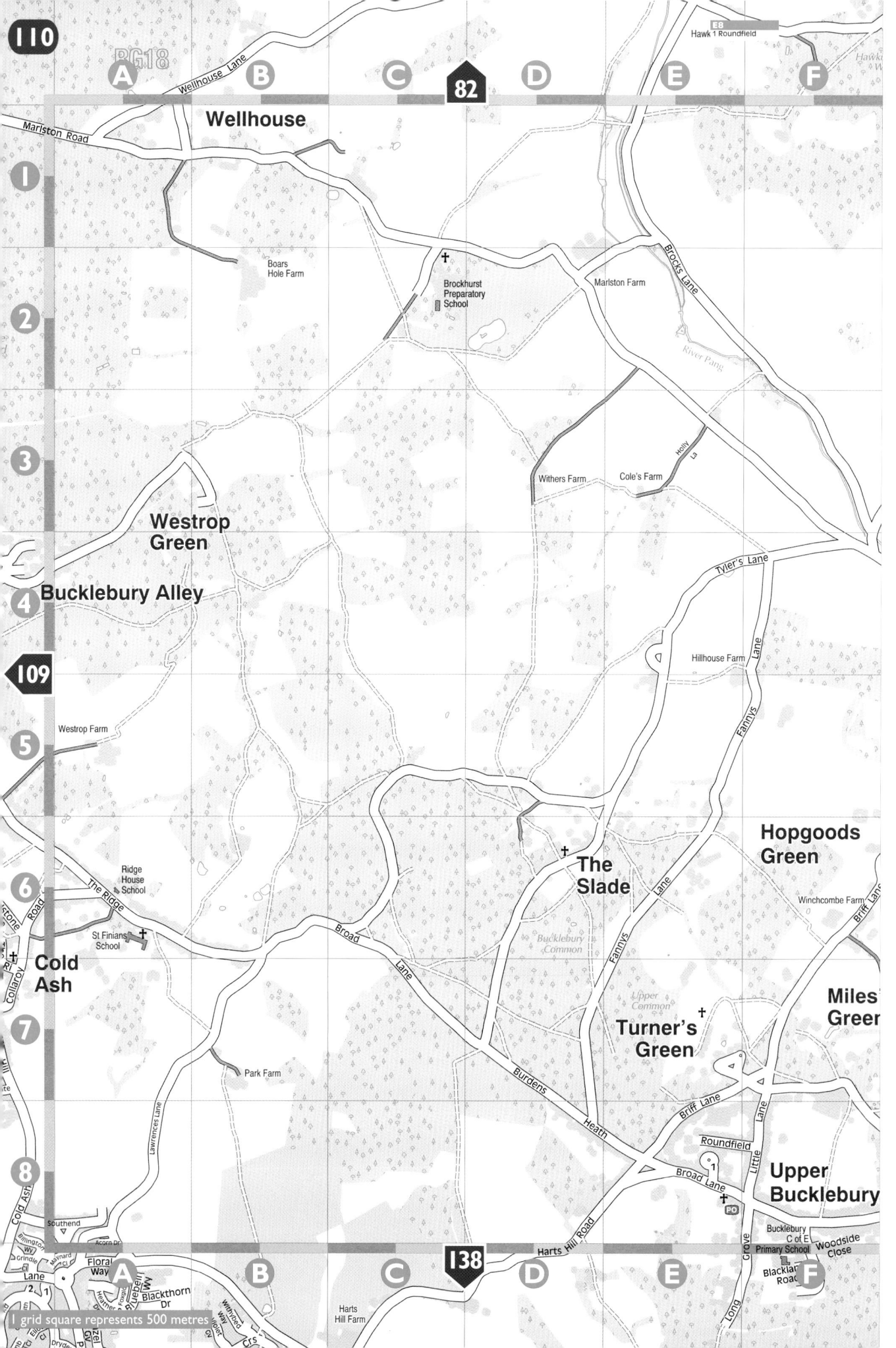

RG18

E8

Hawk 1 Roundfield

Wellhouse Lane

Wellhouse

Marlston Road

Hawk...W

I

Boars
Hole Farm

✝
Brockhurst
Preparatory
School

Marlston Farm

Brocks Lane

2

River Pang

3

Withers Farm   Cole's Farm

Holly La

**Westrop
Green**

Tyler's Lane

Bucklebury Alley

4

Hillhouse Farm

Fannys Lane

Westrop Farm

5

**Hopgoods
Green**

✝
**The
Slade**

Winchcombe Farm

Briff Lane

6

Ridge
House
School

The Ridge

Broad

Lane

Bucklebury
Common

...stone
Road

✝
St Finians
School

**Miles
Green**

Fannys
Lane

✝
Upper
Common

Collaroy...

✝

**Cold
Ash**

**Turner's
Green**

7

Lawrences Lane

Park Farm

Burdens

Heath

Briff Lane

Roundfield

Little Lane

**Upper
Bucklebury**

8

Cold Ash...

Broad Lane

1

✝
PO

Bucklebury
C of E
Primary School

Woodside
Close

Southend

Elmington
Wy

Grove

Blacklan...
Road

...maynard
Cl

...Grindle

Floral
Way

Blackthorn
Dr

Harts Hill Road

2 1

Bluebell Wy

Withybed

Way

Crs

Harts
Hill Farm

Lane

Gazel...

Heather...

GV

Bryde...

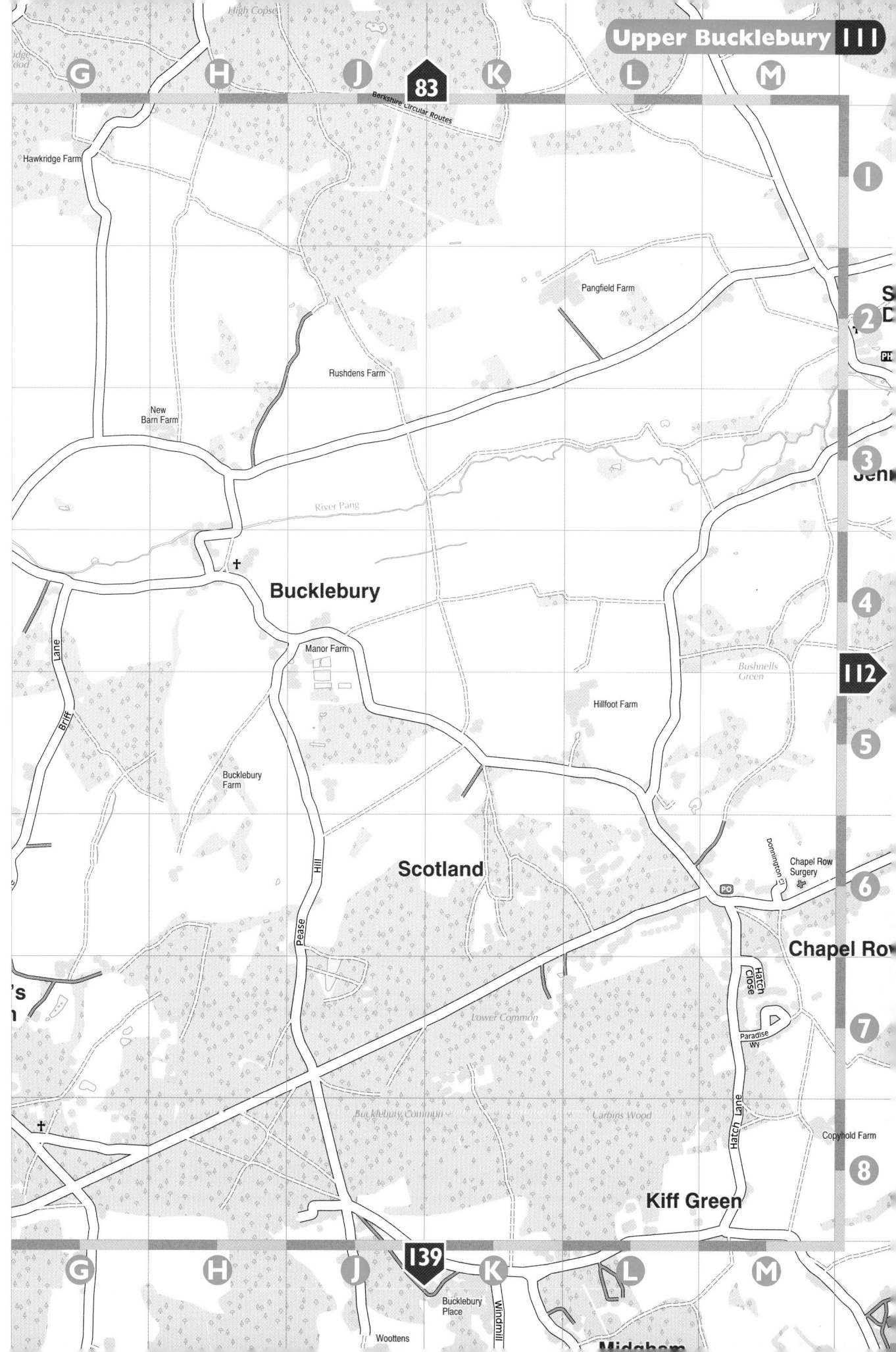

G   H   J   K   L   M

83
Berkshire Circular Routes

Hawkridge Farm

Pangfield Farm

1

S
D

2

PH

Rushdens Farm

Jen

3

New
Barn Farm

River Pang

4

112

Bucklebury

Manor Farm

Bushnells
Green

Hillfoot Farm

5

Lane

Briff

Bucklebury
Farm

Scotland

Donnington Cl

Chapel Row
Surgery

6

Pease

PO

Chapel Row

Hill

Hatch
Close

Lower Common

Paradise
Wy

7

Bucklebury Common

Larkins Wood

Copyhold Farm

8

Hatch Lane

Kiff Green

139

Bucklebury
Place

Windmill

Wootens

Midgham

G   H   J   K   L   M

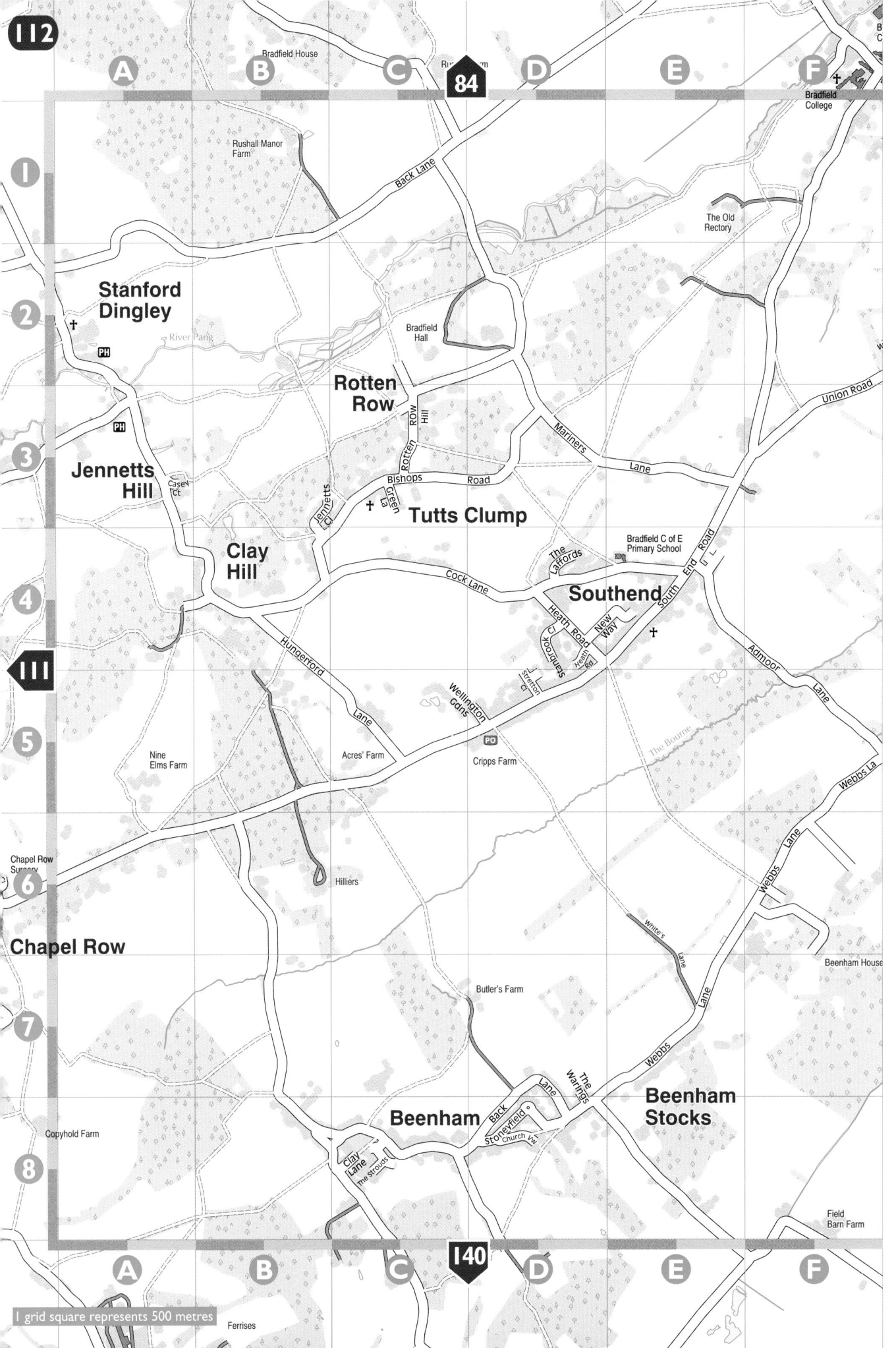

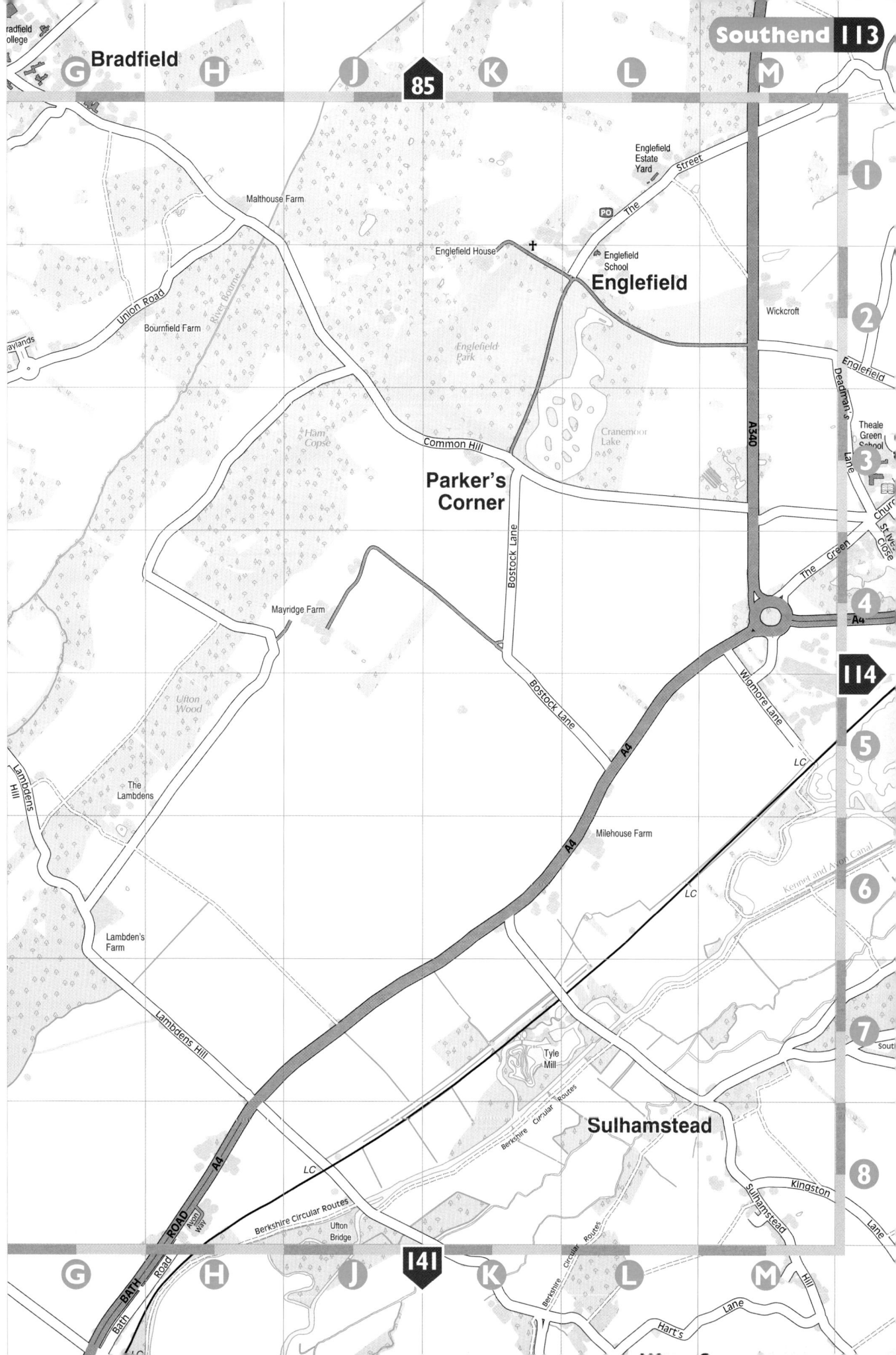

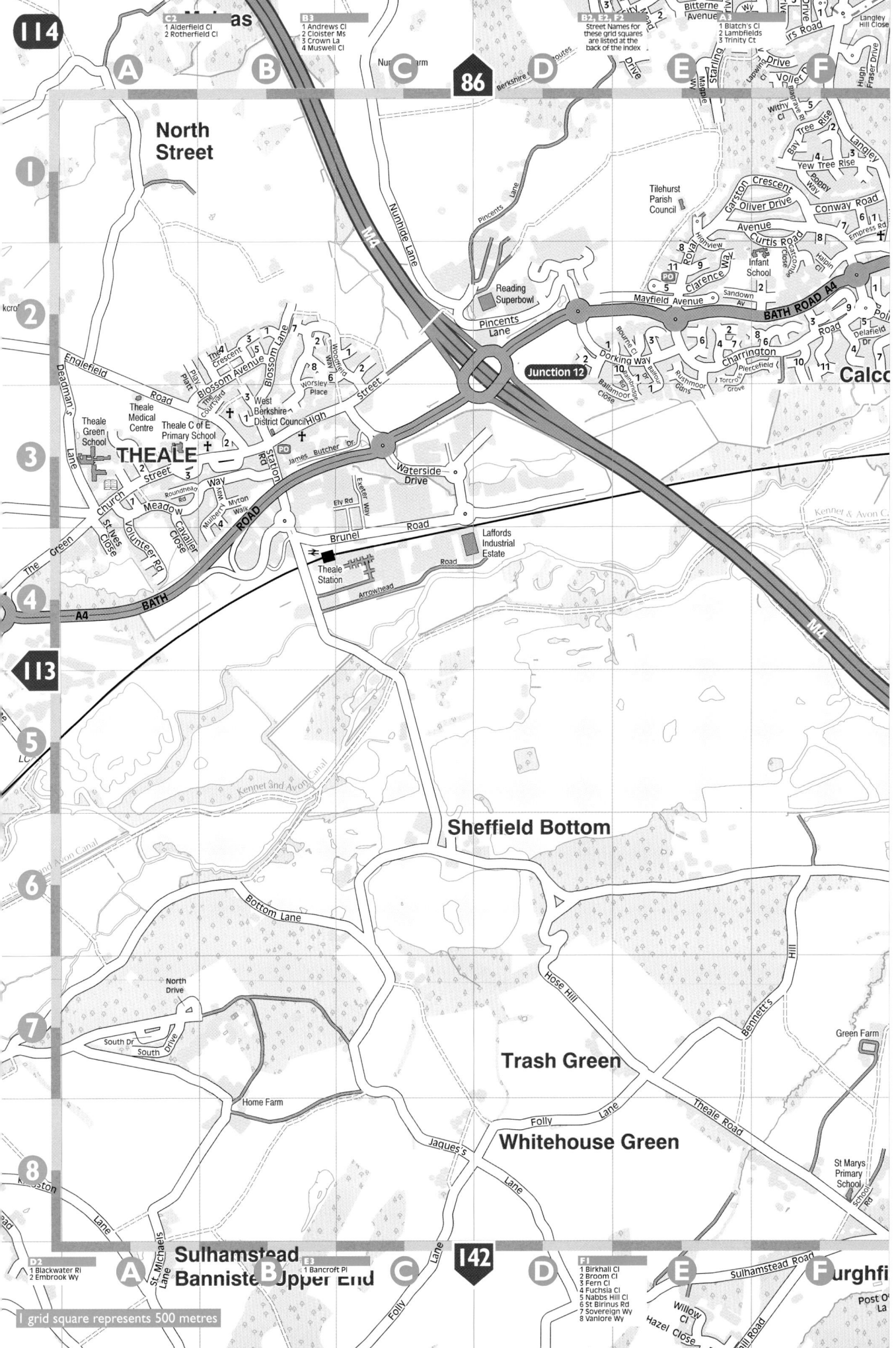

C2
1 Alderfield Cl
2 Rotherfield Cl

B3
1 Andrews Cl
2 Cloister Ms
3 Crown La
4 Muswell Cl

B2, E2, F2
Street Names for
these grid squares
are listed at the
back of the index

A3
1 Blatch's Cl
2 Lambfields
3 Trinity Ct

A **B** **C** **86** **D** **E** **F**

I

North Street

Tilehurst
Parish
Council

2

Reading
Superbowl

Pincents
Lane

BATH ROAD A4

Mayfield Avenue

Calco

Junction 12

Dorking Way

3

Englefield
Road

Deadman's
Lane

Theale
Green
School

THEALE

Theale
Medical
Centre

Theale C of E
Primary School

West
Berkshire
District Council

High

PO

James Butcher Dr

Waterside
Drive

Church

St Ives
Close

Meadow

Roundhead
Rd

Cavalier
Close

Mulbery

Myton
Walk

Station Rd

Elv Rd

Exeter Way

113

4

A4 **BATH**

Brunel

Road

Theale
Station

Arrowhead

Road

Laffords
Industrial
Estate

M4

Kennet & Avon

5

Kennet and Avon Canal

Sheffield Bottom

6

Bottom Lane

Hose Hill

7

North
Drive

South Dr

South Drive

Home Farm

Trash Green

Bennett's

HIII

Green Farm

Theale Road

8

Kingston
Lane

Jaques's

Lane

Folly
Lane

Whitehouse Green

Folly Lane

St Marys
Primary
School

School

D2
1 Blackwater Ri
2 Embrook Wy

A

St Michaels
Lane

Sulhamstead
Bannister Upper End

B

1 Bancroft Pl

C

Lane

Folly

142

D

F1
1 Birkhall Cl
2 Broom Cl
3 Fern Cl
4 Fuchsia Cl
5 Nabbs Hill Cl
6 St Birinus Rd
7 Sovereign Wy
8 Vanlore Wy

E

Willow
Cl

Hazel Close

Sulhamstead Road

F

Furghfi

Post O

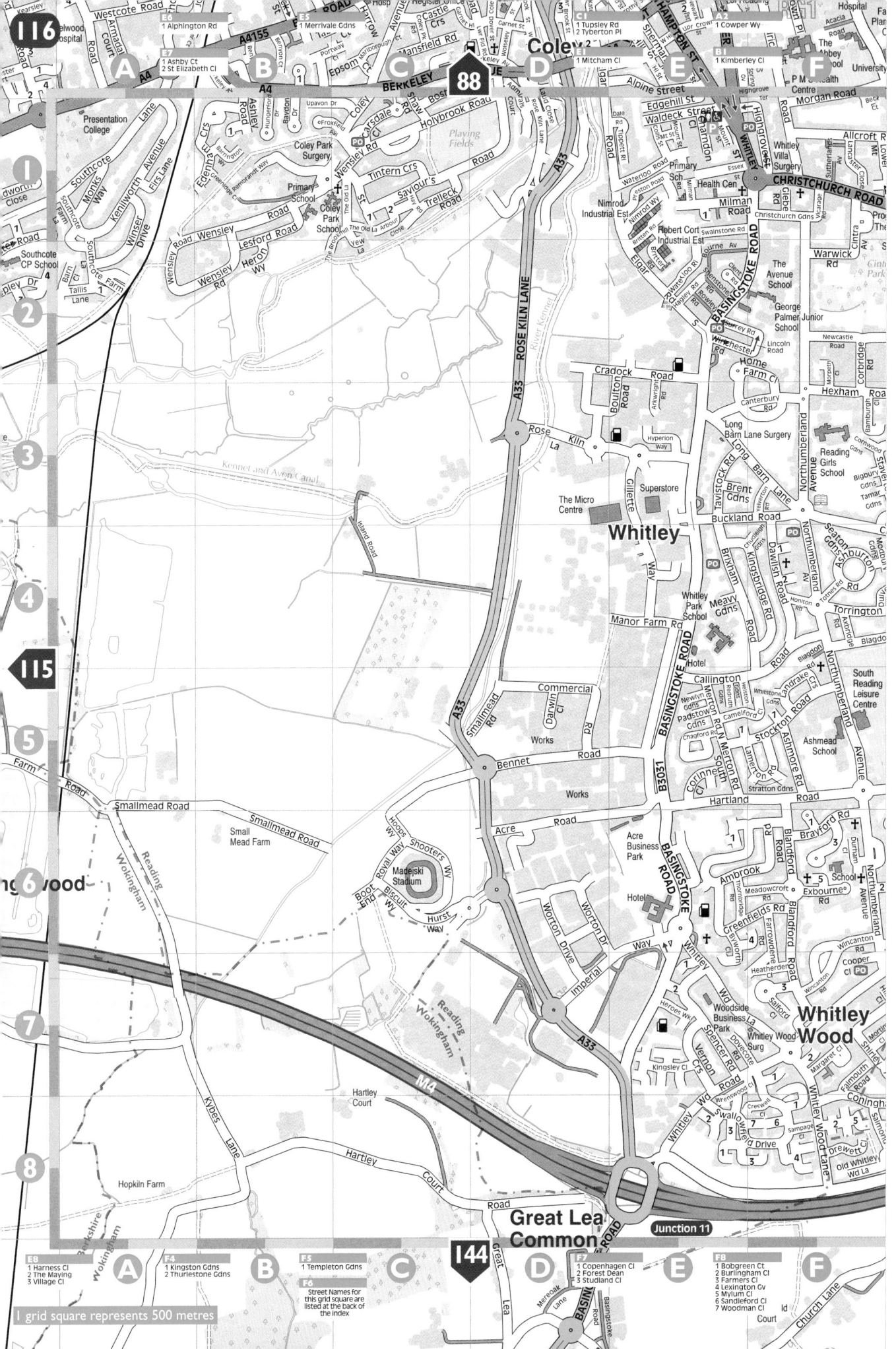

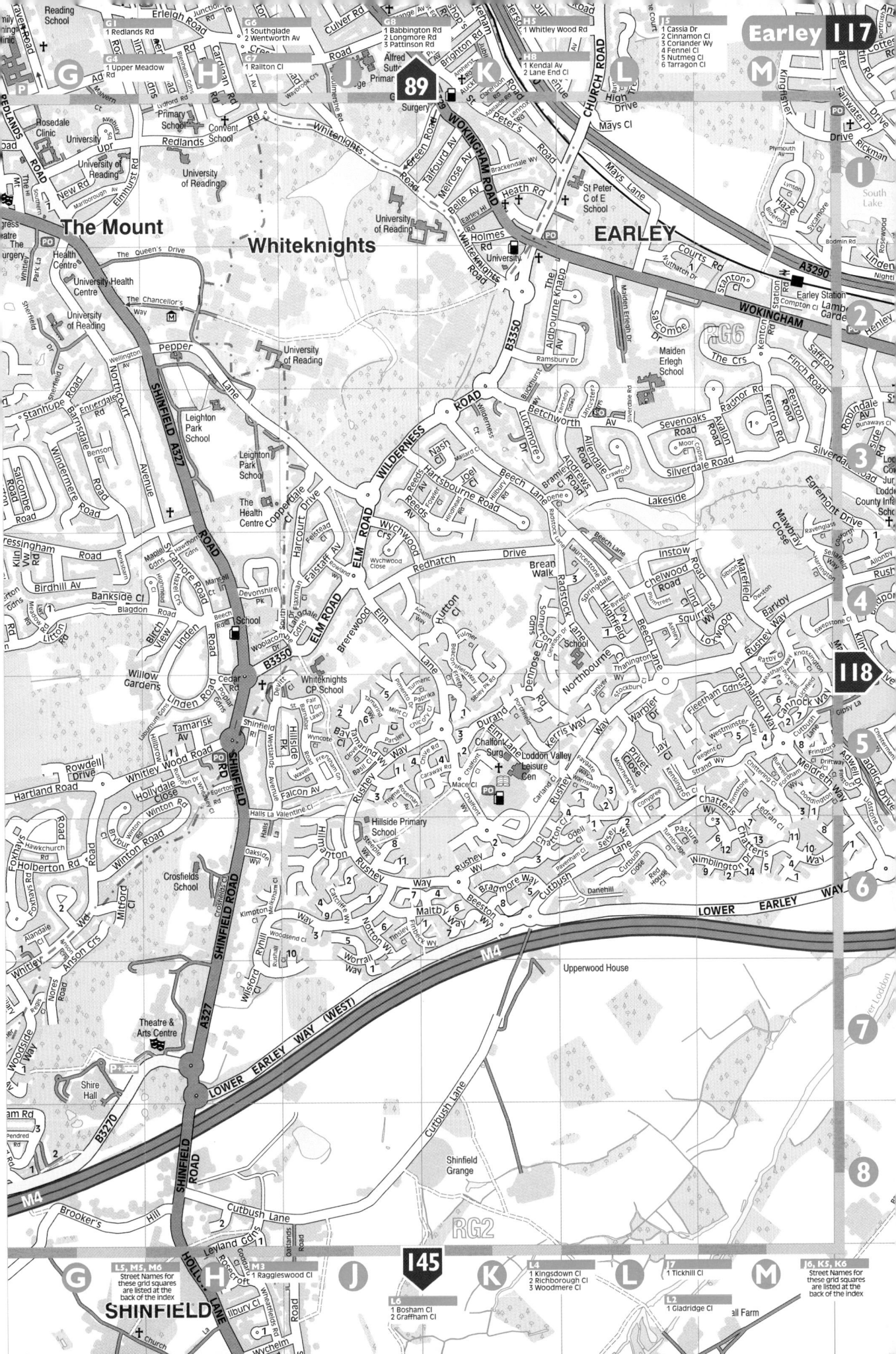

The Mount

Whiteknights

University of Reading

EARLEY

RG6

SHINFIELD

RG2

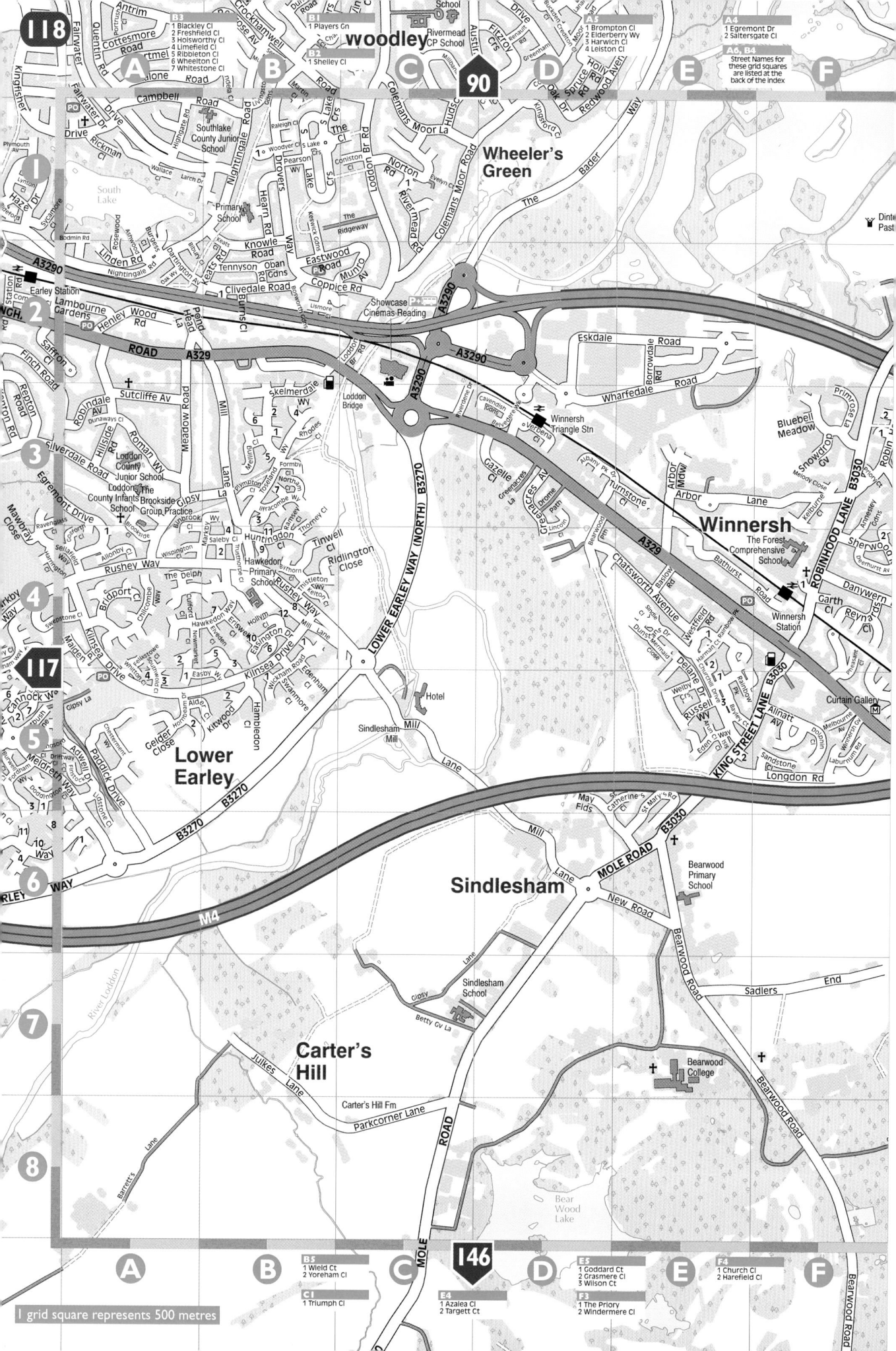

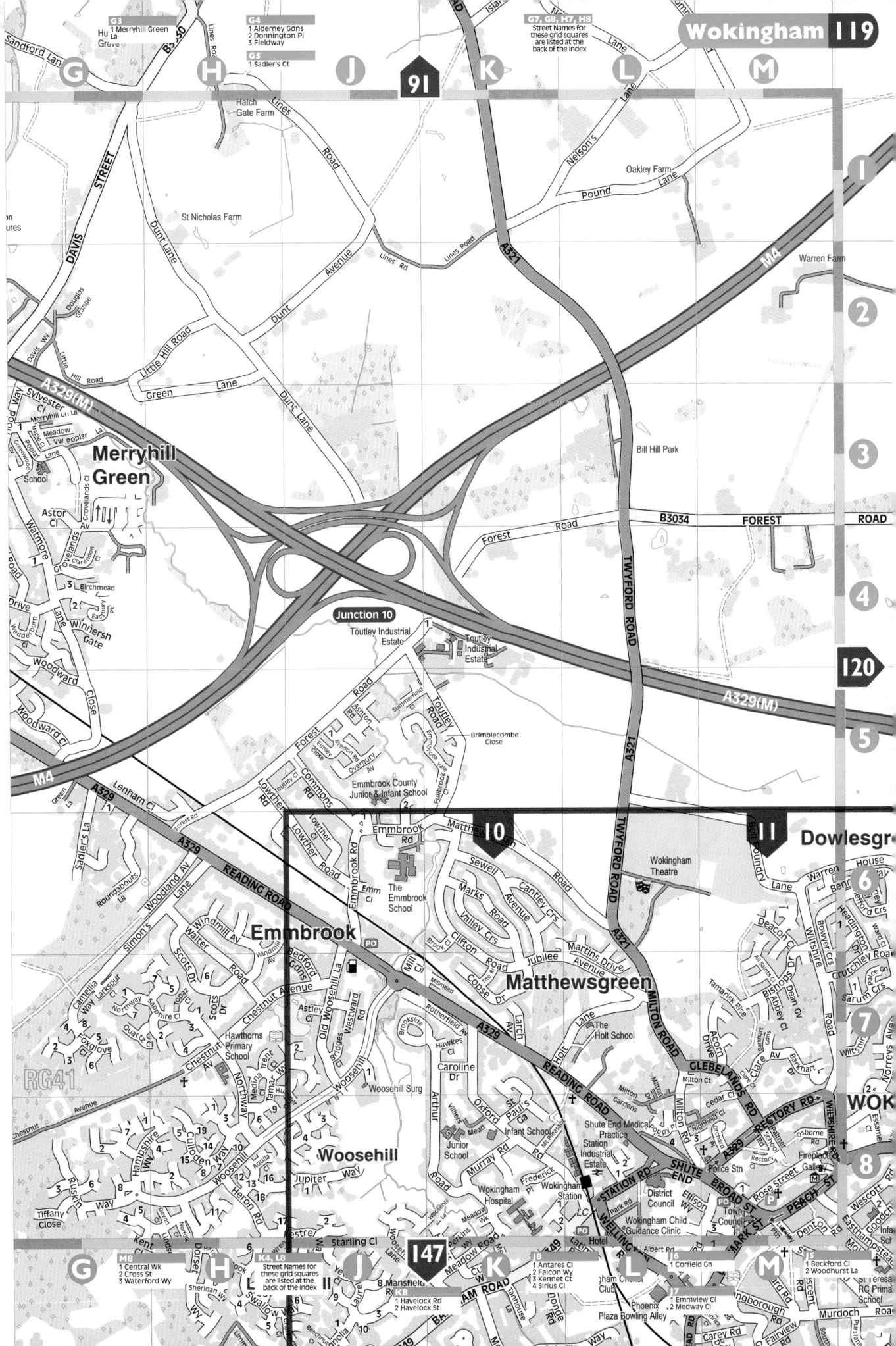

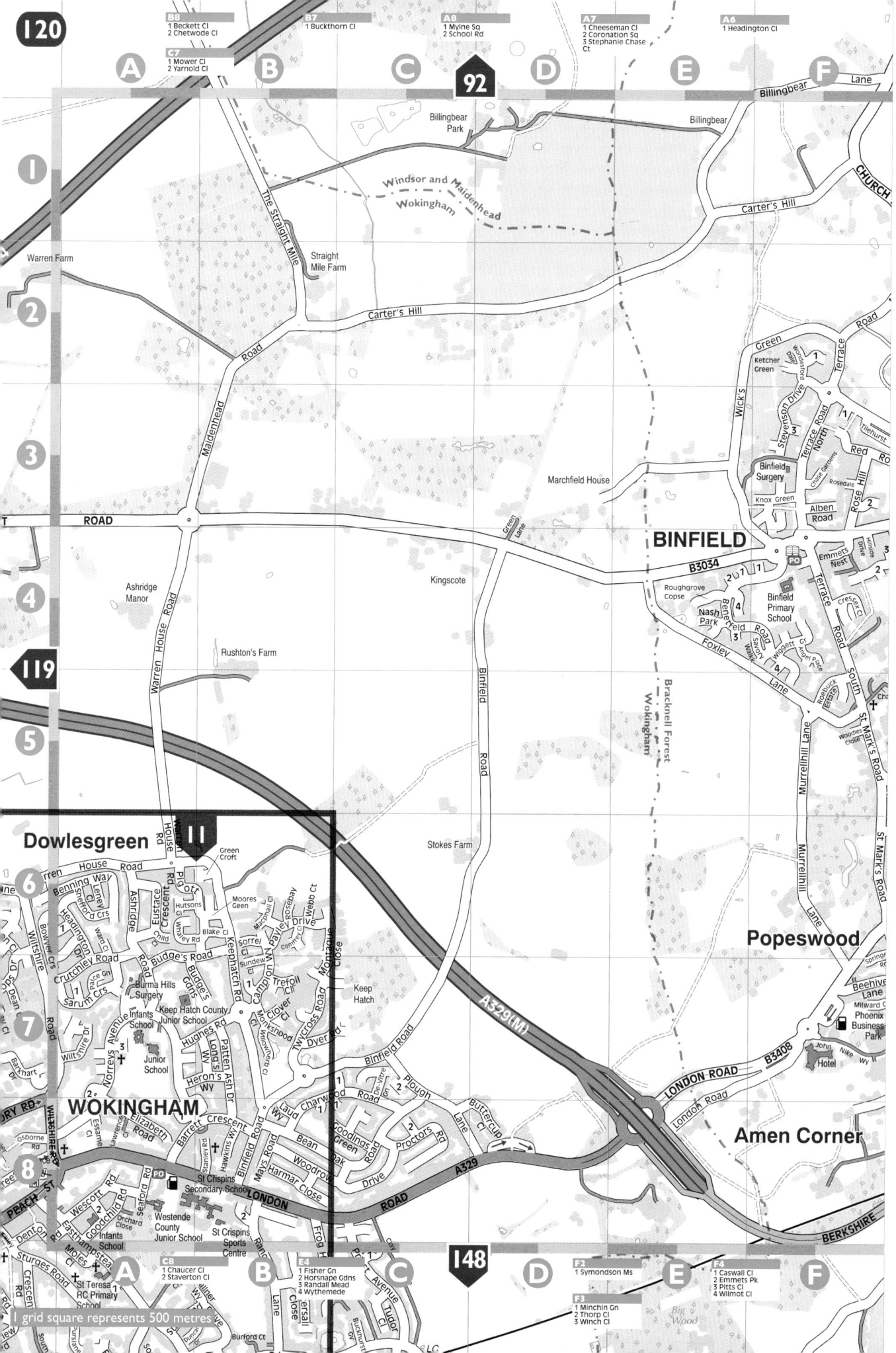

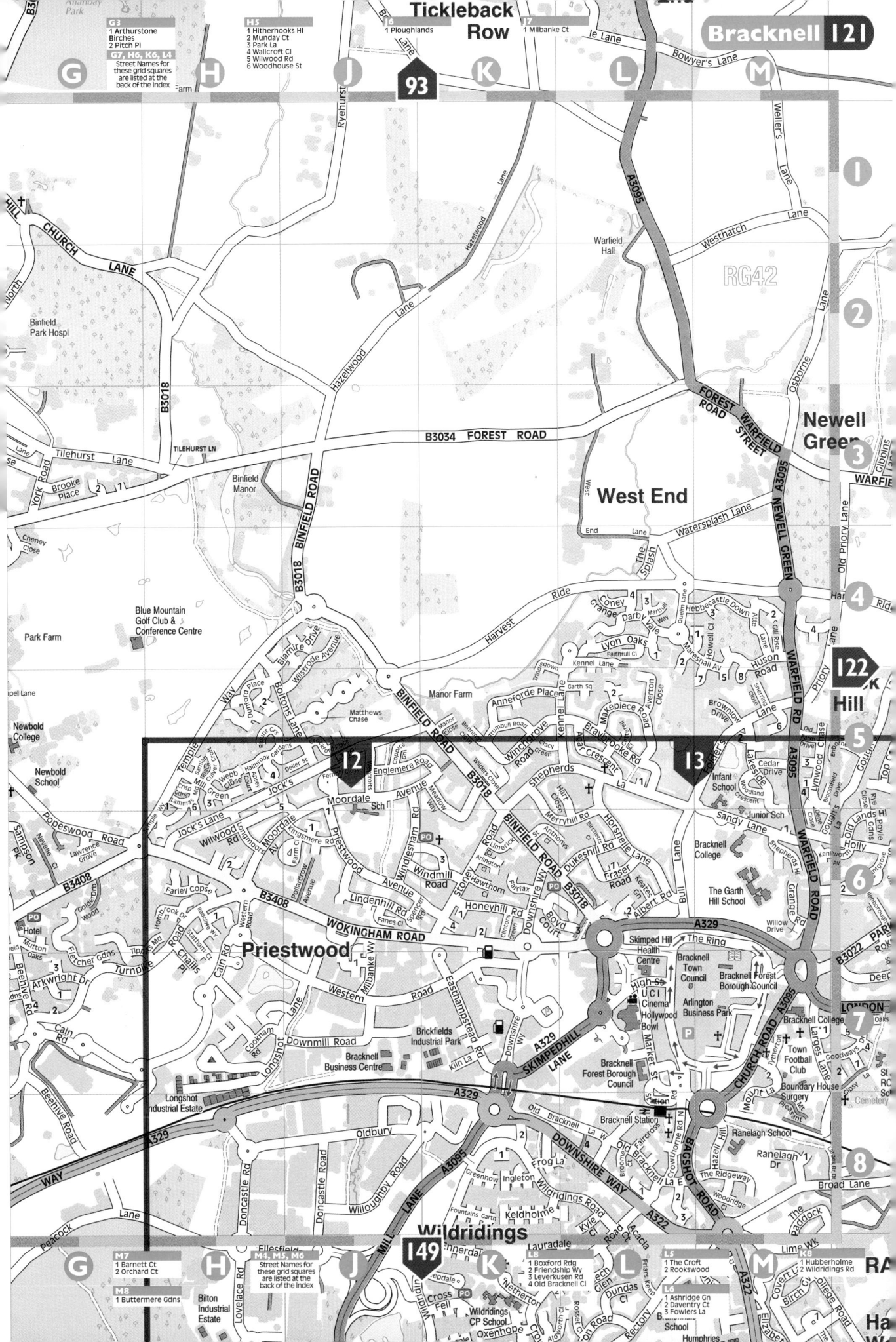

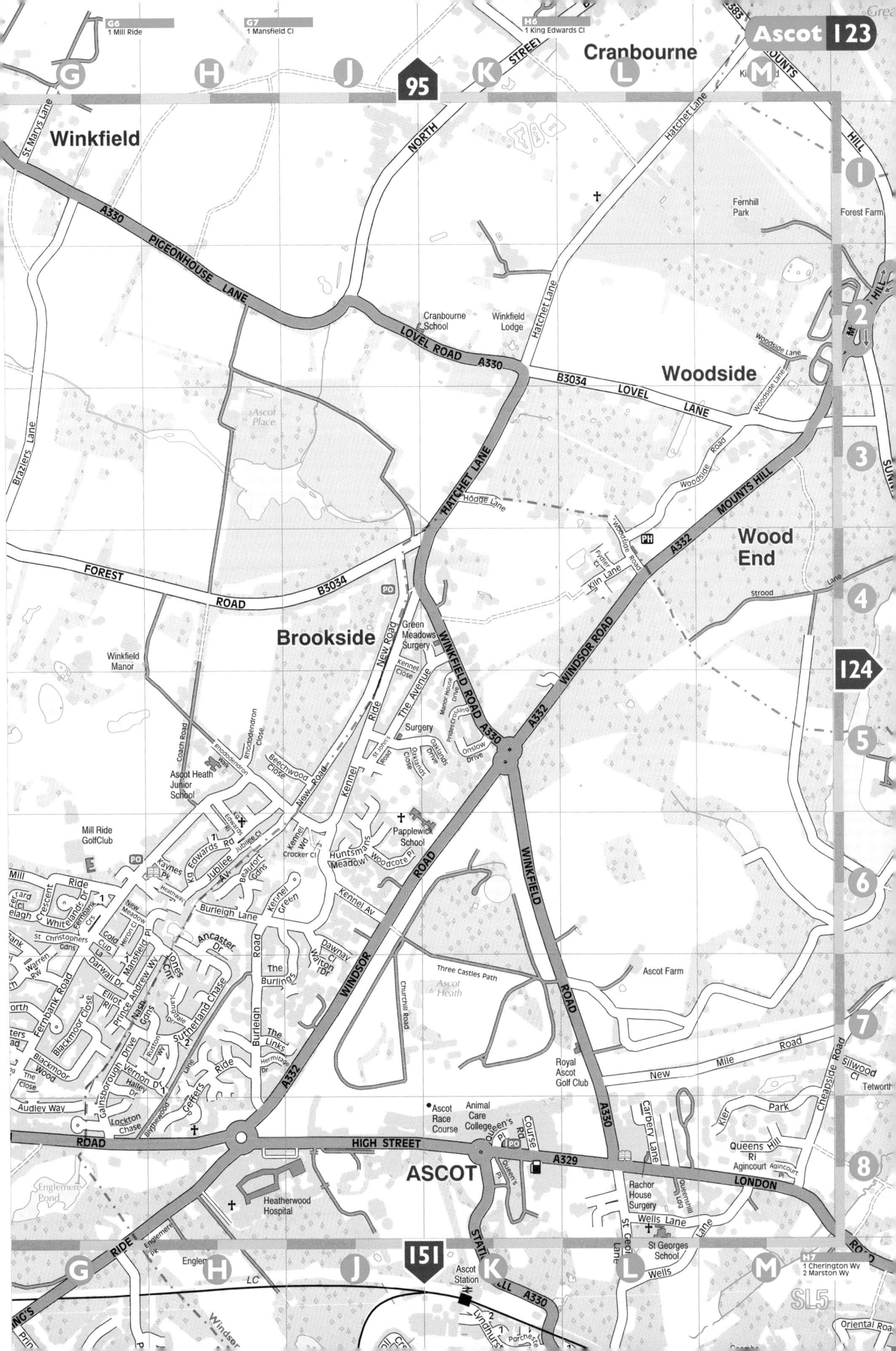

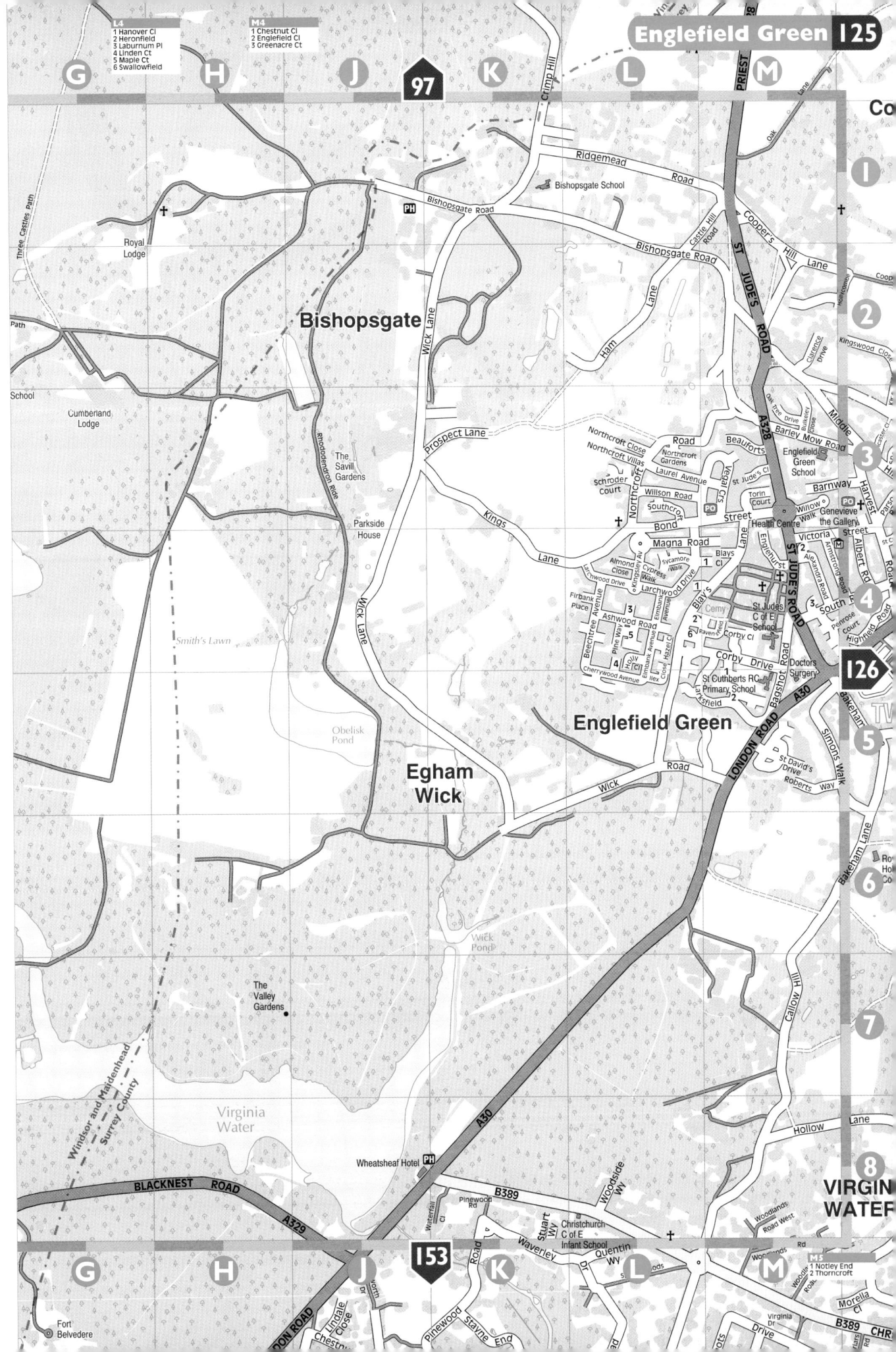

L4
1 Hanover Cl
2 Heronfield
3 Laburnum Pl
4 Linden Ct
5 Maple Ct
6 Swallowfield

M4
1 Chestnut Cl
2 Englefield Cl
3 Greenacre Ct

G H J 97 K L M

Crimp Hill

I

PRIEST

Ridgemead Road

Bishopsgate School

2

Bishopsgate Road

Castle Hill Road

Cooper's Hill Lane

Kingswood Close

Clarence Drive

Blukesley Close

Royal Lodge

Bishopsgate Road

Ham Lane

ST JUDE'S ROAD

Oak Lane

Coop

Three Castles Path

Bishopsgate

Oak Tree Drive

A328

Barley Mow Road

Middle

3

Path

Northcroft Close

Road

Northcroft Villas

Beauforts

Englefield Green School

Barnway

School

Northcroft Gardens

Vegal Crs

St Jude's Cl

Harvest

Cumberland Lodge

Prospect Lane

Schroder Court

Laurel Avenue

Wilson Road

Torin Court

PO

Willow Walk

Genevieve the Gallery

Street

Rhododendron Ride

The Savill Gardens

Northcroft

Southcroft

Bond

PO

Health Centre

Victoria

M

Albert Rd

4

Parkside House

Kings

Magna Road

Almond Cl

Sycamore Walk

Blays Cl

Blays

Alexandra Road

Armstrong Road

street

St Jude's Cl

Penrose Court

Highfield Road

Kingsley Av

Cypress Close

1

Larchwood Drive

Larchwood Drive

Cemy

Corby Cl

South R

126

Wick Lane

Lane

Firbank Place

3

Timbank Avenue

St Judes C of E School

Raven's

3

Beechtree Avenue

Ashwood Road

2

Corby Drive

Doctors Surgery

TW

Pine Way

Holly

Hazel Cl

1

Corby Drive

Road

5

Cherrywood Avenue

Ilex

St Cuthberts RC Primary School

Larksfield

2

Bagshot Road

Simons Walk

Bakeham

5

Englefield Green

Lane

Smith's Lawn

Wick

Road

St David's Drive

LONDON ROAD

A30

Roberts Way

6

Obelisk Pond

Egham Wick

Callow Hill

Bakeham Lane

Ro Hol Co

7

Wick Pond

A30

The Valley Gardens

Hollow Lane

Windsor and Maidenhead
Surrey County

Virginia Water

8

Wheatsheaf Hotel PH

VIRGIN
WATE

BLACKNEST ROAD

Woodside

B389

Woodlands Road West

M5
1 Notley End
2 Thorncroft

A329

Waterfall Rd

Pinewood Rd

B389

Stuart Wy

Christchurch C of E Infant School

Woodlands Rd

Morella

G H J 153 K L M CHR

Fort Belvedere

Lindale Close

Chestn

Pinewood Stayne End

Waverley

Quentin Wy

Loods

Virginia Dr

B389

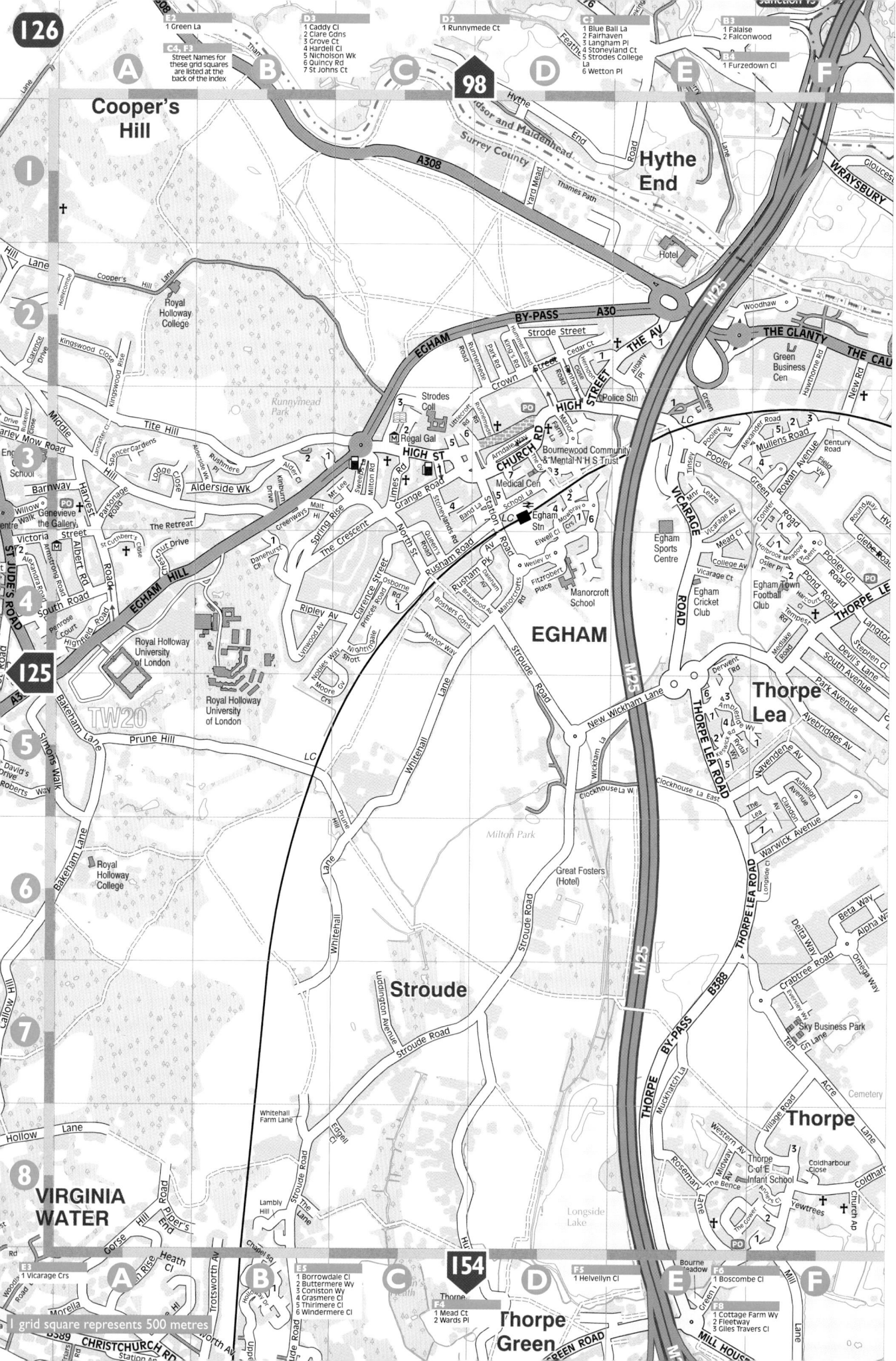

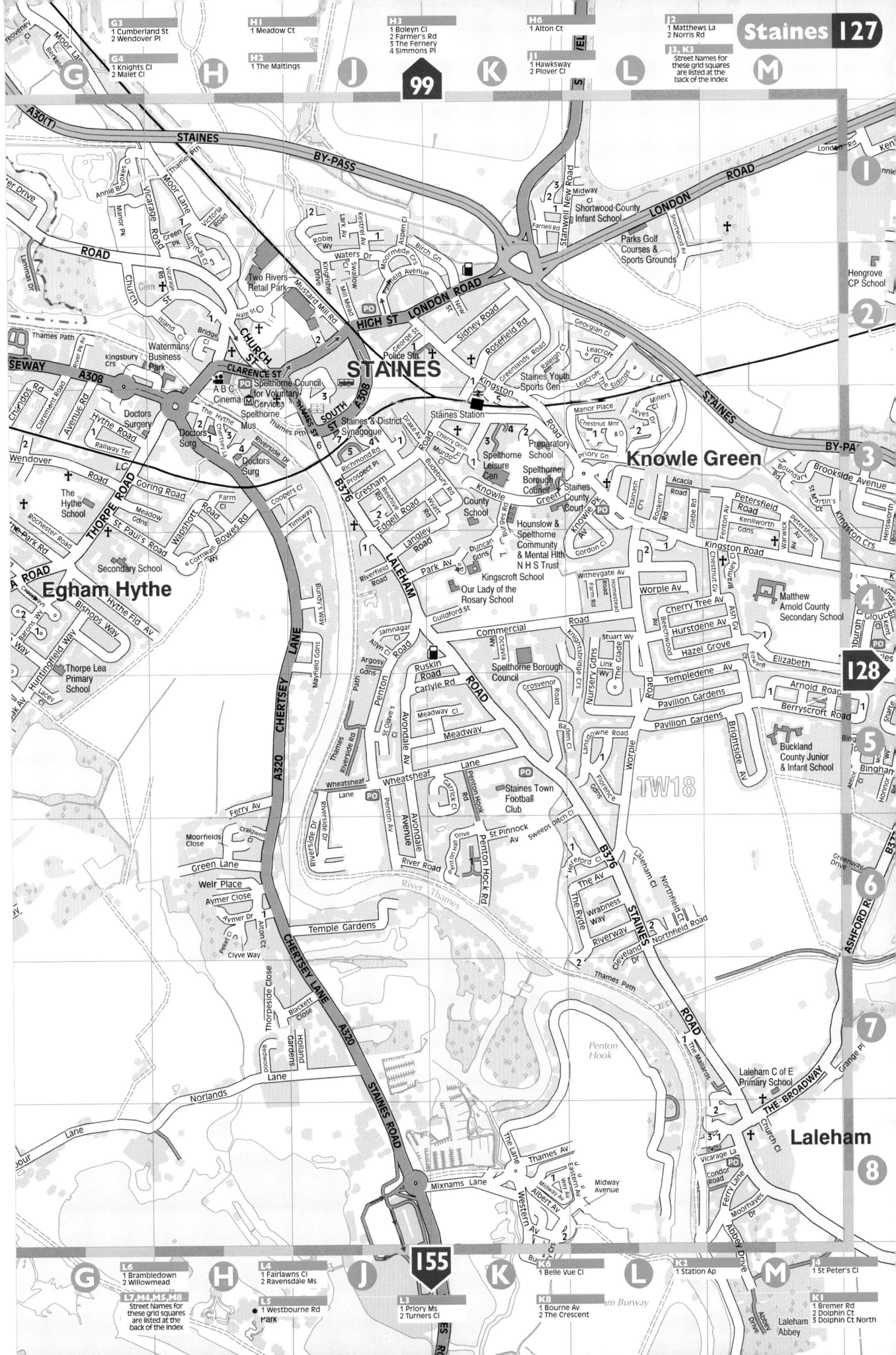

99

128

155

STAINES BY-PASS

A30(T)

STAINES BY-PASS

LONDON ROAD

STAINES BY-PASS

STAINES

Knowle Green

Egham Hythe

TW18

Laleham

River Thames

Penton Hook

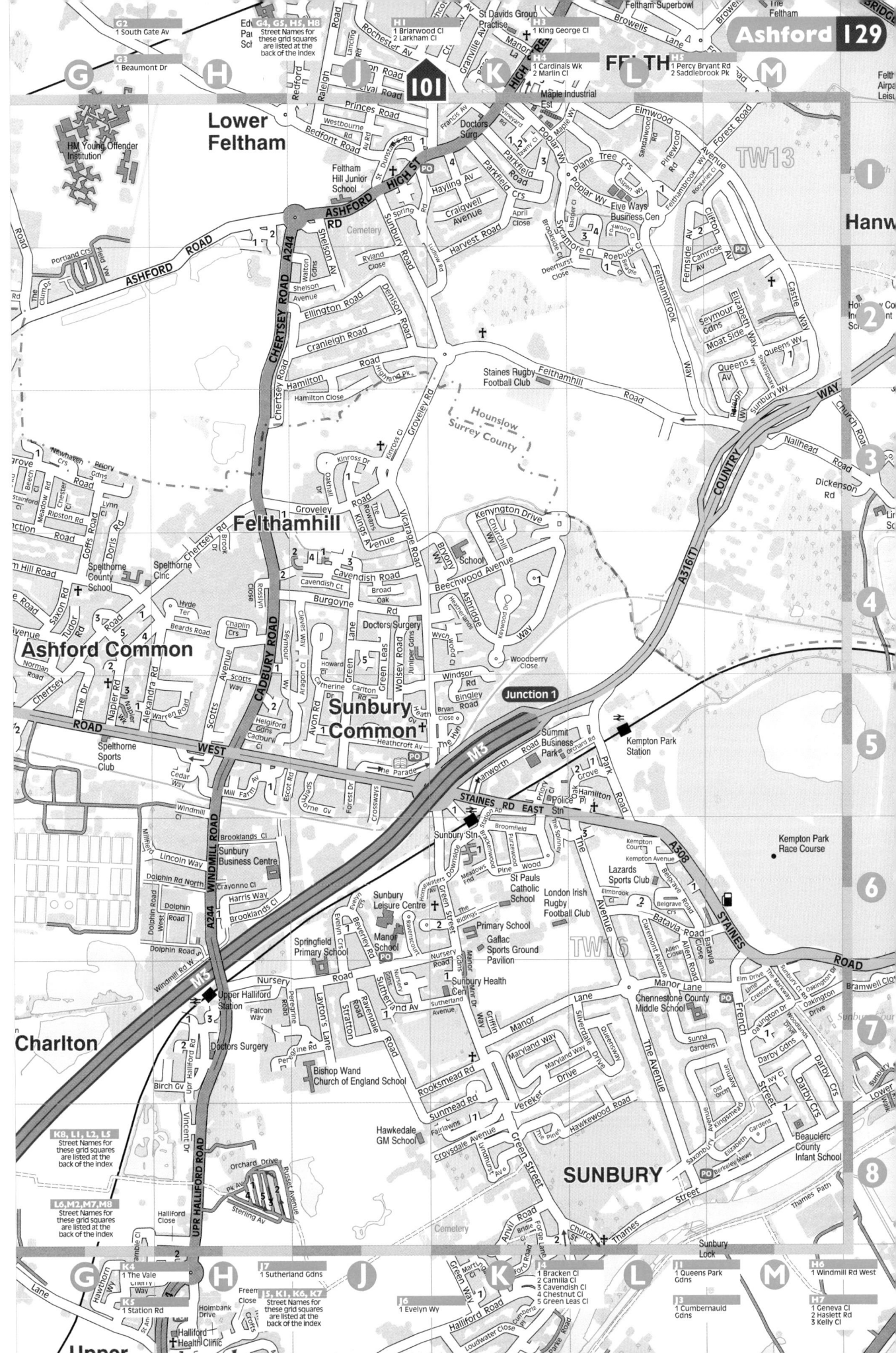

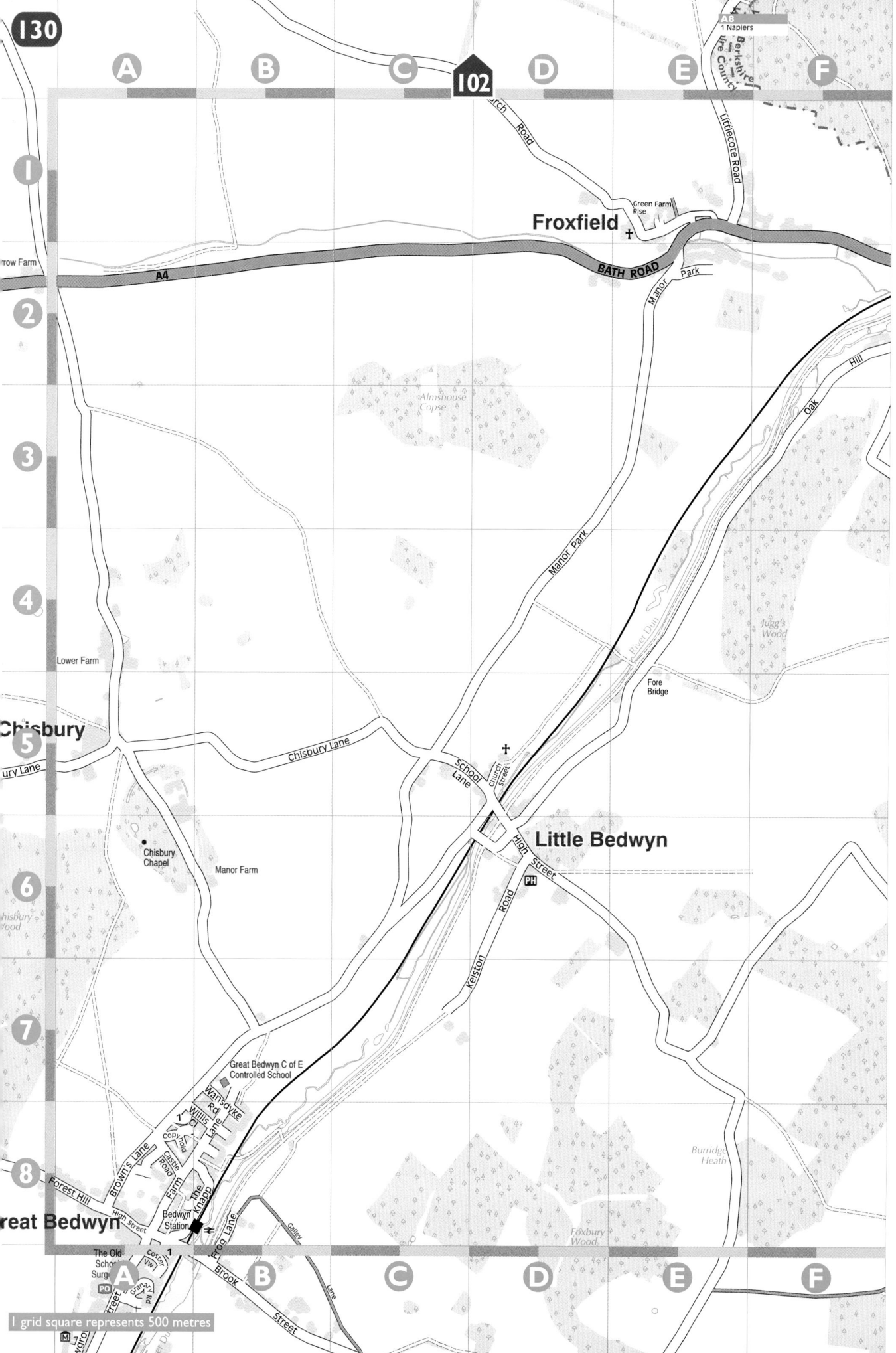

102

I

A B C D E F

Froxfield

Green Farm Rise

Littlecote Road

BATH ROAD

A4

Manor Park

2

Almshouse Copse

Oak Hill

3

River Dun

Jugg's Wood

4

Lower Farm

Fore Bridge

Chisbury

Chisbury Lane

5

ury Lane

School Lane

Church Street

Little Bedwyn

Chisbury Chapel

Manor Farm

High Street

PH

6

hisbury Wood

Kelston Road

Burridge Heath

7

Great Bedwyn C of E Controlled School

Wansdyke Rd

Willis Lane

Copyhold

Foxbury Wood

8

Forest Hill

Brown's Lane

Castle Road

Farm

The Knapp

Frog Lane

Gatley Lane

reat Bedwyn

High Street

Bedwyn Station

Brook Street

The Old School Surg

PO

Coster (VW)

A B C D E F

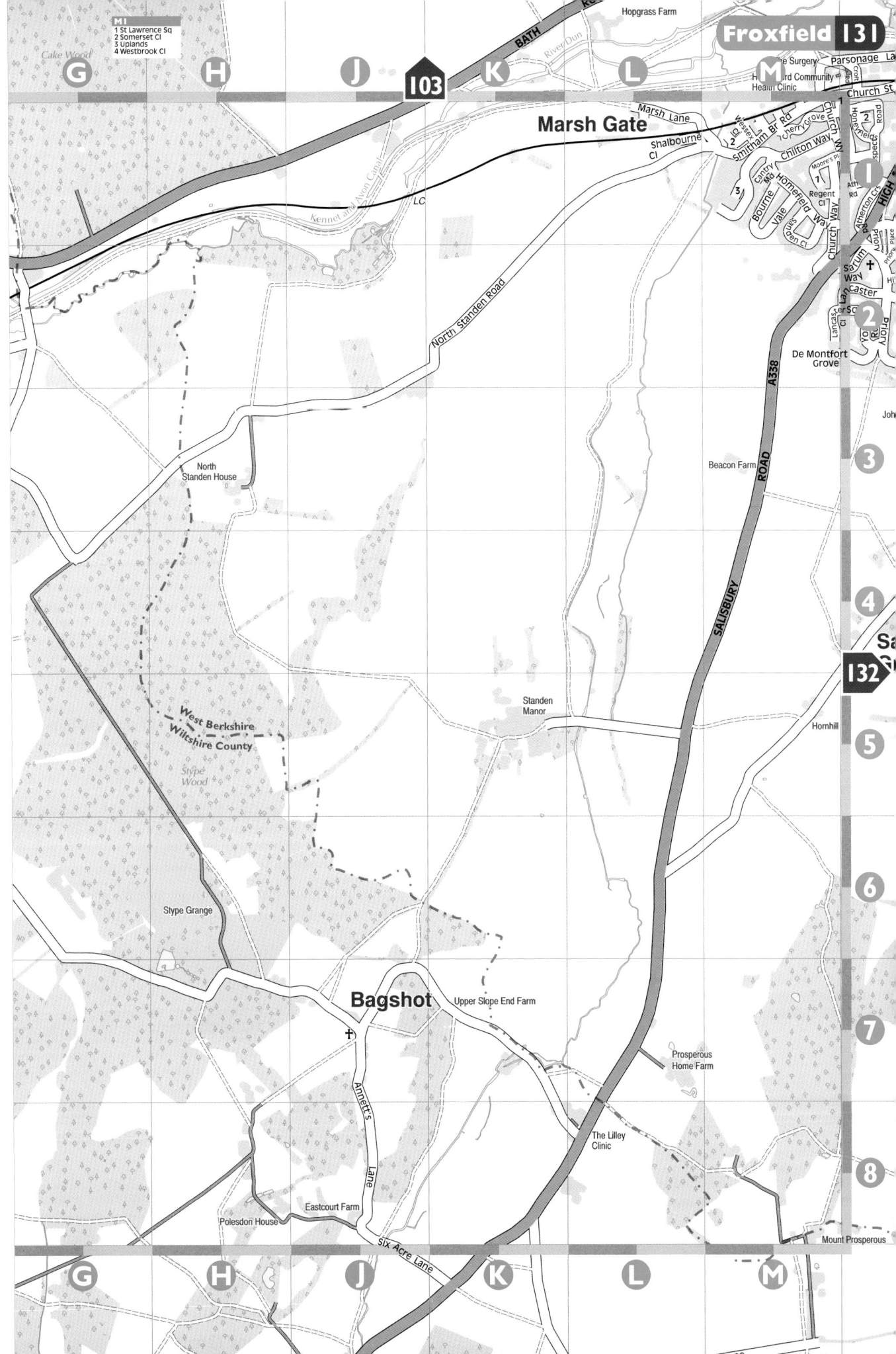

G H J 103 K L M

MI
1 St Lawrence Sq
2 Somerset Cl
3 Uplands
4 Westbrook Cl

Cake Wood

BATH

River Dun

Hopgrass Farm

The Surgery
Parsonage La
Community
Health Clinic
Church St

Marsh Lane
Marsh Gate
Shalbourne Cl
Smitham Br Rd
Wessex Cl
Cherry Grove
Chilton Way

Kennet and Avon Canal

LC

North Standen Road

Cantry Mdw
Bourne Vale
Homefield Way
Regent Cl
Moore's Pl
Sarum Way
Lancaster
Caster
Priory Place
Priory Rd

HIGH

De Montfort Grove

John

North
Standen House

Beacon Farm

SALISBURY ROAD A358

132

Standen Manor

Hornhill

West Berkshire
Wiltshire County

Stype Wood

Stype Grange

Bagshot

Upper Slope End Farm

Prosperous
Home Farm

Annett's Lane

The Lilley
Clinic

Eastcourt Farm

Polesdon House

Six Acre Lane

Mount Prosperous

Sa
S

G H J K L M

I
2
3
4
5
6
7
8

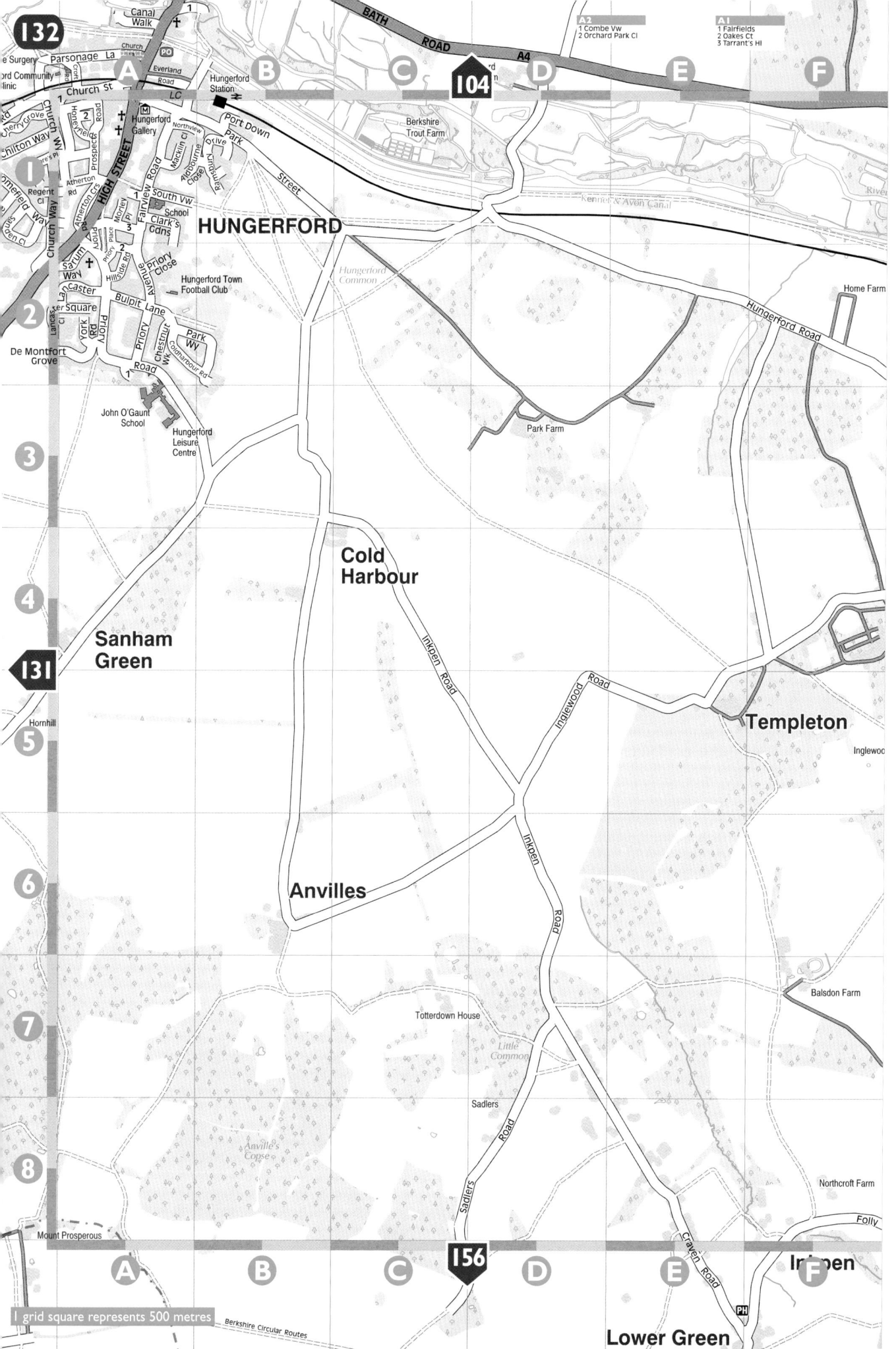

K4
1 Great Severals
2 Kintbury Sq

L4
1 Ashton Pl
2 Barn Cl
3 Gladstone Cl

Barn

G H J **105** K L M

I

Avington
Manor

Avington

Kennet

Barton Court

River Kennet

Wawce

2

Withybed Lane

LC

LC

High Street

Kintbury
Station

PH

Kennet & Av

3

Inglewood Road

Kintbury Farm

Inglewood

Wallingtons Road

Titcombe
Way

The
Croft

PO

Church Street

Mill Bank

Forge Cl

Newbury St

Kintbury St Marys
C of E Primary School

Harold Road

Irish Hill

Hill Road

The Pentlands

4

134

Hemste

5

d Farm

Kintbury

The Haven

Linden

Lawrence Mead

Gainsborough
Av

Long Cl

Burtons

Holt

Craven Wy

Queen's Way

Dunn
Crs

Bradley
Cl

The
Green

Road

Layland's Green

Craven Close

**Layland's
Green**

Kintbu
Fa

6

St Cassian's
College

Titcomb
Manor

Wergs
Copse

Hill

Pebble

Hightree Copse

Titcomb

Back Lane

Cemetery

Forbury Lane

7

Forbury House

Kintbury Cross Ways

The
Folly

Kintbury

Road

New Mill

Holt
Lodge

8

Inkpen
Primary
School

Robins Hill

The Old
Sawmills

Road

Pottery Lane

Office Road

G H J **157** K L M

Toksnest Lane

Heads Lane

Burgess Lane

**Inkpen
Common**

Hell Corner

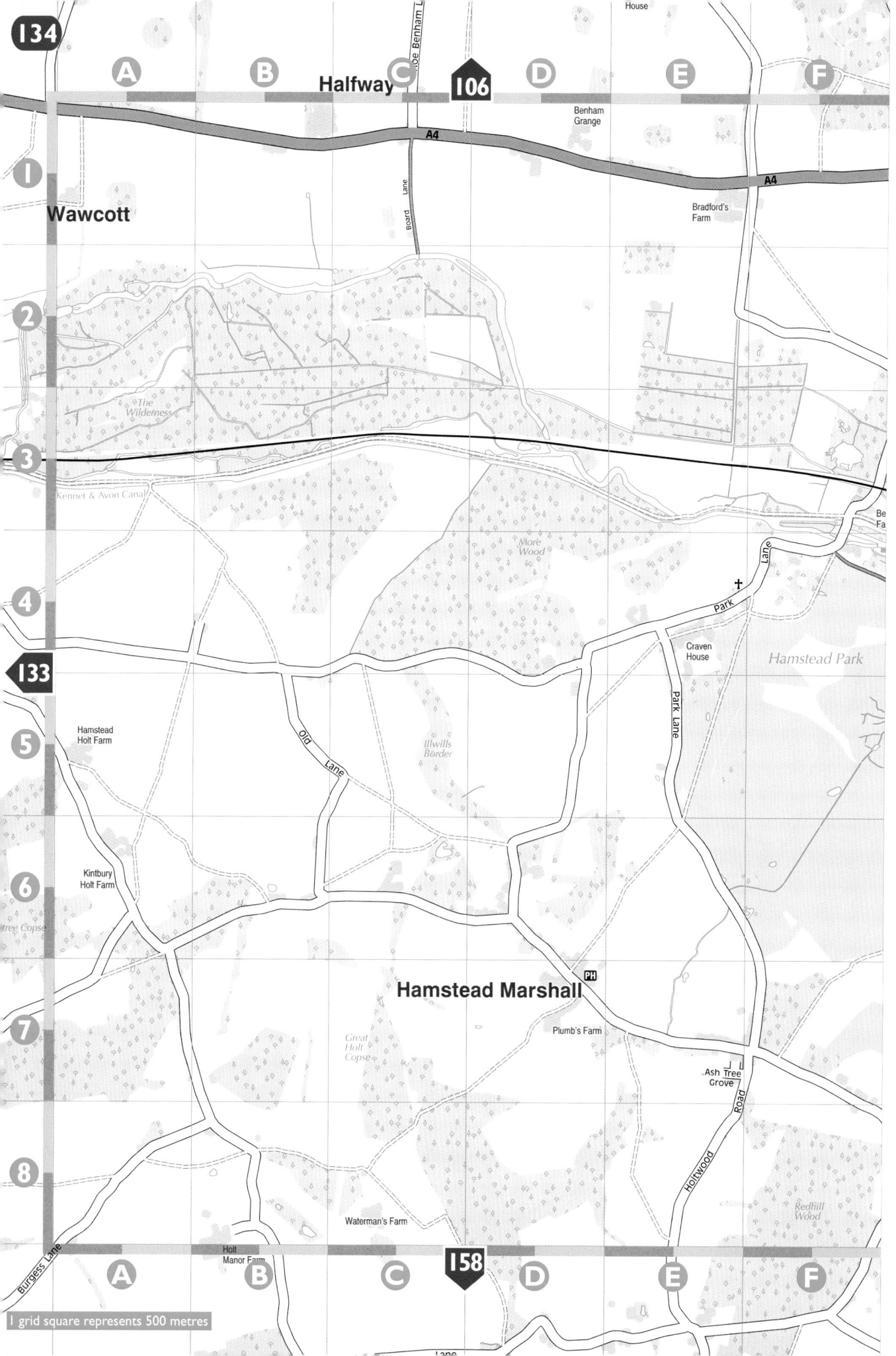

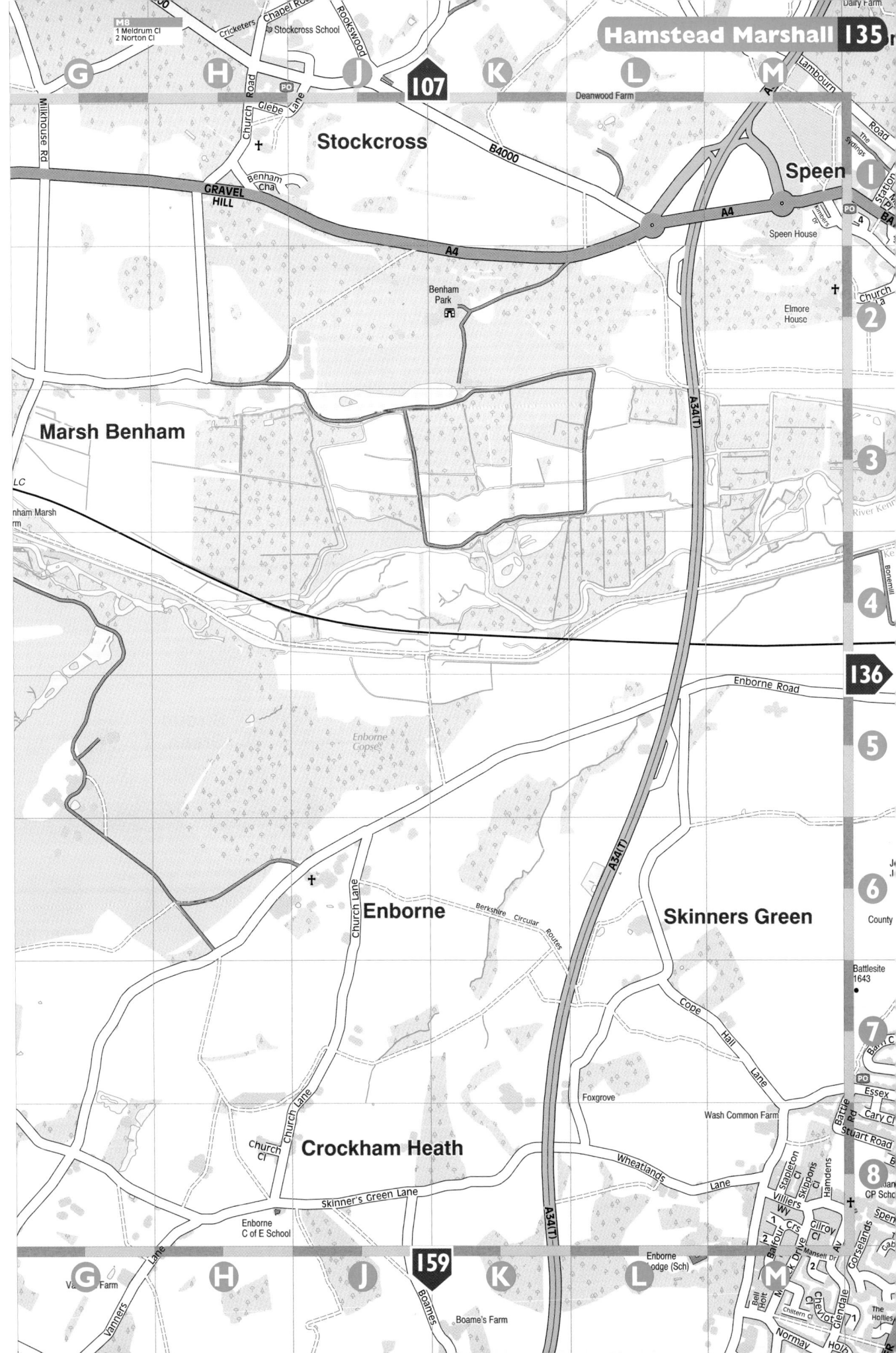

G H J **107** K L M

1 Meldrum Cl
2 Norton Cl

Cricketers Chapel Road
Stockcross School
Rookswood

Dairy Farm

Lambourn

Tatton

Stockcross

B4000

Deanwood Farm

PO

Glebe

Church Road

Benham Cha

Speen

GRAVEL HILL

A4

A4

Speen House

I

The Sidings

Road

PO

Benham Park

Church

Elmore House

2

Marsh Benham

A34(T)

River Kenn

3

Benham Marsh
Farm

LC

4

Bonemill

136

Enborne Road

5

Enborne Copse

Berkshire Circular Routes

Church Lane

† **Enborne**

Skinners Green

A34(T)

6

County

Battlesite 1643

Cope Hall Lane

7

PO

Essex Cl

Battle Rd

Cary Cl

Stuart Road

Foxgrove

Wash Common Farm

Church Lane

Church Cl

Crockham Heath

Wheatlands Lane

Skinner's Green Lane

8

CP Sch

Spen

Stapleton Cl

Skippons Cl

Hamdens

Villiers Wy

Gilroy Cl

Barfour Cl

Enborne C of E School

Enborne Lodge (Sch)

Mark Drive

Mansell Dr

Corslands

The Hollies

Boames

G H J **159** K L M

Vanners Lane

Va Farm

Boame's Farm

Bell Holt

Chiltern Cl

Chevlot Cl

Glendale

Normay

Holb

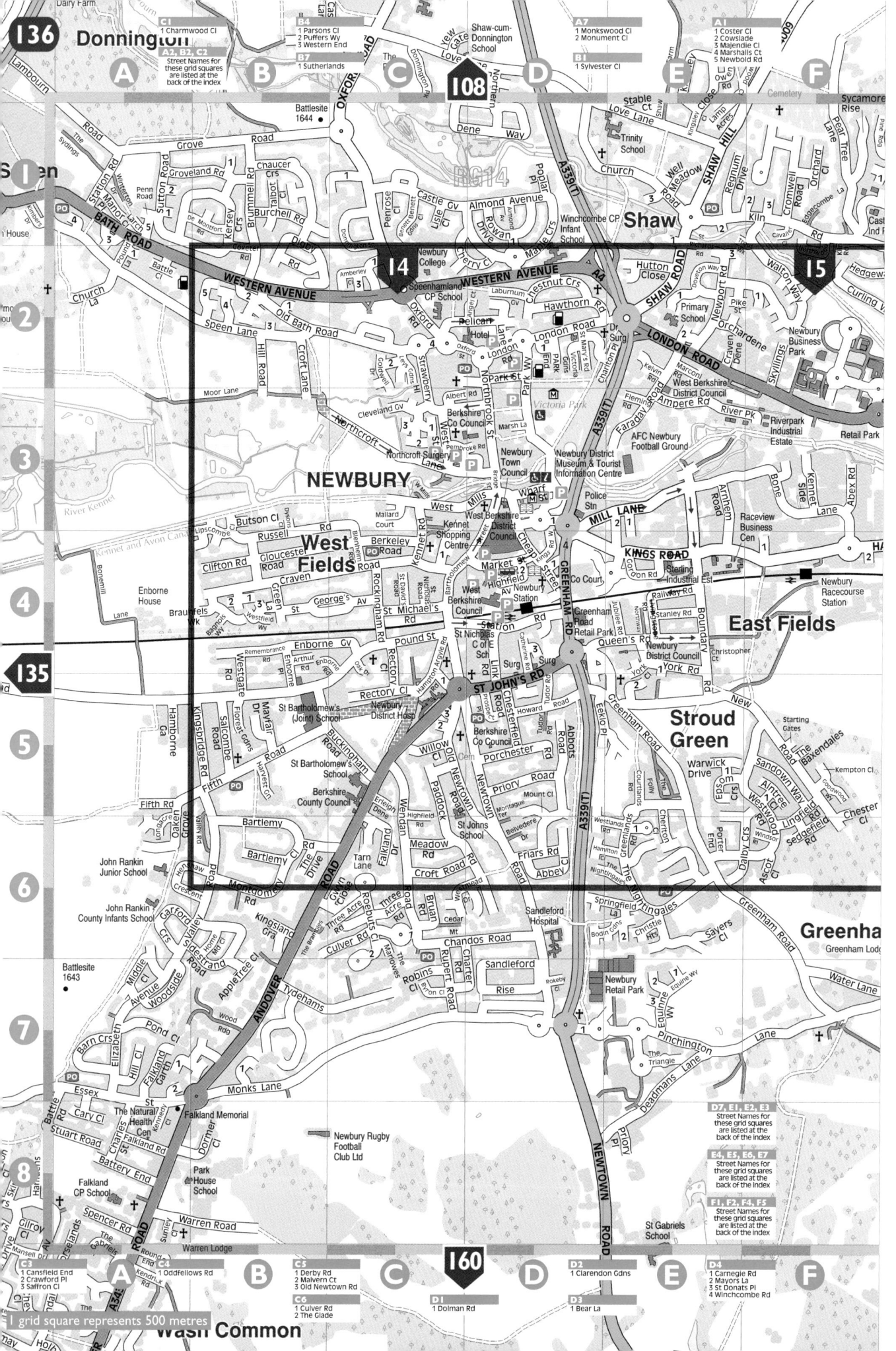

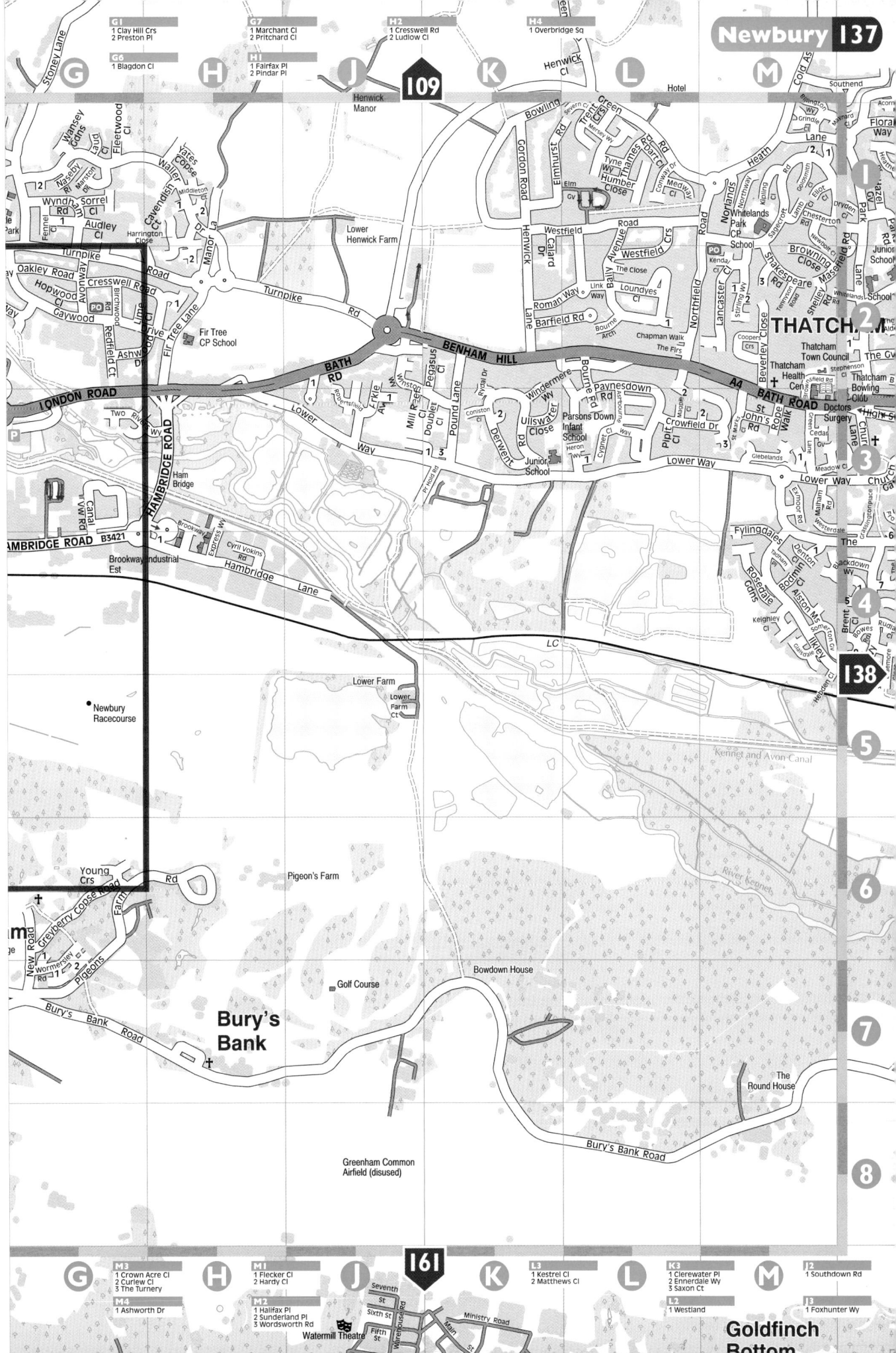

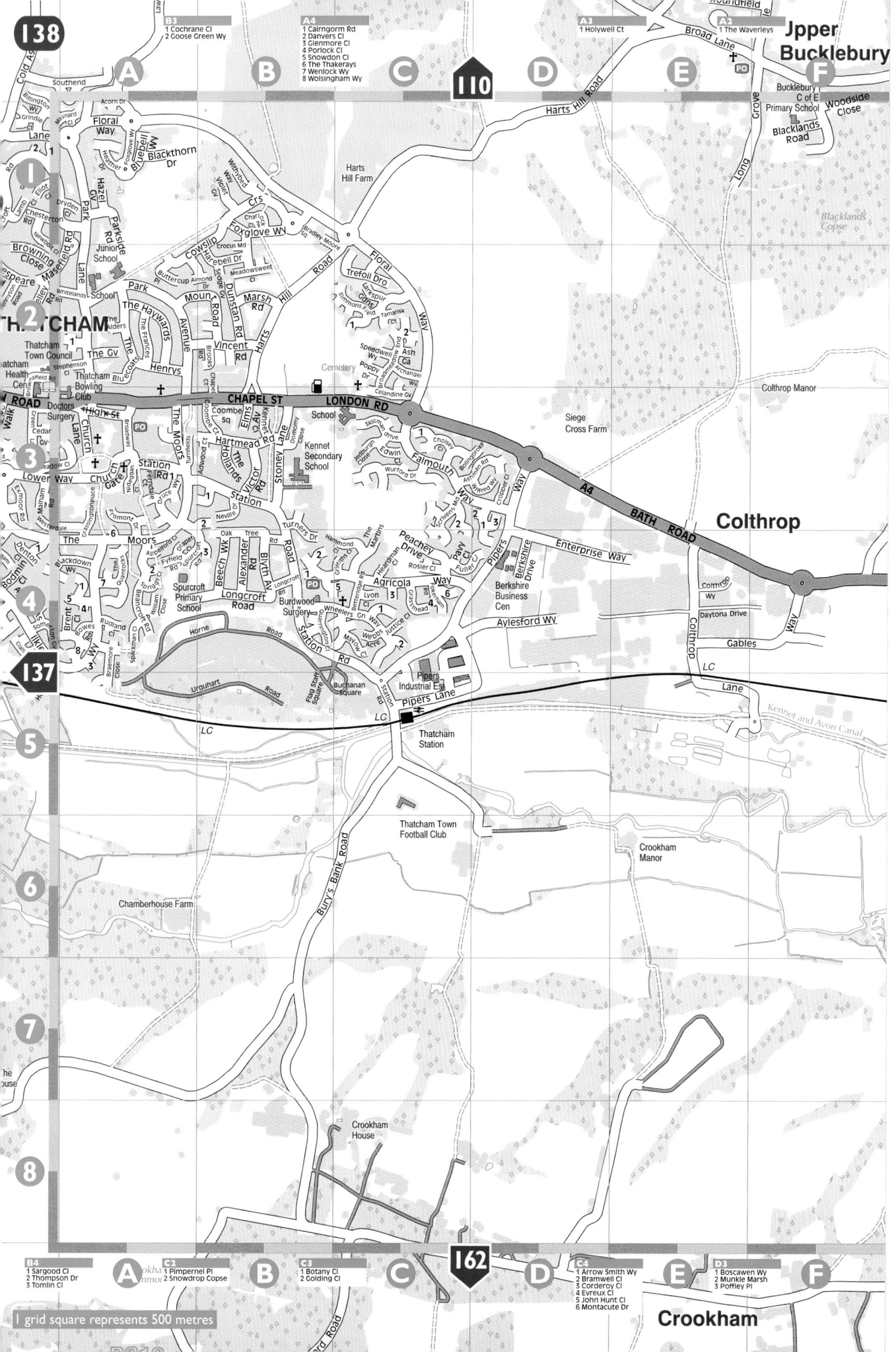

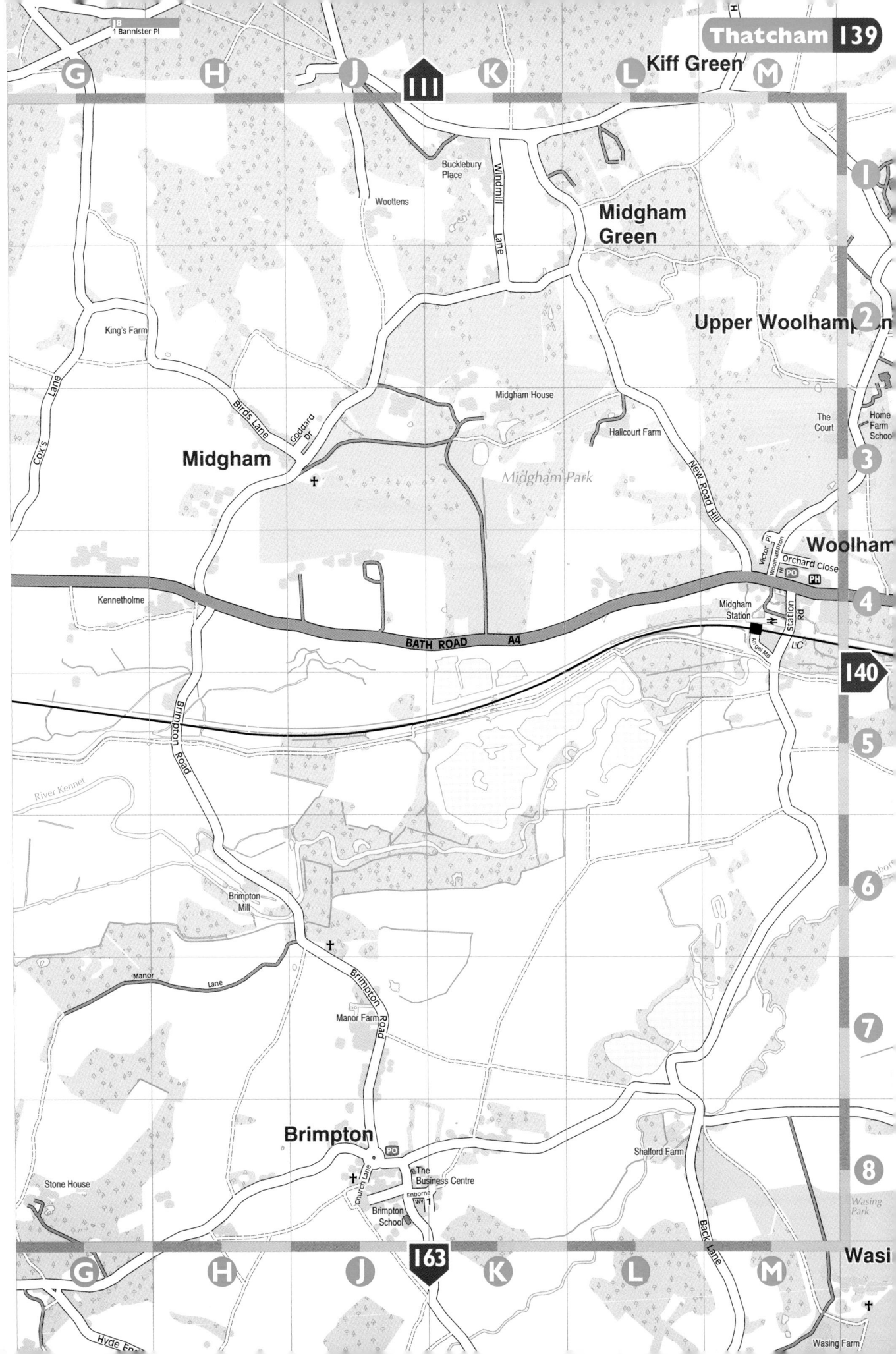

G H J III K L **Kiff Green** M

I

1 Bannister Pl

Bucklebury Place

Woottens

Windmill Lane

Midgham Green

2

Upper Woolhampton

King's Farm

Cox's Lane

Birds Lane

Goddard Dr

Midgham

Midgham House

Midgham Park

Hallcourt Farm

New Road Hill

The Court

Home Farm School

3

Victor Pl

Woolhampton

Orchard Close

PO

PH

Woolham

Kennetholme

BATH ROAD   A4

Midgham Station

Station Rd

Angel Mead

LC

4

140

River Kennet

5

6

Brimpton Mill

Manor Lane

Brimpton Road

7

Manor Farm

Brimpton

PO

The Business Centre

Enborne Wy 1

Stone House

Church Lane

Brimpton School

Shalford Farm

Back Lane

Wasing Park

8

Wasi

G H J **163** K L M

Hyde End

Wasing Farm

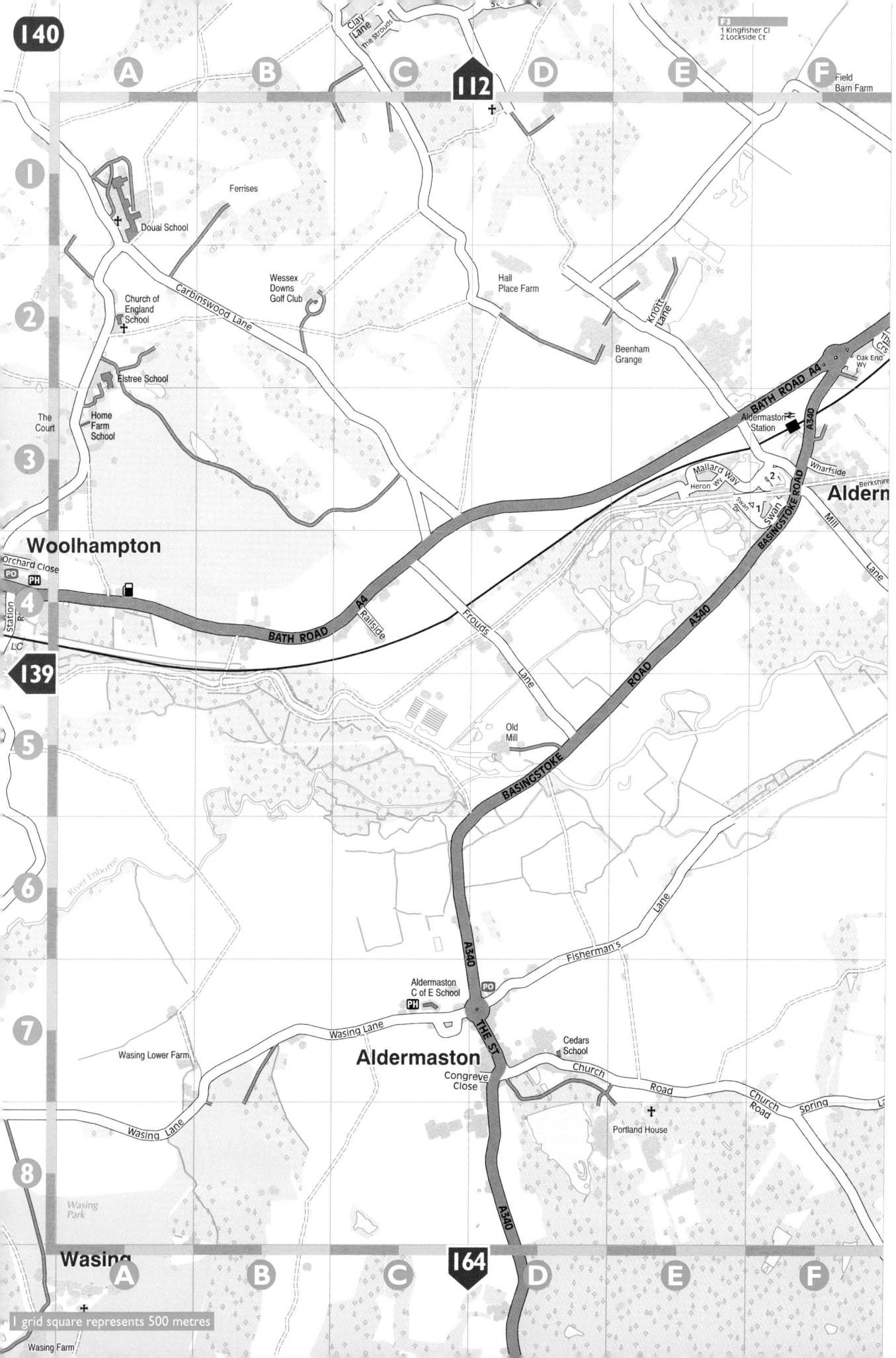

A B C **112** D E F

F3
1 Kingfisher Cl
2 Lockside Ct

Field
Barn Farm

1

Ferrises

Douai School

Church of
England
School

Carbinswood Lane

Wessex
Downs
Golf Club

Hall
Place Farm

Knott Lane

2

Elstree School

Beenham
Grange

The Crs

Oak End Wy

BATH ROAD A4

Aldermaston
Station

A340

Wharfside

Berkshire

3

The
Court

Home
Farm
School

Mallard Way

Heron Wy

Swan Dr

Swan

2

BASINGSTOKE ROAD

Alderm

Mill Lane

Woolhampton

Orchard Close

PO PH

Station Rd

BATH ROAD

A4

Railside

Frouds Lane

A340

ROAD

4

LC

139

Old
Mill

BASINGSTOKE

5

River Enborne

6

Fisherman's

Lane

7

Aldermaston
C of E School

PH

PO

A340

Wasing Lane

Wasing Lower Farm

Aldermaston

THE ST

Congreve
Close

Cedars
School

Church

Road

Church

Road

Spring La

Portland House

Wasing Lane

8

Wasing
Park

Wasing

A B **164** C D E F

A340

1 grid square represents 500 metres

Wasing Farm

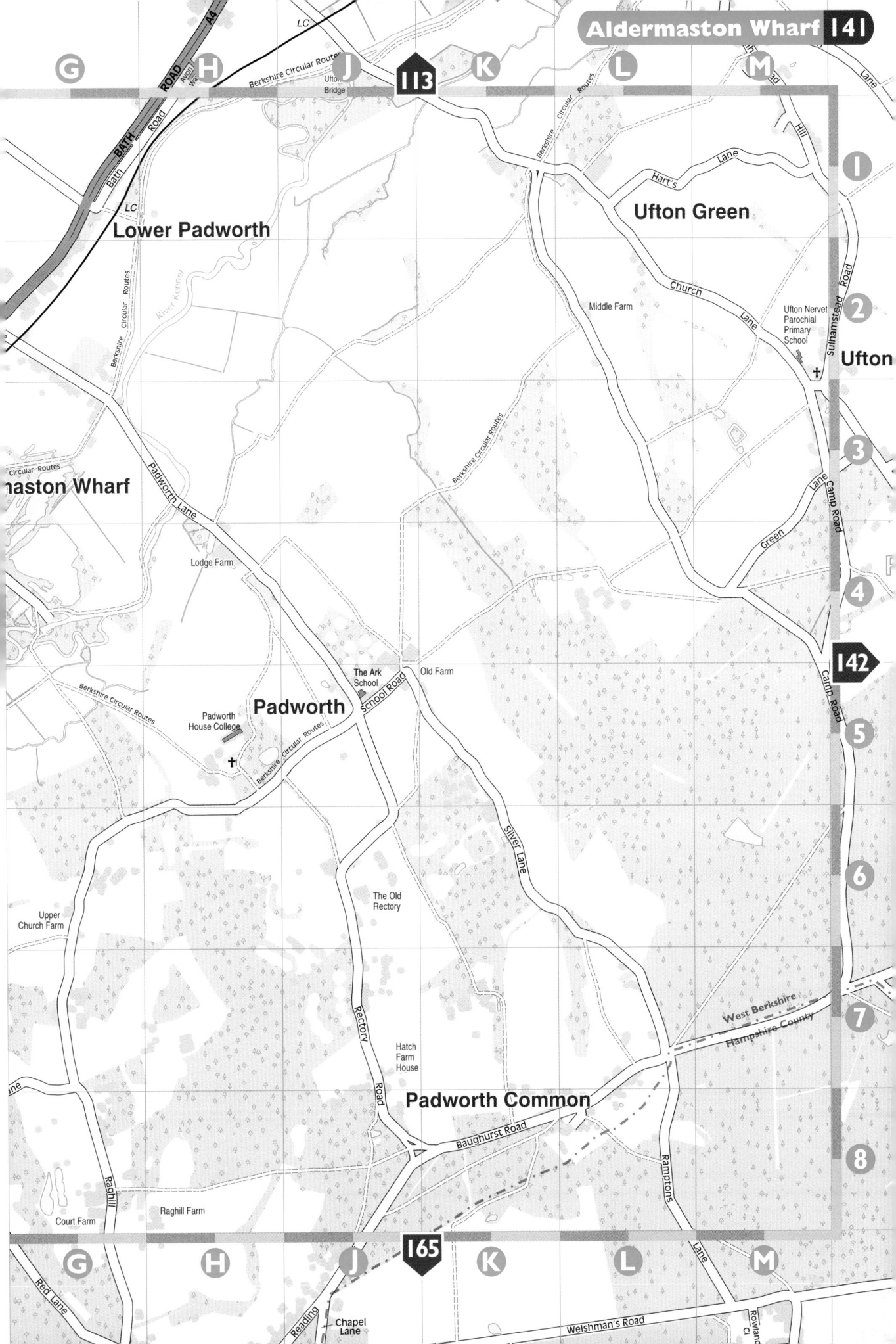

G H J 113 K L M

1

LC

Berkshire Circular Routes
Ufton
Bridge

BATH ROAD A4

Avon Wa

Hart's Lane

Ufton Green

Hill

I

ROAD
Bath

LC

Lower Padworth

Berkshire Circular Routes

River Kennet

Church Lane

Middle Farm

Sulhamstead Road

2

Ufton Nervet
Parochial
Primary
School

Ufton

3

Berkshire Circular Routes

Circular Routes

...maston Wharf

Padworth Lane

Green

Camp Road

4

Lodge Farm

142

Berkshire Circular Routes

The Ark
School

Old Farm

Camp Road

5

Padworth

Padworth
House College

School Road

Berkshire Circular Routes

6

Upper
Church Farm

Silver Lane

The Old
Rectory

7

West Berkshire
Hampshire County

Rectory Road

Hatch
Farm
House

Padworth Common

Ramptons

8

Lane

Raghill

Baughurst Road

165

Court Farm

Raghill Farm

G H J K L M

Red Lane

Reading

Chapel
Lane

Welshman's Road

Rowlan
Cl

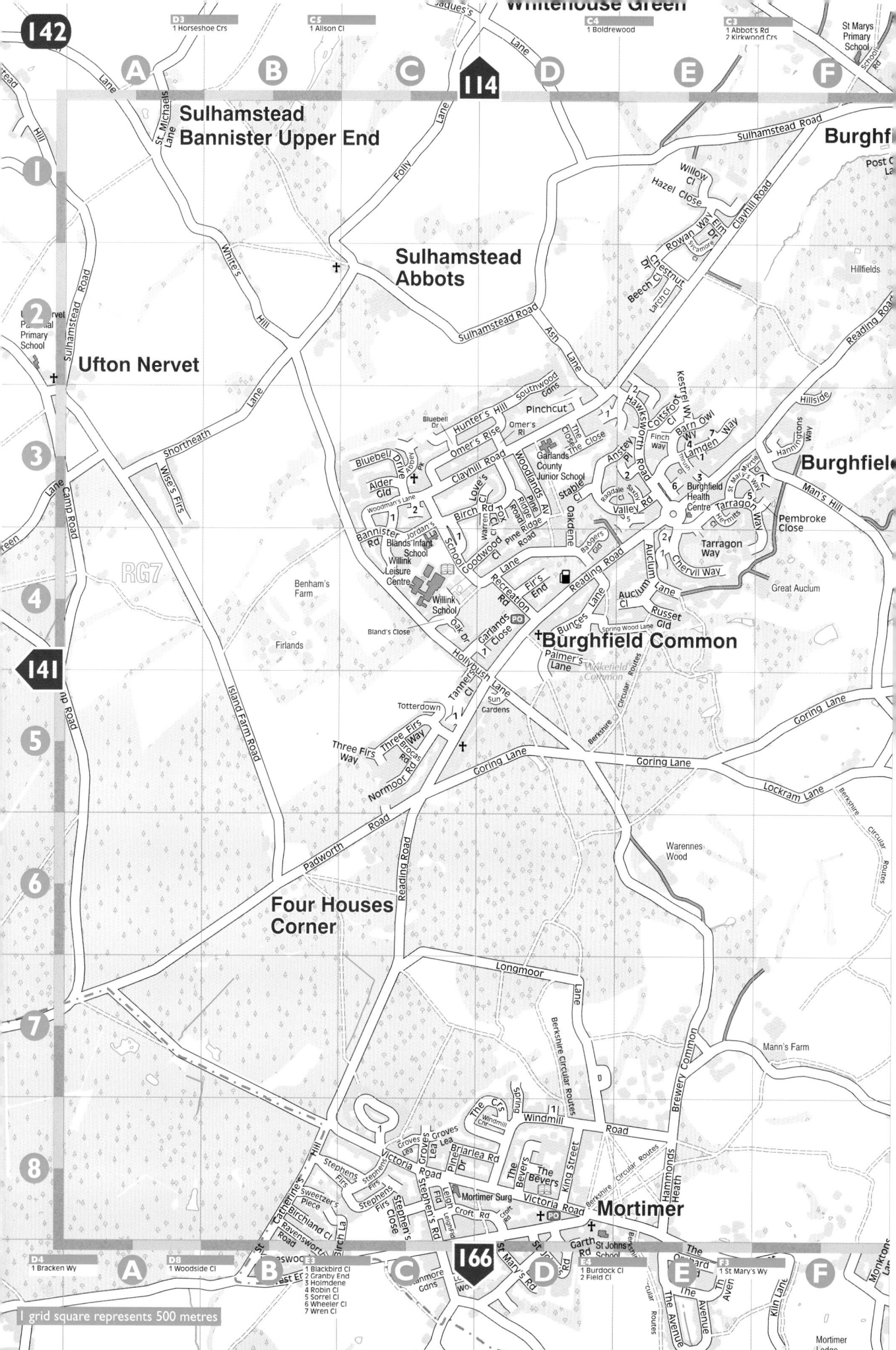

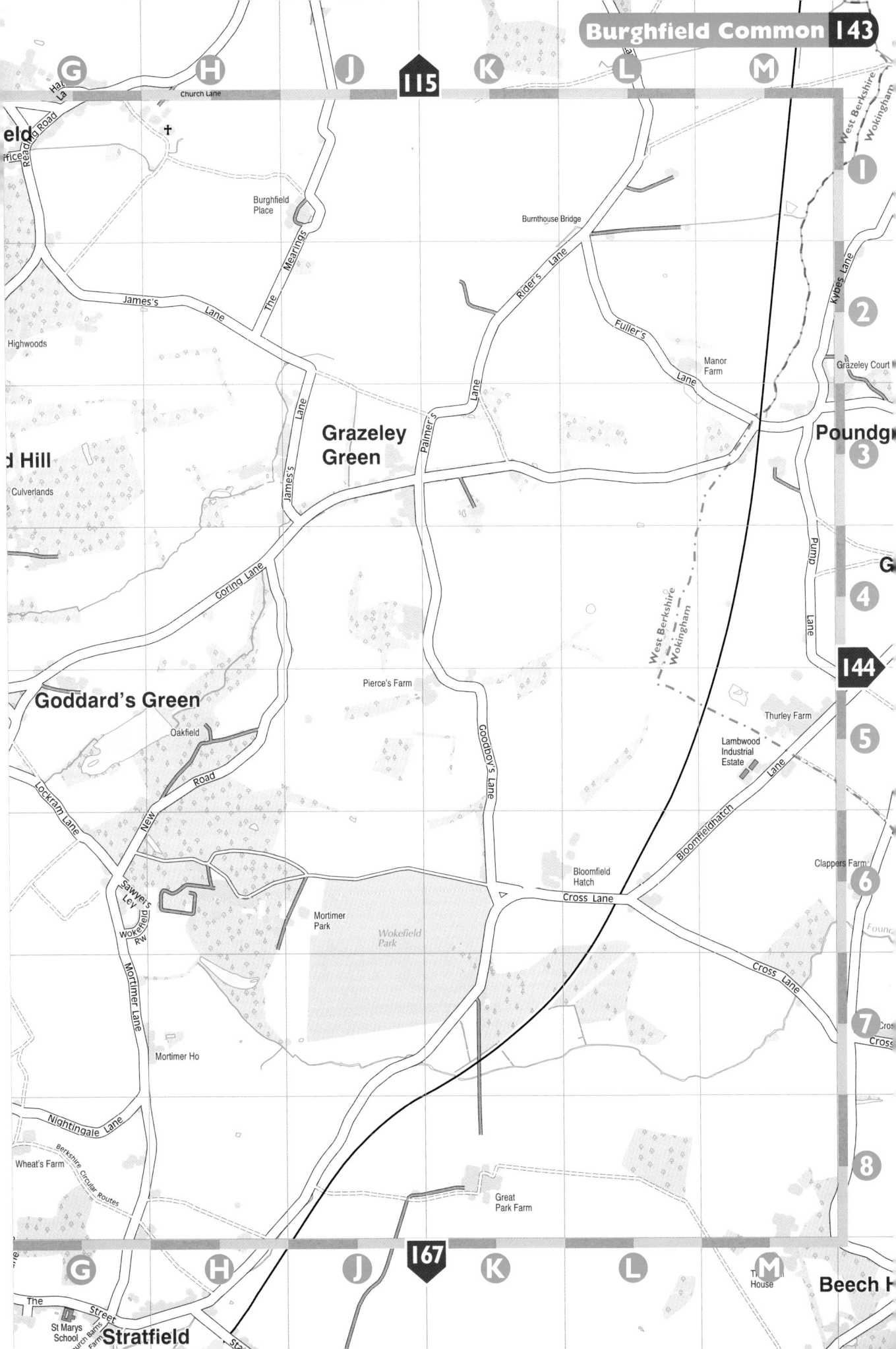

G H J `115` K L M

I

2

3

4

`144`

5

6

7

8

Church Lane

Reading Road

office

Burghfield
Place

James's Lane

The Mearings

Highwoods

Grazeley
Green

Palmer's Lane

James's Lane

Goring Lane

Culverlands

Burnthouse Bridge

Rider's Lane

Fuller's Lane

Manor
Farm

Grazeley Court

Poundg

G

West Berkshire
Wokingham

Kybes Lane

Pump Lane

Goddard's Green

Oakfield

Road

New

Lockram Lane

Pierce's Farm

Goodboy's Lane

Thurley Farm

Lambwood
Industrial
Estate

Bloomfieldhatch Lane

Clappers Farm

Founc

Cross

Bloomfield
Hatch

Cross Lane

Cross Lane

Sawyer's Ley

Wokefield Rw

Mortimer Lane

Mortimer
Park

Wokefield
Park

Mortimer Ho

Nightingale Lane

Berkshire Circular Routes

Wheat's Farm

Great
Park Farm

G H J `167` K L M

The
Street

St Marys
School

Church Barns
Farm

Stratfield

St

Th
House

Beech H

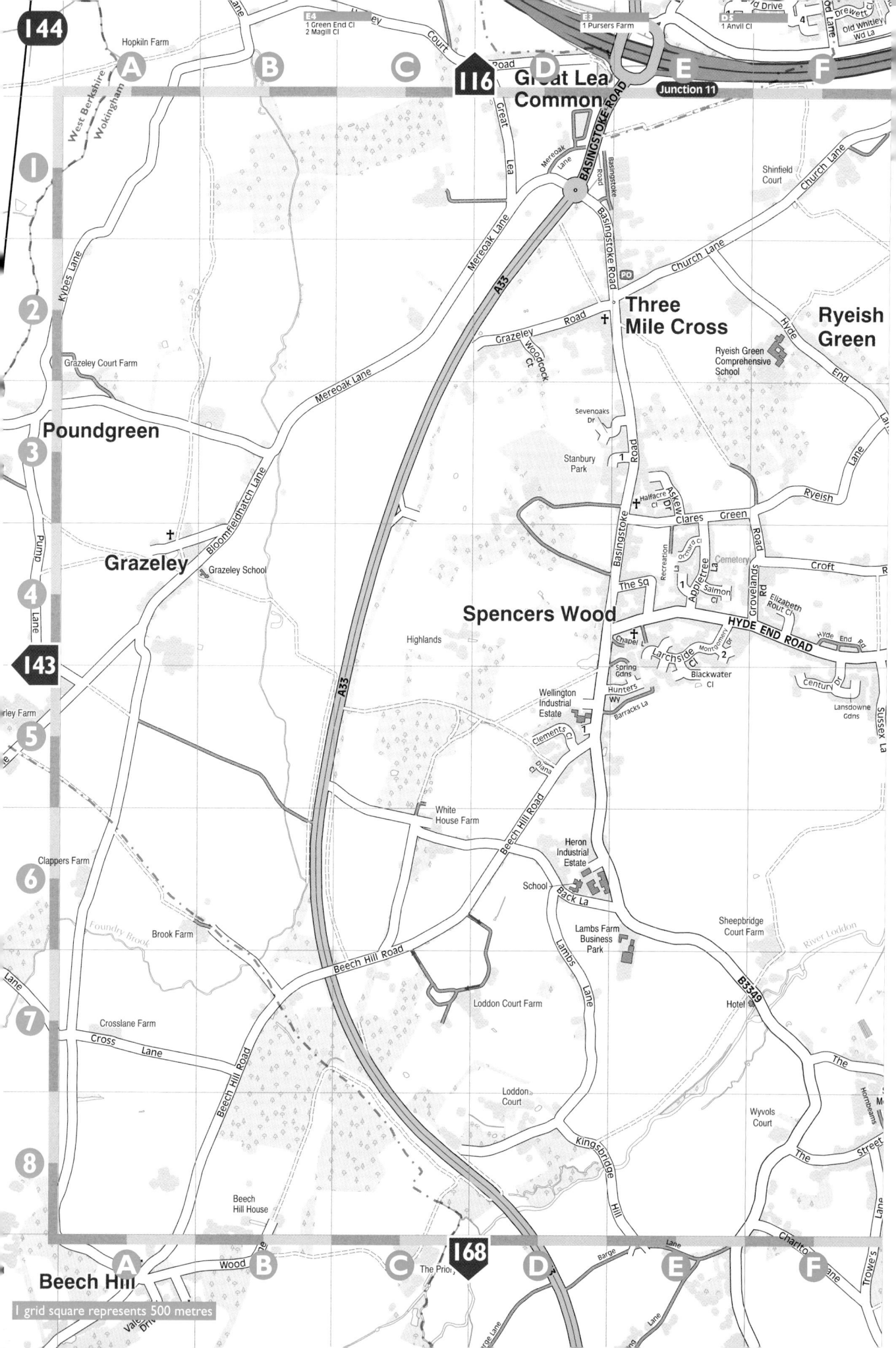

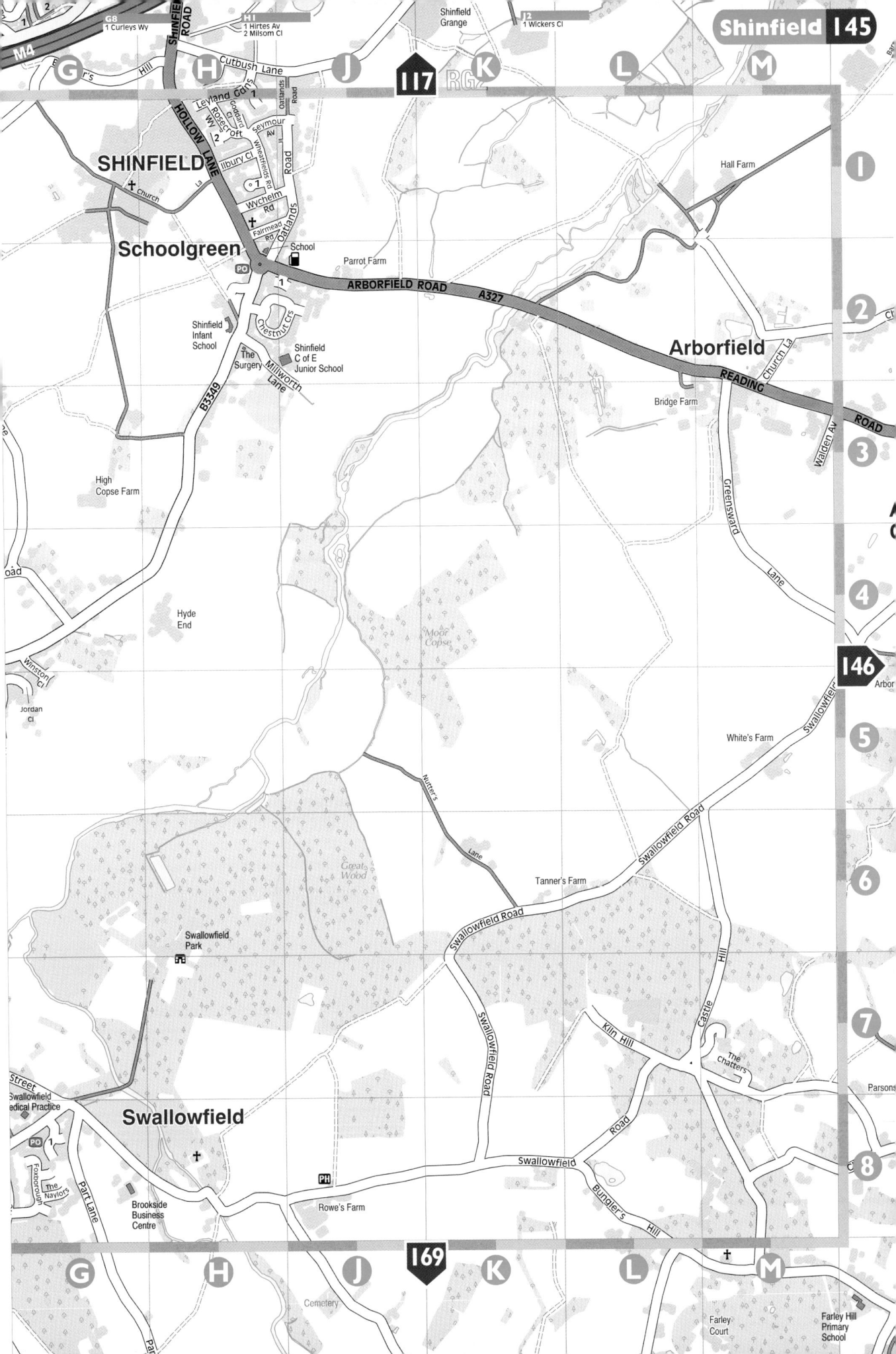

M4

G8
1 Curleys Wy

H1
1 Hirtes Av
2 Milsom Cl

Shinfield
Grange

J2
1 Wickers Cl

Cutbush Lane

G **H** **J** 117 RG2 **K** **L** **M**

Hall Farm

I

SHINFIELD

Leyland Gdns

Rosecroft

Seymour Av

Oatlands Road

Wheatfields Rd

Ilbury Cl

Wychelm Rd

Fairmead Rd

church

SHINFIELD ROAD

HOLLOW LANE

Schoolgreen

PO

School

Parrot Farm

ARBORFIELD ROAD A327

Arborfield

READING ROAD

2

Shinfield
Infant
School

Chestnut Crs

The
Surgery

Shinfield
C of E
Junior School

Millworth Lane

B3349

Church La

Walden Av

Bridge Farm

3

High
Copse Farm

Greensward Lane

4

Hyde
End

Moor
Copse

146 Arbor

Winston

5

Jordan
Cl

White's Farm

Swallowfield Road

Nurter's

6

Great
Wood

Lane

Tanner's Farm

Swallowfield Road

Castle Hill

7

Swallowfield
Park

Swallowfield Road

Kiln Hill

The
Chatters

Street

Swallowfield
Medical Practice

Swallowfield

Part Lane

PO

Foxborough

The
Naylors

church

PH

Rowe's Farm

Swallowfield

Road

Swallowfield

Bungler's Hill

Parsons

8

Brookside
Business
Centre

G **H** **J** 169 **K** **L** **M**

Cemetery

Farley
Court

Farley Hill
Primary
School

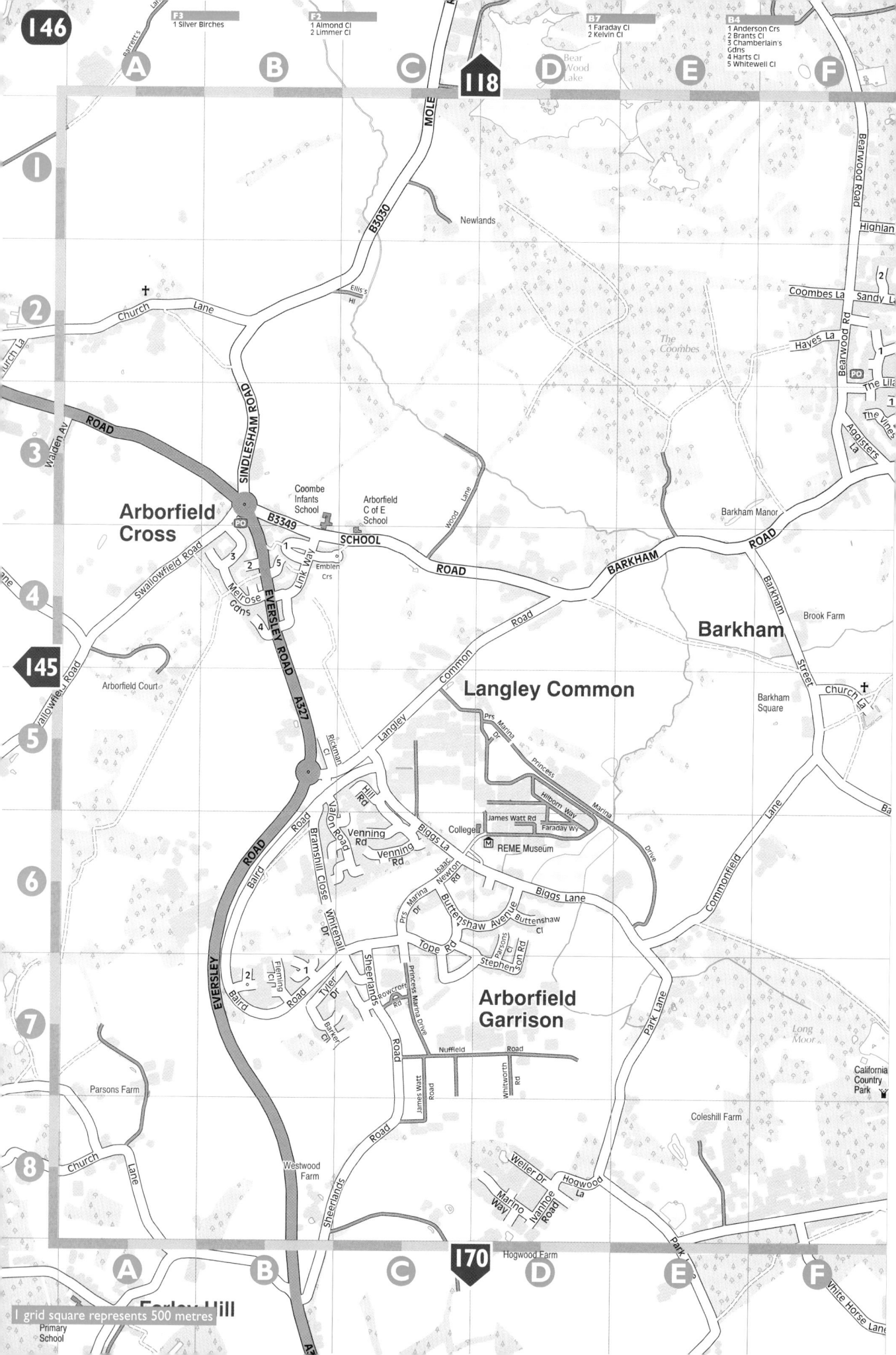

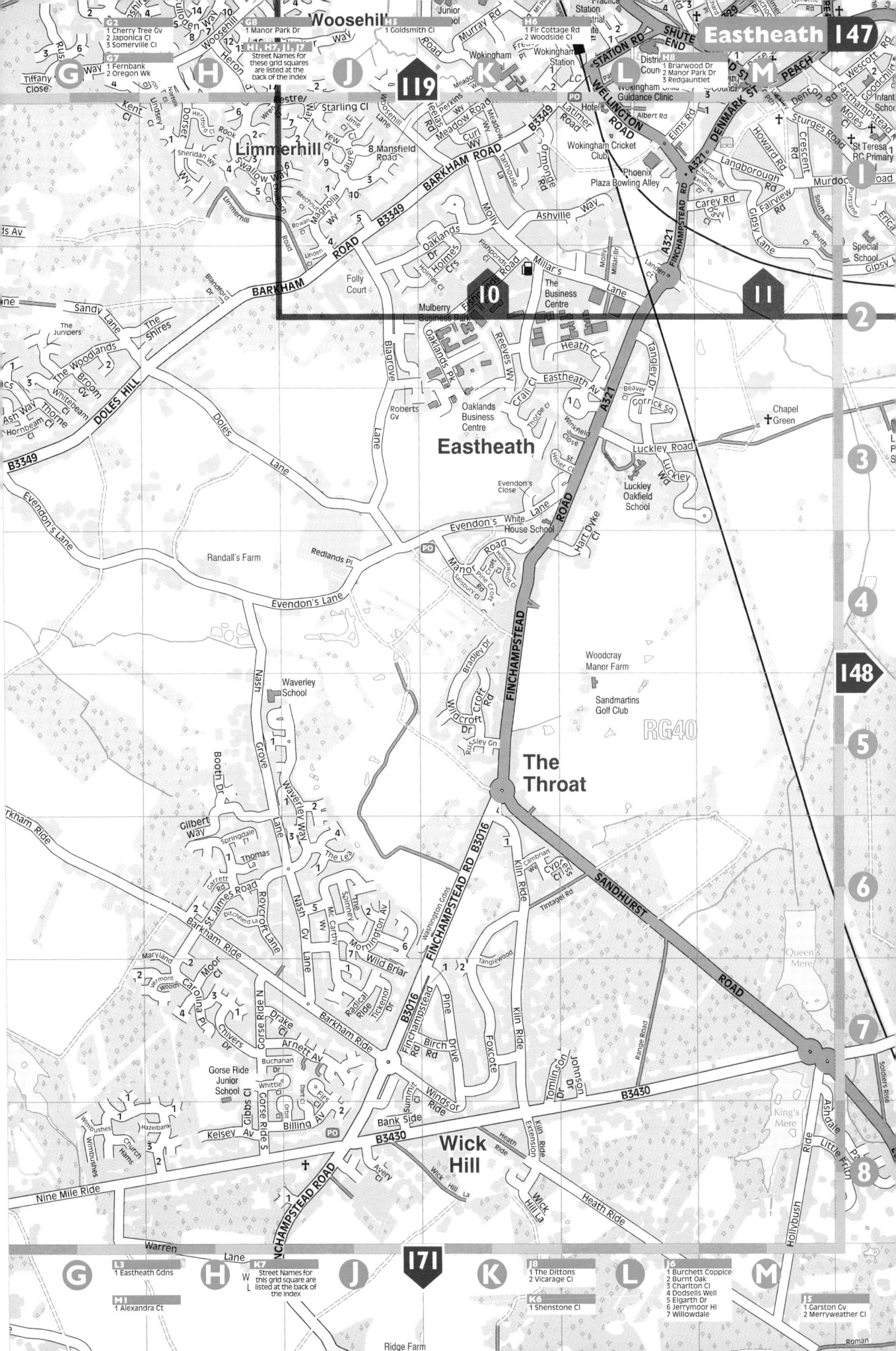

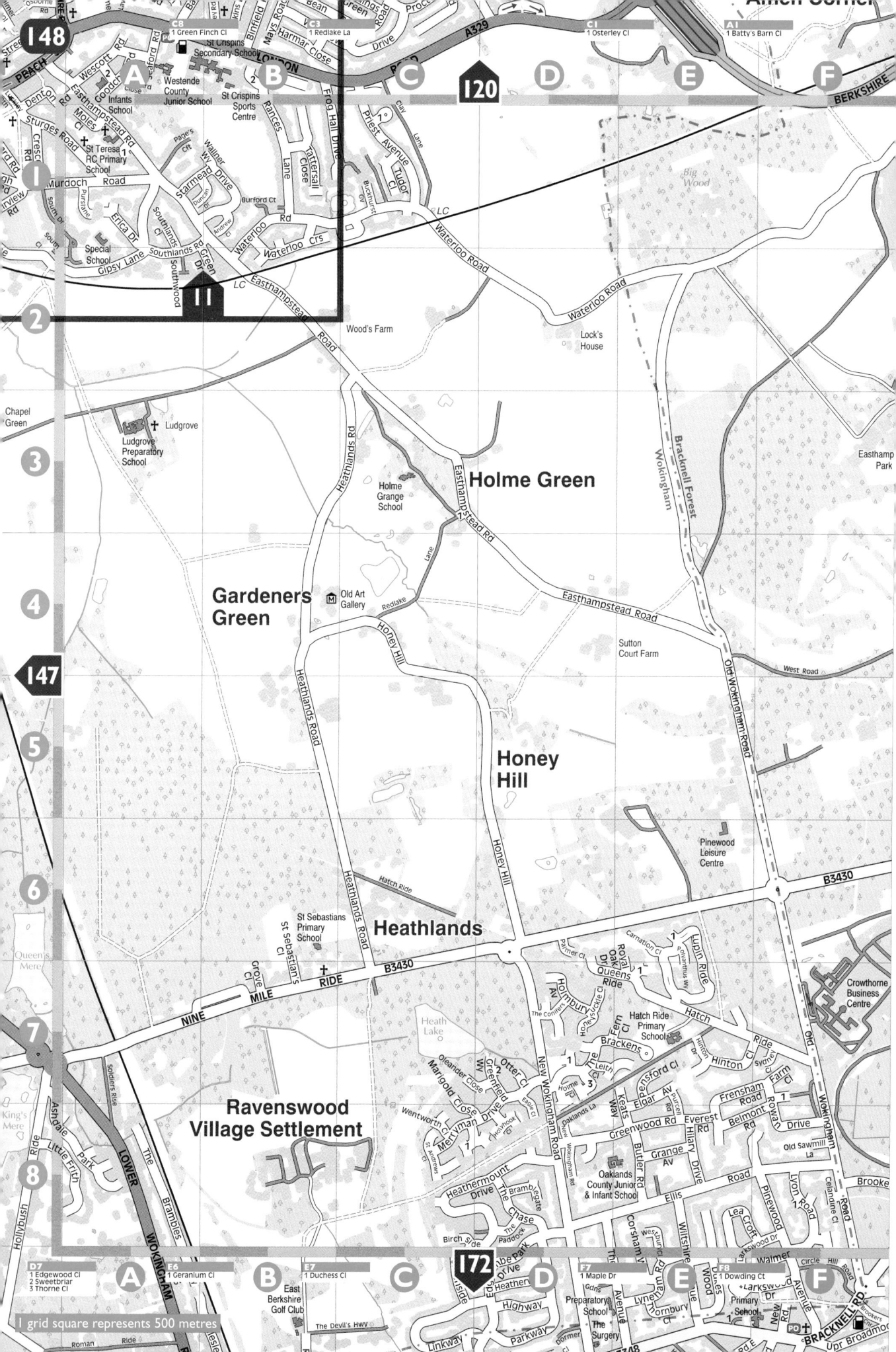

PEACH

BERKSHIRE

Amen Corner

A329

C1 Osterley Cl

A1 Batty's Barn Cl

C8 1 Green Finch Cl

St Crispins
Secondary School

Westende
County
Junior School

Infants
School

St Crispins Sports
Centre

Mays Road

Harmar Close

1 Redlake La

Bean

Frog Hall Drive

LONDON

Priest Avenue

Clay Lane

Buckhurst

Tudor

Proctor

Green Drive

LC

Waterloo Road

Big Wood

Denton Rd

Wescott Rd

Goodce

Easthampstead Rd

Moles

St Teresa's
RC Primary
School

Murdoch Road

Erica Dr

Special
School

Gipsy Lane

Southwood

Southlands Rd

Southlands Cl

Starmead Dr

Duncan Dr

Pane's

Frances Lane

Tattersall Close

Burford Ct

Green Dr

Waterloo Rd

Waterloo Crs

LC

Easthampstead Road

Wood's Farm

Waterloo Road

Lock's
House

Wokingham

Bracknell Forest

Easthamp
Park

147

Chapel
Green

Ludgrove
Preparatory
School

Ludgrove

Heathlands Rd

Easthampstead Rd

Holme Green

Holme
Grange
School

Lane

Redlake

**Gardeners
Green**

Old Art
Gallery

Easthampstead Road

Sutton
Court Farm

Honey Hill

West Road

**Honey
Hill**

Heathlands Road

Pinewood
Leisure
Centre

B3430

Hatch Ride

St Sebastians
Primary
School

St Sebastian's Cl

Heathlands

GROVE

NINE MILE RIDE

B3430

Heath
Lake

Queen's
Mere

Crowthorne
Business
Centre

Soldiers Rise

King's
Mere

Ashdale Park

LOWER

The Brambles

Hollybush

Little Frith

**Ravenswood
Village Settlement**

Wentworth

Marigold Close

Oleander Close

Merryman Drive

St Andrews

Holybrook

Heathermount
Drive

New Wokingham Road

Otter Cl

Greenfield W

Greenend

Esta Cl

The Conifers

Holmbury Av

Honeysuckle Cl

Fern Cl

Brackens

The Leith

Holme

Carnation Cl

Royal Oak Dr

Queens Ride

Pyramids Wy

Lupin Ride

Primrose Wy

Hatch Ride
Primary
School

Hatch Ride

Hinton

Pensford Cl

Elgar Av

Sydney

Frensham
Road

Farm Rd

Keats Way

Hilary Drive

Purcell Rd

Greenwood Rd

Oaklands La

Butler Rd

Grange Av

Everest Rd

Belmont Rd

Ellis

Oaklands
County Junior
& Infant School

Corsham Rd

Lea Croft

Wiltshire Rd

Pinewood Dr

Lyon Road

Old Sawmill La

Brooke

Rowan Road

Celandine Dr

Wokingham Rd

B3430

Old Wokingham Road

WOKINGHAM

D7 1 Edgewood Cl
2 Sweetbriar
3 Thorne Cl

E6 1 Geranium Cl

E7 1 Duchess Cl

F7 1 Maple Dr

F8 1 Dowding Ct

East
Berkshire
Golf Club

The Devil's Hwy

Linkway

The Paddock

Birch Side

Edgedale

Glebe Park Drive

The Chase

Heather Highway

Parkway

Larkswood
Primary
School

Lynten

Thornbury

Preparatory
School

Gdns

The
Surgery

Avenue

Wood

Clues

Walmer

Larkswood

Circle

BRACKNELL RD

Upr Broadmoor

1 grid square represents 500 metres

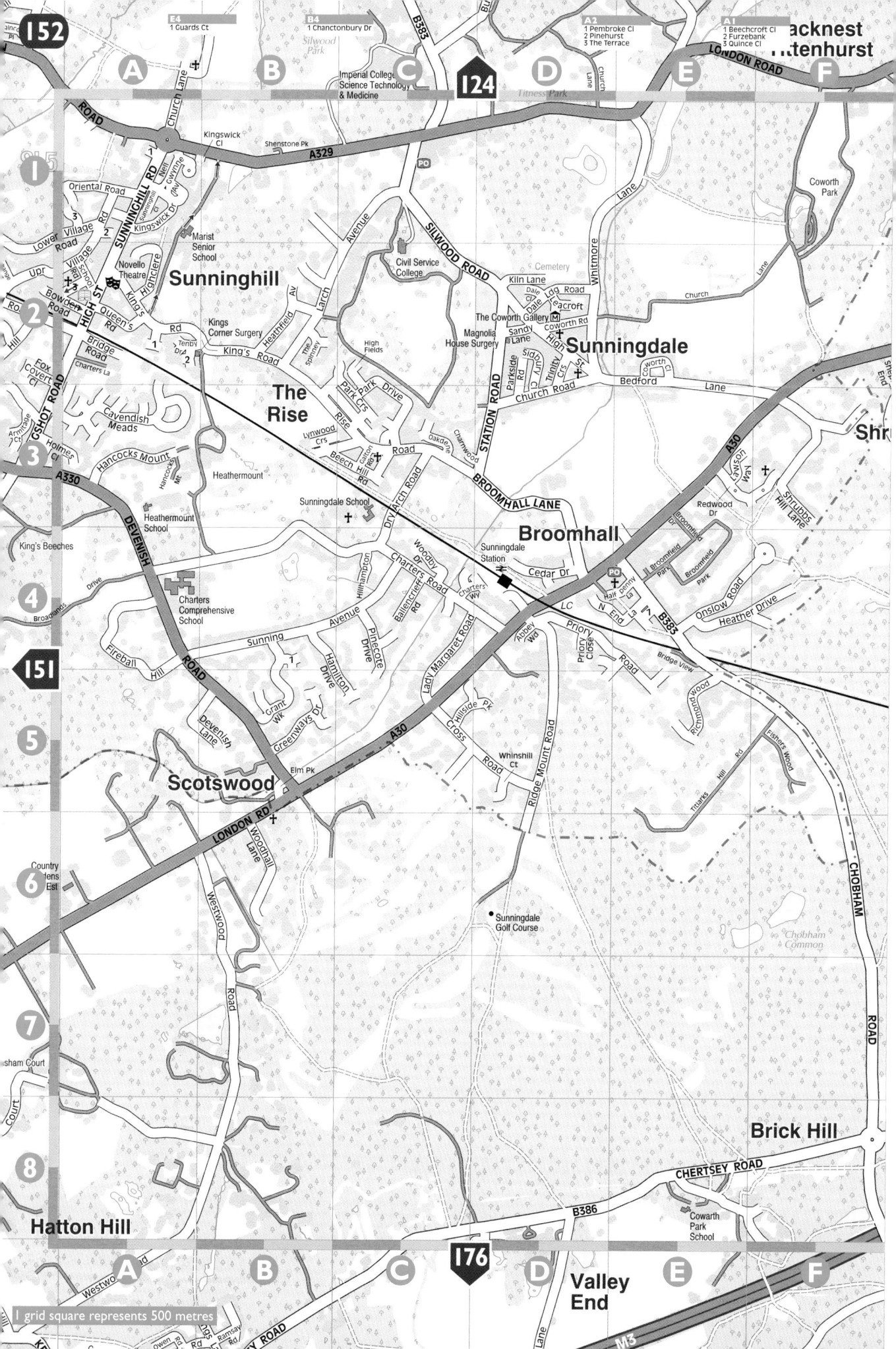

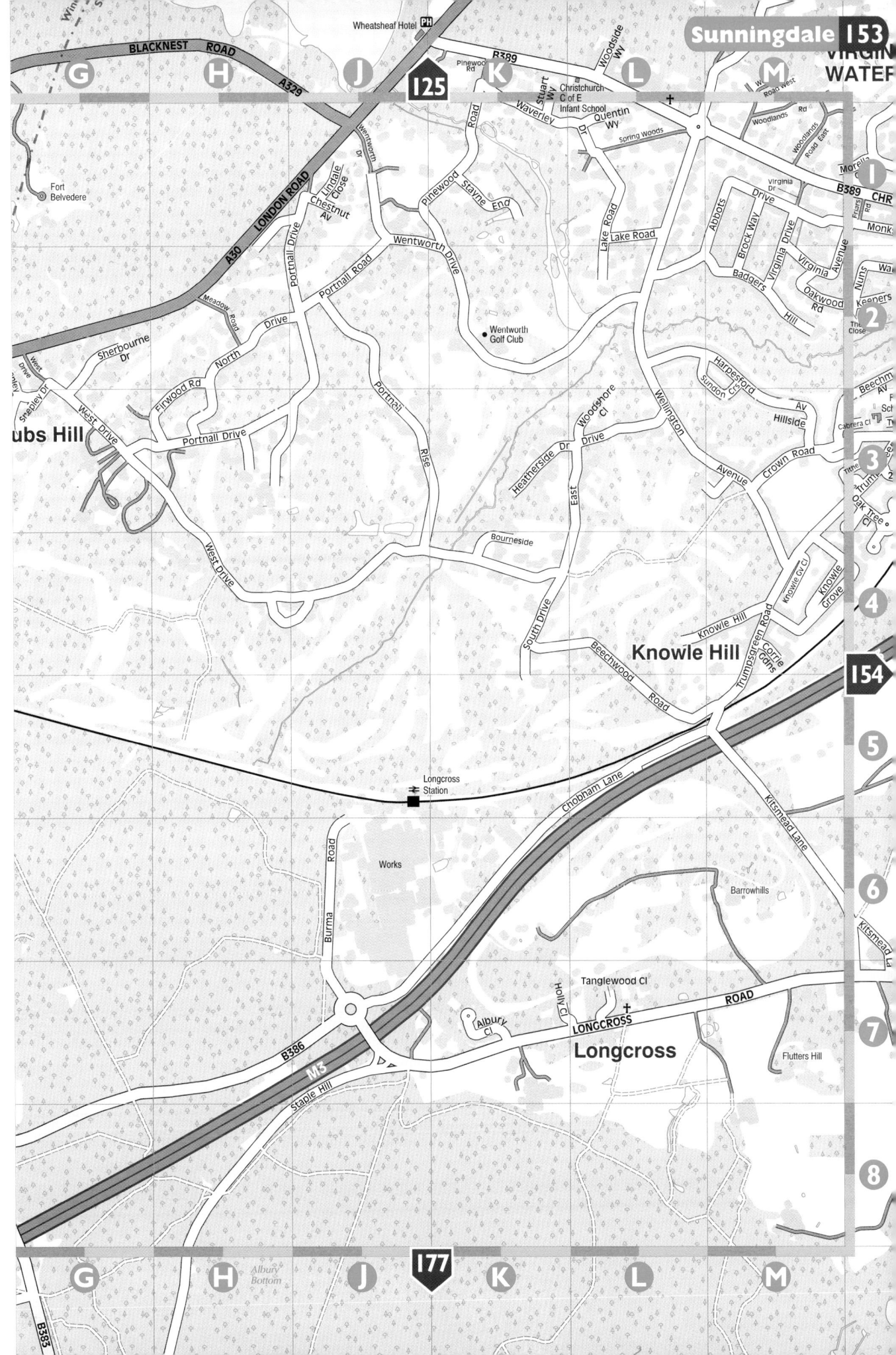

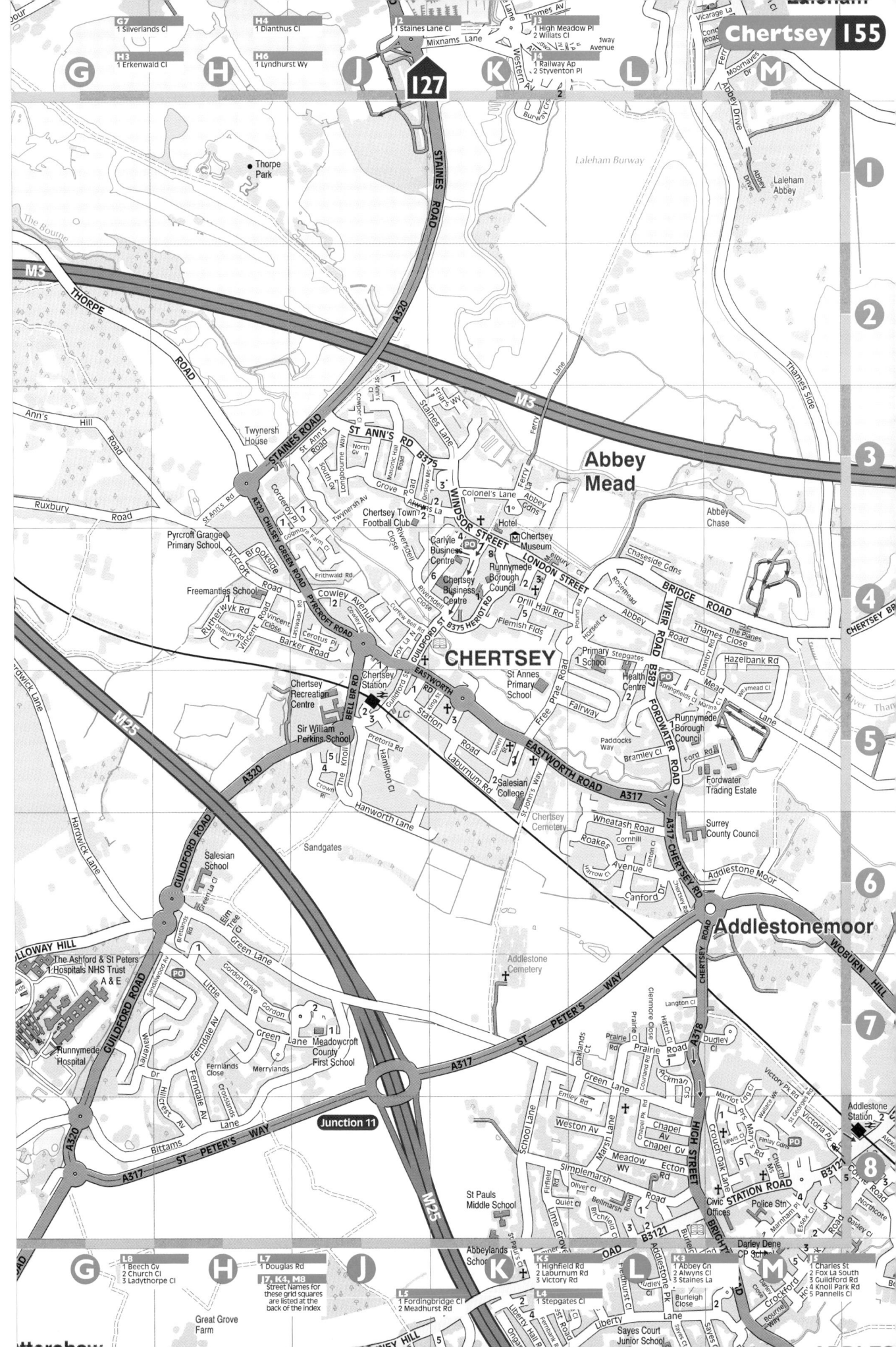

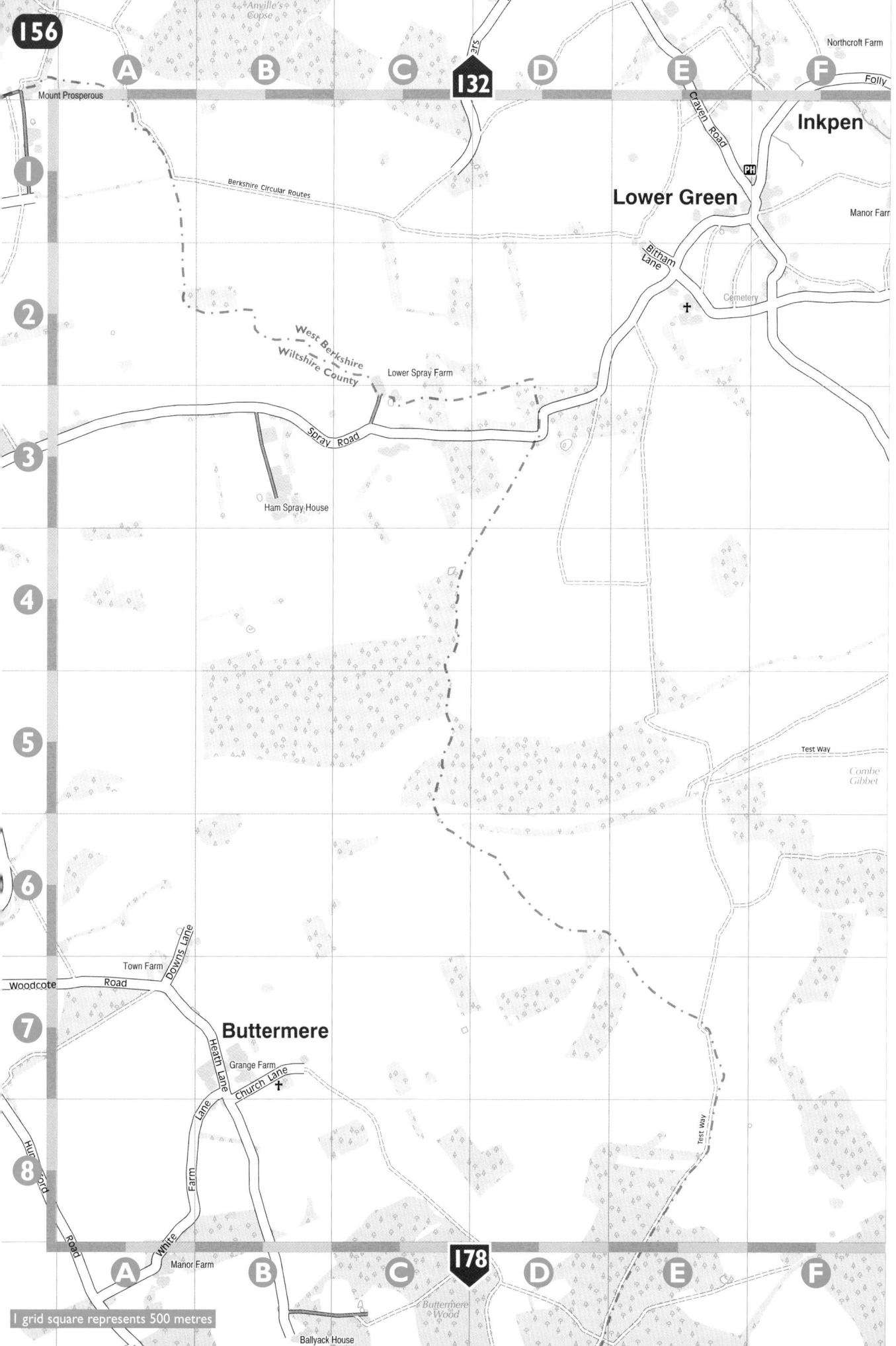

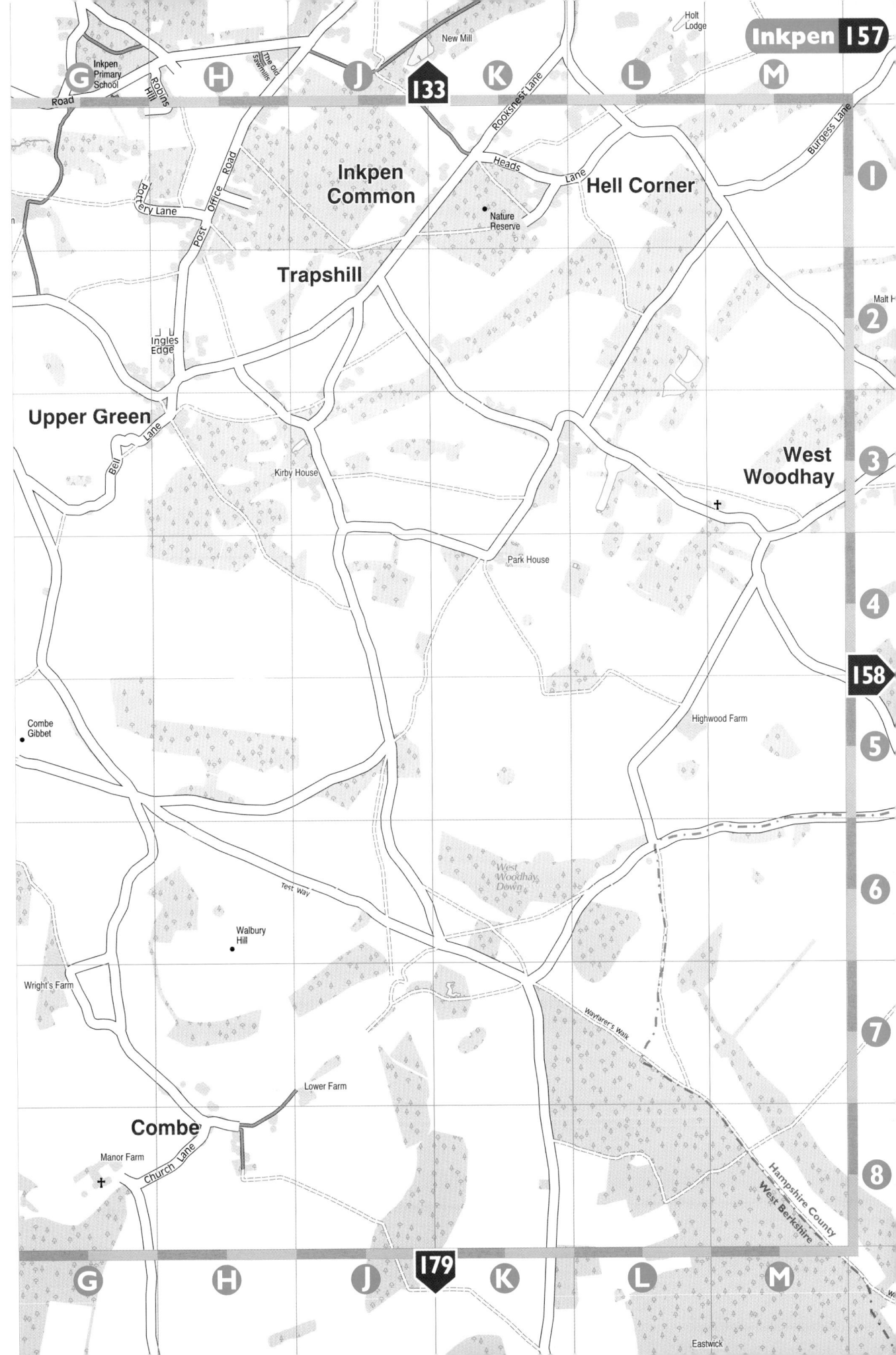

133

158

179

G   H   J   K   L   M

I
2
3
4
5
6
7
8

Inkpen Primary School

Inkpen Common

Trapshill

Ingles Edge

Upper Green

Kirby House

Combe Gibbet

Wright's Farm

Walbury Hill

Lower Farm

Combe

Manor Farm

New Mill

Holt Lodge

Hell Corner

Nature Reserve

West Woodhay

Park House

Highwood Farm

West Woodhay Down

Wayfarer's Walk

Hampshire County
West Berkshire

Eastwick

Malt H

Road
Robins Hill
Pottery Lane
Post Office Road
The Old Sawmills
Rooksnest Lane
Heads Lane
Burgess Lane
Bell Lane
Test Way
Church Lane

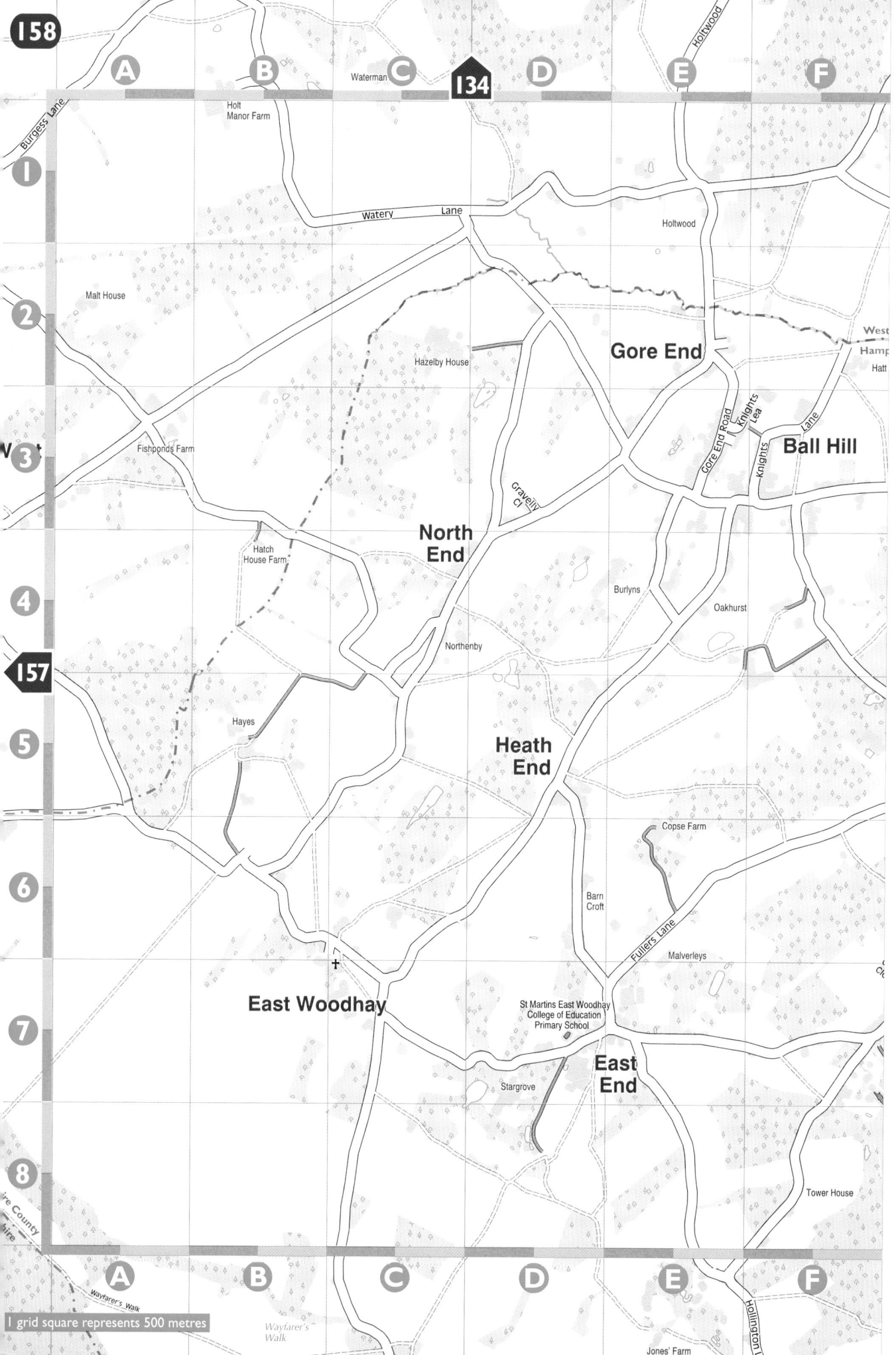

A   B   Waterman   C   134   D   E   F

I

Burgess Lane

Holt
Manor Farm

Watery   Lane

Holtwood

2

Malt House

West
Hamp

Hazelby House

Gore End

Hatt

3

W   t

Fishponds Farm

Knights
Lea

Gore End Road

Knights   Lane

Ball Hill

Gravelly Ct

North
End

4

Hatch
House Farm

Burlyns

Oakhurst

157

Northenby

5

Hayes

Heath
End

Copse Farm

6

Barn
Croft

Fullers Lane

Malverleys

Ch

East Woodhay

St Martins East Woodhay
College of Education
Primary School

7

East
End

Stargrove

8

re County
hire

Tower House

A   B   C   D   E   F

Wayfarer's Walk

Wayfarer's
Walk

Jones' Farm

Hollington L

1 grid square represents 500 metres

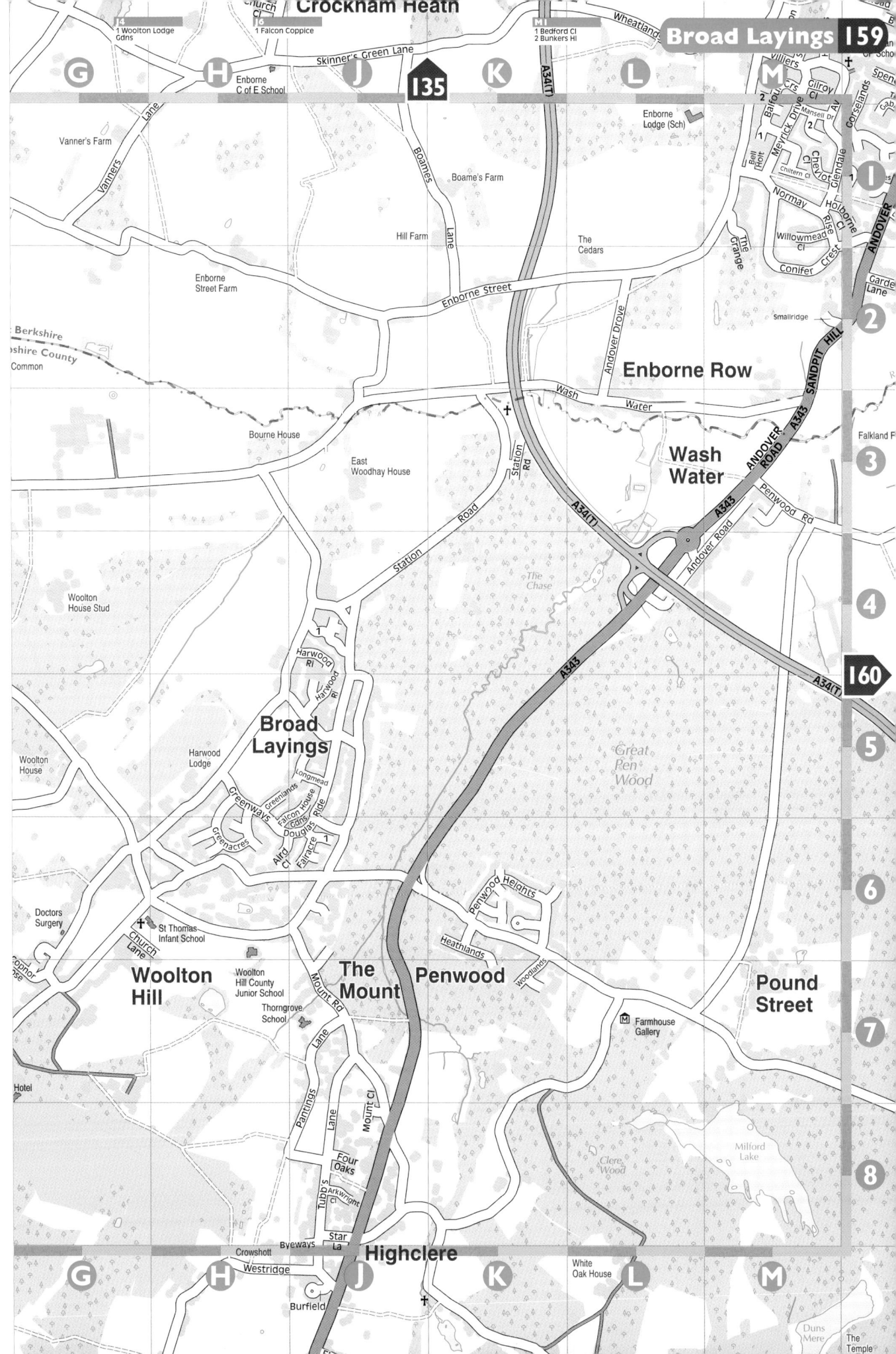

Crockham Heath

G   H   J   135   K   L   M

1 Woolton Lodge
Gdns

1 Falcon Coppice

Skinner's Green Lane

Enborne
C of E School

1 Bedford Cl
2 Bunkers Hi

Wheatlands

M1

A34(T)

Villiers

Gilroy Av

Corselands

Spen

Balfour

Meyrick Drive

Mansell Dr

Cheviot Cl

Glendale

Bell Holt

Chiltern Cl

1

2

Vanner's Farm

Vanners Lane

Enborne Lodge (Sch)

The Grange

Willowmead Cl

Normay Rise

Conifer

Falkland Crest

ANDOVER

I

Boames Lane

Boame's Farm

Hill Farm

The Cedars

Smallridge

Garden Lane

2

Enborne
Street Farm

Enborne Street

Andover Drove

SANDPIT HILL

ANDOVER ROAD

A343

Falkland F

3

Berkshire
shire County
Common

Bourne House

East
Woodhay House

Enborne Row

Wash
Water

Wash Water

Penwood Rd

A343

Andover Road

3

Woolton House Stud

Station Road

Station

The Chase

A34(T)

A343

Andover Road

4

Woolton
House

Harwood Rd

Harwood Rd

1

Broad
Layings

Harwood
Lodge

Longmead

Greenlands

Falcon House Gdns

Douglas Ride

Greenways

Greenacres

Airs Cl

Fairacre

1

Great
Pen
Wood

A34(T)

160

5

Doctors
Surgery

Ophor se

St Thomas
Infant School

Church
Lane

Woolton
Hill County
Junior School

Thorngrove
School

Woolton
Hill

Woolton
Hill County
Junior School

The
Mount

Mount Rd

Penwood Heights

Heathlands

Penwood

Woodlands

Farmhouse
Gallery

Pound
Street

6

Hotel

Pantings Lane

Mount Cl

Lane

Four
Oaks

Tubbs

Arkwright

Byeways

Star La

Crowshott

Westridge

Highclere

Burfield

Clere
Wood

Milford
Lake

Duns
Mere

The
Temple

White
Oak House

7

8

G   H   J   K   L   M

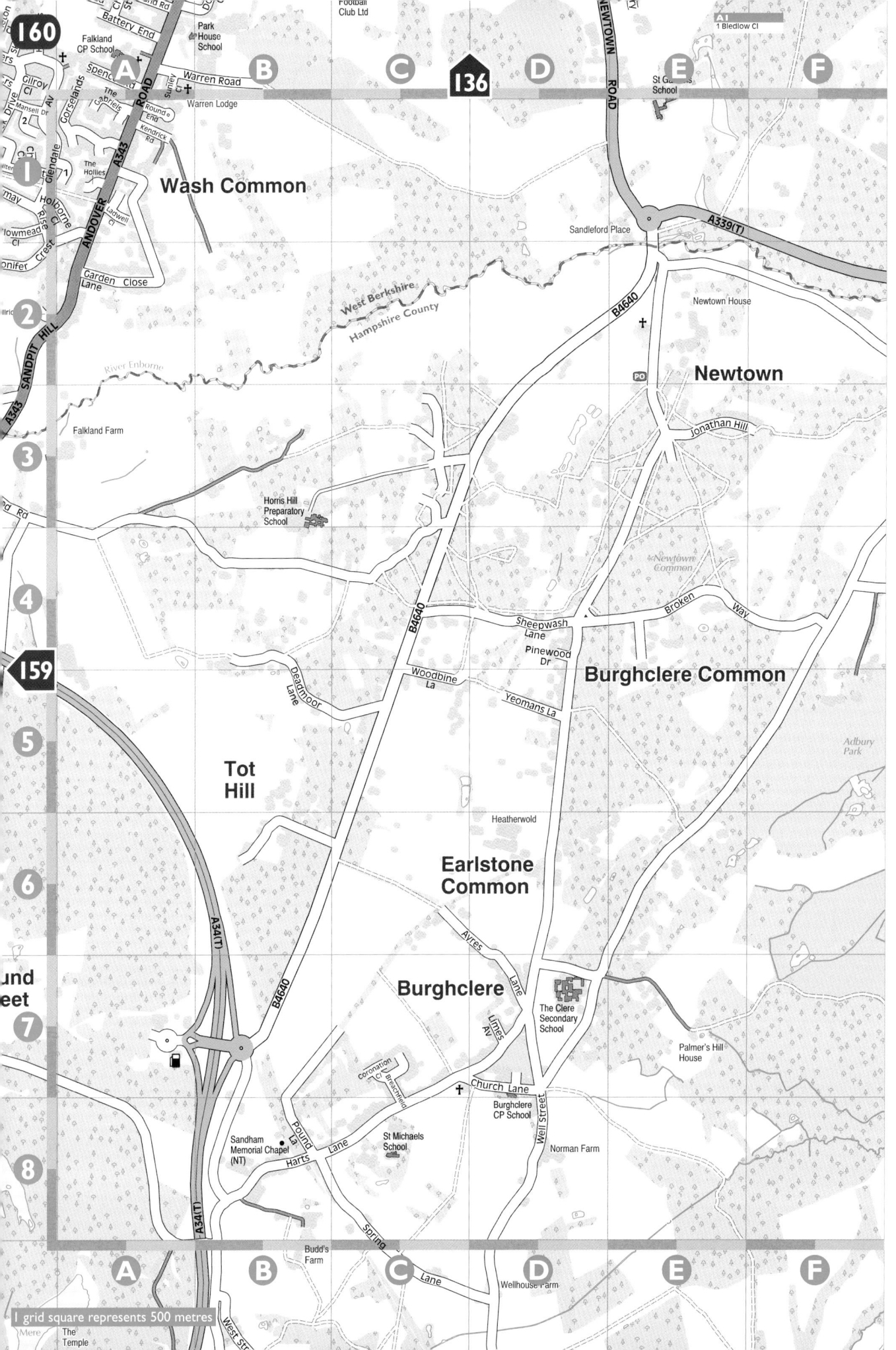

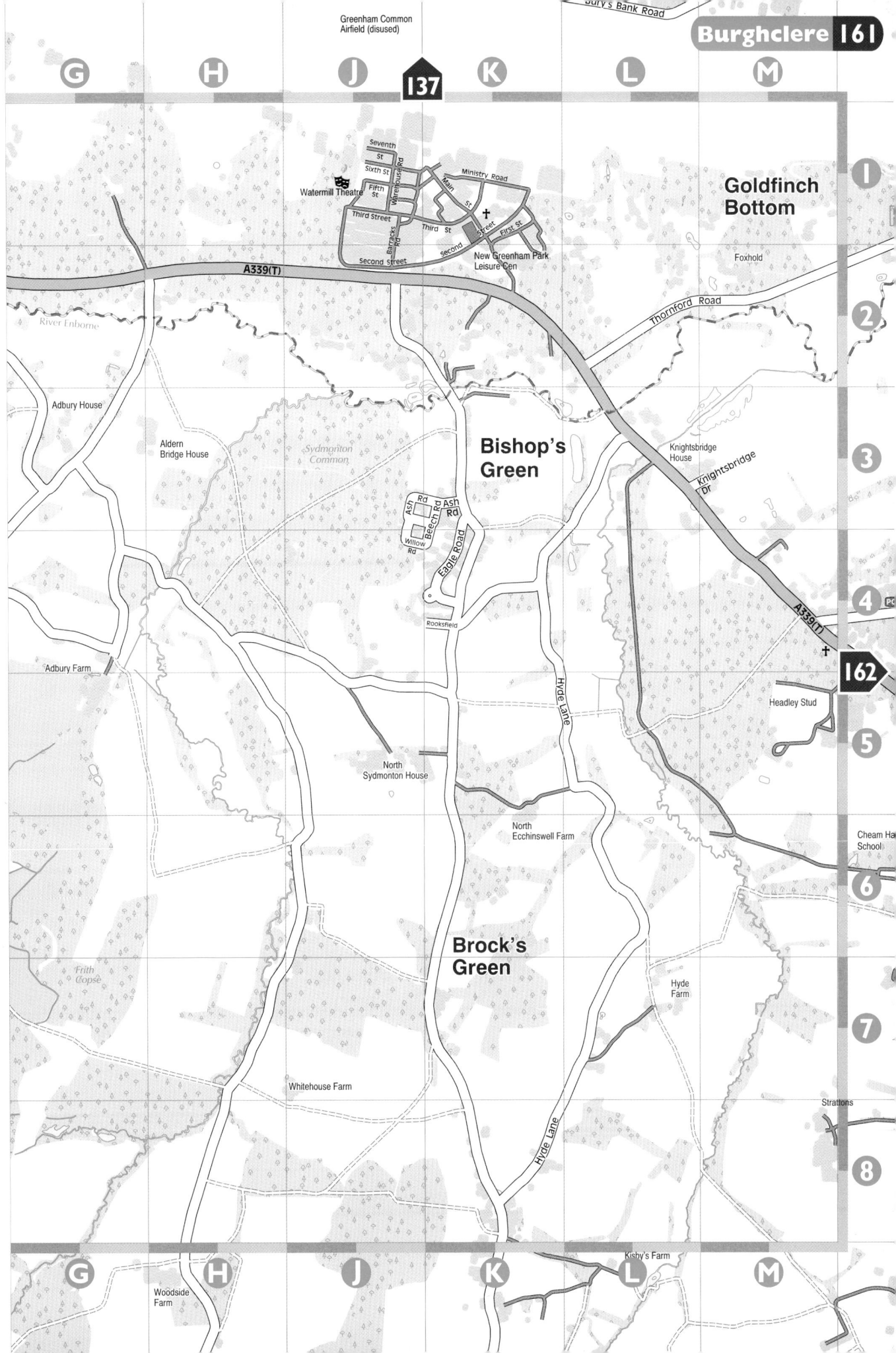

Greenham Common
Airfield (disused)

G   H   J   **137**   K   L   M

Seventh St
Sixth St
Fifth St
Watermill Theatre
Third Street
Warehouse Rd
Main St
Ministry Road
Third St
Barracks Rd
First St
Second Street
Second Street
New Greenham Park
Leisure Cen

A339(T)

River Enborne

Goldfinch Bottom

Foxhold

Thornford Road

Adbury House

Aldern Bridge House

Sydmonton Common

Bishop's Green

Knightsbridge House

Knightsbridge Dr

A339(T)

Ash Rd
Beech Rd
Ash Rd
Willow Rd

Eagle Road

Rooksfield

Adbury Farm

North Sydmonton House

Hyde Lane

North Ecchinswell Farm

Headley Stud

162

Cheam Ha School

Brock's Green

Frith Copse

Hyde Farm

Whitehouse Farm

Hyde Lane

Strattons

Woodside Farm

Kisby's Farm

G   H   J   K   L   M

I
2
3
4
5
6
7
8

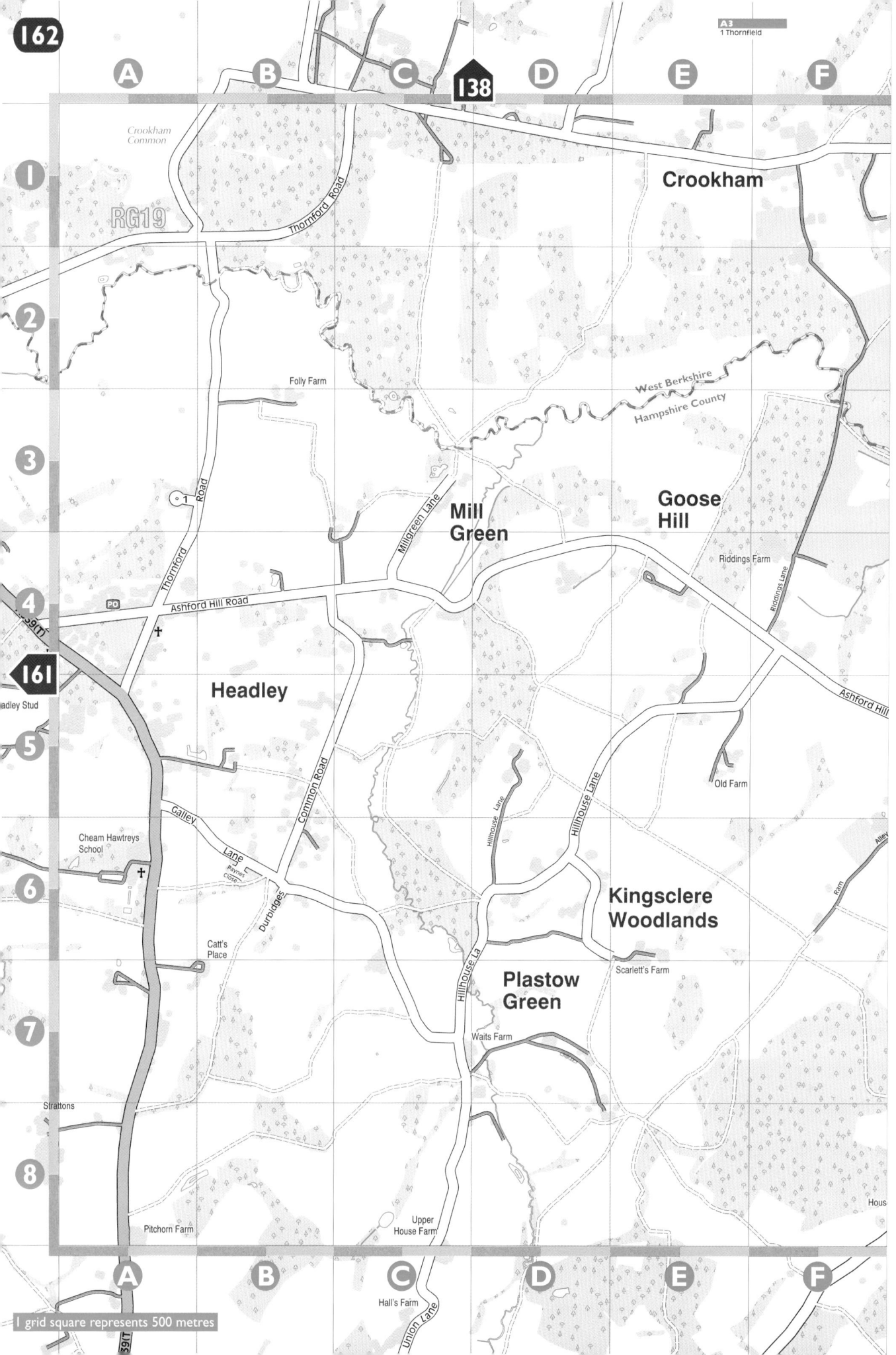

A3
1 Thornfield

A   B   C   138   D   E   F

I

Crookham Common

RG19

Crookham

2

Thornford Road

Folly Farm

West Berkshire
Hampshire County

3

Thornford Road

1

Millgreen Lane

Mill Green

Goose Hill

Riddings Farm

Riddings Lane

PO

4

Ashford Hill Road

Ashford Hill

A339(T)

161

Headley Stud

Headley

5

Common Road

Hillhouse Lane

Hillhouse Lane

Old Farm

Galley

Cheam Hawtreys School

Lane

Paynes Close

6

Durbidges

Kingsclere Woodlands

Catt's Place

Scarlett's Farm

Hillhouse La

Plastow Green

7

Waits Farm

Ram

Alley

Strattons

8

Hous

Pitchorn Farm

Upper House Farm

A   B   C   D   E   F

Hall's Farm

Union Lane

A339(T)

Stone House

Wasing Park

Wasi

Shalford Farm

PO

The Business Centre

Brimpton School

139

G **H** **J** **K** **L** **M**

1

Wasing Farm

Little Park House

Hyde End Lane

Oak Cott

Hyde End

Boot Farm

2

Wasi

River Enborne

Back Lane

3

Blacknest Farm

Woodhouse Lane

Hockford Lane

Brimpton Common

4

Woodhouse Farm

Aldershot

Brimpton Road

164

The Co Sc

Road

Old Lane

B3051

Inhurst Lane

Stokes Lane

Inhurst House School

5

Ashford Hill

Chapel La

Ashford Hill Primary School

Haughurst Hill

Haughur Hill

Tucker's Hill Stud

6

Inhurst

The Holt

Holt Cottages

Inhurst Farm

7

Fair Oak

Wolverton Road

Axmansford

LITTLE KNOWLE HILL

Wheat Hold

Little Ham Farm

Hook Lane

Violet Lane

8

B3051

Dairy Farm

Ham Lane

Wolverton Road

Wol

G **H** **J** **K** **L** **M**

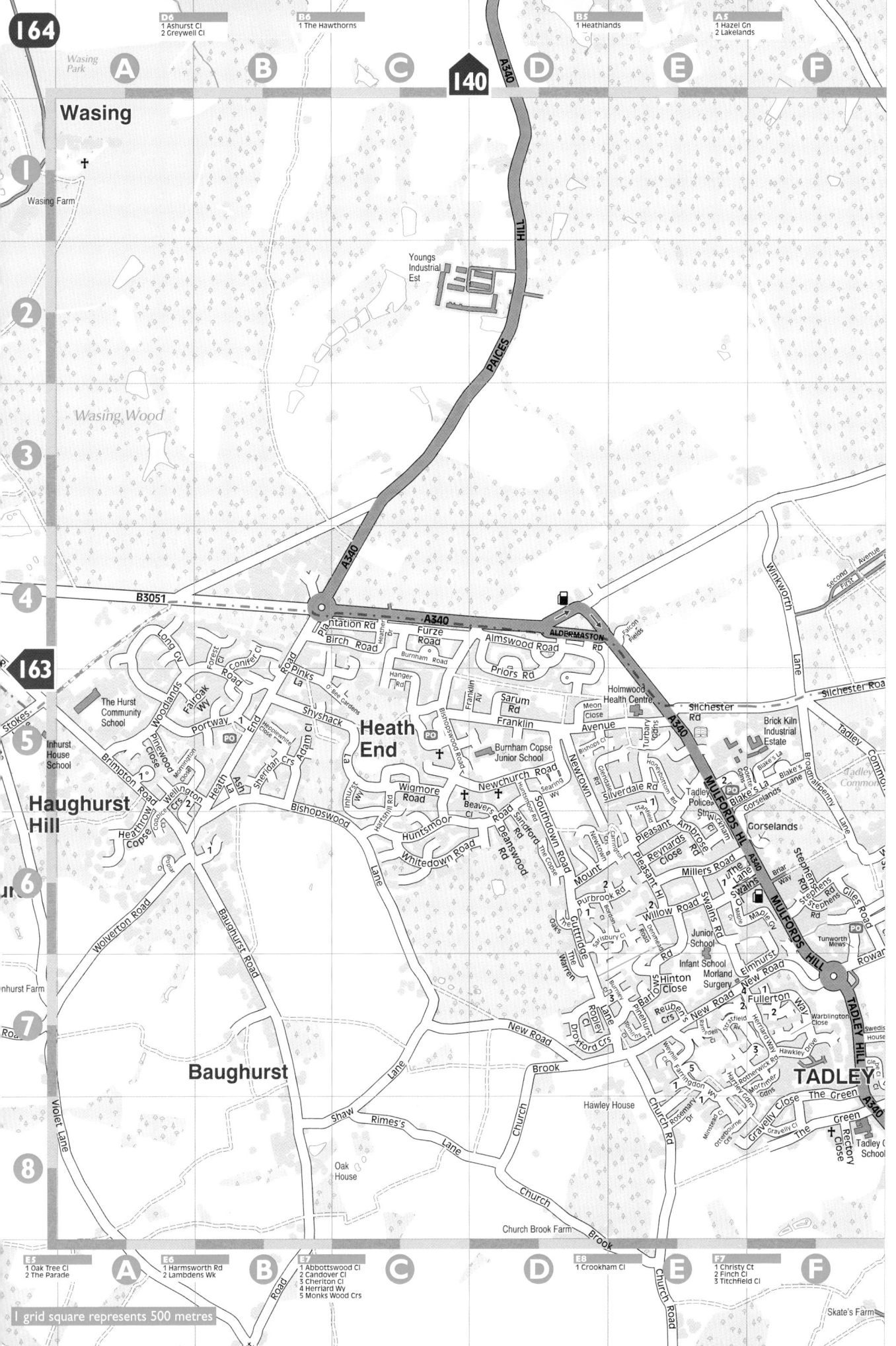

140

D6
1 Ashurst Cl
2 Greywell Cl

B6
1 The Hawthorns

B5
1 Heathlands

A5
1 Hazel Gn
2 Lakelands

A | B | C | D | E | F

Wasing

Wasing Park

✝
Wasing Farm

1

Wasing Wood

2

3

Youngs
Industrial
Est

PACES

TILL

A340

4

B3051

A340

163

Long Cv
Forest Cl
Conifer Cl

Woodlands
Faircak Wy

The Hurst
Community
School

Stokes

Inhurst
House
School

Portway

Plantation Rd
Birch Road
Pinks La

Furze
Road
Burnham
Road

Hanger
Rd

Almswood Road

Priors Rd

Franklin
Av
Sarum
Rd
Franklin

Meon
Close

ALDERMASTON
RD

Falcon
Fields

Holmwood
Health Centre

Turbary
Gdns

A340

Silchester
Rd

Brick Kiln
Industrial
Estate

Silchester Road

Tadley
Common

Tadley
Common

Heath
End

Road
End

Shyshack
La

Hepplewhite
Close

Adam Cl

Sheridan
Crs

Bishopswood

Inhurst
Wy

Wigmore
Road

Hartshill Rd

Beavers
Cl

Newchurch Road

Southdown Road

Searing
Wy

Deanswood
Rd

Sandford
Rd

Bishops Cl

Clarabelle Rd

Hozleton Rd

Silverdale
Rd

Newtown
Rd

Avenue

Bishopswood Road

Haughurst
Hill

Brimpton
Road

Pinewood
Close

Wellington
Rd

Heath
La
Ash

Heathrow
Copse

Huntsmoor

The Copse
Oaks

Whitedown Road

Lane

Mount

Newtown

Carrington

Pleasant
Hi

Stanford
Rd

Pleasant
Rd

Reynards
Close

Ambrose
Rd

Amport
Rd

Tadley
Police

Blake's La

Blake's St

Gorselands

Brockmainpenny
Lane

Giles
Rd

Gorselands

Stephens
Rd
Stephens
Rd

Stephens
Rd

MULFORDS HILL

PO

Wolverton Road

Baughurst Road

Purbrook Rd

Cuttridge

The
Warren

Willow Road

Swains
Rd

Millers Road

The
Swains
Cl

Magpie
Ct

Briar
Wy

Tunworth
Mews

Rowan

6

Salisbury Cl

Junior
School

Infant School
Morland
Surgery

Hinton
Close

Barlows
Rd

Droxford Crs

Ropley
Lane

Pinehurst

Reuben's
Crs

New Road

New Road
Fullerton
Way

Elmhurst
Cl

Warblington
Close

Hawkley Drive

Stephens
Rd

7

inhurst Farm

Road

7

Baughurst

New Road

Lane

Brook

Shaw
Lane

Rimes's
Lane

Oak
House

church

Church Brook Farm

Hawley House

Church Rd

Rosemary
Dr

Minstead Cl

Ottenbourne
Crs

Gravelly Cl

Hannigton Way
Hatch
Gdns

Monteagle Wy

Farringdon
Rd

Rotherwick Rd

Herriard Way

Gravelly Close

Gravelly
Close

TADLEY

✝
Tadley C
School

The Green

The
Green

Swedish
House

TADLEY HILL

A340

Violet Lane

Church
Brook

Skate's Farm

8

A | B | C | D | E | F

E8
1 Oak Tree Cl
2 The Parade

E6
1 Harmsworth Rd
2 Lambdens Wk

E7
1 Abbottswood Cl
2 Candover Cl
3 Cheriton Cl
4 Herriard Wy
5 Monks Wood Crs

E8
1 Crookham Cl

F7
1 Christy Ct
2 Finch Cl
3 Titchfield Cl

1 grid square represents 500 metres

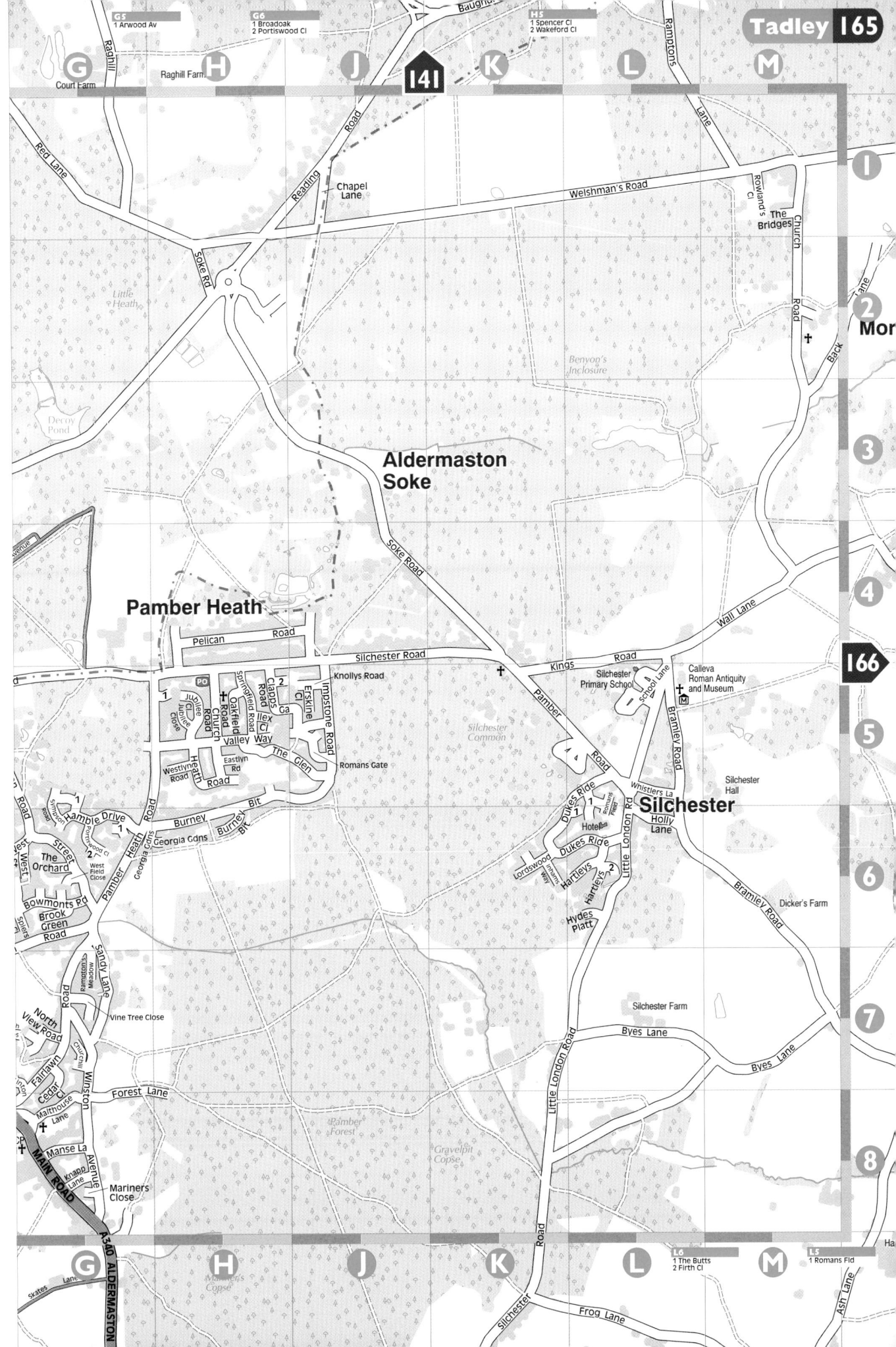

G5
1 Arwood Av

G6
1 Broadoak
2 Portiswood Cl

H5
1 Spencer Cl
2 Wakeford Cl

G **H** **J** **141** **K** **L** **M**

Raghill Farm

Court Farm

Red Lane

Raghill Lane

Soke Rd

Little Heath

Reading Road

Chapel Lane

Welshman's Road

Rowland's Cl

The Bridges

Church Road

Back Lane

1

2 Mor

Decoy Pond

Benyon's Inclosure

3

Aldermaston Soke

Soke Road

Wall Lane

4

166

Pamber Heath

Pelican Road

Silchester Road

Knollys Road

Kings Road

Silchester Primary School

School Lane

Calleva Roman Antiquity and Museum

PO

Springfield Road

Oakfield Road

Clapps Ga

Erskine Cl

Impstone Road

Jubilee Close

Church Road

Ilex Cl

Valley Way

Eastlyn Rd

The Glen

Romans Gate

Silchester Common

Pamber Road

Bramley Road

Silchester Hall

5

Westlyn Road

Heath Road

Syspron Road

Hamble Drive

Portiswood Cl

Burney Road

Georgia Gdns

Burney Bk

Heath Bit

West Field Close

Dukes Ride

Whistlers La

Hotel

Holly Lane

Lordswood

Dukes Ride

Hartleys

Little London Rd

Romans Field

Silchester

6

The Orchard

West Street

Bowmonts Rd

Brook Green Road

Spiers

Pamber Road

Sandy Lane

Hydes Platt

Dicker's Farm

Ramsdon's Meadow

Vine Tree Close

Silchester Farm

Byes Lane

Byes Lane

7

North View Road

Fairlawn

Cedar

Winston Avenue

Churchill

Malthouse Lane

Forest Lane

Pamber Forest

Gravelpit Copse

8

CP

MAIN ROAD

Manse La

Knapp Lane

Mariners Close

Little London Road

Silchester Road

G **A340 ALDERMASTON** **H** **J** **K** **L** **M**

L6
1 The Butts
2 Firth Cl

L5
1 Romans Fld

Skates Lane

Mariner's Copse

Frog Lane

Ash Lane

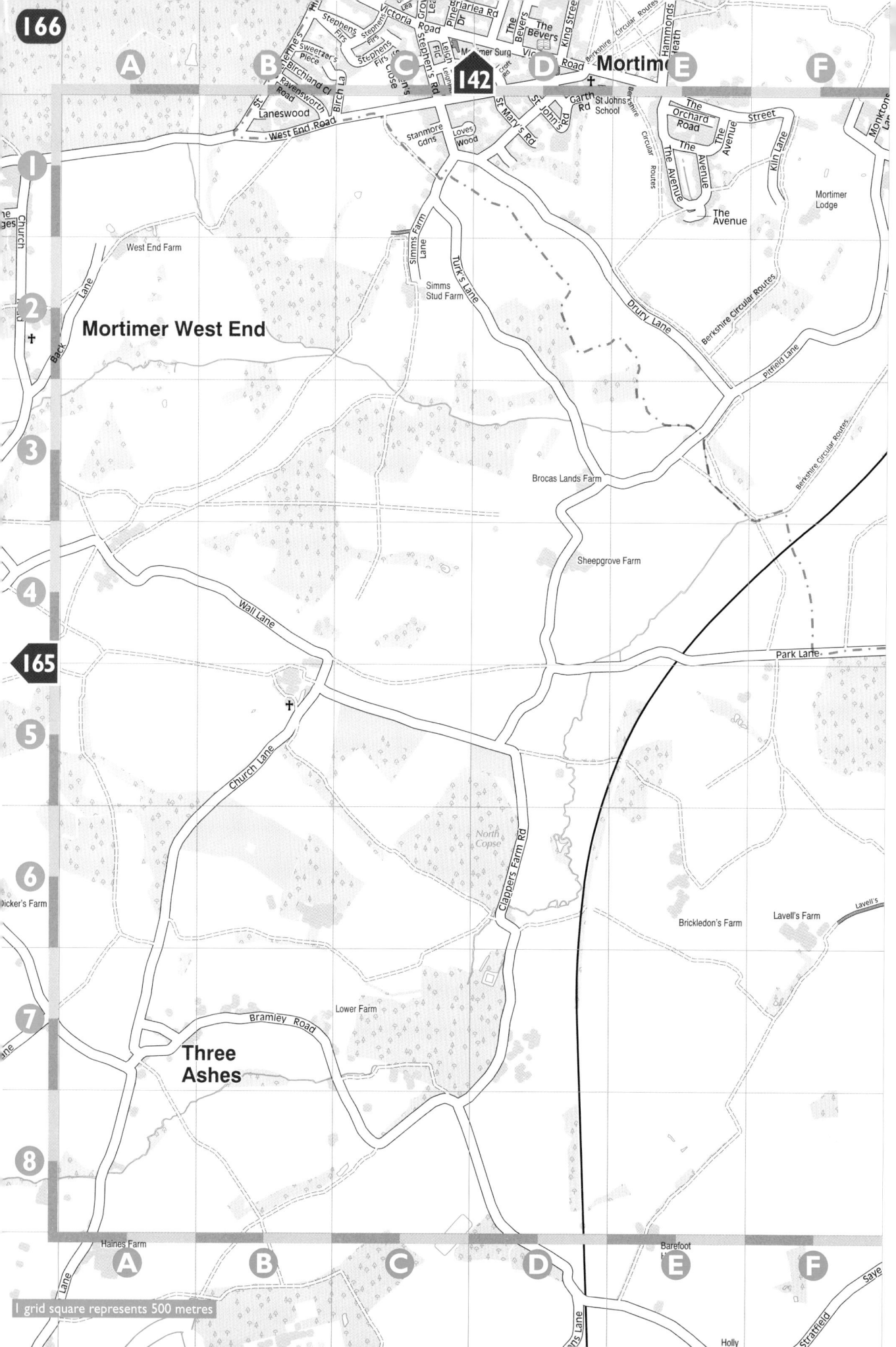

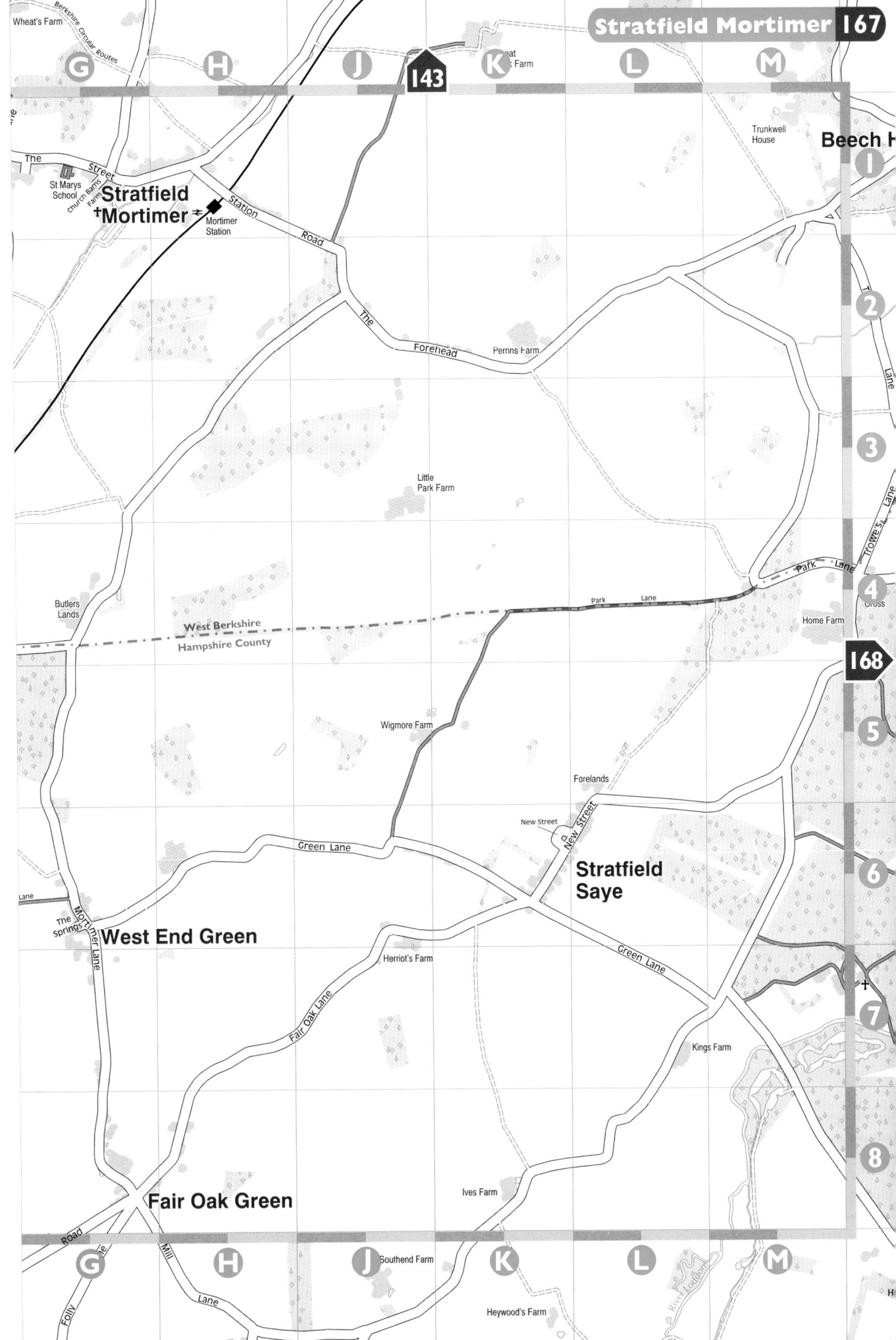

G H J 143 K L M

Wheat's Farm

Berkshire Circular Routes

Trunkwell
House

Beech H

The
Street

St Marys
School

Church Barns
Farm

Stratfield
†**Mortimer**

Mortimer
Station

Station Road

I

2

The

Forehead

Perrins Farm

3

Little
Park Farm

Tromp's Lane

Park   Lane

4

Butlers
Lands

West Berkshire

Park   Lane

Cross

Home Farm

Hampshire County

168

5

Wigmore Farm

Forelands

New Street

New Street

6

Green Lane

**Stratfield
Saye**

Lane

The
springs

Mortimer Lane

West End Green

Herriot's Farm

Green Lane

7

Fair Oak Lane

Kings Farm

8

Ives Farm

Fair Oak Green

Road

Mill

Southend Farm

G H J K L M

Lane

Heywood's Farm

River Loddon

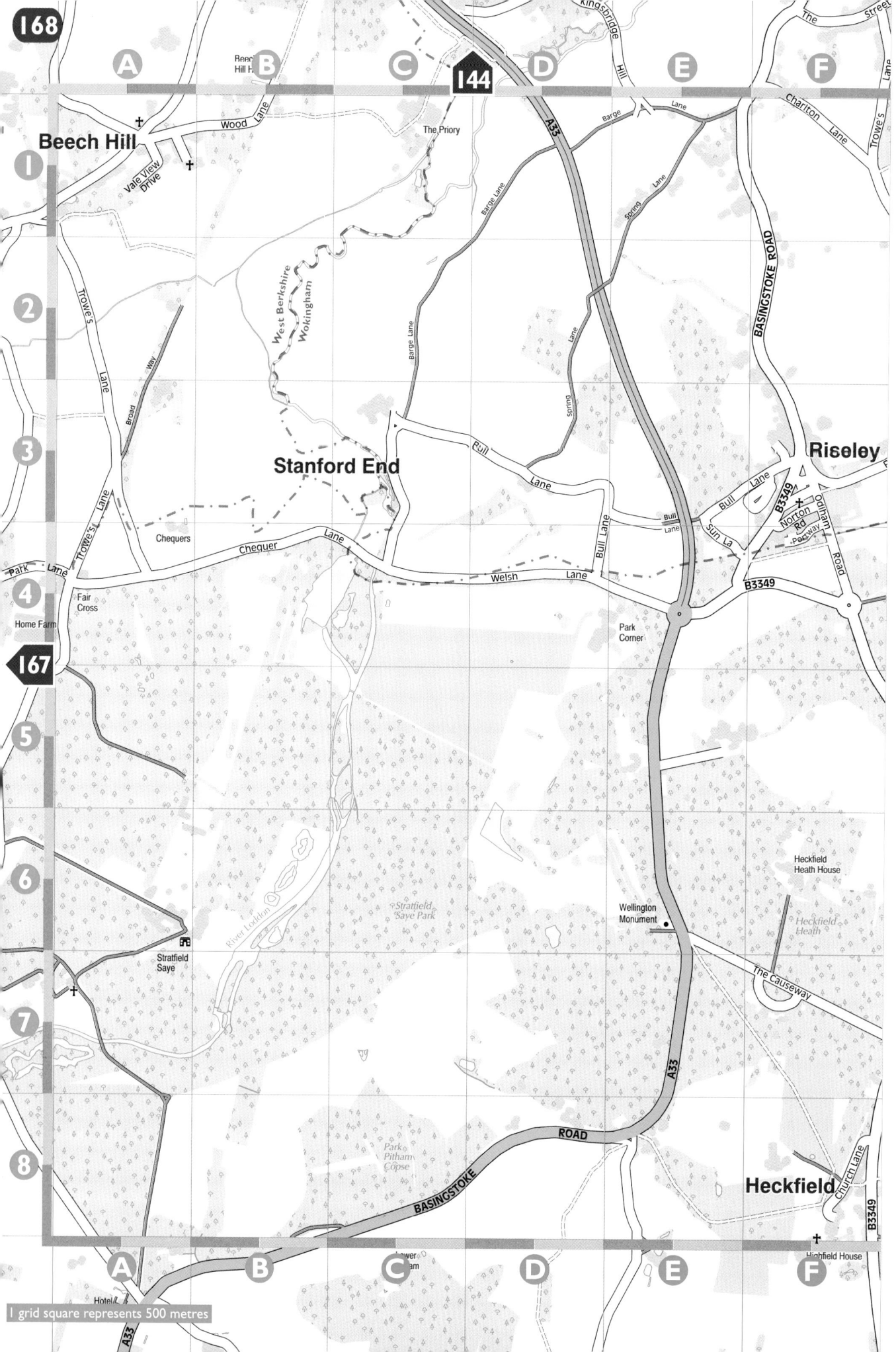

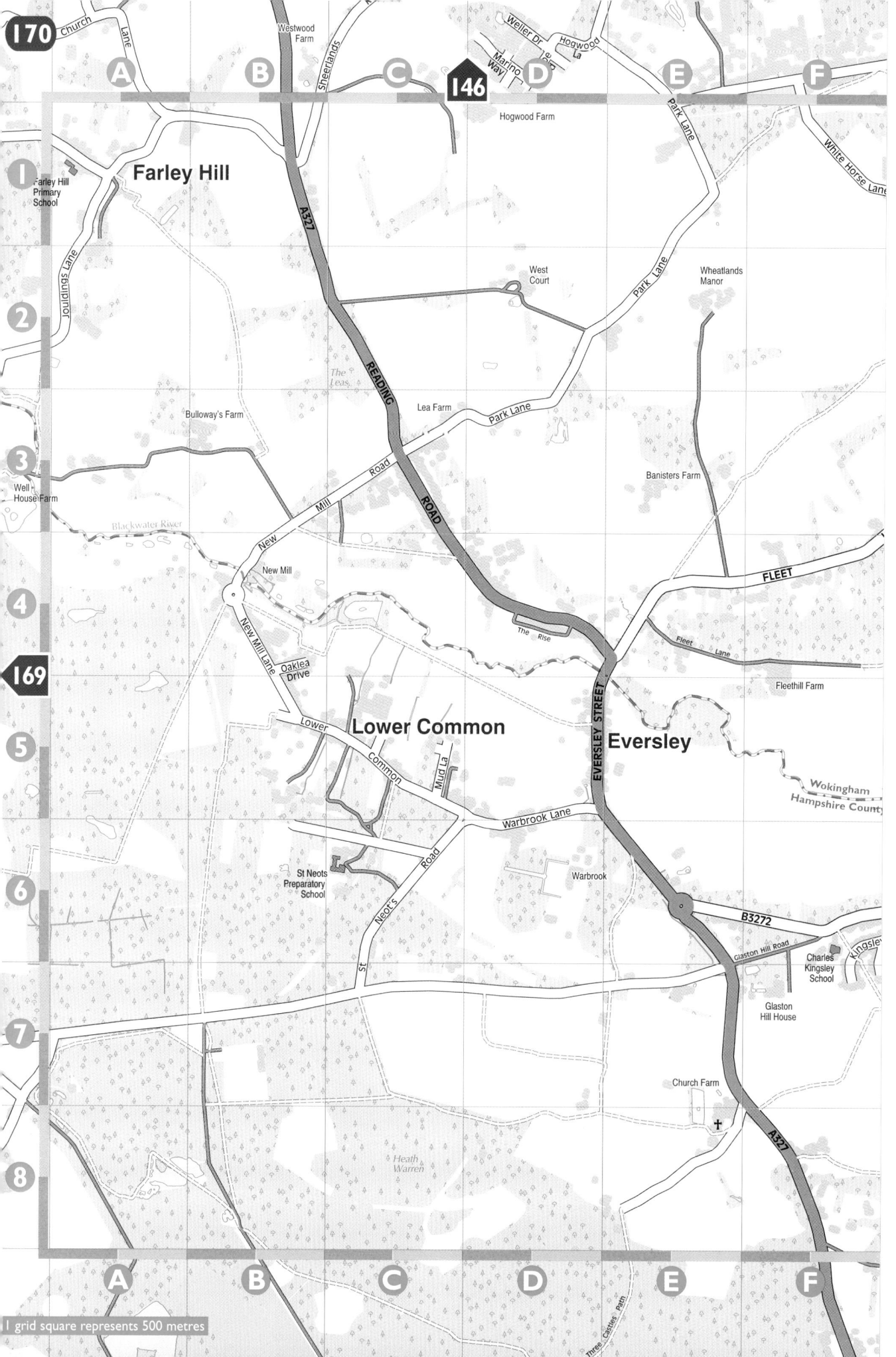

Westwood Farm

Sheerlands

Weller Dr
Hogwood La
Marino Way

146

Hogwood Farm

A321

Hogwood Farm

Farley Hill

Farley Hill Primary School

Johnson's Lane

Park Lane

West Court

Wheatlands Manor

READING

Park Lane

The Leas

Bulloway's Farm

Lea Farm

Park Lane

Banisters Farm

Well House Farm

Blackwater River

New Mill Road

New Mill

FLEET

New Mill Lane

Oaklea Drive

The Rise

Fleet Lane

Fleethill Farm

169

EVERSLEY STREET

Lower Common

Lower Common

Eversley

Wokingham Hampshire County

Muddie La

St Neots Preparatory School

Warbrook Lane

St Neot's Road

Warbrook

B3272

Glaston Hill Road

Kingsley

Charles Kingsley School

Glaston Hill House

Church Farm

A327

Heath Warren

Three Castles Path

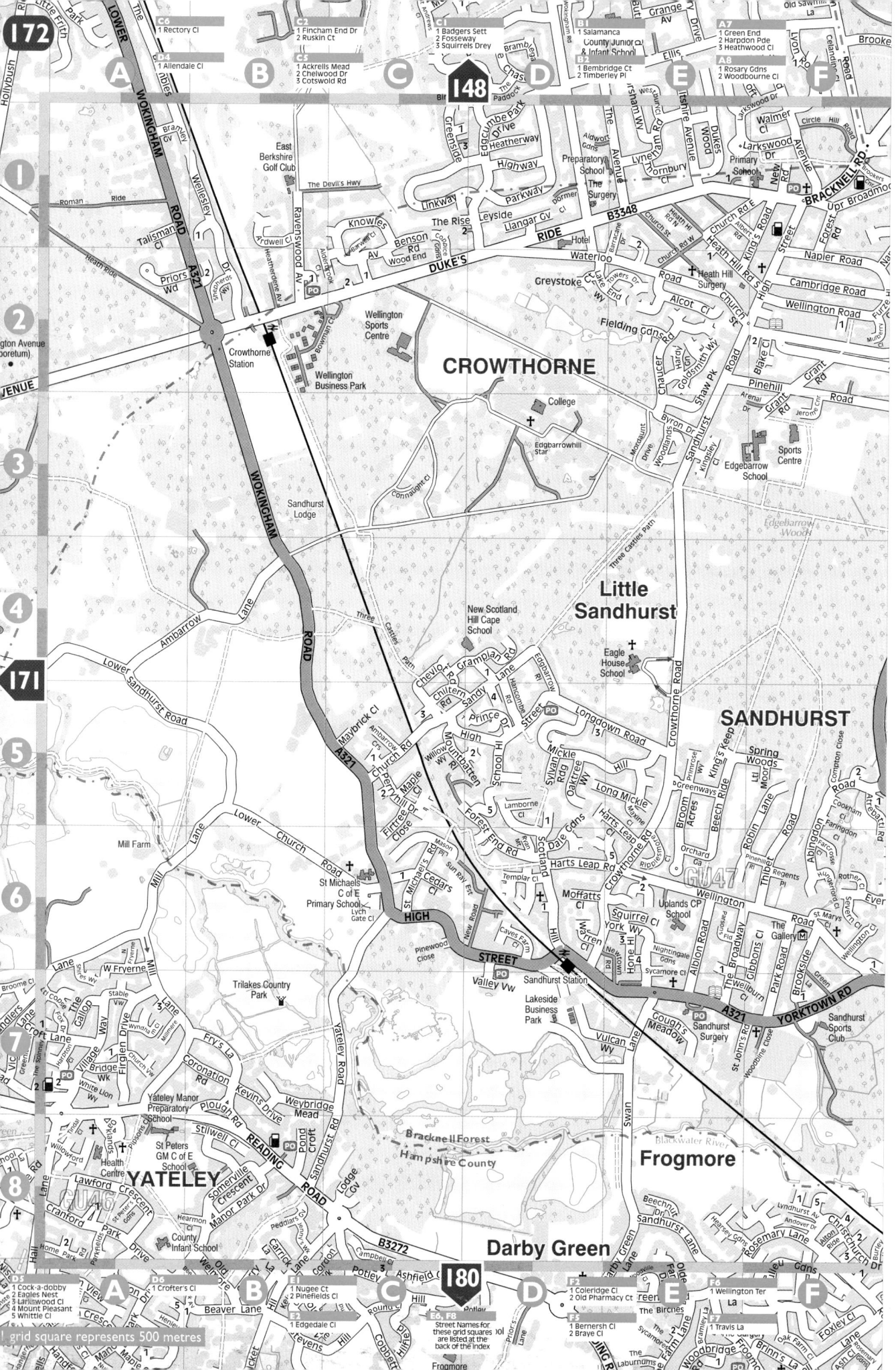

G4
1 Darleydale Cl
2 Georgeham Rd
3 Kirkham Cl

G6
1 Centurion Cl
2 Cornbunting Cl
3 Mulberry Cl
4 Rockfield Wy
5 Shrivenham Cl
6 Sonninge Cl
7 Tarbat Ct

G8
1 Bacon Cl
2 Reynolds Gn

H4
1 Barkis Mead
2 Frodsham Wy
3 Peggotty Pl
4 Steerforth Copse
5 Trotwood Cl

149

174

181

H8
1 Hepworth Cft
2 Maddox Brown
End
3 Seebys Oak
4 Thorburn Cha

H7
1 Rosedene La

M6
1 Overlord Cl

M8
1 St Mary's Rd

L8
1 Willington Cl

K6
1 Dawnay Rd

M
1 Crown Pl
2 Grantham Cl
3 Rugby Cl

H6
1 Bluethroat Cl
2 Bullfinch Cl
3 Chaffinch Cl

RG45

Owlsmoor

College Town

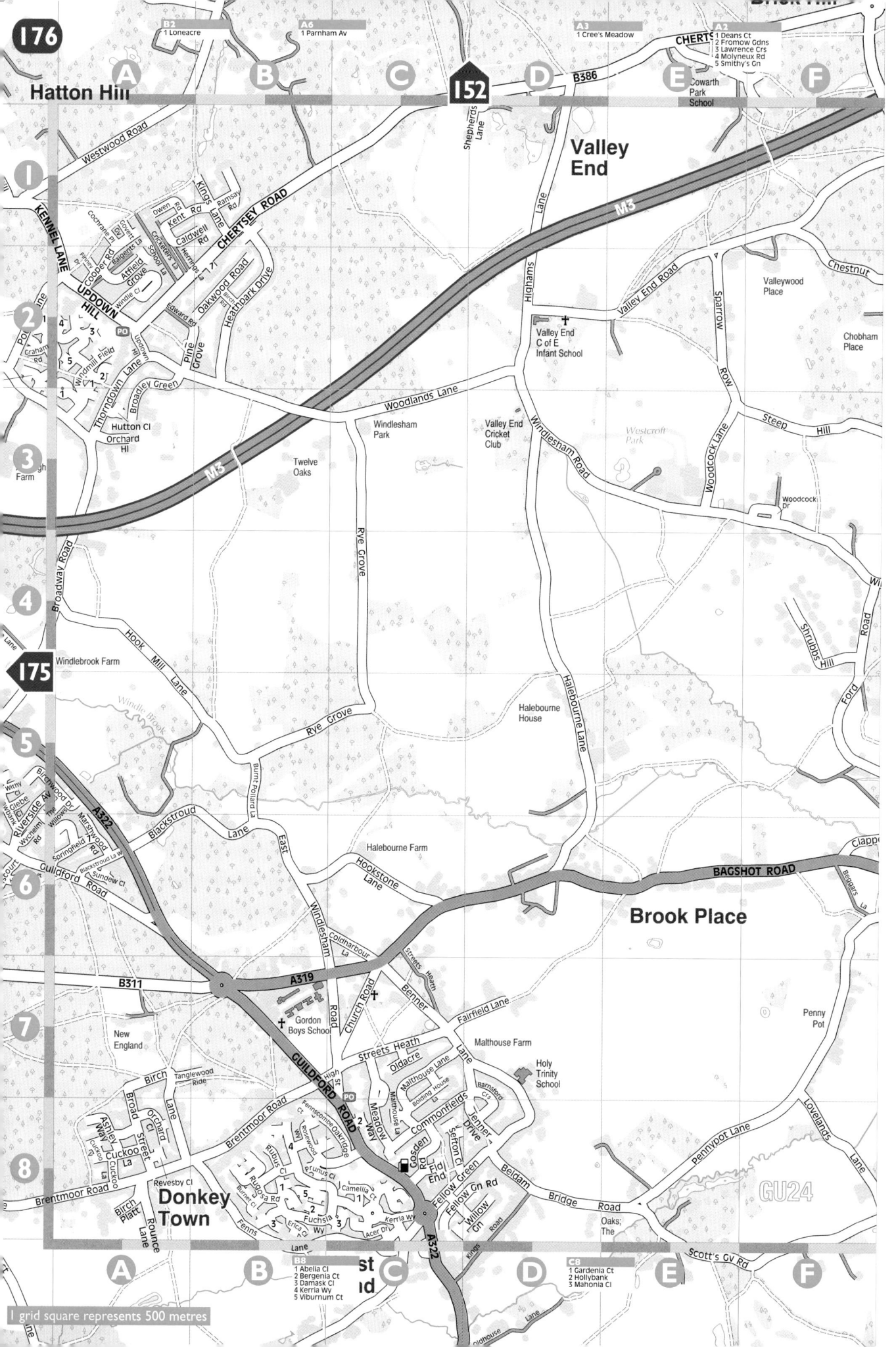

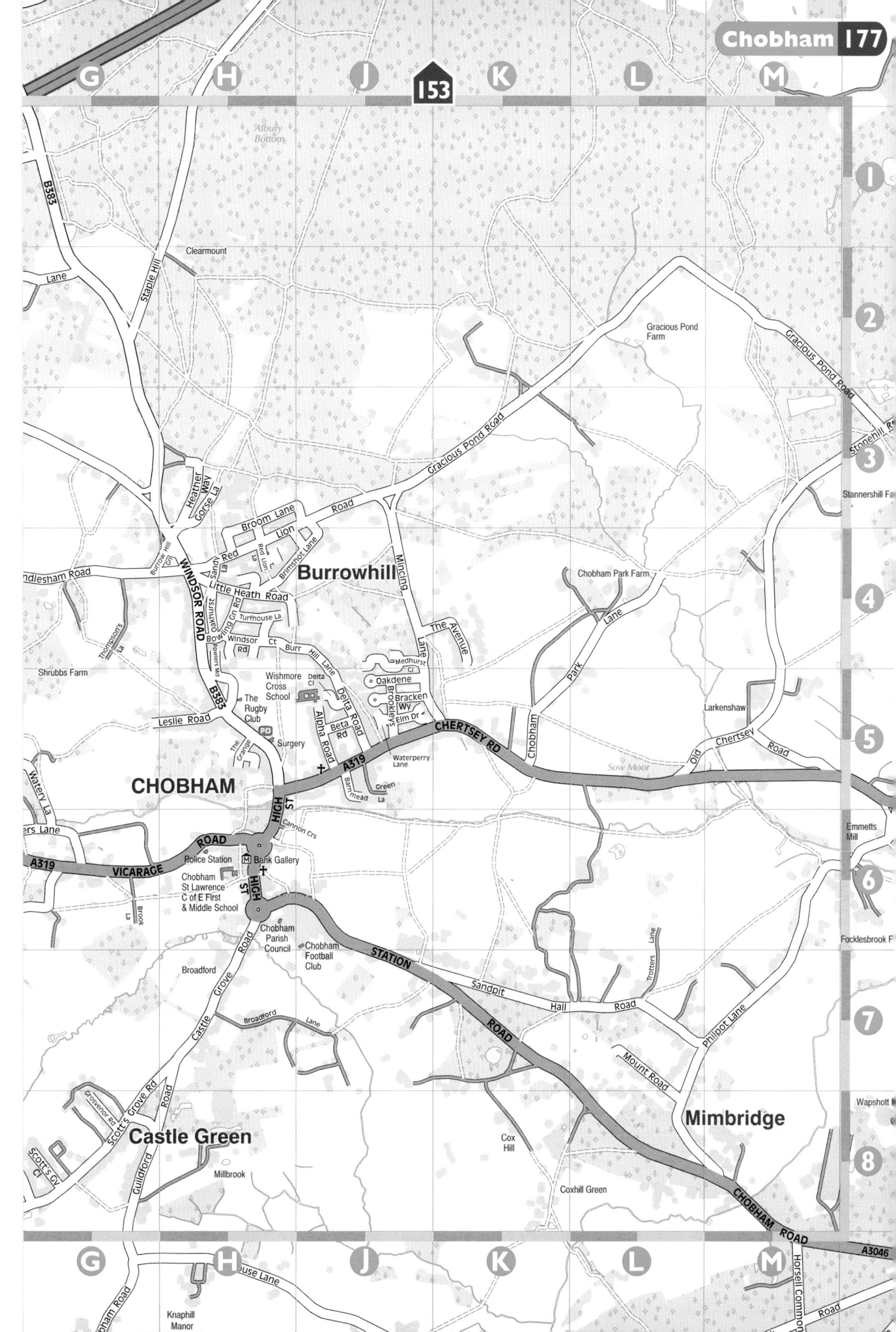

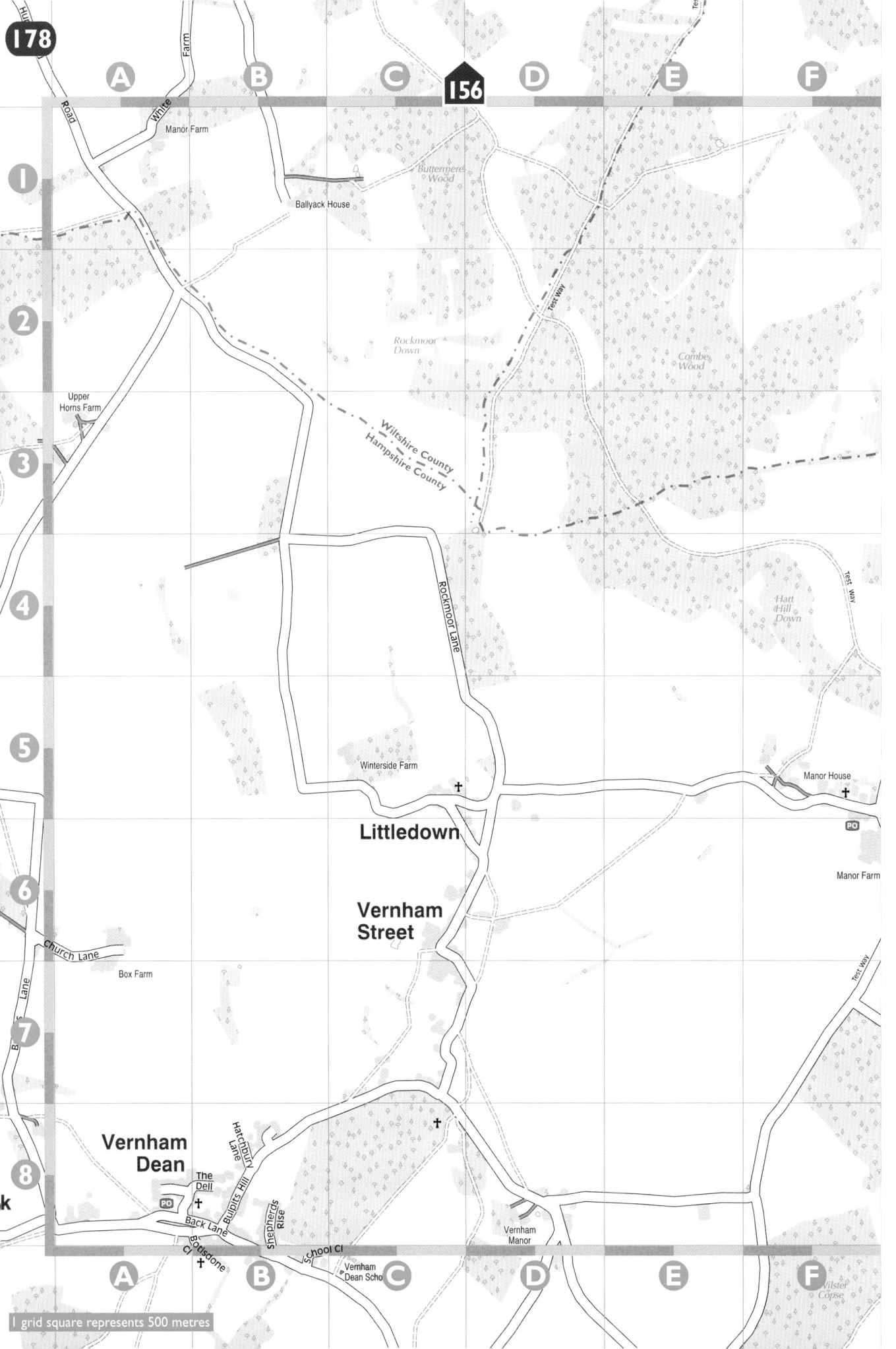

156

A B C D E F

1

2

3

4

5

6

7

8

Manor Farm

White

Road

Ballyack House

Buttermere
Wood

Test Way

Upper
Horns Farm

Rockmoor
Down

Combe
Wood

Wiltshire County
Hampshire County

Rockmoor Lane

Hart
Hill
Down

Test Way

Winterside Farm

Manor House

PO

Littledown

**Vernham
Street**

Manor Farm

Church Lane

Box Farm

Bs Lane

Test Way

**Vernham
Dean**

Hatchbury Lane

Bulpits Hill Lane

The
Dell

PO

Shepherds Rise

Back Lane

Bodsdone Cl

School Cl

Vernham
Dean Scho

Vernham
Manor

Vilster
Copse

k

A B C D E F

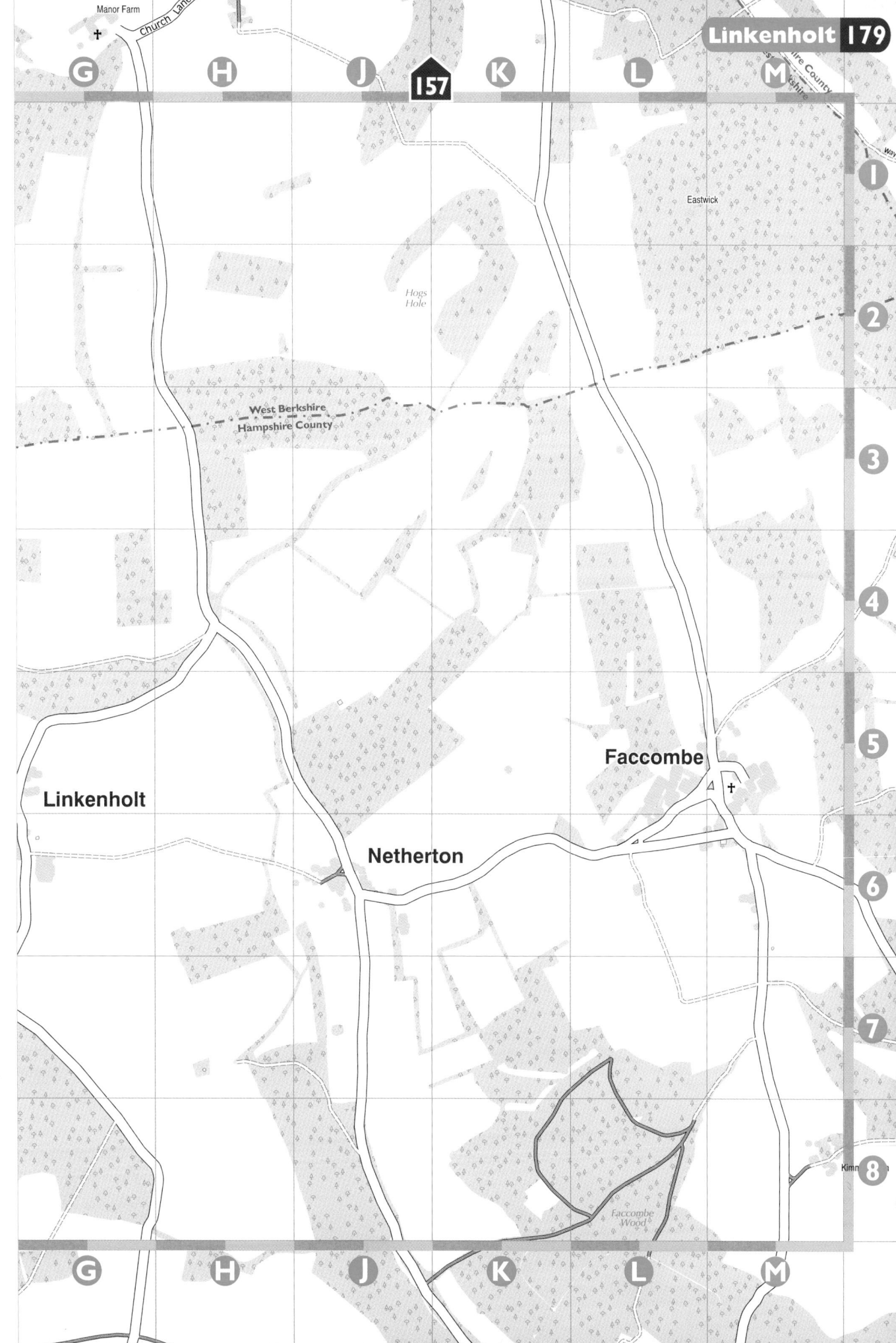

G H J K 157 L M

Manor Farm

Church Lane

I

Eastwick

2

Hogs Hole

West Berkshire
Hampshire County

3

4

5

Faccombe

Linkenholt

Netherton

6

7

Faccombe Wood

8

G H J K L M

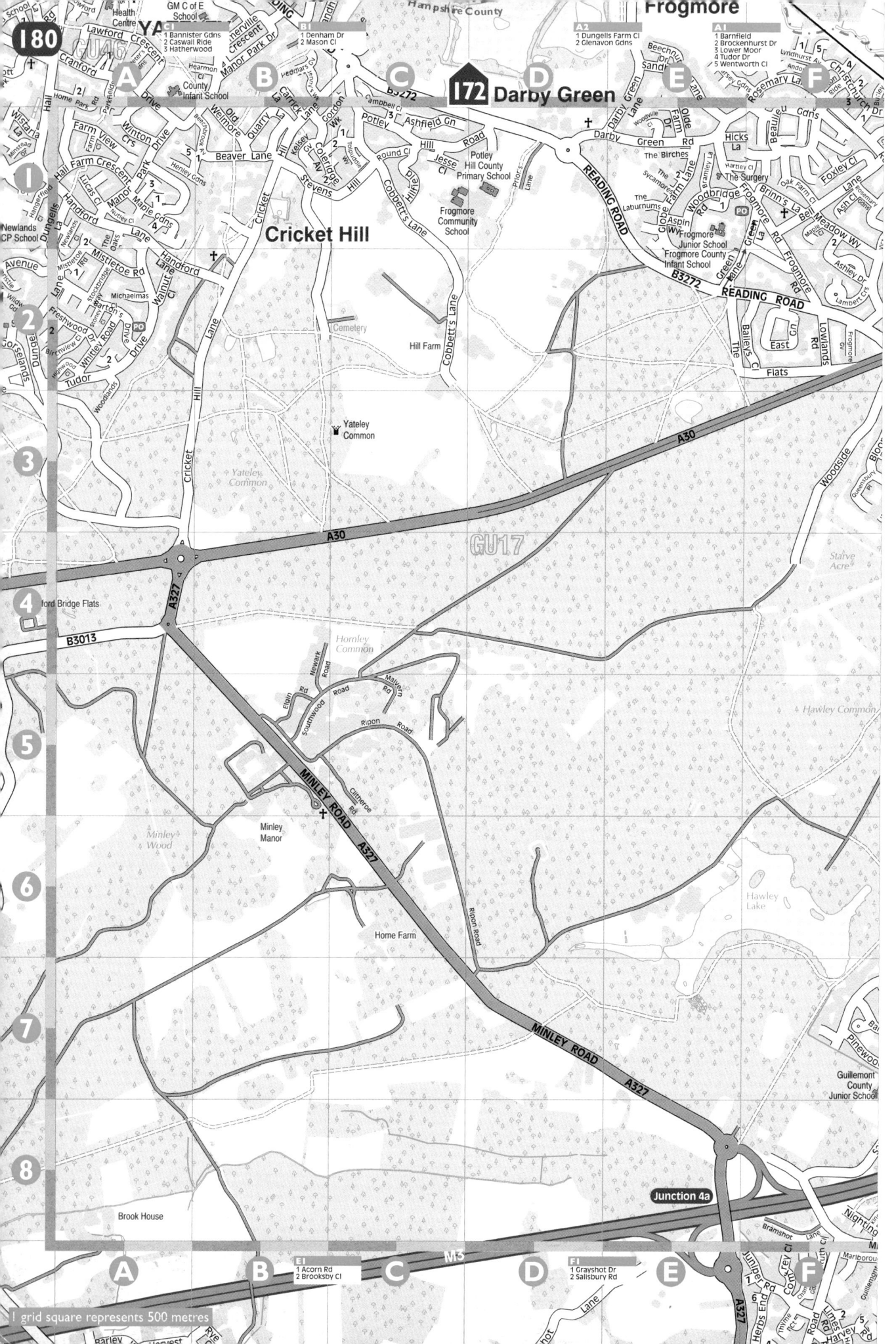

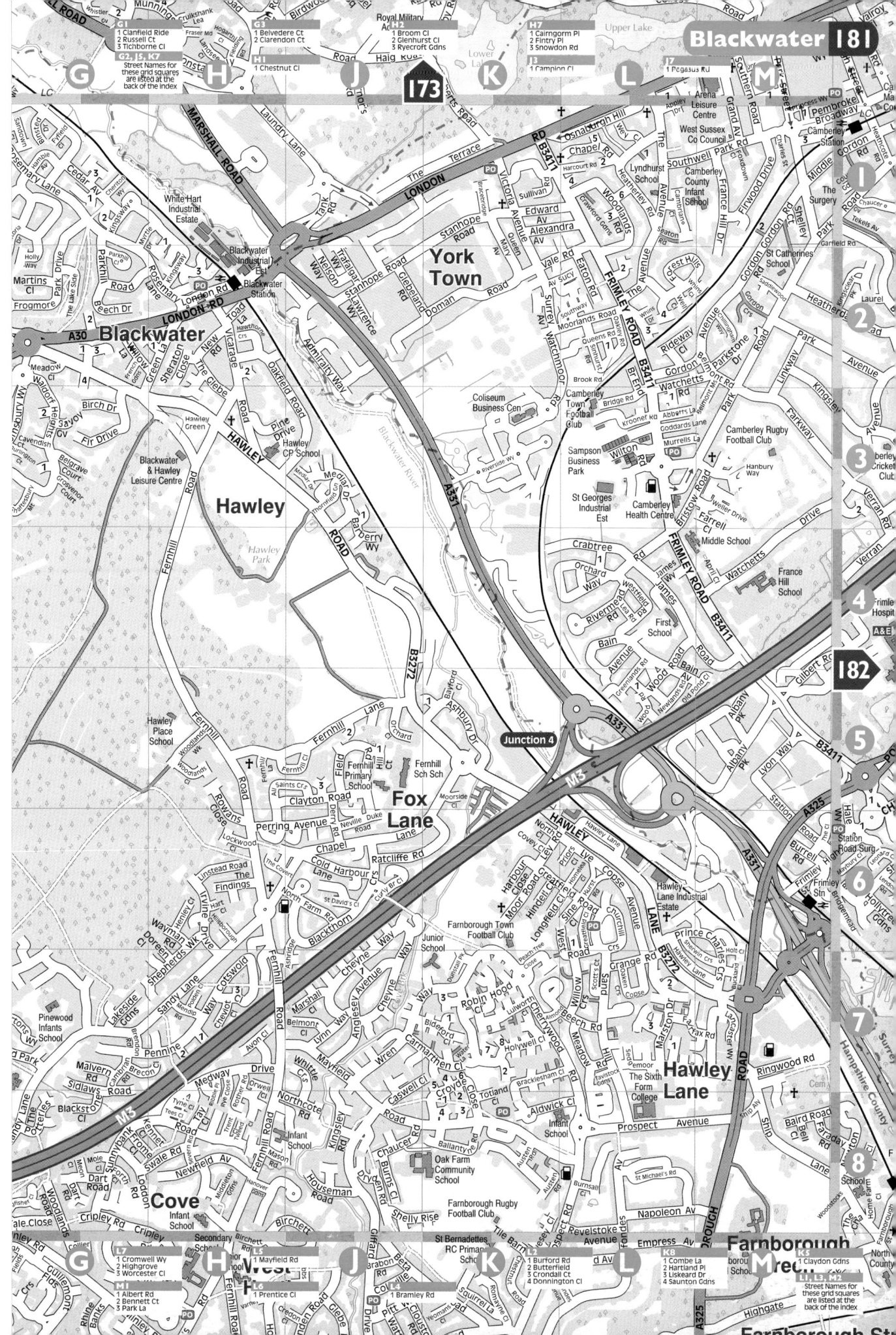

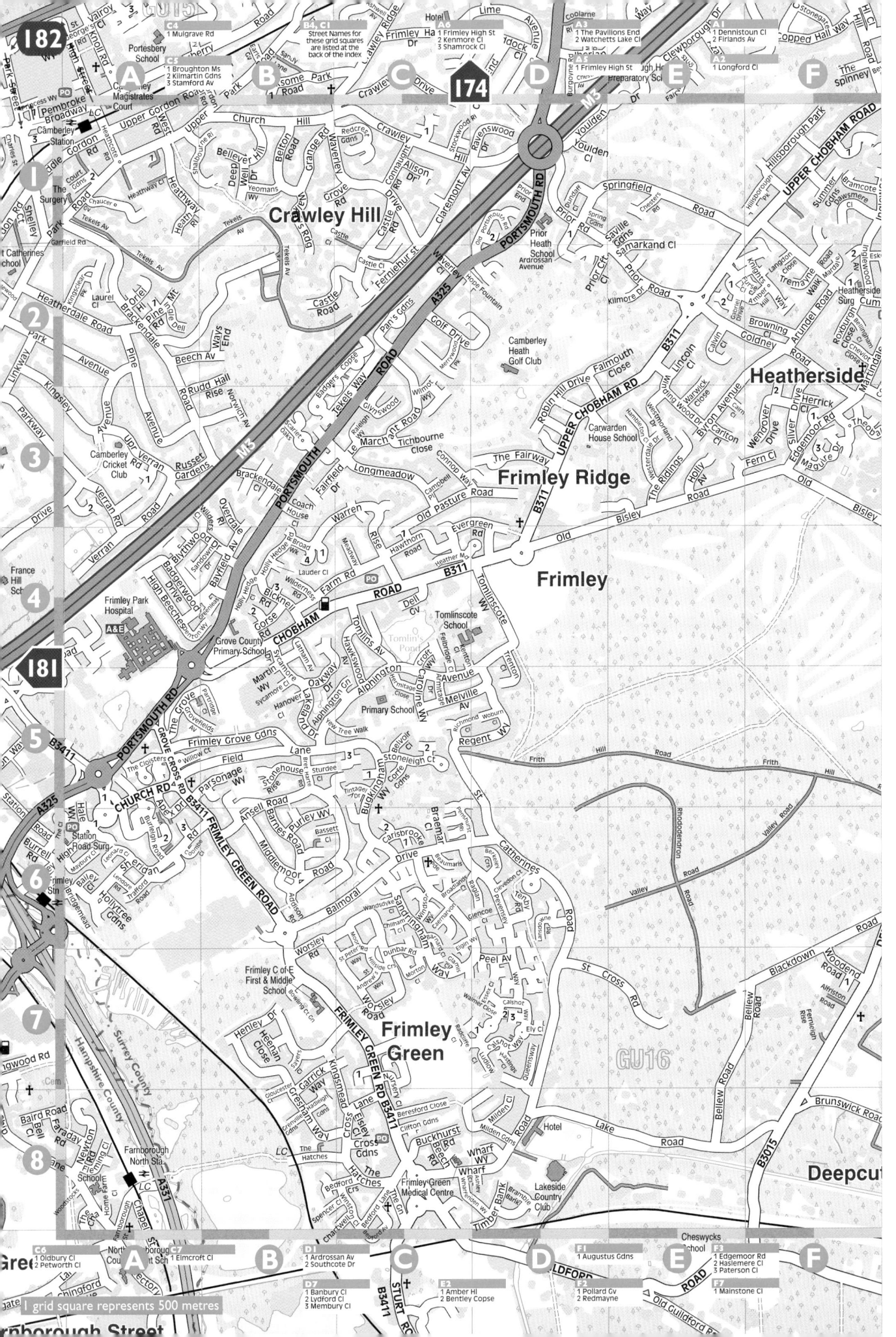

G1
1 Brackenwood
2 Englesfield
3 Greenholme

G3
1 Gosnell Cl

G4
1 Marshall Cl
2 Myers Wy

175

Lucas

Westend Common

Strawberry Bottom

Pirbright Common

Cow Moor

Colony Gate

Minorca Road

Alsne Road

Dettingen Road

Alma Gardens

Malta Rd

Crimea Road

Canada Rd

Union Rd

Newfoundland Road

Newfoundland

Blackdown Primary School

Normandy Close

Royal Logistics Corps Museum

Pirbright Camp

Greenwood Road

Alexander Barracks

Army Training Regiment

Union St

George Street

Argyle Street

Parliamentary Road

Lothian Road

Moore Rd

Elizabeth Barracks

The Princess Royal Barracks

Blackdown Barracks

Brunswick Road

Basingstoke Canal

Curzon Bridge

Brunswick Road

Stanley Pool

Mazamboni Farm

Heather Ridge County Infants School

THE MAULTWAY

Wingfield Gdns

Chevismore Drive

SHEEPCUT BRIDGE ROAD

B3015

B3012

B3012

STANLEY HILL

GRANGE RD

Brontmoor Road

Priest Lane

Hook La

Beech Gv

Coopers Hill

Adams Croft

North Dr

South Drive

Beech

Billesden

Mainstone Crs

Herons

Slade Road

Brunsw

Bisley Range

Cherrydale Rd

Ravenstone Rd

Rydal Pvl

Kental Pvl

Copelands Close

Keswick

Buttermere Dr

Brandon Cl

Pendragon Way

Kirkstone Close

Shilton Close

Redwood Drive

Ripon

Dalston Close

Barbon Close

Thicket Close

Ridgemount Rd

Abbey Mead 155 L3
Addlestonemoor 155 M6
Aldermaston 140 C7
Aldermaston Soke 165 J3
Aldermaston Wharf 140 F3
Aldworth 57 H2
Altmore 67 H2
Amen Corner 120 E8
Anvilles 132 B6
Applehouse Hill 40 D5
Arborfield 145 L2
Arborfield Cross 146 A3
Arborfield Garrison 146 D7
Ascot 123 J8
Ashampstead 57 H2
Ashampstead Green 57 K7
Ashford 128 C3
Ashford Common 129 G4
Ashford Hill 163 H5
Ashmore Green 109 L6
Aston 38 F1
Avington 133 H1
Axmansford 163 M7
Bagnor 107 L6
Bagshot 131 J7
Bagshot 174 F3
Bagshot Heath 175 H5
Ball Hill 158 F3
Barkham 146 E4
Baughurst 164 A7
Baydon 48 C6
Beaumont 97 L7
Beech Hill 167 M1
Beedon 55 G7
Beedon Hill 54 F7
Beenham 112 C8
Beenham's Heath 92 F3
Beenham Stocks 112 E8
Berghers Hill 21 H2
Bigfrith 19 K8
Binfield 120 E3
Binfield Heath 63 K5
Birch Hill 149 M4
Bisham 19 H7
Bishopsgate 125 J2
Bishop's Green 161 K3
Blacknest 124 F8
Blackwater 181 G2
Bockmer End 17 M5
Borough Marsh 64 D6
Bothampstead 81 L2
Bourne End 20 C2
Boveney 69 M6
Bovingdon Green 18 D3
Boxford 107 G3
Boyn Hill 2 C7
Bracknell 13 H5
Bradfield 85 G8
Bramshill 169 L7
Brands Hill 72 E7
Bray 69 G3
Bray Wick 68 D2
Braywoodside 93 M3
Brick Hill 152 F8
Brightwalton 53 G3
Brightwalton Green 53 G4
Brightwalton Holt 53 H6
Brimpton 139 H8
Brimpton Common 163 M4
Britwell 44 C5
Broad Layings 159 H5
Broadplat 37 H2
Brock's Green 161 K7
Brook Place 176 E6
Brookside 123 H4
Broomhall 152 D4
Bucklebury 111 H4
Bucklebury Alley 109 M4
Bullbrook 122 C7
Burchett's Green 40 F7
Burghclere 160 C7
Burghclere Common 160 D5
Burghfield 142 F1
Burghfield Common 142 D4
Burghfield Hill 142 F3
Burnham 43 M3
Burnt Hill 85 L5
Burrowhill 177 J4
Bury's Bank 137 H7
Buttermere 156 B7
Calcot 114 F2
Calcot Row 115 G1
Camberley 174 B7
Cane End 61 J3
Carter's Hill 118 B7
Castle Green 177 G8
Catmore 53 L1
Caversham 88 C3
Caversham Heights 88 C2
Chaddleworth 52 D6
Chalkhouse Green 62 D5
Chalvey 70 F3
Chapel Row 111 M6
Charlton 128 F7
Charvil 90 D1
Chattern Hill 128 E2
Chavey Down 122 E7
Chazey Heath 61 M7
Cheapside 124 B7
Checkendon 35 G3
Chertsey 155 K4
Chieveley 80 E4
Chilton Foliat 103 J4
Chobham 177 G5
Churchend 87 H8
Cippenham 70 A1
Clapton 105 K5
Clay Hill 112 B4
Cleeve 32 F6
Clewer Green 96 B2
Clewer New Town 6 D9
Clewer Village 6 C5
Cockpole Green 39 J6
Cold Ash 109 M7
Cold Harbour 59 L2
Cold Harbour 66 D3
Coley 8 E9
College Town 173 H6

Collins End 60 E4
Colnbrook 72 F8
Colstrope 16 F1
Colthrop 138 E3
Combe 157 G8
Compton 56 A1
Cookham 20 D6
Cookham Dean 19 L7
Cookham Rise 42 A1
Cooper's Hill 126 A1
Cores End 20 F2
Court Garden 19 G5
Cowley 47 M5
Cowley Peachy 47 M7
Cox Green 67 M3
Cranbourne 95 L8
Crawley Hill 182 B1
Cray's Pond 34 A8
Crazies Hill 39 H8
Cricket Hill 180 B1
Crockham Heath 135 J8
Crooked Soley 75 H8
Crookham 162 E1
Cross Lanes 61 H5
Crown Wood 150 A3
Crowsley 62 F2
Crowthorne 172 C2
Curridge 109 G1
Danesfield 18 A8
Darby Green 172 D8
Datchet 71 L8
Datchet Common 97 M1
Dedworth 70 A8
Deepcut 182 F8
Donkey Town 176 A8
Donnington 108 A8
Dorney 69 L3
Dorney Reach 69 J3
Dowlesgreen 11 J2
Downend 80 D3
Dunsden Green 63 J7
Earley 117 L1
Earlstone Common 160 C6
East Bedfont 100 E6
East Burnham 44 C2
Eastbury 50 B7
East End 158 D7
East Fields 15 G6
East Garston 51 G8
Easthampstead 13 H9
Eastheath 147 K3
East Ilsley 29 J8
Easton 106 E1
East Woodhay 158 B7
Eddington 104 B7
Egham 126 D4
Egham Hythe 127 G4
Egham Wick 125 J5
Egypt 53 K8
Elcot 106 A6
Eling 82 B3
Emmbrook 119 H6
Emmer Green 62 D8
Enborne 135 J6
Enborne Row 159 L2
Englefield 113 L2
Englefield Green 125 L5
Eton 7 J3
Eton Wick 70 C4
Eversley 170 E5
Eversley Centre 171 G6
Eversley Cross 171 J6
Exlade Street 34 E6
Faccombe 179 L5
Fair Oak 163 H7
Fair Oak Green 167 G8
Farley Hill 170 A1
Farnborough 27 J5
Farnham Park 44 F2
Farnham Royal 44 F3
Fawley 25 L7
Feltham 101 L8
Felthamhill 129 H3
Fern 20 B1
Fifield 69 G8
Finchampstead 171 G3
Fishery 3 M6
Four Houses Corner 142 B6
Four Points 57 H4
Fox Lane 181 J5
Frilsham 82 F7
Frimley 182 D4
Frimley Green 182 C7
Frimley Ridge 182 D3
Frogmore 172 E8
Froxfield 130 D1
Furze Platt 42 A4
Gallowstree Common 61 K1
Gardeners Green 148 B4
George Green 46 B7
Goddard's Green 143 G5
Goldfinch Bottom 161 M1
Goose Hill 162 E3
Gore End 158 E2
Goring 32 F8
Goring Heath 60 D3
Grazeley 144 A4
Grazeley Green 143 J3
Great Hollands 149 H3
Great Lea Common 116 D8
Great Shefford 77 L3
Greenham 136 F6
Greenlands 16 D6
Greys Green 37 G4
Halfway 106 B8
Hambleden 16 E5
Hampstead Norreys 56 B8
Hamstead Marshall 134 C7
Hanworth 149 K4
Hare Hatch 65 K6
Harmans Water 13 L9
Harmondsworth 73 M6
Harpsden 38 B8
Harpsden Bottom 37 L8
Hatton 101 H3
Haughurst Hill 163 M5
Hawks Hill 21 G3

Hawley 181 H3
Hawley Lane 181 L7
Hawthorn Hill 93 M5
Headley 162 B5
Heath End 158 D5
Heath End 164 C5
Heatherside 182 F2
Heathlands 148 C6
Heckfield 168 F8
Hedsor 21 J3
Hell Corner 157 L1
Henley-on-Thames 38 A5
Hermitage 81 L8
High Curley 175 G6
Highmoor Cross 35 M1
Highway 41 K8
Hill Bottom 60 B3
Hillgreen 79 M1
Hoe Benham 106 D7
Holloway 66 F1
Holly Cross 39 K8
Holme Green 148 C3
The Holt 65 L5
Holyport 68 D7
Honey Hill 148 D5
Hook End 35 G6
Hopgoods Green 110 F6
Horncastle 115 H1
Horton 98 D2
Hungerford 92 A4
Hungerford 132 B1
Hungerford Green 57 J3
Hungerford Newtown 104 D2
Hunt's Green 107 G5
Hurley 40 B2
Hurley Bottom 40 A3
Hurst 91 J6
Hyde End 163 H2
Hythe End 126 E1
Inhurst 163 M6
Inkpen 156 F1
Inkpen Common 157 J1
Iver 47 J7
Iver Heath 47 G2
Jealott's Hill 93 L6
Jennetts Hill 112 A3
Kidmore End 61 M3
Kiff Green 111 L8
Kiln Green 65 M5
Kingsclere Woodlands 162 D6
Kintbury 133 K4
Knighton 102 D3
Knowle Green 127 L3
Knowle Hill 153 L4
Knowl Hill 66 C2
Lake End 69 L2
Laleham 127 M8
Lambourn 49 M4
Lambourn Woodlands 75 J1
Langley 72 C3
Langley Common 146 C5
Layland's Green 133 L5
Leckhampstead 79 J1
Leckhampstead Thicket 53 G7
Lent 43 K5
Lent Rise 43 K6
Leverton 103 M5
Lightwater 175 M6
Lilley 53 K3
Limmerhill 147 H1
Linkenholt 179 G5
Little Bedwyn 130 D6
Littledown 178 C6
Littlefield Green 67 H8
Little Heath 86 D6
Little Hungerford 81 M6
Little Marlow 19 M1
Little Sandhurst 172 D4
Littlestead Green 63 H8
Littleton 128 E8
Littleton Common 128 E5
Littlewick Green 66 F1
Longcross 153 K7
Longford 73 M8
Longlane 109 K2
Love Green 47 G6
Lower Basildon 59 G4
Lower Caversham 9 M2
Lower Common 170 C5
Lower Earley 118 A5
Lower Feltham 129 H1
Lower Green 156 E1
Lower Padworth 141 G1
Lower Shiplake 64 C3
Lower Woodend 18 B3
Maidenhead 2 D5
Maidenhead Court 42 F2
Maiden's Green 94 D8
Malpas 86 A8
Manor Park 44 F5
Mapledurham 61 H8
Marlow 18 F3
Marsh Benham 135 G3
Marsh Gate 131 K1
Matthewsgreen 10 D3
Mays Green 63 L1
Medmenham 39 L1
Mell Green 53 M6
Merryhill Green 119 G3
Middle Green 46 B8
Midgham 139 H3
Midgham Green 139 L1
Miles's Green 110 F7
Mill End 16 F7
Mill Green 162 C3
Mimbridge 177 L8
Moneyrow Green 68 D7
Mortimer 142 D8
Mortimer West End 166 A2
Moss End 93 L8
Moulsford 32 C2
The Mount 117 G1
The Mount 159 J7
Netherton 179 J7
Newbury 14 C4
New Cross 64 B4
Newell Green 121 M3
Newtown 38 B6

New Town 84 F2
New Town 89 H7
New Town 102 B2
Newtown 160 E2
Nodmore 52 E7
North Ascot 122 F7
North End 158 C4
North Feltham 101 L4
North Heath 80 A4
North Street 114 A1
North Town 3 G1
Nuney Green 61 H3
Nuptown 94 B7
Oakley Green 95 K1
Oare 81 L5
Old Windsor 97 J6
Owlsmoor 173 G4
Ownham 106 F5
Padworth 141 H5
Padworth Common 141 J8
Paley Street 93 L1
Pamber Heath 165 G4
Pangbourne 85 L1
Parker's Corner 113 K3
Peasemore 54 A7
Penwood 159 J7
Pheasant's Hill 16 F3
Pingewood 115 M6
Pinkneys Green 41 J5
Plastow Green 162 D7
Play Hatch 89 J1
Popeswood 120 E6
Poundgreen 143 M3
Pound Street 159 M7
Poyle 73 H8
Priestwood 12 D2
Purley on Thames 86 D2
Purton 54 F6
Quick's Green 84 A1
Ragnal 75 J6
Ramsbury 102 A3
Ravenswood Village
   Settlement 148 B8
Reading 8 F6
Remenham 38 C1
Remenham Hill 38 F4
Richings Park 73 H3
The Ridges 171 L2
Riseley 168 F3
The Rise 152 B3
Rockwell End 17 J1
Rose Hill 43 K1
Rotherfield Greys 36 F5
Rotherfield Peppard 36 C7
Rotten Row 112 C3
Ruscombe 91 H1
Ryeish Green 144 F2
Salt Hill 4 D6
Sandhurst 172 E5
Sanham Green 132 A4
Satwell 36 C2
Schoolgreen 145 G2
Scotland 111 J6
Scotswood 152 A5
Shaw 136 E1
Sheepdrove 50 A2
Sheffield Bottom 114 C6
Shefford Woodlands 77 G7
Shepherd's Green 36 D3
Shinfield 145 G1
Shiplake 64 B4
Shiplake Bottom 36 B8
Shiplake Row 63 L4
Shreding Green 46 E7
Shrubs Hill 152 F3
Shurlock Row 92 D4
Silchester 165 L6
Sindlesham 118 C6
Skinners Green 135 L6
The Slade 110 D6
Slough 5 J7
Slough 71 M2
Sonning 90 A2
Sonning Common 36 B8
Sonning Eye 89 M1
South Ascot 151 K3
Southcote 115 L2
Southend 52 F5
Southend 112 D4
South Fawley 51 M1
South Field 6 D1
South Stoke 32 D2
Speen 135 M1
Spencers Wood 144 C4
Spinfield 18 D5
Spital 96 E3
Staines 127 J2
Stanford Dingley 112 A2
Stanford End 168 B3
Stanmore 54 D4
Stanwell 99 M5
Stanwell Moor 99 K5
Stockcross 135 J1
Stoke Green 45 K5
Stoke Poges 45 J3
Stoke Row 35 K1
Stoney Ware 19 G6
Straight Soley 75 K8
Stratfield Mortimer 167 G1
Stratfield Saye 167 L6
Streatley 32 D7
Stroude 126 C7
Stroud Green 15 G7
Stubbings 41 G6
Stubbles 83 M1
Stud Green 68 B6
Sulham 86 B5
Sulhampstead Abbots 142 C2
Sulhampstead Bannister
   Upper End 142 A1
Sulhampstead 113 L8
Sunbury 129 K8
Sunbury Common 129 J5
Sunningdale 152 D2
Sunninghill 152 A2
Sunnymeads 98 B3
Sutton 72 F5
Swallowfield 145 G8

Tadley 164 F7
Taplow 43 H5
Temple 40 F1
Templeton 132 E5
Thatcham 137 M2
Theale 114 A3
Thorney 73 L2
Thorpe 126 F8
Thorpe Green 154 D1
Thorpe Lea 126 F5
Three Ashes 166 A7
Three Mile Cross 144 E2
The Throat 147 K5
Tickleback Row 93 J8
Tidmarsh 85 L4
Tilehurst 87 H5
Titcomb 133 H7
Tittenhurst 124 F8
Tittle Row 41 L8
Tokers Green 62 A7
Tot Hill 160 B5
Touchen-end 68 A3
Trapshill 157 H2
Trash Green 114 D7
Trench Green 61 K7
Trumps Green 154 A3
Turner's Green 110 E7
Tutts Clump 112 C3
Twyford 91 H1
Ufton Green 141 L1
Ufton Nervet 142 A2
Up Green 171 H8
Upper Basildon 84 D1
Upper Bucklebury 110 F8
Upper Green 157 G3
Upper Lambourn 23 J8
Upper Woolhampton 139 L2
Upton 71 K3
Upton Lea 5 M3
Uxbridge 47 M2
Uxbridge Moor 47 L2
Valley End 176 D1
Vernham Dean 178 A8
Vernham Street 178 C6
The Village 124 E1
Virginia Water 125 M8
Waltham St Lawrence 66 B7
Warfield 122 B1
Wargrave 64 F5
Warren Row 39 M8
Wash Common 160 A1
Wash Water 159 L3
Wasing 164 A1
Wawcott 133 M1
Welford 78 D7
Well End 20 C1
Wellhouse 110 B1
West Bedfont 100 C6
Westbrook 106 F2
West End 92 B2
West End Green 167 G6
West Fields 14 B5
West Ilsley 28 D4
Weston 78 A6
Westridge Green 57 K2
Westrop Green 110 A3
West Woodhay 157 M3
Wether Down 23 M8
Wexham Street 45 M2
Wheat Hold 163 H8
Wheeler's Green 118 D1
Whistley Green 91 H5
Whitchurch Hill 60 B4
Whitchurch-on-Thames 59 L7
Whitehouse Green 114 D8
Whiteknights 117 H2
White Waltham 67 H7
Whitley 116 D4
Whitley Wood 116 F7
Whittonditch 102 C1
Wickham 105 M2
Wickham Green 105 M2
Wickham Heath 106 E7
Wick Hill 122 A5
Wick Hill 147 K8
Widmoor 21 H3
Wildridings 12 E8
Windlesham 175 L2
Windsor 7 G7
Winkfield 123 G1
Winkfield Place 95 K6
Winkfield Row 122 D5
Winnersh 118 E4
Winterbourne 107 M1
Witheridge Hill 35 M1
Wokingham 11 K7
Wooburn 20 F2
Woodburn Common 21 K3
Woodcote 34 B6
Wood End 123 M4
Woodlands 38 B4
Woodlands Park 67 J4
Woodlands St Mary 76 A4
Woodley 90 C8
Woodley Green 90 C7
Woodside 123 L2
Woodspeen 107 K7
Woodway 30 D1
Woolhampton 139 M4
Woolley Green 67 H1
Woolton Hill 159 H7
Woose Hill 10 A5
World's End 54 F8
Wraysbury 98 B6
Yateley 172 A8
Yattendon 83 H5
York Town 181 K2

USING THE STREET INDEX

Street names are listed alphabetically. Each street name is followed by its postal town or area locality, the Postcode District, the page number, and the reference to the square in which the name is found.

Example: **Abbey Gn** *CHERT* KT16 .... **155** K3 1

Some entries are followed by a number in a blue box. This number indicates the location of the street within the referenced grid square. The full street name is listed at the side of the map page.

GENERAL ABBREVIATIONS

ACC	ACCESS
ALY	ALLEY
AP	APPROACH
AR	ARCADE
ASS	ASSOCIATION
AV	AVENUE
BCH	BEACH
BLDS	BUILDINGS
BND	BEND
BNK	BANK
BR	BRIDGE
BRK	BROOK
BTM	BOTTOM
BUS	BUSINESS
BVD	BOULEVARD
BY	BYPASS
CATH	CATHEDRAL
CEM	CEMETERY
CEN	CENTRE
CFT	CROFT
CH	CHURCH
CHA	CHASE
CHYD	CHURCHYARD
CIR	CIRCLE
CIRC	CIRCUS
CL	CLOSE
CLFS	CLIFFS
CMP	CAMP
CNR	CORNER
CO	COUNTY
COLL	COLLEGE
COM	COMMON
COMM	COMMISSION
CON	CONVENT
COT	COTTAGE
COTS	COTTAGES
CP	CAPE
CPS	COPSE
CR	CREEK
CREM	CREMATORIUM
CRS	CRESCENT
CSWY	CAUSEWAY
CT	COURT
CTRL	CENTRAL
CTS	COURTS
CTYD	COURTYARD
CUTT	CUTTINGS
CV	COVE
CYN	CANYON
DEPT	DEPARTMENT
DL	DALE
DM	DAM
DR	DRIVE
DRO	DROVE
DRY	DRIVEWAY
DWGS	DWELLINGS
E	EAST
EMB	EMBANKMENT
EMBY	EMBASSY
ESP	ESPLANADE
EST	ESTATE
EX	EXCHANGE
EXPY	EXPRESSWAY
EXT	EXTENSION
F/O	FLYOVER
FC	FOOTBALL CLUB
FK	FORK
FLD	FIELD
FLDS	FIELDS
FLS	FALLS
FLS	FLATS
FM	FARM
FT	FORT
FWY	FREEWAY
FY	FERRY
GA	GATE
GAL	GALLERY
GDN	GARDEN
GDNS	GARDENS
GLD	GLADE
GLN	GLEN
GN	GREEN
GND	GROUND
GRA	GRANGE
GRG	GARAGE
GT	GREAT
GTWY	GATEWAY
GV	GROVE
HGR	HIGHER
HL	HILL
HLS	HILLS
HO	HOUSE
HOL	HOLLOW
HOSP	HOSPITAL
HRB	HARBOUR
HTH	HEATH
HTS	HEIGHTS
HVN	HAVEN
HWY	HIGHWAY
IMP	IMPERIAL
IN	INLET
IND EST	INDUSTRIAL ESTATE
INF	INFIRMARY
INFO	INFORMATION
INT	INTERCHANGE
IS	ISLAND
JCT	JUNCTION
JTY	JETTY
KG	KING
KNL	KNOLL
L	LAKE
LA	LANE
LDG	LODGE
LGT	LIGHT
LK	LOCK
LKS	LAKES
LNDG	LANDING
LTL	LITTLE
LWR	LOWER
MAG	MAGISTRATE
MAN	MANSIONS
MD	MEAD
MDW	MEADOWS
MEM	MEMORIAL
MKT	MARKET
MKTS	MARKETS
ML	MALL
ML	MILL
MNR	MANOR
MS	MEWS
MSN	MISSION
MT	MOUNT
MTN	MOUNTAIN
MTS	MOUNTAINS
MUS	MUSEUM
MWY	MOTORWAY
N	NORTH
NE	NORTH EAST
NW	NORTH WEST
O/P	OVERPASS
OFF	OFFICE
ORCH	ORCHARD
OV	OVAL
PAL	PALACE
PAS	PASSAGE
PAV	PAVILION
PDE	PARADE
PH	PUBLIC HOUSE
PK	PARK
PKWY	PARKWAY
PL	PLACE
PLN	PLAIN
PLNS	PLAINS
PLZ	PLAZA
POL	POLICE STATION
PR	PRINCE
PREC	PRECINCT
PREP	PREPARATORY
PRIM	PRIMARY
PROM	PROMENADE
PRS	PRINCESS
PRT	PORT
PT	POINT
PTH	PATH
PZ	PIAZZA
QD	QUADRANT
QU	QUEEN
QY	QUAY
R	RIVER
RBT	ROUNDABOUT
RD	ROAD
RDG	RIDGE
REP	REPUBLIC
RES	RESERVOIR
RFC	RUGBY FOOTBALL CLUB
RI	RISE
RP	RAMP
RW	ROW
S	SOUTH
SCH	SCHOOL
SE	SOUTH EAST
SER	SERVICE AREA
SH	SHORE
SHOP	SHOPPING
SKWY	SKYWAY
SMT	SUMMIT
SOC	SOCIETY
SP	SPUR
SPR	SPRING
SQ	SQUARE
ST	STREET
STN	STATION
STR	STREAM
STRD	STRAND
SW	SOUTH WEST
TDG	TRADING
TER	TERRACE
THWY	THROUGHWAY
TNL	TUNNEL
TOLL	TOLLWAY
TPK	TURNPIKE
TR	TRACK
TRL	TRAIL
TWR	TOWER
U/P	UNDERPASS
UNI	UNIVERSITY
UPR	UPPER
V	VALE
VA	VALLEY
VIAD	VIADUCT
VIL	VILLA
VIS	VISTA
VLG	VILLAGE
VLS	VILLAS
VW	VIEW
W	WEST
WD	WOOD
WHF	WHARF
WK	WALK
WKS	WALKS
WLS	WELLS
WY	WAY
YD	YARD
YHA	YOUTH HOSTEL

POSTCODE TOWNS AND AREA ABBREVIATIONS

ADL/WDHM	Addlestone/Woodham
ASC	Ascot
ASHF	Ashford (Surrey)
BAGS	Bagshot
BFOR	Bracknell Forest/Windlesham
BLKW	Blackwater
BNEND	Bourne End
BNFD	Binfield
BRAK	Bracknell
CAV/SC	Caversham/Sonning Common
CBLY	Camberley
CHOB/PIR	Chobham/Pirbright
CHTSY	Chertsey
CWTH	Crowthorne
DEN/HRF	Denham/Harefield
DID	Didcot
DTCH/LGLY	Datchet/Langley
E/WMO/HCT	East & West Molesey/Hampton Court
EARL	Earley
EBED/NFELT	East Bedfont/North Feltham
EGH	Egham
EWKG	Wokingham east
FARN	Farnborough
FELT	Feltham
FLKWH	Flackwell Heath
FRIM	Frimley
GOR/PANG	Goring/Pangbourne
HEN	Henley-on-Thames
HEST	Heston
HGHW	Highworth
HSLWW	Hounslow west
HTHAIR	Heathrow Airport
HTWY	Hartley Wintney
HUNG	Hungerford/Lambourn
IVER	Iver
KSCL	Kingsclere/Rural Newbury
LTWR	Lightwater
MARL	Marlborough
MDHD	Maidenhead
MLW	Marlow
NTHA	Thatcham north
NWBY	Newbury
RAND	Rural Andover
RDGW	Reading west
READ	Reading
SHPTN	Shepperton
SHST	Sandhurst
SL	Slough
SLN	Slough north
STA	Staines
STHA	Thatcham south
STWL/WRAY	Stanwell/Wraysbury
SUN	Sunbury
TADY	Tadley
THLE	Theale/Rural Reading
TLHT	Tilehurst
UX/CGN	Uxbridge/Colham Green
VW	Virginia Water
WANT	Wantage
WAR/TWY	Wargrave/Twyford
WDR/YW	West Drayton/Yiewsley
WDSR	Windsor
WGFD	Wallingford
WHIT	Whitley/Arborfield
WODY	Woodley
WOKN/KNAP	Woking north/Knaphill
WOT/HER	Walton-on-Thames/Hersham
WWKG	Wokingham west
YTLY	Yateley

Index - streets

A

Abattoirs Rd *READ* RG1 8 E4
Abbetts La *CBLY* GU15 181 L3
Abbey Cl *BRAK* RG12 150 A2
EWKG RG40 11 H3
NWBY RG14 14 F9
SL SL1 44 B8
Abbey Dr *STA* TW18 127 M8
STA TW18 155 M1
Abbey Gdns *CHERT* KT16 155 K3
Abbey Gn *CHERT* KT16 155 K3 1
Abbey Pk *THLE* RG7 142 C3
Abbey Rd *BNEND* SL8 20 C1
CHERT KT16 155 L4
VW GU25 154 A2
Abbey Sq *READ* RG1 9 H6
Abbey St *READ* RG1 9 H6
Abbey Wy *MLW* SL7 19 G8
Abbey Wd *ASC* SL5 152 D4
Abbot Cl *STA* TW18 128 A5
Abbotsbury *BRAK* RG12 149 J2
Abbots Cl *GOR/PANG* RG8 34 C6 1
Abbots Dr *VW* GU25 153 M1
Abbotsmead Pl *READ* RG1 8 E1
Abbots Rd *NWBY* RG14 14 F7
THLE RG7 142 C3 1
Abbot's Wk *READ* RG1 9 H5
WDSR SL4 96 B1
Abbotts Wy *SL* SL1 70 A1
Abbottswood Cl *TADY* RG26 164 E7 1
Abelia Cl *CHOB/PIR* GU24 176 B8 1
Abell Gdns *MDHD* SL6 41 K5
Aberaman *CAV/SC* RG4 62 C8
Aberdeen Av *SL* SL1 44 D8
Aberford Cl *TLHT* RG30 87 M7 1
Abex Rd *NWBY* RG14 15 K4
Abingdon Cl *BRAK* RG12 150 B2 1
Abingdon Dr *CAV/SC* RG4 62 F8
Abingdon Rd *KSCL* RG20 29 H7
SHST GU47 172 F6
Abney Court Dr *BNEND* SL8 20 D4
Abrahams Rd *HEN* RG9 37 M3
Acacia Av *SHST* GU47 173 G5
STWL/WRAY TW19 98 B3
Acacia Ct *BRAK* RG12 13 G7
Acacia Rd *READ* RG1 9 K9
STA TW18 127 L3
Academy Cl *CBLY* GU15 174 B6
Accommodation La
WDR/YW UB7 73 M6
CHERT KT16 154 A7
Accommodation Rd
CHERT KT16 154 B8
Acer Dr *CHOB/PIR* GU24 176 C8
Ackrells Md *SHST* GU47 172 C5 1
Acorn Dr *EWKG* RG40 11 G4
NTHA RG18 138 A1
Acorn Rd *BLKW* GU17 180 E1 1
Acre Pas *WDSR* SL4 7 J7
Acre Rd *WHIT* RG2 116 D6
The Acre *MLW* SL7 19 J4
Adam Cl *SL* SL1 70 D1 1
TADY RG26 164 B5
Adam Ct *HEN* RG9 38 A4
Adams Cft *CHOB/PIR* GU24 183 M7
Adams Wy *EARL* RG6 117 J4
Addington Cl *WDSR* SL4 96 D2
Addington Rd *READ* RG1 9 L9
Addiscombe Cha *CALC* RG31 86 E3 1
Addiscombe Rd *CWTH* RG45 172 F2
Addison Cl *IVER* SL0 47 H8 1
Addison Ct *MDHD* SL6 3 L1
Addison Rd *FRIM* GU16 182 B6
READ RG1 8 E2
Addlestone Moor
ADL/WDHM KT15 155 M6
Adelaide Cl *SL* SL1 70 D2
Adelaide Rd *ASHF* TW15 128 A3
EARL RG6 117 K1
WDSR SL4 71 J8
Adelaide Sq *WDSR* SL4 7 J9
Adelphi Gdns *SL* SL1 4 E8
Adey's Cl *NWBY* RG14 15 G7
Adkins Rd *WAR/TWY* RG10 66 B7
Admirals Ct *WHIT* RG2 8 E9
Admiralty Wy *CBLY* GU15 181 J2
Admoor La *THLE* RG7 112 F4
Adwell Dr *EARL* RG6 118 A5
Adwell Sq *HEN* RG9 38 A4 1
Adwood Ct *STHA* RG19 138 B3
Agar Crs *BNFD* RG42 13 G1
BNFD RG42 121 L5
Agars Pl *DTCH/LGLY* SL3 71 K6
Agate Cl *WWKG* RG41 119 H7 1
Aggisters La *WWKG* RG41 146 F3
Agincourt Cl *WWKG* RG41 119 H8 1
Agincourt Pl *ASC* SL5 123 M8
Agricola Wy *STHA* RG19 138 C4
Ainsdale Crs *TLHT* RG30 115 K2 1
Aintree *HUNG* RG17 49 L4
Aintree Cl *DTCH/LGLY* SL3 73 H8
NWBY RG14 15 J8
Aird Cl *KSCL* RG20 159 H6
Airport Wy *STWL/WRAY* TW19 99 K3
Aisne Rd *FRIM* GU16 183 H5
Ajax Av *SL* SL1 44 E8
Alandale Cl *WHIT* RG2 117 G6
Alan Wy *DTCH/LGLY* SL3 46 B7 1
Albain Crs *ASHF* TW15 100 B8
Albany Pk *DTCH/LGLY* SL3 73 G7
FRIM GU16 181 M5
Albany Park Dr *WWKG* RG41 118 D3
Albany Pl *EGH* TW20 126 E2
Albany Rd *TLHT* RG30 88 A7
WDSR SL4 7 H8
WDSR SL4 97 K4
Alben Rd *BNFD* RG42 120 F3
Albert Av *CHERT* KT16 127 K8
Albert Illsley Cl *CALC* RG31 87 G6
Albert Pl *WDSR* SL4 70 D5
Albert Rd *ASHF* TW15 128 C3 1
BAGS GU19 175 H5
BNFD RG42 13 H3
CAV/SC RG4 88 C2
CBLY GU15 181 M1 1
CWTH RG45 172 E1
EGH TW20 126 A4
EWKG RG40 10 F7
HEN RG9 38 B5
NWBY RG14 14 D3
WDSR SL4 97 H3
Albert St *MDHD* SL6 3 G5
SL SL1 71 H3
WDSR SL4 6 E7
Albion Cl *SLN* SL2 5 J7
Albion Rd *SHST* GU47 172 E7
Albury Cl *CHERT* KT16 153 K7
TLHT RG30 87 M5
Albury Gdns *CALC* RG31 115 H3
Alcot Cl *CWTH* RG45 172 E2
Aldborough Sp *SL* SL1 4 E3
Aldbourne Av *EARL* RG6 117 K2
Aldbourne Cl *HUNG* RG17 132 A1
Aldbourne Rd *SL* SL1 43 L6
Aldeburgh Cl *CAV/SC* RG4 62 F6 1
Aldebury Rd *MDHD* SL6 42 B4
Aldenham Cl *CAV/SC* RG4 62 F8
Aldenham Ter *BRAK* RG12 149 M3 1
Alden Vw *WDSR* SL4 70 A8
Alderbrook Cl *CWTH* RG45 172 B2
Alderbury Rd *DTCH/LGLY* SL3 72 C2
Alderbury Rd West
DTCH/LGLY SL3 72 C2
Alder Cl *EGH* TW20 126 B3
SL SL1 70 C1
Alder Dr *CALC* RG31 86 F8
Alderfield Cl *THLE* RG7 114 C2 1
Alder Gld *THLE* RG7 142 C3
Alderley Cl *WODY* RG5 90 C5
Alderman Willey Cl *WWKG* RG41 10 E5
Aldermaston Rd *TADY* RG26 164 D4
Alderney Gdns *WWKG* RG41 119 G4 1
Alder Rd *IVER* SL0 46 F3
Alderside Wk *EGH* TW20 126 A3
The Alders *NTHA* RG18 138 A2
Aldin Av North *SL* SL1 5 K8
Aldin Av South *SL* SL1 5 K9
Aldridge Pk *BNFD* RG42 122 E4
Aldridge Rd *SLN* SL2 44 D5
Aldwick Cl *FARN* GU14 181 K8
Aldwick Dr *MDHD* SL6 2 C6
Aldworth Cl *BRAK* RG12 12 F9
TLHT RG30 115 M1
Aldworth Gdns *CWTH* RG45 172 D1
Aldworth Rd *GOR/PANG* RG8 58 D8
KSCL RG20 56 B2
Alexander Rd *EGH* TW20 126 E3
STHA RG19 138 B4
Alexandra Av *CBLY* GU15 181 K1
Alexandra Cl *ASHF* TW15 129 G5 1
STA TW18 128 A4
Alexandra Ct *ASHF* TW15 129 G4 1
EWKG RG40 11 G7
Alexandra Rd *ASHF* TW15 129 G5
EGH TW20 125 M4
MDHD SL6 2 C3
READ RG1 9 M8
SL SL1 71 G3
WDSR SL4 7 J9
Alford Cl *TLHT* RG30 87 G6 1
Alfred Rd *FELT* TW13 101 M8
Alfred St *READ* RG1 8 D6
Alfriston Rd *FRIM* GU16 182 F7
Alice La *SL* SL1 43 L5
Alison Cl *THLE* RG7 142 C5 1
Alison Dr *CBLY* GU15 182 C1
Allanson Rd *MLW* SL7 19 J3
Allcot Cl *EBED/NFELT* TW14 101 J7 1
Allcroft Rd *READ* RG1 116 F1
Allenby Rd *CBLY* GU15 173 K8
MDHD SL6 41 L7
Allen Cl *SUN* TW16 129 L6
Allendale Cl *SHST* GU47 172 D4 1
Allendale Rd *EARL* RG6 117 L3
Allen Rd *SUN* TW16 129 L6
Allerds Rd *SLN* SL2 44 C2
Alleyns La *MDHD* SL6 20 A6
All Hallows Rd *CAV/SC* RG4 89 G3
Allington Av *SHPTN* TW17 129 H8 1
Allison Gdns *GOR/PANG* RG8 86 F1
Allnatt Av *WWKG* RG41 118 F5
Allonby Cl *EARL* RG6 118 A4
All Saints Av *MDHD* SL6 2 B3
All Saints Cl *EWKG* RG40 11 G3
All Saints Crs *FARN* GU14 181 H5
All Saints Ri *BNFD* RG42 122 B5 1
All Saints Rd *LTWR* GU18 175 M5
Allsmoor La *BRAK* RG12 122 C8
All Souls' Rd *ASC* SL5 151 K2
Allyn Cl *STA* TW18 127 J4
Alma Gdns *FRIM* GU16 183 G6
Alma Gn *HEN* RG9 35 K2
Alma Rd *WDSR* SL4 7 G8
WDSR SL4 70 C4
Alma St *TLHT* RG30 87 M6
Almners Rd *CHERT* KT16 154 E5
CHERT KT16 154 F3
Almond Av *NWBY* RG14 136 D1
Almond Cl *EGH* TW20 125 L4
FARN GU14 181 K7
SHPTN TW17 128 F7
WDSR SL4 6 E8

WWKG RG41 .... 146 F2
Almond Dr *CAV/SC* RG4 .... 89 J2
   NTHA RG18 .... 138 A2
Almond Rd *SL* SL1 .... 43 L4
Almons Wy *SL* SL1 .... 44 E7
Alpha Dr *CHOB/PIR* GU24 ...... 177 J3
Alpha St North *SL* SL1 .... 5 J9
Alpha St South *SL* SL1 .... 71 J3
Alpha Wy *EGH* TW20 .... 126 F6
Alphington Av *FRIM* GU16 ...... 182 C5
Alphington Gn *FRIM* GU16 ...... 182 C5
Alphington Rd *WHIT* RG2 ...... 116 E6
Alpine St *READ* RG1 .... 9 G9
Alsford Cl *LTWR* GU18 .... 175 J7
Alston Gdns *MDHD* SL6 .... 2 F4
Alston Ms *STHA* RG19 .... 137 M4
Altmore *MDHD* SL6 .... 67 H2
Altona Wy *SL* SL1 .... 44 E7
Alton Ct *STA* TW18 .... 127 H6
Alton Ride *BLKW* GU17 .... 172 F8
Altwood Bailey *MDHD* SL6 ...... 67 L1
Altwood Cl *MDHD* SL6 .... 67 L1
   SL SL1 .... 44 B6
Altwood Dr *MDHD* SL6 .... 67 L1
Altwood Rd *MDHD* SL6 .... 2 A8
   MDHD SL6 .... 67 L1
Alvista Av *MDHD* SL6 .... 43 L7
Alwyn Rd *MDHD* SL6 .... 41 L6
Alwyns Cl *CHERT* KT16 .... 155 K3
Alwyns La *CHERT* KT16 .... 155 J3
Amanda Ct *DTCH/LGLY* SL3 ...... 72 A3
Ambarrow Crs *SHST* GU47 ...... 172 C5
Ambarrow La *CWTH* RG45 ...... 172 A4
Ambassador *BRAK* RG12 .... 149 J2
Amber Hl *CBLY* GU15 .... 182 E2
Amberley Cl *NWBY* RG14 .... 14 C1
Amberley Ct *MDHD* SL6 .... 42 F3
Amberley Dr *WAR/TWY* RG10 ...... 65 C8
Amberley Rd *SLN* SL2 .... 44 B6
Amberley Wy *HSLWW* TW4 ...... 101 M4
Amberwood Dr *CBLY* GU15 ...... 174 C7
Amblecote Rd *TLHT* RG30 .... 87 L7
Ambleside *WODY* RG5 .... 90 B7
Ambleside Dr
   EBED/NFELT TW14 .... 101 J7
Ambleside Rd *LTWR* GU18 ...... 175 K6
Ambleside Wy *EGH* TW20 ...... 126 E5
Ambrook Rd *WHIT* RG2 .... 116 E6
Ambrose Pl *READ* RG1 .... 8 D6
Ambrose Rd *TADY* RG26 .... 164 G6
Ambury Rd *GOR/PANG* RG8 ...... 57 J2
Amerden Cl *MDHD* SL6 .... 43 C7
Amerden La *MDHD* SL6 .... 69 C2
Amerden Wy *SL* SL1 .... 70 D2
Amersham Rd *CAV/SC* RG4 ...... 9 L1
Amethyst Cl *WWKG* RG41 ...... 119 G7
Amethyst La *TLHT* RG30 .... 87 M8
Amherst Rd *EARL* RG6 .... 89 K8
Amity St *READ* RG1 .... 89 H7
Amity St *READ* RG1 .... 89 H7
Ammanford *CAV/SC* RG4 .... 88 C1
Amners Farm Rd *TLHT* RG30 ...... 115 J6
Ampere Rd *NWBY* RG14 .... 15 G3
Ancaster Dr *ASC* SL5 .... 123 H6
Ancastle Gn *HEN* RG9 .... 37 M5
Andermans *WDSR* SL4 .... 70 A8
Anderson Av *EARL* RG6 .... 89 K8
Anderson Crs *WHIT* RG2 .... 146 B4
Anderson Dr *ASHF* TW15 .... 128 C4
Anderson Pl *BAGS* GU19 .... 175 H2
Andover Cl *CALC* RG31 .... 87 G5
   EBED/NFELT TW14 .... 101 J7
   UX/CGN UB8 .... 47 L3
Andover Dro *KSCL* RG20 .... 159 L2
Andover Rd *BLKW* GU17 .... 172 F8
   KSCL RG20 .... 159 L4
   NWBY RG14 .... 136 B7
Andrew Cl *EWKG* RG40 .... 11 L8
Andrews Cl *THLE* RG7 .... 114 B3
Andrews Rd *EARL* RG6 .... 117 J3
Angel Ct *NWBY* RG14 .... 14 E2
Angel Md *THLE* RG7 .... 139 M4
Angel Pl *BNFD* RG42 .... 120 F4
Angle Field Rd *CAV/SC* RG4 ...... 88 F3
Anglers Wy *READ* RG1 .... 9 L6
Anglesey Av *FARN* GU14 .... 181 J7
Anglesey Cl *ASHF* TW15 .... 128 D2
Angus Cl *CALC* RG31 .... 115 H2
Annadale *NTHA* RG18 .... 109 M5
Anne Cl *MDHD* SL6 .... 42 B4
Anneforde Pl *BNFD* RG42 .... 121 K5
Anners Cl *EGH* TW20 .... 126 F8
Annesley Gdns *WWKG* RG41 ...... 118 F3
Annett's La *HUNG* RG17 .... 131 J7
Annie Brookes Cl *STA* TW18 ...... 127 C1
Anscuff Rd *SLN* SL2 .... 44 D4
Ansell Rd *FRIM* GU16 .... 182 B6
Anslow Gdns *IVER* SL0 .... 47 G3
Anson Crs *WHIT* RG2 .... 117 G7
Anstey Pl *THLE* RG7 .... 142 D3
Anstey Rd *READ* RG1 .... 8 B4
Anston Cl *EARL* RG6 .... 117 K6
Antares Cl *WWKG* RG41 .... 10 A6
Anthian Cl *WODY* RG5 .... 90 E6
Anthony Wy *SL* SL1 .... 44 A8
Antrim Rd *WODY* RG5 .... 90 A8
Anvil Cl *THLE* RG7 .... 144 D5
Anvil Cl *SUN* TW16 .... 129 K8
Apex Dr *FRIM* GU16 .... 182 A5
Aplin Wy *LTWR* GU18 .... 175 K6
Appelford Cl *STHA* RG19 .... 138 A4
Appleby End *TLHT* RG30 .... 87 L7
Appleby Gdns
   EBED/NFELT TW14 .... 101 J7
Apple Cl *CALC* RG31 .... 86 C2
   WWKG RG41 .... 10 A8
Applecroft *MDHD* SL6 .... 67 M3
Appledore *BRAK* RG12 .... 149 J2
Appledore Ms *FARN* GU14 ...... 181 K7
Appleford Rd *TLHT* RG30 .... 115 K2
Apple Tree Cl *NWBY* RG14 ...... 136 B7
Appletree Cl *CAV/SC* RG4 ...... 36 B8
Appletree La *DTCH/LGLY* SL3 ...... 71 M3
   THLE RG7 .... 144 E4
Appletree Pl *BNFD* RG42 .... 12 E1
Apple Tree Wy *SHST* GU47 ...... 173 C5
Appley Dr *CBLY* GU15 .... 181 L1

Approach Rd *ASHF* TW15 .... 128 F4
   MDHD SL6 .... 43 H7
April Cl *CBLY* GU15 .... 181 M4
   FELT TW13 .... 129 K1
Apsey Ct *BRAK* RG12 .... 12 B1
Aquila Cl *WWKG* RG41 .... 119 H8
Aragon Cl *SUN* TW16 .... 129 J5
Arborfield Cl *SL* SL1 .... 71 H3
Arborfield Rd *WHIT* RG2 .... 145 J2
Arbor La *WWKG* RG41 .... 118 E3
Arbor Mdw *WWKG* RG41 .... 118 E3
Arbour Cl *READ* RG1 .... 116 C1
Archangel Wy *NTHA* RG18 ...... 138 C2
Archer Cl *MDHD* SL6 .... 2 C5
Archway Rd *READ* RG1 .... 8 F1
Arden Cl *BRAK* RG12 .... 122 D7
Ardingly *BRAK* RG12 .... 149 K3
Ardrossan Av *CBLY* GU15 ...... 182 D7
Ardrossan Cl *SLN* SL2 .... 44 F5
Ardwell Cl *CWTH* RG45 .... 172 B1
Arenal Dr *CWTH* RG45 .... 172 E5
Argent Cl *EGH* TW20 .... 126 F4
Argosy Gdns *STA* TW18 .... 127 J4
Argosy La *STWL/WRAY* TW19 ...... 100 A6
Argyle Rd *NWBY* RG14 .... 14 D6
   READ RG1 .... 8 B7
Argyle St *CHOB/PIR* GU24 ...... 183 K8
   READ RG1 .... 8 B6
Argyll Av *SL* SL1 .... 44 D8
Ariel Wy *HSLWW* TW4 .... 101 L2
Arkle Av *STHA* RG19 .... 137 J3
Arkley Ct *MDHD* SL6 .... 68 E5
Arkwright Cl *KSCL* RG20 .... 159 J8
Arkwright Dr *BNFD* RG42 .... 121 C7
Arkwright Rd *DTCH/LGLY* SL3 ...... 99 H1
   WHIT RG2 .... 116 E3
Arlington Cl *BNFD* RG42 .... 12 E2
   MDHD SL6 .... 41 J6
Arlington Rd *ASHF* TW15 .... 128 C3
Armadale Ct *TLHT* RG30 .... 88 A8
Armadale Rd
   EBED/NFELT TW14 .... 101 K4
Armitage Ct *ASC* SL5 .... 151 M3
Armitage Dr *FRIM* GU16 .... 182 C5
Armour Hl *CALC* RG31 .... 87 C5
Armour Rd *CALC* RG31 .... 87 C5
Armour Wk *CALC* RG31 .... 87 C5
Armstrong Rd *EGH* TW20 ...... 125 M4
Armstrong Wy *WODY* RG5 ...... 90 D7
Arncliffe *BRAK* RG12 .... 12 E9
   BRAK RG12 .... 149 K2
Arndale Wy *EGH* TW20 .... 126 D3
Arnett Av *EWKG* RG40 .... 147 H7
Arnhem Rd *NWBY* RG14 .... 15 H4
Arnold Rd *STA* TW18 .... 127 M5
Arnside Cl *WAR/TWY* RG10 ...... 65 C7
Arrowhead Rd *THLE* RG7 .... 114 C4
Arrow Smith Wy *STHA* RG19 ...... 138 C4
Arthur Cl *BAGS* GU19 .... 175 H5
Arthur Rd *NWBY* RG14 .... 14 B6
   SL SL1 .... 4 D8
   WDSR SL4 .... 7 G6
   WWKG RG41 .... 10 C4
Arthurstone Birches
   BNFD RG42 .... 121 C3
Arun Cl *WWKG* RG41 .... 118 E5
Arundel Cl *MDHD* SL6 .... 41 K6
Arundel Ct *DTCH/LGLY* SL3 ...... 72 A4
Arundel Rd *CBLY* GU15 .... 182 F2
   HSLWW TW4 .... 101 M2
   UX/CGN UB8 .... 47 L3
   WODY RG5 .... 90 B8
Arwood Av *TADY* RG26 .... 165 C5
Ascot Cl *NWBY* RG14 .... 15 J9
Ascot Rd *ASHF* TW15 .... 100 D7
   BRAK RG12 .... 94 B6
   MDHD SL6 .... 68 C7
Ashampstead Rd
   GOR/PANG RG8 .... 58 B8
   THLE RG7 .... 84 F7
   TLHT RG30 .... 115 C2
Ashbourne *BRAK* RG12 .... 149 J3
Ashbourne Gv *MDHD* SL6 ...... 67 M3
Ashbourne Wy *STHA* RG19 ...... 137 L3
Ashbrook Rd *WDSR* SL4 .... 97 L6
Ashburton Rd *WHIT* RG2 .... 116 F4
Ashbury Dr *CALC* RG31 .... 86 F7
   FARN GU14 .... 181 K5
Ash Cl *BLKW* GU17 .... 180 F1
   DTCH/LGLY SL3 .... 72 E3
Ashcroft Cl *CAV/SC* RG4 .... 88 B1
Ashcroft Cl *SL* SL1 .... 43 L3
Ashcroft Rd *MDHD* SL6 .... 2 A3
Ashdale Cl *STWL/WRAY* TW19 ...... 100 B8
Ashdale Pk *EWKG* RG40 .... 147 M7
Ashdene Cl *ASHF* TW15 .... 128 F5
Ashdown *MDHD* SL6 .... 42 E3
Ashdown Cl *BRAK* RG12 .... 122 C7
Asher Dr *ASC* SL5 .... 122 F6
Ashfield Av *FELT* TW13 .... 101 L7
Ashfield Gn *YTLY* GU46 .... 180 C1
Ashford Av *ASHF* TW15 .... 128 E4
   CAV/SC RG4 .... 62 B1
Ashford Cl *ASHF* TW15 .... 128 B2
Ashford Crs *ASHF* TW15 .... 128 B1
Ashford Hill Rd *STHA* RG19 ...... 162 A4
Ashford La *MDHD* SL6 .... 69 L2
   FELT TW13 .... 129 G2
Ashford Rd *FELT* TW13 .... 129 J1
   IVER SL0 .... 46 F2
   SHPTN TW17 .... 128 F5
   STA TW18 .... 128 A6
Ash Ga *NTHA* RG18 .... 138 C2
Ash Gv *EBED/NFELT* TW14 ...... 101 H7
   SLN SL2 .... 45 J1
   STA TW18 .... 127 M4
Ashgrove Rd *ASHF* TW15 .... 128 F3
Ash La *TADY* RG26 .... 164 B5
   THLE RG7 .... 142 D2
   WDSR SL4 .... 96 A1
Ashlee Wk *GOR/PANG* RG8 ...... 34 C6
Ashleigh Av *EGH* TW20 .... 126 F5
Ashley Cl *EARL* RG6 .... 117 L4
   FRIM GU16 .... 182 D8
Ashley Dr *BLKW* GU17 .... 180 F2
Ashley Pk *MDHD* SL6 .... 42 E4
Ashley Piece *MARL* SN8 .... 102 A1

Ashley Rd *UX/CGN* UB8 .... 47 L3
Ashley Wy *CHOB/PIR* GU24 ...... 176 A8
Ashley Rd *STHA* RG19 .... 138 C3
Ashmead Rd
   EBED/NFELT TW14 .... 101 K7
Ashmere Ter *TLHT* RG30 .... 8 A4
Ashmere Cl *CALC* RG31 .... 114 F2
Ashmere Ter *TLHT* RG30 .... 8 A4
Ashmore Green Rd *NTHA* RG18 ...... 109 K7
Ashmore Rd *WHIT* RG2 .... 116 F5
Ashridge Gn *BNFD* RG42 .... 13 C2
Ashridge Rd *EWKG* RG40 ...... 11 K2
Ashridge Wy *SUN* TW16 .... 129 K4
Ash Rd *KSCL* RG20 .... 161 J3
   TLHT RG30 .... 87 H7
Ash Ter *NTHA* RG18 .... 109 L6
Ashton Cl *CALC* RG31 .... 86 F6
Ashton Pl *HUNG* RG17 .... 133 L4
   MDHD SL6 .... 41 H8
Ashton Rd *WWKG* RG41 .... 119 J5
Ash Tree Gv *KSCL* RG20 .... 134 E7
Ashtrees Rd *WODY* RG5 .... 90 C6
Ashurst Cl *TADY* RG26 .... 164 D6
Ashview Cl *ASHF* TW15 .... 128 B4
Ashview Gdns *ASHF* TW15 ...... 128 B3
Ashville Wy *WWKG* RG41 .... 10 D8
Ash Wy *WWKG* RG41 .... 147 C3
Ashwell Ct *CBLY* GU15 .... 174 C8
Ashwood *WODY* RG5 .... 90 A6
Ashwood Cl *CALC* RG31 .... 86 E8
Ashwood Dr *NWBY* RG14 ...... 15 M2
Ashwood Rd *EGH* TW20 .... 125 L4
Ashworth Dr *STHA* RG19 ...... 137 M4
Askew Dr *THLE* RG7 .... 144 F3
Aspen Cl *SL* SL1 .... 44 E6
   STA TW18 .... 127 J1
Aspen Wy *FELT* TW13 .... 129 L1
Aspin Wy *BLKW* GU17 .... 180 E1
Astleham Wy *SHPTN* TW17 ...... 128 B8
Astley Dr *WWKG* RG41 .... 10 A3
Aston Av *CALC* RG31 .... 86 E6
Aston Cl *GOR/PANG* RG8 .... 86 A1
Aston Ferry La *HEN* RG9 .... 38 F1
Aston La *HEN* RG9 .... 38 F3
Aston Md *WDSR* SL4 .... 70 B8
Astor Cl *MDHD* SL6 .... 3 M7
   WWKG RG41 .... 119 C3
Astra Md *BNFD* RG42 .... 122 E4
Atfield Gv *BFOR* GU20 .... 176 A2
Atherton Cl *MARL* SN8 .... 102 A2
   STWL/WRAY TW19 .... 100 A5
   TLHT RG30 .... 87 J6
Atherton Crs *HUNG* RG17 ...... 132 A1
Atherton Pl *HUNG* RG17 .... 49 L3
Atherton Rd *HUNG* RG17 .... 132 A1
Athlone Cl *MDHD* SL6 .... 42 B5
Atrebatti Rd *SHST* GU47 .... 150 A4
Atte La *BNFD* RG42 .... 121 M4
Auckland Cl *MDHD* SL6 .... 3 L3
Auckland Rd *EARL* RG6 .... 89 K8
Auclum Cl *THLE* RG7 .... 142 E4
Auclum La *THLE* RG7 .... 142 E4
Audley Cl *NWBY* RG14 .... 137 C1
Audley Dr *MDHD* SL6 .... 41 L8
Audley Wy *ASC* SL5 .... 123 C8
Augur Cl *STA* TW18 .... 127 J3
August End *DTCH/LGLY* SL3 ...... 46 B7
   TLHT RG30 .... 87 M6
Augustine Cl *DTCH/LGLY* SL3 ...... 99 H2
Augustine Wk *BNFD* RG42 ...... 122 B5
Augustus Gdns *CBLY* GU15 ...... 182 F1
Austen Rd *FARN* GU14 .... 181 K8
Austin Rd *WODY* RG5 .... 90 C8
Austinsgate *MDHD* SL6 .... 41 J6
Australia Av *MDHD* SL6 .... 3 G2
Australia Cl *SL* SL1 .... 5 L8
Autumn Cl *CAV/SC* RG4 .... 62 F7
   SL SL1 .... 70 C1
Autumn Wk *MDHD* SL6 .... 41 K8
   WAR/TWY RG10 .... 65 C4
Avalon Rd *BNEND* SL8 .... 20 E1
   EARL RG6 .... 117 M3
Avebury *BRAK* RG12 .... 149 K3
   SL SL1 .... 70 D1
Avebury Sq *READ* RG1 .... 117 G1
Avenue Dr *DTCH/LGLY* SL3 ...... 46 C6
Avenue Rd *FELT* TW13 .... 129 J1
   MDHD SL6 .... 3 M8
   STA TW18 .... 127 C3
Avenue Sucy *CBLY* GU15 .... 181 K2
The Avenue *ASC* SL5 .... 123 J5
   BNEND SL8 .... 20 C2
   CBLY GU15 .... 181 C2
   CHOB/PIR GU24 .... 177 J4
   CWTH RG45 .... 172 D1
   DTCH/LGLY SL3 .... 71 L8
   EGH TW20 .... 126 E2
   LTWR GU18 .... 175 K5
   MDHD SL6 .... 42 E4
   STA TW18 .... 127 L6
   STWL/WRAY TW19 .... 98 A2
   STWL/WRAY TW19 .... 98 B3
   SUN TW16 .... 129 L6
   THLE RG7 .... 166 E1
   WDSR SL4 .... 97 L4
Averil Ct *SL* SL1 .... 43 M7
Averton Cl *BNFD* RG42 .... 121 L5
Avery Cl *EWKG* RG40 .... 147 J8
Avington Cl *CALC* RG31 .... 86 E6
Avocet Crs *SHST* GU47 .... 173 G6
Avon Cl *FARN* GU14 .... 181 H7
   SL SL1 .... 44 B8
Avondale *MDHD* SL6 .... 41 M5
Avondale Av *STA* TW18 .... 127 J5
Avondale Rd *ASHF* TW15 .... 128 A1
Avon Gv *BRAK* RG12 .... 13 K1
Avon Pl *READ* RG1 .... 9 M5
Avon Rd *SUN* TW16 .... 129 J5
Avonway *NWBY* RG14 .... 15 M1
Avon Wy *THLE* RG7 .... 113 H6
Axbridge *BRAK* RG12 .... 150 B2
Axbridge Rd *WHIT* RG2 .... 116 F4
Ayebridges Av *EGH* TW20 ...... 126 F5
Aylesbury Crs *SL* SL1 .... 4 D3
Aylesford Wy *STHA* RG19 ...... 138 D4

Aylesham Wy *YTLY* GU46 .... 171 L8
Baber Dr *EBED/NFELT* TW14 ...... 101 M5
Back La *HUNG* RG17 .... 133 J7
   RAND SP11 .... 178 A8
   THLE RG7 .... 112 C1
   THLE RG7 .... 112 D8
   THLE RG7 .... 144 D6
   THLE RG7 .... 163 L3
   THLE RG7 .... 165 M2
Backsideans *WAR/TWY* RG10 ...... 65 C4
Back St *HUNG* RG17 .... 50 F8
Bacon Cl *SHST* GU47 .... 173 C8
Baden Cl *STA* TW18 .... 127 K5
Bader Gdns *SL* SL1 .... 70 D2
The Bader Wy *WODY* RG5 ...... 118 D1
Badgemore La *HEN* RG9 .... 38 A3
Badger Cl *FELT* TW13 .... 129 L1
   HSLWW TW4 .... 101 M1
   MDHD SL6 .... 68 A2
Badger Dr *LTWR* GU18 .... 175 K5
   WAR/TWY RG10 .... 65 G1
Badgers Cl *ASHF* TW15 .... 128 C3
Badgers Copse *CBLY* GU15 ...... 182 B3
Badgers Gld *THLE* RG7 .... 142 D4
Badgers Hl *VW* GU25 .... 153 M2
Badgers Ri *CAV/SC* RG4 .... 88 D1
Badgers Sett *CWTH* RG45 ...... 172 C1
Badgers Wk *HEN* RG9 .... 64 D3
Badgers Wy *BRAK* RG12 .... 122 C6
Badgerwood Dr *FRIM* GU16 ...... 182 A4
Bad Godesberg Wy *MDHD* SL6 ...... 3 C5
Badminton Rd *MDHD* SL6 ...... 41 L8
Bagnols Wy *NWBY* RG14 ...... 14 A6
Bagshot Gn *BAGS* GU19 .... 175 H4
Bagshot Rd *ASC* SL5 .... 151 L5
   BRAK RG12 .... 13 H7
   CHOB/PIR GU24 .... 176 E6
   EGH TW20 .... 125 M5
Baigents La *FRIM* GU16 .... 182 A6
Bailey Cl *FRIM* GU16 .... 182 A6
   MDHD SL6 .... 3 G4
   WDSR SL4 .... 6 C9
Baileys Cl *BLKW* GU17 .... 180 E2
Bailey's La *WAR/TWY* RG10 ...... 92 B2
Baily Av *NTHA* RG18 .... 137 L2
Bain Av *CBLY* GU15 .... 181 L5
Bainbridge Rd *CALC* RG31 ...... 114 E2
Baird Cl *SL* SL1 .... 70 E2
Baird Rd *FARN* GU14 .... 181 M8
   WHIT RG2 .... 146 B6
Bakeham La *EGH* TW20 .... 126 A6
Bakers La *MDHD* SL6 .... 41 J6
Bakers Orch *FLKWH* HP10 ...... 21 H1
Baker St *READ* RG1 .... 8 C7
Baldons Cl *GOR/PANG* RG8 ...... 34 C5
Baldwin Rd *SL* SL1 .... 43 M4
Baldwin's Shore *WDSR* SL4 .... 7 J2
Balfour Crs *BRAK* RG12 .... 149 L2
   NWBY RG14 .... 159 M1
Balfour Dr *CALC* RG31 .... 114 E2
Balfour Pl *MLW* SL7 .... 18 F2
Balintore Ct *SHST* GU47 .... 173 C7
Ballamoor Cl *CALC* RG31 ...... 114 D2
Ballantyne Rd *FARN* GU14 ...... 181 K8
Ballard Gn *WDSR* SL4 .... 70 B7
Ballard Rd *CBLY* GU15 .... 174 D6
Ballencrieff Rd *ASC* SL5 .... 152 C4
Balliol Rd *CAV/SC* RG4 .... 88 A3
Balliol Wy *SHST* GU47 .... 173 H5
Ball Pit Rd *KSCL* RG20 .... 54 D3
Balme Cl *WAR/TWY* RG10 ...... 90 E3
Balmoral *MDHD* SL6 .... 41 L5
Balmoral Cl *SL* SL1 .... 44 B7
Balmoral Dr *FRIM* GU16 .... 182 B6
Balmoral Gdns *WDSR* SL4 ...... 97 C2
Balmore Dr *CAV/SC* RG4 .... 88 E2
Balmore Pk *CAV/SC* RG4 .... 88 D2
Bamburgh Cl *WHIT* RG2 .... 116 F3
Bamford Pl *CALC* RG31 .... 114 E2
Banbury *BRAK* RG12 .... 150 B4
Banbury Av *SL* SL1 .... 44 C6
Banbury Cl *FRIM* GU16 .... 182 D7
Banbury Gdns *CAV/SC* RG4 ...... 88 F3
Bancroft Cl *ASHF* TW15 .... 128 D3
Bancroft Pl *CALC* RG31 .... 114 E3
Band La *EGH* TW20 .... 126 C3
Bangors Cl *IVER* SL0 .... 47 J7
Bangors Rd North *IVER* SL0 ...... 47 C2
Bangors Rd South *IVER* SL0 ...... 47 H5
Bank Side *EWKG* RG40 .... 147 J8
Bankside Cl *WHIT* RG2 .... 117 C4
Banks Sp *SL* SL1 .... 70 E2
Bannard Rd *MDHD* SL6 .... 67 K1
Bannister Cl *DTCH/LGLY* SL3 ...... 72 C2
Bannister Gdns *HTWY* RG27 ...... 171 H6
   YTLY GU46 .... 180 C1
Bannister Pl *THLE* RG7 .... 139 J8
Bannister Rd *THLE* RG7 .... 142 C4
Barbara's Meadow *CALC* RG31 ...... 86 E4
Barbel Cl *EARL* RG6 .... 89 K6
Barber Cl *WAR/TWY* RG10 ...... 91 H7
Barberry Wy *BLKW* GU17 ...... 181 J3
Barbon Cl *CBLY* GU15 .... 183 C3
Barbrook Cl *CALC* RG31 .... 87 C3
Barchester Rd *DTCH/LGLY* SL3 ...... 72 C2
Barclay Rd *CALC* RG31 .... 115 C2
Barclose Av *CAV/SC* RG4 .... 88 F3
Bardney Cl *MDHD* SL6 .... 68 A3
Bardolph's Cl *CAV/SC* RG4 ...... 62 A6
Bardown *KSCL* RG20 .... 80 D3

Barefoot Cl *CALC* RG31 .... 86 E5
Barfield Rd *NTHA* RG18 .... 137 K2
Barge La *THLE* RG7 .... 168 D7
Bargeman Rd *MDHD* SL6 .... 68 B2
Barholm Cl *EARL* RG6 .... 118 A3
Barkby EARL RG6 .... 117 M4
Barker Cl *WHIT* RG2 .... 146 B7
Barker Ct *WAR/TWY* RG10 ...... 91 J6
Barker Rd *CHERT* KT16 .... 155 H4
Barkham Ride *EWKG* RG40 ...... 146 F5
   EWKG RG40 .... 147 J7
Barkham Rd *WHIT* RG2 .... 146 B3
   WWKG RG41 .... 146 D4
Barkham St *EWKG* RG40 .... 146 F4
Barkhart Dr *EWKG* RG40 .... 11 H4
Barkhart Gdns *EWKG* RG40 ...... 11 H4
Barkis Md *SHST* GU47 .... 173 H4
Barkwith Cl *EARL* RG6 .... 118 B4
Barlee Crs *UX/CGN* UB8 .... 47 M6
Barley Md *BNFD* RG42 .... 122 B5
Barley Mow Cl *EGH* TW20 ...... 125 M3
Barlows Rd *TADY* RG26 .... 164 E7
Barnard Cl *CAV/SC* RG4 .... 62 F8
   FRIM GU16 .... 182 C6
   SUN TW16 .... 129 L5
Barnards Hl *MLW* SL7 .... 18 F4
Barn Cl *ASHF* TW15 .... 128 E3
   BRAK RG12 .... 13 M4
   CBLY GU15 .... 174 B8
   HUNG RG17 .... 133 L4
   MDHD SL6 .... 42 C1
   TLHT RG30 .... 116 A2
Barn Crs *NWBY* RG14 .... 136 A7
Barn Dr *MDHD* SL6 .... 67 K2
Barnes Rd *FRIM* GU16 .... 182 B6
Barnes Wy *IVER* SL0 .... 47 J8
Barnett Ct *BRAK* RG12 .... 13 K4
Barnett Gn *BRAK* RG12 .... 149 L3
Barnett La *LTWR* GU18 .... 175 J7
Barnfield *IVER* SL0 .... 47 H7
   SL SL1 .... 70 A1
   YTLY GU46 .... 180 A3
Barnfield Cl *MDHD* SL6 .... 42 C1
Barnhill Cl *MLW* SL7 .... 19 C2
Barnhill Gdns *MLW* SL7 .... 19 C2
Barnhill Rd *MLW* SL7 .... 19 C2
Barn La *HEN* RG9 .... 37 M2
Barnmead *CHOB/PIR* GU24 ...... 177 J5
Barn Owl Wy *THLE* RG7 .... 142 F4
Barnsdale Rd *WHIT* RG2 .... 117 C3
Barnsfield Pl *UX/CGN* UB8 ...... 47 M2
Barnsford Crs *CHOB/PIR* GU24 ...... 176 D7
Barnway *EGH* TW20 .... 125 M3
Barnwood Cl *TLHT* RG30 .... 8 A4
Baron Cl *TLHT* RG30 .... 8 A7
Baronsmead *HEN* RG9 .... 38 A4
Barons Wy *EGH* TW20 .... 127 C4
Barossa Rd *CBLY* GU15 .... 174 A7
Barracane Dr *CWTH* RG45 ...... 172 C2
Barrack La *WDSR* SL4 .... 7 K7
Barracks La *THLE* RG7 .... 144 C5
Barracks Rd *STHA* RG19 .... 161 J2
Barrett Crs *EWKG* RG40 .... 11 K5
Barrett's La *WHIT* RG2 .... 118 A8
Barrington Cl *EARL* RG6 .... 89 L8
Barrington Wy *READ* RG1 ...... 116 B1
Barr's Rd *MDHD* SL6 .... 43 L7
Barry Av *WDSR* SL4 .... 6 F5
Barry Pl *READ* RG1 .... 8 E3
Barry Sq *BRAK* RG12 .... 150 A4
Bartelotts Rd *SLN* SL2 .... 44 A5
Bartholomew Pl *BNFD* RG42 ...... 122 B5
Bartholomew St *NWBY* RG14 ...... 14 D6
Bartlemy Cl *NWBY* RG14 .... 14 A9
Bartlemy Rd *NWBY* RG14 .... 14 A9
Bartletts La *MDHD* SL6 .... 68 D7
Barton Rd *CALC* RG31 .... 86 E8
   DTCH/LGLY SL3 .... 72 C2
Barton's Dr *YTLY* GU46 .... 180 A2
Bartons Wy *FARN* GU14 .... 180 F7
Barwell Cl *CWTH* RG45 .... 172 C2
Basemoors *BRAK* RG12 .... 122 B7
Basford Wy *WDSR* SL4 .... 96 A2
Basil Cl *EARL* RG6 .... 117 J5
Basingstoke Rd *HTWY* RG27 ...... 168 C3
   THLE RG7 .... 140 D5
   THLE RG7 .... 144 D1
   THLE RG7 .... 144 D1
   THLE RG7 .... 144 E4
   THLE RG7 .... 144 E7
   WHIT RG2 .... 116 E6
Baskerville La *HEN* RG9 .... 64 D3
Baskerville Rd *CAV/SC* RG4 ...... 62 B1
Baslow Rd *WWKG* RG41 .... 118 E4
Bassett Cl *EARL* RG6 .... 117 M6
   FRIM GU16 .... 182 B6
Bassett Rd *UX/CGN* UB8 .... 47 M1
Bass Md *MDHD* SL6 .... 42 C1
Batavia Cl *SUN* TW16 .... 129 L6
Batavia Rd *SUN* TW16 .... 129 L6
Batcombe Md *BRAK* RG12 ...... 150 B4
Bates Cl *DTCH/LGLY* SL3 .... 46 B7
Bath Ct *MDHD* SL6 .... 66 E1
Bath Rd *CALC* RG31 .... 115 G1
   CALC RG31 .... 89 M5
   CAV/SC RG4 .... 90 A5
   CBLY GU15 .... 173 M8
   DTCH/LGLY SL3 .... 73 H8
   HUNG RG17 .... 103 K8
   HUNG RG17 .... 104 C8
   MARL SN8 .... 130 D2
   MDHD SL6 .... 43 J7
   MDHD SL6 .... 66 E1
   NTHA RG18 .... 137 J2
   NWBY RG14 .... 136 A1
   READ RG1 .... 8 B9
   SL SL1 .... 4 A5
   SL SL1 .... 44 A8
   SL SL1 .... 5 J1
   THLE RG7 .... 114 A4
   THLE RG7 .... 139 J4
   THLE RG7 .... 140 F3
   THLE RG7 .... 141 G1
   WAR/TWY RG10 .... 65 K6
   WAR/TWY RG10 .... 66 B3
   WDR/YW UB7 .... 73 L8
Bathurst Cl *IVER* SL0 .... 73 J2

Bathurst Rd *WWKG* RG41 .... 118 E4
Bathurst Wk *IVER* SL0 .... 73 H2
Battery End *NWBY* RG14 .... 136 A8
Battle Cl *NWBY* RG14 .... 136 A2
Battlemead Cl *MDHD* SL6 .... 42 F3
Battle Rd *GOR/PANG* RG8 .... 33 J7
   NWBY RG14 .... 135 M8
Battle St *READ* RG1 .... 8 C5
Batty's Barn Cl *EWKG* RG40 ...... 11 J7
The Baxendales *NWBY* RG14 ..... 15 J8
Bay Cl *EARL* RG6 .... 117 J5
Baydon Dr *READ* RG1 .... 116 B1
   HUNG RG17 .... 48 E8
Baydon Rd *HUNG* RG17 .... 48 F6
   HUNG RG17 .... 75 K2
   HUNG RG17 .... 76 A4
   HUNG RG17 .... 76 F7
Bayfield Av *FRIM* GU16 .... 182 B4
Bayford Cl *FARN* GU14 .... 181 K5
Bayford Dr *CALC* RG31 .... 115 J2
Bayley Ct *WWKG* RG41 .... 118 E5
Bayley Crs *SL* SL1 .... 43 K6
Baylis Rd *SL* SL1 .... 4 D5
Bayliss Rd *WAR/TWY* RG10 .... 65 C5
Bay Rd *BRAK* RG12 .... 122 B6
Baysfarm Ct *WDR/YW* UB7 .... 73 M8
Bay Tree Cl *SL* SL1 .... 43 M4 ⊡
Bay Tree Ri *CALC* RG31 .... 114 F1
Beacon Ct *DTCH/LGLY* SL3 .... 72 F7
Beacon Rd *HTHAIR* TW6 .... 100 D5
Beaconsfield Wy *EARL* RG6 ...... 117 K4
Beagle Cl *FELT* 129 L2
Beales Farm Rd *HUNG* RG17 ..... 49 L4 ⊡
Beancroft Rd *STHA* RG19 .... 138 A4
Bean Oak Rd *EWKG* RG40 .... 11 M5
Beards Rd *ASHF* TW15 .... 129 H4
Bearfield La *HUNG* RG17 .... 75 L6
Bear La *NWBY* RG14 .... 14 E4
   WAR/TWY RG10 .... 65 L4
Bearwood Pth *WWKG* RG41 ..... 118 D4
Bearwood Rd *WWKG* RG41 .... 118 E6
Beattie Cl *EBED/NFELT* TW14 .... 101 J7
Beatty Dr *TLHT* RG30 .... 87 H6
Beauchief Cl *EARL* RG6 .... 117 J6 ⊡
Beauclerk Ct *FELT* TW13 .... 101 L7 ⊡
Beaufield Cl *WODY* RG5 .... 90 A7
Beaufort Gdns *ASC* SL5 .... 123 H6
   MLW SL7 .... 19 H4 ⊡
Beaufort Pl *MDHD* SL6 .... 69 G2
Beauforts *EGH* TW20 .... 125 M3
Beaufront Cl *CBLY* GU15 .... 174 D7
Beaufront Rd *CBLY* GU15 .... 174 D7
Beaulieu Cl *BRAK* RG12 .... 122 C8
   DTCH/LGLY SL3 .... 97 M1 ⊡
Beaulieu Gdns *BLKW* GU17 ...... 180 F1
Beaumaris Pde *FRIM* GU16 ...... 182 C6
Beaumont Cl *MDHD* SL6 .... 67 K3 ⊡
Beaumont Dr *ASHF* TW15 .... 129 G3 ⊡
Beaumont Gdns *BRAK* RG12 ..... 150 B2 ⊡
Beaumont Ri *MLW* SL7 .... 19 H4
Beaumont Rd *SLN* SL2 .... 45 G6
   WDSR SL4 .... 7 H9
Beaver Ct *WWKG* RG41 .... 147 L3
Beaver La *YTLY* GU46 .... 180 B1
Beavers La *HSLWW* TW4 .... 101 M2
Beaver Wy *WODY* RG5 .... 90 E7
Beck Ct *READ* RG1 .... 9 K9
   READ RG1 .... 116 F1
Beckett Cl *EWKG* RG40 .... 11 M5
Beckford Av *BRAK* RG12 .... 149 L3
Beckford Rd *WWKG* RG41 .... 119 J5 ⊡
Beckfords *GOR/PANG* RG8 .... 84 D1
Beckley *GOR/PANG* RG8 .... 34 C6 ⊡
Bec Tithe *GOR/PANG* RG8 .... 60 B3
Bedfont Cl *EBED/NFELT* TW14 ... 100 F5
Bedfont Ct *STWL/WRAY* TW19 ... 99 K2
Bedfont Green Cl
   EBED/NFELT TW14 .... 100 F7
Bedfont La *EBED/NFELT* TW14 ... 101 H6
Bedfont Rd *EBED/NFELT* TW14 .. 100 F7
   FELT TW13 .... 129 J1
   STWL/WRAY TW19 .... 100 C3
Bedford Av *SL* SL1 .... 44 D7
Bedford Cl *MDHD* SL6 .... 67 K3
   NWBY RG14 .... 159 M1 ⊡
Bedford Crs *FRIM* GU16 .... 182 B8
Bedford Gdns *WWKG* RG41 ...... 10 A3
Bedford La *ASC* SL5 .... 152 C2
   FRIM GU16 .... 182 C8
Bedford Rd *READ* RG1 .... 8 C5
Bedfordshire Down
   BNFD RG42 .... 122 C4
Bedfordshire Wy
   WWKG RG41 .... 119 H8 ⊡
Bedwins La *MDHD* SL6 .... 19 L1
Beecham Rd *TLHT* RG30 .... 87 M7
Beech Av *CBLY* GU15 .... 182 A2
Beechbrook Av *YTLY* GU46 ...... 180 A1
Beech Cl *ASHF* TW15 .... 129 G3
   MDHD SL6 .... 41 L6 ⊡
   NTHA RG18 .... 82 D1
   STWL/WRAY TW19 .... 100 A6
   TLHT RG30 .... 142 E2
Beechcroft *NTHA* RG18 .... 82 D1
Beechcroft Cl *ASC* SL5 .... 152 A1 ⊡
Beech Dr *BLKW* GU17 .... 181 G2
The Beeches *CALC* RG31 .... 87 G3 ⊡
   GOR/PANG RG8 .... 58 E1
Beeches Wy *BNEND* SL8 .... 20 E6
   MDHD SL6 .... 21 H4
   SL SL1 .... 43 L4 ⊡
Beech Gln *BRAK* RG12 .... 13 G8
Beech Gv *ADL/WDHM* KT15 ..... 155 L8 ⊡
   CHOB/PIR GU24 .... 183 M7
   THLE RG7 .... 144 B8
Beech Hill Rd *ASC* SL5 .... 152 B3
Beechingstoke *MLW* SL7 .... 19 J3 ⊡
Beech La *EARL* RG6 .... 117 K3
   GOR/PANG RG8 .... 33 J5
   GOR/PANG RG8 .... 34 B6
Beechmont Av *GU25* 154 A3
Beechnut Dr *BLKW* GU17 .... 172 E8
Beech Ride *SHST* GU47 .... 172 E6
Beech Ri *CAV/SC* RG4 .... 36 B8

Beech Rd *CAV/SC* RG4 .... 62 A7
   DTCH/LGLY SL3 .... 72 B2
   EBED/NFELT TW14 .... 101 H6
   FARN GU14 .... 181 L7
   FRIM GU16 .... 182 C8
   GOR/PANG RG8 .... 86 D1
   KSCL RG20 .... 161 K4
   WHIT RG2 .... 117 H4
Beechtree Av *EGH* TW20 .... 125 L4
   MLW SL7 .... 19 G1
Beech Tree La *STA* TW18 .... 127 L7 ⊡
Beech Wk *STHA* RG19 .... 138 B4
Beechwood Av *CALC* RG31 ...... 87 G6
   STA TW18 .... 127 L4
   SUN TW16 .... 129 K4
   WODY RG5 .... 90 A7
Beechwood Cl *ASC* SL5 .... 123 H5
   GOR/PANG RG8 .... 34 A8 ⊡
Beechwood Dr *MDHD* SL6 .... 41 K8
   MLW SL7 .... 18 E6
Beechwood Gdns *SL* SL1 .... 4 F9
Beechwood Rd *SLN* SL2 .... 45 G6
   VW GU25 .... 153 L4
Beedon Dr *BRAK* RG12 .... 149 G3
Beehive La *BRAK* RG12 .... 120 F7
Beehive Rd *BRAK* RG12 .... 121 G7
   STA TW18 .... 127 J3
Beeson Cl *GOR/PANG* RG8 .... 34 C6 ⊡
Beeston Wy *EARL* RG6 .... 117 K6
   EBED/NFELT TW14 .... 101 M5
Beggars Hill Rd *WODY* RG5 ...... 90 E5
Beggars La *CHOB/PIR* GU24 ..... 176 F6
Behoes La *GOR/PANG* RG8 .... 34 A5
Beighton Cl *EARL* RG6 .... 117 J6 ⊡
Beldam Bridge Rd
   CHOB/PIR GU24 .... 176 D8
Belfast Av *SL* SL1 .... 4 B3
   SL SL1 .... 4 C2
Belgrave Ct *BLKW* GU17 .... 181 G3
Belgrave Crs *SUN* TW16 .... 129 L6
Belgrave Rd *SL* SL1 .... 4 F5
   SL SL1 .... 5 G5
   SUN TW16 .... 129 L6
Bell Bridge Rd *CHERT* KT16 ..... 155 J5
Bell Cl *FARN* GU14 .... 181 M8
   SLN SL2 .... 5 M1
Bell Ct *MDHD* SL6 .... 40 C3
   WAR/TWY RG10 .... 91 G1 ⊡
Belle Av *EARL* RG6 .... 117 K1
Bellever Hl *CBLY* GU15 .... 182 B1
Belle Vue La *STA* TW18 .... 127 K6 ⊡
Belle Vue Pl *SL* SL1 .... 71 J3 ⊡
Belle Vue Rd *HEN* RG9 .... 38 A6
   READ RG1 .... 8 C7
   FRIM GU16 .... 182 E8
Bellew Rd *FRIM* GU16 .... 182 F7
Bell Holt *NWBY* RG14 .... 159 M1
Bell House Gdns *WWKG* RG41 ... 10 E5
Bellingham Cl *CBLY* GU15 .... 182 F2
Bellisle *GOR/PANG* RG8 .... 86 E1 ⊡
Bell La *BLKW* GU17 .... 180 F1 ⊡
   GOR/PANG RG8 .... 57 J2
   HEN RG9 .... 38 B3
   HUNG RG17 .... 157 G3
   WDSR SL4 .... 70 C4
Bellmarsh Rd *ADL/WDHM* KT15 .. 155 L8
Bell Pl *BAGS* GU19 .... 175 J3
Bells Hl *SLN* SL2 .... 45 K2
Bells Hill Gn *SLN* SL2 .... 45 K1
Bells La *DTCH/LGLY* SL3 .... 98 E2
Bell St *HEN* RG9 .... 38 B4
   MDHD SL6 .... 3 H6
Bellswood La *IVER* SL0 .... 46 E6
Bell Vw *WDSR* SL4 .... 96 C2
Bell View Cl *WDSR* SL4 .... 6 A9
Belmont *SLN* SL2 .... 44 D6
Belmont Cl *FARN* GU14 .... 181 J7
Belmont Crs *MDHD* SL6 .... 2 B3
Belmont Dr *MDHD* SL6 .... 2 C2
Belmont Ms *CBLY* GU15 .... 181 M3
Belmont Park Av *MDHD* SL6 ...... 2 D1
Belmont Park Rd *MDHD* SL6 ...... 2 C2
Belmont Rd *CBLY* GU15 .... 181 M2
   CWTH RG45 .... 148 E8
   MDHD SL6 .... 2 D3
   TLHT RG30 .... 88 A7
Belmont V *MDHD* SL6 .... 2 C3
Belstone Ms *FARN* GU14 .... 181 K7 ⊡
Belton Rd *CBLY* GU15 .... 182 B1
Belvedere Ct *BLKW* GU17 .... 181 G3 ⊡
Belvedere Dr *NWBY* RG14 .... 14 E9
Belvedere Wk *WWKG* RG41 ..... 118 D3
Belvoir Cl *FRIM* GU16 .... 182 C5
Bembridge Cl *CWTH* RG45 ...... 172 B2 ⊡
Bembridge Pl *READ* RG1 .... 9 J6 ⊡
Benares Gv *HEN* RG9 .... 35 K2 ⊡
Benbow Wy *UX/CGN* UB8 .... 47 M6
The Bence *EGH* TW20 .... 126 E8
Bencombe Rd *MLW* SL7 .... 19 L1
Benedict Dr *EBED/NFELT* TW14 . 101 G6
Benedict Gn *BRAK* RG12 .... 122 B5 ⊡
Benen-stock Rd
   STWL/WRAY TW19 .... 99 K5
Benetfeld Rd *BNFD* RG42 .... 120 E4
Benett Cl *NWBY* RG14 .... 136 C1
Benett Gdns *NWBY* RG14 .... 136 C1
Benham Cha *KSCL* RG20 .... 135 H1
Benham Hl *NTHA* RG18 .... 137 K2
Benham La *THLE* RG7 .... 169 G3
Benhams Cl *HEN* RG9 .... 16 A4
Benner La *CHOB/PIR* GU24 ...... 176 C7
Benner Rd *WHIT* RG2 .... 116 D5
Bennet Cl *CBLY* GU15 .... 181 M1 ⊡
Bennet's Hl *TLHT* RG30 .... 114 E7
Benning Cl *WDSR* SL4 .... 96 A2
Bennings Cl *BNFD* RG42 .... 121 K5
Bennings Rd *EWKG* RG40 .... 11 K7
Bensgrove Cl *GOR/PANG* RG8 ... 34 C6 ⊡
Benson Cl *SLN* SL2 .... 5 J6
   WHIT RG2 .... 117 G3
Benson Rd *CWTH* RG45 .... 172 C1
Bentley Pk *SL* SL1 .... 188 A3
Bentley Rd *SL* SL1 .... 70 C1
Benwell Ct *SUN* TW16 .... 129 K6 ⊡
Benyon Ct *READ* RG1 .... 8 A9
Beomonds Rw *CHERT* KT16 ..... 155 K4 ⊡

Bere Court Rd *GOR/PANG* RG8 .. 85 J4
Bere Rd *BRAK* RG12 .... 150 B3
Beresford Av *SLN* SL2 .... 45 M8
Beresford Cl *FRIM* GU16 .... 182 C8
Beresford Rd *TLHT* RG30 .... 8 A5
Bergenia Ct *CHOB/PIR* GU24 .... 176 B8 ⊡
Berkeley Av *READ* RG1 .... 8 A9
   WHIT RG2 .... 8 F9
Berkeley Cl *STWL/WRAY* TW19 .. 99 G3
Berkeley Crs *FRIM* GU16 .... 182 D6
Berkeley Dr *WDSR* SL4 .... 95 L7
Berkeley Ms *MLW* SL7 .... 19 J4 ⊡
   SUN TW16 .... 129 M8
Berkeley Rd *NWBY* RG14 .... 14 C5
Berkley Cl *MDHD* SL6 .... 41 K6
Berks Av *SL* SL1 .... 44 E7
Berkshire Av *SL* SL1 .... 44 B8
Berkshire Circular Route
   KSCL RG20 .... 28 E6
   KSCL RG20 .... 56 C1
Berkshire Circular Routes
   HUNG RG17 .... 156 B1
   KSCL RG20 .... 135 K6
   THLE RG7 .... 83 J8
   THLE RG7 .... 113 H8
   THLE RG7 .... 142 E8
   WAR/TWY RG10 .... 65 L2
Berkshire Dr *CALC* RG31 .... 86 F6
   STHA RG19 .... 138 D4
Berkshire Rd *CBLY* GU15 .... 174 C6
   HEN RG9 .... 38 A6
Berkshire Wy *BRAK* RG12 .... 12 C6
   EWKG RG40 .... 120 F8
Bernadine Cl *BNFD* RG42 .... 122 B5 ⊡
Berners Cl *SL* SL1 .... 44 B8
Bernersh Cl *SHST* GU47 .... 172 F5 ⊡
Berries Rd *MDHD* SL6 .... 20 D7
Berrybank *SHST* GU47 .... 173 H8
Berrycroft *BNFD* RG42 .... 13 M2
Berry Fld *SLN* SL2 .... 45 M7
Berry Hl *MDHD* SL6 .... 43 G7
Berrylands *CAV/SC* RG4 .... 88 C3
Berryscroft Rd *STA* TW18 .... 127 M5
   TLHT RG30 .... 115 J5
Berrys La *TLHT* RG30 .... 115 L6
Berstead Cl *EARL* RG6 .... 117 L5 ⊡
Berwick Av *SL* SL1 .... 44 E8
Berwick Cl *MLW* SL7 .... 18 F3
Berwick La *MLW* SL7 .... 19 G3 ⊡
Berwick Rd *MLW* SL7 .... 18 F3
Bestobell Rd *SL* SL1 .... 4 C2
Beswick Gdns *BRAK* RG12 ...... 122 C6 ⊡
Betam Rd *READ* RG1 .... 9 L6
Beta Rd *CHOB/PIR* GU24 .... 177 J5
Beta Wy *EGH* TW20 .... 126 F6
Betchworth Av *EARL* RG6 .... 117 K3
Bethany Waye
   EBED/NFELT TW14 .... 101 H6
Bethesda Cl *GOR/PANG* RG8 .... 58 D8
Bethesda St *GOR/PANG* RG8 .... 58 D8
Betteridge Rd *STHA* RG19 ...... 138 C4
Bettles Cl *UX/CGN* UB8 .... 47 M3 ⊡
Betty Grove La *WWKG* RG41 .... 118 C7
Beverley Cl *CBLY* GU15 .... 174 F8
   MLW SL7 .... 18 F4
   NTHA RG18 .... 137 M2
Beverley Gdns *MDHD* SL6 .... 41 L5
   WAR/TWY RG10 .... 65 H5
Beverley Rd *CALC* RG31 .... 86 F5
   SUN TW16 .... 129 J6
The Bevers *THLE* RG7 .... 142 D8
Bexley Ct *TLHT* RG30 .... 88 A3
Bexley St *WDSR* SL4 .... 6 F7
Bibury Cl *WODY* RG5 .... 118 A2
Bicknell Rd *FRIM* GU16 .... 182 B4
Biddles Cl *SL* SL1 .... 70 B7
Bideford Cl *FARN* GU14 .... 181 K7
   WODY RG5 .... 117 M1
Bideford Sp *SLN* SL2 .... 44 E4
Big Barn Gv *BNFD* RG42 .... 13 M1
Bigbury Gdns *WHIT* RG2 .... 116 F3
Bigfrith La *MDHD* SL6 .... 19 K8
Biggs La *EWKG* RG40 .... 146 C6
Big La *HUNG* RG17 .... 49 L3
Biko Cl *UX/CGN* UB8 .... 47 M7 ⊡
Billesden Rd *CHOB/PIR* GU24 .. 183 M8
Billet La *DTCH/LGLY* SL3 .... 46 E7
   IVER SL0 .... 46 E4
Billing Av *EWKG* RG40 .... 147 H8
Billingbear La *BNFD* RG42 .... 92 F8
Billington Wy *NTHA* RG18 ...... 109 M8
Binbrook Cl *EARL* RG6 .... 118 A4
Binfield Rd *BNFD* RG42 .... 12 E1
   BNFD RG42 .... 121 J4
   EWKG RG40 .... 11 L6
   EWKG RG40 .... 120 C7
   EWKG RG40 .... 120 D4
Bingham Dr *STA* TW18 .... 128 A5
Bingham Rd *SL* SL1 .... 43 K6
The Binghams *MDHD* SL6 .... 68 E3
Bingley Gv *WODY* RG5 .... 90 C5
Bingley Rd *SUN* TW16 .... 129 K5
Binsted Dr *BLKW* GU17 .... 181 G1
Birch Av *TLHT* RG30 .... 87 K6
Birch Cl *CAV/SC* RG4 .... 62 C2
   CBLY GU15 .... 174 B6
   IVER SL0 .... 47 G3
Birch Dr *BLKW* GU17 .... 181 G3
Birchen Cl *GOR/PANG* RG8 ...... 34 C6 ⊡
Birch Gn *STA* TW18 .... 127 J2
Birch Gv *BRAK* RG12 .... 13 K8
   SHPTN TW17 .... 129 H7
   SL SL1 .... 44 E6
   WDSR SL4 .... 70 A8
Birch Hill Rd *BRAK* RG12 .... 149 L4
Birchington Rd *WDSR* SL4 .... 6 D8
Birchland Cl *THLE* RG7 .... 142 B8
Birch La *ASC* SL5 .... 123 M4
   CHOB/PIR GU24 .... 176 A7
   THLE RG7 .... 166 C1
Birchmead *WWKG* RG41 .... 119 G4
Birch Platt *CHOB/PIR* GU24 .... 176 A8
Birch Rd *BFOR* GU20 .... 176 B2
   EWKG RG40 .... 147 K7

TADY RG26 .... 164 B4
THLE RG7 .... 142 C3
Birch Side *CWTH* RG45 .... 148 C8
Birch Tree Vw *LTWR* GU18 ...... 175 K5
Birch Vw *WHIT* RG2 .... 117 H4
Birchwood Cl *CAV/SC* RG4 ...... 62 B1
Birchwood Dr *LTWR* GU18 ...... 175 M5
Birchwood Rd *NWBY* RG14 ..... 15 M1
The Birchwoods *CALC* RG31 .... 86 E6
Birdhill Av *WHIT* RG2 .... 117 G4
Bird Ms *EWKG* RG40 .... 10 F5
Birds La *THLE* RG7 .... 139 H3
Bird Wood Ct *CAV/SC* RG4 ...... 62 D2
Birdwood Rd *CBLY* GU15 .... 173 J8
   SHST GU47 .... 173 H5
Birkbeck Pl *SHST* GU47 .... 173 H5
Birkdale *BRAK* RG12 .... 149 H3
Birkhall Cl *CALC* RG31 .... 114 F1 ⊡
Birley Rd *SL* SL1 .... 4 C3
Biscuit Wy *WHIT* RG2 .... 116 C6
Bisham Ct *MLW* SL7 .... 19 H8
Bisham Rd *MLW* SL7 .... 19 G7
Bishop Ct *MDHD* SL6 .... 2 D6
Bishopdale *BRAK* RG12 .... 12 E9
Bishops Ct *TADY* RG26 .... 164 D5
Bishops Dr
   EBED/NFELT TW14 .... 101 G5 ⊡
   EWKG RG40 .... 11 G3
Bishops Farm Cl *WDSR* SL4 ..... 95 L1
Bishopsgate Rd *WDSR* SL4 ..... 125 K1
Bishops Gv *BFOR* GU20 .... 175 M2 ⊡
Bishop's La *BNFD* RG42 .... 94 D7
Bishops Orch *SLN* SL2 .... 44 E4 ⊡
Bishop's Rd *EARL* RG6 .... 89 K8
   SL SL1 .... 5 J9
   THLE RG7 .... 112 C3
Bishops Wk *FLKWH* HP10 .... 21 H1 ⊡
Bishops Wy *EGH* TW20 .... 127 G4
Bishopswood La *TADY* RG26 ... 164 B5
Bishopswood Rd *TADY* RG26 ... 164 C5
Bissley Dr *MDHD* SL6 .... 67 K3
Bitham La *HUNG* RG17 .... 156 C2
Bittams La *CHERT* KT16 .... 155 G8
Bittern Cl *SHST* GU47 .... 173 G6
Bitterne Av *CALC* RG31 .... 86 E8
Bix La *MDHD* SL6 .... 41 L7
Blackamoor La *MDHD* SL6 .... 3 J1
Blackbird Cl *SHST* GU47 .... 173 G6
   THLE RG7 .... 142 E3 ⊡
Blackbird La *MDHD* SL6 .... 94 D1
Black Boy La *WAR/TWY* RG10 ... 39 M3
Black Butts Cottages *MDHD* SL6 .. 20 E7
Blackcap Pl *SHST* GU47 .... 173 H6
Blackdown Rd *FRIM* GU16 ...... 182 F7
Blackdown Wy *STHA* RG19 ..... 137 M4
Blackett Cl *EGH* TW20 .... 143 M4
Black Horse La *WDSR* SL4 .... 96 A1 ⊡
Blacklands Rd *THLE* RG7 .... 138 F1
Blackley Cl *EARL* RG6 .... 118 B3 ⊡
Blackmeadows *BRAK* RG12 .... 149 M3 ⊡
Blackmoor Cl *ASC* SL5 .... 123 G7
Blackmoor Wd *ASC* SL5 .... 123 G7
Blackmore La *CAV/SC* RG4 ...... 62 D1
Black Park Rd *DTCH/LGLY* SL3 ... 46 C3
Blackpond La *SLN* SL2 .... 44 E2
Blacksmith Rw
   DTCH/LGLY SL3 .... 72 B4 ⊡
Blacksmiths La *CHERT* KT16 .... 155 K4 ⊡
   STA TW18 .... 127 M8 ⊡
Blackstone Cl *FARN* GU14 ...... 181 G8
Blackstroud La East
   LTWR GU18 .... 176 A3
Blackstroud La West
   LTWR GU18 .... 176 A3
Blackthorn Cl *CALC* RG31 .... 86 E4
   EARL RG6 .... 89 K7
Blackthorn Crs *FARN* GU14 .... 181 J6
Blackthorn Dell *DTCH/LGLY* SL3 .. 71 M3
Blackthorn Dr *LTWR* GU18 ..... 175 L7
   NTHA RG18 .... 105 M7
Blackthorne Crs *DTCH/LGLY* SL3 ... 99 H1
Blackthorne Rd *DTCH/LGLY* SL3 .. 99 G1
Blackwater Cl *CAV/SC* RG4 ...... 89 H2
   THLE RG7 .... 144 E5
Blackwater Ri *CALC* RG31 ...... 114 D2 ⊡
Blackwater Vw *EWKG* RG40 .... 171 K4
Blaenavon *CAV/SC* RG4 .... 88 C1
Blagdon Cl *STHA* RG19 .... 137 G6 ⊡
Blagdon Rd *WHIT* RG2 .... 116 F4
   WHIT RG2 .... 117 G4
Blagrave Farm La *CAV/SC* RG4 .. 88 A1
Blagrave La *CAV/SC* RG4 .... 87 M3
Blagrave Ri *CALC* RG31 .... 86 F8
Blagrave St *READ* RG1 .... 9 G5
Blagrove La *WWKG* RG41 .... 10 B9
   WWKG RG41 .... 147 J2
Blaire Pk *YTLY* GU46 .... 171 L6
Blair Rd *SL* SL1 .... 4 E1
Blake Cl *CWTH* RG45 .... 172 F2
   EWKG RG40 .... 11 L3
Blakeney Flds *HUNG* RG17 ...... 77 L2
Blake's La *TADY* RG26 .... 164 E5
Blake's Ride *YTLY* GU46 .... 171 L8
Blakes Rd *WAR/TWY* RG10 ...... 65 H3
Blakewood Cl *FELT* TW13 ...... 129 M2 ⊡
Blamire Dr *BNFD* RG42 .... 121 H4
Blanchard Cl *WODY* RG5 .... 90 E6
Blandford Cl *DTCH/LGLY* SL3 ... 72 A3
Blandford Dr *WWKG* RG41 ..... 147 H2
Blandford Rd *FELT* TW13 .... 116 F6
Blandford Rd North
   DTCH/LGLY SL3 .... 72 A3
Blandford Rd South
   DTCH/LGLY SL3 .... 72 A4 ⊡
Bland's Cl *THLE* RG7 .... 142 C4
Blandy Rd *HEN* RG9 .... 38 A6
Blandy's La *GOR/PANG* RG8 ..... 58 D3
Blane's La *ASC* SL5 .... 150 C2
Blatch's Cl *THLE* RG7 .... 114 A3 ⊡
Blays Cl *EGH* TW20 .... 125 M4
Blay's La *EGH* TW20 .... 125 L4
Bledlow Cl *NWBY* RG14 .... 160 A1 ⊡
Blenheim Cl *WWKG* RG41 ...... 119 H8 ⊡
Blenheim Gdns *READ* RG1 .... 89 H8
Blenheim Rd *CAV/SC* RG4 .... 88 D2
   DTCH/LGLY SL3 .... 72 A4

MDHD SL6 .... 41 L6
NWBY RG14 .... 14 C4
READ RG1 .... 9 M7
Blewburton Wk *BRAK* RG12 .... 150 B1 ⊡
Blewbury Dr *CALC* RG31 .... 86 E7
Blinco La *DTCH/LGLY* SL3 .... 46 E3
Blind La *BNEND* SL8 .... 20 D2
Blomfield Dl *BNFD* RG42 .... 121 G7 ⊡
Bloomfield Dr *BRAK* RG12 .... 13 K1
Bloomfield Gdns *MDHD* SL6 .... 67 K1
Bloomfieldhatch La *THLE* RG7 .. 143 L6
Bloomsbury Wy *BLKW* GU17 .. 180 F3
Blossom Av *THLE* RG7 .... 114 B3
Blossom La *THLE* RG7 .... 114 B3
Blount Crs *BNFD* RG42 .... 12 B1
Bloxworth Cl *BRAK* RG12 ...... 150 C1 ⊡
Blue Ball La *EGH* TW20 .... 126 C3
Bluebell Dr *THLE* RG7 .... 142 C3
Bluebell Hl *BRAK* RG12 .... 122 B6
Bluebell Meadow *WWKG* RG41 .. 118 F3
Bluebell Ri *LTWR* GU18 .... 175 L6 ⊡
Bluebell Wy *NTHA* RG18 .... 138 A1
Bluecoats *NTHA* RG18 .... 138 A2
Blue Coat Wk *BRAK* RG12 ...... 150 A2
Bluethroat Cl *SHST* GU47 .... 173 H6 ⊡
Blumfield Crs *SL* SL1 .... 44 A6
Blundells Rd *TLHT* RG30 .... 87 H6
Blunden Dr *DTCH/LGLY* SL3 .... 72 E4
Blyth Av *STHA* RG19 .... 138 B4
Blythe La *IVER* SL0 .... 47 J7
Blythewood La *ASC* SL5 .... 123 G8
Blythwood Dr *FRIM* GU16 ...... 182 A4
Boames La *KSCL* RG20 .... 159 J1
Board La *KSCL* RG20 .... 134 C1
Boarlands Cl *SL* SL1 .... 44 C8 ⊡
Bobgreen Ct *WHIT* RG2 .... 116 F8 ⊡
Bobmore La *MLW* SL7 .... 19 H2
Bockhampton Rd *HUNG* RG17 .. 49 L4
Bockmer La *MLW* SL7 .... 17 L8
Bodens Ride *ASC* SL5 .... 151 J5
Bodin Gdns *NWBY* RG14 .... 136 D6
Bodmin Av *SL* SL1 .... 44 D6
Bodmin Cl *STHA* RG19 .... 137 M4
Bodmin Rd *WODY* RG5 .... 117 M1
Body Rd *READ* RG1 .... 8 E7
Bog La *ASC* SL5 .... 122 D8
   ASC SL5 .... 150 D1
   BRAK RG12 .... 150 D1
Boham's Rd *DID* OX11 .... 29 M3
Bolding House La
   CHOB/PIR GU24 .... 176 C8
Boldrewood *THLE* RG7 .... 142 C4 ⊡
Boleyn Cl *STA* TW18 .... 127 H3 ⊡
Bolingbroke Wy *STHA* RG19 ... 138 C3
Bolney La *HEN* RG9 .... 64 D1
Bolney Rd *HEN* RG9 .... 64 E2
Bolney Trevor Dr *HEN* RG9 ...... 64 D2
Bolton Av *WDSR* SL4 .... 97 G2
Bolton Crs *WDSR* SL4 .... 96 F2
Bolton Rd *WDSR* SL4 .... 96 F2
Boltons La *BNFD* RG42 .... 121 H5
Bolwell Cl *WAR/TWY* RG10 ...... 91 J2
Bomford Cl *NTHA* RG18 .... 81 J8 ⊡
Bond St *EGH* TW20 .... 125 L4
Bone La *NWBY* RG14 .... 15 H4
Bonemill La *KSCL* RG20 .... 136 A4
Bones La *HEN* RG9 .... 63 K3
Boot End *WHIT* RG2 .... 116 C6
Booth Dr *EWKG* RG40 .... 147 H5
   STA TW18 .... 128 A4
Borderside *SLN* SL2 .... 5 K3
   YTLY GU46 .... 171 K8
Bordon Cl *TADY* RG26 .... 164 D6
Borrowdale Cl *EGH* TW20 .... 126 E5 ⊡
Borrowdale Rd *WWKG* RG41 ... 118 C2
Boscawen Wy *STHA* RG19 ..... 138 D3 ⊡
Boscombe Cl *EGH* TW20 .... 126 F6 ⊡
Bosham Cl *EARL* RG6 .... 117 L6 ⊡
Boshers Gdns *EGH* TW20 .... 126 C4
Bosman Dr *BFOR* GU20 .... 151 L7
Bostock La *THLE* RG7 .... 113 K4
Boston Av *READ* RG1 .... 8 D9
   READ RG1 .... 116 C1
Boston Dr *BNEND* SL0 .... 20 E3
Boston Gv *SL* SL1 .... 4 A2
Boston Rd *HEN* RG9 .... 38 B6
Bosworth Gdns *WODY* RG5 ..... 118 B2
Botany Cl *STHA* RG19 .... 138 C3 ⊡
The Bothy *WAR/TWY* RG10 ...... 65 G4
Botisdone Cl *RAND* SP11 .... 178 A3
Botmoor Wy *KSCL* RG20 .... 52 B8
Bottisham Cl *EARL* RG6 .... 117 M6 ⊡
Bottle La *BNFD* RG42 .... 93 J8
   SL SL6 .... 66 C2
Bottom Harrow Rd *VW* GU25 .. 154 C3
Bottom La *GOR/PANG* RG8 ...... 34 D2
   THLE RG7 .... 114 B6
Bouldish Farm Rd *ASC* SL5 ..... 151 J2
Boulmer Rd *UX/CGN* UB8 .... 47 M4
Boulters Cl *SL* SL1 .... 70 D2
   MDHD SL6 .... 42 F5
Boulters Gdns *MDHD* SL6 .... 42 F5 ⊡
Boulters La *MDHD* SL6 .... 42 F5
Boulton Rd *WHIT* RG2 .... 116 E3
Boult St *READ* RG1 .... 9 J7
Boundaries Rd *FELT* TW13 ..... 101 M7
Boundary Cl *CALC* RG31 .... 86 F8 ⊡
Boundary La *CAV/SC* RG4 .... 88 B3
Boundary Rd *ASHF* TW15 ...... 127 M3
   MDHD SL6 .... 43 J6
   NWBY RG14 .... 15 H5
Bourn Cl *EARL* RG6 .... 117 M5 ⊡
Bourne Arch *NTHA* RG18 .... 137 L2
Bourne Cl *CHERT* KT16 .... 127 K8 ⊡
   CALC RG31 .... 114 C2
Bourne End Rd *MDHD* SL6 ...... 21 G6
Bourne Meadow *EGH* TW20 ... 154 E1
Bourne Rd *GOR/PANG* RG8 ..... 86 B1
   SL SL1 .... 4 B8
   STHA RG19 .... 137 L2
   VW GU25 .... 154 A2
Bourneside *VW* GU25 .... 153 K4
Bourne-stevens Cl *READ* RG1 .... 9 H7
Bourne V *HUNG* RG17 .... 131 M1

Bourton Cl *TLHT* RG30 ..... 87 J7
Bouverie Wy *DTCH/LGLY* SL3 ..... 72 B5
Boveney Cl *SL* SL1 ..... 70 D2
Boveney New Rd *WDSR* SL4 ..... 70 B4
Boveney Rd *WDSR* SL4 ..... 69 M4
Bovingdon Hts *MLW* SL7 ..... 18 E4
Bowden Cl *EBED/NFELT* TW14 ..... 101 H7
Bowden Rd *ASC* SL5 ..... 151 M2
Bower Wy *SL* SL1 ..... 44 B8
Bowes Rd *STA* TW18 ..... 127 H4
STHA RG19 ..... 138 A4
Bowfell Cl *CALC* RG31 ..... 86 F4
Bowland Dr *BRAK* RG12 ..... 150 B4
Bowling Ct *HEN* RG9 ..... 37 M3
Bowling Court Gn *FRIM* GU16 ..... 182 B7
Bowling Green La
GOR/PANG RG8 ..... 86 E1
Bowling Green Rd
CHOB/PIR GU24 ..... 177 H4
NTHA RG18 ..... 137 K1
Bowman Ct *CWTH* RG45 ..... 172 B2
Bowmans Cl *SL* SL1 ..... 43 L2
Bowmonts Rd *TADY* RG26 ..... 165 G6
Bowry Dr *STWL/WRAY* TW19 ..... 98 C5
Bowsley Ct *FELT* TW13 ..... 101 K8
Bowyer Crs *EWKG* RG40 ..... 11 J3
Bowyer Dr *SL* SL1 ..... 44 B8
Bowyer's La *BNFD* RG42 ..... 93 L8
Boxford Rdg *BRAK* RG12 ..... 13 H7
Boyd Ct *BNFD* RG42 ..... 12 F3
BNFD RG42 ..... 13 G3
Boyndon Rd *MDHD* SL6 ..... 2 D5
Boyn Hill Av *MDHD* SL6 ..... 2 D6
Boyn Hill Cl *MDHD* SL6 ..... 2 C6
Boyn Hill Rd *MDHD* SL6 ..... 2 B8
Boyn Valley Rd *MDHD* SL6 ..... 2 D7
Bracebridge *CBLY* GU15 ..... 181 K1
Bracken Bank *ASC* SL5 ..... 122 F6
Bracken Cl *CALC* RG31 ..... 86 F5
SUN TW16 ..... 129 J4
Brackendale Cl *FRIM* GU16 ..... 182 B3
Brackendale Rd *CBLY* GU15 ..... 182 A2
Brackendale Wy *EARL* RG6 ..... 117 K1
Brackenforde *DTCH/LGLY* SL3 ..... 71 M2
Bracken La *YTLY* GU46 ..... 171 K8
Bracken Rd *MDHD* SL6 ..... 67 M2
The Brackens *CWTH* RG45 ..... 148 D7
Bracken Wy *CHOB/PIR* GU24 ..... 177 J5
THLE RG7 ..... 142 D4
Brackenwood *CBLY* GU15 ..... 183 G1
SUN TW16 ..... 129 K6
Bracklesham Cl *FARN* GU14 ..... 181 K7
Bracknell Cl *CBLY* GU15 ..... 174 C5
Bracknell Rd *BAGS* GU19 ..... 151 G8
BNFD RG42 ..... 122 C2
CBLY GU15 ..... 174 D4
CWTH RG45 ..... 149 G8
CWTH RG45 ..... 149 H6
Brackstone Cl *CAV/SC* RG4 ..... 9 J1
Bradcutts La *MDHD* SL6 ..... 20 A5
Bradenham La *MLW* SL7 ..... 40 F1
Bradfields *BRAK* RG12 ..... 150 A2
Bradford Rd *SL* SL1 ..... 44 D7
Brading Wy *GOR/PANG* RG8 ..... 87 G1
Bradley Cl *HUNG* RG17 ..... 133 L5
Bradley Dr *EWKG* RG40 ..... 147 K5
Bradley-Moore Sq *NTHA* RG18 ..... 138 B1
Bradley Rd *SL* SL1 ..... 4 E5
Bradley's St *GOR/PANG* RG8 ..... 34 E2
Bradmore Wy *EARL* RG6 ..... 117 K6
Bradshaw Cl *WDSR* SL4 ..... 70 B8
Bradwell Rd *CALC* RG31 ..... 86 F3
Braemar Cl *FRIM* GU16 ..... 182 C5
Braemar Gdns *SL* SL1 ..... 70 D2
Braemore Cl *STHA* RG19 ..... 138 A5
Brainton Av *EBED/NFELT* TW14 ..... 101 L6
Bramber Ct *SL* SL1 ..... 70 D1
Bramber Ms *CAV/SC* RG4 ..... 89 H2
Bramble Bank *FRIM* GU16 ..... 182 D8
Bramble Crs *TLHT* RG30 ..... 87 H7
Brambledown *STA* TW18 ..... 127 L6
Bramble Dr *MDHD* SL6 ..... 67 K2
Bramblegate *CWTH* RG45 ..... 148 D8
The Brambles *CWTH* RG45 ..... 148 A8
NWBY RG14 ..... 136 B6
Bramblings *CAV/SC* RG4 ..... 62 B8
Bramcote *CBLY* GU15 ..... 182 F1
Bramley Av *SHPTN* TW17 ..... 129 H8
Bramley Cha *MDHD* SL6 ..... 67 M2
Bramley Cl *CHERT* KT16 ..... 155 L5
EARL RG6 ..... 117 K3
MDHD SL6 ..... 67 M3
STA TW18 ..... 127 M4
Bramley Crs *CAV/SC* RG4 ..... 62 B1
Bramley Gv *CWTH* RG45 ..... 172 A1
Bramley La *BLKW* GU17 ..... 180 E1
Bramley Rd *CBLY* GU15 ..... 181 L4
THLE RG7 ..... 165 L5
Bramling Av *YTLY* GU46 ..... 171 L8
Brammas Cl *SL* SL1 ..... 70 F3
Brampton Cha *HEN* RG9 ..... 64 D2
Brampton Ct *MDHD* SL6 ..... 3 M3
Bramshaw Rd *TLHT* RG30 ..... 87 K5
Bramshill Cl *WHIT* RG2 ..... 146 B6
Bramshot La *FARN* GU14 ..... 180 F8
Bramwell Cl *STHA* RG19 ..... 138 C4
Bran Cl *TLHT* RG30 ..... 87 H6
Brandon Av *WODY* RG5 ..... 90 D5
Brandon Cl *CBLY* GU15 ..... 183 G2
Brands Rd *DTCH/LGLY* SL3 ..... 72 E6
Branksome Cl *CBLY* GU15 ..... 174 B8
Branksome Hill Rd *SHST* GU47 ..... 173 H7
Branksome Park Rd *CBLY* GU15 ..... 174 B8
Brants Br *BRAK* RG12 ..... 122 B7
Brants Cl *WHIT* RG2 ..... 146 B4
Brassey Cl *EBED/NFELT* TW14 ..... 101 K7
Braunfels Wk *KSCL* RG20 ..... 14 A6
KSCL RG20 ..... 136 A4
NWBY RG14 ..... 14 A5
Braybank *MDHD* SL6 ..... 69 G2
Braybrooke Dr *WAR/TWY* RG10 ..... 91 J6
Braybrooke Gdns
WAR/TWY RG10 ..... 65 G5
Braybrooke Rd *BNFD* RG42 ..... 121 L5
WAR/TWY RG10 ..... 65 G5
Bray Cl *MDHD* SL6 ..... 68 F3
Bray Ct *MDHD* SL6 ..... 68 F4
Braye Cl *SHST* GU47 ..... 172 F5
Brayfield Rd *MDHD* SL6 ..... 68 F2
Brayford Rd *WHIT* RG2 ..... 116 F6
Bray Rd *MDHD* SL6 ..... 3 M8
MDHD SL6 ..... 68 E2
TLHT RG30 ..... 115 L2
Braywick Rd *MDHD* SL6 ..... 3 H9
MDHD SL6 ..... 68 D2
Braywood Av *EGH* TW20 ..... 126 C4
Braziers La *ASC* SL5 ..... 123 G3
GOR/PANG RG8 ..... 34 B1
Breachfield *KSCL* RG20 ..... 160 C7
Breadcroft La *MDHD* SL6 ..... 67 H3
Breadcroft Rd *MDHD* SL6 ..... 67 J3
Bream Cl *MLW* SL7 ..... 18 F6
Brean Wk *EARL* RG6 ..... 117 K4
Brecon Cl *FARN* GU14 ..... 181 G7
Brecon Rd *WODY* RG5 ..... 90 C6
Bredon Rd *WWKG* RG41 ..... 119 J5
Bredward Cl *SL* SL1 ..... 43 L4
The Breech *CBLY* GU15 ..... 173 H7
Breedons Hl *GOR/PANG* RG8 ..... 85 M1
Bremer Rd *STA* TW18 ..... 127 K1
Brendon Cl *TLHT* RG30 ..... 87 H5
Brent Cl *STHA* RG19 ..... 138 A4
Brent Gdns *WHIT* RG2 ..... 116 E3
Brentmoor Rd *CHOB/PIR* GU24 ..... 175 M8
Brent Rd *BNEND* SL8 ..... 20 D2
Brerewood *EARL* RG6 ..... 117 J4
Bret Harte Rd *FRIM* GU16 ..... 182 B5
Bretlands Rd *CHERT* KT16 ..... 155 H6
Brewery Common *THLE* RG7 ..... 142 E8
Briant's Av *CAV/SC* RG4 ..... 88 F4
Briants Piece *NTHA* RG18 ..... 81 L8
LTWR GU18 ..... 175 J7
Briar Av *LTWR* GU18 ..... 175 K6
Briar Cl *CAV/SC* RG4 ..... 88 D2
MDHD SL6 ..... 43 L7
Briar Dene *MDHD* SL6 ..... 41 M5
Briar Gln *MDHD* SL6 ..... 20 B8
Briarlea Rd *THLE* RG7 ..... 142 C8
Briars Cl *GOR/PANG* RG8 ..... 86 B1
The Briars *DTCH/LGLY* SL3 ..... 72 C5
STWL/WRAY TW19 ..... 99 K4
Briar Wy *SLN* SL2 ..... 44 E6
TADY RG26 ..... 164 F6
Briarwood Cl *FELT* TW13 ..... 129 H1
Briarwood Dr *EWKG* RG40 ..... 147 H8
Brickfield La *SL* SL1 ..... 43 K2
Bridge Av *MDHD* SL6 ..... 3 J5
MDHD SL6 ..... 42 B1
Bridge Cl *SL* SL1 ..... 44 C8
STA TW18 ..... 127 H2
Bridge End *CBLY* GU15 ..... 181 L2
Bridge Gdns *ASHF* TW15 ..... 128 F5
Bridge La *VW* GU25 ..... 154 B3
Bridgeman Dr *WDSR* SL4 ..... 6 D8
Bridgemead *FRIM* GU16 ..... 182 A6
Bridge Rd *ASC* SL5 ..... 152 A2
BAGS GU19 ..... 175 H2
CBLY GU15 ..... 181 L3
CHERT KT16 ..... 155 L4
MDHD SL6 ..... 3 K4
MDHD SL6 ..... 3 M4
UX/CGN UB8 ..... 47 M3
Bridges Cl *WWKG* RG41 ..... 10 A4
The Bridges *THLE* RG7 ..... 165 M1
Bridgestone Dr *BNEND* SL8 ..... 20 E3
Bridge St *DTCH/LGLY* SL3 ..... 73 G7
MDHD SL6 ..... 3 J4
NWBY RG14 ..... 14 E4
READ RG1 ..... 8 E1
READ RG1 ..... 8 F7
Bridge Vw *ASC* SL5 ..... 152 E4
Bridge Wk *YTLY* GU46 ..... 172 A7
TLHT RG30 ..... 87 M5
Bridgewater Cl *TLHT* RG30 ..... 87 M6
Bridgewater Ct *DTCH/LGLY* SL3 ..... 72 D5
Bridgewater Ter *WDSR* SL4 ..... 7 J5
Bridgewater Wy *WDSR* SL4 ..... 7 J7
Bridle Cl *MDHD* SL6 ..... 2 E1
SUN TW16 ..... 129 K8
Bridle Pth *GOR/PANG* RG8 ..... 34 B6
Bridlepath Wy
EBED/NFELT TW14 ..... 101 H6
Bridle Rd *GOR/PANG* RG8 ..... 60 B3
MDHD SL6 ..... 2 E1
MDHD SL6 ..... 42 B5
Bridlington Sp *SL* SL1 ..... 70 E3
Bridport Cl *EARL* RG6 ..... 118 A4
Bridport Wy *SLN* SL2 ..... 44 E5
Brierley Pl *CALC* RG31 ..... 86 F2
Briff La *THLE* RG7 ..... 110 E8
THLE RG7 ..... 111 G5
Brigham Rd *READ* RG1 ..... 8 F3
Brighton Rd *ADL/WDHM* KT15 ..... 155 M8
EARL RG6 ..... 89 K8
Brighton Sp *SLN* SL2 ..... 44 E5
Brightside Av *STA* TW18 ..... 127 M5
Brill Cl *CAV/SC* RG4 ..... 88 D2
MDHD SL6 ..... 68 A2
MLW SL7 ..... 18 F4
Brimblecombe Cl *WWKG* RG41 ..... 119 K5
THLE RG7 ..... 140 B5
Brimpton Rd *THLE* RG7 ..... 139 J7
THLE RG7 ..... 163 M4
TLHT RG30 ..... 115 L2
Brimshot La *CHOB/PIR* GU24 ..... 177 H4
Brinds Cl *CAV/SC* RG4 ..... 62 C1
Brinn's La *BLKW* GU17 ..... 180 F1
Brisbane Rd *TLHT* RG30 ..... 87 L6
Bristol Cl *STWL/WRAY* TW19 ..... 100 B5
Bristol Wy *SL* SL1 ..... 5 G6
Bristow Rd *CBLY* GU15 ..... 181 L3
Britannia Wy
STWL/WRAY TW19 ..... 100 A6
Britten Rd *WHIT* RG2 ..... 116 E2
Britwell Rd *SL* SL1 ..... 43 M4
Brixham Rd *WHIT* RG2 ..... 116 E4
Broadacre *STA* TW18 ..... 127 K3
Broadford La *CHOB/PIR* GU24 ..... 177 H7
Broadhalfpenny La *TADY* RG26 ..... 164 F5
Broad Hinton *WAR/TWY* RG10 ..... 91 J3
Broadlands *FRIM* GU16 ..... 182 C6
Broadlands Cl *CALC* RG31 ..... 86 F1
Broadlands Dr *ASC* SL5 ..... 151 M4
Broad La *BRAK* RG12 ..... 13 K7
FLKWH HP10 ..... 21 J2
NTHA RG18 ..... 110 C6
THLE RG7 ..... 110 E8
Broadley Gn *BFOR* GU20 ..... 176 A3
Broadmark Rd *SLN* SL2 ..... 5 L5
Broadmeadow End *NTHA* RG18 ..... 138 C3
Broadmoor La *CAV/SC* RG4 ..... 90 B2
WAR/TWY RG10 ..... 66 E8
Broad Oak *SLN* SL2 ..... 44 F5
SUN TW16 ..... 129 J4
Broadoak *TADY* RG26 ..... 165 G6
Broad Oak Ct *SLN* SL2 ..... 44 F5
Broad Platts *DTCH/LGLY* SL3 ..... 72 A3
Broadrick Heath *BNFD* RG42 ..... 13 M1
Broad St *CHOB/PIR* GU24 ..... 176 A7
EWKG RG40 ..... 11 G6
KSCL RG20 ..... 29 H7
READ RG1 ..... 8 F6
Broad Wk *FRIM* GU16 ..... 182 B4
Broadwater Cl
STWL/WRAY TW19 ..... 98 C6
Broadwater La *WAR/TWY* RG10 ..... 91 H5
Broadwater Pk *MDHD* SL6 ..... 69 H5
Broadwater Rd *WAR/TWY* RG10 ..... 91 H3
Broad Wy *THLE* RG7 ..... 168 A3
Broadway *MDHD* SL6 ..... 3 H5
STHA RG19 ..... 138 A3
WDSR SL4 ..... 95 L7
Broadway Rd *CHOB/PIR* GU24 ..... 176 A4
The Broadway *HUNG* RG17 ..... 49 L3
SHST GU47 ..... 172 E7
STA TW18 ..... 127 M8
Brocas Rd *THLE* RG7 ..... 142 C5
Brocas St *WDSR* SL4 ..... 7 J4
Brockenhurst Dr *YTLY* GU46 ..... 180 A1
Brockenhurst Rd *ASC* SL5 ..... 151 L2
BRAK RG12 ..... 122 C8
Brock Gdns *TLHT* RG30 ..... 87 M6
Brock La *MDHD* SL6 ..... 3 H5
Brockley Cl *TLHT* RG30 ..... 87 K6
Brocks La *NTHA* RG18 ..... 110 E1
Brocks Wy *HEN* RG9 ..... 64 D3
Brock Wy *VW* GU25 ..... 153 M2
Broken Furlong *WDSR* SL4 ..... 6 F1
Broken Wy *KSCL* RG20 ..... 160 E4
Brompton Cl *EARL* RG6 ..... 118 A5
Brompton Dr *MDHD* SL6 ..... 41 M5
Bromycroft Rd *SLN* SL2 ..... 44 D4
Brookbank *FLKWH* HP10 ..... 20 F3
FLKWH HP10 ..... 21 G3
Brook Cl *SHST* GU47 ..... 173 H5
STWL/WRAY TW19 ..... 100 C6
WWKG RG41 ..... 10 B2
Brook Crs *SL* SL1 ..... 44 B7
Brookdene Cl *MDHD* SL6 ..... 42 C4
Brook Dr *BRAK* RG12 ..... 150 B1
SUN TW16 ..... 129 H4
Brookers Cnr *CWTH* RG45 ..... 172 F1
Brooker's Hl *WHIT* RG2 ..... 117 G8
Brookers Rw *CWTH* RG45 ..... 148 F8
Brookfield Rd *FLKWH* HP10 ..... 21 G3
Brook Gn *TADY* RG26 ..... 165 G6
Brookhouse Dr *BNEND* SL8 ..... 20 F3
Brooklands Cl *SUN* TW16 ..... 129 H6
Brook La *CHOB/PIR* GU24 ..... 177 G6
WAR/TWY RG10 ..... 92 C4
Brookleys *CHOB/PIR* GU24 ..... 177 J5
Brooklyn Dr *CAV/SC* RG4 ..... 62 E7
The Brookmill *READ* RG1 ..... 116 B2
Brook Pth *SL* SL1 ..... 44 C8
Brook Rd *BAGS* GU19 ..... 175 H4
CBLY GU15 ..... 181 L2
Brooksby Cl *BLKW* GU17 ..... 180 E1
Brooksby Rd *CALC* RG31 ..... 87 G4
Brookside *CHERT* KT16 ..... 155 H4
DTCH/LGLY SL3 ..... 72 F7
SHST GU47 ..... 172 F7
WWKG RG41 ..... 10 B4
Brookside Av *ASHF* TW15 ..... 127 M3
STWL/WRAY TW19 ..... 98 A2
Brookside Cl *EARL* RG6 ..... 118 A3
FELT TW13 ..... 129 K1
Brooks Rd *NTHA* RG18 ..... 138 B2
Brook St *WAR/TWY* RG10 ..... 91 G2
WDSR SL4 ..... 7 K8
Brook St West *READ* RG1 ..... 8 E8
Brookway *NWBY* RG14 ..... 137 H3
Broom Acres *SHST* GU47 ..... 172 E6
Broom Cl *BLKW* GU17 ..... 181 H2
CALC RG31 ..... 114 F1
Broome Cl *YTLY* GU46 ..... 171 M7
Broome Ct *BRAK* RG12 ..... 13 G7
Broom Fld *LTWR* GU18 ..... 175 K7
Broomfield *SUN* TW16 ..... 129 K6
Broomfield Dr *ASC* SL5 ..... 152 E3
Broomfield Pk *ASC* SL5 ..... 152 E4
Broomfield Rd *TLHT* RG30 ..... 87 J6
Broom Gv *WWKG* RG41 ..... 147 G2
Broomhall La *ASC* SL5 ..... 152 C3
Broom Hl *MDHD* SL6 ..... 20 B8
SLN SL2 ..... 45 K1
Broom La *CHOB/PIR* GU24 ..... 177 H4
Broomsquires Rd *BAGS* GU19 ..... 175 H4
Broughton Cl *TLHT* RG30 ..... 87 M5
Broughton Ms *FRIM* GU16 ..... 182 C5
Browells La *FELT* TW13 ..... 101 M8
Browning Cl *CBLY* GU15 ..... 182 F2
NTHA RG18 ..... 137 M2
Brownlow Dr *BNFD* RG42 ..... 121 M5
Brownlow Rd *READ* RG1 ..... 8 B7
Brownrigg Crs *BRAK* RG12 ..... 122 B6
Brownrigg Rd *ASHF* TW15 ..... 128 D2
Brownsfield Rd *NTHA* RG18 ..... 137 M3
Brown's La *MARL* SN8 ..... 130 A8
Bruan Rd *NWBY* RG14 ..... 136 C6
Bruce Cl *SL* SL1 ..... 70 D1
Bruce Rd *WODY* RG5 ..... 90 A7
Brudenell *WDSR* SL4 ..... 96 C2
Brummell Rd *NWBY* RG14 ..... 14 A1
NWBY RG14 ..... 136 B1
Brunel Cl *MDHD* SL6 ..... 2 E8
Brunel Dr *WODY* RG5 ..... 90 C5
Brunel Rd *MDHD* SL6 ..... 2 D8
THLE RG7 ..... 114 B4
TLHT RG30 ..... 115 K2
Brunel Wy *SL* SL1 ..... 5 G7
Brunswick *BRAK* RG12 ..... 149 K4
Brunswick Hl *READ* RG1 ..... 8 A7
Brunswick Rd *FRIM* GU16 ..... 182 F8
FRIM GU16 ..... 183 G8
Brunswick St *READ* RG1 ..... 8 B8
Bruton Wy *BRAK* RG12 ..... 150 B4
Bryan Cl *SUN* TW16 ..... 129 K5
Bryant Av *SLN* SL2 ..... 45 G6
Bryant Pl *GOR/PANG* RG8 ..... 86 E1
Brybur Cl *WHIT* RG2 ..... 117 G6
Bryer Pl *WDSR* SL4 ..... 96 A2
Bryony Wy *SUN* TW16 ..... 129 K4
Buccaneer Cl *WODY* RG5 ..... 90 E6
Buccleuch Rd *DTCH/LGLY* SL3 ..... 71 K7
Buchanan Dr *EWKG* RG40 ..... 147 H7
Buchanan Sq *STHA* RG19 ..... 138 B5
Buchan Cl *UX/CGN* UB8 ..... 47 M4
The Buchan *CBLY* GU15 ..... 174 D6
Buckden Cl *WODY* RG5 ..... 90 D8
Buckham Hl *HUNG* RG17 ..... 51 M8
Buckhurst Gv *EWKG* RG40 ..... 148 C1
Buckhurst Hl *BRAK* RG12 ..... 150 C1
Buckhurst La *ASC* SL5 ..... 124 D8
Buckhurst Rd *ASC* SL5 ..... 124 C7
FRIM GU16 ..... 182 C8
Buckhurst Wy *EARL* RG6 ..... 117 K3
Buckingham Av
EBED/NFELT TW14 ..... 101 L5
SL SL1 ..... 4 A3
SL SL1 ..... 44 D7
Buckingham Av East *SL* SL1 ..... 4 A3
Buckingham Dr *CAV/SC* RG4 ..... 88 E1
Buckingham Gdns *SL* SL1 ..... 5 G9
Buckingham Ga *MLW* SL7 ..... 18 A7
Buckingham Rd *NWBY* RG14 ..... 14 B7
Buckland Av *DTCH/LGLY* SL3 ..... 71 L3
Buckland Cl *FARN* GU14 ..... 181 M7
Buckland Crs *WDSR* SL4 ..... 6 B6
Buckland Rd *WHIT* RG2 ..... 116 E3
Bucklebury *BRAK* RG12 ..... 149 K4
Bucklebury Cl *MDHD* SL6 ..... 68 F6
Buckle La *BNFD* RG42 ..... 93 L8
Bucknell Av *GOR/PANG* RG8 ..... 86 B1
Bucknell Cl *CALC* RG31 ..... 115 J2
Buck Side *READ* RG1 ..... 8 E1
Buckthorn Cl *EWKG* RG40 ..... 11 L3
Budebury Rd *STA* TW18 ..... 127 J3
Budge's Gdns *EWKG* RG40 ..... 11 K3
Budge's Rd *EWKG* RG40 ..... 11 K3
Budham Wy *BRAK* RG12 ..... 149 L3
Buffins *MDHD* SL6 ..... 43 H4
Bugkingham Wy *FRIM* GU16 ..... 182 C6
Bulkeley Av *WDSR* SL4 ..... 96 E2
Bulkeley Cl *EGH* TW20 ..... 125 M3
Bullbrook Dr *BRAK* RG12 ..... 122 B6
Bullfinch Cl *SHST* GU47 ..... 173 H6
Bull La *BRAK* RG12 ..... 13 H3
THLE RG7 ..... 168 D3
The Bull Meadow
GOR/PANG RG8 ..... 32 D8
Bullrush Gv *UX/CGN* UB8 ..... 47 M5
Bulmershe Ct *EARL* RG6 ..... 89 L8
READ RG1 ..... 89 H8
Bulmershe Rd *READ* RG1 ..... 89 J8
Bulpit La *HUNG* RG17 ..... 132 A2
Bulpits Hl *RAND* SP11 ..... 178 B8
Bunby Rd *SLN* SL2 ..... 45 J1
Bunces Cl *WDSR* SL4 ..... 6 F1
Bunce's La *GOR/PANG* RG8 ..... 60 D4
THLE RG7 ..... 142 D4
Bundy's Wy *STA* TW18 ..... 127 L8
Bungler's Hl *THLE* RG7 ..... 145 L8
Bunkers Hl *NWBY* RG14 ..... 159 M1
Bunten Meade *SL* SL1 ..... 70 E1
Burbage Gn *BRAK* RG12 ..... 150 C2
Burbidge Cl *CALC* RG31 ..... 115 J3
Burchell Rd *NWBY* RG14 ..... 136 B1
Burchett Coppice
EWKG RG40 ..... 147 J6
Burchetts Green La *MDHD* SL6 ..... 40 F8
Burchett's Green Rd *MDHD* SL6 ..... 66 D1
Burcombe Wy *CAV/SC* RG4 ..... 88 E2
Burcot Gdns *MDHD* SL6 ..... 42 B3
Burdens Heath *NTHA* RG18 ..... 110 D7
Burdock Cl *LTWR* GU18 ..... 175 L6
THLE RG7 ..... 142 E4
Burfield Rd *WDSR* SL4 ..... 97 K6
Burford Cl *MLW* SL7 ..... 18 F1
Burford Ct *EWKG* RG40 ..... 11 L8
Burford Gdns *SL* SL1 ..... 43 M6
Burford Rd *CBLY* GU15 ..... 181 L2
Burford's *HUNG* RG17 ..... 50 F8
Burges Rd *STA* TW18 ..... 127 K4
Burgess Cl *WODY* RG5 ..... 118 A1
Burgess La *KSCL* RG20 ..... 157 M1
Burgett Rd *SL* SL1 ..... 70 E3
Burghead Cl *SHST* GU47 ..... 173 G7
Burghfield Rd *TLHT* RG30 ..... 115 K2
Burgoyne Rd *CBLY* GU15 ..... 174 D8
SUN TW16 ..... 129 J4
Burleigh Gdns *ASHF* TW15 ..... 128 F3
Burleigh La *ASC* SL5 ..... 123 H6
Burleigh Ms *CAV/SC* RG4 ..... 62 F8
Burleigh Rd *ADL/WDHM* KT15 ..... 155 L8
ASC SL5 ..... 123 H7
FRIM GU16 ..... 182 A6
Burley Wy *BLKW* GU17 ..... 172 F8
Burlingham Cl *WHIT* RG2 ..... 116 F8
The Burlings *ASC* SL5 ..... 123 H7
Burlington Av *SL* SL1 ..... 4 E8
Burlington Cl
EBED/NFELT TW14 ..... 101 G6
Burlington Ct *BLKW* GU17 ..... 180 F3
Burlington Rd *SL* SL1 ..... 4 E8
SL SL1 ..... 43 L6
Burlsdon Wy *BRAK* RG12 ..... 122 B6
Burma Rd *CHOB/PIR* GU24 ..... 153 J6
Burne-jones Dr *SHST* GU47 ..... 173 G8
Burnet Cl *CHOB/PIR* GU24 ..... 176 B8
Burnetts Rd *WDSR* SL4 ..... 70 B8
Burney Bit *TADY* RG26 ..... 165 H6
Burnham Cl *BNEND* SL8 ..... 20 D3
WDSR SL4 ..... 96 A1
Burnham Gv *BNFD* RG42 ..... 13 J1
SL SL1 ..... 44 A6
Burnham La *SL* SL1 ..... 44 B7
Burnham Ri *CAV/SC* RG4 ..... 62 F7
Burnham Rd *TADY* RG26 ..... 164 C4
Burniston Cl *EARL* RG6 ..... 118 B4
Burnley Cl *TADY* RG26 ..... 164 E7
Burn Moor Cha *BRAK* RG12 ..... 150 B4
Burnmoor Meadow
EWKG RG40 ..... 171 H4
Burnsall Cl *FARN* GU14 ..... 181 L8
Burns Av *EBED/NFELT* TW14 ..... 101 K5
Burns Cl *FARN* GU14 ..... 181 J8
WODY RG5 ..... 118 B2
Burnthouse Br *TLHT* RG30 ..... 143 K1
Burnthouse Gdns
BNFD RG42 ..... 122 B5
Burnthouse La *TLHT* RG30 ..... 115 L7
Burnt Oak *EWKG* RG40 ..... 147 J6
MDHD SL6 ..... 20 C7
Burnt Pollard La
CHOB/PIR GU24 ..... 176 B5
Burrcroft Rd *TLHT* RG30 ..... 115 K1
Burrell Rd *FRIM* GU16 ..... 181 M6
KSCL RG20 ..... 56 B2
Burr Hill La *CHOB/PIR* GU24 ..... 177 H4
Burroughs Crs *BNEND* SL8 ..... 20 D2
Burroway Rd *DTCH/LGLY* SL3 ..... 72 E3
Burrow Hill Gn *CHOB/PIR* GU24 ..... 177 G4
Burrows Hill Cl
STWL/WRAY TW19 ..... 99 L3
Burton Cl *WAR/TWY* RG10 ..... 91 H4
Burtons Hl *HUNG* RG17 ..... 133 L4
Burton Wy *WDSR* SL4 ..... 96 B2
Burway Crs *CHERT* KT16 ..... 155 K1
Burwell Cl *EARL* RG6 ..... 117 M5
Bury's Bank Rd *STHA* RG19 ..... 137 G7
STHA RG19 ..... 138 B6
Busgrove La *GOR/PANG* RG8 ..... 35 J3
Butchers La *MDHD* SL6 ..... 66 F5
Bute St *TLHT* RG30 ..... 115 L1
Butler Rd *BAGS* GU19 ..... 175 J4
CWTH RG45 ..... 148 E8
Butlers Cl *WDSR* SL4 ..... 96 A1
Butlers Orch *CAV/SC* RG4 ..... 62 A3
Butlers Pond *GOR/PANG* RG8 ..... 60 A4
Butson Cl *NWBY* RG14 ..... 14 A4
Buttenshaw Av *WHIT* RG2 ..... 146 C6
Buttenshaw Cl *WHIT* RG2 ..... 146 D6
Buttercup Cl *EWKG* RG40 ..... 120 C8
Buttercup Pl *NTHA* RG18 ..... 138 A2
Buttercup Sq
STWL/WRAY TW19 ..... 100 A7
Butterfield *CBLY* GU15 ..... 181 L2
FLKWH HP10 ..... 21 G2
Butter Market *READ* RG1 ..... 9 G6
Buttermere Av *SL* SL1 ..... 43 M6
Buttermere Cl
EBED/NFELT TW14 ..... 101 J7
Buttermere Dr *CBLY* GU15 ..... 183 G2
Buttermere Gdns *BRAK* RG12 ..... 13 K6
Buttermere Wy *EGH* TW20 ..... 126 E5
Buttersteep Ri *ASC* SL5 ..... 150 F5
Butts Hill Rd *WODY* RG5 ..... 90 B5
The Butts *THLE* RG7 ..... 165 L6
Buxton Av *CAV/SC* RG4 ..... 88 C2
Buxton Rd *ASHF* TW15 ..... 128 A3
Bybend Cl *SLN* SL2 ..... 44 E2
Byefield Rd *TLHT* RG30 ..... 115 K2
Byes La *THLE* RG7 ..... 165 L7
Byland Dr *MDHD* SL6 ..... 68 E5
Byreton Cl *EARL* RG6 ..... 117 L4
Byron Av *FRIM* GU16 ..... 182 E3
HSLWW TW4 ..... 101 L1
Byron Cl *MLW* SL7 ..... 19 J3
NWBY RG14 ..... 136 C7
Byron Dr *CWTH* RG45 ..... 172 E3
Byron Rd *EARL* RG6 ..... 89 K7
WAR/TWY RG10 ..... 91 H2
Bythorn Cl *EARL* RG6 ..... 118 B4
Byward Av *EBED/NFELT* TW14 ..... 101 M5
Byways *SL* SL1 ..... 43 K6
Bywood *BRAK* RG12 ..... 149 K4
Byworth Cl *WHIT* RG2 ..... 116 E6

C

Cabbell Pl *ADL/WDHM* KT15 ..... 155 M8
Cabin Moss *BRAK* RG12 ..... 150 B4
Cabrera Av *VW* GU25 ..... 154 A2
Cabrera Cl *VW* GU25 ..... 153 M3
Cadbury Cl *SUN* TW16 ..... 129 H5
Cadbury Rd *SUN* TW16 ..... 129 H5
Caddy Cl *EGH* TW20 ..... 126 D3
Cadogan Cl *CAV/SC* RG4 ..... 89 H2
MDHD SL6 ..... 68 D6
TLHT RG30 ..... 87 H7
Cadwell Dr *MDHD* SL6 ..... 68 A3
Caernarvon *FRIM* GU16 ..... 182 C6
Caesar's Camp Rd *CBLY* GU15 ..... 174 D6
Caesar's Cl *CBLY* GU15 ..... 174 D6
Caesars Ga *BNFD* RG42 ..... 122 B5
Cain Rd *BNFD* RG42 ..... 121 G7
BRAK RG12 ..... 12 B4
Cain's La *EBED/NFELT* TW14 ..... 101 G4
Cairn Cl *FRIM* GU16 ..... 182 E3
Cairngorm Pl *FARN* GU14 ..... 181 H7
Cairngorm Rd *STHA* RG19 ..... 138 A4
Caistor Cl *CALC* RG31 ..... 114 E2
Calard Dr *NTHA* RG18 ..... 137 K1
Calbourne Dr *CALC* RG31 ..... 115 G2
Calbroke Rd *SLN* SL2 ..... 44 C4
Calcot Place Dr *CALC* RG31 ..... 115 H2
Calcott Pk *YTLY* GU46 ..... 171 M8
Caldbeck Dr *WODY* RG5 ..... 90 C8
Calder Cl *MDHD* SL6 ..... 2 E1
TLHT RG30 ..... 87 J6
Calder Ct *DTCH/LGLY* SL3 ..... 72 C5
MDHD SL6 ..... 2 D1
Calder Wy *DTCH/LGLY* SL3 ..... 99 H2
Caldwell Rd *BFOR* GU20 ..... 176 A1
Caledonia Rd *STWL/WRAY* TW19 ..... 100 B7
Caleta Cl *CAV/SC* RG4 ..... 89 G4
Calfridus Wy *BRAK* RG12 ..... 122 B8
Callington Rd *WHIT* RG2 ..... 116 E5
Callin's La *WAR/TWY* RG10 ..... 92 E3
Callis Farm Cl *STWL/WRAY* TW19 ..... 100 B5
Callow Hl *VW* GU25 ..... 125 M7
Calshot Pl *CALC* RG31 ..... 115 G2
Calshot Rd *HTHAIR* TW6 ..... 100 E1
Calshot Wy *FRIM* GU16 ..... 182 D7
HTHAIR TW6 ..... 100 D1
Calvin Cl *CBLY* GU15 ..... 182 E2
Camberley Rd *HTHAIR* TW6 ..... 100 D2

Camborne Cl *HTHAIR* TW6 .... 100 D2
Cambria Ct *EBED/NFELT* TW14 .. 101 L6 🖪
Cambria Gdns *STWL/WRAY* TW19.. 100 B6
Cambrian Cl *CBLY* GU15 .... 181 L1
Cambrian Rd *FARN* GU14 .... 181 G7
Cambrian Wy *CALC* RG31 ...... 115 G2
 EWKG RG40 .... 147 K6
 SL SL1 .... 43 L3
Cambridge Av *SL* SL1 .... 44 D7
Cambridge Rd *ASHF* TW15 ...... 128 F5
 CWTH RG45 .... 172 F2
 MLW SL7 .... 19 G4
 SHST GU47 .... 173 H5
Cambridgeshire Cl *BNFD* RG42.... 122 C5
 WWKG RG41 .... 119 H8 🖪
Cambridge St *READ* RG1 .... 8 B5
Camden Av *FELT* TW13.......... 101 M8
 CALC RG31 .... 114 E2 🖪
Camden Pl *BNEND* SL8.......... 20 D3
Camden Rd *MDHD* SL6 .... 42 A5
Camelford Cl *WHIT* RG2 .... 116 E5
Camellia Ct *CHOB/PIR* GU24 .... 176 C8
Camellia Wy *WWKG* RG41 ...... 119 G7 🖪
Camilla Cl *SUN* TW16 .... 129 J4 🖪
Camley Gdns *MDHD* SL6 .... 41 K6
Camley Park Dr *MDHD* SL6 .... 41 J6
Campbell Cl *YTLY* GU46 .... 172 C8
Campbell Pl *FRIM* GU16 .... 182 C3
Campbell Rd *WODY* RG5 .... 118 A1
Camperdown *MDHD* SL6.......... 3 M1
Campion Cl *BLKW* GU17 .... 181 J3 🖪
Campion Wy *EWKG* RG40 .... 11 L3
Camp Rd *THLE* RG7.......... 141 M3
Camrose Av *FELT* TW13 .... 129 L2
Canada Rd *FRIM* GU16 .... 183 G6
 SL SL1 .... 5 L8
Canal View Rd *NWBY* RG14 ...... 15 M4
Canal Wk *HUNG* RG17 .... 104 A8
Canal Wy *READ* RG1 .... 9 L6
Canal Whf *DTCH/LGLY* SL3........ 72 D2
Canberra Cl *HTWY* RG27 .... 171 K7
Candleford Cl *BRAK* RG12 .... 13 K1
Candover Cl *TADY* RG26 ...... 164 E7 🖪
Canford Ct *ADL/WDHM* KT15 .... 155 L6
Canhurst La *WAR/TWY* RG10...... 66 A3
Cannock Cl *MDHD* SL6 .... 3 L7
Cannock Wy *EARL* RG6 .... 117M5
Cannon Cl *SHST* GU47 .... 173 J6
Cannon Court Rd *MDHD* SL6 ...... 42 A3
Cannon Crs *CHOB/PIR* GU24 .... 177 H6
Cannondown Rd *MDHD* SL6 ...... 42 B1
Cannon Hl *BRAK* RG12 .... 149M3
Cannon Hill Cl *MDHD* SL6 ...... 68 F4
Cannon La *MDHD* SL6 .... 67 J3
Cannon St *READ* RG1 .... 8 B5
Canon Hill Dr *MDHD* SL6 .... 68 E3
Canon Hill Wy *MDHD* SL6 .... 68 E4
Canopus Wy *STWL/WRAY* TW19.. 100 B6
Cansfield End *NWBY* RG14 ...... 14 D3
Canterbury Av *SLN* SL2 .... 44 F5
Canterbury Rd *WHIT* RG2 .... 116 E5
Cantley Crs *WWKG* RG41 .... 10 D2
Capper Rd *CBLY* GU15 .... 173 K7
Captains Gorse *GOR/PANG* RG8 .. 58 C8
Caraway Rd *EARL* RG6 .... 117 K5
Carbery La *ASC* SL5 .... 123 L8
Carbinswood La *THLE* RG7 ...... 140 A2
Cardiff Rd *READ* RG1 .... 8 D3
Cardigan Cl *SL* SL1 .... 44 C8
Cardigan Rd *READ* RG1 .... 89 H8
Cardinal Cl *READ* RG1........ 9 G1
Cardinal Rd *FELT* TW13 .... 101 L7
Cardinals Wk *MDHD* SL6 .... 43M7
 SUN TW16 .... 129 H4 🖪
Cardwell Crs *ASC* SL5 .... 151M2
Carew Cl *CALC* RG31 .... 86 E2 🖪
Carew Rd *ASHF* TW15.......... 128 F4
Carey Cl *WDSR* SL4 .... 96 E2
Carey Rd *EWKG* RG40 .... 11 G8
Carey St *READ* RG1 .... 8 D7
Carisbrooke *FRIM* GU16.......... 182 C6
Carisbrooke Cl *CAV/SC* RG4 .... 62 F8 🖪
 MDHD SL6 .... 2 A8
Carland Cl *EARL* RG6 .... 117 K5
Carlile Gdns *WAR/TWY* RG10...... 65 G7
Carling Rd *CAV/SC* RG4 .... 36 B8
Carlinwark Dr *CBLY* GU15 ...... 174 C7
Carlisle Rd *CALC* RG31 .... 87 H3
 SL SL1 .... 4 C4
Carlton Av *EBED/NFELT* TW14 ...... 101M5
Carlton Cl *FRIM* GU16 .... 182 E3 🖪
 WODY RG5 .... 90 B8
Carlton Rd *CAV/SC* RG4 .... 88 A1
 SLN SL2 .... 5M5
 SUN TW16 .... 129 J5
Carlyle Rd *STA* TW18........ 127 J5
Carmarthen Ct *FARN* GU14 ...... 181 J7
Carmarthen Rd *SL* SL1 .... 4 E5
Carnarvon Rd *READ* RG1 .... 89 H7
Carnation Cl *EWKG* RG40 ...... 148 E6
Carnation Dr *BNFD* RG42.......... 122 D4
Carnegie Rd *NWBY* RG14.......... 14 F5
Carnoustie *BRAK* RG12.......... 149 H4
Carolina Pl *EWKG* RG40 .... 147 H7
Caroline Ct *ASHF* TW15 .... 128 E4
Caroline Dr *WWKG* RG41 .... 10 C4
Caroline St *READ* RG1 .... 8 D5
Caroline Wy *FRIM* GU16.......... 182 C5
Carrick Gdns *WODY* RG5 .... 90 A8
Carrick La *YTLY* GU46 .... 172 B8
Carrington Crs *TADY* RG26 ...... 164 E6
Carrington Rd *SL* SL1 .... 4 F4
Carroll Crs *ASC* SL5 .... 151 J1
Carron Cl *TLHT* RG30 .... 87 K7
Carsdale Cl *READ* RG1 .... 116 C1
Carshalton Rd *CBLY* GU15 ...... 174 D5
Carshalton Wy *EARL* RG6 ...... 117M4
Carston Gv *CALC* RG31 .... 115 J2
Carter Cl *WDSR* SL4 .... 6 C8
Carter's Hl *EWKG* RG40 .... 120 C2
Carters Ri *CALC* RG31 .... 115 H3
Cartmel Dr *WODY* RG5 .... 90 A8
Cary Cl *NWBY* RG14 .... 136 A4
Casey Ct *THLE* RG7.......... 112 A3
Cassia Dr *EARL* RG6 .... 117 J5
Cassiobury Av *EBED/NFELT* TW14 101 J6
Castle Av *DTCH/LGLY* SL3........ 71 K6

Castle Cl *CBLY* GU15 .... 182 C2
Castle Ct *MDHD* SL6 .... 2 D4
Castlecraig Ct *SHST* GU47 ...... 173 G7 🖪
Castle Crs *READ* RG1 .... 8 D8
Castle Dr *MDHD* SL6 .... 2 D4
Castle End Rd *WAR/TWY* RG10.... 65 J8
Castle Gv Rd *CHOB/PIR* GU24 .. 177 H7
Castle Grove Rd *CHOB/PIR* GU24 177 H7
 READ RG1 .... 8 D8
 THLE RG7 .... 145M7
 WDSR SL4 .... 7 K6
Castle Hill Rd *EGH* TW20 .... 125 L2
Castle Hill Ter *MDHD* SL6 .... 2 E5
Castle La *NWBY* RG14.......... 108 B8
Castle Ms *MDHD* SL6 .... 2 E5
Castle Rd *CBLY* GU15 .... 182 B2
 MARL SN8 .... 130 A8
Castle St *READ* RG1 .... 8 E7
 SL SL1 .... 71 J3
Castleview Rd *DTCH/LGLY* SL3 .... 71 M4
Castle Wy *FELT* TW13 .... 129 M2
Castor Ct *YTLY* GU46 .... 171 L7
Caswall Cl *BNFD* RG42 .... 120 F4 🖪
Caswall Ride *YTLY* GU46 ...... 180 C1 🖪
Caswell Cl *FARN* GU14 .... 181 J8
Catalina Cl *WODY* RG5 .... 90 E7
Catalina Rd *HTHAIR* TW6 ...... 100 D2
Catcliffe Wy *EARL* RG6 .... 117 J6
Catena Ri *LTWR* GU18.......... 175 K5
Catherine Dr *SUN* TW16 .... 129 J5
Catherine Rd *NWBY* RG14........ 14 E6
Catherine St *TLHT* RG30.......... 88 A6
Catmore Rd *KSCL* RG20 .... 27M7
 KSCL RG20 .... 28 B6
Caunter Rd *NWBY* RG14 ...... 136 A2 🖪
Causeway *EBED/NFELT* TW14...... 101 L3
The Causeway *CAV/SC* RG4...... 9 L2
 HTWY RG27 .... 168 F7
 MDHD SL6 .... 68 F2
 MLW SL7 .... 19 H5 🖪
 STA TW18 .... 126 F2
 STA TW18 .... 127 G2
Causmans Wy *CALC* RG31 ...... 86 F5
Cavalier Cl *NWBY* RG14 .... 136 F1
 THLE RG7 .... 114 A3
Cavalry Crs *WDSR* SL4 .... 96 E2
Cavendish Cl *MDHD* SL6 .... 43 K7
 SUN TW16 .... 129 J4 🖪
Cavendish Ct *BLKW* GU17 ...... 181 G3
 NWBY RG14 .... 137 H1
 SUN TW16 .... 129 J4
Cavendish Gdns *WWKG* RG41.... 118 D3
Cavendish Meads *ASC* SL5 ...... 152 A3
Cavendish Rd *CAV/SC* RG4 ...... 62 F8
 SUN TW16 .... 129 J4
Caversham Br *READ* RG1.......... 8 D1
Caversham Park Dr *CAV/SC* RG4 .. 63 G8
Caversham Park Rd *CAV/SC* RG4 .. 63 G8
 READ RG1 .... 8 E5
Caversham Rd *READ* RG1 .... 8 E5
Caves Farm Cl *SHST* GU47 ...... 172 D6
Cawcott Dr *WDSR* SL4 .... 70 B8
Cawsam Gdns *CAV/SC* RG4 ...... 88 F2
Caxton Cl *TLHT* RG30 .... 87M5
Caxton Dr *UX/CGN* UB8 .... 47 M3 🖪
Cecil Cl *ASHF* TW15 .... 128 E5
Cecil Rd *ASHF* TW15 .... 128 F5
 IVER SL0 .... 47 H7
 SLN SL2 .... 44 C5
Cedar Av *BLKW* GU17 .... 181 G1
Cedar Cha *MDHD* SL6 .... 43 G5
Cedar Cl *BAGS* GU19 .... 175 H3
 EWKG RG40 .... 11 G5
 NWBY RG14 .... 46 F2
 STA TW18 .... 127 M8 🖪
 TADY RG26 .... 165 G8
Cedar Ct *ADL/WDHM* KT15 ...... 155 M8 🖪
 EGH TW20 .... 126 D2
Cedar Dr *ASC* SL5 .... 152 D4
 BNFD RG42 .... 13 J1
 GOR/PANG RG8 .... 85M2
 MDHD SL6 .... 20 C8
Cedar Gv *STHA* RG19 .... 137M3
Cedar Mt *NWBY* RG14 .... 136 C6
Cedar Rd *EBED/NFELT* TW14...... 101 M1
 HEST TW5 .... 101 M1
Cedars Cl *SHST* GU47 .... 172 C6
Cedars Rd *MDHD* SL6 .... 3 K5
Cedar Wy *DTCH/LGLY* SL3........ 72 B4
 SUN TW16 .... 129 H5
Cedar Wood Crs *CAV/SC* RG4 .... 88 E2
Celandine Cl *CWTH* RG45 ...... 148 F8
Celandine Ct *YTLY* GU46 .... 171 K7
Celandine Gv *NTHA* RG18 ...... 138 C3
Celia Crs *ASHF* TW15 .... 128 A4
Cell Farm Av *WDSR* SL4 .... 97 L4
Central Dr *SL* SL1 .... 44 C8
Central La *WDSR* SL4 .... 95 M4
Central Wk *EWKG* RG40 .... 11 G6
Central Wy *EBED/NFELT* TW14 .... 101 L4
 WDSR SL4 .... 95 K7
The Centre *FELT* TW13 .... 101 K8
Centurion Cl *SHST* GU47 .... 173 G6 🖪
Century Dr *THLE* RG7 .... 144 F5
Century Rd *EGH* TW20 .... 126 F3
Cerotus Pl *CHERT* KT16 .... 155 J4
Chaffinch Cl *CALC* RG31 ...... 86 E7 🖪
 SHST GU47 .... 173 H6 🖪
 WWKG RG41 .... 10 A8
 WWKG RG41 .... 147 H1
Chagford Rd *WHIT* RG2 .... 116 C5
Chain St *READ* RG1 .... 8 F6
Chalcraft Cl *HEN* RG9 .... 37 M6
Chalfont Cl *EARL* RG6 .... 117 K5
Chalfont Wy *EARL* RG6 .... 117 K6 🖪
Chalford Rd *NWBY* RG14........ 14 A5
Chalgrove Cl *MDHD* SL6 .... 3 L7
Chalgrove Wy *CAV/SC* RG4 ...... 62 E8
Chalk Hl *HEN* RG9 .... 63 M1
Chalkhouse Green La
 CAV/SC RG4.......... 62 D5
Chalkhousegreen La
 CAV/SC RG4.......... 62 E6

Chalkhouse Green Rd
 CAV/SC RG4.......... 62 A3
Chalklands *BNEND* SL8.......... 20 D2
Chalkpit La *MLW* SL7 .... 18 E3
Chalk Pit La *SL* SL1 .... 43 L2
Challenge Rd *ASHF* TW15 ...... 128 F1
Challenor Cl *EWKG* RG40 ...... 147 J7 🖪
Challis Rd *BNFD* RG42 .... 12 A3
Challow Ct *MDHD* SL6 .... 2 D1
Chalmers Rd *ASHF* TW15 ...... 128 E2
Chalmers Rd East *ASHF* TW15 .... 128 E2
Chalmers Wy
 EBED/NFELT TW14.......... 101 L4
Chalvey Gdns *SL* SL1 .... 4 E9
Chalvey Gv *SL* SL1 .... 70 E3
Chalvey Pk *SL* SL1 .... 4 F9
Chalvey Rd East *SL* SL1 .... 4 E9
Chalvey Rd West *SL* SL1 .... 4 D9
Chamberlain's Gdns
 WHIT RG2 .... 146 B4 🖪
Champion Rd *CAV/SC* RG4 ...... 62 A3
The Chancellor's Wy *EARL* RG6 .. 117 G2
Chanctonbury Dr *ASC* SL5 ...... 152 B4 🖪
Chandlers Cl *EBED/NFELT* TW14.. 101 J6
Chandlers La *YTLY* GU46 .... 171 M7
Chandos Rd *NWBY* RG14 ...... 136 C6
 STA TW18 .... 127 G3
Chantry Cl *WDSR* SL4 .... 6 D6
Chantry Md *HUNG* RG17 .... 131 M1
Chantry Rd *BAGS* GU19 .... 175 G4
 CHERT KT16 .... 155 L5
Chapel La *GOR/PANG* RG8 ...... 32 F3 🖪
Chapel Ct *HUNG* RG17 .... 104 B8 🖪
 NTHA RG18 .... 138 B2
Chapel Gv *ADL/WDHM* KT15 .... 155 L8
Chapel Hl *CALC* RG31 .... 86 E6
Chapel La *BAGS* GU19 .... 175 G4
 BNFD RG42 .... 120 F5
 FARN GU14 .... 181 J6
 GOR/PANG RG8 .... 57 K8
 HUNG RG17 .... 49 L4
 MARL SN8 .... 102 A2
 NTHA RG18 .... 81 M6
 NTHA RG18 .... 83 H5
 NTHA RG18 .... 109 H2
 SLN SL2 .... 45 L1
 STHA RG19 .... 163 J5
 THLE RG7 .... 144 E4
 THLE RG7 .... 165 J1
Chapel Ms *HTWY* RG27 .... 171 H6 🖪
Chapel Park Rd
 ADL/WDHM KT15.......... 155 L8
Chapel Rd *CBLY* GU15 .... 181 L1
 KSCL RG20 .... 107 H8
Chapels Cl *SL* SL1 .... 70 B1 🖪
Chapel Sq *CBLY* GU15 .... 173 J8
 VW GU25 .... 126 B8
Chapel St *FARN* GU14 .... 182 A8
 MLW SL7 .... 19 G4
 NTHA RG18 .... 138 B3
 SL SL1 .... 5 G9
Chaplain's Hl *CWTH* RG45 ...... 173 G2
Chaplin Crs *SUN* TW16 .... 129 H4
Chapman La *BNEND* SL8 .... 20 D1
Chapman Wk *NTHA* RG18 ...... 137 L2
Chapter Ms *WDSR* SL4 .... 7 K5
Chard Cl *WODY* RG5 .... 90 B8
Charlbury Cl *BRAK* RG12 ...... 150 C1 🖪
Charles Evans Wy *CAV/SC* RG4.... 89 G4
Charles Rd *STA* TW18 .... 128 A4
Charles St *CBLY* GU15 .... 181 M1
 CHERT KT16 .... 155 J5 🖪
 NWBY RG14 .... 136 A8
 READ RG1 .... 8 C5
 WDSR SL4 .... 7 H7
Charleston Cl *FELT* TW15 ...... 129 K1 🖪
Charlock Cl *NTHA* RG18 .... 138 B1
Charlotte Cl *NTHA* RG18.......... 81 K8
Charlton Cl *EWKG* RG40 .... 147 J6 🖪
 SL SL1 .... 70 E2
Charlton Ct *SHST* GU47 .... 173 G5
Charlton La *SHPTN* TW17 ...... 128 F8
 THLE RG7 .... 168 F1
Charlton Pl *NWBY* RG14........ 14 F2
Charlton Rd *SHPTN* TW17 ...... 128 F8
Charlville Dr *CALC* RG31 .... 114 E2 🖪
Charmwood Cl *NWBY* RG14 .... 136 C1 🖪
Charndon Cl *WHIT* RG2 .... 116 E1
Charnham La *HUNG* RG17 ...... 104 A8
Charnham Pk *HUNG* RG17........ 104 A7
Charnham St *HUNG* RG17........ 103 M8
 HUNG RG17 .... 104 A8
Charnwood *ASC* SL5.......... 152 C3
Charrington Rd *CALC* RG31...... 114 E2
Charta Rd *EGH* TW20 .... 126 F3 🖪
Charter Cl *SL* SL1 .... 71 J3 🖪
Charterhouse Cl *BRAK* RG12 .. 150 B2
Charter Rd *NWBY* RG14 .... 136 C6
 SL SL1 .... 44 B8
Charters La *ASC* SL5 .... 152 A2
Charters Rd *ASC* SL5 .... 152 C4
Charters Wy *ASC* SL5 .... 152 C4
Charvil House Rd
 WAR/TWY RG10.......... 90 D1
Charvil La *CAV/SC* RG4 .... 90 B2
Charvil Meadow Rd
 WAR/TWY RG10.......... 90 E1
Charwood Rd *EWKG* RG40 ...... 11 M5
Chase Gdns *BNFD* RG42 .... 120 F3
Chaseside Av *WAR/TWY* RG10.... 65 G4
Chaseside Gdns *CHERT* KT16 .... 155 L4
The Chase *CALC* RG31 .... 115 G2
 CWTH RG45 .... 148 D8
 FARN GU14 .... 182 A8
 MDHD SL6 .... 42 A3
 MLW SL7 .... 19 K3
 NWBY RG14 .... 108 C7 🖪
 SUN TW16 .... 129 L6 🖪
Chatfield *SLN* SL2 .... 44 D8
Chatham St *READ* RG1.......... 8 C5
Chatsworth Av *WWKG* RG41...... 118 D4
Chatsworth Cl *CAV/SC* RG4 ...... 62 F8
 MDHD SL6 .... 2 A8
Chatsworth Hts *CBLY* GU15 .... 174 F2
Chatteris La *SLN* SL2 .... 44 C5
Chattern Hl *ASHF* TW15 .... 128 E2 🖪

Chattern Rd *ASHF* TW15 .... 128 F2
The Chatters *THLE* RG7.......... 145 M7
Chatton Cl *EARL* RG6 .... 117 K6
Chaucer Av *HSLWW* TW4 .... 101 L1
Chaucer Cl *CAV/SC* RG4 .... 88 D1
 EWKG RG40 .... 11 M4
 EWKG RG40 .... 120 C1
 WDSR SL4 .... 97 G2
Chaucer Crs *NWBY* RG14 ...... 136 B1
Chaucer Gv *CBLY* GU15 .... 182 A1
Chaucer Rd *ASHF* TW15 .... 128 B2
 CWTH RG45 .... 172 E2
 FARN GU14 .... 181 J8
Chaucer Wy *WWKG* RG41 ...... 147 H1 🖪
Chauntry Cl *MDHD* SL6 .... 42 F8
Chauntry Rd *MDHD* SL6 .... 3 L6
Chavey Down Rd *BNFD* RG42.... 122 C3
Chawridge La *WDSR* SL4 .... 94 F7
Chazey Cl *CAV/SC* RG4 .... 61 M6
Chazey Rd *CAV/SC* RG4 .... 88 A2
Cheam Ct *BRAK* RG12.......... 150 A2
Cheapside *READ* RG1 .... 8 E5
Cheapside Rd *ASC* SL5 .... 123 M8
Cheap St *KSCL* RG20 .... 56 B1
 NWBY RG14 .... 14 E4
Cheddington Cl *TLHT* RG30 ...... 87 J8 🖪
Cheeseman Cl *EWKG* RG40 ...... 11 J3
Chelsea Cl *TLHT* RG30.......... 87 J5
Chelwood Dr *SHST* GU47 ...... 172 C5 🖪
Chelwood Rd *EARL* RG6 .... 117 L4
Cheney Cl *BNFD* RG42 .... 121 G4
Cheniston Gv *MDHD* SL6 .... 41 J7
Chepstow Rd *CALC* RG31 .... 86 F4
Chequer La *THLE* RG7 .... 168 B4
Chequers La *HTWY* RG27 .... 171 H7
Chequers Orch *IVER* SL0 .... 47 J7 🖪
Chequers Wy *WODY* RG5 .... 89 M7
Cherbury Cl *BRAK* RG12 .... 122 B8
Cherington Ga *MDHD* SL6 .... 41 L5 🖪
Cherington Wy *ASC* SL5 .... 123 H7 🖪
Cheriton Av *WAR/TWY* RG10...... 65 C8
Cheriton Cl *NWBY* RG14.......... 15 G4
Cheriton Pl *CAV/SC* RG4 .... 62 C1 🖪
Cheriton Wy *BLKW* GU17 ...... 181 G1
The Cherries *SLN* SL2 .... 5 M2
 SLN SL2 .... 45 M7
Cherry Av *DTCH/LGLY* SL3 ...... 72 A2
Cherry Cl *CAV/SC* RG4 .... 62 F6
 NWBY RG14 .... 14 D1
Cherrydale Rd *CBLY* GU15 ...... 183 G1
Cherry Garden La *MDHD* SL6 .... 67 H3
 MDHD SL6 .... 67 H6
Cherry Gv *HUNG* RG17 .... 131 M1
Cherry Orch *HUNG* RG17 ...... 77 L2 🖪
 SLN SL2 .... 45 L1
 STA TW18 .... 127 K3
Cherry Tree Av *STA* TW18 ...... 127 L4
Cherry Tree Cl *HEN* RG9 .... 35 K1 🖪
 SHST GU47 .... 173 G5 🖪
Cherry Tree Dr *BRAK* RG12 ...... 13 L1
Cherry Tree Gv *WWKG* RG41 .... 147 G2 🖪
Cherrytree La *IVER* SL0 .... 47 K2
Cherry Tree Rd *SLN* SL2 .... 44 E1
Cherry Wy *DTCH/LGLY* SL3 ...... 98 F2
Cherrywood Av *EGH* TW20 ...... 125 L5
Cherrywood Gdns *CAV/SC* RG4.. 181 K7
Chertsey La *STA* TW18 .... 127 H3
 STA TW18 .... 127 H3
 STA TW18 .... 127 H6
Chertsey Rd *ADL/WDHM* KT15 .. 155 L6
 ADL/WDHM KT15 .... 155M7
 ASHF TW15 .... 129 G5
 BFOR GU20 .... 176 B2
 CHOB/PIR GU24 .... 177 K5
 FELT TW13 .... 129 H3
 SUN TW16 .... 129 H5
Chertsey Wk *CHERT* KT16 ...... 155 K4 🖪
Chervil Cl *FELT* TW13 .... 129 K1 🖪
Chervil Wy *THLE* RG7 .... 142 E4
Cherwell Cl *DTCH/LGLY* SL3 .... 72 E6 🖪
 MDHD SL6 .... 3 J3
Cherwell Rd *BNEND* SL8 .... 20 E2
 CAV/SC RG4.......... 62 D8
Chesleridge Rd *KSCL* RG20 ...... 55 L4
Cheshire Pk *DNFD* RG42.......... 122 B8
Chessholme Rd *ASHF* TW15 .... 128 F4
Chesterblade La *BRAK* RG12 .. 150 A4
Chester Cl *ASHF* TW15 .... 129 G4
 NWBY RG14 .... 15 K9
Chesterfield Rd *ASHF* TW15 .... 128 B3
 NWBY RG14 .... 14 E7
Chesterman St *READ* RG1 ...... 9 G9
Chesterment Wy *EARL* RG6 .... 118 A5
Chester Rd *HSLWW* TW4 .... 101 L2
 HTHAIR TW6 .... 100 D3 🖪
 SL SL1 .... 4 D2
Chesters Rd *CBLY* GU15 .... 182 E1
Chester St *CAV/SC* RG4 .... 88 D4
 TLHT RG30 .... 88 A6
Chesterton Dr
 STWL/WRAY TW19.......... 100 C7 🖪
Chesterton Rd *NTHA* RG18 ...... 137M1
Chestnut Av *CAV/SC* RG4 .... 89 H2 🖪
 CBLY GU15 .... 174 D8
 DTCH/LGLY SL3.......... 72 B2
 VW GU25 .... 153 J1
 WWKG RG41 .... 118 E4
 WWKG RG41 .... 119 H7
Chestnut Cl *ASHF* TW15 .... 128 E2
 BLKW GU17 .... 181 H1 🖪
 EGH TW20 .... 125 M4 🖪
 MDHD SL6 .... 42 E5
 MLW SL7 .... 18 A7 🖪
 SUN TW16 .... 129 J4 🖪
 THLE RG7 .... 114 B2 🖪
Chestnut Crs *NWBY* RG14 ...... 14 E1
 WHIT RG2 .... 145 H2
Chestnut Dr *EGH* TW20 .... 126 A4
 TLHT RG30 .... 142 E2
 WDSR SL4 .... 96 B3
Chestnut Gv *GOR/PANG* RG8...... 87 G1
 STA TW18 .... 127M4
Chestnut La *CHOB/PIR* GU24 .. 176 F2
 HUNG RG17 .... 50 D7
Chestnut Manor Cl *STA* TW18.... 127 L3
Chestnut Rd *ASHF* TW15 .... 128 D2
The Chestnuts *HEN* RG9 .... 64 D3

Chestnut Wk *HUNG* RG17 ...... 132 A2
Chestnut Wy *FELT* TW13 .... 129 L1 🖪
Chetwode Cl *EWKG* RG40 .... 11 L6
Cheviot Cl *CBLY* GU15 .... 182 C2
 FARN GU14 .... 181 H7
 MDHD SL6 .... 3 L7
Cheviot Dr *WAR/TWY* RG10 ...... 90 E2
Cheviot Rd *DTCH/LGLY* SL3 ...... 72 C5
 SHST GU47 .... 172 C5
Chewter La *BFOR* GU20 .... 151 L3
Cheylesmore Dr *FRIM* GU16 ...... 183 G3
Cheyne Rd *ASHF* TW15 .... 129 G4 🖪
Cheyne Wy *FARN* GU14 .... 181 J7
Chichester Rd *TLHT* RG30 ...... 87 H6
Chichester Wy
 EBED/NFELT TW14.......... 101 M6 🖪
Chicory Cl *EARL* RG6 .... 117 J5
Chieveley Cl *CALC* RG31 .... 86 F6
Chilcombe Wy *EARL* RG6.......... 118 A4
Child Cl *EWKG* RG40 .... 11 K2
Childrey Wy *CALC* RG31 .... 86 E6
Child St *HUNG* RG17 .... 49 K3
Chilham Cl *FRIM* GU16 .... 182 C6
Chillingham Wy *CBLY* GU15...... 181 M2
Chilsey Green Rd *CHERT* KT16 .. 155 H3
Chiltern Cl *HEN* RG9 .... 37 L6
 NWBY RG14 .... 159 M1
 STA TW18 .... 127 K3 🖪
Chiltern Ct *CAV/SC* RG4 .... 62 E8
Chiltern Crs *EARL* RG6 .... 89 K7
Chiltern Dr *WAR/TWY* RG10 ...... 90 E2
Chiltern Rd *CAV/SC* RG4.......... 88 F2
 HEN RG9 .... 36 B7
 MDHD SL6 .... 3 L7
 MLW SL7 .... 18 F4
 SHST GU47 .... 172 C5
 SL SL1 .... 43 L6
Chilterns Pk *BNEND* SL8 .... 20 E1
Chiltern Vw *GOR/PANG* RG8 .... 87 G1
Chiltern View Rd *UX/CGN* UB8 .. 47M3
Chilton Wy *HUNG* RG17 .... 131 M1
Chilwick Rd *SLN* SL2 .... 44 C5
Chinchilla Dr *HSLWW* TW4 ...... 101 M1
Chippenham Cl *EARL* RG6 ...... 117 J6 🖪
Chisbury Cl *BRAK* RG12 .... 150 B3
Chisbury La *MARL* SN8.......... 130 B5
Chittering Cl *EARL* RG6 .... 117M5
Chive Rd *EARL* RG6 .... 117 K5
Chivers Dr *EWKG* RG40 .... 147 H2 🖪
Chives Pl *BNFD* RG42 .... 122 A5 🖪
Chobham La *CHERT* KT16 ...... 153 K5
Chobham Park La
 CHOB/PIR GU24 .... 177 K5
Chobham Rd *CHOB/PIR* GU24 .. 152 F6 🖪
 CHOB/PIR GU24 .... 177M8
 FRIM GU16 .... 182 B4
Choke La *MDHD* SL6.......... 41 K2
Cholmeley Pl *READ* RG1 .... 89 H7 🖪
Cholmeley Rd *READ* RG1 .... 89 H6
Cholmeley Ter *READ* RG1 .... 89 H7 🖪
Cholsey Cl *STHA* RG19 .... 138 C3
Choseley Cl *WAR/TWY* RG10 .... 66 B2
Choseley Rd *WAR/TWY* RG10 .... 66 B2
Chrislaine Cl
 STWL/WRAY TW19.......... 100 A5 🖪
Christchurch Dr *BLKW* GU17 .... 172 F8
Christchurch Gdns *WHIT* RG2 .. 116 F1
Christchurch Rd *VW* GU25 ...... 154 A1
 WHIT RG2 .... 116 F1
Christie Cl *LTWR* GU18 .... 175 L5
Christie Hts *NWBY* RG14 ...... 136 B6
Christopher Ct *NWBY* RG14 .... 15 H6
Christy Ct *TADY* RG26 .... 164 F7 🖪
Chudleigh Gdns *WHIT* RG2 ...... 116 F4
Church Ap *EGH* TW20 .... 126 F8
Church Barns Farm *THLE* RG7 .. 167 G1
Church Brook *TADY* RG26 ...... 164 D8
Church Cl *ADL/WDHM* KT15 .... 155 L8 🖪
 HEN RG9 .... 37 G5
 HUNG RG17 .... 49 L3 🖪
 KSCL RG20 .... 135 H8
 STA TW18 .... 127M4
 UX/CGN UB8 .... 47 L3
 WDSR SL4 .... 7 J3
 WWKG RG41 .... 118 F4 🖪
Church Dr *MDHD* SL6 .... 68 F2
Church End La *TLHT* RG30 ...... 87 J7
Churchfield Ms *SLN* SL2.......... 5 K2
Church Ga *STHA* RG19 .... 138 A3
Church Gv *DTCH/LGLY* SL3 ...... 45 M6
Church Hams *EWKG* RG40 ...... 147 G8
Church Hl *CBLY* GU15 .... 182 B1
 KSCL RG20 .... 29 H8
 KSCL RG20 .... 105 M4
 WAR/TWY RG10 .... 91 H7
Churchill Cl
 EBED/NFELT TW14.......... 101 J7 🖪
 TADY RG26 .... 165 G7
Churchill Crs *CAV/SC* RG4 ...... 36 C8
 FARN GU14 .... 181 L7
Churchill Dr *MLW* SL7 .... 19 J3
 WWKG RG41 .... 118 E4
Churchill Rd *ASC* SL5 .... 123 J7
 DTCH/LGLY SL3.......... 72 C4
Churchill Wy *SUN* TW16 .... 129 K3
Church La *CBLY* GU15 .... 124 D8
 ASC SL5 .... 152 A1
 ASC SL5 .... 152 E2
 BNFD RG42 .... 121 G1
 BNFD RG42 .... 122 A1
 EGH TW20 .... 146 F5
 EWKG RG40 .... 171 H2
 GOR/PANG RG8 .... 57 K8
 HEN RG9 .... 36 C6
 HEN RG9 .... 64 C5
 HTWY RG27 .... 168 F4
 HUNG RG17 .... 157 G8
 KSCL RG20 .... 80 D5
 KSCL RG20 .... 135 H8
 KSCL RG20 .... 159 C6
 KSCL RG20 .... 160 D7
 MARL SN8 .... 156 B8
 MDHD SL6 .... 68 F2
 NTHA RG18 .... 83 H5
 NWBY RG14 .... 136 A2

READ RG1 .... 9 C8
SLN SL2 .... 45 J5
SLN SL2 .... 45 L5
STHA RG19 .... 138 A3
THLE RG7 .... 139 J8
THLE RG7 .... 141 L2
THLE RG7 .... 144 E2
THLE RG7 .... 146 A8
THLE RG7 .... 166 B5
TLHT RG30 .... 115 H8
WAR/TWY RG10 .... 91 J1
WDSR SL4 .... 7 K6
WHIT RG2 .... 145 C1
WHIT RG2 .... 145 M2
Church Ms ADL/WDHM KT15 ... 155 M8
GOR/PANG RG8 .... 87 G1 ⊡
WODY RG5 .... 90 C6
Church Rd ASC SL5 .... 122 E6
ASC SL5 .... 151 K1
ASC SL5 .... 152 D3
ASHF TW15 .... 128 C2
ASHF TW15 .... 128 C2
ASHF TW15 .... 128 D3
BAGS GU19 .... 175 C3
BFOR GU20 .... 175 L2
BRAK RG12 .... 13 J5
CBLY GU15 .... 173 J7 ⊡
CHOB/PIR GU24 .... 176 C7
EARL RG6 .... 117 L1
EGH TW20 .... 126 D3
FELT TW13 .... 129 M3
FRIM GU16 .... 182 A6
IVER SL0 .... 46 F3
KSCL RG20 .... 135 H1
MARL SN8 .... 102 D8
MDHD SL6 .... 3 M9
MDHD SL6 .... 19 L8
MLW SL7 .... 19 M1
NWBY RG14 .... 136 D1
SHST GU47 .... 172 C5
SHST GU47 .... 173 C5
SLN SL2 .... 44 F4
TADY RG26 .... 164 E8
TADY RG26 .... 165 H5
THLE RG7 .... 140 D7
THLE RG7 .... 140 F7
THLE RG7 .... 165 M1
WDSR SL4 .... 94 E8
WDSR SL4 .... 97 L4
WDSR SL4 .... 122 F1
WODY RG5 .... 90 C6
Church Rd East CWTH RG45 ... 172 E1
Church Rd West CWTH RG45 ... 172 E2
Church St CAV/SC RG4 .... 88 D4
CWTH RG45 .... 172 E1
HEN RG9 .... 38 A5
HUNG RG17 .... 77 K3
HUNG RG17 .... 104 A8
HUNG RG17 .... 133 K4
MARL SN8 .... 130 D5
NTHA RG18 .... 82 C1
READ RG1 .... 9 C8
SL SL1 .... 4 B9
SL SL1 .... 43 M5
SL SL1 .... 71 J3
STA TW18 .... 127 G2
SUN TW16 .... 129 K8
THLE RG7 .... 114 A3
WAR/TWY RG10 .... 64 F4
WAR/TWY RG10 .... 91 G2
WDSR SL4 .... 7 K6
Church Vw HEN RG9 .... 35 J1 ⊡
MDHD SL6 .... 67 H6
THLE RG7 .... 112 D8
YTLY GU46 .... 172 A7
Church Wy HUNG RG17 .... 131 M2
Churchway KSCL RG20 .... 28 D5
Churn Rd KSCL RG20 .... 29 M7
Cinnamon Cl EARL RG6 .... 117 J5 ⊡
Cintra Av WHIT RG2 .... 116 F2
Cippenham Cl SL SL1 .... 44 C8 ⊡
SL SL1 .... 44 C8
Circle Hill Rd CWTH RG45 ...... 172 F1
Circuit La TLHT RG30 .... 115 M1
City Rd CALC RG31 .... 86 E8
Clacy Gn BNFD RG42 .... 12 F1
Clammas Wy UX/CGN UB8 ...... 47 M6
Clandon Av EGH TW20 .... 126 F5
Clanfield Crs CALC RG31 .... 86 F4
Clanfield Ride BLKW GU17 .... 181 G1 ⊡
Clappers Farm Rd THLE RG7 ... 166 D6
Clappers La CHOB/PIR GU24 ... 176 F6
Clappers Meadow MDHD SL6 ... 42 E5
Clapps Gate Rd TADY RG26 ... 165 H5
Clare Av EWKG RG40 .... 11 C4
Clare Ct EWKG RG40 .... 11 C4
Clarefield Cl MDHD SL6 .... 41 K5
Clarefield Dr MDHD SL6 .... 41 K5
Clarefield Rd MDHD SL6 .... 41 L5 ⊡
Clare Gdns EGH TW20 .... 126 D3 ⊡
Claremont Av CBLY GU15 ..... 182 C1
SUN TW16 .... 129 L6
Claremont Gdns MLW SL7 .... 19 H4
Claremont Rd MLW SL7 .... 19 H4
STA TW18 .... 127 C3
WDSR SL4 .... 7 G8
Clarence Crs WDSR SL4 .... 7 H7
Clarence Dr CBLY GU15 .... 174 E7
EGH TW20 .... 125 M2
Clarence Rd HEN RG9 .... 38 A4
WDSR SL4 .... 6 F7
Clarence St EGH TW20 .... 126 C4
STA TW18 .... 127 H2
Clarence Wy CALC RG31 .... 114 E2
Clarendon Cl WWKG RG41 .... 119 C4
Clarendon Ct BLKW GU17 .... 181 G3 ⊡
SLN SL2 .... 5 M4 ⊡
Clarendon Gdns NWBY RG14 ... 14 F2
Clarendon Rd ASHF TW15 .... 128 C2
EARL RG6 .... 89 C8
Clare Rd MDHD SL6 .... 2 E7
MDHD SL6 .... 43 M7
STWL/WRAY TW19 .... 100 A7
Clares Green Rd THLE RG7 .... 144 E3
Clarewood Dr CBLY GU15 ..... 174 D8
Clarke Crs CBLY GU15 .... 173 H7
Clark's Gdns HUNG RG17 ..... 132 A1

The Classics HUNG RG17 .... 49 L5
Claverdon BRAK RG12 .... 149 K4
Clay Cl CALC RG31 .... 86 E5
Claydon Gdns FARN GU14 ... 181 K5 ⊡
Clayhall La WDSR SL4 .... 97 J4
Clayhill Cl BRAK RG12 .... 122 C8
Clay Hill Crs NWBY RG14 ... 137 G1 ⊡
Clayhill Rd THLE RG7 .... 142 C3
Clay La EWKG RG40 .... 120 C8
THLE RG7 .... 112 C8
Clayton Gv BRAK RG12 .... 122 B6
Clayton Rd FARN GU14 .... 181 J5
Claytons Meadow BNEND 20 E4
Cleares Pasture SL SL1 .... 43 L4 ⊡
Clearsprings LTWR GU18 ..... 175 J6
Cleeve Down GOR/PANG RG8 ... 33 G7
Cleeve Rd GOR/PANG RG8 ..... 32 E7
Clements Cl SL SL1 .... 5 L9
THLE RG7 .... 144 D5
Clements Md CALC RG31 .... 86 E6
Clements Rd HEN RG9 .... 37 M3
Clent Rd WHIT RG2 .... 116 E2
Cleopatra Pl BNFD RG42 .... 122 B5 ⊡
Clerewater Pl STHA RG19 ... 137 K3 ⊡
WDSR SL4 .... 96 C2
Clevedon Ct FRIM GU16 ...... 182 D6
Clevedon Dr EARL RG6 .... 117 K4
Clevedon Gdns HEST TW5 ... 101 L1
Clevedon Rd CALC RG31 .... 87 H3
Cleveland WAR/TWY RG10 .... 90 E2 ⊡
Cleveland Cl MDHD SL6 .... 3 M7
Cleveland Dr STA TW18 .... 127 L7
Cleveland Gv NWBY RG14 .... 14 D3
Clevemede GOR/PANG RG8 ... 32 F7 ⊡
Cleves Wy SUN TW16 .... 129 J4
Clewborough Dr CBLY GU15 ... 174 E8
Clewer Av WDSR SL4 .... 6 E8
Clewer Court Rd WDSR SL4 .... 6 E5
Clewer Hill Rd WDSR SL4 ...... 96 B1
Clewer New Town WDSR SL4 ... 6 D5
Clewer Pk WDSR SL4 .... 6 D5
Clifford Gv ASHF TW15 .... 128 C2
Cliffords Wy BNEND SL8 .... 20 D1
Clifton Av FELT TW13 .... 129 M1
Clifton Cl ADL/WDHM KT15 ... 155 L6
MDHD SL6 .... 68 C2
Clifton Gdns FRIM GU16 ...... 182 C8
Clifton Park Rd CAV/SC RG4 ... 88 C3
Clifton Ri WAR/TWY RG10 .... 65 H5
WDSR SL4 .... 70 A8
Clifton Rd HTHAIR TW6 ...... 100 E3 ⊡
NWBY RG14 .... 14 A5
SL SL1 .... 5 L9
WWKG RG41 .... 10 C2
Clifton St READ RG1 .... 8 C7
Clintons Gn BNFD RG42 .... 12 F3
Clitheroe Rd FARN GU14 ...... 180 C5
Clive Ct SL SL1 .... 4 C9
Clivedale Rd WODY RG5 ...... 118 B2
Cliveden Md MDHD SL6 .... 42 F4
Cliveden Rd MDHD SL6 .... 43 C4
Clive Gn BRAK RG12 .... 149 L2
Clivemont Rd MDHD SL6 .... 2 F1
Clive La EBED/NFELT TW14 ... 101 K5
NWBY RG14 .... 14 A5
SL SL1 .... 5 L9
WWKG RG41 .... 10 C2
Clifton St READ RG1 .... 8 C7
Clintons Gn BNFD RG42 .... 12 F3
Close End HUNG RG17 .... 49 L4
The Close ASC SL5 .... 123 C7
BRAK RG12 .... 13 K9
FRIM GU16 .... 181 M6
GOR/PANG RG8 .... 34 C6 ⊡
HEN RG9 .... 38 A6
HUNG RG17 .... 77 K3
IVER SL0 .... 46 F4
LTWR GU18 .... 175 K5
NTHA RG18 .... 82 C1
NTHA RG18 .... 137 L2
SHST GU47 .... 173 H6
SL SL1 .... 44 A8
THLE RG7 .... 142 D3
VW GU25 .... 154 A2
WODY RG5 .... 118 B1
Clough Dr NTHA RG18 .... 81 J8 ⊡
Clove Cl EARL RG6 .... 117 J5
Clover Cl EWKG RG40 .... 11 M3
Clover La YTLY GU46 .... 171 K8
Cloves Wy BNFD RG42 .... 121 G7 ⊡
Club La CWTH RG45 .... 173 G1
The Clumps ASHF TW15 ...... 129 G2
Clyde Rd STWL/WRAY TW19 ... 100 A7
Clymping Dene
EBED/NFELT TW14 .... 101 L4
Clyve Wy STA TW18 .... 127 H6
Coach House Cl FRIM GU16 ... 182 B3
Coachman's Ct NWBY RG14 ... 136 E1 ⊡
Coach Ride MLW SL7 .... 19 G2
Coach Rd ASC SL5 .... 123 H5
Coalport Wy TLHT RG30 .... 87 H5
Cobb Cl DTCH/LGLY SL3 .... 72 A8
Cobbett's La BLKW GU17 .... 180 C2
YTLY GU46 .... 180 C1
Cobblers Cl SLN SL2 .... 44 E3
Cobden Cl UX/CGN UB8 .... 47 M2
Cobham Cl SL SL1 .... 70 C1 ⊡
Cobham Rd WODY RG5 .... 90 C7
Cochrane Cl STHA RG19 ..... 138 B3 ⊡
Cochrane Pl BFOR GU20 ...... 176 A1
Cock-a-dobby SHST GU47 ... 172 D5 ⊡
Cockett Rd DTCH/LGLY SL3 ... 72 B3
Cock La THLE RG7 .... 112 C4
Cockney Hl TLHT RG30 .... 87 J8
Cock's La BNFD RG42 .... 94 D8
Cody Cl WODY RG5 .... 90 E6
Coe Sp SL SL1 .... 70 E2
Coftards SLN SL2 .... 45 M7
Cold Ash HI NTHA RG18 ...... 109 M6
Coldharbour Cl EGH TW20 ... 126 F8 ⊡
HEN RG9 .... 37 M6
Coldharbour La
CHOB/PIR GU24 .... 176 C6
EGH TW20 .... 126 F8
Cold Harbour La FARN GU14 ... 181 J6
Coldharbour Rd HUNG RG17 ... 132 A2

Coldicutt St CAV/SC RG4 .... 9 J2
Coldmoorholme La BNEND SL8 ... 20 B3
Colemans Moor La WODY RG5 ... 90 B2
Colemans Moor Rd WODY RG5 ... 90 C1 ⊡
WODY RG5 .... 118 C1
Colenorton Crs WDSR SL4 ..... 70 B4
Coleridge Av YTLY GU46 ..... 180 B1
Coleridge Cl EWKG RG45 .... 172 F2 ⊡
WAR/TWY RG10 .... 91 J3 ⊡
Coleridge Crs DTCH/LGLY SL3 ... 73 H8
Coleridge La GOR/PANG RG8 ... 85 C2
Coleridge Rd ASHF TW15 .... 128 B2
Coley Av READ RG1 .... 8 C9
READ RG1 .... 116 C1
Coley HI READ RG1 .... 8 D8
Coley Park Rd READ RG1 .... 8 D8
Coley Rd READ RG1 .... 8 E8
Colin Wy WDSR SL4 .... 70 E3
Collaroy Rd NTHA RG18 ...... 109 M7
College Av EGH TW20 .... 126 E4
MDHD SL6 .... 2 E4
SL SL1 .... 71 H3
College Cl CBLY GU15 .... 174 A6
College Crs SHST GU47 .... 173 H6
WDSR SL4 .... 6 F9
College Gln MDHD SL6 .... 2 D4
College Piece THLE RG7 .... 142 C8
College Ride BAGS GU19 .... 174 F4
CBLY GU15 .... 174 A7
College Ri MDHD SL6 .... 2 D4
College Rd BRAK RG12 .... 13 K8
EARL RG6 .... 89 J8
MDHD SL6 .... 2 D3
SHST GU47 .... 173 H7
SL SL1 .... 70 C1
College Wy ASHF TW15 .... 128 C2 ⊡
HUNG RG17 .... 51 C8
Colleton Dr WAR/TWY RG10 ... 91 H4
Collier Cl MDHD SL6 .... 3 C1
Colliers La HEN RG9 .... 36 B6
Colliers Wy TLHT RG30 .... 87 L7
Collingwood Grange Cl
CBLY GU15 .... 174 E6
Collingwood Ri CBLY GU15 ... 174 D7
Collins Cl NWBY RG14 .... 15 J1
Collins Dr NTHA RG18 .... 81 J8
Collis St WHIT RG2 .... 116 E1
Colmore La HEN RG9 .... 36 B6
Colmworth Cl EARL RG6 .... 117 K6 ⊡
DTCH/LGLY SL3 .... 72 E6 ⊡
Colnbrook By-pass
DTCH/LGLY SL3 .... 72 F7
WDR/YW UB7 .... 73 L7
Coln Cl MDHD SL6 .... 3 H3
Colndale Rd DTCH/LGLY SL3 ... 99 H1
Colne Av WDR/YW UB7 .... 73 M2
Colne Bank STWL/WRAY TW19 ... 98 F2
Colne Orch IVER SL0 .... 47 K7
Colne Valley Wy IVER SL0 ..... 47 K7
STWL/WRAY TW19 .... 99 H7
Colonel's La CHERT KT16 .... 155 K3
Colonial Rd EBED/NFELT TW14 ... 101 H6
SL SL1 .... 5 K8
Colston Cl CALC RG31 .... 115 C2 ⊡
Coithrop La STHA RG19 ...... 138 E4
Coltsfoot Cl THLE RG7 .... 142 E3 ⊡
Columbia Ct EWKG RG40 .... 147 H7 ⊡
Colville Gdns LTWR GU18 ... 175 L6
Colwyn Cl YTLY GU46 .... 171 J3
Colyer Cl YTLY GU46 .... 171 K8
Colyton Wy GOR/PANG RG8 ... 86 F1
Combe La FARN GU14 .... 181 K6 ⊡
Combermere Cl WDSR SL4 ..... 6 E9
Combe Rd TLHT RG30 .... 87 J7
Combe Vw HUNG RG17 .... 132 A2 ⊡
Comet Rd STWL/WRAY TW19 ... 100 A6
Comet Wy WODY RG5 .... 90 D7
Comfrey Cl EWKG RG40 .... 11 M2
Commercial Rd STA TW18 ... 127 K4
WHIT RG2 .... 116 D5
Commonfield La EWKG RG40 ... 146 E6
Commonfields CHOB/PIR GU24 ... 176 C3
Common HI THLE RG7 .... 113 J3
Common La KSCL RG20 .... 53 C2
WANT OX12 .... 53 C1
WDSR SL4 .... 7 J1
Common Rd DTCH/LGLY SL3 ... 72 D4
STHA RG19 .... 162 B6
WDSR SL4 .... 70 A4
WDSR SL4 .... 70 D3
WDSR SL4 .... 70 D5
Commons Rd WWKG RG41 ... 119 J5
Compton Av CALC RG31 .... 86 E7
Compton Cl BRAK RG12 ...... 149 H5 ⊡
EARL RG6 .... 117 M2
SHST GU47 .... 172 F5
Compton Dr MDHD SL6 .... 41 K6
Compton Wk BRAK RG12 .... 149 M2 ⊡
Concorde Rd MDHD SL6 .... 68 A2
Concorde Wy SL SL1 .... 4 A9
WODY RG5 .... 90 D7
Condor Cl CALC RG31 .... 86 F3
Condor Rd STA TW18 .... 127 M8
Conduit La DTCH/LGLY SL3 ... 72 B5
Conegar Ct SL SL1 .... 4 E7
Coney Gra BNFD RG42 .... 121 L4
Congreve Cl THLE RG7 .... 140 C7
Conifer Cl TADY RG26 .... 164 B5
Conifer Crest NWBY RG14 ... 159 M2
Conifer Dr CALC RG31 .... 86 E4
CBLY GU15 .... 174 D8
Conifer La EGH TW20 .... 126 F5
The Conifers CWTH RG45 .... 148 D7
MDHD SL6 .... 41 K6
Coningham Rd WHIT RG2 .... 116 F8
Coningsby BRAK RG12 .... 13 J8
Coningsby Cl MDHD SL6 .... 68 A3 ⊡
Coningsby La MDHD SL6 ...... 68 F8
Conisboro Av CAV/SC RG4 ..... 88 B1
Conisboro Wy CAV/SC RG4 ... 88 B1
Coniston Cl CBLY GU15 ...... 182 F3
STHA RG19 .... 137 K3
WODY RG5 .... 118 B1
Coniston Crescent SL SL1 ...... 43 M6
Coniston Dr TLHT RG30 .... 87 J4
Coniston Wy EGH TW20 ...... 126 E5 ⊡
Connaught Av ASHF TW15 ... 128 B2 ⊡
Coronation Av DTCH/LGLY SL3 ... 46 B7

Connaught Cl MDHD SL6 ...... 42 B5 ⊡
TLHT RG30 .... 88 A7 ⊡
YTLY GU46 .... 171 L8
Connaught Rd BAGS GU19 ... 174 F3
CBLY GU15 .... 182 C1
NWBY RG14 .... 15 H4
SL SL1 .... 5 L8 ⊡
TLHT RG30 .... 88 A7
Conniston Cl MLW SL7 .... 18 E4 ⊡
Connop Wy FRIM GU16 ...... 182 C3
Consort Dr CBLY GU15 .... 174 F7 ⊡
Constable Cl WODY RG5 ...... 90 E6 ⊡
Constable Wy SHST GU47 ... 173 H8
Constitution Rd TLHT RG30 ... 87 L6 ⊡
Consul Cl WODY RG5 .... 118 D1
Control Tower Rd HTHAIR TW6 ... 100 D2
Convent Cl ASHF TW15 .... 128 C3
WDSR SL4 .... 6 C9
Conway Dr ASHF TW15 .... 128 F4
NTHA RG18 .... 137 L1
Conway Rd CALC RG31 .... 114 F1
MDHD SL6 .... 43 J7
Conygree Cl EARL RG6 .... 117 L5
Cooke Ri BNFD RG42 .... 121 M4 ⊡
Cookham Cl SHST GU47 ...... 173 H8
Cookham Dean Bottom
MDHD SL6 .... 19 M6
Cookham Rd BRAK RG12 ...... 12 B5
MDHD SL6 .... 42 B4
Coolarne Ri CBLY GU15 ...... 174 D8
Coolgardie Rd ASHF TW15 ... 128 F3
Coombe Cl FRIM GU16 .... 182 A6
Coombe Ct NTHA RG18 ...... 138 B3
Coombe Hill Ct WDSR SL4 .... 96 A3
Coombe Pine BRAK RG12 ... 150 A3
Coombe Rd KSCL RG20 .... 56 C4
YTLY GU46 .... 171 L7
Coombesbury La KSCL RG20 ... 106 F5
Coombes La WWKG RG41 ... 146 F2
Coombe Sq STHA RG19 ...... 138 B3
The Coombe GOR/PANG RG8 ... 32 C8
Cooper Cl WHIT RG2 .... 116 F7
Cooper Rd BFOR GU20 ...... 176 A2 ⊡
HEN RG9 .... 37 M3
Coopers Cl STA TW18 .... 127 H3
Coopers Crs NTHA RG18 .... 137 M2
Coopers Hill Dr CHOB/PIR GU24 ... 183 M7
Cooper's Hill La EGH TW20 ... 126 A2
Coopers Pightle CAV/SC RG4 ... 62 A3
Coopers Rw IVER SL0 .... 46 F5
Cooper Wy SL SL1 .... 70 E3
Cope Ct MDHD SL6 .... 2 A4
Cope Hall La NWBY RG14 .... 135 L7
Copelands Cl CBLY GU15 .... 183 C2
Copenhagen Cl WHIT RG2 .. 116 F7 ⊡
Copes La THTWY RG27 ...... 169 K7
Copnor Cl KSCL RG20 .... 158 F6
Copped Hall Dr CBLY GU15 ... 174 F8
Copped Hall Wy CBLY GU15 ... 174 F8
Copperage Rd WANT OX12 ... 27 H5
Copper Beech Cl WDSR SL4 ... 70 A8 ⊡
Copperdale Cl WHIT RG2 .... 117 H3
Copperfield Av SHST GU47 ... 173 H4
Coppermill Rd
STWL/WRAY TW19 .... 98 E5
Coppice Cl NWBY RG14 .... 15 C9
TADY RG26 .... 164 A6
Coppice Gdns CWTH RG45 ... 172 C1
Coppice Gn BNFD RG42 .... 12 D1
Coppice Rd WODY RG5 .... 118 B2
The Coppice ASHF TW15 .... 128 E4 ⊡
Coppins La IVER SL0 .... 47 J6
Copse Av CAV/SC RG4 .... 89 C3
Copse Cl CALC RG31 .... 87 C3
CBLY GU15 .... 182 D1
SL SL1 .... 70 C1
Copse Dr WWKG RG41 .... 10 C3
Copse End CBLY GU15 .... 174 C8
Copse Md WODY RG5 .... 90 C5
The Copse TADY RG26 .... 164 D6
WAR/TWY RG10 .... 65 H3
Copse Wy EWKG RG40 .... 147 H7 ⊡
Copse Wd IVER SL0 .... 47 G2
Copthorn Cl MDHD SL6 .... 67 K2 ⊡
Copthorne Dr LTWR GU18 ... 175 L5
Copyhold MARL SN8 .... 130 A8
Corbett Dr LTWR GU18 ...... 175 J7
Corbett Gdns WODY RG5 ...... 90 B7
Corbridge Rd WHIT RG2 .... 116 F3
Corby Cl EGH TW20 .... 125 M4
WODY RG5 .... 90 D5
Corby Dr EGH TW20 .... 125 M4
Cordelia Cft BNFD RG42 .... 122 B6 ⊡
Cordelia Gdns
STWL/WRAY TW19 .... 100 B6
Cordelia Rd STWL/WRAY TW19 ... 100 B6
Corderoy Cl STHA RG19 ...... 138 C4 ⊡
Corderoy Pl CHERT KT16 .... 155 H3
Cordwalles Rd CBLY GU15 ... 174 C6
Cordwallis Rd MDHD SL6 ...... 2 F3
Cordwallis St MDHD SL6 .... 2 F2
Cores End Rd BNEND SL8 ...... 20 D3
Corfe Gdns FRIM GU16 .... 182 C5
Corfe Ms CAV/SC RG4 .... 89 H2
Corfe Pl MDHD SL6 .... 2 A4
Corfield Rd EWKG RG40 ...... 171 H3
Corfield Gn WWKG RG41 ...... 10 A1
Coriander Wy EARL RG6 .... 117 J5 ⊡
Corinne Cl WHIT RG2 .... 116 E5
Cormorant Pl SHST GU47 ... 173 H6
Cornbunting Cl SHST GU47 ... 173 G6 ⊡
Corn Cft BNFD RG42 .... 13 M1
Cornerside ASHF TW15 .... 128 F5 ⊡
Cornfield Rd WODY RG5 .... 90 D6
Cornflower Cl WWKG RG41 ... 119 G7 ⊡
Cornhill Cl ADL/WDHM KT15 ... 155 L6
Cornwall Av SLN SL2 .... 44 F5
Cornwall Cl BNFD RG42 ..... 122 C4
CBLY GU15 .... 174 C7
MDHD SL6 .... 42 B3 ⊡
WDSR SL4 .... 70 B5
WWKG RG41 .... 119 G8 ⊡
Cornwall Wy STA TW18 ...... 127 H4
Cornwell Rd WDSR SL4 .... 97 K5
Cornwood Gdns WHIT RG2 ... 116 F3
Coronation Av DTCH/LGLY SL3 ... 46 B7

WDSR SL4 .... 97 J1
Coronation Cl KSCL RG20 .... 160 C7
Coronation Rd ASC SL5 .... 151 K5
MDHD SL6 .... 66 E2
YTLY GU46 .... 172 A7
Coronation Sq EWKG RG40 ... 11 J5
TLHT RG30 .... 115 L2 ⊡
Corrie Gdns VW GU25 .... 153 M4
Corsair Cl STWL/WRAY TW19 ... 100 A6
Corsair Rd STWL/WRAY TW19 ... 100 B6
Corsham Rd CALC RG31 ...... 115 J3
Corsham Wy CWTH RG45 ... 148 E8
Corwen Rd TLHT RG30 .... 87 G6
Coster Cl NWBY RG14 .... 136 A1 ⊡
Cotswold Cl FARN GU14 .... 181 H7
MDHD SL6 .... 3 L7
STA TW18 .... 127 K3 ⊡
UX/CGN UB8 .... 47 M2
Cotswold Rd SHST GU47 .... 172 C5 ⊡
Cotswold Wy CALC RG31 ...... 86 F4
Cottage Farm Wy EGH TW20 ... 126 F8 ⊡
Cotterell Cl BNFD RG42 .... 12 G1
Cotterell Gdns WAR/TWY RG10 ... 91 J3
Cottesbrooke Cl DTCH/LGLY SL3 ... 73 G8
Cottesmore BRAK RG12 ...... 149 K4
Cottesmore Rd WODY RG5 ... 90 A8
Coulson Wy SL SL1 .... 43 L6
Country Wy FELT TW13 ...... 129 M3
County La BNFD RG42 .... 122 B4
Courage Ct TLHT RG30 .... 115 L1 ⊡
Courland Rd ADL/WDHM KT15 ... 155 L7
Course Rd ASC SL5 .... 123 K8
Court Cl MDHD SL6 .... 68 F4
Court Crs SL SL1 .... 4 D2
Court Dr MDHD SL6 .... 42 F3
Courtenay Dr CAV/SC RG4 .... 62 E7
Courtfield Dr MDHD SL6 .... 2 A6
Courtfield Rd ASHF TW15 .... 128 E4
Court Gdns CBLY GU15 ...... 182 A1
MDHD SL6 .... 2 A5
Courthouse Rd MDHD SL6 ...... 2 C1
Courtlands Av HTHAIR TW6 ... 72 A4
Courtlands Rd NWBY RG14 ... 15 C8
Court La IVER SL0 .... 73 K1
SL SL1 .... 44 A4
WDSR SL4 .... 69 K3
Courtney Rd HTHAIR TW6 ... 100 D2 ⊡
Courtney Wy HTHAIR TW6 ... 100 D2 ⊡
Court Rd MDHD SL6 .... 42 F3
Courts Rd EARL RG6 .... 117 L2
The Courtyard THLE RG7 .... 114 B5
Coventry Rd READ RG1 .... 89 H7
Coverdale Wy SLN SL2 .... 44 B5 ⊡
Covert La BRAK RG12 .... 13 K8
The Covert ASC SL5 .... 151 L4
FARN GU14 .... 181 H6
Covey Cl FARN GU14 .... 181 K6
Cow La GOR/PANG RG8 .... 32 C3
KSCL RG20 .... 29 H7
READ RG1 .... 8 B2
TLHT RG30 .... 8 B4
Cowley Av CHERT KT16 ...... 155 J4
Cowley Crs UX/CGN UB8 .... 47 M6
Cowley La CHERT KT16 ...... 155 J4
Cowley Mill Rd UX/CGN UB8 ... 47 L3
UX/CGN UB8 .... 47 L4
Cowley Rd UX/CGN UB8 ...... 47 M4 ⊡
UX/CGN UB8 .... 47 M4 ⊡
UX/CGN UB8 .... 47 M5 ⊡
Coworth Cl ASC SL5 .... 152 E2
Coworth Rd ASC SL5 .... 152 D2
Cowper Cl CHERT KT16 .... 155 J3
Cowper Rd SLN SL2 .... 44 D5
Cowper Wy TLHT RG30 ...... 116 A2 ⊡
Cowslade NWBY RG14 .... 136 A1 ⊡
Cowslip Crs NTHA RG18 ..... 138 A2
Coxborrow Cl MDHD SL6 ...... 20 B7
Coxeter Rd NWBY RG14 .... 14 A1
Coxgreen SHST GU47 .... 173 G8
Cox Green La MDHD SL6 .... 67 L3
Cox Green Rd MDHD SL6 ...... 67 J3
Coxs Av SHPTN TW17 .... 129 H8 ⊡
Cox's La HEN RG9 .... 35 J1
THLE RG7 .... 139 C3
Crabtree Cl NTHA RG18 .... 81 J8
Crabtree La NTHA RG18 .... 81 J8
Crabtree Rd CBLY GU15 ..... 181 L4
EGH TW20 .... 126 F7
Cradock Rd WHIT RG2 .... 116 D2
Craig Av TLHT RG30 .... 87 L6
Craigwell Av FELT TW13 ..... 129 K1
Craigwell Cl STA TW18 ...... 127 H6
Crail Cl WWKG RG41 .... 147 K3
Crake Pl SHST GU47 .... 173 G6
Cranbourne Av CALC RG31 ... 114 F2 ⊡
WDSR SL4 .... 6 A9
Cranbourne Cl SL SL1 .... 4 A7
Cranbourne Gdns TLHT RG30 ... 87 J4
Cranbourne Rd SL SL1 .... 4 A7
Cranbrook Dr MDHD SL6 ...... 41 L5
Cranbury Rd TLHT RG30 .... 88 A7
Crane Ct SHST GU47 .... 173 G6
Crane Rd STWL/WRAY TW19 ... 100 D5
Crane Whf READ RG1 .... 9 H6
Cranford Av STWL/WRAY TW19 ... 100 B6
Cranford Cl
STWL/WRAY TW19 .... 100 B6 ⊡
Cranford Dr WAR/TWY RG10 ... 91 J6
Cranford La HTHAIR TW6 ... 100 J2
Cranford Park Dr YTLY GU46 ... 172 A8
Cranleigh Rd FELT TW13 .... 129 J2
Cranmer Cl CALC RG31 .... 86 E3
Cranwell Gv LTWR GU18 .... 175 J6
Craufurd Ri MDHD SL6 .... 2 F3
Cravan Av FELT TW13 .... 101 K8
Craven Cl HUNG RG17 .... 133 L5
Craven Dene NWBY RG14 ... 15 H2
Craven Rd HUNG RG17 .... 132 E3 ⊡
NWBY RG14 .... 14 A5
READ RG1 .... 9 L8
Craven Wy HUNG RG17 .... 133 L4
Crawford Cl EARL RG6 .... 117 L3
Crawford Gdns CBLY GU15 ... 181 L1
Crawford Pl NWBY RG14 ...... 14 D3
Crawley Cha BNFD RG42 .... 122 E4
Crawley Dr CBLY GU15 .... 174 C8

Crawley HI *CBLY* GU15 .... 182 C1
Crawley Rdg *CBLY* GU15 .... 174 C8
Crawley Wood CI *CBLY* GU15 .. 182 C1 🔲
Crawshay Dr *CAV/SC* RG4 .... 62 E7
Crayle St *SLN* SL2 .... 44 D4
Craysleaze *CAV/SC* RG4 .... 62 A3
Crecy CI *WWKG* RG41 .... 119 H8 🔲
Creden CI *MDHD* SL6 .... 2 D2
Crediton Wy *WODY* RG5 .... 90 D8
Cree's Meadow *BFOR* GU20 .... 176 A3 🔲
Cremyll Rd *READ* RG1 .... 8 C2
Crescent Dr *MDHD* SL6 .... 2 F3
Crescent PI *CALC* RG31 .... 87 C5
  EWKG RG40 .... 11 H7
  READ RG1 .... 89 H8
The Crescent *ASHF* TW15 ...... 128 C3
  BRAK RG12 .... 13 K9
  CHERT KT16 .... 127 K8 🔲
  EARL RG6 .... 117M2
  EGH TW20 .... 126 B4
  HEN RG9 .... 64 E2
  MDHD SL6 .... 2 F4
  SL SL1 .... 4 E9
  THLE RG7 .... 114 B2
  THLE RG7 .... 140 F1
  THLE RG7 .... 142 D8
Cressex CI *BNFD* RG42 .... 120 F4
Cressida Cha *BNFD* RG42 ...... 122 B5 🔲
Cressingham Rd *WHIT* RG2 ..... 116 F4
Cressington PI *BNEND* SL8 .... 20 D2
Cress Rd *SL* SL1 .... 70 C2
Cresswell Rd *NWBY* RG14 ...... 15 M1
  NWBY RG14 .... 137 H2 🔲
Cresswells Md *MDHD* SL6 ...... 68 E5
Crest Ct *WAR/TWY* RG10 .... 65 H8
Creswell CI *WHIT* RG2 .... 116 C0
Cricketers *KSCL* RG20 .... 107 H8
Cricketers La *BFOR* GU20 ..... 176 A1
  BNFD RG42 .... 122 D3
Cricket Field Gv *CWTH* RG45 .. 173 G2
Cricketfield Rd *WDR/YW* UB7 .. 73 M4
Cricket HI *EWKG* RG40 .... 171 J4
Cricket Hill La *BLKW* GU17 ... 180 A3
  YTLY GU46 .... 180 B1
Crimea Rd *FRIM* GU16 .... 183 G6
Crimp HI *EGH* TW20 .... 97 K8
  WDSR SL4 .... 97 J6
Cripley Rd *FARN* GU14 .... 181 G8
Crisp Gdns *BNFD* RG42 .... 12 A1
Crispin CI *CAV/SC* RG4 .... 88 A1
Crisp Rd *HEN* RG9 .... 37 M3
Crocker CI *ASC* SL5 .... 123 H6
Crockford CI
  ADL/WDHM KT15 .... 155 M8 🔲
Crockford PI *BNFD* RG42 ...... 12 C1
Crockhamwell Rd *WODY* RG5 .... 90 B8
Crocus Md *NTHA* RG18 .... 138 B2
Crocus Wy *WWKG* RG41 .... 119 C7 🔲
Croft CI *WWKG* RG41 .... 147 K4
Crofters *WDSR* SL4 .... 97 K5
Crofter's CI *SHST* GU47 .... 172 D6 🔲
Crofthill Rd *SLN* SL2 .... 44 E5
Croft La *NWBY* RG14 .... 14 B2
  YTLY GU46 .... 171 M7
Crofton CI *BRAK* RG12 .... 150 B2
Croft Rd *EWKG* RG40 .... 147 K5
  GOR/PANG RG8 .... 32 F8
  HUNG RG17 .... 104 A8
  NWBY RG14 .... 14 D9
  THLE RG7 .... 142 C8
  THLE RG7 .... 144 F4
The Croft *BNFD* RG42 .... 13 H1
  HUNG RG17 .... 133 K4
  MDHD SL6 .... 2 B9
  MLW SL7 .... 19 K3
Croft Wy *FRIM* GU16 .... 182 C1
  GOR/PANG RG8 .... 34 C6
Cromer CI *CALC* RG31 .... 86 F5 🔲
Cromer Rd *HTHAIR* TW6 .... 100 D2
Cromwell CI *HEN* RG9 .... 38 K6 🔲
Cromwell Dr *SL* SL1 .... 4 F2
Cromwell Gdns *MLW* SL7 .... 19 H8
Cromwell Rd *ASC* SL5 .... 151 L1
  CAV/SC RG4 .... 88 E4
  CBLY GU15 .... 174 A7
  FELT TW13 .... 101 L7
  HEN RG9 .... 38 B6
  MDHD SL6 .... 2 C2
  MLW SL7 .... 19 H4 🔲
  NWBY RG14 .... 136 F1
Cromwell Wy *FARN* GU14 .... 181 L7 🔲
Crondall Ct *CBLY* GU15 .... 181 L2 🔲
Crondall End *YTLY* GU46 ...... 171 M7
Crookham CI *TADY* RG26 .... 164 E8 🔲
Cropper CI *STHA* RG19 .... 138 D3
Crosby Gdns *YTLY* GU46 .... 171 K7
Crosby Hill Dr *CBLY* GU15 .... 174 C7
Crosfields CI *WHIT* RG2 .... 117 H6
Cross Fell *BRAK* RG12 .... 12 E9
Cross Gdns *FRIM* GU16 .... 182 C8
Cross Gates CI *BRAK* RG12 .... 122 C8
Cross Keys Rd *GOR/PANG* RG8 .. 32 F3
Crossland Rd *READ* RG1 .... 9 G7
Crosslands *CHERT* KT16 .... 155 H7
Cross La *FRIM* GU16 .... 182 C8
  THLE RG7 .... 143 K6
  THLE RG7 .... 144 A7
Cross Oak *WDSR* SL4 .... 6 C8
Cross Rd *ASC* SL5 .... 152 C5
Cross St *EWKG* RG40 .... 11 H5
  READ RG1 .... 9 G6
Crossways *EGH* TW20 .... 127 G4
  SUN TW16 .... 129 J6
Crosswell CI *SHPTN* TW17 ..... 128 F7 🔲
Crosthwaite Wy *SL* SL1 .... 44 N8
Crouch La *BRAK* RG12 .... 95 H7
Crouch Oak La
  ADL/WDHM KT15 .... 155 M8 🔲
Crowfield Dr *STHA* RG19 ...... 137 L3
Crowle Rd *HUNG* RG17 .... 49 K4
Crown Acre CI *STHA* RG19 ..... 137 M3 🔲
Crown CI *DTCH/LGLY* SL3 ...... 72 F7
Crown Hill Ct *ASC* SL5 .... 151 L2
Crown La *MDHD* SL6 .... 3 J4
  SLN SL2 .... 44 E1
  THLE RG7 .... 114 B3 🔲
  VW GU25 .... 154 A3
Crown Meadow *DTCH/LGLY* SL3 .. 72 E7

Crown PI *READ* RG1 .... 9 J8
  SHST GU47 .... 173 H5 🔲
Crown Ri *CHERT* KT16 .... 155 J5
Crown Rd *MLW* SL7 .... 19 G4
  VW GU25 .... 153M8
Crown Rw *BRAK* RG12 .... 150 A3
Crown Sq *MDHD* SL6 .... 3 L4 🔲
Crown St *EGH* TW20 .... 126 D3
  READ RG1 .... 9 J8
Crowood La *MARL* SN8 .... 102 A2
Crow Piece La *SLN* SL2 .... 44 C1
Crowsley Rd *HEN* RG9 .... 64 D2
Crowsley Wy *CAV/SC* RG4 ...... 62 B1
Crowthorne Rd *BRAK* RG12 ..... 149 J5
  BRAK RG12 .... 149 K2
  SHST GU47 .... 172 E6
Crowthorne Rd North
  BRAK RG12 .... 13 H7
Croxley Ri *MDHD* SL6 .... 2 C7
Croyde CI *FARN* GU14 .... 181 K8
Croysdale Av *SUN* TW16 .... 129 K8
Cruch La *BNFD* RG42 .... 94 B5
Cruikshank Lea *SHST* GU47 .... 173 H8 🔲
Crummock CI *SL* SL1 .... 43 M7 🔲
Crutchley Rd *EWKG* RG40 ...... 11 J5
Cuckoo La *CHOB/PIR* GU24 ..... 176 A8
Cuckoo V *CHOB/PIR* GU24 ...... 176 A8
Cuddesdon CI *GOR/PANG* RG8 ... 34 C6 🔲
Culford CI *EARL* RG6 .... 118 A4
Culham CI *MDHD* SL6 .... 42 B4
Cullen's Pas *MDHD* SL6 .... 3 H5
Culley Wy *MDHD* SL6 .... 67 K2
Culloden Wy *WWKG* RG41 .... 119 H8
Culver Cft *BNFD* RG42 .... 12 A1
Culver La *EARL* RG6 .... 89 K8
Culver Rd *NWBY* RG14 .... 136 C6 🔲
  READ RG1 .... 89 J8
  SHST GU47 .... 173 G5
Culvert La *UX/CGN* UB8 .... 47 L3
Cumberland Dr *BRAK* RG12 ..... 13 M3
  BRAK RG12 .... 122 B6 🔲
  CBLY GU15 .... 174 A7
  READ RG1 .... 9 M6
Cumberland Rd *ASHF* TW15 ..... 128 A1
Cumberland St *STA* TW18 ...... 127 C3 🔲
Cumberland Wy *WWKG* RG41 ..... 119 C8 🔲
Cumbernauld Gdns
  SUN TW16 .... 129 J3 🔲
Cumbrae CI *SLN* SL2 .... 5 K6
Cumbria CI *MDHD* SL6 .... 67 M2 🔲
Cumnor Wy *BRAK* RG12 .... 150 B1
Curfew Bell Rd *CHERT* KT16 ... 155 J4
Curlew CI *STHA* RG19 .... 137 M3 🔲
Curlew Dr *CALC* RG31 .... 86 F8
Curley Hill Rd *LTWR* GU18 .... 175 H7
Curleys Wy *THLE* RG7 .... 145 L2
Curling Wy *NWBY* RG14 .... 15 K1
Curls La *MDHD* SL6 .... 68 B2
Curls Rd *MDHD* SL6 .... 68 A2
Curl Wy *WWKG* RG41 .... 10 C7
Curly Bridge CI *FARN* GU14 ... 181 J6
Curran CI *UX/CGN* UB8 .... 47 M5
Curridge Gn *NTHA* RG18 .... 109 H2
Curridge Rd *NWBY* RG14 .... 108 F3
Curtis CI *CBLY* GU15 .... 174 F7 🔲
Curtis Rd *CALC* RG31 .... 114 L1
Cutbush CI *EARL* RG6 .... 117 L6
  EARL RG6 .... 117 K6
Cutbush La *EARL* RG6 .... 117M5
  WHIT RG2 .... 117 H8
The Cuttings *NTHA* RG18 ...... 82 C1
Cwmcarn *CAV/SC* RG4 .... 62 C8
Cygnet Av *EBED/NFELT* TW14 ... 101 M6
Cygnet CI *STHA* RG19 .... 137 L3
The Cygnets *STA* TW18 .... 127 J3 🔲
Cypress *FARN* GU14 .... 181 J5 🔲
Cypress CI *EWKG* RG40 .... 147 K6
Cypress Rd *WODY* RG5 .... 90 D8
Cypress Wk *EGH* TW20 .... 125 L4
Cyprus Rd *FRIM* GU16 .... 183 G6
Cyril Vokins Rd *NWBY* RG14 ... 137 H4

D

Dacre Av *CAV/SC* RG4 .... 89 G2
Dagmar Rd *WDSR* SL4 .... 7 J8
Dagnall Crs *UX/CGN* UB8 ...... 47 M6
Dairy Ct *MDHD* SL6 .... 68 D7
Dairy La *HEN* RG9 .... 16 E5
Dalby CI *WAR/TWY* RG10 .... 91 J6
Dalby Crs *NWBY* RG14 .... 15 H9
Dalcross *BRAK* RG12 .... 150 B3
Dale CI *ASC* SL5 .... 152 D2
Dale Gdns *SHST* GU47 .... 172 D6
Daleham Av *EGH* TW20 .... 126 D4
Dale Lodge Rd *ASC* SL5 .... 152 C2
Dale Rd *SUN* TW16 .... 129 J5 🔲
  WHIT RG2 .... 116 E1
Dalley Ct *SHST* GU47 .... 173 G7
Dalston CI *CBLY* GU15 .... 183 G3
Dalton CI *TLHT* RG30 .... 87 H6 🔲
Damar Gdns *HEN* RG9 .... 38 B6
Damask CI *CHOB/PIR* GU24 ..... 176 B3 🔲
Damson Gv *SL* SL1 .... 4 B9
Dandridge CI *DTCH/LGLY* SL3 .. 72 A4
Dandridge Dr *BNEND* SL8 ...... 20 F3 🔲
Danehurst CI *EGH* TW20 .... 126 B4
Dane Rd *ASHF* TW15 .... 128 F4
Danesbury Rd *FELT* TW13 ...... 101 L7
Danes Gdns *MDHD* SL6 .... 20 C8 🔲
Danvers CI *STHA* RG19 .... 138 A4 🔲
Danywern Dr *WWKG* RG41 ...... 118 F4
Darby Crs *SUN* TW16 .... 129M7
Darby Gdns *SUN* TW16 .... 129M7
Darby Green La *BLKW* GU17 .... 180 L1
Darby Green Rd *BLKW* GU17 ... 180 D1
Darby La *GOR/PANG* RG8 .... 84 L1
Darell Rd *CAV/SC* RG4 .... 88 C3
Dark La *CALC* RG31 .... 86 E4
  HUNG RG17 .... 104 D8
  THLE RG7 .... 84 F7
  WAR/TWY RG10 .... 65 G4
Darleydale CI *SHST* GU47 ..... 173 C4 🔲
Darling's La *MDHD* SL6 .... 41 H6
Darracott CI *CBLY* GU15 ...... 174 E7 🔲

Darrell CI *DTCH/LGLY* SL3 ..... 72 C4
Dart CI *DTCH/LGLY* SL3 .... 72 E6
  EWKG RG40 .... 147 J7
  NTHA RG18 .... 137 L1
Dartington Av *WODY* RG5 ...... 118 A2
Dartmouth CI *BRAK* RG12 ...... 122 B8 🔲
Dart Rd *FARN* GU14 .... 181 G8
Darvill's La *SL* SL1 .... 4 D9
  WAR/TWY RG10 .... 92 C5
Darwall Dr *ASC* SL5 .... 123 G7
Darwin CI *WHIT* RG2 .... 116 D5
Darwin Rd *DTCH/LGLY* SL3 ..... 72 C2
Dashwood CI *BRAK* RG12 .... 13 L3
  DTCH/LGLY SL3 .... 71 M4
Datchet PI *DTCH/LGLY* SL3 .... 71 L8
Datchet Rd *DTCH/LGLY* SL3 .... 98 C2
  WDSR SL4 .... 7 K5
  WDSR SL4 .... 97 K4
Dauntless Rd *THLE* RG7 .... 142 E3
Davenport Rd *BRAK* RG12 ...... 122 B6
Daventry CI *DTCH/LGLY* SL3 ... 73 J8
Daventry Ct *BNFD* RG42 .... 13 G3
David Rd *DTCH/LGLY* SL3 ...... 99 J1
Davis CI *MLW* SL7 .... 19 H5
Davis Gdns *SHST* GU47 .... 173 H7
Davis St *WAR/TWY* RG10 .... 119 G2
Davis Wy *WAR/TWY* RG10 .... 119 G2
Davy CI *EWKG* RG40 .... 11 G8
Dawes East Rd *SL* SL1 .... 43 M5
Dawes Moor CI *SLN* SL2 .... 45 M7
Dawley Ride *DTCH/LGLY* SL3 ... 73 H8
Dawlish Rd *WHIT* RG2 .... 116 F4
Dawnay CI *ASC* SL5 .... 123 J6
Dawnay Rd *CBLY* GU15 .... 173 K6 🔲
Dawn Redwood CI
  DTCH/LGLY SL3 .... 98 D2
Dawsmere CI *CBLY* GU15 .... 182 F1
Dawson CI *WDSR* SL4 .... 6 C8
Deacon CI *EWKG* RG40 .... 11 H3
Deaconfield *GOR/PANG* RG8 .... 32 F3 🔲
Deacons La *NTHA* RG18 .... 81 M7
Deacon Wy *TLHT* RG30 .... 87 K4
Deadman's La *GOR/PANG* RG8 ... 60 F1
  STHA RG19 .... 136 E8
  THLE RG7 .... 113M2
Deadmoor La *KSCL* RG20 .... 160 B4
Deal Av *SL* SL1 .... 44 C7
Deal CI *WDSR* SL4 .... 96 A2
Deanfield Av *HEN* RG9 .... 38 A5
Deanfield CI *MLW* SL7 .... 19 G3
Deanfield Rd *HEN* RG9 .... 37 M5
Dean Gv *EWKG* RG40 .... 11 H3
Dean La *MDHD* SL6 .... 45 L2
Deans CI *WDSR* SL4 .... 96 A2
Deans Ct *BFOR* GU20 .... 176 A2 🔲
Deansgate *BRAK* RG12 .... 149 K4
Deansgate Rd *READ* RG1 .... 9 G8
Dean St *MLW* SL7 .... 19 G4
Deanswood Rd *TADY* RG26 ...... 164 D6
De Beauvoir Rd *READ* RG1 ..... 89 H7
De Bohun Rd *READ* RG1 .... 9 G4
De Broome Rd *FELT* TW13 ...... 101 M7
Decies Wy *SLN* SL2 .... 45 K2 🔲
Dedmere Ct *MLW* SL7 .... 19 H4
Dedmere Ri *MLW* SL7 .... 19 H4
Dedmere Rd *MLW* SL7 .... 19 H4
Dedworth Dr *WDSR* SL4 .... 70 B8
Dedworth Rd *WDSR* SL4 .... 6 A8
  WDSR SL4 .... 95 L1
Deena CI *SL* SL1 .... 44 B8
Deepcut Bridge Rd *FRIM* GU16 . 183 G7
Deepdale *BRAK* RG12 .... 12 E8
Deepdene CI *READ* RG1 .... 8 B7
Deep Fld *DTCH/LGLY* SL3 ...... 71 L7
Deepfield Rd *BRAK* RG12 ...... 13 L4
Deep Well Dr *CBLY* GU15 ...... 182 B1
Deerhurst Av *WWKG* RG41 ...... 118 F4
Deerhurst CI *FELT* TW13 ...... 129 K2
Deer Leap *LTWR* GU18 .... 175 K6
Dee Rd *TLHT* RG30 .... 87 K7
Deer Rock HI *BRAK* RG12 ...... 149M3
Deer Rock Rd *CBLY* GU15 ...... 174 C7
Deer's La *GOR/PANG* RG8 ...... 34 F4
Deerswood CI *MDHD* SL6 .... 3 K1
De Havilland Wy
  STWL/WRAY TW19 .... 100 A5
Delafield Dr *CALC* RG31 ...... 114 F2
Delaford CI *IVER* SL0 .... 47 K7 🔲
Delamere *EARL* RG6 .... 89 L6
Delane Dr *WWKG* RG41 .... 118 E4
Delaney CI *TLHT* RG30 .... 87 J6
Delft CI *TLHT* RG30 .... 87 J6 🔲
Dellbow Rd *EBED/NFELT* TW14 .. 101 L4
Deller St *BNFD* RG42 .... 12 C1
Dellfield Crs *UX/CGN* UB8 .... 47 M5
Dell Gv *FRIM* GU16 .... 183 G6
Dell Rd *CALC* RG31 .... 86 F4
  EWKG RG40 .... 171 K3
The Dell *EBED/NFELT* TW14 .... 101 L6
  MDHD SL6 .... 67 J3 🔲
  RAND SP11 .... 178 B8
  READ RG1 .... 9 J8
The Delph *EARL* RG6 .... 118 A4
Delta CI *CHOB/PIR* GU24 ...... 177 J5
Delta Rd *CHOB/PIR* GU24 ...... 177 J5
Delta Wy *EGH* TW20 .... 126 F6
De Montfort Gv *HUNG* RG17 .... 131M2
De Montfort Rd *NWBY* RG14 .... 136 A1
  READ RG1 .... 8 F3
Denbigh PI *READ* RG1 .... 8 D2
Denbury Gdns *WHIT* RG2 .... 116 F6 🔲
Denby Wy *TLHT* RG30 .... 87 J5
Dene CI *BRAK* RG12 .... 13 K2
Denford La *HUNG* RG17 .... 104 F6
Denham Dr *YTLY* GU46 .... 180 B1 🔲
Denham Gv *BRAK* RG12 .... 149 M3 🔲
Denham Rd *EBED/NFELT* TW14 .. 101 M6
  EGH TW20 .... 126 D2
  IVER SL0 .... 47 G2
Denison Rd *FELT* TW13 .... 129 J2
Denly Wy *LTWR* GU18 .... 175M5
Denman Dr *ASHF* TW15 .... 128 E4
Denmark Av *WODY* RG5 .... 90 D5

Denmark Rd *NWBY* RG14 .... 15 G4
  READ RG1 .... 9 L7
Denmark St *EWKG* RG40 .... 11 G7
  MDHD SL6 .... 2 F2
Denmead Ct *BRAK* RG12 .... 150 B3
Denmead Rd *TADY* RG26 .... 164 E6
Dennisford Rd *KSCL* RG20 ..... 55 J1
Dennistoun CI *CBLY* GU15 ..... 182 A1 🔲
Dennis Wy *SL* SL1 .... 44 A8
Dennose CI *EARL* RG6 .... 117 K5
Denny Rd *DTCH/LGLY* SL3 ...... 72 C4 🔲
Denton CI *STHA* RG19 .... 137M4
Denton Rd *EWKG* RG40 .... 11 H7
Denton Wy *FRIM* GU16 .... 182 A4
Depot Rd *MDHD* SL6 .... 3 J7
Derby CI *HUNG* RG17 .... 49 K4
Derby Rd *CAV/SC* RG4 .... 88 E3
  NWBY RG14 .... 14 D7
  UX/CGN UB8 .... 47 M3
Derbyshire Gn *BNFD* RG42 ..... 122 C5
Derby St *READ* RG1 .... 8 C5
Derek Rd *MDHD* SL6 .... 42 F6
Deri Dene CI
  STWL/WRAY TW19 .... 100 B5
Derrick CI *CALC* RG31 .... 114 F2 🔲
Derry Rd *FARN* GU14 .... 181 J5
Derwent CI *EBED/NFELT* TW14 .. 101 J7
  WWKG RG41 .... 119 H8
Derwent Dr *MDHD* SL6 .... 2 C2
Derwent Rd *EGH* TW20 .... 126 E4
  LTWR GU18 .... 175 L6
  STHA RG19 .... 137 K3
Desborough Crs *MDHD* SL6 ..... 2 B9
Desford Wy *ASHF* TW15 .... 100 C8
Dettingen Rd *FRIM* GU16 ...... 183 H6
Devenish La *ASC* SL5 .... 152 A5
Devenish Rd *ASC* SL5 .... 152 A3
Devereux Rd *WDSR* SL4 .... 7 J8
Deverills Wy *DTCH/LGLY* SL3 .. 72 F4
Deveron Dr *TLHT* RG30 .... 87 K6
The Devil's Hwy *CWTH* RG45 ... 172 B1
Devil's La *EGH* TW20 .... 126 F4
De-vitre Gn *EWKG* RG40 .... 120 C7
Devitt CI *WHIT* RG2 .... 117 H5
Devon Av *SL* SL1 .... 4 B2
Devon Cha *BNFD* RG42 .... 122 B4 🔲
  BNFD RG42 .... 122 C4 🔲
Devon CI *SHST* GU47 .... 173 C4 🔲
  WWKG RG40 .... 119 H8
Devon Dr *CAV/SC* RG4 .... 89 H2
Devonshire Dr *CBLY* GU15 ..... 174 C7
Devonshire Gdns *CALC* RG31 ... 86 E2
Devonshire Gn *SLN* SL2 .... 44 E3
Devonshire Pk *WHIT* RG2 ...... 117 H5
Dewe La *THLT* RG30 .... 115 H4
Dhoon Ri *MDHD* SL6 .... 3 H7
Diamedes Av
  STWL/WRAY TW19 .... 100 A6 🔲
Diamond HI *CBLY* GU15 .... 174 A7
Diamond Rdg *CBLY* GU15 .... 174 A7
Diamond Rd *SL* SL1 .... 5 K8
Diamond Wy *WWKG* RG41 .... 119 H7 🔲
Diana CI *DTCH/LGLY* SL3 ...... 46 B7
  THLE RG7 .... 144 D5
Dianthus CI *CHERT* KT16 ...... 155 H4 🔲
Dianthus PI *BNFD* RG42 .... 122 E4
Dickens CI *CAV/SC* RG4 .... 9 L1
Dickenson Rd *FELT* TW13 ...... 129M3
Dick Turpin Wy
  EBED/NFELT TW14 .... 101 J3
Dieppe CI *WWKG* RG41 .... 119 H8 🔲
Digby Rd *NWBY* RG14 .... 14 B1
  NWBY RG14 .... 136 B1
Dines Wy *NTHA* RG18 .... 81 L7
Dingle Rd *ASHF* TW15 .... 128 E3
Disraeli Ct *DTCH/LGLY* SL3 ... 72 E6 🔲
Ditchfield La *EWKG* RG40 ..... 147 H6
Ditchling *BRAK* RG12 .... 149 K4
Ditton Mace *MDHD* SL6 .... 41 K5
Ditton Park Rd *DTCH/LGLY* SL3 . 72 B6
Ditton Rd *DTCH/LGLY* SL3 ..... 72 A4
  DTCH/LGLY SL3 .... 72 C6
The Dittons *EWKG* RG40 .... 147 J8 🔲
Dockwell CI *EBED/NFELT* TW14 . 101 K3
Doctors La *NTHA* RG18 .... 81 K8
Doddington CI *EARL* RG6 ...... 117M5
Doddsfield Rd *SLN* SL2 .... 44 D4
Dodsells Well *EWKG* RG40 ..... 147 J6 🔲
Dogkennel La *WANT* OX12 ...... 51M2
Dog La *GOR/PANG* RG8 .... 57 K8
  HEN RG9 .... 36 D6
Doles HI *WWKG* RG41 .... 147 G3
Doles La *WWKG* RG41 .... 147 H3
Dolman Rd *NWBY* RG14 .... 14 E1
  NWBY RG14 .... 136 D1 🔲
Dolphin CI *WWKG* RG41 .... 118 F5
Dolphin Ct *SL* SL1 .... 5 M9
  STWL/WRAY TW19 .... 127 K1 🔲
Dolphin Ct North
  STWL/WRAY TW19 .... 127 K1 🔲
Dolphin Rd *SL* SL1 .... 5 M8
Doman Rd *CBLY* GU15 .... 181 K2
Domomy CI *STHA* RG19 .... 138 B3
Donaldson Wy *WODY* RG5 .... 90 D6
Doncastle Rd *BRAK* RG12 ...... 12 B7
Don CI *TLHT* RG30 .... 87 K6
Donegal CI *CAV/SC* RG4 .... 88 F3
Donkin HI *CAV/SC* RG4 .... 88 F3
Donnington CI *CBLY* GU15 ..... 181 L2 🔲
  THLE RG7 .... 111M6
Donnington Gdns *MDHD* SL6 .... 3 G1
  READ RG1 .... 9 M8
Donnington Pk *NWBY* RG14 ..... 108 C3
Donnington PI *WWKG* RG41 ..... 119 G4 🔲
Donnington Rd *READ* RG1 ...... 9 M7
Donnington Sq *NWBY* RG14 ..... 136 C1
Donnybrook *BRAK* RG12 .... 149 K4
Dorcas Ct *CBLY* GU15 .... 181 L3 🔲
Dorchester CI *MDHD* SL6 ...... 41 L5
Dorchester Ct *TLHT* RG30 ..... 87M8
Dorchester Dr
  EBED/NFELT TW14 .... 101 H5
Doreen CI *FARN* GU14 .... 181 C6
Dorian Dr *ASC* SL5 .... 124 B6
Doris Rd *ASHF* TW15 .... 129 G4
Dorking Wy *CALC* RG31 .... 114 D2

Dormer CI *CWTH* RG45 .... 172 D1
  NWBY RG14 .... 136 B8
Dornels *SLN* SL2 .... 45 M7
Dorney Reach Rd *MDHD* SL6 ... 69 J3
Dorney Wood Rd *SL* SL1 .... 21 M5
Dorothy St *READ* RG1 .... 9 G8
Dorset Rd *ASHF* TW15 .... 128 A1
  WDSR SL4 .... 7 H8
Dorset St *TLHT* RG30 .... 87M6
Dorset V *BNFD* RG42 .... 122 B4
Dorset Wy *WWKG* RG41 .... 147 H1
Doublet CI *STHA* RG19 .... 137 K3
Douglas Gra *WAR/TWY* RG10 ... 119 G2
Douglas La *STWL/WRAY* TW19 ... 98 C4
Douglas Ride *KSCL* RG20 ...... 159 H6
Douglas Rd *ADL/WDHM* KT15 ... 155 L7 🔲
  SLN SL2 .... 45 G6 🔲
  STWL/WRAY TW19 .... 100 A5 🔲
Dove CI *EARL* RG6 .... 117 J6 🔲
Dovecote Rd *WHIT* RG2 .... 116 E7
Dovedale CI *CAV/SC* RG4 ...... 88 C3
  SHST GU47 .... 173 C4 🔲
Dove House Crs *SLN* SL2 ...... 44 B4
Dove La *HEN* RG9 .... 36 A6
Dover Rd *SL* SL1 .... 44 C7
Dover St *READ* RG1 .... 8 E5
Doveton Wy *NWBY* RG14 .... 15 H1
Dowding CI *WODY* RG5 .... 90 D7
Dowding Ct *CWTH* RG45 .... 148 F8 🔲
Dower Pk *WDSR* SL4 .... 96 B3
Downend La *KSCL* RG20 .... 80 C3
Downfield La *WAR/TWY* RG10 ... 92 E2
Downfield Rd *WAR/TWY* RG10 ... 92 D2
Downing Rd *CALC* RG31 .... 86 F6
Downlands *HUNG* RG17 .... 50 F8 🔲
Downmill Rd *BRAK* RG12 .... 12 D5
Downs CI *HUNG* RG17 .... 50 C7
Downshire CI *HUNG* RG17 ...... 77 K2
Downshire Sq *READ* RG1 .... 8 B8
Downshire Wy *BNFD* RG42 ...... 12 F3
  BRAK RG12 .... 12 F5
Downside *SUN* TW16 .... 129 K6
Downs La *MARL* SN8 .... 156 A7
Downsmead *MARL* SN8 .... 48 A6
Downs Rd *DTCH/LGLY* SL3 ...... 72 A2
  KSCL RG20 .... 56 D2
Downs Wy *CALC* RG31 .... 86 F4
  STA TW18 .... 127 J3
Drake Av *DTCH/LGLY* SL3 ...... 72 A4
Drake CI *EWKG* RG40 .... 147 H7
Draper CI *STHA* RG19 .... 138 A4
Draycott *BRAK* RG12 .... 150 B2
Drayhorse Dr *BAGS* GU19 ...... 175 H4
Dray's La *HEN* RG9 .... 36 C9
Drayton CI *BRAK* RG12 .... 13 L5
Drayton Rd *TLHT* RG30 .... 87 L6
Dresden Wy *TLHT* RG30 .... 87 J5 🔲
Drewett CI *WHIT* RG2 .... 116 F8
Drift Rd *WDSR* SL4 .... 94 D3
Drift Wy *DTCH/LGLY* SL3 ...... 72 F8
Driftway CI *EARL* RG6 .... 117M5
Drill Hall Rd *CHERT* KT16 .... 155 K4
The Drive *ASHF* TW15 .... 129 G5
  BNEND SL8 .... 20 C2
  DTCH/LGLY SL3 .... 71 J8
  DTCH/LGLY SL3 .... 72 B2
  EARL RG6 .... 89 K7
  EBED/NFELT TW14 .... 101M6
  NWBY RG14 .... 14 B9
  STWL/WRAY TW19 .... 98 A4
Droitwich CI *BRAK* RG12 ...... 13M7
  BRAK RG12 .... 122 B8 🔲
Drome Pth *WWKG* RG41 .... 118 D3
Dropmore Rd *SL* SL1 .... 43 M3
Drove La *NTHA* RG18 .... 109 L4
Drovers Wy *BRAK* RG12 .... 122 C8
  WODY RG5 .... 118 B1
Droxford Crs *TADY* RG26 ...... 164 D7
Druce Wy *STHA* RG19 .... 138 A3
Drummond CI *BRAK* RG12 .... 122 C6 🔲
Drury La *THLE* RG7 .... 166 E2
Dry Arch Rd *ASC* SL5 .... 152 C4
Dryden *BRAK* RG12 .... 149 K4
Dryden CI *NTHA* RG18 .... 137 K1
Dryden Rd *FARN* GU14 .... 181 J8
Duchess CI *CWTH* RG45 .... 148 E7 🔲
Duchess St *SL* SL1 .... 70 B1 🔲
  CALC RG31 .... 87 H5
Dudley Ms *CALC* RG31 .... 87 H5 🔲
Dudley Rd *ASHF* TW15 .... 128 C4
  EBED/NFELT TW14 .... 101 C7
Duffield La *SLN* SL2 .... 45 J1
Duffield Pk *SLN* SL2 .... 45 J4
Duffield Rd *WODY* RG5 .... 90 C5
Duke of Cornwall Av
  CBLY GU15 .... 174 A5
Dukes CI *ASHF* TW15 .... 128 F2
Dukes Covert *BAGS* GU19 ...... 151 H8
Dukes HI *BAGS* GU19 .... 175 H1
Dukeshill Rd *BNFD* RG42 ...... 13 G2
Duke's La *ASC* SL5 .... 124 C5
Dukes PI *MLW* SL7 .... 19 G4 🔲
Duke's Ride *CWTH* RG45 .... 172 C2
  THLE RG7 .... 165 L6
Duke St *HEN* RG9 .... 38 B4
  READ RG1 .... 9 G5
  WDSR SL4 .... 7 G6
Dukes Wd *CWTH* RG45 .... 172 E1
Dulnan CI *TLHT* RG30 .... 87 K6
Dulverton Gdns *WHIT* RG2 ..... 116 F4
Dumbarton Wy *CAV/SC* RG4 ..... 89 H7
Dunaways CI *EARL* RG6 .... 118 A3
Dunbar CI *SLN* SL2 .... 5 J4
Dunbar Dr *WODY* RG5 .... 90 D8
Dunbar Rd *NWBY* RG14 .... 182 C7
Duncan Dr *EWKG* RG40 .... 11 K8
  STA TW18 .... 127 K4
Duncannon Crs *WDSR* SL4 ...... 96 A2
Duncan Rd *WODY* RG5 .... 90 D8
Duncroft *WDSR* SL4 .... 96 C2
Dundaff CI *CBLY* GU15 .... 182 D1
Dundas CI *BRAK* RG12 .... 13 G8
Dundee Rd *SL* SL1 .... 44 C7
Dundela CI *WODY* RG5 .... 90 B8

Dunford Pl *BNFD* RG42 .... 121 H5
Dungells Farm Cl *YTLY* GU46 ... 180 A2 1
Dungrove Hill La *MDHD* SL6......... 40 F3
Dunholme Cl *EARL* RG6 .... 118 B4 4
Dunholme End *MDHD* SL6 .... 68 A3 3
Dunkirk Cl *WWKG* RG41 .... 119 H8 3
Dunluce Gdns *GOR/PANG* RG8 .. 86 B1 1
Dunn Crs *HUNG* RG17................ 133 L5
Dunnock Wy *WAR/TWY* RG10 ... 65 H3 1
Dunoon Cl *CALC* RG31 .... 115 H2 2
Dunsfold Rd *TLHT* RG30................. 87 J7
Dunstall Cl *CALC* RG31 .... 87 G6 2
Dunstall Pk *FARN* GU14 .... 181 K7
Dunstan Rd *NTHA* RG18................. 138 B2
Dunstans Dr *WWKG* RG41 .... 118 E4
Dunster Cl *CAV/SC* RG4 .... 62 F8
Dunster Gdns *SL* SL1 .... 44 D8 2
Dunt Av *WAR/TWY* RG10 .... 119 H2
Dunt La *WAR/TWY* RG10 .... 119 H1
Dupre Cl *SL* SL1.............................. 70 B2
Durand Rd *EARL* RG6 .... 117 K5
Durant Wy *CALC* RG31 .... 87 G3
Durbidges *STHA* RG19 .... 162 B6
Durham Av *SL* SL1 .... 44 D7 2
Durham Cl *WHIT* RG2 .... 116 F6
Durham Rd *EBED/NFELT* TW14.... 101 M6
SHST GU47 .... 173 H4
Durley Md *BRAK* RG12 .... 150 C2
Dutch Barn Cl
STWL/WRAY TW19 .... 100 A5
Dutton Wy *IVER* SL0........................ 47 H7
Duval Pl *BAGS* GU19 .... 175 H3
Dwyer Rd *TLHT* RG30 .... 115 J2
Dyer Rd *EWKG* RG40........................ 11 M4
Dyson Cl *WDSR* SL4 .... 96 E2
Dysons Cl *NWBY* RG14 .... 14 B4
Dysonswood La *CAV/SC* RG4 .... 62 B6

E

Eagle Cl *CWTH* RG45........................ 148 D7
Eagle Rd *KSCL* RG20 .... 161 K4
Eagles Nest *SHST* GU47 .... 172 D5 2
Earle Cft *BNFD* RG42 .... 121 M5 3
Earleydene *ASC* SL5 .... 151 L5
Earley Hill Rd *EARL* RG6 .... 117 K1
Earley Pl *READ* RG1 .... 9 G6
Earlsfield *MDHD* SL6 .... 68 F4
Earlsfield Cl *CAV/SC* RG4 .... 89 H2
Earls Gv *CBLY* GU15 .... 174 B8
Earls La *SL* SL1.................................. 70 C1
Earlswood *BRAK* RG12..................... 149 L4
Easby Wy *EARL* RG6 .... 118 A5
Easington Dr *EARL* RG6 .... 118 B4
Eastbourne Rd *SL* SL1 .... 44 D7 3
Eastbridge *SLN* SL2 .... 5 M7 1
East Burnham La *SLN* SL2 .... 44 D2
Eastbury Av *CALC* RG31 .... 86 E6
Eastbury Pk *WWKG* RG41 .... 119 G4
Eastbury Shute *HUNG* RG17 .... 76 B4
Eastchurch Rd *HTHAIR* TW6 .... 101 H2
Eastcourt Av *EARL* RG6 .... 89 K8
Eastcroft *SLN* SL2 .... 44 E5
East Dr *CALC* RG31 .... 115 H1
VW GU25.. 153 L3
Eastern Av *CHERT* KT16 .... 127 K8
READ RG1 .... 89 H8
Eastern Dr *BNEND* SL8..................... 20 F2
Eastern La *CWTH* RG45 .... 173 J2
Eastern Perimeter Rd
HTHAIR TW6 .... 101 H1
HTHAIR TW6 .... 101 J2
Eastern Rd *BRAK* RG12 .... 13 M5
Eastfield Cl *SL* SL1 .... 71 K3 1
Eastfield La *GOR/PANG* RG8 .... 34 B8
GOR/PANG RG8 .... 60 A7
Eastfield Rd *SL* SL1.......................... 43 K6
East Gn *BLKW* GU17 .... 180 F2
Easthampstead Rd *BRAK* RG12 ..... 12 E4
EWKG RG40.. 11 J6
Eastheath Av *WWKG* RG41 .... 147 K2
Eastheath Gdns *WWKG* RG41 ... 147 L3 1
East La *KSCL* RG20 .... 80 E5
Eastleigh Wy
EBED/NFELT TW14 .... 101 K7 2
Eastlyn Rd *TADY* RG26 .... 165 H5
Easton Hl *KSCL* RG20 .... 106 E1
East Paddock *MDHD* SL6 .... 19 J8
East Park Farm Dr
WAR/TWY RG10 .... 90 E2
East Rdg *BNEND* SL8 .... 20 E2
East Rd *EBED/NFELT* TW14 .... 101 G6
MDHD SL6.. 2 F5
East Stanley Gn *DTCH/LGLY* SL3.... 72 C4
East Stratton Cl *BRAK* RG12 .... 150 C2 2
East St *READ* RG1 .... 9 H7
East View Cl *WAR/TWY* RG10 .... 65 H4
East View Rd *WAR/TWY* RG10.......... 65 H4
Eastwood Rd *WODY* RG5 .... 118 B2
Eastworth Rd *CHERT* KT16 .... 155 J5
Eaton Pl *READ* RG1............................. 8 D6
Eaton Rd *CBLY* GU15 .... 181 L2
Ebborn Sq *EARL* RG6 .... 117 M6 3
Ebsworth Cl *MDHD* SL6 .... 42 F3
Eccles Cl *CAV/SC* RG4 .... 88 F4 1
Echelforde Dr *ASHF* TW15.............. 128 D2
Ecton Rd *ADL/WDHM* KT15 .... 155 L8
Eddington Hl *HUNG* RG17 .... 104 B7
Eddington Rd *BRAK* RG12 .... 149 H3
Eden Cl *DTCH/LGLY* SL3 .... 72 D5
Edenhall Cl *CALC* RG31 .... 87 G3
Edenham Cl *EARL* RG6 .... 118 B4
Edenham Crs *READ* RG1 .... 116 B1
Eden Wy *WWKG* RG41 .... 118 E5
Edgar Milward Cl *TLHT* RG30 .... 87 K5
Edgbarrowhill Star *CWTH* RG45.. 172 D3
Edgbarrow Ri *SHST* GU47 .... 172 D4
Edgcumbe Park Dr *CWTH* RG45.. 172 D1
Edgecombe La *NWBY* RG14 .... 136 F1
Edgedale Cl *CWTH* RG45 .... 172 E2 1
Edgehill St *READ* RG1..................... 116 E1
Edgell Cl *VW* GU25 .... 126 C8
Edgell Rd *STA* TW18 .... 127 J4
Edgemoor Rd *FRIM* GU16 .... 182 F3 1
Edgewood Cl *CWTH* RG45 .... 148 D7 1
Edinburgh Av *SL* SL1 .... 44 D7
Edinburgh Dr *STA* TW18 .... 128 A4
Edinburgh Gdns *WDSR* SL4.............. 7 K9
Edinburgh Rd *MDHD* SL6 .... 42 B5
MLW SL7 .... 19 H3 1
TLHT RG30... 8 A6
TLHT RG30 .... 88 A7 2
Edith Rd *MDHD* SL6 .... 41 K7
Edmonds Ct *BRAK* RG12 .... 13 K2
Edmunds Wy *SLN* SL2 .... 5 M1
Edward Av *CBLY* GU15..................... 181 K1
Edward Ct *STA* TW18 .... 127 M4
Edward Rd *BFOR* GU20 .... 176 A2
EBED/NFELT TW14............................ 101 G4
WAR/TWY RG10 .... 90 E1
Edwards Ct *SL* SL1 .... 4 E9
Edwards Hl *HUNG* RG17..................... 49 L4
Edward Wy *ASHF* TW15 .... 100 C8
Edwin Cl *STHA* RG19 .... 138 C3
Eeklo Pl *NWBY* RG14 .... 14 F8
Egerton Rd *CBLY* GU15 .... 173 J8
SHST GU47 .... 173 H8
SLN SL2 .... 44 B5
WHIT RG2 .... 117 H5
Egham By-pass *EGH* TW20 .... 126 C2
Egham Hl *EGH* TW20 .... 126 A4
Egremont Dr *EARL* RG6 .... 118 A4 1
Egremont Gdns *SL* SL1 .... 70 D1 2
Eight Acres *SL* SL1 .... 43 L5
Eisenhower Av *KSCL* RG20 .... 78 D2
Elan Cl *TLHT* RG30............................. 87 J7
Elcho Rd *CHOB/PIR* GU24 .... 183 M6
Eldart Cl *TLHT* RG30 .... 87 L7
Elderberry Wy *EARL* RG6 .... 118 A5 2
Elder Cl *CALC* RG31 .... 86 F5
Eldon Pl *READ* RG1 .... 9 K7
Eldon Rd *READ* RG1 .... 9 K7
Eldon Sq *READ* RG1 .... 9 K7
Eldon St *READ* RG1 .... 9 L7
Eldon Ter *READ* RG1 .... 9 K7
Eldridge Cl *EBED/NFELT* TW14 .... 101 K7
Elford Cl *EARL* RG6 .... 117 M5 2
Elgar Av *CWTH* RG45 .... 148 E8
Elgar Rd South *WHIT* RG2 .... 116 E2
Elgarth Dr *EWKG* RG40 .... 147 J6 3
Elgin Av *ASHF* TW15 .... 128 F4
Elgin Crs *HTHAIR* TW6 .... 101 H1 1
Elgin Rd *BLKW* GU17 .... 180 B5
Elgin Wy *FRIM* GU16....................... 182 C7
Eliot Cl *CAV/SC* RG4.......................... 88 D2
CBLY GU15 .... 174 E7
NTHA RG18 .... 137 M1
Eliot Dr *MLW* SL7............................... 19 J2
Elizabethan Wy
STWL/WRAY TW19 .... 100 A6
Elizabeth Av *BAGS* GU19 .... 175 J4
NWBY RG14 .... 136 A7
STA TW18 .... 127 M4
Elizabeth Cl *BRAK* RG12 .... 13 K9
HEN RG9 .... 37 K5
Elizabeth Gdns *ASC* SL5 .... 151 L2
SUN TW16 .... 129 M8
Elizabeth Rd *EWKG* RG40 .... 11 J5
HEN RG9 .... 37 L6
MLW SL7 .... 19 H3
Elizabeth Rout Cl *THLE* RG7 .... 144 F4
Elizabeth Wy *FELT* TW13 .... 129 M2
SLN SL2 .... 45 J2
Ellenborough Cl *BRAK* RG12 .... 13 L3
Ellerton Cl *THLE* RG7 .... 114 B2 2
Ellesfield Av *BRAK* RG12 .... 12 B8
Ellesmere Cl *CAV/SC* RG4................ 88 E3
Ellies Ms *ASHF* TW15....................... 100 B8
Elliman Av *SL* SL1 .... 4 F4
Ellington Gdns *MDHD* SL6 .... 42 F7 1
Ellington Pk *MDHD* SL6 .... 2 F1
Ellington Rd *FELT* TW13.................. 129 J2
MDHD SL6.. 42 F7
Elliot Ri *ASC* SL5 .... 123 G7
Elliots Wy *READ* RG1 .... 9 G1
Ellis Av *SL* SL1 .... 4 E8
Ellison Cl *WDSR* SL4 .... 96 C2
Ellison Wy *EWKG* RG40...................... 10 F6
Ellis Rd *CWTH* RG45 .... 148 E8
Ellis's Hl *WHIT* RG2 .... 146 C2
Elmar Gn *SLN* SL2 .... 44 D4 1
Elm Bank *YTLY* GU46 .... 171 M7 1
Elmbank Av *EGH* TW20 .... 125 L5
Elmbrook Cl *SUN* TW16 .... 129 L6
Elm Cl *STWL/WRAY* TW19................ 100 A7
Elm Ct *CAV/SC* RG4 .... 62 C2
Elm Cft *DTCH/LGLY* SL3 .... 71 M8
Elmcroft *GOR/PANG* RG8 .... 58 F1 1
Elmcroft Cl *EBED/NFELT* TW14 .... 101 J5
FRIM GU16 .... 182 C7 1
Elmcroft Dr *ASHF* TW15 .... 128 D3 2
Elmdon Rd *HTHAIR* TW6 .... 101 J2
Elm Dr *CHOB/PIR* GU24 .... 177 J5
SUN TW16 .... 129 M7
TLHT RG30.. 142 E1
WDSR SL4 .... 95 L7
Elmgate Av *FELT* TW13 .... 129 L1 2
Elm Gv *MDHD* SL6.............................. 2 F4
NTHA RG18 .... 137 L1
Elmhurst *TADY* RG26 .... 164 E7
Elmhurst Rd *DTCH/LGLY* SL3.......... 72 D3
GOR/PANG RG8 .... 32 F7
NTHA RG18 .... 137 K1
READ RG1 .... 117 G1
Elm La *BNEND* SL8 .... 20 C1
EARL RG6 .... 117 J4
Elmleigh Ct *CAV/SC* RG4 .... 88 F4 2
Elmley Cl *WWKG* RG41 .... 119 J5
Elm Lodge Av *TLHT* RG30................. 88 A6
Elm Pk *ASC* SL5 .... 152 B5
Elm Park Rd *TLHT* RG30 .... 88 A7
Elm Rd *CAV/SC* RG4 .... 62 A7
EARL RG6 .... 117 J4
EBED/NFELT TW14........................... 101 G7
WDSR SL4 .... 96 E2
Elms Av *STHA* RG19......................... 138 B3
Elms Dr *BNEND* SL8 .... 20 F3 2
Elmshott La *SL* SL1 .... 44 B8
Elmsleigh Rd *STA* TW18 .... 127 J3 3
Elms Rd *EWKG* RG40.......................... 10 F7
Elmstone Dr *CALC* RG31.................... 86 F5
Elmsway *ASHF* TW15 .... 128 C3 2
Elm Tree Cl *ASHF* TW15 .... 128 E3
CHERT KT16 .... 155 H6
Elmwood *MDHD* SL6 .... 42 E2
Elmwood Av *FELT* TW13 .... 129 L1
Elmwood Rd *SLN* SL2 .... 5 M5
Elsenwood Crs *CBLY* GU15 .... 174 D8
Elsenwood Dr *CBLY* GU15 .... 174 D7
Elsinore Av
STWL/WRAY TW19 .... 100 B6 2
Elsley Cl *FRIM* GU16 .... 182 C8
Elsley Rd *CALC* RG31........................ 87 G3
Elstow Av *CAV/SC* RG4...................... 62 F8
Elstree Cl *CALC* RG31 .... 87 G4
Elsworth Cl *EBED/NFELT* TW14.... 101 H7
Eltham Av *CAV/SC* RG4..................... 89 H1
SL SL1 .... 70 E3
Elthorne Ct *FELT* TW13 .... 101 M7
Elton Dr *MDHD* SL6 .... 2 D2
Elvaston Wy *TLHT* RG30.................... 87 J7
Elveden Cl *EARL* RG6 .... 118 B4
Elvendon La *GOR/PANG* RG8.......... 33 M7
Elvendon Rd *GOR/PANG* RG8 .... 33 G7
Elwell Cl *EGH* TW20......................... 126 D4
Ely Av *SL* SL1 .... 4 B1
Ely Cl *FRIM* GU16............................. 182 D7
Elyham *GOR/PANG* RG8 .... 86 E1 1
Ely Rd *HSLWW* TW4........................ 101 M2
HTHAIR TW6 .... 101 J1 1
The Embankment
STWL/WRAY TW19 .... 97 M6
Ember Rd *DTCH/LGLY* SL3 .... 72 E3
Emblen Crs *WHIT* RG2 .... 146 B4
Embrook Wy *CALC* RG31 .... 114 D2 2
Emerald Cl *WWKG* RG41 .... 119 H7 3
Emerald Ct *SL* SL1 .... 4 F9 1
Emery Acres *GOR/PANG* RG8 .... 58 D8
Emery Down Cl *BRAK* RG12 ...... 122 D8 1
Emley Rd *ADL/WDHM* KT15............ 155 K7
Emma La *WAR/TWY* RG10 .... 65 H4
Emmbrook Ga *WWKG* RG41 .... 10 B1
Emmbrook Rd *WWKG* RG41 .... 10 A2
Emmbrook V *WWKG* RG41 .... 119 K5
Emm Cl *WWKG* RG41 .... 10 B2
Emmens Cl *GOR/PANG* RG8............. 35 G3
Emmens La *GOR/PANG* RG8 .... 35 H4
Emmer Green Ct *CAV/SC* RG4.......... 88 F1
Emmets Nest *BNFD* RG42 .... 120 F4
Emmets Pk *BNFD* RG42 .... 120 F4 2
Emmview Cl *WWKG* RG41 .... 10 B4
Empress Rd *CALC* RG31 .... 114 F1
Enborne Cl *CALC* RG31 .... 86 F6 1
Enborne Gdns *BRAK* RG12............... 13 L1
Enborne Gv *NWBY* RG14 .... 14 B6
Enborne Pl *NWBY* RG14..................... 14 B6
Enborne Rd *KSCL* RG20 .... 135 M5
NWBY RG14 .... 14 B6
Enborne St *KSCL* RG20.................... 159 K2
Enborne Wy *THLE* RG7..................... 139 J8
Enfield Rd *HTHAIR* TW6 .... 101 H1 2
Englefield Cl *EGH* TW20 .... 125 M4 2
Englefield Rd *THLE* RG7................. 114 A2
Engleheart Dr
EBED/NFELT TW14............................ 101 J5
Englehurst *EGH* TW20 .... 125 M4
Englemere Pk *ASC* SL5................... 151 G1
Englemere Rd *BNFD* RG42 .... 12 D1
Englesfield *CBLY* GU15 .... 183 G1 2
English Gdns *STWL/WRAY* TW19.... 98 A3
Ennerdale *BRAK* RG12 .... 12 E8
Ennerdale Cl
EBED/NFELT TW14 .... 101 J7 7
Ennerdale Crs *SL* SL1 .... 43 M6
Ennerdale Rd *WHIT* RG2 .... 117 G3
Ennerdale Wy *STHA* RG19 .... 137 K3 3
Ensign Cl *STWL/WRAY* TW19 .... 100 A7
Ensign Wy *STWL/WRAY* TW19......... 100 A7
Enstone Rd *WODY* RG5 .... 90 D6
Enterprise Wy *STHA* RG19.............. 138 D4
Epping Cl *READ* RG1 .... 8 D7
Epping Wy *BRAK* RG12.................... 150 C1
Epsom Cl *CBLY* GU15 .... 173 M6
Epsom Ct *READ* RG1........................... 8 C9
Epsom Crs *NWBY* RG14 .... 15 H8
Epsom Sq *HTHAIR* TW6 .... 101 J1 2
Equine Wy *NWBY* RG14 .... 136 E7
Equinne Wy *NWBY* RG14 .... 136 E7
Erica Cl *CHOB/PIR* GU24.................. 176 B8
SL SL1 .... 44 B8
Erica Dr *EWKG* RG40.......................... 11 J8
Eric Av *CAV/SC* RG4............................ 62 D8
Eriswell Cl *EARL* RG6 .... 118 B4
Erkenwald Cl *CHERT* KT16 .... 155 H3 1
Erleigh Court Dr *EARL* RG6 .... 89 K7
Erleigh Court Gdns *EARL* RG6......... 89 K7
Erleigh Dene *NWBY* RG14 .... 14 C8
Erleigh Rd *READ* RG1 .... 9 L8
Ermin Cl *MARL* SN8............................ 48 B6
Ermine Cl *HSLWW* TW4 .... 101 M1 3
Errington Dr *WDSR* SL4 .... 6 D6
Erskine Cl *TADY* RG26 .... 165 J5
Escot Rd *SUN* TW16 .... 129 H5
Esher Crs *HTHAIR* TW6 .... 101 J1
Esher Rd *CBLY* GU15...................... 174 D5
Eskdale Gdns *MDHD* SL6 .... 68 E4
Eskdale Rd *IVER* SL0.......................... 47 L3
WWKG RG41 .... 118 D2
Eskdale Wy *CBLY* GU15 .... 182 F2
Eskin Cl *TLHT* RG30 .... 87 K7
Essame Cl *EWKG* RG40 .... 11 J5
Essex Av *SL* SL1 .... 44 F6
Essex Cl *ADL/WDHM* KT15 .... 155 M8
FRIM GU16 .... 182 D7
Essex Pl *HUNG* RG17......................... 49 L3
Essex Ri *BNFD* RG42 .... 122 C5
Essex St *NWBY* RG14 .... 136 A7
WHIT RG2 .... 116 E1
Essex Wy *CAV/SC* RG4 .... 62 D3
Ester Carling La *HEN* RG9 .... 36 A6
Ethel Rd *ASHF* TW15....................... 128 B3
Eton Cl *DTCH/LGLY* SL3 .... 71 K6
Eton Ct *STA* TW18 .... 127 J3 2
WDSR SL4 .... 7 J4
Eton Pl *MLW* SL7................................ 19 G4
Eton Rd *DTCH/LGLY* SL3.................... 71 K6
Eton Sq *WDSR* SL4 .... 7 K4
Eton Wick Rd *WDSR* SL4 .... 70 C5 1
Eustace Crs *EWKG* RG40 .... 11 K2
Evedon *BRAK* RG12.......................... 149 L4
Evelyn Ct *WODY* RG5 .... 118 C1
Evelyn Crs *SUN* TW16..................... 129 J6
Evelyn Wy *SUN* TW16 .... 129 J6 1
Evendon's Cl *WWKG* RG41 .... 147 K3
Evendon's La *WWKG* RG41 .... 147 G3
Evenlode *MDHD* SL6 .... 3 H3
Evenlode Rd *BNEND* SL8 .... 20 E2
Evenlode Wy *SHST* GU47 .... 172 F6
Everard Av *SL* SL1 .... 4 E8
Everest Rd *CBLY* GU15 .... 174 A6
CWTH RG45 .... 148 E8
STWL/WRAY TW19 .... 100 A6
Evergreen Dr *CALC* RG31 .... 115 J2 1
Evergreen Oak Av *WDSR* SL4 .... 97 K2
Evergreen Rd *FRIM* GU16 .... 182 C4
Evergreen Wy
STWL/WRAY TW19 .... 100 A6 2
WWKG RG41 .... 10 B8
Everington La *NTHA* RG18................ 82 D5
Everland Rd *HUNG* RG17 .... 104 A8
Eversley Rd *WHIT* RG2 .... 146 B4
Eversley St *HTWY* RG27 .... 170 D5
Eversley Wy *EGH* TW20 .... 126 F7
Evesham Rd *CAV/SC* RG4.................. 88 E1
Evesham Wk *SHST* GU47 .... 172 F5
Evreham Rd *IVER* SL0........................ 47 H7
Evreux Cl *STHA* RG19 .... 138 C4 4
Exbourne Rd *WHIT* RG2.................. 116 F6
Exchange Rd *ASC* SL5 .... 151 M2
Exeforde Av *ASHF* TW15 .... 128 D2
Exeter Gdns *YTLY* GU46 .... 171 L7
Exeter Rd *HTHAIR* TW6 .... 101 H2
Exeter Wy *HTHAIR* TW6 .... 101 H1
Exmoor Rd *STHA* RG19 .... 137 M3
Explorer Av *STWL/WRAY* TW19.... 100 B7
Express Wy *NWBY* RG14 .... 137 H4
Eynsford Cl *CAV/SC* RG4 .... 89 H1 1
Eynsham Cl *WODY* RG5 .... 90 B6

F

Faggs Rd *EBED/NFELT* TW14 ...... 101 J3
EBED/NFELT TW14.......................... 101 K3
Fairacre *KSCL* RG20 .... 159 J6
Faircroft *SLN* SL2 .... 44 E5
Faircross *BRAK* RG12 .... 13 H7
Faircross Quarters *NTHA* RG18 .... 81 J8
Faircross Rd *TLHT* RG30 .... 115 M1 1
Fairfax *BNFD* RG42 .... 12 F3
Fairfax Cl *CAV/SC* RG4 .... 88 E4
Fairfax Pl *NWBY* RG14 .... 137 H1 1
Fairfax Rd *FARN* GU14 .... 181 L7
Fairfield *KSCL* RG20 .... 56 A2
Fairfield Ap *STWL/WRAY* TW19...... 98 A5
Fairfield Av *DTCH/LGLY* SL3............ 71 M7
STA TW18 .... 127 J2
Fairfield Cl *BNEND* SL8 .... 20 C2 1
Fairfield Dr *FRIM* GU16 .... 182 B3
Fairfield La *CHOB/PIR* GU24 .... 176 C7
SLN SL2 .... 44 F3
Fairfield Rd *GOR/PANG* RG8 .... 33 G7
SL SL1 .... 43 M4
STWL/WRAY TW19 .... 98 A5
Fairfields *HUNG* RG17 .... 132 A1 1
Fairford Rd *CALC* RG31 .... 86 F4
MDHD SL6.. 2 F3
Fairhaven *EGH* TW20 .... 126 C3 2
Fairholme
EBED/NFELT TW14 .... 101 G6 1
Fairholme Rd *ASHF* TW15 .... 128 B3
Fair Lawn Gn *WHIT* RG2................. 117 J5
Fairlawn Pk *WDSR* SL4 .... 96 B3
Fairlawn Rd *TADY* RG26.................. 165 G7
Fairlawns *SUN* TW16 .... 129 K8
Fairlawns Cl *STA* TW18 .... 127 L4 1
Fairlea *MDHD* SL6.............................. 67 K2
Fairlie Rd *SL* SL1 .... 44 D7
Fairlight Av *WDSR* SL4 .... 7 J9
Fairlop Cl *CALC* RG31 .... 115 G2 3
Fairmead Cl *SHST* GU47 .... 173 H7
Fairmead Rd *WHIT* RG2 .... 145 H1
Fair Mile *HEN* RG9............................. 37 L1
Fair Oak La *THLE* RG7..................... 167 H7
Fairoak Wy *TADY* RG26 .... 164 A5
Fairsted Cl *TLHT* RG30 .... 87 K6 1
Fairview Av *EARL* RG6 .... 89 L8
Fairview Rd *EWKG* RG40 .... 11 G8
HUNG RG17 .... 132 A1
MDHD SL6... 43 K7
SLN SL2 .... 44 C5
Fairwater Dr *WODY* RG5 .... 90 A8
Fairway *CHERT* KT16 .... 155 L5
Fairway Av *TLHT* RG30..................... 87 G8
WDR/YW UB7 .... 73 M1
Fairway Dr *WAR/TWY* RG10 .... 90 D1 1
Fairway Hts *CBLY* GU15 .... 174 E8
Fairways *ASHF* TW15 .... 128 D4
The Fairway *FRIM* GU16 .... 182 D3
MDHD SL6.. 67 L3
SL SL1 .... 43 M4
Faithfull Cl *BNFD* RG42 .... 121 L4
Fakenham Cl *EARL* RG6 .... 117 K6 1
Fakenham Wy *SHST* GU47............ 173 G5
Falaise *EGH* TW20 .... 126 B3 1
Falcon Av *WHIT* RG2....................... 117 J5
Falcon Cl *LTWR* GU18 .... 175 J6
Falcon Coppice *KSCL* RG20 ...... 159 J6 1
Falcon Dr *STWL/WRAY* TW19 .... 100 A5
Falcon Flds *TADY* RG26 .... 164 E4
Falcon House Gdns *KSCL* RG20..... 159 H6
Falcon Wy *SUN* TW16..................... 129 H7
WWKG RG41 .... 10 A6
YTLY GU46 .... 171 L8 1
Falconwood *EGH* TW20 .... 126 B3 2
Falkland Dr *NWBY* RG14 .... 14 C9
Falkland Garth *NWBY* RG14 .... 136 A7
Falkland Rd *NWBY* RG14 .... 136 A8
Fallowfield *YTLY* GU46.................... 171 L7
Fallowfield Cl *CAV/SC* RG4 .... 88 E2
Falmouth Cl *CBLY* GU15.................. 182 D2
Falmouth Rd *SL* SL1 .... 44 D7 1
WHIT RG2 .... 116 F7
Falmouth Wy *STHA* RG19 .... 138 C3
Falstaff Av *EARL* RG6 .... 117 J4
Fanes Cl *BNFD* RG42 .... 12 D3
Fane Wy *MDHD* SL6 .... 2 D9
MDHD SL6.. 68 A2
Fannys La *THLE* RG7....................... 110 E5
Faraday Cl *SLN* SL2 .... 44 E6 1
WHIT RG2 .... 146 B7 1
Faraday Rd *FARN* GU14 .... 181 M8
NWBY RG14 .... 15 G3
SLN SL2 .... 44 E6
Faraday Wy *EWKG* RG40 .... 146 D6
Farcrosse Cl *SHST* GU47 .... 172 F6
Fareham Dr *YTLY* GU46 .... 171 L7 1
Fareham Rd *EBED/NFELT* TW14.. 101 M6
Faringdon Cl *SHST* GU47 .... 172 F5
Faringdon Dr *BRAK* RG12 .... 150 A2
Farleigh Ms *CAV/SC* RG4 .... 89 H1
Farman Cl *WODY* RG5 .... 90 E6
Farm Cl *ASC* SL5 .... 151 M2
BNFD RG42 .... 12 C2
CHERT KT16 .... 154 D3
CWTH RG45 .... 148 F7
GOR/PANG RG8 .... 86 F1
MDHD SL6 .... 41 K7
MDHD SL6... 68 F5
STA TW18 .... 127 H3
YTLY GU46 .... 180 A1
Farm Crs *SLN* SL2 .... 5 M1
Farm Dr *CALC* RG31 .... 86 E8
WDSR SL4 .... 97 L5
Farmers Cl *MDHD* SL6 .... 67 K2
WHIT RG2 .... 116 F8 1
Farmers End *WAR/TWY* RG10.......... 90 E2
Farmer's Rd *STA* TW18 .... 127 H3 2
Farmers Wy *MDHD* SL6 .... 67 K2
Farm La *MARL* SN8 .... 130 A8
Farm Rd *BNEND* SL8......................... 20 C2
FRIM GU16 .... 182 B4
GOR/PANG RG8 .... 32 F8
MDHD SL6... 41 K7
MDHD SL6... 43 K8
STA TW18 .... 127 L4
Farm Vw *YTLY* GU46....................... 180 A1
Farm Wy *STWL/WRAY* TW19 .... 99 J5
Farm Yd *WDSR* SL4............................. 7 K5
Farnborough Rd *FARN* GU14 .... 181 M7
Farnburn Av *SL* SL1 .... 44 E6
Farnell Rd *STA* TW18 .... 127 K1
Farnham Cl *BRAK* RG12 .... 13 L5
Farnham Dr *CAV/SC* RG4 .... 89 H2
Farnham La *SLN* SL2 .... 44 C3
Farnham Park La *SLN* SL2............... 44 F1
Farnham Rd *SL* SL1 .... 4 A1
SL SL1 .... 4 A1 1
SL SL1 .... 4 A3 1
SL SL1 .... 4 A5
SL SL1 .... 4 B6
Farningham *BRAK* RG12 .... 150 B3
Farnsfield Cl *EARL* RG6 .... 117 K6 1
Farrell Cl *CBLY* GU15..................... 181 M3
Farriers Cl *WODY* RG5 .... 90 B7
Farriers La *KSCL* RG20 .... 29 H7
Farringdon Wy *TADY* RG26 .... 164 E7
Far Rd *HEN* RG9 .... 38 C6
Farrowdene Rd *WHIT* RG2 .... 116 F6
The Farthingales *MDHD* SL6............. 3 L5
Farthing Green La *SLN* SL2 .... 45 K3
Fatherson Rd *READ* RG1 .... 9 L7
Faulkner Pl *BAGS* GU19 .... 175 H2
Faversham Rd *SHST* GU47 .... 173 G5 2
Fawcett Crs *WODY* RG5 .... 90 A8
Fawcett Rd *WDSR* SL4 .... 6 F7
Fawler Md *BRAK* RG12 .... 150 C1 4
Fawley Cl *MDHD* SL6 .... 42 A4
Fawley Rd *TLHT* RG30 .... 115 M1
Fawns Manor Rd
EBED/NFELT TW14............................ 101 G7
Fawsley Cl *DTCH/LGLY* SL3 .... 73 H7
Faygate Wy *EARL* RG6 .... 117 L5
Feathers La *STWL/WRAY* TW19....... 98 D8
Felbridge Cl *FRIM* GU16 .... 182 C4
Felixstowe Cl *EARL* RG6................. 118 A4
Fellow Gn *CHOB/PIR* GU24 .... 176 C8
Fellow Green Rd
CHOB/PIR GU24 .... 176 C8
The Fells *CALC* RG31 .... 86 D8 1
Felstead Cl *EARL* RG6 .... 117 J4
Felthambrook Wy *FELT* TW13 ...... 129 L1
ASHF TW15 .... 128 D3
Feltham Hill Rd *ASHF* TW15 .... 128 F4
Felthamhill Rd *FELT* TW13............ 129 K2
Feltham Rd *ASHF* TW15.................. 128 E2
Felthorpe Cl *EARL* RG6 .... 117 K6 1
Felton Wy *CALC* RG31...................... 86 F6
Fencote *BRAK* RG12 .... 150 A4
Fennel Cl *EARL* RG6 .... 117 J5 4
NWBY RG14 .... 137 G1
Fennscombe Ct
CHOB/PIR GU24 .... 176 B8
Fenns La *CHOB/PIR* GU24 .... 176 B8
Fenton Av *STA* TW18 .... 127 M4
Fernbank *EWKG* RG40 .... 147 G7 1
Fernbank Crs *ASC* SL5 .... 123 G6
Fernbank Pl *ASC* SL5 .... 122 F6
Fernbank Rd *ASC* SL5.................... 123 G7
Fernbrook Rd *CAV/SC* RG4 .... 88 A1
Fern Cl *CALC* RG31 .... 114 F1 3
CWTH RG45....................................... 148 E7
FRIM GU16 .... 182 F3
Ferndale Av *CHERT* KT16.............. 155 H7
Ferndale Cl *CALC* RG31 .... 87 H3 1
Ferndale Ct *STHA* RG19 .... 138 A3
Ferndale Crs *UX/CGN* UB8............. 47 M4
Ferndale Rd *ASHF* TW15 .... 128 A3
Fern Dr *MDHD* SL6 .... 43 L7
Ferne Cl *GOR/PANG* RG8 .... 32 F7 2
The Fernery *STA* TW18 .... 127 H3 3
Fernes Cl *UX/CGN* UB8.................... 47 M7
Fern Gln *CALC* RG31 .... 86 F5 3
Fern Gv *EBED/NFELT* TW14 .... 101 L6
Fernhill Cl *BNFD* RG42 .... 12 C1
FARN GU14 .... 181 H5
Fernhill La *FARN* GU14................... 181 H5
FARN GU14 .... 181 J5
Fernhill Rd *BLKW* GU17 .... 181 H4
FARN GU14 .... 181 H7
Fernhill Wk *FARN* GU14 .... 181 J5 2
Fernhurst Rd *ASHF* TW15 .... 128 F2
CALC RG31 .... 114 F2 4
Ferniehurst *CBLY* GU15 .... 182 C2
Fernlands Cl *CHERT* KT16 .... 155 H7
Fern La *MLW* SL7.............................. 20 B1
Fernleigh Ri *FRIM* GU16................ 182 F7

Fernley Ct *MDHD* SL6 .... 2 D1
Fernside Av *FELT* TW13 .... 129 L2
Fern Wk *ASHF* TW15 .... 128 A3
Ferrard Cl *ASC* SL5 .... 123 G6
Ferrers Cl *SL* SL1 .... 70 B1
Ferry Av *STA* TW18 .... 127 H5
Ferry La *BNEND* SL8 .... 20 E5
  CHERT KT16 .... 155 K3
  GOR/PANG RG8 .... 32 E2
  HEN RG9 .... 17 G8
  MDHD SL6 .... 20 E7
  MLW SL7 .... 39 L1
  STA TW18 .... 127 M8
  STWL/WRAY TW19 .... 98 E3
  WAR/TWY RG10 .... 64 F4
Ferry Rd *GOR/PANG* RG8 .... 32 F2
  MDHD SL6 .... 68 F2
Fettiplace *HUNG* RG17 .... 77 L3 🔲
Fetty Pl *MDHD* SL6 .... 68 A2
Fidler's La *KSCL* RG20 .... 29 H7
Fidlers Wk *WAR/TWY* RG10 .... 65 H4
Field Cl *THLE* RG7 .... 142 E4
Field End *CHOB/PIR* GU24 .... 176 E6
Fielden Pl *BRAK* RG12 .... 13 M4
The Fielders *HTWY* RG27 .... 171 H6
Fieldfare Av *YTLY* GU46 .... 171 K8
Fieldhead Gdns *CWTH* RG45 .... 172 D2
Field House Cl *ASC* SL5........... 151 K5
Fieldhouse La *MLW* SL7 .... 19 J4
Fieldhouse Wy *MLW* SL7 .... 19 J4 🔲
Field Hurst *DTCH/LGLY* SL3 .... 72 C4
Fielding Gdns *CWTH* RG45 .... 172 D2
  DTCH/LGLY SL3 .... 71 M2
Fielding Rd *MDHD* SL6 .... 41 L7
  SHST GU47 .... 173 H8
The Fieldings *MDHD* SL6 .... 68 C7
Field La *FRIM* GU16 .... 182 B5
Field Pk *DRAK* RG12 .... 13 M2
Fieldridge *NWBY* RG14 .... 136 F1 🔲
  FARN GU14 .... 181 J5
  KSCL RG20 .... 54 A6
  READ RG1 .... 8 D8
Field Vw *CAV/SC* RG4 .... 88 E3
  EGH TW20 .... 126 F3
  FELT TW13 .... 129 C2
Fieldway *WWKG* RG41 .... 119 G4 🔲
Fifehead Cl *ASHF* TW15 .... 128 A4
Fifield La *WDSR* SL4 .... 95 G2
Fifield Rd *MDHD* SL6 .... 69 H6
Fifth Rd *NWBY* RG14 .... 14 A8
Fifth St *STHA* RG19 .... 161 J1
Filbert Dr *CALC* RG31 .... 86 F6
Filey Rd *READ* RG1 .... 89 H7
Filey Sp *SL* SL1 .... 70 E2 🔲
Filmer Rd *WDSR* SL4 .... 96 A1
Finbeck Wy *EARL* RG6 .... 117 C6
Fincham End Dr *CWTH* RG45 .... 172 C2 🔲
Finchampstead Rd *EWKG* RG40 ...... 10 F9
  EWKG RG40 .... 147 K5
  EWKG RG40 .... 147 K7 🔲
Finch Cl *TADY* RG26 .... 164 F7 🔲
Finch Ct *MDHD* SL6 .... 2 D9
Finches La *MARL* SN8 .... 48 B5
Finch Rd *EARL* RG6 .... 117 M2
Finch Wy *THLE* RG7 .... 142 E3
Findhorn Cl *SHST* GU47 .... 173 C7 🔲
The Findings *FARN* GU14 .... 181 H6
Finlay Gdns *ADL/WDHM* KT15...... 155 M8 🔲
Finmere *BRAK* RG12 .... 149 M3
Finney Dr *BFOR* GU20 .... 176 A2
Finstock Cl *EARL* RG6 .... 118 A5
Finstock Gn *BRAK* RG12 .... 150 C1 🔲
Fintry Pl *FARN* GU14 .... 181 H7 🔲
Firbank Pl *EGH* TW20 .... 125 L4
Fir Cottage Rd *EWKG* RG40 ...... 147 H6 🔲
Fircroft Cl *CALC* RG31 .... 86 F5
Fir Dr *BLKW* GU17 .... 181 C5
Fireball Hl *ASC* SL5 .... 152 A4
Firfield Rd *ADL/WDHM* KT15....... 155 K8
Firglen Dr *YTLY* GU46 .... 172 A2
Firgrove Rd *HTWY* RG27 .... 171 H8
  YTLY GU46 .... 171 L8
Firlands *BRAK* RG12 .... 149 M2
Firlands Av *CBLY* GU15 .... 182 A1 🔲
Firmstone Cl *EARL* RG6 .... 117 M5
Firs Av *WDSR* SL4 .... 96 C3
Firs Cl *EWKG* RG40 .... 147 J7
Firs Dr *DTCH/LGLY* SL3 .... 72 C1
Fir's End *THLE* RG7 .... 142 D4
Firs La *MDHD* SL6 .... 67 J2
  TLHT RG30 .... 116 A1
Firs Rd *CALC* RG31 .... 86 F8
First Av *MLW* SL7 .... 19 K4
  THLE RG7 .... 164 F4
First Crs *SL* SL1 .... 4 A1
The Firs *NTHA* RG18 .... 137 L2
First St *STHA* RG19 .... 161 K1
Firth Cl *THLE* RG7 .... 165 L6 🔲
Fir Tree Av *SLN* SL2 .... 45 J5
Fir Tree Cl *ASC* SL5 .... 151 K4
Firtree Cl *SHST* GU47 .... 172 C6
Fir Tree La *NWBY* RG14 .... 137 H2
Fir Tree Paddock *KSCL* RG20 ..... 28 D4
Firview Cl *MLW* SL7 .... 19 J5
Firwood Dr *CBLY* GU15 .... 181 M1
Firwood Rd *VW* GU25 .... 153 H3
Fisher Gn *BNFD* RG42 .... 120 E4 🔲
Fisherman's La *THLE* RG7 .... 140 D7
Fishermans Retreat *MLW* SL7 .. 19 H5 🔲
Fisherman's Wy *BNEND* SL8 .... 20 E2
Fishers Ct *CAV/SC* RG4 .... 62 F8
Fisher's Wd *ASC* SL5 .... 152 F5
Fishery Rd *MDHD* SL6 .... 68 F1
Fishguard Sp *SL* SL1 .... 5 M9 🔲
Fishponds Cl *WWKG* RG41 .... 10 C9
Fitzrobert Pl *EGH* TW20 .... 126 D4
Fitzroy Crs *WODY* RG5 .... 90 D8
Five Acre *CALC* RG31 .... 86 E5
Flag Staff Sq *STHA* RG19 .... 138 B5
Flambards *CAV/SC* RG4 .... 88 F4
Flamborough Cl *EARL* RG6 .... 118 B4 🔲
Flamborough Sp *SL* SL1 .... 70 D2
Flamingo Cl *WWKG* RG41 .... 147 H1 🔲
The Flats *BLKW* GU17 .... 180 E2
Flaxman Cl *EARL* RG6 .... 117 J4
Flecker Cl *NTHA* RG18 .... 137 M1 🔲

Fleet Cl *WWKG* RG41 .... 119 H8 🔲
Fleetham Gdns *EARL* RG6 .... 117 L5
Fleet Hl *EWKG* RG40 .... 170 F4
Fleet La *EWKG* RG40 .... 170 E4
Fleetway *EGH* TW20 .... 126 F8 🔲
Fleetwood Cl *NWBY* RG14 .... 137 G1
Fleetwood Rd *SLN* SL2 .... 5 H6
Fleming Cl *FARN* GU14 .... 182 A8
  WHIT RG2 .... 146 B7
Fleming Rd *NWBY* RG14 .... 15 G3
Flemish Flds *CHERT* KT16 .... 155 K4
Fletcher Gdns *BNFD* RG42 .... 121 G6
Flexford Gn *BRAK* RG12 .... 149 H3 🔲
Floral Wy *NTHA* RG18 .... 138 A1
Floreat Gdns *NWBY* RG14 .... 14 A7
Florence Av *MDHD* SL6 .... 3 J2
Florence Cl *YTLY* GU46 .... 171 M8 🔲
Florence Gdns *STA* TW18 .... 127 L5
Florence Rd *FELT* TW13 .... 101 L7
  SHST GU47 .... 173 H7
Florence Wk *READ* RG1 .... 9 M4
Florian Gdns *READ* RG1 .... 115 L1 🔲
Flower's Hl *GOR/PANG* RG8........ 85 M2
Flowers Piece *GOR/PANG* RG8 ..... 57 L8
Fobney St *READ* RG1 .... 8 F7
Fokerham Rd *STHA* RG19 .... 138 C4
Folder's La *BNFD* RG42 .... 13 J1
Foliejohn Wy *MDHD* SL6 .... 67 J4 🔲
Folkestone Ct *DTCH/LGLY* SL3 ..... 72 D5
Follet Cl *WDSR* SL4 .... 97 L5 🔲
Folly Gn *GOR/PANG* RG8 .... 34 B6
Folly La *SLN* SL2 .... 44 E6
Folly Orchard Rd
  GOR/PANG RG8 .... 34 B6
Folly Rd *HUNG* RG17 .... 49 H4
  HUNG RG17 .... 132 F8
The Folly *NWBY* RG14 .... 15 G8
Fontmell Cl *ASHF* TW15 .... 128 D3
Fontmell Pk *ASHF* TW15 .... 128 D3 🔲
Fontwell Cl *MDHD* SL6 .... 41 J6
Fontwell Dr *TLHT* RG30 .... 115 J1
Fontwell Rd *NWBY* RG14 .... 15 H8
Forbes Cha *SHST* GU47 .... 173 G7
Forbury La *HUNG* RG17 .... 133 L7
Forbury Rd *READ* RG1 .... 9 G5
The Forbury *READ* RG1 .... 9 G5
Fordbridge Rd *ASHF* TW15 .... 128 B4
Ford Cl *ASHF* TW15 .... 128 B4
Ford Rd *ASHF* TW15 .... 128 C2
  CHOB/PIR GU24 .... 176 F5
Fordwater Rd *CHERT* KT16 .... 155 L5
Fordwells Dr *BRAK* RG12 .... 150 C1
The Forehead *THLE* RG7 .... 167 J2
Forest Cl *ASC* SL5 .... 122 F8
  TADY RG26 .... 164 B5
Forest Dean *WHIT* RG2 .... 116 F7 🔲
Forest Dr *SUN* TW16 .... 129 J5
Forest End Rd *SHST* GU47 .... 172 C5
Foresters Sq *BRAK* RG12 .... 122 B8 🔲
Foresters Wy *CWTH* RG45 .... 149 H6
  CWTH RG45 .... 149 J7
Forest Gn *MDHD* SL6 .... 68 C8
Forest Green Rd *MDHD* SL6 .... 94 F1
Forest Hills *CBLY* GU15 .... 181 L2
Forest La *TADY* RG26 .... 165 G8
Forest Rd *ASC* SL5 .... 123 G4
  BNFD RG42 .... 120 E4
  BNFD RG42 .... 121 M3
  CWTH RG45 .... 172 F1
  EWKG RG40 .... 119 K4
  FELT TW13 .... 101 M8
  FELT TW13 .... 129 M1
  WDSR SL4 .... 96 A1
  WDSR SL4 .... 96 A6
  WDSR SL4 .... 119 H6
Forge Cl *CAV/SC* RG4 .... 9 K2
  HUNG RG17 .... 133 H4
Forge Hl *NTHA* RG18 .... 82 D1
Forge La *SUN* TW16 .... 129 K8
The Forge *HUNG* RG17 .... 104 A8 🔲
Forlease Cl *MDHD* SL6 .... 3 K6
Forlease Dr *MDHD* SL6 .... 3 K6
Forlease Rd *MDHD* SL6 .... 3 J5
  MDHD SL6 .... 3 K6
Formby Cl *DTCH/LGLY* SL3 .... 72 F4 🔲
  EARL RG6 .... 118 B3
Forndon Cl *EARL* RG6 .... 118 B4 🔲
Forth Cl *FARN* GU14 .... 181 D3
Fortrose Cl *SHST* GU47 .... 173 G7 🔲
Forty Green Dr *MLW* SL7 .... 18 E4
Fosseway *CWTH* RG45 .... 172 C1 🔲
Fossewood Dr *CBLY* GU15......... 174 A6
Foster Av *WDSR* SL4 .... 96 B2
Fosters Gv *BFOR* GU20 .... 151 L8
Fosters La *WODY* RG5 .... 90 B8
Fosters Pth *SLN* SL2 .... 44 C5 🔲
Fotherby Ct *MDHD* SL6 .... 3 J5
Fotheringay Gdns *SL* SL1 .... 44 D8 🔲
Foundry Ct *CHERT* KT16 .... 155 K4 🔲
Foundry La *DTCH/LGLY* SL3 .... 98 E2
Fountain Gdns *WDSR* SL4 .... 97 G2
Fountains Garth *BRAK* RG12...... 12 E7
Four Oaks *KSCL* RG20 .... 159 J8
Fourth Av *MLW* SL7 .... 19 K4
Fowler Cl *EARL* RG6 .... 117 K3
Fowlers La *BNFD* RG42 .... 13 C3
Fowlers Md *CHOB/PIR* GU24...... 177 H4
Foxborough Cl *THLE* RG7 .... 145 C8
Foxborough Cl *DTCH/LGLY* SL3 .... 72 D5
Foxbury *HUNG* RG17 .... 49 L4
Fox Cl *THLE* RG7 .... 142 D3
Foxcombe Dr *CALC* RG31 .... 86 F7
Foxcote *EWKG* RG40 .... 147 K7
Fox Covert *LTWR* GU18 .... 175 K6
Fox Covert Cl *ASC* SL5 .... 151 M2
Foxdown Cl *CBLY* GU15 .... 181 M1
Fox Dr *YTLY* GU46 .... 172 A7
Foxes Piece *MLW* SL7 .... 19 H4
Foxes Wy *WAR/TWY* RG10 .... 90 D3

Foxglove Cl *BNFD* RG42 .... 122 D4
  STWL/WRAY TW19 .... 100 A7
  WWKG RG41 .... 119 G7
Foxglove Gdns *READ* RG1 .... 8 B5
Foxhays Rd *WHIT* RG2 .... 117 G6
Foxherne *DTCH/LGLY* SL3 .... 71 M2
Foxhill Cl *CAV/SC* RG4 .... 89 L1
Foxhill Crs *CBLY* GU15 .... 174 E6
Foxhill La *CAV/SC* RG4 .... 63 G7
Foxhill Rd *READ* RG1 .... 89 H8
Foxhunter Wy *STHA* RG19 .... 137 J3 🔲
Foxhunt Gv *CALC* RG31 .... 115 J2
Fox La *HTWY* RG27 .... 171 J6
Fox La North *CHERT* KT16 ...... 155 J4
Fox La South *CHERT* KT16 ...... 155 J5 🔲
Foxley Cl *BLKW* GU17 .... 180 F1
Foxley La *BNFD* RG42 .... 120 E4
Fox Rd *BRAK* RG12 .... 13 K9
  DTCH/LGLY SL3 .... 72 A4
Foxwood Cl *FELT* TW13 .... 129 L4
Framewood Rd *DTCH/LGLY* SL3 ... 45 M1
Framlingham Dr *CAV/SC* RG4 ..... 89 H1 🔲
Frampton Cl *WODY* RG5 .... 90 B5
France Hill Dr *CBLY* GU15 ...... 181 M1
Frances Av *MDHD* SL6 .... 42 F5
Frances Rd *WDSR* SL4 .... 7 J9
The Frances *NTHA* RG18 .... 138 A2
Francis Av *FELT* TW13 .... 129 K1
Francis Chichester Cl *ASC* SL5 ... 151 L2
Francis Gdns *BNFD* RG42 .... 122 A4
Francis St *READ* RG1 .... 9 G9
Francis Wy *SL* SL1 .... 44 A8
Francomes Fld *HUNG* RG17 .... 49 L5
Franklin Av *SLN* SL2 .... 44 E6
  TADY RG26 .... 164 D5
Franklin St *READ* RG1 .... 0 C7
Franklyn Crs *WDSR* SL4 .... 96 A2
Frank Lunnon Cl *BNEND* SL8 ...... 20 F3
Frank Sutton Wy *SL* SL1 .... 4 C5
Frascati Wy *MDHD* SL6 .... 3 G5
Fraser Av *CAV/SC* RG4 .... 62 F8
Fraser Md *SHST* GU47 .... 173 H8
Fraser Rd *BNFD* RG42 .... 13 G2
Frayslea *UX/CGN* UB8 .... 47 M3
Fray's Waye *UX/CGN* UB8 .... 47 M2
Frederick Pl *WWKG* RG41 .... 10 D6
Freeborn Wy *BRAK* RG12 .... 122 B7 🔲
Freemantle Rd *BAGS* GU19 ...... 175 J3 🔲
Free Prae Rd *CHERT* KT16 ...... 155 K5
Freesia Cl *WWKG* RG41 .... 119 G7 🔲
French Gdns *BLKW* GU17 .... 181 G2
French St *SUN* TW16 .... 129 M7
Frenchum Gdns *SL* SL1 .... 70 B1
Frensham *BRAK* RG12 .... 150 A3
Frensham Cl *YTLY* GU46 .... 171 L8
Frensham Gn *WHIT* RG2 .... 117 J5
Frensham Rd *CWTH* RG45 .... 148 F2
Freshfield Cl *EARL* RG6 .... 118 B3 🔲
Freshfields La *KSCL* RG20 .... 80 D4
Freshwater Rd *READ* RG1 .... 89 H5
Friars Keep *BRAK* RG12 .... 13 H8
Friars Rd *NWBY* RG14 .... 14 E9
  VW GU25 .... 154 A1
Friar St *READ* RG1 .... 8 E5
  READ RG1 .... 9 G5
Friars Wy *CHERT* KT16 .... 155 K3
Friary Rd *ASC* SL5 .... 151 K3
  STWL/WRAY TW19 .... 97 M5
The Friary *STWL/WRAY* TW19 ...... 97 M5
Friday St *HEN* RG9 .... 38 B5
Friendship Wy *BRAK* RG12 .... 13 H7
Frieth Cl *EARL* RG6 .... 117 K4
Frilsham Rd *TLHT* RG30 .... 115 J2
Frimley Cl *WODY* RG5 .... 90 A6
Frimley Green Rd *FRIM* GU16 .... 182 A6
Frimley Grove Gdns *FRIM* GU16.. 182 A5
Frimley Hall Dr *CBLY* GU15 ..... 174 C8
Frimley High St *FRIM* GU16..... 181 M6
  FRIM GU16 .... 182 A5 🔲
  FRIM GU16 .... 182 A6 🔲
Frimley Rd *CBLY* GU15 .... 181 K1
  FRIM GU16 .... 181 M5
  FRIM GU16 .... 181 M5
Fringford Cl *EARL* RG6 .... 117 M5
  SLN SL2 .... 5 L2
The Frithe *SLN* SL2 .... 5 M4
Frith Hill Rd *FRIM* GU16 .... 182 D5
Frithwald Rd *CHERT* KT16 .... 155 J4
Frobisher *BRAK* RG12 .... 149 M4
Frobisher Crs
  STWL/WRAY TW19 .... 100 B6
Frodsham Wy *SHST* GU47 .... 173 H4 🔲
Frog Hall Dr *EWKG* RG40 .... 11 M6
Frog La *BRAK* RG12 .... 12 F6
Frogmill *MDHD* SL6 .... 39 M3
Frogmore Dr *WDSR* SL4 .... 7 L6
Frogmore Gv *BLKW* GU17 .... 180 F2
Frogmore Park Dr *BLKW* GU17 ... 181 G2
Frogmore Rd *BLKW* GU17 .... 180 E1
Frogmore Wy *TLHT* RG30 .... 115 L1
Frome Cl *FARN* GU14 .... 181 D3
Fromer Rd *FLKWH* HP10 .... 21 G2
Fromont Dr *STHA* RG19 .... 138 A3
Fromow Gdns *BFOR* GU20 .... 176 A2 🔲
Front St *HUNG* RG17 .... 50 F8
Frouds La *THLE* RG7 .... 140 C4
Froxfield Av *READ* RG1 .... 116 B1
Froxfield Down *BRAK* RG12 ...... 150 C2 🔲
Fruen Rd *EBED/NFELT* TW14 ...... 101 J5
Frymley Vw *WDSR* SL4 .... 70 A8
Fry's La *YTLY* GU46 .... 172 B7
Fuchsia Cl *CALC* RG31 .... 114 F1 🔲
Fuchsia La *CHOB/PIR* GU24 ...... 176 B8
Fullbrook Cl *MDHD* SL6 .... 3 J2
  WWKG RG41 .... 119 K5
Fullbrook Crs *CALC* RG31 .... 87 G3
Fuller Cl *STHA* RG19 .... 138 C4
Fullers La *KSCL* RG20 .... 158 E7
  THLE RG7 .... 143 L2
Fullerton Wy *TADY* RG26 .... 164 F7
Fulmead Rd *TLHT* RG30 .... 87 M6
Fulmer Cl *EARL* RG6 .... 117 K4
Furlong Cl *BNEND* SL8 .... 20 E5
Furlong Rd *BNEND* SL8 .... 20 E5
Furness *WDSR* SL4 .... 95 M1
Furnival Av *SLN* SL2 .... 44 E6
Furnival Cl *VW* GU25 .... 154 A1

Furrow Wy *MDHD* SL6 .... 67 K2
Furse Cl *CBLY* GU15 .... 182 E2
Furzebank *ASC* SL5 .... 152 A1 🔲
Furzedown Cl *EGH* TW20 .... 126 B4 🔲
Furze Hill Crs *CWTH* RG45 ...... 172 F2
Furzen Cl *SLN* SL2 .... 44 D4
Furze Platt Rd *MDHD* SL6 .... 41 L5
Furze Rd *MDHD* SL6 .... 42 A5
  TADY RG26 .... 164 C4
Furzewood *SUN* TW16 .... 129 K6
Fuzzens Wk *WDSR* SL4 .... 96 B1
Fydlers Cl *ASC* SL5 .... 123 L4
Fyfield Cl *BLKW* GU17 .... 181 G1
Fyfield Rd *STHA* RG19 .... 138 A4
Fylingdales *STHA* RG19 .... 137 M4

G

Gables Av *ASHF* TW15 .... 128 C3
Gables Cl *DTCH/LGLY* SL3 .... 71 K6
  MDHD SL6 .... 3 M2
Gables Wy *STHA* RG19 .... 138 E4
Gabriel Dr *CBLY* GU15 .... 182 E2
The Gabriels *NWBY* RG14 .... 136 A8
Gage Rd *MDHD* SL6 .... 68 B2
Gainsborough *BRAK* RG12........ 149 M3
  MDHD SL6 .... 42 C1 🔲
Gainsborough Av *HUNG* RG17 .... 133 L4
Gainsborough Cl *CBLY* GU15 .... 174 C7 🔲
  WODY RG5 .... 90 D3
Gainsborough Crs *HEN* RG9 .... 37 M6
Gainsborough Dr *ASC* SL5 .... 123 G8
Gainsborough Hl *HEN* RG9 .... 38 A6
Gainsborough Ru *HEN* RG9 .... 37 M6
  TLHT RG30 .... 115 L1
Cairn Cl *TLHT* RG30 .... 87 K7
Galahad Cl *SL* SL1 .... 70 D2
Gale Dr *LTWR* GU18 .... 175 K5
Galleons La *DTCH/LGLY* SL3 ...... 73 J8
The Gallops *KSCL* RG20 .... 29 H8
The Gallop *YTLY* GU46 .... 172 A7
Galloway Cha *SLN* SL2 .... 5 J5
Gallys Rd *WDSR* SL4 .... 70 A8
Galsworthy Dr *CAV/SC* RG4 ...... 89 C1
Galsworthy Rd *CHERT* KT16 ..... 155 K4 🔲
Galton Rd *ASC* SL5 .... 152 C3
Calvin Rd *SL* SL1 .... 4 A6
Gap Wy *GOR/PANG* RG8 .... 34 C6
Garden Cl *ASHF* TW15 .... 128 F4
  MDHD SL6 .... 67 K1
Garden Close La *NWBY* RG14 .... 160 A2
Gardeners La *GOR/PANG* RG8 ..... 84 F2
Gardenia Ct *CHOB/PIR* GU24 .... 176 C8 🔲
The Gardens *EBED/NFELT* TW14... 101 C5
  GOR/PANG RG8 .... 32 F5
  WHIT RG2 .... 90 D3
Gardner Pl
  EBED/NFELT TW14 .... 101 L5 🔲
Gardner Rd *MDHD* SL6 .... 42 A4
Gardners Rd *BNFD* RG42 .... 122 D4
Garfield Rd
  ADL/WDHM KT15 .... 155 M8 🔲
  CBLY GU15 .... 181 M1
Garford Crs *NWBY* RG14 .... 136 A6
Garlands Cl *THLE* RG7 .... 142 D4
Garnet Cl *SL* SL1 .... 70 D2
Garnet Ct *MLW* SL7 .... 18 E5 🔲
Garnet St *READ* RG1 .... 8 D8
Garrard Rd *SLN* SL2 .... 44 B5
Garrard St *READ* RG1 .... 9 G5
Garrett Rd *EWKG* RG40 .... 147 H6
Garrick Cl *STA* TW18 .... 127 K5
Garrick Wy *FRIM* GU16 .... 182 B8
Garson La *STWL/WRAY* TW19 ...... 98 A6
Garson's La *BNFD* RG42 .... 94 D3
Garston Cl *TLHT* RG30 .... 115 K2 🔲
Garston Crs *CALC* RG31 .... 114 E1
Garston Gv *EWKG* RG40 .... 147 J5 🔲
Garswood *BRAK* RG12 .... 150 A3
Garth Cl *WWKG* RG41 .... 118 F4
Garthlands *MDHD* SL6 .... 42 A4
Garth Rd *THLE* RG7 .... 166 D1
Garth Sq *BNFD* RG42 .... 121 L5
Gascon's Gv *SLN* SL2 .... 44 E5
Gaskells End *CAV/SC* RG4 .... 62 A6
Gas La *MDHD* SL6 .... 68 D3
  WAR/TWY RG10 .... 91 G2
Gas Works Rd *READ* RG1 .... 9 K6
Gatcombe Cl *CALC* RG31 .... 114 F2
Gatehampton Rd
  GOR/PANG RG8 .... 32 F8
Gatewick Cl *SL* SL1 .... 4 E7
Gatward Av *MDHD* SL6 .... 67 L3 🔲
Gaveston Rd *SLN* SL2 .... 44 C4
Gayhurst Cl *CAV/SC* RG4 .... 63 G8
Gaywood Dr *NWBY* RG14 .... 15 L1
Gazelle Cl *WWKG* RG41 .... 118 C3
Geffers Ride *ASC* SL5 .... 123 H8
Gelder Cl *EARL* RG6 .... 118 A5
Genesis Cl *STWL/WRAY* TW19 .... 100 C7
Geneva Cl *SHPTN* TW17 .... 129 H7
Geoffreyson Rd *CAV/SC* RG4 ..... 88 A1
George Cl *MLW* SL7 .... 19 J2
George Green Dr *DTCH/LGLY* SL3.. 46 C7
George Green Rd
  DTCH/LGLY SL3 .... 46 B7
Georgeham Rd *SHST* GU47 .... 173 G4 🔲
George St *CHOB/PIR* GU24 .... 183 K8
  READ RG1 .... 8 F5
  READ RG1 .... 9 H3
  STA TW18 .... 127 K5
Georgia Gdns *TADY* RG26 .... 165 H6
Georgian Cl *CBLY* GU15 .... 174 B7
  STA TW18 .... 127 L2
Geranium Cl *CWTH* RG45 .... 148 E6 🔲
Gervaise Cl *SL* SL1 .... 70 C1
Gibbet La *CBLY* GU15 .... 174 D7
Gibbins La *BNFD* RG42 .... 122 A3
Gibbons Cl *SHST* GU47 .... 172 F7
Gibbs Cl *EWKG* RG40 .... 147 H8
Gibraltar La *MDHD* SL6 .... 19 L5

Gibson Ct *DTCH/LGLY* SL3 .... 72 C5
Gibson Pl *STWL/WRAY* TW19 ...... 99 M5
Gidley La *KSCL* RG20 .... 80 B5
Giffard Dr *FARN* GU14 .... 181 J8
Gifford Cl *CAV/SC* RG4 .... 89 H1 🔲
Gilbert Rd *FRIM* GU16 .... 181 M5
Gilbert Wy *EWKG* RG40 .... 147 H6
Giles Rd *TADY* RG26 .... 164 F6
Giles Travers Cl *EGH* TW20 .... 126 E8 🔲
Gillette Wy *WHIT* RG2 .... 116 E3
Gilliat Rd *SL* SL1 .... 4 F5
Gilliatt Cl *IVER* SL0 .... 47 K7 🔲
Gillotts La *HEN* RG9 .... 37 L7
Gillott's La *HEN* RG9 .... 37 L7
Gill Ri *BNFD* RG42 .... 121 M4
Gilman Crs *WDSR* SL4 .... 96 A2
Gilmore Cl *SLN* SL2 .... 71 🔲
Gilmore Crs *ASHF* TW15 .... 128 C3
Gilroy Cl *NWBY* RG14 .... 135 M8
Gilson Cl *STWL/WRAY* TW19 ...... 97 M6 🔲
Gingells Farm Rd
  WAR/TWY RG10 .... 90 E1 🔲
Gipsy La *BRAK* RG12 .... 13 L5
  EARL RG6 .... 118 A3
  EARL RG6 .... 118 A5
  EWKG RG40 .... 11 G8
  HUNG RG17 .... 104 B6
  TLHT RG30 .... 87 H5
  WWKG RG41 .... 118 C7
Girling Wy *EBED/NFELT* TW14 ... 101 K2
Girton Cl *SHST* GU47 .... 173 H5
Glade Rd *MLW* SL7 .... 19 H4
The Glade *ASC* SL5 .... 151 M2
  CALC RG31 .... 86 F2
  NWBY RG14 .... 136 C5
  STA TW18 .... 127 L5
Gladridge Cl *EARL* RG6 .... 117 L2 🔲
Gladstone Av
  EBED/NFELT TW14 .... 101 K5
Gladstone Cl *HUNG* RG17 .... 133 L4 🔲
Gladstone La *NTHA* RG18........ 109 M6
Gladstone Wy *SL* SL1 .... 70 D2
Glaisdale *STHA* RG19 .... 137 M4
Glaisyer Wy *IVER* SL0 .... 46 F3 🔲
Glamis Av *CALC* RG31 .... 114 E2 🔲
Glamis Wy *CALC* RG31 .... 114 E2 🔲
Glanmor Rd *SLN* SL2 .... 5 M5
The Glanty *EGH* TW20 .... 126 F2
Glasgow Rd *SL* SL1 .... 44 D7 🔲
Glaston Hill Rd *HTWY* RG27 .... 170 E6
Glebe Cl *LTWR* GU18 .... 175 M5
  MDHD SL6 .... 69 J2
  TADY RG26 .... 164 F7
  WGFD OX10 .... 32 C1
Glebe Flds *KSCL* RG20 .... 52 D7
Glebefields *NWBY* RG14 .... 136 E1 🔲
Glebe Gdns *CAV/SC* RG4 .... 90 B3
Glebeland Cl *CBLY* GU15 .... 181 J2
Glebelands *STHA* RG19 .... 137 M4
Glebelands Rd
  EBED/NFELT TW14 .... 101 K6 🔲
  EWKG RG40 .... 11 G4
Glebe La *CAV/SC* RG4 .... 90 B3
  KSCL RG20 .... 135 H1
Glebe Pl *HUNG* RG17 .... 103 K4
Glebe Ride *GOR/PANG* RG8 .... 32 E8
Glebe Rd *EGH* TW20 .... 126 F4
  GOR/PANG RG8 .... 86 E1
  MDHD SL6 .... 3 M8
  STA TW18 .... 127 L3
  UX/CGN UB8 .... 47 M3
  WDSR SL4 .... 97 L4
  WHIT RG2 .... 116 F1
The Glebe *BLKW* GU17 .... 181 H2
  BNFD RG42 .... 57 J3
  HEN RG9 .... 36 B1
Glebewood *BRAK* RG12 .... 149 M2
Glen Av *ASHF* TW15 .... 128 C2
Glenavon Gdns *DTCH/LGLY* SL3 ... 71 M4
  YTLY GU46 .... 180 A2 🔲
Glenbeigh Ter *READ* RG1 .... 8 A8
Glencoe Cl *FRIM* GU16 .... 182 C6
Glendale Av *NWBY* RG14 .... 159 M4
Glendale Rd *TADY* RG26 .... 164 D5
Glendevon Rd *WODY* RG5 .... 90 C6
Gleneagles *HTHAIR* TW6 .... 99 M4
Glenfield Rd *ASHF* TW15 .... 128 C4
Glenhurst Cl *BLKW* GU17 .... 181 H2 🔲
Glen Innes *SHST* GU47 .... 173 J5
Glen Miller Cl *KSCL* RG20 ...... 78 D2
Glenmore Cl *ADL/WDHM* KT15 .... 155 L7
  STHA RG19 .... 138 A4
Glennon Cl *TLHT* RG30 .... 115 M2 🔲
Glenrhondda *CAV/SC* RG4 .... 88 C1
Glenrosa Rd *TLHT* RG30 .... 87 J6
The Glen *DTCH/LGLY* SL3 .... 71 M4
  TADY RG26 .... 165 H5
Glentworth Pl *SL* SL1 .... 4 B7
Glenwood *BRAK* RG12 .... 13 M9
Glenwood Dr *CALC* RG31 .... 86 F7
Globe Farm La *BLKW* GU17 ...... 180 E1
Gloucester Av *SL* SL1 .... 4 B1
Gloucester Cl *FRIM* GU16 ...... 182 B8
Gloucester Crs *STA* TW18........ 128 A4
Gloucester Dr
  STWL/WRAY TW19 .... 126 F1
Gloucester Pl *BNFD* RG42 ...... 122 C5
  WDSR SL4 .... 7 K9
Gloucester Rd *BAGS* GU19 ...... 175 M7
  FELT TW13 .... 101 M7
  MDHD SL6 .... 42 B4
  NWBY RG14 .... 14 B5
  TLHT RG30 .... 88 A7
Glyncastle *CAV/SC* RG4 .... 88 C1
Glynswood *CBLY* GU15 .... 182 C3
Goaters Rd *ASC* SL5 .... 122 F8
Goddard Cl *WWKG* RG41 .... 118 E5 🔲
Goddard Dr *THLE* RG7 .... 139 J3
Goddards La *CBLY* GU15 .... 181 L3
Goddington Rd *BNEND* SL8 .... 20 D1
Godolphin Rd *SL* SL1 .... 4 C4
Goffs Rd *ASHF* TW15 .... 129 G4
Gogmore Farm Cl *CHERT* KT16... 155 H4

Gogmore La CHERT KT16 155 K4
Goldcrest Cl YTLY GU46 171 L8
Goldcrest Wy CALC RG31 86 E8
Gold Cup La ASC SL5 123 G6
Golden Ball La MDHD SL6 41 J3
Golden Orb Wd BNFD RG42 121 G6
Golding Cl STHA RG19 138 C3
Goldney Rd CBLY GU15 182 E2
Goldsmid Rd READ RG1 8 C7
Goldsmith Cl EWKG RG40 147 H5
NTHA RG18 137 M1
Goldsmith Wy CWTH RG45 172 E2
Goldsworthy Wy SL SL1 43 M7
Goldthorpe Gdns EARL RG6 117 J6
Goldwell Dr NWBY RG14 14 C2
Golf Dr CBLY GU15 182 C2
Gooch Cl WAR/TWY RG10 91 J3
Goodboy's La THLE RG7 143 K5
Goodchild Rd EWKG RG40 11 J6
Goodings La HUNG RG17 76 D5
Goodliffe Gdns CALC RG31 86 F2
Goodman Pk SLN SL2 71 M2
Goodrich Cl CAV/SC RG4 89 H1
Goodways Dr BRAK RG12 13 K5
Goodwin Cl CALC RG31 115 H2
Goodwin Rd SLN SL2 44 C4
Goodwood Cl CBLY GU15 173 M6
THLE RG7 142 C4
Goodwood Wy NWBY RG14 15 K8
Goose Gn HUNG RG17 49 L3
SLN SL2 44 E3
Goose Green Wy STHA RG19 138 B3
Goose La KSCL RG20 79 H1
Gordon Av CBLY GU15 181 L2
Gordon Cl CHERT KT16 155 H7
STA TW18 127 L4
Gordon Crs CBLY GU15 181 M2
KSCL RG20 56 A2
Gordon Dr CHERT KT16 155 H7
Gordon Pl TLHT RG30 87 M6
Gordon Rd ASHF TW15 128 B1
CBLY GU15 174 B8
CBLY GU15 181 M2
CWTH RG45 173 G3
MDHD SL6 2 C4
NTHA RG18 137 K1
NWBY RG14 15 G5
WDSR SL4 6 B9
Gordon Wk YTLY GU46 180 B1
Gore End Rd KSCL RG20 158 E3
Gore Rd SL SL1 43 L4
Goring La THLE RG7 142 C5
Goring Rd GOR/PANG RG8 34 A7
STA TW18 127 G3
Gorrick Sq WWKG RG41 147 L3
Gorse Bank LTWR GU18 175 K6
Gorse Cottage Dr NTHA RG18 109 L5
Gorse Dr WODY RG5 90 D6
Gorse Hill La VW GU25 154 A1
Gorse Hill Rd VW GU25 154 A1
Gorselands CAV/SC RG4 62 D8
NWBY RG14 160 A1
TADY RG26 164 F6
Gorse La CHOB/PIR GU24 177 H3
Gorse Meade SL SL1 70 E1
Gorse Ride North EWKG RG40 147 H7
Gorse Ride South EWKG RG40 147 H7
Gorse Rd FRIM GU16 182 B4
MDHD SL6 20 B8
Gosbrook Rd CAV/SC RG4 9 K1
READ RG1 9 G1
Gosden Rd CHOB/PIR GU24 176 C8
Gosforth Cl EARL RG6 118 A4
Goslar Wy WDSR SL4 6 F8
Gosling Gn DTCH/LGLY SL3 72 B3
Gosling Rd DTCH/LGLY SL3 72 B3
Gosnell Cl FRIM GU16 183 G3
Gossmore Cl MLW SL7 19 J5
Gossmore La MLW SL7 19 J5
Gossmore Wk MLW SL7 19 J5
Goswell Hl WDSR SL4 7 J6
Goswell Rd WDSR SL4 7 J6
Gough's Barn La BNFD RG42 93 K6
Gough's La BRAK RG12 13 L1
Gough's Meadow SHST GU47 172 E7
Gould Rd EBED/NFELT TW14 101 H6
Governor's Rd CBLY GU15 173 J8
Govett Gv BFOR GU20 176 A1
Gower Pk SHST GU47 173 G7
Gower St READ RG1 8 B6
The Gower EGH TW20 126 E8
Grace Bennett Cl FARN GU14 181 K7
Grace Ct SL SL1 4 B6
Graces La KSCL RG20 80 E6
Gracious Pond Rd
CHOB/PIR GU24 177 J3
Graffham Cl EARL RG6 117 L6
Grafton Cl DTCH/LGLY SL3 46 B7
MDHD SL6 42 B4
Grafton Rd TLHT RG30 87 G7
Graham Cl CALC RG31 115 H2
MDHD SL6 2 A9
Grahame Av GOR/PANG RG8 86 A1
Graham Rd BFOR GU20 175 M2
MDHD SL6 20 B8
Grampian Rd SHST GU47 172 C4
Grampian Wy DTCH/LGLY SL3 72 D5
Gramp's Hl WANT OX12 25 G2
Granby Ct READ RG1 89 H7
Granby End THLE RG7 142 E3
Granby Gdns EARL RG6 89 H7
Grand Av CBLY GU15 173 M8
DTCH/LGLY SL3 72 A1
Grand Union Canal Wk
DTCH/LGLY SL3 72 C2
SLN SL2 5 J5
Grange Av CWTH RG45 148 E8
EARL RG6 89 J8
HEN RG9 36 D6
Grange Cl GOR/PANG RG8 58 E1
STWL/WRAY TW19 98 B5
Grange Dr FLKWH HP10 21 G3
Grange La MDHD SL6 20 C6
Grangely Cl CALC RG31 115 G2
Grange Pl STA TW18 127 M7
Grange Rd BRAK RG12 13 K3
CBLY GU15 182 B1
EGH TW20 126 C3
FARN GU14 181 L7
HEN RG9 38 B5
MDHD SL6 20 C7
The Grange CHOB/PIR GU24 177 H5
NWBY RG14 159 M1
WDSR SL4 97 L4
Grange Wy IVER SL0 47 J7
Grangewood DTCH/LGLY SL3 45 M6
Grant Av SL SL1 4 F3
Grantham Cl SHST GU47 173 H5
Grantham Rd CALC RG31 115 J2
The Granthams HUNG RG17 49 L3
Grantley Rd HSLWW TW4 101 M1
Grant Rd CWTH RG45 172 F3
Grant Wk ASC SL5 152 B5
Granville Av FELT TW13 101 K8
SLN SL2 45 G6
Granville Rd TLHT RG30 115 L1
Grasholm Wy DTCH/LGLY SL3 72 F4
Grasmere Av SLN SL2 5 J5
TLHT RG30 87 J4
Grasmere Cl
EBED/NFELT TW14 101 J7
EGH TW20 126 E5
WWKG RG41 118 E5
Grasmere Rd LTWR GU18 175 L5
Grass Hl CAV/SC RG4 88 B3
Grassington Pl STHA RG19 138 A3
Grassmead STHA RG19 138 C4
Grassy La MDHD SL6 2 E4
Gratton Dr WDSR SL4 96 B3
Gratton Rd WHIT RG2 116 F6
Gratwicke Rd TLHT RG30 87 H6
Gravel Hl CAV/SC RG4 62 B8
HEN RG9 36 C8
KSCL RG20 135 H1
Gravel Hill Crs HEN RG9 36 C8
Gravelly Cl KSCL RG20 158 D3
TADY RG26 164 F8
Gravel Rd CAV/SC RG4 63 J5
Graveney Dr CAV/SC RG4 88 B3
Gravett Cl HEN RG9 37 M6
Grayling Cl MLW SL7 18 F6
Grays Crs WODY RG5 89 M6
Grayshot Dr BLKW GU17 180 F1
Grays La ASHF TW15 128 E2
Grays Park Rd SLN SL2 45 K3
Grays Pl SLN SL2 5 H6
Grays Rd SL SL1 5 G6
Grazeley Rd THLE RG7 144 D2
Greatfield Cl FARN GU14 181 L6
Greatfield Rd FARN GU14 181 K6
Great Hill Crs MDHD SL6 67 L1
Great Hollands Rd BRAK RG12 149 J3
Great Hollands Sq
BRAK RG12 149 J3
Great Knollys St READ RG1 8 C5
Great Lea THLE RG7 144 D1
Great Severals HUNG RG17 133 K4
Great South-west Rd
EBED/NFELT TW14 100 F6
Greenacre WDSR SL4 96 B1
Greenacre Ct EGH TW20 125 M4
Green Acre Mt TLHT RG30 87 G6
Greenacres KSCL RG20 159 H6
Green Acres MARL SN8 102 A2
Greenacres Av WWKG RG41 118 D4
Greenacres La WWKG RG41 118 D3
Green Cl MDHD SL6 3 H1
MDHD SL6 43 K7
Green Cft EWKG RG40 11 L1
Greendale Ms SLN SL2 5 J5
Green Dr EWKG RG40 11 K9
Greene Fielde End STA TW18 128 A5
Green End YTLY GU46 172 A7
Green End Cl THLE RG7 144 E4
Green Farm Ri MARL SN8 130 E1
Green Farm Rd BAGS GU19 175 J3
Greenfern Av SL SL1 43 M7
Greenfields MDHD SL6 3 J7
Greenfields Rd WHIT RG2 116 E6
Greenfield Wy CWTH RG45 148 D7
Greenfinch Cl CALC RG31 86 E8
Green Finch Cl CWTH RG45 148 C8
Greenham Cl WODY RG5 90 D8
Greenham Rd NWBY RG14 14 F6
Green Hill Cl CBLY GU15 174 F8
Green Hill Rd CBLY GU15 174 F8
Greenholme CBLY GU15 183 G1
Greenhow BRAK RG12 12 E7
Greenidge Cl READ RG1 116 B1
Greenlands CHERT KT16 154 F7
KSCL RG20 159 H5
Greenlands Rd CBLY GU15 181 L5
NWBY RG14 15 G9
STA TW18 127 K2
Green La ASC SL5 124 B6
BAGS GU19 175 J4
BLKW GU17 180 E2
BLKW GU17 181 H2
CAV/SC RG4 62 C1
CAV/SC RG4 63 K5
CHERT KT16 155 H6
CHOB/PIR GU24 177 J5
DTCH/LGLY SL3 71 L8
EGH TW20 126 E1
EGH TW20 126 E3
EGH TW20 126 F7
EWKG RG40 120 D4
GOR/PANG RG8 34 C7
GOR/PANG RG8 85 M1
HEN RG9 38 A6
HSLWW TW4 101 M3
KSCL RG20 80 E6
MDHD SL6 3 K8
MDHD SL6 66 E1
MDHD SL6 68 E2
MDHD SL6 93 K1
NWBY RG14 14 B5
SHST GU47 172 F7
SL SL1 43 M4
STA TW18 127 H6
STHA RG19 137 M3
SUN TW16 129 J5
THLE RG7 112 C3
THLE RG7 141 M4
THLE RG7 167 J6
TLHT RG30 115 K4
WAR/TWY RG10 119 H3
WDSR SL4 6 E8
WWKG RG41 119 G5
YTLY GU46 171 L7
Green Lane Cl CBLY GU15 173 M7
CHERT KT16 155 H6
Green Lane Ct SL SL1 43 M4
Greenleaf Ct DTCH/LGLY SL3 71 K6
Greenleas FRIM GU16 182 B4
Green Leas SUN TW16 129 J5
Greenleas Av CAV/SC RG4 62 E7
Green Leas Cl SUN TW16 129 J4
Greenleas Cl YTLY GU46 171 M7
Green Man La
EBED/NFELT TW14 101 K3
Greenmoor GOR/PANG RG8 34 C6
Greenock Rd SL SL1 44 D7
Green Pk STA TW18 127 H1
Green Rd CHERT KT16 154 E1
EARL RG6 117 J1
EGH TW20 154 D1
Greenside BNEND SL8 20 D1
SLN SL2 44 D6
Green St SUN TW16 129 K6
Greensward La WHIT RG2 145 M3
The Green BRAK RG12 13 G9
FELT TW13 101 L8
FLKWH HP10 21 H1
FRIM GU16 182 C8
HUNG RG17 133 L5
SL SL1 4 C9
STWL/WRAY TW19 98 B5
TADY RG26 164 F8
THLE RG7 113 M4
WWKG RG41 119 H7
Green Verges MLW SL7 19 H3
Green Wy SL SL1 43 L3
Greenway Dr STA TW18 127 M6
Greenways EGH TW20 126 B4
HUNG RG17 49 L4
KSCL RG20 159 H5
SHST GU47 172 E5
Greenways Dr ASC SL5 152 B5
MDHD SL6 41 K6
The Greenway SL SL1 70 A1
Green Wd ASC SL5 122 F6
Greenwood Gv WWKG RG41 119 G3
Greenwood Rd CHOB/PIR GU24 183 L8
CWTH RG45 148 D8
TLHT RG30 115 J1
Gregory Cl EARL RG6 117 M6
Gregory Dr WDSR SL4 97 L5
Grenfell Av MDHD SL6 3 G6
Grenfell Pl MDHD SL6 3 G6
Grenfell Rd MDHD SL6 2 E5
MDHD SL6 3 G6
Grensell Cl HTWY RG27 171 H6
Grenville Cl SL SL1 43 L3
Grenville Gdns FRIM GU16 182 B8
Gresham Rd SL SL1 44 D7
STA TW18 127 J3
Gresham Wy FRIM GU16 182 B8
TLHT RG30 87 K4
Greyberry Copse Rd
STHA RG19 137 G6
Greyfriars Dr ASC SL5 151 L2
Greyfriars Rd READ RG1 8 F5
Greys Ct READ RG1 9 J7
Greys Hl HEN RG9 38 A5
Greys Rd HEN RG9 37 K6
Greystoke Ct CWTH RG45 172 D2
Greystoke Rd CAV/SC RG4 88 F2
SL SL1 44 C6
Greywell Cl TADY RG26 164 D6
Griffin Cl MDHD SL6 2 E9
SL SL1 4 A9
Griffin Wy SUN TW16 129 K7
Griffiths Cl STHA RG19 138 C4
Grimmer Wy GOR/PANG RG8 34 C6
Grindle Cl NTHA RG18 137 M1
Gringer Hl MDHD SL6 2 D2
Grosvenor Ct BLKW GU17 181 G3
Grosvenor Rd CAV/SC RG4 88 F3
CHOB/PIR GU24 177 G8
STA TW18 127 K5
Grove Cl EWKG RG40 148 B7
SL SL1 71 K3
WDSR SL4 97 L6
Grove Ct EGH TW20 126 D3
Grove Cross Rd FRIM GU16 182 A5
Grovefields Av FRIM GU16 182 A5
Grove Hl CAV/SC RG4 88 D2
Groveland Pl TLHT RG30 87 L6
Groveland Rd NWBY RG14 136 A1
Grovelands Av WWKG RG41 119 G4
Grovelands Cl WWKG RG41 119 G3
Grovelands Rd THLE RG7 144 F4
TLHT RG30 87 L6
Grove La BNFD RG42 122 E3
Groveley Rd SUN TW16 129 J3
Grove Rd CAV/SC RG4 62 C1
CAV/SC RG4 88 D1
CBLY GU15 182 B1
CHERT KT16 155 J3
HEN RG9 38 B5
MDHD SL6 3 H5
NWBY RG14 136 A1
SL SL1 44 B1
WDSR SL4 7 J8
Groves Cl BNEND SL8 20 F3
Groves Lea THLE RG7 142 C8
Grovestile Waye
EBED/NFELT TW14 101 G6
Groves Wy MDHD SL6 20 B8
The Grove ASC SL5 122 F6
EGH TW20 126 D3
FRIM GU16 182 A5
NTHA RG18 138 A2
READ RG1 9 J7
SL SL1 5 J9
WAR/TWY RG10 91 G1
Grubwood La MDHD SL6 19 K7
Guards Club Rd MDHD SL6 42 F7
Guards Ct ASC SL5 152 E4
Guards Rd WDSR SL4 95 M1
Guerdon Pl BRAK RG12 150 A4
Guildford Av FELT TW13 101 K8
Guildford Rd BAGS GU19 175 H3
BAGS GU19 175 J4
CHERT KT16 155 G7
CHERT KT16 155 J5
CHOB/PIR GU24 176 B7
CHOB/PIR GU24 177 G8
CHERT KT16 155 J5
Guildford St CHERT KT16 155 K4
STA TW18 127 K4
Gun St READ RG1 8 F6
Gunthorpe Rd MLW SL7 19 J3
Gurney Cl CAV/SC RG4 88 A1
Gurney Dr CAV/SC RG4 88 A2
Guttridge La TADY RG26 164 D6
Gwendale MDHD SL6 41 M5
Gwent Cl MDHD SL6 67 L2
Gwyn Cl NWBY RG14 136 C6
Gwynne Cl CALC RG31 87 G3
WDSR SL4 70 B8
Gwyns Piece HUNG RG17 49 L3
Gypsy La MLW SL7 19 H2

H

Habershon Dr FRIM GU16 183 G4
Haddon Dr WODY RG5 90 B6
Hadfield Rd STWL/WRAY TW19 100 A5
Hadleigh Ri CAV/SC RG4 89 H1
Hadlow Ct SL SL1 4 A6
Hadrian Cl STWL/WRAY TW19 100 B6
Hadrian Wy
STWL/WRAY TW19 100 B6
Hafod CAV/SC RG4 62 C8
Hagbourne Cl GOR/PANG RG8 34 C6
Hag Hill La MDHD SL6 43 K7
Hagley Rd WHIT RG2 116 E2
Haig Dr SL SL1 70 E2
Haig Rd CBLY GU15 173 J8
Hailey La KSCL RG20 54 A6
Hailsham Cl SHST GU47 173 G5
Halcyon Ter TLHT RG30 87 H6
Haldane Rd CAV/SC RG4 88 B1
Halebourne La CHOB/PIR GU24 176 D5
Hale End BRAK RG12 150 C1
Hale St STA TW18 127 H2
Hale Wy FRIM GU16 182 A5
Halewood BRAK RG12 149 J3
Halfacre Cl THLE RG7 144 E3
Half Mile Rd HUNG RG17 75 K5
Halfpenny La ASC SL5 152 D4
WGFD OX10 32 B1
Halfway La MARL SN8 102 B2
Halifax Cl MDHD SL6 41 K6
Halifax Pl NTHA RG18 137 M2
Halifax Rd MDHD SL6 41 K6
Halifax Wy MDHD SL6 41 K6
Halkingcroft DTCH/LGLY SL3 71 M2
Hallbrook Gdns BNFD RG42 12 B1
Hall Cl CBLY GU15 174 B8
Hall Ct DTCH/LGLY SL3 71 L7
Halldore Hl MDHD SL6 20 B7
Halley Dr ASC SL5 123 G7
Halliford Cl SHPTN TW17 129 H8
Hallmark Cl SHST GU47 173 H6
Hall Meadow SL SL1 43 M3
Hall Place La MDHD SL6 40 E6
Halls La WAR/TWY RG10 66 D8
WHIT RG2 117 H6
Halls Rd TLHT RG30 86 F8
Halpin Cl CALC RG31 114 F2
Halstead Cl WODY RG5 90 B7
The Halters NWBY RG14 136 E7
Hamble Av BLKW GU17 181 G1
Hambledon Cl EARL RG6 118 B5
Hamble Dr TADY RG26 165 G6
Hambleton Cl CBLY GU15 182 E3
Hamblin Meadow
HUNG RG17 104 B7
Hamborne Ga NWBY RG14 136 A5
Ham Br STHA RG19 137 H3
NWBY RG14 15 M4
Hambridge La NWBY RG14 137 H4
Hambridge Rd NWBY RG14 15 J5
Hamdens NWBY RG14 135 M8
Hamilton Av HEN RG9 38 B5
Hamilton Cl CHERT KT16 155 J5
FELT TW13 129 J3
NWBY RG14 14 F9
Hamilton Dr ASC SL5 152 B4
Hamilton Gdns SL SL1 43 L4
Hamilton Pk MDHD SL6 41 K8
Hamilton Pl SUN TW16 129 L5
Hamilton Rd FELT TW13 129 H3
READ RG1 89 H8
SL SL1 44 D7
WAR/TWY RG10 65 H4
Ham La EGH TW20 125 L2
TADY RG26 163 L8
WDSR SL4 97 M3
Hamlet St BNFD RG42 122 B6
The Hamlet CAV/SC RG4 61 L1
Hammond Cl STHA RG19 138 B4
Hammonds Heath THLE RG7 142 E8
Hammond Wy LTWR GU18 175 L5
Hampden Cl SLN SL2 45 K4
Hampden Rd CAV/SC RG4 88 E4
DTCH/LGLY SL3 72 C3
MDHD SL6 41 L6
Hampshire Av SL SL1 4 A1
Hampshire Ri BNFD RG42 122 C4
Hampshire Rd CBLY GU15 174 C6
Hampshire Wy WWKG RG41 119 G8
Hampstead Norreys Rd
NTHA RG18 81 L7
Hampton Rd NWBY RG14 14 D7
Hanbury Cl SL SL1 43 L5
Hanbury Dr CALC RG31 115 G2
Hanbury Wy CBLY GU15 181 M3
Hancocks Mt ASC SL5 152 A3
Hancombe Rd SHST GU47 172 D4
Handford La YTLY GU46 180 A2
Hanger Rd TADY RG26 164 C5
Hangman's Stone La KSCL RG20 78 C1
Hanley Cl WDSR SL4 70 A8
Hannibal Rd STWL/WRAY TW19 100 B6
Hanningtons Wy THLE RG7 142 F3
Hanover Av FELT TW13 101 K7
Hanover Cl EGH TW20 125 L4
FRIM GU16 182 B5
SL SL1 71 K3
WDSR SL4 6 A7
Hanover Gdns BRAK RG12 149 J4
FARN GU14 181 H8
Hanover Md MDHD SL6 68 F3
Hanover Wy WDSR SL4 6 A7
Hanson Cl CBLY GU15 174 E7
Hanwood Cl WODY RG5 89 M6
Hanworth Cl BRAK RG12 149 M3
Hanworth La CHERT KT16 155 J5
Hanworth Rd BRAK RG12 149 K4
FELT TW13 101 L7
SUN TW16 129 K5
Harbour Cl FARN GU14 181 K6
Harcourt STWL/WRAY TW19 98 B5
Harcourt Cl EGH TW20 126 F4
HEN RG9 37 M5
MDHD SL6 69 J3
Harcourt Dr EARL RG6 117 J4
Harcourt Rd BRAK RG12 149 L3
CBLY GU15 181 L1
MDHD SL6 69 J3
WDSR SL4 70 B8
Hardell Cl EGH TW20 126 D3
Harding Rd WODY RG5 89 M6
Hardings Rw IVER SL0 46 F4
Hardwell Wy BRAK RG12 150 B1
Hardwick Cl MDHD SL6 41 J6
Hardwick La CHERT KT16 154 F4
Hardwick Rd GOR/PANG RG8 60 A7
TLHT RG30 87 J7
Hardy Cl CAV/SC RG4 9 J1
CAV/SC RG4 88 F4
NTHA RG18 137 M1
Hardy Gn CWTH RG45 172 E2
Harebell Dr NTHA RG18 138 B2
Harefield Cl WWKG RG41 118 F4
Harefield Rd MDHD SL6 41 K7
Hare Shoots MDHD SL6 2 E9
Harewood Dr NTHA RG18 109 M6
Harewood Pl SL SL1 71 K3
Hargrave Rd MDHD SL6 2 D2
Harkness Rd SL SL1 43 L6
Harlech Av CAV/SC RG4 89 H1
Harlech Rd BLKW GU17 181 G2
Harleyford La MLW SL7 18 E7
Harley Rd READ RG1 9 G1
Harlington Rd East
EBED/NFELT TW14 101 L6
Harlington Rd West
EBED/NFELT TW14 101 L5
Harlton Cl EARL RG6 117 M6
Harman Ct WWKG RG41 118 E4
Harmans Water Rd BRAK RG12 150 A2
Harmar Cl EWKG RG40 11 M6
Harmsworth Rd TADY RG26 164 E6
Harness Cl WHIT RG2 116 E8
Harold Rd HUNG RG17 133 M4
Harpdon Pde YTLY GU46 172 A7
Harpesford Av VW GU25 153 M2
Harpsden Rd HEN RG9 38 B6
Harpsden Wy HEN RG9 38 B7
Harpton Cl YTLY GU46 172 A7
Harrier Cl WODY RG5 90 D8
Harrington Cl EARL RG6 117 M4
NWBY RG14 137 G1
WDSR SL4 96 C3
Harris Cl HUNG RG17 49 L3
WODY RG5 90 E6
Harrison Cl WAR/TWY RG10 91 J3
Harrison Wy SL SL1 70 A1
Harris Wy SUN TW16 129 H6
Harrogate Ct DTCH/LGLY SL3 72 D5
Harrogate Rd CAV/SC RG4 88 B2
Harrow Cl ADL/WDHM KT15 155 L6
MDHD SL6 42 B5
Harrow Ct READ RG1 8 C8
Harrow La MDHD SL6 2 D1
Harrow Rd ASHF TW15 100 D7
DTCH/LGLY SL3 72 C3
Harrow Wy SHPTN TW17 128 F7
Hart Cl BNFD RG42 13 G1
FARN GU14 181 H6
Hart Dene Ct BAGS GU19 175 H3
Hart Dyke Cl WWKG RG41 147 L4
Hartford Ri CBLY GU15 174 A8
Hartigan Pl WODY RG5 90 D6
Hartland Cl SL SL1 4 C7
Hartland Pl FARN GU14 181 K8
Hartland Rd WHIT RG2 116 E5
Hartley Cl BLKW GU17 180 E1
DTCH/LGLY SL3 45 M2
Hartley Copse WDSR SL4 97 K5
Hartley Court Rd THLE RG7 116 C8
Hartley Gdns TADY RG26 164 E7
Hartleys THLE RG7 165 K6
Hartmead Rd STHA RG19 138 B3
Hartsbourne Rd EARL RG6 117 K3
Harts Cl WHIT RG2 146 B4
Harts Hill Rd NTHA RG18 138 B2
Hartshill Rd TADY RG26 164 C6
Harts La KSCL RG20 160 B8
THLE RG7 141 L1
Harts Leap Cl SHST GU47 172 D5
Harts Leap Rd SHST GU47 172 D6
Hartslock Ct GOR/PANG RG8 59 L8
Hartslock Vw GOR/PANG RG8 59 H4
Hartslock Wy CALC RG31 86 F4
Hart St READ RG1 8 B5
Harvard Cl WODY RG5 90 E6
Harvard Rd SHST GU47 173 J5
Harvest Cl CALC RG31 86 E8
Harvest Gn NWBY RG14 14 B8
Harvest Hl BNEND SL8 21 G4
Harvest Hill Rd MDHD SL6 68 B2
Harvest Ride BNFD RG42 121 K4
Harvest Rd EGH TW20 126 A3
FELT TW13 129 K2
Harvey Rd DTCH/LGLY SL3 72 E3
Harwich Cl EARL RG6 118 A5
Harwich Rd SL SL1 44 D7
Harwood Gdns WDSR SL4 97 L6
Harwood Ri KSCL RG20 159 J5
Harwood Rd MLW SL7 18 F5
Haslemere Av HEST TW5 101 M1
Haslemere Cl FRIM GU16 182 F3

Haslemere Rd *WDSR* SL4 .... 6 C7
Haslett Rd *SHPTN* TW17 .... 129 H7 🔲
Hasting Cl *MDHD* SL6 .... 68 F4
Hastings Cl *FRIM* GU16 .... 182 D7
TLHT RG30 .... 115 K2 🔲
Hatchbury La *RAND* SP11 .... 178 B8
Hatch Cl *ADL/WDHM* KT15 .... 155 L7
THLE RG7 .... 111 M7
Hatch End *BFOR* GU20 .... 175 M2
The Hatches *FRIM* GU16 .... 182 C8
Hatchet La *ASC* SL5 .... 123 K3
WDSR SL4 .... 123 K2
Hatchets La *NTHA* RG18 .... 82 F7
Hatchett Rd *EBED/NFELT* TW14 .. 100 F7
Hatchgate Cl *NTHA* RG18 .... 109 M8
Hatchgate Copse *BRAK* RG12 .. 149 H3
Hatchgate Gdns *SL* SL1 .... 44 A4
Hatch Gate La *WAR/TWY* RG10 .. 39 J7
Hatch La *THLE* RG7 .... 111 M8
TLHT RG30 .... 115 C8
WDSR SL4 .... 96 D2
Hatch Ride *CWTH* RG45 .... 148 E7
EWKG RG40 .... 148 C6
The Hatch *NTHA* RG18 .... 69 M7
Hatfield Cl *MDHD* SL6 .... 2 A6
Hatfield Ct *CALC* RG31 .... 114 E2 🔲
CBLY GU15 .... 181 L1 🔲
Hatfield Rd *SL* SL1 .... 5 J9
Hatford Rd *TLHT* RG30 .... 115 L2
Hatherley Rd *READ* RG1 .... 89 H8
Hatherwood *YTLY* GU46 .... 180 C1 🔲
Hatton Av *SLN* SL2 .... 45 G5
Hatton Ct *WDSR* SL4 .... 7 G9
Hatton Gn *EBED/NFELT* TW14 .. 101 K3
Hatton Hl *BFOR* GU20 .... 175 M1
GOR/PANG RG8 .... 57 L7
Hatton Rd *EBED/NFELT* TW14 .. 100 F6
HTHAIR TW6 .... 101 J3
Haughurst Hl *STHA* RG19 .... 163 L6
Havelock Crs *MDHD* SL6 .... 41 L7
Havelock Rd *MDHD* SL6 .... 41 L7
WWKG RG41 .... 10 D6
Havelock St *WWKG* RG41 .... 10 D6
Haven Rd *ASHF* TW15 .... 128 E2
SUN TW16 .... 129 K5
Haversham Dr *BRAK* RG12 .... 149 L3
Hawkchurch Rd *WHIT* RG2 .... 117 G6
Hawkedon Wy *EARL* RG6 .... 118 A4
Hawker Wy *WODY* RG5 .... 90 D8
Hawkesbury Dr *CALC* RG31 .... 115 H3
Hawkes Cl *WWKG* RG41 .... 10 C4
Hawkes Leap *BFOR* GU20 .... 151 L8
Hawkes Rd *EBED/NFELT* TW14 .. 101 K6
Hawkesworth Dr *BAGS* GU19 .. 175 G5
Hawkewood Rd *SUN* TW16 .... 129 L8
Hawkins Cl *BRAK* RG12 .... 122 D7
Hawkins Wy *EWKG* RG40 .... 11 L5
Hawk La *BRAK* RG12 .... 13 L9
Hawkley Dr *TADY* RG26 .... 164 F7
Hawks Hl *BNEND* SL8 .... 20 F4
Hawkshill Rd *SLN* SL2 .... 44 D4
Hawksway *STA* TW18 .... 127 J1 🔲
Hawksworth Av *FRIM* GU16 .... 182 C4
Hawksworth Rd *THLE* RG7 .... 142 E3
Haw La *GOR/PANG* RG8 .... 57 H7
Hawley Cl *CALC* RG31 .... 114 F2 🔲
Hawley La *BLKW* GU17 .... 181 H3
Hawley La *FARN* GU14 .... 181 L6
Hawley Rd *BLKW* GU17 .... 181 H3
Hawley Wy *ASHF* TW15 .... 128 E3 🔲
Hawthorn Cl *BNFD* RG42 .... 12 E2
IVER SL0 .... 46 F4 🔲
Hawthorne Av *WDSR* SL4 .... 95 L8
Hawthorne Cl *MLW* SL7 .... 19 H2 🔲
Hawthorne Crs *BLKW* GU17 .... 181 H2 🔲
SL SL1 .... 4 F3
Hawthorne Dr *WDSR* SL4 .... 95 L7 🔲
Hawthorne Rd *CAV/SC* RG4 .... 89 H3
EGH TW20 .... 126 F3
Hawthornes *CALC* RG31 .... 86 E4 🔲
Hawthorne Wy *HUNG* RG17 .... 77 L2 🔲
WDSR SL4 .... 95 K7
Hawthorn Gdns *MDHD* SL6 .... 2 D9
WHIT RG2 .... 117 H4
Hawthorn La *BNFD* RG42 .... 94 A6
SLN SL2 .... 44 C1
Hawthorn Rd *FRIM* GU16 .... 182 C4
NWBY RG14 .... 14 E1
The Hawthorns *DTCH/LGLY* SL3 .. 73 J8
TADY RG26 .... 164 B6 🔲
WAR/TWY RG10 .... 90 D3
Hawthorn Wy *CAV/SC* RG4 .... 90 B4
Hawtrey Cl *SL* SL1 .... 5 M9
Hawtrey Rd *WDSR* SL4 .... 7 H8
Haydon La *KSCL* RG20 .... 29 H7
Hayes La *WWKG* RG41 .... 146 F2
Hayfield Cl *CALC* RG31 .... 86 F6
Hayley Gn *BNFD* RG42 .... 122 C3
Hayling Av *FELT* TW13 .... 129 K1
Haymill Rd *SL* SL1 .... 44 A5
SLN SL2 .... 44 A5
Haynes Cl *DTCH/LGLY* SL3 .. 72 C5 🔲
Hay Rd *READ* RG1 .... 116 C1
Hayse Hl *WDSR* SL4 .... 70 A8
Haywards Cl *HEN* RG9 .... 37 M5
Haywards Md *WDSR* SL4 .... 70 C5
The Haywards *NTHA* RG18 .... 138 A2
Haywood *BRAK* RG12 .... 149 M4
Haywood Ct *EARL* RG6 .... 89 J7
Haywood Wy *TLHT* RG30 .... 115 J1
Hazelbank *EWKG* RG40 .... 147 C8
Hazelbank Rd *CHERT* KT16 .... 155 M4
Hazel Cl *EGH* TW20 .... 125 L4
TLHT RG30 .... 142 E1
WWKG RG41 .... 10 A9
Hazel Crs *WHIT* RG2 .... 117 H4
Hazeldene *KSCL* RG20 .... 80 E5 🔲
Hazel Dr *WODY* RG5 .... 117 M1
Hazel Gdns *CAV/SC* RG4 .... 36 C8
Hazel Gn *TADY* RG26 .... 164 A5 🔲
Hazel Gv *NTHA* RG18 .... 138 A1
STA TW18 .... 127 L4
Hazelhurst Rd *SL* SL1 .... 43 M3
Hazell Cl *MDHD* SL6 .... 3 H2
Hazell Hl *BRAK* RG12 .... 13 J7
Hazelmere Cl
EBED/NFELT TW14 .... 101 G5

Hazelmere Rd *SLN* SL2 .... 5 M6
Hazelmoor La *CAV/SC* RG4 .... 61 M2
Hazel Rd *CALC* RG31 .... 86 F2
Hazelwood Cl *CALC* RG31 .... 86 F5 🔲
Hazelwood La *BNFD* RG42 .... 121 K2
Heacham Cl *EARL* RG6 .... 117 K6 🔲
Headington Cl *EWKG* RG40 .... 11 H2
MDHD SL6 .... 41 K7
Headington Dr *EWKG* RG40 .... 11 J2
Headington Rd *MDHD* SL6 .... 41 K6
Headley Cl *WODY* RG5 .... 90 D6
Headley Rd *WODY* RG5 .... 90 B7
Headley Rd East *WODY* RG5 .... 90 D7
Heads La *HUNG* RG17 .... 157 K1
Heardman Cl *STHA* RG19 .... 138 C4
Hearmon Cl *YTLY* GU46 .... 172 A3
Hearn Rd *WODY* RG5 .... 118 B1
Hearns La *CAV/SC* RG4 .... 61 M1
Hearn Wk *BRAK* RG12 .... 122 B6 🔲
Hearsey Gdns *BLKW* GU17 .... 172 E8
Heath Cl *STWL/WRAY* TW19 .... 99 M5
VW GU25 .... 154 A1
WWKG RG41 .... 147 L2
Heathcote *MDHD* SL6 .... 68 E4 🔲
Heathcote Rd *CBLY* GU15 .... 182 A1
Heathcroft Av *SUN* TW16 .... 129 J5
Heath Dr *CAV/SC* RG4 .... 63 K5
Heath End Rd *TADY* RG26 .... 164 B5
Heather Cl *CAV/SC* RG4 .... 62 C1
EWKG RG40 .... 147 H7 🔲
Heatherdale Rd *CBLY* GU15 .... 181 M2
Heatherden Cl *WHIT* RG2 .... 116 F7
Heatherdene Av *CWTH* RG45 .... 172 B2
Heatherden Gn *IVER* SL0 .... 46 F7
Heather Dr *ASC* SL5 .... 152 K4
NTHA RG18 .... 138 B4
TADY RG26 .... 164 C4
Heatherlands *SUN* TW16 .... 129 J4
Heatherley Cl *CBLY* GU15 .... 181 L1 🔲
Heatherley Rd *CBLY* GU15 .... 181 L1
Heather Md *FRIM* GU16 .... 182 C4
Heathermount *BRAK* RG12 .... 150 B1 🔲
Heathermount Dr *CWTH* RG45 .. 148 C8
Heatherside Dr *VW* GU25 .... 153 K3
The Heathers
STWL/WRAY TW19 .... 100 C6 🔲
Heather Wy *CHOB/PIR* GU24 .. 177 H3
Heatherway *CWTH* RG45 .... 172 D1
Heathfield Av *ASC* SL5 .... 152 B2
HEN RG9 .... 63 L4
TLHT RG30 .... 87 G7
Heathfield Cl *HEN* RG9 .... 63 L4
Heathfield Rd *MDHD* SL6 .... 21 J6
Heathfields *KSCL* RG20 .... 80 D6
Heath Gv *SUN* TW16 .... 129 J5
Heath Hill Rd North
CWTH RG45 .... 172 E1
Heath Hill Rd South
CWTH RG45 .... 172 E1
Heathlands *KSCL* RG20 .... 159 K6
Heathlands Cl *SLN* SL2 .... 44 C4
Heathlands Dr *MDHD* SL6 .... 41 K8
Heathlands Rd *EWKG* RG40 .. 148 C3
Heath La *MARL* SN8 .... 156 B7
NTHA RG18 .... 137 M1
Heathmoors *BRAK* RG12 .... 149 M2 🔲
Heathpark Dr *BFOR* GU20 .... 176 B2
Heath Ride *CWTH* RG45 .... 172 A2
EWKG RG40 .... 147 L8
Heath Ri *CBLY* GU15 .... 182 A1
VW GU25 .... 154 A1
Heath Rd *BAGS* GU19 .... 175 J3
EARL RG6 .... 117 K1
TADY RG26 .... 165 H5
THLE RG7 .... 112 D4
Heathrow Cl *WDR/YW* UB7 .... 73 L8
Heathrow Copse *TADY* RG26 .. 164 A6
Heathside Pk *CBLY* GU15 .... 174 F7
Heathway *ASC* SL5 .... 123 H6
CALC RG31 .... 86 F6 🔲
CBLY GU15 .... 182 A1
Heath Wy *IVER* SL0 .... 47 G3
Heathway Cl *CBLY* GU15 .... 182 A1
Heathwood Cl *YTLY* GU46 .... 172 A7 🔲
Heavens Lea *BNEND* SL8 .... 20 F4
Hebbecastle Down *BNFD* RG42 .. 121 L4
Hebden Ct *STHA* RG19 .... 137 M5
Heddon Wk *FARN* GU14 .... 181 K7 🔲
Hedgeway *NWBY* RG14 .... 15 K1
Hedsor Hl *MDHD* SL6 .... 21 G5
Hedsor La *FLKWH* HP10 .... 21 J4
Hedsor Rd *BNEND* SL8 .... 20 E4
Heelas Rd *WWKG* RG41 .... 10 C6
Heenan Cl *FRIM* GU16 .... 182 B7
Helena Rd *WDSR* SL4 .... 95 K7
Helen Av *EBED/NFELT* TW14 .. 101 L6
Helgiford Gdns *SUN* TW16 .. 129 K5
Helksham Ct *SHST* GU47 .... 173 G5 🔲
Hellyer Wy *BNEND* SL8 .... 20 F4
Helmsdale *BRAK* RG12 .... 150 B2
Helmsdale Cl *TLHT* RG30 .... 87 L6
Helston Gdns *WHIT* RG2 .... 116 E5
Helston La *WDSR* SL4 .... 95 J7
Helvellyn Cl *EGH* TW20 .... 126 F5 🔲
Hemdean Hl *CAV/SC* RG4 .... 88 D3
Hemdean Ri *CAV/SC* RG4 .... 88 D3
Hemdean Rd *CAV/SC* RG4 .... 88 D2
Hemmyng Cnr *BNFD* RG42 .. 121 M4 🔲
Hempson Av *DTCH/LGLY* SL3 .. 71 M3
Hemsdale *MDHD* SL6 .... 41 L5
Hemwood Rd *WDSR* SL4 .... 96 A2
Hencroft St North *SL* SL1 .... 5 H9
Hencroft St South *SL* SL1 .... 71 J3
Hendons Wy *MDHD* SL6 .... 68 E5
Hendon Wy *STWL/WRAY* TW19 .. 100 A4
Hengrave Cl *EARL* RG6 .... 118 B4 🔲
Hengrove Crs *ASHF* TW15 .... 128 A1
Henley Cl *FARN* GU14 .... 181 H6
Henley Dr *FRIM* GU16 .... 182 B7
Henley Gdns *YTLY* GU46 .... 180 A1
Henley Rd *CAV/SC* RG4 .... 88 B7
HEN RG9 .... 63 M6
MDHD SL6 .... 40 F5
MLW SL7 .... 18 E6
MLW SL7 .... 18 F5
SL SL1 .... 44 B7

WAR/TWY RG10 .... 39 L4
Henley Wood Rd *EARL* RG6 .. 118 A2
Henry Rd *SL* SL1 .... 4 D8
The Henrys *NTHA* RG18 .... 138 A2
Henry St *READ* RG1 .... 9 G8
Henshaw Crs *NWBY* RG14 .... 136 A6
Hensworth Rd *ASHF* TW15 .. 128 A4
Henwick Cl *NTHA* RG18 .... 109 K8
Henwick La *NTHA* RG18 .... 137 K1
Henwood Copse *GOR/PANG* RG8 .. 58 D8
Hepplewhite Cl *TADY* RG26 .. 164 B5
Hepworth Cft *SHST* GU47 .... 173 H8 🔲
Herald Wy *WODY* RG5 .... 90 D8
Herbert Cl *BRAK* RG12 .... 149 L2
Hereford Cl *STA* TW18 .... 127 L6
Hereford Rd *FELT* TW13 .... 101 M7
Herewood Cl *NWBY* RG14 .... 14 C1
Heriot Rd *CHERT* KT16 .... 155 K4
Heritage Cl *UX/CGN* UB8 .... 47 M5
Hermitage Dr *DTCH/LGLY* SL3 .. 71 M3
FRIM GU16 .... 182 C5
Hermitage Dr *ASC* SL5 .... 123 H7
WAR/TWY RG10 .... 91 G1
Hermitage La *WDSR* SL4 .... 96 D2
Hermitage Rd *NTHA* RG18 .... 109 L4
Hermits Cl *THLE* RG7 .... 142 E3
Herndon Cl *EGH* TW20 .... 126 D2
Heroes Wk *WHIT* RG2 .... 116 F7
Heron Cl *ASC* SL5 .... 123 G6
Herondale *BRAK* RG12 .... 149 M4
Heron Dr *DTCH/LGLY* SL3 .... 72 E4
WAR/TWY RG10 .... 65 H8
Heronfield *EGH* TW20 .... 125 L4 🔲
Herongate *HUNG* RG17 .... 104 A7
Heron Island *CAV/SC* RG4 .... 9 J2
Heron Rd *WWKG* RG41 .... 119 J10
Heronscourt *LTWR* GU18 .... 175 M6
Heronscroft *LTWR* GU18 .... 175 M6
Heron Shaw *GOR/PANG* RG8 .. 32 F7 🔲
Heron's Wy *EWKG* RG40 .... 11 K4
Heron Wy *READ* RG1 .... 116 B2
STHA RG19 .... 137 L3
THLE RG7 .... 140 F3
Herriard Wy *TADY* RG26 .... 164 E7 🔲
Herrick Cl *FRIM* GU16 .... 182 F3
Herrings La *BFOR* GU20 .... 176 A2
Herschel Park Dr *SL* SL1 .... 5 G9
Herschel St *SL* SL1 .... 5 G9
Hertford Cl *CAV/SC* RG4 .... 63 G8
WWKG RG41 .... 147 H1
Hetherington Cl *SLN* SL2 .... 44 C4
Hetherington Rd *SHPTN* TW17 .. 128 F7
Hever Cl *MDHD* SL6 .... 2 A6
Hewett Av *CAV/SC* RG4 .... 88 A2
Hewett Cl *CAV/SC* RG4 .... 88 A2
Hewlett Pl *BAGS* GU19 .... 175 H3
Hexham Cl *SHST* GU47 .... 173 G4
Hexham Rd *WHIT* RG2 .... 116 F3
Heynes Gn *MDHD* SL6 .... 67 J3
Heywood Av *MDHD* SL6 .... 67 K5
Heywood Court Cl *MDHD* SL6 .. 67 K4 🔲
Heywood Dr *BAGS* GU19 .... 174 F4
Hibbert Rd *MDHD* SL6 .... 68 E2
Hicks La *BLKW* GU17 .... 180 E1
Higgs La *BAGS* GU19 .... 175 G4
Highams La *CHOB/PIR* GU24 .. 176 D2
High Beech *BRAK* RG12 .... 150 C1 🔲
High Beeches *FRIM* GU16 .... 182 A4
Highbridge Cl *CAV/SC* RG4 .... 89 H1
Highbridge Whf *READ* RG1 .... 9 H6
Highbury Crs *CBLY* GU15 .... 174 D7
Highbury Rd *CALC* RG31 .... 86 D5
Highclere *ASC* SL5 .... 152 A2
Highclere Dr *CBLY* GU15 .... 174 D7
Highcliffe Cl *WODY* RG5 .... 90 C5
Highdown Av *CAV/SC* RG4 .... 62 D8
Higher Alham *BRAK* RG12 .. 150 B4 🔲
BRAK RG12 .... 150 B4 🔲
BRAK RG12 .... 150 B4 🔲
Highfield *BRAK* RG12 .... 149 J3
EARL RG6 .... 117 L4
Highfield Av *NWBY* RG14 .... 14 E5
Highfield Cl *EWKG* RG40 .... 10 F5
Highfield La *MDHD* SL6 .... 67 K2
Highfield Pk *MLW* SL7 .... 18 E6
WAR/TWY RG10 .... 65 J4
Highfield Rd *BNEND* SL8 .... 20 E3
CALC RG31 .... 86 E4
CHERT KT16 .... 155 K5 🔲
EGH TW20 .... 126 A4
FELT TW13 .... 101 K7
MDHD SL6 .... 41 L7
NWBY RG14 .... 14 D9
WDSR SL4 .... 96 C2 🔲
High Flds *ASC* SL5 .... 152 C2
Highgate Rd *WODY* RG5 .... 118 A1
Highgrove *FARN* GU14 .... 181 L7 🔲
Highgrove Pk *MDHD* SL6 .... 2 E2
Highgrove St *READ* RG1 .... 116 F1
Highgrove Ter *READ* RG1 .... 9 H9
Highland Pk *FELT* TW13 .... 129 J2
Highland Rd *CBLY* GU15 .... 174 B6
Highlands Av *WWKG* RG41 .... 146 F1
Highlands La *HEN* RG9 .... 37 K7
Highmead Cl *WHIT* RG2 .... 117 H4
High Meadow *CAV/SC* RG4 .... 88 A3
High Meadow Pl *CHERT* KT16 .. 155 J5 🔲
Highmoor Rd *CAV/SC* RG4 .... 88 C3
High Rd *MDHD* SL6 .... 20 B7
UX/CGN UB8 .... 47 M6
High St *ADL/WDHM* KT15 .. 155 L8
ASC SL5 .... 123 J8
ASC SL5 .... 152 A2
BAGS GU19 .... 175 H3
BRAK RG12 .... 13 H4
CAV/SC RG4 .... 90 A3
CBLY GU15 .... 174 A8
CHOB/PIR GU24 .... 176 B7
CHOB/PIR GU24 .... 177 H6
CWTH RG45 .... 172 C2
DTCH/LGLY SL3 .... 71 L8
DTCH/LGLY SL3 .... 72 D4
DTCH/LGLY SL3 .... 72 F7
EGH TW20 .... 126 C3
FELT TW13 .... 101 K8
FELT TW13 .... 129 J1
GOR/PANG RG8 .... 32 D8

GOR/PANG RG8 .... 60 A7
HUNG RG17 .... 49 G1
HUNG RG17 .... 49 L4
HUNG RG17 .... 132 A1
HUNG RG17 .... 133 L3
IVER SL0 .... 47 J7
KSCL RG20 .... 29 H8
KSCL RG20 .... 56 A2
KSCL RG20 .... 80 E5
KSCL RG20 .... 106 D5
MARL SN8 .... 130 A8
MARL SN8 .... 130 D6
MDHD SL6 .... 3 G5
MDHD SL6 .... 20 D7
MDHD SL6 .... 43 H5
MDHD SL6 .... 68 F2
MLW SL7 .... 19 G5
SHST GU47 .... 172 C6
SL SL1 .... 4 F8
SL SL1 .... 5 H8
SL SL1 .... 5 J9
SL SL1 .... 43 M4
SL SL1 .... 71 C3
STA TW18 .... 127 J2
STHA RG19 .... 138 A3
STWL/WRAY TW19 .... 98 B5
STWL/WRAY TW19 .... 100 A3
UX/CGN UB8 .... 47 M1
UX/CGN UB8 .... 47 M5
WAR/TWY RG10 .... 65 G5
WAR/TWY RG10 .... 91 G1
WDSR SL4 .... 7 J2
WDSR SL4 .... 7 K6
High Town Rd *MDHD* SL6 .... 2 F6
MDHD SL6 .... 3 G5 🔲
High Tree Dr *EARL* RG6 .... 89 L8
Highview *CALC* RG31 .... 114 E1
Highview Crs *CBLY* GU15 .... 174 C5
High View Rd *LTWR* GU18 .... 175 H6
Highway *WHIT* RG2 .... 172 D1
Highway Av *MDHD* SL6 .... 41 K7
Highwayman's Rdg
BFOR GU20 .... 151 L8
Highway Rd *MDHD* SL6 .... 41 L8
Highwood Cl *NWBY* RG14 .... 108 E8
Highworth Wy *CALC* RG31 .... 86 E4
Hilary Cl *WHIT* RG2 .... 116 F7
Hilary Dr *CWTH* RG45 .... 148 E8
Hilborn Wy *EWKG* RG40 .... 146 D5
Hilbury Rd *EARL* RG6 .... 117 K3
Hilcot Rd *TLHT* RG30 .... 88 A6
Hildens Dr *CALC* RG31 .... 86 F7
Hilfield *BLKW* GU17 .... 180 C1
Hillary Rd *DTCH/LGLY* SL3 .... 72 B3
Hillberry *BRAK* RG12 .... 149 J8
Hill Bottom Cl *GOR/PANG* RG8 .. 60 B3
Hillbrow *WHIT* RG2 .... 117 H5
Hill Cl *NWBY* RG14 .... 136 A7
Hill Copse Vw *BRAK* RG12 .. 122 B6
Hill Ct *FARN* GU14 .... 181 J5
Hillcrest Av *CHERT* KT16 .... 155 H7
Hillcrest La *HEN* RG9 .... 36 C7
Hillcrest Rd *CBLY* GU15 .... 174 E7
Hilldrop La *HUNG* RG17 .... 75 J2
Hillersdon *SLN* SL2 .... 5 M1
Hill Farm Rd *MDHD* SL6 .... 43 H4
Hill Gdns *GOR/PANG* RG8 .... 32 D8
Hillgreen La *KSCL* RG20 .... 53 M7
Hillhampton *ASC* SL5 .... 152 C4
Hillhouse La *STHA* RG19 .... 162 D6
Hillingdon Av
STWL/WRAY TW19 .... 100 B7
Hill Lands *WAR/TWY* RG10 .. 65 G4
Hillmead Ct *MDHD* SL6 .... 43 J6
Hill Pl *SLN* SL2 .... 44 E1 🔲
Hillrise *DTCH/LGLY* SL3 .... 72 D6
Hill Rd *NWBY* RG14 .... 14 A2
WHIT RG2 .... 146 C5
Hillsborough Ct *FARN* GU14 .. 181 H6
Hillsborough Pk *CBLY* GU15 .. 182 F1
Hillside *CBLY* GU15 .... 173 J7
GOR/PANG RG8 .... 60 A6
MDHD SL6 .... 2 D9
SL SL1 .... 4 E8
THLE RG7 .... 142 F3
WAR/TWY RG10 .... 153 M3
Hillside Crs *FRIM* GU16 .... 182 C1
Hillside Dr *BNFD* RG42 .... 120 F4
Hillside Pk *ASC* SL5 .... 152 C5
WHIT RG2 .... 117 J5
Hillside Rd *EARL* RG6 .... 118 A3
HUNG RG17 .... 132 A2
WHIT RG2 .... 19 H2
Hills La *MDHD* SL6 .... 19 M7
Hill St *READ* RG1 .... 9 G9
Hillswood Dr *CHERT* KT16 .. 154 F8
Hilltop Cl *ASC* SL5 .... 124 B7
Hilltop Rd *CAV/SC* RG4 .... 88 A1
EARL RG6 .... 89 L6
WAR/TWY RG10 .... 91 J6
Hillview Cl *CALC* RG31 .... 86 A3
Hill View Rd *STWL/WRAY* TW19 .. 98 A5
Hilmanton *EARL* RG6 .... 117 J6
Hilperton Rd *SL* SL1 .... 4 E8
Hilton Cl *UX/CGN* UB8 .... 47 L3 🔲
Hindell Cl *FARN* GU14 .... 181 K6
Hindhay La *MDHD* SL6 .... 41 L3
Hindhead Rd *EARL* RG6 .... 117 K3
Hinksey Cl *DTCH/LGLY* SL3 .... 72 E3
Hinton Cl *CWTH* RG45 .... 148 E7
TADY RG26 .... 164 E7
Hinton Dr *CWTH* RG45 .... 148 E7
Hinton Rd *SL* SL1 .... 44 B8
UX/CGN UB8 .... 47 M2
WAR/TWY RG10 .... 91 J6
Hirstwood *TLHT* RG30 .... 87 H5 🔲
Hirtes Av *WHIT* RG2 .... 145 H1 🔲
Hitcham La *SL* SL1 .... 43 K4
Hitcham Rd *SL* SL1 .... 43 K5
Hitchcock Cl *SHPTN* TW17 .. 128 C8
Hitherhooks Hl *BNFD* RG42 .. 12 A3
Hithermoor Rd
STWL/WRAY TW19 .... 99 M4
Hobbis Dr *MDHD* SL6 .... 41 K8
Hockett La *MDHD* SL6 .... 19 J8

Hocketts Cl *GOR/PANG* RG8 .. 60 B3
Hockford La *THLE* RG7 .... 163 K3
Hockham Rd *KSCL* RG20 .... 56 A1
Hockley La *SLN* SL2 .... 45 L1
Hodgedale La *WAR/TWY* RG10 .. 40 A8
Hodge La *ASC* SL5 .... 123 K3
Hodsoll Rd *READ* RG1 .... 8 D1
Hoe Benham La *KSCL* RG20 .. 106 C3
Hogarth Av *ASHF* TW15 .... 128 F4
TLHT RG30 .... 115 J1
Hogarth Cl *SHST* GU47 .... 173 H8
SL SL1 .... 44 B8
Hogfair La *SL* SL1 .... 43 M5
Hogmoor La *WAR/TWY* RG10 .. 91 J5
Hogoak La *BNFD* RG42 .... 94 D6
Hogwood La *EWKG* RG40 .... 146 D8
Holbeck *BRAK* RG12 .... 149 J3
Holberton Rd *WHIT* RG2 .... 117 G6
Holborne Cl *NWBY* RG14 .... 159 M1
Holbrook Meadow *EGH* TW20 .. 126 F4
Holford Cl *CALC* RG31 .... 86 F6
Holkam Cl *TLHT* RG30 .... 87 J5 🔲
Holland Gdns *EGH* TW20 .... 127 J7
Holland Pines *BRAK* RG12 .. 149 J4
Holland Rd *MLW* SL7 .... 19 J4
TLHT RG30 .... 87 G7
The Hollands *STHA* RG19 .... 138 B3
Hollicombe Cl *TLHT* RG30 .... 87 H7 🔲
The Hollies *NWBY* RG14 .... 160 A1
Holloway Dr *VW* GU25 .... 154 B1
Holloway Hl *CHERT* KT16 .... 154 F7
Hollow Hill La *DTCH/LGLY* SL3 .. 72 F2
IVER SL0 .... 46 E7
Hollow La *VW* GU25 .... 125 M8
WDSR SL4 .... 145 H1
Holly Av *FRIM* GU16 .... 182 F3
Hollybank *CHOB/PIR* GU24 .. 176 C3 🔲
Hollybush Hl *SLN* SL2 .... 45 L1
Hollybush La *HTWY* RG27 .... 171 L6
IVER SL0 .... 46 E7
MDHD SL6 .... 19 L8
THLE RG7 .... 142 C4
Hollybush Ride *BFOR* GU20 .. 151 J3
EWKG RG40 .... 171 M1
Holly Cl *CHERT* KT16 .... 153 K7
EGH TW20 .... 125 L4
HEN RG9 .... 36 B1
Hollycombe *EGH* TW20 .... 126 A2
Holly Crs *WDSR* SL4 .... 96 A1
Hollydale Cl *WHIT* RG2 .... 117 C5
Holly Dr *MDHD* SL6 .... 3 H2
WDSR SL4 .... 97 H4
Hollyfields Cl *CBLY* GU15 .... 181 L1 🔲
Holly Hedge Cl *FRIM* GU16 .. 182 B4
Holly Hedge Rd *FRIM* GU16 .. 182 B4
Holly La *GOR/PANG* RG8 .... 57 L8
NTHA RG18 .... 110 E3
THLE RG7 .... 165 L6
Hollym Cl *EARL* RG6 .... 118 B4
Holly Orch *WWKG* RG41 .... 10 A8
Holly Rd *WODY* RG5 .... 90 D8
Holly Spring La *BRAK* RG12 .. 13 L2
Hollytree Gdns *FRIM* GU16 .. 182 A6
Holly Wk *WDSR* SL4 .... 124 B2
Holly Wy *BLKW* GU17 .... 181 G2
Holmanleaze *MDHD* SL6 .... 3 J4
Holmbury Av *CWTH* RG45 .... 148 D7
Holmdale *SL* SL2 .... 45 M8
Holmdene *THLE* RG7 .... 142 E3 🔲
Holme Cl *CWTH* RG45 .... 148 D7
Holmemoor Dr *CAV/SC* RG4 .. 90 A4
Holme Park Farm La
CAV/SC RG4 .... 89 M4
Holmes Cl *ASC* SL5 .... 151 M3
WWKG RG41 .... 10 B9
Holmes Crs *WWKG* RG41 .... 10 B9
Holmes Rd *EARL* RG6 .... 117 K1
WWKG RG41 .... 147 K4
Holmlea Rd *DTCH/LGLY* SL3 .. 72 A8
GOR/PANG RG8 .... 58 F1
Holmlea Wk *DTCH/LGLY* SL3 .. 71 M8
Holmsdale Cl *IVER* SL0 .... 47 J7
Holmwood Av *TLHT* RG30 .... 115 J1
Holmwood Cl *MDHD* SL6 .... 67 L1 🔲
Holsworthy Cl *EARL* RG6 .. 118 B3 🔲
Holt Cl *FARN* GU14 .... 181 M7
Holt Cottages *STHA* RG19 .. 163 J6
Holt La *KSCL* RG20 .... 53 C5
WWKG RG41 .... 10 E4
Holton Heath *BRAK* RG12 .. 150 C1 🔲
Holt Rd *HUNG* RG17 .... 133 L4
Holtwood Rd *KSCL* RG20 .... 134 E8
Holybrook Crs *TLHT* RG30 .. 115 K2 🔲
Holybrook Rd *READ* RG1 .... 116 C1
Holyhook Cl *CWTH* RG45 .. 148 D8
Holyport Rd *MDHD* SL6 .... 68 E6
Holyport St *MDHD* SL6 .... 68 D6
Holyrood Cl *CAV/SC* RG4 .... 63 C8
Holywell Cl *FARN* GU14 .... 181 K7
STWL/WRAY TW19 .... 100 B7
Holywell Ct *STHA* RG19 .... 138 A3
Holywell Wy *STWL/WRAY* TW19 .. 100 B7
Hombrook Dr *BNFD* RG42 .... 12 A3
Home Cl *VW* GU25 .... 154 A3
Home Cft *CALC* RG31 .... 86 E5
Home Farm Cl *FARN* GU14 .. 182 A8
WHIT RG2 .... 116 E2
Home Farm Wy
DTCH/LGLY SL3 .... 45 M2 🔲
Homefield Wy *HUNG* RG17 .. 131 M1
Homelands Wy *HEN* RG9 .... 38 A5 🔲
Homelea Cl *FARN* GU14 .... 181 L6
Home Mead Cl *NWBY* RG14 .. 136 B6
Home Meadow *SLN* SL2 .... 44 F3 🔲
Home Park Rd *YTLY* GU46 .. 171 M8
Homers Rd *WDSR* SL4 .... 70 A8
Homestead Rd *MDHD* SL6 .. 68 A2 🔲
STA TW18 .... 127 L4
Homewaters Av *SUN* TW16 .. 129 J8
Homewood *DTCH/LGLY* SL3 .. 46 A7
Hone Hl *SHST* GU47 .... 172 F7
Honesty Bottom *KSCL* RG20 .. 53 G4
Honeybottom Rd *TADY* RG26 .. 164 E5
Honey End La *TLHT* RG30 .... 87 K8
Honeyfields *HUNG* RG17 .... 132 A1
Honey Hl *HUNG* RG17 .... 49 L3
Honeyhill Rd *BNFD* RG42 .... 12 E3
Honey La *MDHD* SL6 .... 40 B4

Honey Meadow Cl *CAV/SC* RG4 .... **89** H4
Honeysuckle Cl *CWTH* RG45 ...... **148** D7
  IVER SL0 .... **46** F7
  YTLY GU46 .... **171** K8 ⑤
Honiton Rd *WHIT* RG2 .... **116** F4
Honnor Rd *STA* TW18 .... **128** A5
Hookend La *GOR/PANG* RG8 ...... **35** G5
  GOR/PANG RG8 .... **58** D7
Hook End La *GOR/PANG* RG8 ...... **58** F3
Hook La *CHOB/PIR* GU24 ...... **175** M8
  TADY RG26 .... **163** L8
Hook Mill La *CHOB/PIR* GU24 .. **176** A4
Hookstone La *CHOB/PIR* GU24 .. **176** A4
Hoops Wy *WHIT* RG2 .... **116** C6
Hope Av *BRAK* RG12 .... **150** B4
Hope Fountain *CBLY* GU15 ...... **182** C2
Hopeman Cl *SHST* GU47 ...... **173** C7 ①
Hop Gdns *HEN* RG9 .... **38** A4
Hopwood Cl *NWBY* RG14 .... **15** L1
Horatio Av *BNFD* RG42 .... **122** B6
Horewood Rd *BRAK* RG12 ...... **149** L3
Hormer Cl *SHST* GU47 .... **173** G5 ①
Hornbeam Cl *GOR/PANG* RG8 .. **86** F1 ①
  SHST GU47 .... **173** C5 ①
  WWKG RG41 .... **147** G3
Hornbeam Dr *EARL* RG6 ...... **118** A5
Hornbeam Gdns
  DTCH/LGLY SL3 .... **71** K3 ②
Hornbeams *THLE* RG7 .... **144** F3
Hornby Av *BRAK* RG12 .... **150** A4
Horncastle Dr *TLHT* RG30 ...... **115** J1 ②
Horndean Rd *BRAK* RG12 ...... **150** C3 ③
Horne Rd *STHA* RG19 .... **138** A4
Hornsea Cl *TLHT* RG30 .... **87** H5 ①
Horn St *KSCL* RG20 .... **56** B1
Horsebrass Dr *BAGS* GU19 .... **175** H4 ①
The Horse Cl *CAV/SC* RG4 .... **88** F2 ②
Horse Gate Ride *ASC* SL5 ...... **151** K3
Horseguards Dr *MDHD* SL6 ...... **3** M5
Horsell Ct *CHERT* KT16 .... **155** L4
Horsemoor Cl *DTCH/LGLY* SL3 .. **72** D4 ②
Horsepond Rd *CAV/SC* RG4 ...... **61** L1
Horseshoe Cl *CBLY* GU15 ...... **174** C6 ①
Horseshoe Crs *CBLY* GU15 .... **174** C6
  THLE RG7 .... **142** D3
Horseshoe End *NWBY* RG14 .. **136** E7 ①
Horseshoe Hl *SL* SL1 .... **21** M6
Horseshoe Pk *GOR/PANG* RG8 .. **86** A1
Horseshoe Rd *GOR/PANG* RG8 .. **86** A1
Horsham Rd *EBED/NFELT* TW14.. **100** F5
  SHST GU47 .... **173** G5 ①
Horsnape Gdns *BNFD* RG42 .... **120** E4 ③
Horsneile La *BNFD* RG42 .... **13** G2
Horton Cl *MDHD* SL6 .... **42** F5
Horton Rd *DTCH/LGLY* SL3 ...... **71** M8
  DTCH/LGLY SL3 .... **72** E8
  DTCH/LGLY SL3 .... **99** H2
  STWL/WRAY TW19 .... **99** K4
Hose Hl *THLE* RG7 .... **114** D7
Hosier St *READ* RG1 .... **8** F6
Houlton Ct *BAGS* GU19 .... **175** H4
Hounslow Rd
  EBED/NFELT TW14 .... **101** L6
Houseman Rd *FARN* GU14 ...... **181** J8
Howard Av *SLN* SL2 .... **45** G6
Howard Cl *SUN* TW16 .... **129** J4
Howard Ct *BNEND* SL8 .... **20** D3 ④
Howard Rd *EWKG* RG40 .... **11** G7
  NWBY RG14 .... **14** E7
Howard St *READ* RG1 .... **8** D6
Howarth Rd *MDHD* SL6 .... **3** K6
Howe La *BNFD* RG42 .... **93** H6
Howell Cl *BNFD* RG42 .... **121** M4
How's Rd *UX/CGN* UB8 .... **47** M2
Howth Dr *WODY* RG5 .... **90** A7
Hubbard Cl *WAR/TWY* RG10 ...... **91** J3
Hubberholme *BRAK* RG12 .... **12** F6
Hubert Rd *DTCH/LGLY* SL3 ...... **72** A3
Huckleberry Cl
  GOR/PANG RG8 .... **86** F2 ⑤
Hudson Rd *WODY* RG5 .... **118** C1
Hughenden Cl *MDHD* SL6 .... **2** A7
Hughenden Rd *SL* SL1 .... **4** D3
Hughes Rd *ASHF* TW15 .... **127** G5
  EWKG RG40 .... **11** K4
Hugh Fraser Dr *CALC* RG31 ...... **86** F8
Hull Cl *SL* SL1 .... **4** A8
Humber Cl *NTHA* RG18 .... **137** L1
  WWKG RG41 .... **10** A4
  WWKG RG41 .... **119** H7
Humber Wy *DTCH/LGLY* SL3 .... **72** D4
  SHST GU47 .... **173** G4 ①
Hummer Rd *EGH* TW20 .... **126** D2
Humphrey's La *HUNG* RG17 ...... **50** F8
Hungerford Cl *SHST* GU47 .... **172** F6
  READ RG1 .... **116** B1
Hungerford Dr *MDHD* SL6 ...... **42** B3
  READ RG1 .... **116** B1
Hungerford Hl *HUNG* RG17 ...... **49** K5
  HUNG RG17 .... **77** K5
Hungerford La *THLE* RG7 ...... **112** B4
  WAR/TWY RG10 .... **91** M4
Hungerford Rd *HUNG* RG17 .... **132** E2
Hunstanton Cl *DTCH/LGLY* SL3 .. **72** F7
Huntercombe Cl *MDHD* SL6 .... **43** L7
Huntercombe La North *SL* SL1.. **43** M6
Huntercombe La South
  MDHD SL6 .... **69** L1
Hunters Cha *CAV/SC* RG4 .... **88** C1
Hunter's Hl *THLE* RG7 .... **142** C3
Hunters Meadow *HUNG* RG17 .. **77** K3 ①
Hunters Wy *SL* SL1 .... **70** B2
  THLE RG7 .... **144** D5
Huntingdon Cl *EARL* RG6 ...... **118** B4
Huntingfield Wy *EGH* TW20 .... **127** G5
Hunt's La *MDHD* SL6 .... **43** H3
Huntsman Cl *FELT* TW13 ...... **129** L2 ①
Huntsmans Meadow *ASC* SL5 .. **123** J6
Huntsmoor Rd *TADY* RG26 .... **164** C6
Huntswood La *SL* SL1 .... **43** J1
Hurley High St *MDHD* SL6 ...... **40** E3
Hurley La *MDHD* SL6 .... **40** E3
Hurricane Wy *WODY* RG5 .... **90** D7
Hursley Cl *TLHT* RG30 .... **87** H7 ②
Hurstdene Av *STA* TW18 .... **127** L4
Hurstfield Dr *MDHD* SL6 .... **43** L7 ④
Hurst La *EGH* TW20 .... **126** C8
Hurst Park Rd *WAR/TWY* RG10 .. **91** H4
Hurst Rd *FARN* GU14 .... **181** L6

SL *SL1* .... **44** A6 ②
  WAR/TWY RG10 .... **91** H3
Hurst Wy *WHIT* RG2 .... **116** C6
Hurstwood *ASC* SL5 .... **151** K3
Huscarle Wy *CALC* RG31 .... **86** F2 ②
Huson Rd *BNFD* RG42 .... **121** M5
Hutsons Cl *EWKG* RG40 .... **11** K2
Hutton Cl *BFOR* GU20 .... **176** A3
  EARL RG6 .... **117** K4
  NWBY RG14 .... **15** G1
Hyde End La *STHA* RG19 .... **163** G1
  THLE RG7 .... **144** F2
Hyde End Rd *THLE* RG7 .... **144** E4
Hyde Gn *MLW* SL7 .... **19** J5
Hyde La *KSCL* RG20 .... **161** K8
Hydes Platt *THLE* RG7 .... **165** L6
The Hydes *CALC* RG31 .... **86** F2 ②
Hyde Ter *SUN* TW16 .... **129** H4
Hylle Cl *WDSR* SL4 .... **70** B8
Hyperion Wy *WHIT* RG2 .... **116** E3
Hythe Cl *BRAK* RG12 .... **150** B2
Hythe End Rd *STWL/WRAY* TW19.. **98** D8
Hythe Field Av *EGH* TW20 ...... **127** C4
Hythe Park Rd *EGH* TW20 ...... **126** F3
Hythe Rd *STA* TW18 .... **127** G3
The Hythe *STA* TW18 .... **127** H3

I

Iberian Wy *CBLY* GU15 .... **174** D8
Ibstock Cl *TLHT* RG30 .... **87** L7
Ibstone Av *CAV/SC* RG4 .... **89** H4
Icknield Pl *GOR/PANG* RG8 ...... **33** G6
Icknield Rd *GOR/PANG* RG8 ...... **33** G6
Ilbury Cl *WHIT* RG2 .... **145** H1
Ilchester Cl *MDHD* SL6 .... **2** B8
Ilchester Ms *CAV/SC* RG4 .... **63** H8 ③
Ilex Cl *CAV/SC* RG4 .... **62** C2
  EGH TW20 .... **125** L5
  SUN TW16 .... **129** M7 ③
  TADY RG26 .... **165** H5
  YTLY GU46 .... **171** L8
Ilfracombe Wy *EARL* RG6 ...... **118** B3
Ilkley Rd *CAV/SC* RG4 .... **88** B3
Ilkley Wy *STHA* RG19 .... **137** M4
Illingworth *WDSR* SL4 .... **96** B2
Illingworth Av *CAV/SC* RG4 ...... **63** H4
  CAV/SC RG4 .... **89** H1
Illingworth Gv *BRAK* RG12 .... **122** C6
Ilsley Cl *CAV/SC* RG4 .... **62** C1 ③
Ilsley Rd *KSCL* RG20 .... **55** M2
Imperial Ct *WDSR* SL4 .... **96** D2 ②
Imperial Rd *EBED/NFELT* TW14 .. **101** H6
  WDSR SL4 .... **96** D2
Imperial Wy *WHIT* RG2 .... **116** D7
Impstone Rd *TADY* RG26 .... **165** J5
Inchwood *BRAK* RG12 .... **149** M5
India Rd *SL* SL1 .... **5** L8
Ingle Dell *CBLY* GU15 .... **182** A2
Ingle Gln *EWKG* RG40 .... **147** K7 ②
Ingles Edge *HUNG* RG17 .... **157** C2 ③
Ingleside *DTCH/LGLY* SL3 .... **73** J8 ①
Ingleton *BRAK* RG12 .... **12** F7
Inglewood *CHERT* KT16 .... **155** J7 ①
Inglewood Av *CBLY* GU15 ...... **182** F2
Inglewood Cl *CAV/SC* RG4 .... **62** C1
Inglewood Ct *TLHT* RG30 .... **87** M8 ③
Inglewood Rd *HUNG* RG17 .... **132** D5
Inhams Wy *THLE* RG7 .... **165** K6
Inhurst La *STHA* RG19 .... **163** H5
Inhurst Wy *TADY* RG26 .... **164** C5
Inkerman Rd *WDSR* SL4 .... **70** C4
Inkpen Cl *TLHT* RG30 .... **115** K2 ③
Inkpen Rd *HUNG* RG17 .... **132** D6
Innings La *BNFD* RG42 .... **13** M2 ⑤
  MDHD SL6 .... **67** G7
Institute Rd *MDHD* SL6 .... **43** J7
  MLW SL7 .... **19** G5
Instow Gdns *FARN* GU14 ...... **181** K7 ②
Instow Rd *EARL* RG6 .... **117** L4
In the Ray *MDHD* SL6 .... **3** M2
Invergordon Cl *CALC* RG31 .... **115** H2 ②
Inverness Wy *SHST* GU47 ...... **173** C7
Invicta Cl *EBED/NFELT* TW14 .. **101** J7 ②
Inwood Cl *MDHD* SL6 .... **19** L8
Iona Crs *SL* SL1 .... **44** B7
Ipswich Rd *SL* SL1 .... **44** C7
Irish Hill Rd *HUNG* RG17 ...... **133** L4
Irvine Dr *FARN* GU14 .... **181** H6
Irvine Pl *VW* GU25 .... **154** B2
Irvine Wy *EARL* RG6 .... **117** M6 ②
Isaac Newton Rd *WHIT* RG2 .. **146** C6
Isis Cl *WWKG* RG41 .... **118** C5
Isis Wy *BNEND* SL8 .... **20** E2
  SHST GU47 .... **173** G6
Island Cl *STA* TW18 .... **127** H2
Island Farm Rd *THLE* RG7 ...... **142** B5
Island Rd *WHIT* RG2 .... **116** C3
Islandstone La *WAR/TWY* RG10 .. **91** K8
Isles Rd *MARL* SN8 .... **102** A2
Islet Pk *MDHD* SL6 .... **42** F3
Islet Park Dr *MDHD* SL6 .... **42** F3
Islet Rd *MDHD* SL6 .... **42** F3
Ivanhoe Rd *EWKG* RG40 ...... **146** D8
Iverdale Cl *IVER* SL0 .... **46** F8
Iver La *IVER* SL0 .... **47** L6
Iver La *IVER* SL0 .... **47** L6
Iverna Gdns *EBED/NFELT* TW14 .. **101** G4
Ives Cl *YTLY* GU46 .... **171** L7
Ives Rd *DTCH/LGLY* SL3 .... **72** D3
Ivory Ct *FELT* TW13 .... **101** K8 ③
Ivybank *CALC* RG31 .... **86** F5
Ivy Cl *MDHD* SL6 .... **68** D7
  SUN TW16 .... **129** M7
Ivy Crs *SL* SL1 .... **44** C8
Ivydene Rd *TLHT* RG30 .... **87** M5
Ivy Dr *LTWR* GU18 .... **175** K7

J

Jackson Cl *BRAK* RG12 .... **149** L2 ③
Jacksons La *CAV/SC* RG4 .... **87** K1
Jacob Cl *BNFD* RG42 .... **121** G7 ③
  WDSR SL4 .... **70** B8
Jacob Rd *CBLY* GU15 .... **173** K7

James Cl *MLW* SL7 .... **19** J2
James Rd *CBLY* GU15 .... **181** L4
James's La *TLHT* RG30 .... **143** G2
James St *READ* RG1 .... **8** C6
  WDSR SL4 .... **7** J7
Jameston *BRAK* RG12............ **149** M5
James Watt Rd *EWKG* RG40 .. **146** D6
James Wy *CBLY* GU15 .... **181** L4
Jamnagar Cl *STA* TW18 .... **127** J4
Janson Ct *READ* RG1 .... **8** C8
Japonica Cl *WWKG* RG41 ...... **147** G2 ③
Jaques's La *THLE* RG7 .... **114** C8
Jarvis Cl *WWKG* RG41 .... **119** D7 ③
Jarvis Dr *WAR/TWY* RG10 ...... **65** G3
Jasmine Cl *WWKG* RG41 .... **119** D7
Jay Cl *EARL* RG6.................. **117** L5
Jays Nest Cl *BLKW* GU17 ...... **181** G2 ②
Jedburgh Cl *STHA* RG19 .... **138** C3
Jefferson Cl *CAV/SC* RG4 .... **62** F7
  DTCH/LGLY SL3 .... **72** D4 ①
Jeffries Ct *BNEND* SL8 .... **20** D4
Jellicoe Cl *SL* SL1 .... **70** E2
Jenkins Cl *TLHT* RG30 .... **87** M8 ①
Jenkins' Hill London Rd
  BAGS GU19 .... **174** F5
Jenner Dr *CHOB/PIR* GU24 .... **176** D8
Jenner Wk *CALC* RG31 .... **86** D7 ②
Jennery La *SL* SL1 .... **43** M4
Jennetts Cl *THLE* RG7 .... **112** B3
Jenny's Wk *YTLY* GU46 .... **172** B8
Jerome Cl *MLW* SL7 .... **19** J2
Jerome Cnr *CWTH* RG45 .... **172** F3
Jerome Rd *WODY* RG5 .... **90** A8
Jerrymoor Hl *EWKG* RG40 .... **147** J6 ②
Jersey Cl *CHERT* KT16 .... **155** J7 ②
Jesmond Dene *NWBY* RG14 .... **14** C2
Jesse Cl *BLKW* GU17 .... **180** C1
Jesse Ter *READ* RG1 .... **8** D7
Jevington *BRAK* RG12 .... **149** M4
Jig's La North *BNFD* RG42 .... **122** B4 ③
Jig's La South *BNFD* RG42 .... **122** B5 ①
Job's La *MDHD* SL6 .... **19** L6
Jock's La *BNFD* RG42 .... **12** A2
Joel Cl *EARL* RG6 .... **117** K3
John Hunt Cl *STHA* RG19 ...... **138** C4 ②
John Nike Wy *BRAK* RG42 .... **120** F7 ③
Johnson Dr *EWKG* RG40 .... **147** L7
John Taylor Ct *SL* SL1 .... **4** B7
Jonathan Hl *KSCL* RG20 .... **160** E3
Jones Cnr *ASC* SL5 .... **123** H6
Jordan Cl *CAV/SC* RG4 .... **89** H1
  THLE RG7 .... **145** G5
Jordans Cl *STWL/WRAY* TW19 .. **99** M6
Jordan's La *THLE* RG7 .... **142** C4
Joseph Ct *BNFD* RG42 .... **122** B4 ③
Josephine Ct *TLHT* RG30 .... **88** A8 ①
Josey Cl *CAV/SC* RG4 .... **36** C8 ①
Jouldings La *HTWY* RG27 ...... **170** A2
Journeys End *SL* SL1 .... **45** H6
Jubilee Av *ASC* SL5 .... **123** H6
  WWKG RG41 .... **10** D3
Jubilee Cl *ASC* SL5 .... **123** H6
  STWL/WRAY TW19 .... **99** M6
  TADY RG26 .... **165** H5
Jubilee Rd *EARL* RG6 .... **89** K8 ①
  EWKG RG40 .... **171** J3
  MDHD SL6 .... **66** E2
  NWBY RG14 .... **15** G6
Jubilee Sq *READ* RG1 .... **9** H8
Jubilee Wy *EBED/NFELT* TW14 .. **101** K7
Judges Cl *GOR/PANG* RG8 ...... **35** J3
Juliet Gdns *BNFD* RG42 .... **122** C5 ③
Julius Hl *BNFD* RG42 .... **122** C5 ①
Julkes La *WHIT* RG2 .... **118** B7
Junction Rd *ASHF* TW15 .... **128** F3 ③
  LTWR GU18 .... **175** L5
  READ RG1 .... **8** H8 ④
Junction Ter *NWBY* RG14........ **15** J5
Juniper Dr *MDHD* SL6 .... **3** L3
Juniper Gdns *SUN* TW16 ...... **129** J4
Juniper Rd *MLW* SL7................ **19** G1
The Junipers *WWKG* RG41 .... **147** C2
Juniper Wy *CALC* RG31 .... **87** G4
Jupiter Wy *WWKG* RG41 .... **10** A6
Justice Cl *STHA* RG19 .... **138** C4
Jutland Cl *WWKG* RG41 .... **119** H3 ③
Jutland Pl *EGH* TW20 .... **126** F3 ②

K

Katesgrove La *READ* RG1 .... **8** F8
Kathleen Sanders Ct
  THLE RG7 .... **114** B2 ①
Kaynes Pk *ASC* SL5 .... **123** H6
Kaywood Cl *DTCH/LGLY* SL3 .... **71** M3
Keane Cl *WODY* RG5 .... **90** B6
Kearsley Rd *TLHT* RG30 .... **87** M8
Keates Gn *BNFD* RG42 .... **13** H2
Keats Cl *WODY* RG5 .... **118** B1
Keats La *WDSR* SL4.................. **7** H3
Keats Rd *WODY* RG5................ **118** B2
Keats Wy *CWTH* RG45 .... **148** E7
Keble Cl *MDHD* SL6 .... **2** D3
Keble Wy *SHST* GU47 .... **173** H4
Keeler Cl *WDSR* SL4 .... **96** B2
Keensacre *IVER* SL0 .... **47** G3 ②
Keepers Combe *BRAK* RG12 .. **150** A3
Keepers Farm Cl *WDSR* SL4 .... **96** B1 ①
  WDSR SL4 .... **96** B2 ①
Keepers Wk *VW* GU25 .... **154** A2
Keephatch Rd *EWKG* RG40 ...... **11** L4
Keighley Cl *STHA* RG19 .... **137** M4
Kelburne Cl *WWKG* RG41 ...... **118** F3
Keldholme *BRAK* RG12 .... **12** F7
Kelly Cl *SHPTN* TW17 .... **129** H7 ③
Kelmscott Cl *CAV/SC* RG4 .... **88** B3
Kelpatrick Rd *SL* SL1 .... **44** A7
Kelsey Av *EWKG* RG40 .... **147** H8
Kelsey Cl *MDHD* SL6 .... **68** A3
Kelsey Gv *YTLY* GU46 .... **180** B1
Kelston Rd *MARL* SN8 .... **130** D7
Kelton Cl *EARL* RG6 .... **118** B4
Kelvedon Wy *CAV/SC* RG4 .... **88** B3
Kelvin Cl *WHIT* RG2 .... **146** B7 ②
Kelvin Rd *NWBY* RG14 .... **15** C2

Kemble Ct *CALC* RG31 .... **115** G2 ③
Kemerton Cl *CALC* RG31 ...... **115** G2 ③
Kemp Ct *BAGS* GU19 .... **175** J4
Kempton Av *SUN* TW16 .... **129** L6
Kempton Cl *NWBY* RG14 .... **15** K8
Kempton Ct *SUN* TW16 .... **129** L6
Kemsley Cha *SLN* SL2 .... **45** G2 ①
Kenavon Dr *READ* RG1 .... **9** J5
  WHIT RG2 .... **117** H8 ③
Kendal Cl
  EBED/NFELT TW14 .... **101** J7 ⑩
  NTHA RG18 .... **137** M2
Kendal Dr *SLN* SL2 .... **5** K4
Kendal Gv *CBLY* GU15 .... **183** G2
Kendrick Cl *EWKG* RG40 .... **11** K2
Kendrick Rd *DTCH/LGLY* SL3 .... **71** L3
  NWBY RG14 .... **160** A1
  READ RG1 .... **9** J8
Kenilworth Av *BRAK* RG12 ...... **13** K2
  TLHT RG30 .... **116** A1
Kenilworth Cl *SL* SL1 .... **71** J3
Kenilworth Gdns *STA* TW18 .. **127** M3
Kenilworth Rd *ASHF* TW15 .... **128** A1
Kenmore Cl *FRIM* GU16 .... **182** A6 ②
Kenneally *WDSR* SL4 .... **95** M1
Kennedy Cl *MDHD* SL6 .... **2** A7
  MLW SL7 .... **19** H3
  NWBY RG14 .... **136** A8
Kennedy Dr *GOR/PANG* RG8 .... **86** A1
Kennedy Gdns *EARL* RG6 ...... **117** L3
Kennel Av *ASC* SL5 .... **123** J6
Kennel Cl *ASC* SL5 .... **123** J4
Kennel Gn *ASC* SL5 .... **123** H6
Kennel La *BFOR* GU20 .... **175** M1
  BNFD RG42 .... **13** G1
  BRAK RG12 .... **121** L5
Kennel Ride *ASC* SL5 .... **123** J5
Kennel Wd *ASC* SL5 .... **123** J6
Kennet Cl *FARN* GU14 .... **181** G8
  STHA RG19 .... **138** B3
Kennet Ct *WWKG* RG41 .... **10** A5
Kennet Pl *THLE* RG7 .... **142** E3
Kennet Rd *MDHD* SL6 .... **3** H3
  NWBY RG14 .... **14** D5
  READ RG1 .... **9** J4
  READ RG1 .... **89** H6
Kennet Side *NWBY* RG14 .... **15** J4
  READ RG1 .... **9** J6
Kennet St *READ* RG1 .... **9** J6
Kennett Rd *BNEND* SL8 .... **20** D2
  DTCH/LGLY SL3 .... **72** E3
Kennet Wy *HUNG* RG17 .... **104** A7
Kennylands Rd *CAV/SC* RG4 .... **62** C2
Kensington Cl *EARL* RG6 ...... **117** L5
Kensington Rd *TLHT* RG30 ...... **88** A7
Kent Av *SL* SL1 .... **44** F6
Kent Cl *STA* TW18 .... **128** A4
Kent Folly *BNFD* RG42 .... **122** C4
Kentigern Dr *CWTH* RG45 ...... **173** H1
Kenton Cl *BRAK* RG12 .... **13** L5
  FRIM GU16 .... **182** C4
Kenton's La *WAR/TWY* RG10 .... **39** G6
  WDSR SL4 .... **6** B8
Kent Rd *BFOR* GU20 .... **176** A1
  TLHT RG30 .... **88** A7
Kent Wy *MDHD* SL6 .... **42** B5 ①
Kentwood Cl *TLHT* RG30 .... **87** H5
Kentwood Hl *CALC* RG31 .... **87** H5
  TLHT RG30 .... **87** H5
Kenwood Cl *MDHD* SL6 .... **41** K7
Kenworth Gv *LTWR* GU18 .... **175** K5
  LTWR GU18 .... **175** L5
Kenyngton Dr *SUN* TW16 ...... **129** K3
Keppel Sp *WDSR* SL4 .... **97** L6
Keppel St *WDSR* SL4 .... **7** K8
Kepple Pl *BAGS* GU19 .... **175** H3
Kernham Dr *CALC* RG31 .... **86** E4 ③
Kerria Wy *CHOB/PIR* GU24 .... **176** B8 ②
Kerris Wy *EARL* RG6 .... **117** K5
Kersey Crs *NWBY* RG14 .... **136** B1
Kesteven Wy *WWKG* RG41 .... **119** H8 ⑪
Keston Cl *CAV/SC* RG4 .... **88** F3
Kestrel Av *STA* TW18.............. **127** J1
Kestrel Cl *STHA* RG19 .... **137** L3 ③
Kestrel Wy *THLE* RG7 .... **142** E2
  TLHT RG30 .... **115** K2
  WWKG RG41 .... **10** A6
  WWKG RG41 .... **119** H8
Keswick Av *SHPTN* TW17 ...... **129** H8 ③
Keswick Cl *CBLY* GU15 .... **182** F2
  TLHT RG30 .... **87** G7
Keswick Ct *SLN* SL2 .... **5** H5
Keswick Dr *LTWR* GU18 .... **175** L6
Keswick Gdns *WODY* RG5 ...... **118** B1
Ketcher Gn *BNFD* RG42 .... **120** F2
Kettering Cl *CALC* RG31 .... **115** H2
Kevins Dr *YTLY* GU46 .... **172** B7
Keynsham Wy *SHST* GU47 .... **173** G4
Keywood Dr *SUN* TW16 .... **129** K4
Kibble Gn *BRAK* RG12 .... **149** M3
Kibblewhite Crs
  WAR/TWY RG10 .... **65** G8 ①
Kidderminster Rd *SLN* SL2 ...... **44** D4
Kidmore End Rd *CAV/SC* RG4 .. **62** D6
Kidmore La *CAV/SC* RG4 .... **62** A3
Kidmore Rd *CAV/SC* RG4 .... **62** B8
Kidwells Cl *MDHD* SL6 .... **3** H4
Kidwells Park Dr *MDHD* SL6 .... **3** H4
Kier Pk *ASC* SL5 .... **123** M8
Kilburn Cl *CALC* RG31 .... **115** G2 ⑩
Kildare Gdns *CAV/SC* RG4 .... **2** F4
Killarney Dr *MDHD* SL6 .... **2** F4
Killmartin Gdns *FRIM* GU16 .. **182** C5 ②
Kilmington Cl *BRAK* RG12 .... **150** B4 ①
Kilmore Dr *CBLY* GU15 .... **182** E2
Kilmuir Cl *SHST* GU47 .... **173** G7
Kiln Cl *NTHA* RG18 .... **81** L7
Kiln Croft Cl *MLW* SL7 .... **19** K3 ①
Kiln Dr *NTHA* RG18 .... **109** H1
Kiln Hl *THLE* RG7 .... **145** L7
Kiln La *ASC* SL5 .... **123** L4
  ASC SL5 .... **152** D2
  BRAK RG12 .... **12** E5

  CALC RG31 .... **86** D6
  FLKWH HP10 .... **21** H3
  HEN RG9 .... **63** M4
  THLE RG7 .... **166** F1
Kiln Pl *MDHD* SL6 .... **41** K3
Kiln Ride *EWKG* RG40 .... **147** K6
  GOR/PANG RG8 .... **84** C1
Kiln Ride Extension
  EWKG RG40 .... **147** K8
Kiln Rd *CAV/SC* RG4 .... **62** F7
  WHIT RG2 .... **136** F1
Kilnsea Dr *EARL* RG6 .... **118** A4
Kiln View Rd *WHIT* RG2 .... **117** G4
Kilowna Cl *WAR/TWY* RG10 .... **90** D2
Kilross Rd *EBED/NFELT* TW14 .. **101** G7
Kimber Cl *WDSR* SL4 .... **96** C2
Kimberley *BRAK* RG12 .... **149** M5
Kimberley Cl *DTCH/LGLY* SL3 .... **72** C4
  READ RG1 .... **116** B1 ③
Kimbers Dr *NWBY* RG14 ...... **135** M1
  SL SL1 .... **44** A4
Kimber's La *MDHD* SL6 .... **68** B3
Kimmeridge *BRAK* RG12 ...... **150** B3 ③
Kimpton Cl *WHIT* RG2 .... **117** H6
Kinburn Dr *ECH* TW20 .... **126** B3
King Edwards Cl *ASC* SL5 ...... **123** H6 ③
King Edwards Ri *ASC* SL5 ...... **123** H6
King Edwards Rd *ASC* SL5 .... **123** H6
King Edward St *SL* SL1.............. **4** D9
King Edward Vii Av *WDSR* SL4 .... **7** L4
Kingfisher Cl *FARN* GU14 ...... **180** F5 ③
  THLE RG7 .... **140** F3 ③
Kingfisher Ct *WAR/TWY* RG10 .. **91** H3 ③
Kingfisher Dr *STA* TW18 .... **127** J2
  WODY RG5 .... **89** M8
  YTLY GU46 .... **171** L8
Kingfisher Pl *READ* RG1 .... **9** H3
King George Ct *SUN* TW16 .... **129** H3 ③
Kinghorn La *MDHD* SL6 .... **42** A3
Kinghorn Pk *MDHD* SL6 .... **42** A3
King James Wy *HEN* RG9 .... **37** M6
King John's Cl *STWL/WRAY* TW19.. **97** M5
Kings Av *SUN* TW16 .... **129** J3
Kingsbridge Hl *THLE* RG7 ...... **144** D8
Kingsbridge Rd *NWBY* RG14 .... **14** A7
  WHIT RG2 .... **116** E4
Kingsbury Crs *STA* TW18 ...... **127** G2
Kingsbury Dr *WDSR* SL4 .... **97** K6
Kingsclear Pk *CBLY* GU15 ...... **182** A2
King's Cl *STA* TW18 .... **128** A3 ③
King's Crs *CBLY* GU15 .... **173** M6
Kingsdown Cl *EARL* RG6 ...... **117** L4 ①
Kings Farm La *HEN* RG9 .... **37** G8
Kingsfield *WDSR* SL4 .... **70** A8 ③
Kingsford Cl *WODY* RG5 .... **118** D1
Kingsgate St *READ* RG1 .... **9** M7
Kings Gv *MDHD* SL6 .... **2** E6
King's Keep *SHST* GU47 .... **172** E5
Kingsland Gra *NWBY* RG14 .... **136** B6
Kings La *BFOR* GU20 .... **176** B1
  EGH TW20 .... **125** K3
  MDHD SL6 .... **19** L6
Kingsley Av *CBLY* GU15 .... **181** M2
  EGH TW20 .... **125** L4
Kingsley Cl *CWTH* RG45 .... **172** E3
  NWBY RG14 .... **136** E1
  WAR/TWY RG10 .... **90** D1
  WHIT RG2 .... **116** E7
Kingsley Rd *FARN* GU14 .... **181** J8
  HTWY RG27 .... **170** F6
Kingsmead *FRIM* GU16 .... **182** B7
Kingsmead Av *SUN* TW16 .... **129** M8
King's Meadow Rd *READ* RG1 .... **9** H4
Kingsmere Rd *BNFD* RG42 ...... **12** C2
King's Ride *ASC* SL5 .... **150** F1
  CBLY GU15 .... **174** A5
King's Rd *ASC* SL5 .... **152** A2
  CAV/SC RG4 .... **9** H1
  CWTH RG45 .... **172** C2
  EGH TW20 .... **126** D2
  FELT TW13 .... **101** M7
  HEN RG9 .... **38** A4
  HEN RG9 .... **38** A4
  NWBY RG14 .... **14** F5
  NWBY RG14 .... **15** G5
  READ RG1 .... **9** H6
  SL SL1 .... **71** H3
  THLE RG7 .... **165** K5
  WDSR SL4 .... **7** K8
  WDSR SL4 .... **97** G3
Kings Rd West *NWBY* RG14 .... **14** F5
King Stable St *WDSR* SL4 .... **7** J4
Kingston Av *EBED/NFELT* TW14 .. **101** H5
Kingston Crs *ASHF* TW15 ...... **127** M3
Kingston Gdns *WHIT* RG2 ...... **116** F4 ③
Kingston La *THLE* RG7 .... **113** M8
Kingston Rd *ASHF* TW15 ...... **128** B4
  CBLY GU15 .... **174** D6
  SHPTN TW17 .... **128** C4
  STA TW18 .... **127** K2
  STA TW18 .... **127** M4
King St *CHERT* KT16 .... **155** K5
  MDHD SL6 .... **3** G5
  MDHD SL6 .... **3** H6
  READ RG1 .... **9** G6
  THLE RG7 .... **142** D8
Kingsway *BLKW* GU17 .... **181** G1
  CAV/SC RG4 .... **63** H8
  STWL/WRAY TW19 .... **100** A7
Kingswick Cl *ASC* SL5 .... **152** B1
Kingswick Dr *ASC* SL5 .... **152** A1
Kings Wd *MLW* SL7 .... **18** A7 ②
Kingswood Cl *EGH* TW20 ...... **126** A2
Kingswood Ct *MDHD* SL6 .... **68** C2
Kingswood Creek
  STWL/WRAY TW19 .... **98** A4
Kingswood Ri *EGH* TW20 ...... **126** A3
Kinnaird Cl *SL* SL1 .... **43** M7 ⑦
Kinross Av *ASC* SL5 .... **151** J2
Kinross Cl *SUN* TW16 .... **129** J3
Kinross Ct *ASC* SL5 .... **151** J2 ②
Kinross Dr *SUN* TW16 .... **129** J3
Kintbury Rd *HUNG* RG17 ...... **133** J8
Kintbury Sq *HUNG* RG17 ...... **133** K4 ⑥
Kipling Cl *NTHA* RG18 .... **137** M1
Kirfell Cl *CALC* RG31 .... **86** F4
Kirkham Cl *CAV/SC* RG4 .... **63** H4
  SHST GU47 .... **173** G4 ②

Kirkstall Ct CALC RG31 ...... 115 G2
Kirkstone Cl CBLY GU15 ...... 183 G2
Kirkwall Sp SL1 ...... 4 E1
Kirkwood Crs THLE RG7 ...... 142 C3
Kirton Cl TLHT RG30 ...... 87 L7
Kitsmead La CHERT KT16 ...... 153 M5
Kittiwake Cl WODY RG5 ...... 90 E7
Klondyke MLW SL7 ...... 19 C4
Knappe Cl HEN RG9 ...... 37 M6
Knapp La TADY RG26 ...... 165 G8
Knapp Rd ASHF TW15 ...... 128 C2
The Knapp EARL RG6 ...... 117 K2
  MARL SN8 ...... 130 B8
Knighton Cl CAV/SC RG4 ...... 88 D3
Knightsbridge Crs STA TW18 ...... 127 L4
Knightsbridge Dr STHA RG19 ...... 161 L3
Knightsbridge Rd CBLY GU15 ...... 174 B7
Knights Cl EGH TW20 ...... 127 G4
  WDSR SL4 ...... 70 A8
Knights La KSCL RG20 ...... 158 F3
Knights Lea KSCL RG20 ...... 158 E3
Knights Pl WDSR SL4 ...... 96 F2
Knights Wy CAV/SC RG4 ...... 88 L1
  CBLY GU15 ...... 182 F2
Knoll Park Rd CHERT KT16 ...... 155 J5
Knoll Rd CBLY GU15 ...... 174 A8
The Knoll CALC RG31 ...... 86 L4
  CHERT KT16 ...... 155 J5
Knollys Rd THLE RG7 ...... 165 J5
Knolton Wy SLN SL2 ...... 5 L2
  SLN SL2 ...... 45 M8
Knossington Cl EARL RG6 ...... 117 M4
Knott La THLE RG7 ...... 140 E2
Knowle Cl CAV/SC RG4 ...... 88 A2
Knowle Gn STA TW18 ...... 127 K3
Knowle Gv VW GU25 ...... 153 M4
Knowle Grove Cl VW GU25 ...... 153 M4
Knowle Hl VW GU25 ...... 153 L4
Knowle Park Av STA TW18 ...... 127 L4
Knowle Rd WODY RG5 ...... 118 B2
Knowles Av CWTH RG45 ...... 172 C2
Knowsley Cl MDHD SL6 ...... 41 K5
Knowsley Rd CALC RG31 ...... 86 E3
Knox Gn BNFD RG42 ...... 120 F3
Korda Cl SHPTN TW17 ...... 128 C8
Krooner Rd CBLY GU15 ...... 181 L3
Kybes La THLE RG7 ...... 144 A2
Kyle Cl BRAK RG12 ...... 13 G7

L

Laburnham Rd MDHD SL6 ...... 2 D7
Laburnum Cl MLW SL7 ...... 19 H2
Laburnum Crs SUN TW16 ...... 129 L6
Laburnum Gdns WHIT RG2 ...... 117 H5
Laburnum Gv DTCH/LGLY SL3 ...... 72 D6
  NWBY RG14 ...... 14 E1
Laburnum Pl EGH TW20 ...... 125 L4
Laburnum Rd CHERT KT16 ...... 155 K5
  WWKG RG41 ...... 118 F5
The Laburnums BLKW GU17 ...... 180 E1
Laburnum Wy
  STWL/WRAY TW19 ...... 100 C7
Lacey Cl EGH TW20 ...... 127 G5
Lackmore Gdns GOR/PANG RG8 ...... 34 C6
Ladbroke Cl WODY RG5 ...... 90 C8
Ladbrooke Rd SL1 ...... 70 C8
Ladwell Cl NWBY RG14 ...... 160 A1
Ladybank BRAK RG12 ...... 149 L5
Lady Jane Cl CAV/SC RG4 ...... 88 E3
Lady Margaret Rd ASC SL5 ...... 152 C5
Ladymask Cl CALC RG31 ...... 115 J2
Ladythorpe Cl
  ADL/WDHM KT15 ...... 155 L8
The Laffords THLE RG7 ...... 112 D4
Lafone Av FELT TW13 ...... 101 M8
Laggan Rd MDHD SL6 ...... 42 C4
Laggan Sq MDHD SL6 ...... 42 C5
Laird Ct BAGS GU19 ...... 175 H5
Lake Av SL1 ...... 4 C5
Lake End Rd MDHD SL6 ...... 43 L8
  WDSR SL4 ...... 69 L3
Lake End Wy CWTH RG45 ...... 172 C2
Lakeland Dr FRIM GU16 ...... 182 B5
Lakelands TADY RG26 ...... 164 A5
Lake Rd FRIM GU16 ...... 182 D8
  VW GU25 ...... 153 L1
Lakeside BNFD RG42 ...... 13 J1
  EARL RG6 ...... 117 L3
  MDHD SL6 ...... 42 E4
Lakeside Dr SLN SL2 ...... 45 H2
Lakeside Gdns FARN GU14 ...... 181 C7
Lakeside Rd DTCH/LGLY SL3 ...... 73 J7
The Lake Side BLKW GU17 ...... 181 G2
Lake Vw MDHD SL6 ...... 42 D5
Lalande Cl WWKG RG41 ...... 119 H8
Laleham Cl STA TW18 ...... 127 L6
Laleham Rd STA TW18 ...... 127 J4
Lamb Cl NTHA RG18 ...... 137 M1
Lambdens Wk TADY RG26 ...... 164 E6
Lambert Av DTCH/LGLY SL3 ...... 72 B3
Lambert Crs BLKW GU17 ...... 180 F2
Lambeth Ct TLHT RG30 ...... 87 J7
Lambfields THLE RG7 ...... 114 A3
Lambly Hl VW GU25 ...... 126 B8
Lamborne Cl SHST GU47 ...... 172 D5
Lambourn Cl CALC RG31 ...... 87 G6
Lambourne Av UX/CGN UB8 ...... 47 L2
Lambourne Dr BAGS GU19 ...... 175 C4
  MDHD SL6 ...... 67 M3
Lambourne Gdns EARL RG6 ...... 117 M2
Lambourne Gv BRAK RG12 ...... 122 B7
Lambourne Rd CAV/SC RG4 ...... 62 B1
Lambourn Pl HUNG RG17 ...... 49 L3
Lambourn Rd KSCL RG20 ...... 107 M8
Lambourn Valley Wy
  HUNG RG17 ...... 49 K3
  KSCL RG20 ...... 78 D2
  KSCL RG20 ...... 107 L6
  NWBY RG14 ...... 13 G1
Lambridge La HEN RG9 ...... 37 L3
Lambridge Wood Rd HEN RG9 ...... 37 L2
Lambs La THLE RG7 ...... 144 D6
Lamden Wy THLE RG7 ...... 142 E3
Lamerton Rd WHIT RG2 ...... 116 E5

Lammas Cl STA TW18 ...... 127 H1
Lammas Ct WDSR SL4 ...... 7 H9
Lammas Dr STA TW18 ...... 127 G2
Lammas Md BNFD RG42 ...... 12 A1
Lammas Rd SL1 ...... 44 A6
Lamorna Crs CALC RG31 ...... 86 F5
Lamp Acres NWBY RG14 ...... 136 E1
Lanark Cl FRIM GU16 ...... 182 B4
  WODY RG5 ...... 90 D7
Lancashire Hl BNFD RG42 ...... 122 C4
Lancaster Av SLN SL2 ...... 44 F5
Lancaster Cl EGH TW20 ...... 126 A3
  HUNG RG17 ...... 131 M2
  NTHA RG18 ...... 137 M2
  READ RG1 ...... 116 F1
  STWL/WRAY TW19 ...... 100 B5
Lancaster Dr CBLY GU15 ...... 174 A8
Lancaster Gdns EARL RG6 ...... 117 L3
Lancaster Rd MDHD SL6 ...... 41 L8
Lancaster Sq HUNG RG17 ...... 132 A2
Lancaster Cl FARN GU14 ...... 181 M7
Lancastria Ms MDHD SL6 ...... 2 D5
Lancelot Cl SL1 ...... 70 D2
Lancing Cl TLHT RG30 ...... 86 B3
Lancing Rd FELT TW13 ...... 101 J8
Landen Ct EWKG RG40 ...... 10 F9
Landon Wy ASHF TW15 ...... 128 E4
Landrake Crs WHIT RG2 ...... 116 F5
Landseer Cl SHST GU47 ...... 173 H4
Landsend La WODY RG5 ...... 90 E4
Lane End Cl WHIT RG2 ...... 117 H8
Laneswood THLE RG7 ...... 166 B3
The Lane CHERT KT16 ...... 127 K8
  TADY RG26 ...... 164 E6
  VW GU25 ...... 126 B8
Langborough Rd EWKG RG40 ...... 11 G7
Langdale Cl MDHD SL6 ...... 3 K5
Langdale Dr ASC SL5 ...... 123 H7
Langdale Gdns EARL RG6 ...... 117 J4
Langdon Cl CBLY GU15 ...... 182 F2
Langford Cl CAV/SC RG4 ...... 88 F1
Langham Pl EGH TW20 ...... 126 C3
Langhams Wy WAR/TWY RG10 ...... 65 G4
Langley Broom DTCH/LGLY SL3 ...... 72 C5
Langley Common Rd
  EWKG RG40 ...... 146 C5
Langley Dr CBLY GU15 ...... 174 A8
Langley Hl CALC RG31 ...... 114 F1
Langley Hill Cl CALC RG31 ...... 86 F8
Langley Park Rd IVER SLO 46 E8
Langley Rd DTCH/LGLY SL3 ...... 71 M3
  DTCH/LGLY SL3 ...... 72 C3
  STA TW18 ...... 127 J4
Langley Wy MLW SL7 ...... 18 E4
Langton Wy EGH TW20 ...... 126 F4
Langton's End MDHD SL6 ...... 68 E6
  MDHD SL6 ...... 2 C2
  SL SL1 ...... 70 A1
Langworthy End MDHD SL6 ...... 68 E6
Langworthy La MDHD SL6 ...... 68 D6
Laniver Cl EARL RG6 ...... 117 K1
Lansbury Av EBED/NFELT TW14 ...... 101 L5
Lansdowne Cl SL SL1 ...... 4 F7
Lansdowne Gdns THLE RG7 ...... 144 F5
Lansdowne Rd FRIM GU16 ...... 182 D6
  STA TW18 ...... 127 L5
  TLHT RG30 ...... 87 C7
Lapwing Cl CALC RG31 ...... 86 E8
Larch Av ASC SL5 ...... 152 B2
  WWKG RG41 ...... 10 D3
Larch Cl CBLY GU15 ...... 174 B5
  NWBY RG14 ...... 136 A1
  SLN SL2 ...... 44 B4
  TLHT RG30 ...... 142 E2
Larch Dr WODY RG5 ...... 118 A1
Larchfield Rd MDHD SL6 ...... 2 D9
Larchside Cl THLE RG7 ...... 144 E4
Larchwood Dr EGH TW20 ...... 125 H4
Larchwood Gld CBLY GU15 ...... 174 D7
Larges Bridge Dr BRAK RG12 ...... 13 K6
Larges La BRAK RG12 ...... 13 H5
Larissa Cl CALC RG31 ...... 87 H5
Lark Av STA TW18 ...... 127 J1
Larkes-meade EARL RG6 ...... 117 K5
Larkham Cl FELT TW13 ...... 101 H8
Larkings La DTCH/LGLY SL3 ...... 45 L2
Larksfield EGH TW20 ...... 125 L5
Larkspur Cl WWKG RG41 ...... 119 G3
Larkspur Gdns NTHA RG18 ...... 138 C2
Larkswood Cl CALC RG31 ...... 87 C3
  SHST GU47 ...... 172 D5
Larkswood Dr CWTH RG45 ...... 171 M5
La Roche DTCH/LGLY SL3 ...... 71 M3
Lascelles Rd DTCH/LGLY SL3 ...... 71 L3
Lashbrook Rd HEN RG9 ...... 64 E2
Lassell Gdns MDHD SL6 ...... 3 L4
Lasswade Rd CHERT KT16 ...... 155 J4
Latham Av FRIM GU16 ...... 182 B4
Latimer BRAK RG12 ...... 149 L5
Latimer Dr CALC RG31 ...... 114 F2
Latimer Rd WWKG RG41 ...... 10 E7
Laud Cl NWBY RG14 ...... 137 G1
Lauder Cl FRIM GU16 ...... 182 B4
Laud's Cl HEN RG9 ...... 37 M5
Laud Wy EWKG RG40 ...... 11 M5
Launceston Av CAV/SC RG4 ...... 63 H8
Launcestone Cl EARL RG6 ...... 117 L4
Laundry La CBLY GU15 ...... 181 H1
Lauradale BRAK RG12 ...... 12 F8
Laurel Av DTCH/LGLY SL3 ...... 72 B2
  EGH TW20 ...... 125 L3
Laurel Cl CBLY GU15 ...... 182 A2
  DTCH/LGLY SL3 ...... 73 H7
  WWKG RG41 ...... 10 B7
Laurel Dr CALC RG31 ...... 86 E6
The Laurels GOR/PANG RG8 ...... 86 A1
Lauser Rd STWL/WRAY TW19 ...... 99 M6
Lavell's La THLE RG7 ...... 166 F6
Lavenham Dr WODY RG5 ...... 90 C6
Lawford Crs YTLY GU46 ...... 172 A8
Lawkland SL SL1 ...... 44 F4
Lawn Av WDR/YW UB7 ...... 73 M2
Lawn Cl DTCH/LGLY SL3 ...... 71 M7
Lawn Rd UX/CGN UB8 ...... 47 M1
Lawrence Cl EWKG RG40 ...... 11 J5
Lawrence Crs BFOR GU20 ...... 176 A2

Lawrence Gv BNFD RG42 ...... 121 G6
Lawrence Md HUNG RG17 ...... 133 K4
Lawrence Rd HSLWW TW4 ...... 101 M3
  TLHT RG30 ...... 87 K6
Lawrences La NTHA RG18 ...... 110 A8
Lawrence Wy CBLY GU15 ...... 181 J2
  SL1 ...... 43 M6
Lawson Dr CAV/SC RG4 ...... 88 B1
Lawson Wy ASC SL5 ...... 123 K8
Laxton Gn MDHD SL6 ...... 67 M3
Layburn Crs DTCH/LGLY SL3 ...... 72 E6
Layland's Gn HUNG RG17 ...... 133 L5
Layleys Gn NTHA RG18 ...... 109 J2
Laytom Ri CALC RG31 ...... 86 F3
Layton's La SUN TW16 ...... 129 J7
Lea Cl TLHT RG30 ...... 115 K3
Leacroft ASC SL5 ...... 152 D2
Lea Cft CHF RG45 ...... 148 E8
Leacroft STA TW18 ...... 127 L3
Leacroft Cl STA TW18 ...... 127 L2
Leacroft Rd IVER SLO 47 G8
Leafield Copse BRAK RG12 ...... 150 C1
Leaholme Gdns SL SL1 ...... 43 M6
Lea Rd CAV/SC RG4 ...... 62 C2
  CBLY GU15 ...... 181 L4
Leas Dr IVER SLO 47 H7
The Lea EGH TW20 ...... 126 E5
  EWKG RG40 ...... 147 J6
Leaver Rd HEN RG9 ...... 37 M5
Leaves Gn BRAK RG12 ...... 150 A3
Ledbury Cl TLHT RG30 ...... 87 M6
Ledbury Dr CALC RG31 ...... 115 G2
Ledger La MDHD SL6 ...... 69 C8
Ledger's Rd SL SL1 ...... 4 D9
  SL SL1 ...... 44 D1
Ledran Cl EARL RG6 ...... 117 M6
Leeds Rd SL1 ...... 4 E4
Lee La MDHD SL6 ...... 41 H3
Lees Cl MDHD SL6 ...... 67 L2
Lees Gdns MDHD SL6 ...... 67 L1
Leeson Gdns WDSR SL4 ...... 70 B4
Leicester BRAK RG12 ...... 150 A4
Leicester Cl HEN RG9 ...... 38 A3
Leigh Fld THLE RG7 ...... 142 C8
Leigh Pk DTCH/LGLY SL3 ...... 71 M7
Leigh Rd SL SL1 ...... 44 E8
Leigh Sq WDSR SL4 ...... 96 A1
Leighton Gdns MDHD SL6 ...... 67 L1
Leiston Cl EARL RG6 ...... 118 A5
Leiston Sp SL SL1 ...... 4 E2
Leith Cl CWTH RG45 ...... 148 D7
  SL SL1 ...... 5 J7
Lela Av HSLWW TW4 ...... 101 M1
Le Marchant Rd FRIM GU16 ...... 182 C3
Lemart Cl TLHT RG30 ...... 87 H6
Lemington Gv BRAK RG12 ...... 149 L3
Lendore Rd FRIM GU16 ...... 182 A6
Leney Cl EWKG RG40 ...... 11 J1
Lenham Cl WWKG RG41 ...... 119 G5
Lennox Cl CALC RG31 ...... 114 E2
Lennox Rd EARL RG6 ...... 117 K1
Lent Green La SL SL1 ...... 43 M6
Lent Rise Rd MDHD SL6 ...... 43 L7
Leonard Cl FRIM GU16 ...... 182 A6
Leopold Wk READ RG1 ...... 9 L6
Leppington BRAK RG12 ...... 149 L5
Lerwick Dr SL SL1 ...... 44 E1
Lesford Rd READ RG1 ...... 116 B2
Leslie Rd CHOB/PIR GU24 ...... 177 G5
Leslie Southern Ct NWBY RG14 ...... 15 G2
Lesters Rd MDHD SL6 ...... 20 A8
Letchworth Av
  EBED/NFELT TW14 ...... 101 J6
Letcombe Sq BRAK RG12 ...... 150 C1
Letcombe St READ RG1 ...... 9 G7
Leverkusen Rd BRAK RG12 ...... 13 H7
Leverton La HUNG RG17 ...... 103 K5
Lewins Wy SL SL1 ...... 44 C8
Lewis Cl ADL/WDHM KT15 ...... 155 M8
Lewisham Wy SHST GU47 ...... 173 C5
Lexington Av MDHD SL6 ...... 2 C8
Lexington Gv WHIT RG2 ...... 116 F8
Leyburn Cl WODY RG5 ...... 90 D6
Leycester Cl BFOR GU20 ...... 151 L8
Leyland Gdns WHIT RG2 ...... 145 H1
Leylands La STWL/WRAY TW19 ...... 99 J4
Ley Rd FARN GU14 ...... 181 K6
Leys Gdns NWBY RG14 ...... 14 D2
Leyside CWTH RG45 ...... 172 D1
Lichfield Cl EARL RG6 ...... 117 M5
Lichfield Rd HSLWW TW4 ...... 101 M3
Lichfields BRAK RG12 ...... 122 B7
Liddell WDSR SL4 ...... 95 M2
Liddell Cl EWKG RG40 ...... 171 H3
Liddell Wy ASC SL5 ...... 151 J2
Lidstone Cl EARL RG6 ...... 118 A5
Liebenrood Rd TLHT RG30 ...... 87 M8
Lightlands La MDHD SL6 ...... 42 C1
Lightwater Meadow
  LTWR RG18 ...... 175 L6
Lightwater Rd LTWR GU18 ...... 175 L6
Lightwood BRAK RG12 ...... 150 A3
Lilac Cl GOR/PANG RG8 ...... 87 G1
The Lilacs WWKG RG41 ...... 146 F3
Lilley Wy SL SL1 ...... 70 B1
Lillibrooke Crs MDHD SL6 ...... 67 K3
Lillyfee Farm La FLKWH HP10 ...... 21 K2
Lily Hill Dr BRAK RG12 ...... 122 B7
Lily Hill Rd BRAK RG12 ...... 122 C7
Lima Ct READ RG1 ...... 8 C8
Lime Av CBLY GU15 ...... 174 D8
  WDSR SL4 ...... 71 J7
  WDSR SL4 ...... 124 C1
Lime Cl NWBY RG14 ...... 10 A7
  WWKG RG41 ...... 10 A7
Lime Crs SUN TW16 ...... 129 M7
Limefield Cl EARL RG6 ...... 118 B3
Limes Av KSCL RG20 ...... 160 D7
Limes Rd EGH TW20 ...... 126 C3
Lime Tree Wk VW GU25 ...... 154 B1
Lime Wk BRAK RG12 ...... 13 K8
  MDHD SL6 ...... 41 K5
Limmer Cl WWKG RG41 ...... 146 F2

Limmerhill Rd WWKG RG41 ...... 147 H1
Linchfield Rd DTCH/LGLY SL3 ...... 71 M8
Lincoln Cl CBLY GU15 ...... 182 E2
  WWKG RG41 ...... 118 D4
Lincoln Gdns WAR/TWY RG10 ...... 91 K1
Lincoln Hatch La SL SL1 ...... 43 M5
Lincoln Rd MDHD SL6 ...... 41 L6
  WHIT RG2 ...... 116 F2
Lincolnshire Gdns BNFD RG42 ...... 122 B5
Lincoln Wy SL SL1 ...... 44 A8
Lindale Cl VW GU25 ...... 153 J1
Lindberg Wy WODY RG5 ...... 90 E5
Lind Cl EARL RG6 ...... 117 L4
Linden Av MDHD SL6 ...... 2 C1
Linden Cl NWBY RG14 ...... 14 C1
  WWKG RG41 ...... 10 A9
Linden Ct CBLY GU15 ...... 174 C7
  EGH TW20 ...... 125 L4
Linden Dr SL SL2 ...... 44 A8
Linden Hill La WAR/TWY RG10 ...... 65 M4
Lindenhill Rd BNFD RG42 ...... 12 B7
Linden Rd WHIT RG2 ...... 117 H4
  WODY RG5 ...... 118 A2
Lindores Rd MDHD SL6 ...... 68 E6
Lindsay Cl STWL/WRAY TW19 ...... 100 A5
Lindsey Cl WWKG RG41 ...... 119 H8
Lindsey Gdns
  EBED/NFELT TW14 ...... 101 C6
Lines Rd WAR/TWY RG10 ...... 91 H8
Ling Dr LTWR GU18 ...... 175 J7
Lingfield Rd NWBY RG14 ...... 15 J9
Lingholm Cl MDHD SL6 ...... 2 B7
  TLHT RG30 ...... 115 J1
Lingwood BRAK RG12 ...... 149 M3
Link Rd DTCH/LGLY SL3 ...... 71 M7
  EBED/NFELT TW14 ...... 101 J6
  NWBY RG14 ...... 14 E6
Links Dr TLHT RG30 ...... 87 K6
Links Rd ASHF TW15 ...... 128 B3
The Links ASC SL5 ...... 123 H7
Linkswood Rd SL SL1 ...... 43 M3
The Link SLN SL2 ...... 5 M2
  YTLY GU46 ...... 171 M7
Link Wy NTHA RG18 ...... 137 L2
  STA TW18 ...... 127 L4
  WHIT RG2 ...... 146 B4
Linkway CBLY GU15 ...... 181 M2
  CWTH RG45 ...... 172 C1
Linnet Cl CALC RG31 ...... 86 E8
Linstead Rd FARN GU14 ...... 181 H6
Linton Cl TADY RG26 ...... 164 F7
Lintott Ct STWL/WRAY TW19 ...... 100 A5
Lion Cl SHPTN TW17 ...... 128 B8
Lip La KSCL RG20 ...... 106 A6
Lipscomb Cl NTHA RG18 ...... 81 L8
Lipscombe Cl NWBY RG14 ...... 14 A5
Liscombe BRAK RG12 ...... 149 L4
Liskeard Dr FARN GU14 ...... 181 K8
Lisle Cl NWBY RG14 ...... 136 C1
Lismore Cl WODY RG5 ...... 118 B2
Lismore Pk SLN SL2 ...... 5 G3
Lisset Rd MDHD SL6 ...... 3 J6
Liston Rd MLW SL7 ...... 19 H3
Litcham Sp SL SL1 ...... 4 D3
Lithgow's Rd HTHAIR TW6 ...... 101 J1
Littington Cl EARL RG6 ...... 117 M6
Little Bowden La
  GOR/PANG RG8 ...... 85 J1
Littlebrook Av SL SL1 ...... 44 B6
Little Buntings WDSR SL4 ...... 96 C2
Little Copse YTLY GU46 ...... 171 M7
Littlecote Dr READ RG1 ...... 8 B9
Littlecote Rd MARL SN8 ...... 130 E1
Littlecroft Rd EGH TW20 ...... 126 C3
Little Croft Rd GOR/PANG RG8 ...... 58 F1
Littledale Cl BRAK RG12 ...... 122 B8
Littledown Rd SL SL1 ...... 5 C6
Littlefield Gn MDHD SL6 ...... 67 H8
  MDHD SL6 ...... 67 J8
Little Frith EWKG RG40 ...... 147 M8
Little Glebe CAV/SC RG4 ...... 90 B3
Little Green La CHERT KT16 ...... 155 H7
Little Heath Rd CALC RG31 ...... 86 B7
  CHOB/PIR GU24 ...... 177 H4
Little Hill Rd WAR/TWY RG10 ...... 119 G2
Little John's La TLHT RG30 ...... 87 M6
Littlejohn's La TLHT RG30 ...... 88 A5
Little Knowle Hl STHA RG19 ...... 163 G8
Little La THLE RG7 ...... 110 F8
Little London Rd THLE RG7 ...... 165 H8
Little Marlow Rd MLW SL7 ...... 19 H3
Little Moor SHST GU47 ...... 172 F5
Little Oak Dr CALC RG31 ...... 86 F6
Little Paddock CBLY GU15 ...... 174 F6
Littleport Sp SL SL1 ...... 4 E3
Little Ringdale BRAK RG12 ...... 150 B1
Little Rd SL SL1 ...... 21 M5
Littlestead Cl CAV/SC RG4 ...... 63 H8
Little St READ RG1 ...... 8 B5
Little Sutton La DTCH/LGLY SL3 ...... 72 E6
Littleton Rd ASHF TW15 ...... 128 E5
Little Woodlands WDSR SL4 ...... 96 C2
Litton Rd WHIT RG2 ...... 116 F8
Liverpool Rd READ RG1 ...... 89 H6
  SL SL1 ...... 44 E7
Livery Cl READ RG1 ...... 9 H7
Livingstone Gdns WODY RG5 ...... 118 B1
Livingstone Rd NWBY RG14 ...... 15 C5
Llangar Gv CWTH RG45 ...... 172 C1
Llanvair Cl ASC SL5 ...... 151 K3
Llanvair Dr ASC SL5 ...... 151 K3
Llewellyn Pk WAR/TWY RG10 ...... 64 F8
Lochinvar Cl SL SL1 ...... 70 E2
Lochinver BRAK RG12 ...... 149 L4
Lock Av MDHD SL6 ...... 42 F1
Lockbridge Ct MDHD SL6 ...... 42 F6
Lock Bridge Rd BNEND SL8 ...... 20 D2
Lock Gdns SLN SL2 ...... 71 M1
Lockets Cl WDSR SL4 ...... 70 A8
Lock Md MDHD SL6 ...... 42 F4
Lock Pth WDSR SL4 ...... 70 A6
Lock Pl READ RG1 ...... 9 L6
Lockram La THLE RG7 ...... 114 F5
Lock Rd MLW SL7 ...... 19 H5

Lockside Ct THLE RG7 ...... 140 F3
Locks Ride ASC SL5 ...... 122 F5
Lockstile Md GOR/PANG RG8 ...... 32 F7
Lockstile Wy GOR/PANG RG8 ...... 32 F8
Lockton Cha ASC SL5 ...... 123 G8
Lockwood Cl FARN GU14 ...... 181 H6
Loddon Br Rd EARL RG6 ...... 118 C3
Loddon Bridge Rd EARL RG6 ...... 118 C1
  WODY RG5 ...... 118 C1
Loddon Cl CBLY GU15 ...... 174 D8
Loddon Dr MDHD SL6 ...... 2 C2
  WAR/TWY RG10 ...... 64 E5
  WAR/TWY RG10 ...... 64 E8
Loddon Hall Rd WAR/TWY RG10 ...... 91 H1
Loddon Rd BNEND SL8 ...... 20 D2
  FARN GU14 ...... 181 G8
Loddon Sp SL SL1 ...... 4 E4
Lodge Cl EGH TW20 ...... 126 A3
  MLW SL7 ...... 19 H5
  SL SL1 ...... 4 A8
  UX/CGN UB8 ...... 47 M5
Lodge Gv YTLY GU46 ...... 172 C8
Lodge Rd WAR/TWY RG10 ...... 91 H6
Lodge Wy ASHF TW15 ...... 128 F7
  SHPTN TW17 ...... 128 F7
  WDSR SL4 ...... 96 B2
Logan Cl TLHT RG30 ...... 87 J7
Lomond Av CAV/SC RG4 ...... 89 H1
London Rd ASC SL5 ...... 122 C6
  BLKW GU17 ...... 181 H2
  BNFD RG42 ...... 120 E7
  BRAK RG12 ...... 13 L4
  CBLY GU15 ...... 181 J1
  DTCH/LGLY SL3 ...... 71 M3
  DTCH/LGLY SL3 ...... 71 M7
  DTCH/LGLY SL3 ...... 72 C5
  DTCH/LGLY SL3 ...... 72 D6
  EARL RG6 ...... 89 K4
  EGH TW20 ...... 125 M5
  EWKG RG40 ...... 11 K5
  NWBY RG14 ...... 14 E2
  READ RG1 ...... 9 J8
  STA TW18 ...... 127 J2
  STHA RG19 ...... 138 B3
  STWL/WRAY TW19 ...... 100 A8
  STWL/WRAY TW19 ...... 127 M1
  WAR/TWY RG10 ...... 65 H8
London St CHERT KT16 ...... 155 K4
  READ RG1 ...... 9 H6
Loneacre BFOR GU20 ...... 176 B2
Longacre NWBY RG14 ...... 136 A6
Long Barn La WHIT RG2 ...... 116 E3
Longbourne Wy CHERT KT16 ...... 155 J3
Longbridge Wy UX/CGN UB8 ...... 47 L3
Long Cl HUNG RG17 ...... 133 L4
  SLN SL2 ...... 44 E1
Longcroft Rd STHA RG19 ...... 138 B4
Longcross Rd CHERT KT16 ...... 153 L7
  CHERT KT16 ...... 154 B7
  CHERT KT16 ...... 154 E7
Longdon Rd WWKG RG41 ...... 118 F5
Longdown Rd SHST GU47 ...... 172 C5
Long Dr SL SL1 ...... 43 M4
Longfield Cl FARN GU14 ...... 181 K6
Longfield Rd WAR/TWY RG10 ...... 65 G8
Longford Av EBED/NFELT TW14 ...... 101 K5
  STWL/WRAY TW19 ...... 100 B7
Longford Cl CBLY GU15 ...... 182 A2
Longford Wy
  STWL/WRAY TW19 ...... 100 B7
Long Furlong Dr SLN SL2 ...... 44 B5
Long Gv TADY RG26 ...... 164 A4
  THLE RG7 ...... 138 E1
Long Half Acre MDHD SL6 ...... 66 F2
Long Hedge HUNG RG17 ...... 50 A5
Long Hill Rd ASC SL5 ...... 122 E6
  BRAK RG12 ...... 122 D7
Longhurst Cl CAV/SC RG4 ...... 88 F3
Long La CALC RG31 ...... 86 E2
  KSCL RG20 ...... 53 C3
  MDHD SL6 ...... 41 M1
  MDHD SL6 ...... 94 A2
  NTHA RG18 ...... 109 J4
  NWBY RG14 ...... 108 F7
  STWL/WRAY TW19 ...... 100 F7
Longleat Dr CALC RG31 ...... 86 E3
Longleat Gdns MDHD SL6 ...... 2 C8
Longleat Wy EBED/NFELT TW14 ...... 100 F6
Longmead KSCL RG20 ...... 159 J5
  WDSR SL4 ...... 70 B8
Longmead La SL SL1 ...... 44 A1
Longmeadow FRIM GU16 ...... 182 C3
Long Mickle SHST GU47 ...... 172 D5
Longmoor La THLE RG7 ...... 142 D7
Longmoors BNFD RG42 ...... 12 B2
Longmore Rd WHIT RG2 ...... 117 G2
Long Readings La SLN SL2 ...... 44 E4
Longridge Cl TLHT RG30 ...... 87 L7
Longshot La BRAK RG12 ...... 12 B5
Longside Cl EGH TW20 ...... 126 F6
Longstone Rd IVER SLO 46 F3
Long's Wy EWKG RG40 ...... 11 L4
Long Toll GOR/PANG RG8 ...... 60 D1
The Long Wk WDSR SL4 ...... 7 L3
  WDSR SL4 ...... 97 G7
Longwater La EWKG RG40 ...... 171 H4
Longwater Rd BRAK RG12 ...... 149 M3
  EWKG RG40 ...... 171 J4
  HTWY RG27 ...... 171 J4
Longworth Av CALC RG31 ...... 86 E7
Longworth Dr MDHD SL6 ...... 42 F5
Lonsdale Cl MDHD SL6 ...... 42 D5
Lonsdale Rd MDHD SL6 ...... 68 F5
Loosen Dr MDHD SL6 ...... 67 K3
Lord Knyvett Cl
  STWL/WRAY TW19 ...... 100 A5
Lord Knyvetts Ct
  STWL/WRAY TW19 ...... 100 B5
Lordswood THLE RG7 ...... 165 K6
Loring Rd WDSR SL4 ...... 6 A7
Lorne Cl WDSR SL4 ...... 70 E3
Lorne Pl READ RG1 ...... 8 B6
Lorne St READ RG1 ...... 8 B6
Lorraine Rd CBLY GU15 ...... 174 C6
Lory Rdg BAGS GU19 ...... 175 H2
Losfield Rd WDSR SL4 ...... 70 B8
Lossie Dr IVER SLO 46 E8
Lothian Rd CHOB/PIR GU24 ...... 183 K1

Loughborough BRAK RG12 150 B3 2
Loundyes Cl NTHA RG18 137 L2
Lovatt Cl CALC RG31 86 E7
Lovedean Ct BRAK RG12 150 B3
Love Green La IVER SL0 47 G6
Lovegrove's La GOR/PANG RG8 34 F2
Love Hill La DTCH/LGLY SL3 46 D8
Lovejoy La WDSR SL4 96 A1
Lovelace Cl MDHD SL6 40 C1
Lovelace Rd BRAK RG12 12 B9
Lovelands La CHOB/PIR GU24 176 F8
Love La IVER SL0 47 G7
NWBY RG14 108 C8
Lovel La ASC SL5 123 L3
Lovell Cl HEN RG9 37 M6
Lovells Cl LTWR GU18 175 L5
Lovel Rd ASC SL5 123 J2
Loverock Rd TLHT RG30 88 A5
Love's Cl THLE RG7 142 C3
Loves Wd THLE RG7 166 C1
Lovett Gdns MDHD SL6 42 F3 1
Lowbrook Dr MDHD SL6 67 K3
Lowbury BRAK RG12 150 B1
Lower Armour Rd CALC RG31 87 G5
Lower Boyndon Rd MDHD SL6 2 D6
Lower Britwell Rd SL SL1 44 A5
Lower Broadmoor Rd
CWTH RG45 173 G2
Lower Brook St READ RG1 8 F8
Lower Canes YTLY GU46 171 K8
Lower Church Rd SHST GU47 172 B5
Lower Cippenham La SL SL1 70 C1
Lower Common HTWY RG27 170 B5
Lower Cookham Rd MDHD SL6 42 F3
Lower Earley Wy EARL RG6 117 M6
Lower Earley Wy (North)
EARL RG6 118 C4
Lower Earley Wy (West)
WHIT RG2 117 H7
Lower Elmstone Dr CALC RG31 86 F5
Lower Farm Ct STHA RG19 137 J5
Lower Field Rd READ RG1 8 E9
Lower Lees Rd SLN SL2 44 D4
Lower Md IVER SL0 47 G4
Lower Meadow Rd WHIT RG2 117 G4
Lower Mill Fld BAGS GU19 175 G4
Lower Moor YTLY GU46 180 A1 3
Lower Mt READ RG1 116 F1
Lower Pound La MLW SL7 18 F7
Lower Rdg BNEND SL8 20 E2
Lower Rd MDHD SL6 20 B7
Lower Sandhurst Rd
EWKG RG40 171 K4
Lower Village Rd ASC SL5 151 M2
Lower Wy STHA RG19 137 J3
Lower Wokingham Rd
EWKG RG40 148 A8
Lowes Cl HEN RG9 64 E2
Lowestoft Dr SL SL1 43 M7
Lowfield Cl LTWR GU18 175 K6
Lowfield Gn CAV/SC RG4 89 H2
Lowfield Rd CAV/SC RG4 89 G1
Lowlands Rd BLKW GU17 180 F2
STWL/WRAY TW19 100 A4
Lowry Cl SHST GU47 173 G8
Lowther Rd WWKG RG41 119 H5
Loxwood EARL RG6 117 M4
Loxwood Cl EBED/NFELT TW14 101 G7
Lucan Dr STA TW18 128 A5
Lucas Cl YTLY GU46 180 A1
Lucey Cl CALC RG31 86 E3 3
Lucie Av ASHF TW15 128 E4
Luckley Pth EWKG RG40 11 H6
Luckley Rd WWKG RG41 147 L3
Luckley Wd WWKG RG41 147 L3
Luckmore Dr EARL RG6 117 K3
Luddington Av EGH TW20 126 C7
Ludlow BRAK RG12 149 L4
Ludlow Cl FRIM GU16 182 D7
NWBY RG14 137 H2 2
Ludlow Rd FELT TW13 129 K1
MDHD SL6 2 F8
Luff Cl WDSR SL4 96 B2
Luker Av HEN RG9 37 M3
Lulworth Cl FARN GU14 181 K7
Lulworth Rd WHIT RG2 116 F6 3
Lunds Farm Rd WODY RG5 90 D6
Lundy La TLHT RG30 87 M7
Lupin Cl BAGS GU19 174 F5
Lupin Ride CWTH RG45 148 E6
Luscombe Cl CAV/SC RG4 89 G4
Lutman's Hvn WAR/TWY RG10 66 B1
Lutterworth Cl BNFD RG42 121 M5 6
Lych Gate Cl SHST GU47 172 C6
Lycroft Cl GOR/PANG RG8 32 F7
Lydbury BRAK RG12 122 C8
Lydford Av SLN SL2 45 G6
Lydford Cl FARN GU14 181 K7 6
FRIM GU16 182 D7 2
Lydford Rd READ RG1 117 H1
Lydney BRAK RG12 149 L4
Lydsey Cl SLN SL2 44 D4
Lye Copse Av FARN GU14 181 L6
Lyefield Ct CAV/SC RG4 62 E8
Lyell Rd WDSR SL4 95 M2
Lyme Gv CALC RG31 87 G5
Lymington Ga CAV/SC RG4 88 B1
Lynch Cl UX/CGN UB8 47 M1 2
Lynch Hill La SLN SL2 44 B5
Lynch La HUNG RG17 49 L3
The Lynch UX/CGN UB8 47 M1
Lynden Cl MDHD SL6 68 E6 2
Lyndhurst Av BLKW GU17 172 F8
MDHD SL6 20 B8 1
SUN TW16 129 K8
Lyndhurst Cl BRAK RG12 122 D8 2
Lyndhurst Rd ASC SL5 151 K1
GOR/PANG RG8 32 F8
TLHT RG30 87 J5
Lyndhurst Wy CHERT KT16 155 H6 1
Lyndwood Dr WDSR SL4 97 K5
Lyne Cl VW GU25 154 C3
Lyne Crossing Rd CHERT KT16 154 D3
Lynegrove Av ASHF TW15 128 F3
Lyneham Gdns MDHD SL6 41 L5
Lyneham Rd CWTH RG45 172 E1
Lyne La CHERT KT16 154 D3
CHERT KT16 154 D5
Lyne Rd VW GU25 154 A3
Lynmouth Rd READ RG1 8 F3
Lynn Cl ASHF TW15 129 G3
Lynn Wy FARN GU14 181 J7
Lynton Cl WODY RG5 117 M1
Lynton Gn MDHD SL6 2 E4
Lynwood Av DTCH/LGLY SL3 72 A3
EGH TW20 126 B4
Lynwood Cha BRAK RG12 13 K1
Lynwood Crs ASC SL5 152 B3
Lyon Cl STHA RG19 138 C4
Lyon Oaks BNFD RG42 121 L4
Lyon Rd CWTH RG45 148 F8
Lyon Sq TLHT RG30 87 K7
Lyon Wy FRIM GU16 181 M5
Lysander Cl WODY RG5 90 D6
Lytchet Minster Cl
BRAK RG12 150 C2 4
Lytham BRAK RG12 149 H3
Lytham Cl TLHT RG30 115 M2 2
Lytham End CALC RG31 86 E3 4
Lytham Rd WODY RG5 90 B7

M

Macbeth Ct BNFD RG42 122 B6
Macdonald Rd LTWR GU18 175 J6
Mace Cl EARL RG6 117 K5
Macklin Cl HUNG RG17 132 A1
Macphail Cl EWKG RG40 11 L2
Macrae Rd YTLY GU46 171 M8
Maddle Rd HUNG RG17 23 G7
Madingley BRAK RG12 149 L5
Madox Brown End
SHST GU47 173 H8 2
Mafeking Rd STWL/WRAY TW19 98 E8
Magdalene Rd SHPTN TW17 128 C8
SHST GU47 173 J4
Magill Cl THLE RG7 144 E4 2
Magna Carta La
STWL/WRAY TW19 98 A7
Magna Rd EGH TW20 125 L4
Magnolia Cl SHST GU47 173 G5 7
Magnolia Wy WWKG RG41 10 A8
Magpie Cl STHA RG19 137 L3
Magpie Wy CALC RG31 86 E8
Maguire Dr FRIM GU16 182 F3
Mahonia Cl CHOB/PIR GU24 176 C8 3
Maidenhead Court Pk
MDHD SL6 42 E3
Maidenhead Rd BNFD RG42 121 L1
EWKG RG40 120 B3
MDHD SL6 42 B2
WDSR SL4 6 F6
WDSR SL4 69 M7
Maiden Pl EARL RG6 118 A4
Main Dr ASC SL5 122 E6
BNFD RG42 122 E5
IVER SL0 73 H3
Mainprize Rd BRAK RG12 122 B6
Main Rd TADY RG26 165 G8
Mainstone Cl FRIM GU16 182 F7 1
Main St STHA RG19 161 K1
Maise Webster Cl
STWL/WRAY TW19 100 A6 3
Maitland Rd READ RG1 8 B7
Maiwand Gdns TLHT RG30 87 G7 1
Maize La BNFD RG42 122 A4
Majendie Cl NWBY RG14 136 A1 3
Major's Farm Rd DTCH/LGLY SL3 72 A7
Makepiece Rd BNFD RG42 121 L5
Maker Cl TLHT RG30 115 L1
Makins Rd HEN RG9 37 M6
Malders La MDHD SL6 41 L3
Maldon Cl TLHT RG30 88 A8 2
Malet Cl EGH TW20 127 G4 2
Malham Fell BRAK RG12 12 F8
Malham Rd STHA RG19 137 M3
Mallard Cl EARL RG6 117 K3
WAR/TWY RG10 91 H3
Mallard Ct NWBY RG14 14 C4
Mallard Dr SL SL1 44 C8
Mallard Rw READ RG1 8 F8
The Mallards HUNG RG17 77 K3
STA TW18 127 L7
Mallards Wy LTWR GU18 175 K6
Mallard Wy THLE RG7 140 E3
YTLY GU46 171 L8 2
Mallory Av CAV/SC RG4 62 F8
Mallowdale Rd BRAK RG12 150 B4 5
Mallow Pk MDHD SL6 2 A1
Malone Rd WODY RG5 90 A8
Malpas Rd SLN SL2 5 L5
Malta Rd FRIM GU16 183 G6
Maltby Wy EARL RG6 117 J6
Malt Hl BNFD RG42 122 B1
EGH TW20 126 B3
Malt House Cl WDSR SL4 97 L6
Malthouse La CHOB/PIR GU24 176 C7
READ RG1 8 D5
TADY RG26 165 G8
Maltings Pl READ RG1 8 F7
The Maltings KSCL RG20 28 D4
STA TW18 127 H2 1
Malton Av SL SL1 44 E7
Malt Shovel La HUNG RG17 49 J2
Malvern Cl WODY RG5 90 C8
Malvern Ct NWBY RG14 14 D7
READ RG1 9 M9
Malvern Rd BLKW GU17 180 C5
FARN GU14 181 G7
MDHD SL6 42 A5
Malvern Wy WAR/TWY RG10 65 G7
Managua Cl CAV/SC RG4 89 G4
Manchester Rd READ RG1 89 H6
Mandeville Cl TLHT RG30 115 J1
Manea Cl EARL RG6 117 M6 9
Manfield Cl SLN SL2 44 D4
Manners Rd WODY RG5 90 A7
Mannock Wy WODY RG5 90 E6
Manor Cl BNFD RG42 121 K5
Manor Ct MLW SL7 18 F3
SL SL1 70 C1 2
Manor Crs KSCL RG20 56 A2
Manorcrofts Rd EGH TW20 126 D4
Manor Dr SUN TW16 129 K7
Manor Farm Cl WDSR SL4 96 C2
Manor Farm Cottages
WDSR SL4 97 K4
Manor Farm La EGH TW20 126 D3
GOR/PANG RG8 85 M4
Manor Farm Rd WHIT RG2 116 E4
Manor Gdns FLKWH HP10 21 H1
SUN TW16 129 K6
Manor Gv MDHD SL6 69 G8
Manor House Dr ASC SL5 123 K5
Manor House La DTCH/LGLY SL3 71 L8
Manor La FELT TW13 101 K8
KSCL RG20 79 J1
KSCL RG20 80 D5
MARL SN8 48 B6
MDHD SL6 68 B2
NTHA RG18 81 L5
NTHA RG18 137 H2
STHA RG19 139 G7
SUN TW16 129 K7
Manor Leaze EGH TW20 126 E3
Manor Pk MARL SN8 130 D4
STA TW18 127 G1
Manor Park Cl TLHT RG30 86 F8 2
Manor Park Dr EWKG RG40 147 G8 1
EWKG RG40 147 H8 2
YTLY GU46 180 A1
Manor Pl EBED/NFELT TW14 101 K7
NWBY RG14 136 A1
STA TW18 127 L3
Manor Rd ASHF TW15 128 C3
GOR/PANG RG8 32 E8
GOR/PANG RG8 59 M7
HEN RG9 38 A6
MDHD SL6 68 B2
WDSR SL4 96 B1
Manor Wy BAGS GU19 175 H4
EGH TW20 126 C4
MDHD SL6 68 D6 2
Manor Wood Ga HEN RG9 64 D2
Manse La TADY RG26 165 G8
Mansel Cl SLN SL2 5 M1
Mansell Cl WDSR SL4 96 B1
Mansell Ct WHIT RG2 117 H4
Mansell Dr NWBY RG14 159 M1
Mansfield Cl ASC SL5 123 G7 1
Mansfield Crs BRAK RG12 149 L3
Mansfield Pl ASC SL5 123 G7
Mansfield Rd READ RG1 8 D9
WWKG RG41 10 B7
Man's Hl THLE RG7 142 F3
Mansion La IVER SL0 72 F1
Manston Dr BRAK RG12 149 L3
Mant Cl KSCL RG20 106 A2
Maple Cl BLKW GU17 180 F1
CAV/SC RG4 62 D2
MDHD SL6 2 B8
SHST GU47 172 C5
WWKG RG41 119 G3
Maple Ct EGH TW20 125 L4 5
GOR/PANG RG8 32 E8
Maple Crs NWBY RG14 14 E1
SLN SL2 5 M5
Mapledene CAV/SC RG4 88 B3
Maple Dr CWTH RG45 148 F7 1
LTWR GU18 175 J6
Mapledurham Dr
GOR/PANG RG8 86 F1
Mapledurham Vw CALC RG31 87 G4 1
Maple Gdns ASHF TW15 100 B8 1
WHIT RG2 117 H4
YTLY GU46 180 A1
Maple Gv TADY RG26 164 E6
Maple La GOR/PANG RG8 84 E1
Maple Ri MLW SL7 19 H3
Maple Wy FELT TW13 129 K1
Maplin Pk DTCH/LGLY SL3 72 E2
Marathon Cl WODY RG5 90 E6
Marbeck Cl WDSR SL4 70 A8
Marbull Wy BNFD RG42 121 L4
Marchant Cl STHA RG19 137 G7 1
Marcheria Cl BRAK RG12 149 L3 2
Marchwood Av CAV/SC RG4 62 F6
Marcia Ct SL SL1 70 C1 3
Marconi Rd NWBY RG14 15 G2
Mardale CBLY GU15 182 F2
Marefield EARL RG6 117 M4
Marefield Rd MLW SL7 19 G4
Mare La BNFD RG42 93 H3
Marescroft Rd SLN SL2 44 B5
Mareshall Av BNFD RG42 121 L4
Marfleet Cl EARL RG6 118 B4 3
Margaret Cl STA TW18 128 A5
WHIT RG2 116 F7
Marigold Cl CWTH RG45 148 C7
Marina Cl CHERT KT16 155 L5
Marina Wy IVER SL0 47 J8
SL SL1 44 A8 1
Mariners Cl TADY RG26 165 G8
Mariners La THLE RG7 112 D3
Marino Wy EWKG RG40 146 D8
Markby Wy EARL RG6 118 B4
Market La DTCH/LGLY SL3 72 F3
Market Pl HEN RG9 38 A4
READ RG1 9 G6
Market St BRAK RG12 13 H4
MDHD SL6 3 H5
NWBY RG14 14 E5
WDSR SL4 7 K6
Markham Ct CBLY GU15 174 A8 2
Marks Rd WWKG RG41 10 C2
The Markway SUN TW16 129 M7
Marlborough Av READ RG1 117 G1
Marlborough Ct READ RG1 8 C9
Marlborough Ri CBLY GU15 174 B8
Marlborough Rd ASHF TW15 128 B3
DTCH/LGLY SL3 72 A4
MDHD SL6 41 K8
Marlborough Wy CALC RG31 114 E2 3
Marlin Cl SUN TW16 129 H4 2
Marlin Ct MLW SL7 19 G5 1
Marling Cl CALC RG31 86 F4 2
Marlow Common MLW SL7 18 C4
The Marlowes NWBY RG14 136 C6
Marlow Rd HEN RG9 38 B3
MDHD SL6 2 F4
MDHD SL6 41 H2
MLW SL7 19 G7
MLW SL7 19 M1
Marlston Rd NTHA RG18 109 M1
Marmion Rd HEN RG9 38 B6
Marnham Pl ADL/WDHM KT15 155 M8
Marriott Cl EBED/NFELT TW14 101 G5
Marriott Lodge Cl
ADL/WDHM KT15 155 M8
Marsack St CAV/SC RG4 88 F4
Marshall Cl FARN GU14 181 J7
FRIM GU16 183 G4 1
GOR/PANG RG8 87 G2
Marshall Rd SHST GU47 173 G7
Marshalls Ct NWBY RG14 136 A1 4
Marshfield DTCH/LGLY SL3 71 M8
Marshland Sq CAV/SC RG4 88 E1
Marsh La ADL/WDHM KT15 155 L8
HTWY RG27 171 J7
HUNG RG17 131 L1
MDHD SL6 69 J2
NTHA RG18 109 G2
NWBY RG14 14 E3
Marsh Rd NTHA RG18 138 B2
Marshwood Rd LTWR GU18 176 A6
Marston Dr FARN GU14 181 L7
NWBY RG14 137 G1
Marston Wy ASC SL5 123 H7 2
Martel Cl CBLY GU15 174 F7
Marten Pl CALC RG31 86 E3
Martin Cl WDSR SL4 69 M8
WODY RG5 90 B8
Martindale IVER SL0 46 F5
Martindale Av CBLY GU15 182 F3
Martineau La WAR/TWY RG10 91 H7 1
Martin Rd MDHD SL6 3 G2
SL SL1 71 H3
Martins Cl BLKW GU17 181 G2
Martins Dr WWKG RG41 10 E3
Martins La BRAK RG12 122 B8
Martin's Pln SLN SL2 45 J4
Martins St EARL RG6 117 M5 4
The Martins STHA RG19 138 C4
Martin Wy FRIM GU16 182 B5
Marunden Gn SLN SL2 44 C4
Maryland EWKG RG40 147 G7
Maryland Wy SUN TW16 129 K7
Mary Md BNFD RG42 122 A4 1
Maryside DTCH/LGLY SL3 72 B2
Masefield Rd NTHA RG18 137 M2
Masefield Wy
STWL/WRAY TW19 100 C7
Mason Cl YTLY GU46 180 B1 2
Masonic Hall Rd CHERT KT16 155 J3
Mason Pl SHST GU47 172 C6
Mason Rd FARN GU14 181 H8
Masons Rd SL SL1 44 B8
Mason St READ RG1 8 B5
Master Cl WODY RG5 90 E6
Mathisen Wy DTCH/LGLY SL3 73 H8
Matlock Rd CAV/SC RG4 88 B2
Matthew Arnold Cl
STA TW18 127 M4 1
Matthews Cha BNFD RG42 121 J5
Matthews Cl STHA RG19 137 L3 2
Matthewsgreen Rd WWKG RG41 10 C1
Matthews La STA TW18 127 J2 1
Matthews Rd CBLY GU15 173 M6
Maultway Cl CBLY GU15 174 E6 1
Maultway Crs CBLY GU15 174 E6
Maultway North CBLY GU15 174 E5
The Maultway CBLY GU15 174 E6
CBLY GU15 183 G2
Mawbray Cl EARL RG6 117 M3
Maxine Cl SHST GU47 172 E5
Maxwell Cl WODY RG5 90 B6
Maxwell Rd ASHF TW15 128 F4
Maybrick Cl SHST GU47 172 C5
Maybury Cl FRIM GU16 182 A6
SL SL1 44 A6
May Cl SHST GU47 173 G6
Mayfair TLHT RG30 87 G7
Mayfair Dr NWBY RG14 14 A7
Mayfield Av CALC RG31 114 E2
Mayfield Cl ASHF TW15 128 E4
Mayfield Ct HTWY RG27 171 G6
Mayfield Dr CAV/SC RG4 88 F3
Mayfield Gdns STA TW18 127 J5
Mayfield Rd CBLY GU15 181 L5 1
FARN GU14 181 J7
May Flds WWKG RG41 118 D5
Mayflower Dr YTLY GU46 171 K7
The Maying WHIT RG2 116 E8 2
Maynard Cl NTHA RG18 137 M1
Mayors La NWBY RG14 14 E5
Mayow Cl STHA RG19 138 C4
May Pk CALC RG31 115 H2
Maypole Rd MDHD SL6 43 K6
Mays Cl EARL RG6 117 L1
Mays La EARL RG6 117 L1
Mays Rd EWKG RG40 11 M5
Maywood Dr CBLY GU15 174 E7
Mc Carthy Wy EWKG RG40 147 J6
Mccrae's Wk WAR/TWY RG10 65 G4
Mcnair Cl EARL RG6 117 K5 2
Mead Av DTCH/LGLY SL3 72 E2
Mead Cl CALC RG31 86 E8
DTCH/LGLY SL3 72 E2
EGH TW20 126 E4
MLW SL7 19 J3
STWL/WRAY TW19 98 A7
Mead Ct EGH TW20 126 F4 1
Meadfield Av DTCH/LGLY SL3 72 D3
Meadfield Rd DTCH/LGLY SL3 72 E3
Meadhurst Rd CHERT KT16 155 L5 2
Mead La CHERT KT16 155 L5
GOR/PANG RG8 58 F8
Meadowbank Rd LTWR GU18 175 M5
Meadowbrook Cl
DTCH/LGLY SL3 99 H1
Meadow Cl BLKW GU17 181 G2
GOR/PANG RG8 32 F8 1
MLW SL7 19 J5
STHA RG19 137 M3
WDSR SL4 97 L5
Meadow Ct STA TW18 127 H1 1
Meadow Crs KSCL RG20 56 B1
Meadowcroft Rd WHIT RG2 116 E6
Meadow Gdns STA TW18 127 G3
Meadow La WDSR SL4 7 G4
Meadow Rd ASHF TW15 129 G3
DTCH/LGLY SL3 72 B3
EARL RG6 118 A3
FARN GU14 181 L7
HEN RG9 38 B5
NWBY RG14 14 D9
READ RG1 8 D3
VW GU25 153 H2
WWKG RG41 10 C7
Meadows End SUN TW16 129 K6
Meadowside CALC RG31 86 E5 1
Meadowside Rd GOR/PANG RG8 86 A1
Meadowsweet Cl NTHA RG18 138 B2
Meadow Vw STWL/WRAY TW19 99 J4
WWKG RG41 119 G3
Meadow View La MDHD SL6 68 B6
Meadow Wk WWKG RG41 10 C6
Meadow Wy ADL/WDHM KT15 155 L8
BLKW GU17 180 F1
BNEND SL8 20 D1
BNFD RG42 12 E1
CHOB/PIR GU24 176 C8
MDHD SL6 69 G8
MDHD SL6 69 J2
THLE RG7 114 A3
WDSR SL4 97 L5
WWKG RG41 10 C7
Meads Cl KSCL RG20 54 A7
The Mead HUNG RG17 77 L3
Mead Wk DTCH/LGLY SL3 72 E2
Meadway ASHF TW15 128 D2
FRIM GU16 182 C4
Mead Wy SL SL1 44 A6
Meadway STA TW18 127 K5
Meadway Cl STA TW18 127 J5
The Meadway TLHT RG30 87 H7
The Mearings TLHT RG30 143 H2
Measham Wy EARL RG6 117 M5
Meavy Gdns WHIT RG2 116 E4
Medallion Pl MDHD SL6 3 M5
Medhurst Cl CHOB/PIR GU24 177 J4
Medill Cl GOR/PANG RG8 34 B6 1
Medina Cl WWKG RG41 119 H8
Medlake Rd EGH TW20 126 F4
Medlar Dr BLKW GU17 181 J3
Medman Cl UX/CGN UB8 47 M3 4
Medway Cl NTHA RG18 137 L1
WWKG RG41 10 A4
Medway Dr FARN GU14 181 H7
Melbourne Av SL SL1 4 B2
WWKG RG41 118 F5
Melbury Cl CHERT KT16 155 K4
Meldreth Wy EARL RG6 117 M5
Meldrum Cl NWBY RG14 135 M8 1
Melford Gn CAV/SC RG4 63 H8 4
Melksham Cl EARL RG6 117 H6
Melling Cl EARL RG6 118 B3
Melody Cl WWKG RG41 118 F3
Melrose BRAK RG12 149 L5
Melrose Av EARL RG6 117 K1
Melrose Gdns WHIT RG2 146 B4
Melton Ct MDHD SL6 3 H6
Melville Av FRIM GU16 182 C5
Membury Cl FRIM GU16 182 D7 3
Membury Wk BRAK RG12 150 C1 3
Memorial Av HEN RG9 64 B4
Mendip Cl DTCH/LGLY SL3 72 D5
WAR/TWY RG10 90 E2
Mendip Dr CALC RG31 86 D8 2
Mendip Rd BRAK RG12 150 B2
FARN GU14 181 H7
Menpes Rd CALC RG31 86 F2
Meon Cl FARN GU14 181 G8
TADY RG26 164 D5
Merchants Pl READ RG1 8 F5
Mercian Wy SL SL1 70 B1
Mercia Rd MDHD SL6 67 L2 3
Mercury Av WWKG RG41 119 H8 13
Mereoak La THLE RG7 144 B3
Mere Rd SL SL1 71 J3
Merlewood BRAK RG12 150 A2 1
Merlin Cl DTCH/LGLY SL3 72 E6 4
Merlin Clove BNFD RG42 122 E4
Mermaid Cl WWKG RG41 118 E4
Merrivale Gdns WHIT RG2 116 E5 1
Merryhill Green La
WWKG RG41 119 G3 1
Merryhill Rd BNFD RG42 12 F1
Merrylands CHERT KT16 155 H7
Merryman Dr CWTH RG45 148 C8
Merryweather Cl EWKG RG40 147 J5 2
Merrywood Pk CBLY GU15 182 C2
Mersey Wy NTHA RG18 137 L1
Merthyr V CAV/SC RG4 62 D8
Merton Cl MDHD SL6 67 M3 4
SHST GU47 173 J4
Merton Rd SL SL1 71 K3
Merton Rd North WHIT RG2 116 E5
Merton Rd South WHIT RG2 116 E5
Merwin Wy WDSR SL4 96 A2 1
Metcalf Rd ASHF TW15 128 E3
Meteor Cl WODY RG5 90 D7
The Mews READ RG1 89 H8
Meyrick Dr NWBY RG14 159 M1
Michaelmas Cl YTLY GU46 180 A2
Micheldever Wy BRAK RG12 150 C3
Michelet Cl LTWR GU18 175 L5
Micklands Rd CAV/SC RG4 89 G2
Mickle Hl SHST GU47 172 D5
Midcroft SLN SL2 44 E5
Middle Cl CBLY GU15 174 F8
NWBY RG14 136 A7
Middlefields WAR/TWY RG10 65 H8
Middle Gordon Rd CBLY GU15 181 M1
Middle Gn DTCH/LGLY SL3 46 B8
Middlegreen Rd DTCH/LGLY SL3 72 A2
Middle Hl EGH TW20 125 M3
Middlemoor Rd FRIM GU16 182 B6
Middleton Ct NWBY RG14 137 H1
Middleton Gdns FARN GU14 181 H8
Middleton Rd CBLY GU15 174 B8
Middletons Cl HUNG RG17 104 B8
Middle Wk SL SL1 43 L4
Midsummer Meadow
CAV/SC RG4 62 C8 1
Midway Av CHERT KT16 127 L8
EGH TW20 126 E8
Midway Cl STA TW18 127 L1

Midwinter Cl TLHT RG30 ...... 87 H6
Milbanke Ct BRAK RG12 ...... 12 D4
Milbanke Wy BRAK RG12 ...... 12 D4
Milden Cl FRIM GU16 ...... 182 D8
Milden Gdns FRIM GU16 ...... 182 D8
Mildenhall Rd SL SL1 ...... 4 E2
Mile Elm MLW SL7 ...... 19 J3
Miles Pl LTWR GU18 ...... 175 J7
Milestone Av WAR/TWY RG10 ...... 90 D2
Milestone Crs WAR/TWY RG10 ...... 90 D2
Miles Wy WODY RG5 ...... 90 D7
Milford Ct SL SL1 ...... 5 K9
Milkhouse Rd KSCL RG20 ...... 107 G8
Mill Av UX/CGN UB8 ...... 47 M3
Mill Bank HUNG RG17 ...... 133 K3
Millbank Crs WODY RG5 ...... 90 C8
Millboard Rd BNEND SL8 ...... 20 E3
Millbridge Rd YTLY GU46 ...... 171 L6
Millbrook Wy DTCH/LGLY SL3 ...... 99 H1
Mill Cl BAGS GU19 ...... 175 G3
  WWKG RG41 ...... 10 C3
Milldown Av GOR/PANG RG8 ...... 32 F7
Milldown Rd GOR/PANG RG8 ...... 32 F7
Millers Cl GOR/PANG RG8 ...... 32 F7
  STA TW18 ...... 127 L3
Miller's Fld HUNG RG17 ...... 77 K3
Millers Gv CALC RG31 ...... 115 H2
Millers Rd TADY RG26 ...... 164 E6
Milley La WAR/TWY RG10 ...... 65 L6
Milley Rd WAR/TWY RG10 ...... 66 C8
Mill Farm Av SUN TW16 ...... 129 H5
Mill Fld BACS 175 G3
Millfield HUNG RG17 ...... 49 L3
  SUN TW16 ...... 129 C6
Millford Rd RCAD RG1 ...... 8 D3
Mill Gn BNFD RG42 ...... 12 A1
  CAV/SC RG4 ...... 9 K2
Millgreen La SHST GU47 ...... 162 C4
Mill House La CHERT KT16 ...... 154 E1
Millins Cl SHST GU47 ...... 173 G5
Mill La ASC SL5 ...... 124 E7
  BRAK RG12 ...... 149 K2
  CALC RG31 ...... 115 H2
  CAV/SC RG4 ...... 61 M5
  DTCH/LGLY SL3 ...... 98 C2
  EARL RG6 ...... 118 B4
  EGH TW20 ...... 154 F1
  HEN RG9 ...... 38 C6
  HEN RG9 ...... 64 D4
  HUNG RG17 ...... 49 M4
  MDHD SL6 ...... 20 E7
  MDHD SL6 ...... 40 C2
  MDHD SL6 ...... 42 F6
  NWBY RG14 ...... 14 F4
  READ RG1 ...... 9 G7
  THLE RG7 ...... 140 F3
  WDSR SL4 ...... 6 D4
  WWKG RG41 ...... 118 D6
  YTLY GU46 ...... 172 A6
Mill Md STA TW18 ...... 127 J2
Millmead WWKG RG41 ...... 10 C3
Millmere YTLY GU46 ...... 172 A3
Mill Pl DTCH/LGLY SL3 ...... 98 A1
Mill Pond Rd BFOR GU20 ...... 151 L8
Mill Reef Cl STHA RG19 ...... 137 J3
Mill Ride ASC SL5 ...... 123 G6
Mill Rd CAV/SC RG4 ...... 9 J2
  GOR/PANG RG8 ...... 32 F7
  HEN RG9 ...... 64 E3
  MLW SL7 ...... 19 H5
  TLHT RG30 ...... 115 H4
  TLHT RG30 ...... 115 J4
Millside BNEND SL8 ...... 20 F3
Mills Sp WDSR SL4 ...... 97 L6
Millstream La SL SL1 ...... 70 B1
Mill St DTCH/LGLY SL3 ...... 73 C7
  SLN SL2 ...... 5 H6
Mill Wy EBED/NFELT TW14 ...... 101 L4
Millworth La WHIT RG2 ...... 145 H2
Milman Cl BRAK RG12 ...... 122 D7
Milman Rd WHIT RG2 ...... 116 E1
Milner Rd SL SL1 ...... 43 K6
Milsom Cl WHIT RG2 ...... 145 H1
Milton Cl BRAK RG12 ...... 149 L3
  DTCH/LGLY SL3 ...... 98 D2
  HEN RG9 ...... 38 A4
Milton Ct EWKG RG40 ...... 10 F4
Milton Dr EWKG RG40 ...... 10 F4
Milton Gdns EWKG RG40 ...... 10 F5
  STWL/WRAY TW19 ...... 100 C7
Milton Rd EARL RG6 ...... 89 K7
  EGH TW20 ...... 126 C3
  EWKG RG40 ...... 10 F5
  SLN SL2 ...... 45 G5
  WWKG RG41 ...... 10 F3
Milton Wy WAR/TWY RG10 ...... 91 J1
Milverton Cl MDHD SL6 ...... 67 L3
Milward Gdns BRAK RG12 ...... 120 F7
Mina Av DTCH/LGLY SL3 ...... 72 A2
Minchin Gn BNFD RG42 ...... 120 F3
Mincing La CHOB/PIR GU24 ...... 177 J4
Minden Cl WWKG RG41 ...... 119 H8
Minibank Cl EBED/NFELT TW14 ...... 101 K5
Ministry Rd STHA RG19 ...... 161 K1
Mink Ct HSLWW TW4 ...... 101 M1
Minley Rd FARN GU14 ...... 180 B5
Minniecroft Rd SL SL1 ...... 43 L4
Minorca Av FRIM GU16 ...... 183 H4
Minorca Rd FRIM GU16 ...... 183 H5
Minstead Cl BRAK RG12 ...... 122 C8
  TADY RG26 ...... 164 E8
Minster St READ RG1 ...... 8 F6
Minster Wy DTCH/LGLY SL3 ...... 72 C2
Mint Cl EARL RG6 ...... 117 J5
Minton Cl TLHT RG30 ...... 87 J6
Minton Ri MDHD SL6 ...... 43 L7
Mirador Crs SLN SL2 ...... 5 M4
Mire La WAR/TWY RG10 ...... 92 A3
Missenden Cl
  EBED/NFELT TW14 ...... 101 J7
Missenden Gdns SL SL1 ...... 43 L7
Mistletoe Rd YTLY GU46 ...... 180 A2
Mitcham Cl WHIT RG2 ...... 116 E1
Mitcham Rd CBLY GU15 ...... 174 D5
Mitchell Cl SL SL1 ...... 70 D2
Mitchell Wy WODY RG5 ...... 90 D7
Mitford Cl WHIT RG2 ...... 117 G6
Mixnams La CHERT KT16 ...... 127 K8

Moat Dr SLN SL2 ...... 45 M6
Moat Side FELT TW13 ...... 129 M2
Modbury Gdns WHIT RG2 ...... 116 F4
Moffatts Cl SHST GU47 ...... 172 D6
Moffy Hl MDHD SL6 ...... 42 B4
Mohawk Wy WODY RG5 ...... 90 E7
Mole Cl FARN GU14 ...... 181 G8
Mole Rd WHIT RG2 ...... 146 C1
  WWKG RG41 ...... 118 D6
Moles Cl EWKG RG40 ...... 11 J7
Mollison Cl WODY RG5 ...... 90 E6
Molly Millar Br WWKG RG41 ...... 10 E9
Molly Millars Cl WWKG RG41 ...... 10 E9
Molly Millar's La WWKG RG41 ...... 10 C8
Molyneux Rd BFOR GU20 ...... 176 A2
Molyns Ms SL SL1 ...... 70 B1
Monarch Cl EBED/NFELT TW14 ...... 101 H6
Moneyrow Gn MDHD SL6 ...... 68 D7
Monkey Island La MDHD SL6 ...... 69 H4
Monksbarn WHIT RG2 ...... 117 G4
Monks Cl ASC SL5 ...... 151 L3
Monks Dr ASC SL5 ...... 151 L3
Monksfield Wy SLN SL2 ...... 44 D5
Monks Hollow MLW SL7 ...... 19 H1
Monkshood Cl EWKG RG40 ...... 11 L3
Monks La NWBY RG14 ...... 136 B7
Monks Rd VW GU25 ...... 154 A1
  WDSR SL4 ...... 96 A1
Monks Wk ASC SL5 ...... 151 L3
Monks Wy STA TW18 ...... 128 A5
  TLHT RG30 ...... 116 A1
Monkswood Cl NWBY RG14 ...... 136 A7
Monks Wood Crs TADY RG26 ...... 164 F7
Monktons La THLE RG7 ...... 166 F1
Mons Cl WWKG RG41 ...... 119 H8
Mons Wk EGH TW20 ...... 126 F3
Montacute Dr STHA RG19 ...... 138 C4
Montague Cl CBLY GU15 ...... 181 L1
  EWKG RG40 ...... 11 M3
  LTWR GU18 ...... 175 K5
Montague Rd SL SL1 ...... 5 G4
Montague St CAV/SC RG4 ...... 9 J1
  READ RG1 ...... 9 L7
Montague Ter NWBY RG14 ...... 14 A9
Montagu Rd DTCH/LGLY SL3 ...... 71 L8
Montem La SL SL1 ...... 4 B7
Montgomery Cl SHST GU47 ...... 172 E6
Montgomery Dr THLE RG7 ...... 144 E4
Montgomery Pl SLN SL2 ...... 45 M7
Montgomery Rd NWBY RG14 ...... 14 A9
Montpelier Dr CAV/SC RG4 ...... 89 H1
Montpellier Ct WDSR SL4 ...... 97 H3
Montrose Av DTCH/LGLY SL3 ...... 71 M7
  SL SL1 ...... 44 E7
Montrose Cl ASHF TW15 ...... 128 F4
  FRIM GU16 ...... 182 B4
Montrose Dr MDHD SL6 ...... 41 K8
Montrose Rd
  EBED/NFELT TW14 ...... 101 G5
Montrose Wy DTCH/LGLY SL3 ...... 72 A8
Monument Cl WWKG RG41 ...... 136 A7
Monycrower Dr MDHD SL6 ...... 2 E5
Moorbridge Rd MDHD SL6 ...... 3 K4
Moor Cl EWKG RG40 ...... 147 H7
  SHST GU47 ...... 173 H5
Moor Copse Cl EARL RG6 ...... 117 L3
  BNFD RG42 ...... 12 B2
Moordale Av BNFD RG42 ...... 12 D2
  BNFD RG42 ...... 12 E1
Moore Cl SL SL1 ...... 70 E2
Moore Grove Crs EGH TW20 ...... 126 B5
Moor End MDHD SL6 ...... 68 F5
Moor Rd CHOB/PIR GU24 ...... 183 L8
Moores Gn EWKG RG40 ...... 11 L2
Moores La WDSR SL4 ...... 70 C4
Moore's Pl HUNG RG17 ...... 131 M1
Moorfields Cl STA TW18 ...... 127 H6
Moor Furlong SL SL1 ...... 70 B1
Moorhayes Dr STA TW18 ...... 127 M8
Moorhen Dr EARL RG6 ...... 117 L5
The Moorings
  STWL/WRAY TW19 ...... 97 M6
Moorland Rd WDR/YW UB7 ...... 73 M7
Moorlands Dr MDHD SL6 ...... 41 J6
Moorlands Rd CBLY GU15 ...... 181 K2
Moor La MDHD SL6 ...... 42 C5
  STWL/WRAY TW19 ...... 98 F7
  STWL/WRAY TW19 ...... 99 G8
  WDR/YW UB7 ...... 73 M6
Moormede Crs STA TW18 ...... 127 J2
Moor Pl BFOR GU20 ...... 175 L1
Moor Rd FARN GU14 ...... 181 K5
  FRIM GU16 ...... 182 C6
Moorside Cl FARN GU14 ...... 181 K5
  MDHD SL6 ...... 42 C5
The Moors GOR/PANG RG8 ...... 86 A1
  STHA RG19 ...... 138 A4
Moorstown Ct SL SL1 ...... 4 F9
The Moor MLW SL7 ...... 19 M2
Moray Av SHST GU47 ...... 173 G7
Moray Dr SLN SL2 ...... 5 K3
Morden Cl BRAK RG12 ...... 150 C1
Moreau Wk DTCH/LGLY SL3 ...... 46 B7
Morecambe Av CAV/SC RG4 ...... 88 B1
Moreland Cl DTCH/LGLY SL3 ...... 72 F7
Moreleigh Cl WHIT RG2 ...... 116 F6
Morella Cl VW GU25 ...... 153 M1
Morello Dr DTCH/LGLY SL3 ...... 72 C1
Moreton Wy SL SL1 ...... 70 A1
Morgan Rd READ RG1 ...... 116 F1
Moriston Cl TLHT RG30 ...... 87 L6
Morlais CAV/SC RG4 ...... 88 C1
Morlands Ar TLHT RG30 ...... 115 K1
Morley Cl DTCH/LGLY SL3 ...... 72 C2
Morley Pl HUNG RG17 ...... 132 A1
Mornington Av EWKG RG40 ...... 147 J6
Mornington Cl TADY RG26 ...... 164 A5
Mornington Rd ASHF TW15 ...... 128 F3
Morpeth Cl WHIT RG2 ...... 116 F3
Morrice Cl DTCH/LGLY SL3 ...... 72 C4
Morris Pl MLW SL7 ...... 19 G4
Mortaine Rd ASHF TW15 ...... 128 A1
Mortimer Cl WHIT RG2 ...... 116 F7
Mortimer Gdns TADY RG26 ...... 164 F7
Mortimer La THLE RG7 ...... 143 G7
  THLE RG7 ...... 167 G6
Mortimer Rd DTCH/LGLY SL3 ...... 72 A3
Morton Cl FRIM GU16 ...... 182 C7

Moss Cl CAV/SC RG4 ...... 88 F3
Mossy V MDHD SL6 ...... 42 A5
Moulsham Copse La YTLY GU46 ...... 171 L7
Moulsham La YTLY GU46 ...... 171 L7
Mountbatten Cl NWBY RG14 ...... 136 F1
  SL SL1 ...... 71 K3
Mountbatten Ri SHST GU47 ...... 172 C5
Mount Cl MDHD SL6 ...... 42 D4
  NWBY RG14 ...... 14 E8
The Mount Cl VW GU25 ...... 154 A3
Mountfield GOR/PANG RG8 ...... 32 F7
Mount La BRAK RG12 ...... 13 J6
  KSCL RG20 ...... 52 C6
Mount Lee EGH TW20 ...... 126 B3
Mount Pleasant BRAK RG12 ...... 13 K6
  READ RG1 ...... 9 H8
  SHST GU47 ...... 172 D5
  TADY RG26 ...... 164 D6
  WWKG RG41 ...... 10 D5
Mount Pleasant Cl LTWR GU18 ...... 175 K5
Mount Pleasant Gv READ RG1 ...... 9 H9
Mount Rd CHOB/PIR GU24 ...... 177 L7
  KSCL RG20 ...... 159 J7
  NTHA RG18 ...... 138 A2
Mountsfield Cl
  STWL/WRAY TW19 ...... 99 K4
Mounts Hl ASC SL5 ...... 123 M3
  WDSR SL4 ...... 95 M8
Mount St WHIT RG2 ...... 116 E1
The Mount CAV/SC RG4 ...... 88 C3
  READ RG1 ...... 117 G1
  VW GU25 ...... 154 A3
Mount Vw HEN RG9 ...... 38 A3
Mowbray Crs EGH TW20 ...... 126 D3
Mowbray Dr TLHT RG30 ...... 87 H2
Mower Cl EWKG RG40 ...... 120 C7
Moyleen Ri MLW SL7 ...... 18 F5
Muckhatch La EGH TW20 ...... 126 E8
Mud La HTWY RG27 ...... 170 C5
  KSCL RG20 ...... 54 A8
Muirfield Cl READ RG1 ...... 9 M7
Mulberry Av STWL/WRAY TW19 ...... 100 B7
  WDSR SL4 ...... 97 J2
Mulberry Cl CWTH RG45 ...... 172 F2
  SHST GU47 ...... 173 G6
  WODY RG5 ...... 90 B8
Mulberry Dr DTCH/LGLY SL3 ...... 72 B5
Mulberry Wk MDHD SL6 ...... 2 A3
Mulberry Wy THLE RG7 ...... 114 B4
Mulfords Hl TADY RG26 ...... 164 E5
Mulgrave Rd FRIM GU16 ...... 182 C4
Mullens Rd EGH TW20 ...... 126 F3
Mulroy Dr CBLY GU15 ...... 174 D8
Mumbery Hl WAR/TWY RG10 ...... 65 H5
Mumberson Cl ASHF TW15 ...... 128 D2
Muncaster Rd ASHF TW15 ...... 128 C2
Munday Ct BNFD RG42 ...... 121 H5
Mundaydean La MLW SL7 ...... 18 C1
Mundesley Sp SL SL1 ...... 4 E3
Mundesley St READ RG1 ...... 9 L2
Munkle Marsh STHA RG19 ...... 138 D3
Munnings Dr SHST GU47 ...... 173 G8
Murdoch Cl STA TW18 ...... 127 K3
Murdoch Rd EWKG RG40 ...... 11 H8
Murray Ct ASC SL5 ...... 151 M3
Murray Rd WWKG RG41 ...... 10 C5
Murrellhill La BNFD RG42 ...... 120 F6
Murrells La CBLY GU15 ...... 181 L3
Murrin Rd MDHD SL6 ...... 2 A3
Mushroom Castle BNFD RG42 ...... 122 E4
Musquash Wy HSLWW TW4 ...... 101 M1
Mustard La CAV/SC RG4 ...... 90 B5
Mustard Mill Rd STA TW18 ...... 127 J2
Muswell Cl THLE RG7 ...... 114 B3
Mutton Oaks BNFD RG42 ...... 121 G6
Myddleton Rd UX/CGN UB8 ...... 47 M2
Myers Wy FRIM GU16 ...... 183 G4
Mylne Sq EWKG RG40 ...... 11 K5
Mylum Cl WHIT RG2 ...... 116 F8
The Myrke DTCH/LGLY SL3 ...... 71 J4
Myrtle Av EBED/NFELT TW14 ...... 101 H3
Myrtle Cl CALC RG31 ...... 86 F5
  DTCH/LGLY SL3 ...... 73 H8
  LTWR GU18 ...... 175 L6
  THLE RG7 ...... 142 E3
Myrtle Crs SLN SL2 ...... 5 H4
Myrtle Dr BLKW GU17 ...... 181 G2
Myton Wk THLE RG7 ...... 114 B3

N

Nabbs Hill Cl CALC RG31 ...... 114 F1
Nairn Cl FRIM GU16 ...... 182 B4
Nalderhill Rd KSCL RG20 ...... 106 E7
Nallhead Rd FELT TW13 ...... 129 M3
Napier Cl CWTH RG45 ...... 172 F2
Napier Dr CBLY GU15 ...... 174 D7
Napier Rd ASHF TW15 ...... 129 G5
  CWTH RG45 ...... 172 F2
  MDHD SL6 ...... 41 L8
  READ RG1 ...... 9 K4
Napiers MARL SN8 ...... 130 A8
Narromine Dr CALC RG31 ...... 115 J2
Naseby BRAK RG12 ...... 149 L5
Naseby Ri NWBY RG14 ...... 137 G1
Nash Cl EARL RG6 ...... 117 K3
Nashdom La SL SL1 ...... 43 K1
Nash Gdns ASC SL5 ...... 123 G7
Nash Grove La EWKG RG40 ...... 147 H4
Nash Pk BNFD RG42 ...... 120 F4
Nash Rd DTCH/LGLY SL3 ...... 72 C5
Natalie Cl EBED/NFELT TW14 ...... 101 G6
The Naylors THLE RG7 ...... 145 G8
Neals La CAV/SC RG4 ...... 35 L4
Neath Gdns TLHT RG30 ...... 87 J7
Needham Cl WDSR SL4 ...... 70 B8
Neil Cl ASHF TW15 ...... 128 F3
Nell Gwynne Av ASC SL5 ...... 152 A1
Nelson Cl BRAK RG12 ...... 122 B7
  DTCH/LGLY SL3 ...... 73 A4
  EBED/NFELT TW14 ...... 101 J7
Nelson Rd ASHF TW15 ...... 128 B3
  CAV/SC RG4 ...... 9 J1
  WDSR SL4 ...... 96 C2
Nelson's La WAR/TWY RG10 ...... 119 L1
Nelson Wy CBLY GU15 ...... 180 A4
Neptune Cl WWKG RG41 ...... 119 H8
Netherton BRAK RG12 ...... 12 F8
Netley Cl CAV/SC RG4 ...... 63 H8
Nettlecombe BRAK RG12 ...... 150 A2
Nevelle Cl BNFD RG42 ...... 121 G6
Neville Cl WAR/TWY RG10 ...... 66 C8
Neville Dr STHA RG19 ...... 138 B3
Neville Duke Rd FARN GU14 ...... 181 J6
Nevis Rd CALC RG31 ...... 87 G3
Newalls Ri WAR/TWY RG10 ...... 65 H4
Newark Rd BFOR GU20 ...... 151 L8
  BLKW GU17 ...... 180 B5
Newark St READ RG1 ...... 9 H8
New Bath Rd WAR/TWY RG10 ...... 90 D2
Newberry Crs WDSR SL4 ...... 69 M8
Newberry Wy SL SL1 ...... 4 D9
Newbold Rd NWBY RG14 ...... 136 A1
Newbolt Cl NTHA RG18 ...... 137 M1
New Bright St READ RG1 ...... 8 F8
Newbury Cl WAR/TWY RG10 ...... 90 E2
Newbury Dr MDHD SL6 ...... 3 L6
Newbury Hl NTHA RG18 ...... 82 C1
Newbury La KSCL RG20 ...... 56 A2
Newbury Rd HUNG RG17 ...... 49 M4
  HUNG 77 L4
  NTHA RG18 ...... 81 K8
Newbury St HUNG RG17 ...... 49 L4
  HUNG 133 L4
Newcastle Rd WHIT RG2 ...... 116 F2
Newchurch Rd SL SL1 ...... 44 C6
  TADY RG26 ...... 164 D5
New Ct MLW SL7 ...... 19 G4
Newcourt UX/CGN UB8 ...... 47 M3
Newell Gn BNFD RG42 ...... 121 M3
Newell's La CAV/SC RG4 ...... 61 L7
Newfield Av FARN GU14 ...... 181 H8
Newfield Gdns MLW SL7 ...... 19 J3
Newfield Rd CAV/SC RG4 ...... 36 C8
  MLW SL7 ...... 19 J4
Newfield Wy SL SL1 ...... 19 H4
New Forest Ride BRAK RG12 ...... 150 B4
Newfoundland Rd FRIM GU16 ...... 183 G4
Newhaven Crs ASHF TW15 ...... 129 G3
Newhaven Sp SLN SL2 ...... 44 E5
New Hl GOR/PANG RG8 ...... 86 F1
Newhurst Gdns BNFD RG42 ...... 122 A3
Newlands Av CAV/SC RG4 ...... 88 E3
Newlands Cl YTLY GU46 ...... 180 A1
Newlands Dr DTCH/LGLY SL3 ...... 99 H2
  MDHD SL6 ...... 41 K7
Newlands La HEN RG9 ...... 35 M3
Newlands Rd FRIM GU16 ...... 181 L5
New Lane Hl TLHT RG30 ...... 87 H8
Newlyn Gdns WHIT RG2 ...... 116 E5
Newmarket Cl EARL RG6 ...... 118 A4
New Meadow ASC SL5 ...... 123 G6
New Mile Rd ASC SL5 ...... 123 L7
New Mill La HTWY RG27 ...... 170 B4
New Mill Rd HTWY RG27 ...... 170 B4
New Park Rd ASHF TW15 ...... 128 F3
Newport Cl NWBY RG14 ...... 15 H2
Newport Rd NWBY RG14 ...... 15 H1
  READ RG1 ...... 8 E2
  SLN SL2 ...... 44 B5
New Rd ASC SL5 ...... 123 L5
  BAGS GU19 ...... 175 K2
  BLKW GU17 ...... 181 H2
  BNEND SL8 ...... 20 E2
  BRAK RG12 ...... 13 M4
  CWTH RG45 ...... 172 F1
  DTCH/LGLY SL3 ...... 72 A1
  EBED/NFELT TW14 ...... 101 G5
  EBED/NFELT TW14 ...... 101 L7
  HEN RG9 ...... 64 D3
  HTWY RG27 ...... 171 H7
  MDHD SL6 ...... 20 B7
  MDHD SL6 ...... 40 C3
  MDHD SL6 ...... 68 E6
  NWBY RG14 ...... 15 G7
  READ RG1 ...... 117 G1
  SHPTN TW17 ...... 128 D3
  SHST GU47 ...... 172 D6
  STA TW18 ...... 126 F3
  STHA RG19 ...... 137 G7
  TADY RG26 ...... 164 D7
  THLE RG7 ...... 143 G6
  WAR/TWY RG10 ...... 65 G7
  WWKG RG41 ...... 118 D6
New Road Hl THLE RG7 ...... 139 L3
New Sq SL SL1 ...... 5 G8
New St HEN RG9 ...... 38 B4
  STA TW18 ...... 127 K2
  THLE RG7 ...... 167 K6
Newton Av CAV/SC RG4 ...... 89 G1
Newton Cl DTCH/LGLY SL3 ...... 72 C1
Newton Ct WDSR SL4 ...... 95 L4
Newton La WDSR SL4 ...... 97 L5
Newton Rd FARN GU14 ...... 182 A8
  TADY RG26 ...... 164 D5
Newtown Cl SL SL1 ...... 44 D5
Newtown Gdns HEN RG9 ...... 38 C6
Newtown Rd HEN RG9 ...... 38 C6
  MARL SN8 ...... 102 B2
  MLW SL7 ...... 19 J3
  NWBY RG14 ...... 14 E8
  NWBY RG14 ...... 136 D1
  SHST GU47 ...... 172 E6
New Wy THLE RG7 ...... 112 D4
New Wickham La EGH TW20 ...... 126 D5
New Wokingham Rd
  CWTH RG45 ...... 148 D8
Niagara Rd HEN RG9 ...... 38 B6
Nicholas Gdns SL SL1 ...... 70 B1
Nicholas Rd HEN RG9 ...... 37 L6
Nicholls WDSR SL4 ...... 95 M2
Nicholsons La MDHD SL6 ...... 3 G5
Nicholson Wk EGH TW20 ...... 126 D3
Nideggan Cl STHA RG19 ...... 138 A3
Nightingale Cl FARN GU14 ...... 180 F8
Nightingale Crs BRAK RG12 ...... 149 M2
Nightingale Gdns SHST GU47 ...... 172 E8
  THLE RG7 ...... 143 G8
Nightingale La MDHD SL6 ...... 42 A3
Nightingale Pk SLN SL2 ...... 44 C1
Nightingale Rd WODY RG5 ...... 118 A2
Nightingale Shott EGH TW20 ...... 126 C4
The Nightingales NWBY RG14 ...... 14 F4
  STWL/WRAY TW19 ...... 100 C7
Nimrod Cl WODY RG5 ...... 90 D7
Nimrod Wy WHIT RG2 ...... 116 E1
Nine Acres SL SL1 ...... 70 C1
Nine Elms Cl
  EBED/NFELT TW14 ...... 101 J7
Nine Mile Ride CWTH RG45 ...... 149 K5
  EWKG RG40 ...... 147 G8
  EWKG RG40 ...... 148 A7
Nire Rd CAV/SC RG4 ...... 89 H3
Nixey Cl SL SL1 ...... 5 K9
Noakes Hl GOR/PANG RG8 ...... 57 L7
Nobles Wy EGH TW20 ...... 126 B5
  TLHT RG30 ...... 87 H6
Norcot Rd TLHT RG30 ...... 87 J6
Norden Cl MDHD SL6 ...... 67 M2
Norden Mdw MDHD SL6 ...... 2 B9
Norden Rd MDHD SL6 ...... 2 B9
  MDHD SL6 ...... 67 M2
Norelands Dr SL SL1 ...... 43 M3
Nores Rd WHIT RG2 ...... 117 G2
Norfolk Av SL SL1 ...... 44 F6
Norfolk Cha BNFD RG42 ...... 122 C5
Norfolk Cl WWKG RG41 ...... 119 H8
Norfolk Rd FELT TW13 ...... 101 M7
  MDHD SL6 ...... 87 M7
  TLHT RG30 ...... 87 M7
Norlands NTHA RG18 ...... 137 M1
Norlands La EGH TW20 ...... 127 H7
Norman Av HEN RG9 ...... 38 B5
Normandy Cl FRIM GU16 ...... 183 H6
Norman Keep BNFD RG42 ...... 122 C5
Norman Pl READ RG1 ...... 9 G3
Norman Rd ASHF TW15 ...... 129 G4
  CAV/SC RG4 ...... 88 F2
Normanstead Rd CALC RG31 ...... 87 G3
The Normans SLN SL2 ...... 5 L2
Normay Ri NWBY RG14 ...... 159 M1
Normoor Rd THLE RG7 ...... 142 C5
Norreys Av EWKG RG40 ...... 11 K4
Norreys Dr MDHD SL6 ...... 67 M2
  MDHD SL6 ...... 68 A2
Norris Fld KSCL RG20 ...... 52 E6
Norris La KSCL RG20 ...... 52 E6
Norris Rd EARL RG6 ...... 89 J8
  STA TW18 ...... 127 J2
Northam Cl EARL RG6 ...... 118 B3
Northampton Av SL SL1 ...... 4 B2
Northampton Avevue SL SL1 ...... 4 B3
Northampton Cl BRAK RG12 ...... 13 M7
  BRAK RG12 ...... 122 B8
Northborough Rd SLN SL2 ...... 44 D5
Northbourne Cl EARL RG6 ...... 117 L5
Northbrook Copse
  BRAK RG12 ...... 150 C3
Northbrook Rd CAV/SC RG4 ...... 89 G1
Northbrook St NWBY RG14 ...... 14 E3
North Burnham Cl SL SL1 ...... 43 L3
Northbury Av WAR/TWY RG10 ...... 91 H1
North Cl EBED/NFELT TW14 ...... 101 G5
  FARN GU14 ...... 181 K6
  WDSR SL4 ...... 95 M2
Northcote FARN GU14 ...... 181 H8
Northcott BRAK RG12 ...... 149 K5
Northcourt Av WHIT RG2 ...... 117 G2
Northcroft SL SL2 ...... 44 E5
Northcroft Cl EGH TW20 ...... 125 L3
Northcroft Gdns EGH TW20 ...... 125 L3
Northcroft La NWBY RG14 ...... 14 C3
Northcroft Rd EGH TW20 ...... 125 L3
Northcroft Vls EGH TW20 ...... 125 L3
North Dean MDHD SL6 ...... 3 H1
North Dr CHOB/PIR GU24 ...... 183 M8
  THLE RG7 ...... 114 A7
  VW GU25 ...... 153 H8
North End La ASC SL5 ...... 152 D4
Northern Av NWBY RG14 ...... 108 D8
Northern Hts BNEND SL8 ...... 20 E1
Northern Rd SLN SL2 ...... 45 G5
North Farm Cl HUNG RG17 ...... 49 M3
North Farm Rd FARN GU14 ...... 181 H6
Northfield LIWR GU18 ...... 175 L6
Northfield Av HEN RG9 ...... 64 D2
Northfield Ct STA TW18 ...... 127 L6
Northfield End HEN RG9 ...... 38 A3
Northfield Rd HEN RG9 ...... 64 E2
  MDHD SL6 ...... 42 C5
  NTHA RG18 ...... 137 L2
  READ RG1 ...... 8 E3
  STA TW18 ...... 127 L6
  WDSR SL4 ...... 70 C4
Northfields HUNG RG17 ...... 49 L3
  KSCL RG20 ...... 80 D2
North Fryerne YTLY GU46 ...... 172 A6
Northgate Dr CBLY GU15 ...... 174 D7
North Gn BRAK RG12 ...... 13 M3
  MDHD SL6 ...... 3 H1
  SL SL1 ...... 4 F5
North Gv CHERT KT16 ...... 155 J3
Northington Cl BRAK RG12 ...... 150 C3
North Lodge Dr ASC SL5 ...... 122 F7
Northmead SLN SL2 ...... 44 C5
North Pk IVER SL0 ...... 73 H3
North Rd ASC SL5 ...... 122 E6
  EBED/NFELT TW14 ...... 101 G5
  MDHD 2 F5
  WGFD OX10 ...... 32 C2
North Standen Rd HUNG RG17 ...... 131 K2
North Star La MDHD SL6 ...... 2 B7
North St CAV/SC RG4 ...... 88 E4
  EGH TW20 ...... 126 C3
  READ RG1 ...... 8 D5
  WDSR SL4 ...... 123 J1
North Town Cl MDHD SL6 ...... 3 H1
North Town Md MDHD SL6 ...... 3 H1
North Town Moor MDHD SL6 ...... 42 C4
North Town Rd MDHD SL6 ...... 42 C5
Northumberland Av WHIT RG2 ...... 116 F1
Northumberland Cl
  BNFD RG42 ...... 122 C5
  STWL/WRAY TW19 ...... 100 B5
Northumberland Crs
  EBED/NFELT TW14 ...... 101 H5
Northumbria Rd MDHD SL6 ...... 67 G2

Northview *HUNG* RG17 .... 132 A1
North View Rd *TADY* RG26 .... 165 G7
North Wk *THLE* RG7 .... 114 B2
Northway *NTHA* RG18 .... 137 M1
  NWBY RG14 .... 15 G6
  WWKG RG41 .... 119 G7
Northwood Dr *NWBY* RG14 ...... 15 J1
Norton Cl *NWBY* RG14 .... 135 M8 ⓘ
Norton Pk *ASC* SL5 .... 151 M2
Norton Rd *CBLY* RG15 .... 182 F2
  EWKG RG40 .... 11 C7
  READ RG1 .... 89 H7
  THLE RG7 .... 168 F4
  WODY RG5 .... 118 C1
Norway Dr *SLN* SL2 .... 5 L1
Norwich Av *CBLY* GU15 .... 182 B3
Norwich Dr *WODY* RG5 .... 89 M6
Norwood La *IVER* SLO 47 C5
Norwood Rd *READ* RG1 .... 9 M6
Notley End *EGH* TW20 .... 125 M5 ⓘ
Notton Wy *EARL* RG6 .... 117 J6
Nottwood La *HEN* RG9 .... 35 K1
Nuffield Dr *SHST* GU47 .... 173 J3
Nuffield Rd *WHIT* RG2 .... 146 C7
Nugee Ct *CWTH* RG45 .... 172 E1 ⓘ
Nuneaton Brak RG12 .... 150 B3
Nunhide La *GOR/PANG* RG8 .... 86 C5
Nun's Acre *GOR/PANG* RG8 ..... 32 E7
Nuns Wk *VW* GU25 .... 154 A2
Nuptown La *BNFD* RG42 .... 94 C7
Nursery Cl *EBED/NFELT* TW14 .. 101 L6 ⓘ
  FRIM GU16 .... 182 C7
  HEN RG9 .... 64 D2
  WAR/TWY RG10 .... 91 H6
Nursery Gdns *GOR/PANG* RG8 .. 86 C4
  STA TW18 .... 127 L5
  SUN TW16 .... 129 J7
Nursery La *DTCH/LGLY* SL3 ..... 71 M1
Nursery Rd *MDHD* SL6 .... 43 L7
  SUN TW16 .... 129 H7
  SUN TW16 .... 129 H7
Nursery Wy *STWL/WRAY* TW19 .. 98 A5
Nutbean La *THLE* RG7 .... 169 J1
Nuthatch Dr *EARL* RG6 .... 117 L2
Nuthurst *BRAK* RG12 .... 150 B2
Nut La *WAR/TWY* RG10 .... 66 B8
Nutley *BRAK* RG12 .... 149 K5
Nutley Cl *YTLY* GU46 .... 180 A1
Nutmeg Cl *EARL* RG6 .... 117 J5 ⓘ
Nutter's La *WHIT* RG2 .... 145 K5

O

Oak Av *EGH* TW20 .... 126 F5
  SHST GU47 .... 173 G5
Oakdale *BRAK* RG12 .... 150 A3
Oakdale Cl *CALC* RG31 .... 86 F6
Oakdene *ASC* SL5 .... 152 C3
  CHOB/PIR GU24 .... 177 J5
  GOR/PANG RG8 .... 34 C7 ⓘ
  THLE RG7 .... 142 D3
Oakdown Cl *GOR/PANG* RG8 .... 60 B3
Oak Dr *NWBY* RG14 .... 14 C6
  THLE RG7 .... 142 C4
  WODY RG5 .... 90 D8
Oaken Copse *CBLY* GU15 .... 174 F7
Oaken Copse Crs *FARN* GU14 .. 181 L7
Oak End Dr *IVER* SLO 46 F3
Oak End Wy *THLE* RG7 .... 140 F2
Oakengates *BRAK* RG12 .... 149 K5
Oaken Gv *NWBY* RG14 .... 136 A6
Oakes Ct *HUNG* RG17 .... 132 A1 ⓘ
Oak Farm Cl *BLKW* GU17 .... 180 F1
Oakfield Av *SL* SL1 .... 70 E1 ⓘ
Oakfield Rd *ASHF* TW15 .... 128 E3
  BLKW GU17 .... 181 H2
  BNEND SL8 .... 20 D3
  TADY RG26 .... 165 H5
Oak Gv *SUN* TW16 .... 129 L5
Oak Grove Crs *CBLY* GU15 ..... 173 J8
Oakhall Dr *SUN* TW16 .... 129 J3
Oakham Cl *CALC* RG31 .... 87 G4 ⓘ
Oak HI *MARL* SN8 .... 130 F3
Oakhurst *CHOB/PIR* GU24 ...... 177 H4
  MDHD SL6 .... 42 E2 ⓘ
Oakington Dr *SUN* TW16 .... 129 M7
Oaklands *NTHA* RG18 .... 108 F3
  YTLY GU46 .... 172 A8
Oaklands Cl *ASC* SL5 .... 123 J5
Oaklands Ct *ADL/WDHM* KT15 .. 155 L7
Oaklands Dr *ASC* SL5 .... 123 K5
  WWKG RG41 .... 10 B9
Oaklands La *CWTH* RG45 .... 148 D8
Oaklands Pk *WWKG* RG41 ...... 147 K2
Oak La *EGH* TW20 .... 125 M1
  WDSR SL4 .... 6 C7
Oaklea Dr *HTWY* RG27 .... 170 B4
Oakley Crs *SL* SL1 .... 4 E4
Oakley Green Rd *WDSR* SL4 ... 69 L7 ⓘ
Oakley Rd *CAV/SC* RG4 .... 88 C2
  CBLY GU15 .... 181 L2
  NWBY RG14 .... 15 L1
Oakridge *CHOB/PIR* GU24 ...... 176 C8
Oakside Wy *WHIT* RG2 .... 117 H6
The Oaks *BRAK* RG12 .... 13 L4
  TADY RG26 .... 164 D6
  YTLY GU46 .... 180 A1
Oak Stubbs La *MDHD* SL6 ...... 69 J2
Oak Tree Av *MLW* SL7 .... 19 G3
Oak Tree Cl *MLW* SL7 .... 19 G3
  TADY RG26 .... 164 E5 ⓘ
  VW GU25 .... 154 A3
Oak Tree Copse *CALC* RG31 ... 87 H3 ⓘ
Oak Tree Dr *CAV/SC* RG4 .... 62 B1
  EBED/NFELT TW14 .... 101 G4
  SL SL1 .... 44 A6
  WDSR SL4 .... 6 D7
Oak Tree Rd *CALC* RG31 .... 87 G4
  MLW SL7 .... 19 G2
  STHA RG19 .... 138 B4
Oak Tree Wk *GOR/PANG* RG8 .. 87 G1
Oaktree Wy *SHST* GU47 .... 172 D5
Oak Vw *CALC* RG31 .... 86 F6
Oak Wy *EBED/NFELT* TW14 ..... 101 H7
  WODY RG5 .... 118 A2
Oakway Dr *FRIM* GU16 .... 182 B5
Oakwood Rd *BFOR* GU20 .... 176 B2

  BRAK RG12 .... 122 B7
  VW GU25 .... 153 M2
Oareborough *BRAK* RG12 .... 150 B1
Oareborough La *NTHA* RG18 ... 81 K4
Oast House Cl *STWL/WRAY* TW19 .. 98 B6
Oatlands Dr *SL* SL1 .... 4 D3
Oatlands Rd *WHIT* RG2 .... 145 J2
Oban Ct *SL* SL1 .... 4 D8
Oban Gdns *WODY* RG5 .... 118 B2
O'bee Gdns *TADY* RG26 .... 164 B5
Obelisk Wy *CBLY* GU15 .... 173 M8
Oberon Wy *SHPTN* TW17 ...... 128 B8
Octavia *BRAK* RG12 .... 149 K5
Octavia Wy *STA* TW18 .... 127 K4
Oddfellows Rd *NWBY* RG14 .... 14 D5
Odell Cl *EARL* RG6 .... 117 L6
Odencroft Rd *SLN* SL2 .... 44 D4
Odette Gdns *TADY* RG26 .... 164 E5
Odiham Av *CAV/SC* RG4 .... 89 H1
Odiham Rd *HTWY* RG27 .... 169 G5
  THLE RG7 .... 168 F3
Odney La *MDHD* SL6 .... 20 E7
Ogmore Cl *BRAK* RG12 .... 87 H7 ⓘ
Okingham Cl *SHST* GU47 .... 173 G5 ⓘ
Oldacre *CHOB/PIR* GU24 .... 176 C7
Old Acre La *WAR/TWY* RG10 ... 90 E1
Oldacres *MDHD* SL6 .... 3 M5
Old Barn Cl *CAV/SC* RG4 .... 62 D8
Old Bath Rd *CAV/SC* RG4 .... 89 M5
  NWBY RG14 .... 14 C2
Old Bisley Rd *FRIM* GU16 ...... 182 D4
Old Bracknell Cl *BRAK* RG12 ... 13 G6
Old Bracknell La East
  BRAK RG12 .... 13 G6
Old Bracknell La West
  BRAK RG12 .... 12 F6
Oldbury *BRAK* RG12 .... 12 D6
Oldbury Cl *FRIM* GU16 .... 182 C6 ⓘ
Oldbury Rd *CHERT* KT16 .... 155 H4
Old Chertsey Rd
  CHOB/PIR GU24 .... 177 L5
Old Copse Gdns *HEN* RG9 ..... 36 C8
Old Court Cl *MDHD* SL6 .... 67 L3
Old Dean Rd *CBLY* GU15 .... 174 A7
Olde Farm Dr *BLKW* GU17 .... 180 L1
Old Elm Dr *TLHT* RG30 .... 87 G6 ⓘ
Oldershaw Ms *MDHD* SL6 ...... 41 L6 ⓘ
Old Farm Crs *CALC* RG31 ...... 86 F4 ⓘ
Old Farm Dr *BRAK* RG12 ...... 121 M5
Old Ferry Dr *STWL/WRAY* TW19 .. 97 M5
Oldfield Cl *EARL* RG6 .... 89 K8
Oldfield Rd *MDHD* SL6 .... 3 L6
Old Fives Ct *SL* SL1 .... 43 M4
Old Forest Rd *WWKG* RG41 ... 119 K4 ⓘ
Old Forge Cl *MDHD* SL6 .... 68 D3 ⓘ
Old Green La *CBLY* GU15 ...... 173 M7
Old Hayward La *HUNG* RG17 .. 104 A4
Oldhouse La *CHOB/PIR* GU24 .. 175 M4
Old Lands HI *BRAK* RG12 .... 13 L2
Old La *KSCL* RG20 .... 134 B5
  STHA RG19 .... 163 H5
The Old La *READ* RG1 .... 116 C1
Old Marsh La *MDHD* SL6 .... 69 J2
Old Mill Ct *WAR/TWY* RG10 ... 91 G1
Old Mill La *MDHD* SL6 .... 68 F2
  UX/CGN UB8 .... 47 L6
Old Newtown Rd *NWBY* RG14 .. 14 D7
Old Nursery Pl *ASHF* TW15 .... 128 E3
Old Orch *SUN* TW16 .... 129 M7
The Old Orch *CALC* RG31 ...... 115 H2
Old Pasture Rd *FRIM* GU16 .... 182 C5
Old Pharmacy Ct *CWTH* RG45 .. 172 F2 ⓘ
Old Pond Cl *CBLY* GU15 .... 181 L5
Old Portsmouth Rd *CBLY* GU15 .. 182 D2
Old Post Office La *MDHD* SL6 .. 3 H5
Old Priory La *BNFD* RG42 ...... 122 A4
Old Sawmill La *CWTH* RG45 ... 148 F8
The Old Sawmills *HUNG* RG17 .. 133 H8
Old School Ct *WAR/TWY* RG10 .. 91 G1
Old School La *YTLY* GU46 ...... 171 M8
Old Slade La *IVER* SLO 73 J4
Old Station La *STWL/WRAY* TW19 .. 98 C5
Old Station Wy *FLKWH* HP10 .. 21 H1
The Old Station Yd *HUNG* RG17 .. 49 L4
Oldstead *BRAK* RG12 .... 150 A2
Old St *KSCL* RG20 .... 80 F1
  NTHA RG18 .... 81 G5
Old Vicarage Wy *FLKWH* HP10 .. 21 G2 ⓘ
Oldway La *SL* SL1 .... 70 A1
Old Welmore *YTLY* GU46 .... 180 B1
Old Whitley Wood La *WHIT* RG2 .. 116 F8
Old Wokingham Rd
  CWTH RG45 .... 148 F7
  EWKG RG40 .... 148 E4
Old Woosehill La *WWKG* RG41 .. 10 A4
Oleander Cl *CWTH* RG45 .... 148 C7
Oliver Cl *ADL/WDHM* KT15 .... 155 L8
Oliver Dr *CALC* RG31 .... 114 E1
Oliver Rd *ASC* SL5 .... 151 L1
Oliver's Paddock *MLW* SL7 .... 19 G1
Ollerton *BRAK* RG12 .... 149 K5
Omega Wy *EGH* TW20 .... 126 F6
Omer's Ri *THLE* RG7 .... 142 C3
Onslow Dr *ASC* SL5 .... 123 K5
Onslow Gdns *CAV/SC* RG4 ..... 88 F3
Onslow Ms *CHERT* KT16 ...... 155 J3
Onslow Rd *ASC* SL5 .... 152 L4
Opal Ct *DTCH/LGLY* SL3 .... 45 M5
Opal Wy *WWKG* RG41 .... 119 H7 ⓘ
Opendale Rd *SL* SL1 .... 43 L6
Opladen Wy *BRAK* RG12 .... 149 J2
Opossum Wy *HSLWW* TW4 .... 101 M2
Oracle Pkwy *EARL* RG6 .... 89 J6
Orbit Cl *EWKG* RG40 .... 147 J8
Orchard Av *ASHF* TW15 .... 128 F4
  CAV/SC RG4 .... 62 B1
  EBED/NFELT TW14 .... 101 G4
  SL SL1 .... 44 A6
  WDSR SL4 .... 6 D7
Orchard Cha *WAR/TWY* RG10 .. 91 J7
Orchard Cl *ASHF* TW15 .... 128 F4
  CALC RG31 .... 86 E2
  CHOB/PIR GU24 .... 176 A8
  EWKG RG40 .... 11 J6
  FARN GU14 .... 181 J5
  HEN RG9 .... 38 B5
  HEN RG9 .... 64 B4

  MDHD SL6 .... 68 D3
  NTHA RG18 .... 81 M6
  NWBY RG14 .... 136 F1
  THLE RG7 .... 139 M4
  THLE RG7 .... 144 E4
Orchard Coombe
  GOR/PANG RG8 .... 60 A3
Orchard Ct *BRAK* RG12 .... 13 J5
Orchard Dr *FLKWH* HP10 .... 21 G2
  SHPTN TW17 .... 129 H8
Orchardene *NWBY* RG14 .... 15 H2
Orchard Est *WAR/TWY* RG10 .. 91 H1
Orchard Fld *CAV/SC* RG4 .... 61 M1 ⓘ
Orchard Ga *SHST* GU47 .... 172 E6
Orchard Gv *CAV/SC* RG4 .... 89 H2
Orchard HI *BFOR* GU20 .... 176 A3
Orchard MI *BNEND* SL8 .... 20 B5
Orchard Park Cl *HUNG* RG17 .. 132 A2 ⓘ
Orchard Pl *EWKG* RG40 .... 11 G5
  SUN TW16 .... 166 E1
  WAR/TWY RG10 .... 91 J7
  WDSR SL4 .... 97 L6
Orchard St *READ* RG1 .... 8 F8
The Orchard *LTWR* GU18 ...... 175 L6 ⓘ
  MLW SL7 .... 19 H3
  TADY RG26 .... 165 G6
  THLE RG7 .... 114 B2 ⓘ
  VW GU25 .... 154 B2
Orchardville *SL* SL1 .... 43 L5
Orchard Wy *ASHF* TW15 ...... 100 C6
  CBLY GU15 .... 181 L4
  DTCH/LGLY SL3 .... 72 B1
Ordnance Cl *FELT* TW13 ...... 101 K8 ⓘ
Oregon Av *CALC* RG31 .... 86 F3
Oregon Wk *EWKG* RG40 .... 147 G7
Oriel HI *CBLY* GU15 .... 182 A2
Oriental Rd *ASC* SL5 .... 152 A1
Orion *BRAK* RG12 .... 149 K5
Orkney Cl *CALC* RG31 .... 115 H2
Ormathwaites Cnr
  BNFD RG42 .... 122 B5 ⓘ
Ormonde Rd *WWKG* RG41 ..... 10 D7
Ormsby St *READ* RG1 .... 8 B6
Orrin Cl *TLHT* RG30 .... 87 K6
Orts Rd *READ* RG1 .... 9 K6
Orville Cl *WODY* RG5 .... 90 D7
Orwell Cl *CAV/SC* RG4 .... 88 C2
  FARN GU14 .... 181 H7
  WDSR SL4 .... 97 C2
Osborne Av *STWL/WRAY* TW19 .. 100 B7
Osborne Ct *WDSR* SL4 .... 7 H9
Osborne Dr *LTWR* GU18 .... 175 K6
Osborne La *BNFD* RG42 .... 121 M3
Osborne Ms *WDSR* SL4 .... 7 G9
Osborne Rd *EGH* TW20 .... 126 C4
  EWKG RG40 .... 11 H5
  TLHT RG30 .... 87 L6
  WDSR SL4 .... 7 G9
Osborne St *SL* SL1 .... 5 H9
Osborn Rd *UX/CGN* UB8 .... 47 M1
Osier Pl *EGH* TW20 .... 126 F4
Osman's Cl *BNFD* RG42 .... 122 E5
Osnaburgh HI *CBLY* GU15 ..... 181 L1
Osney Rd *MDHD* SL6 .... 42 B4
Osterley Cl *EWKG* RG40 .... 148 C1 ⓘ
Osterley Dr *CAV/SC* RG4 .... 63 H8
Ostler Ga *MDHD* SL6 .... 2 A1
Oswald Cl *BNFD* RG42 .... 122 A4 ⓘ
Othello Gv *BNFD* RG42 .... 122 B6 ⓘ
Otterbourne Crs *TADY* RG26 .. 164 E8
Otter Cl *CWTH* RG45 .... 148 D7
Ouseley Rd *STWL/WRAY* TW19 .. 97 M6
Overbridge Sq *NWBY* RG14 ... 15 M4
  NWBY RG14 .... 137 H4 ⓘ
Overbury Av *WWKG* RG41 .... 119 J5
Overdale Ri *FRIM* GU16 .... 182 B3
Overdown Rd *CALC* RG31 ...... 86 F5
Overlanders End *CALC* RG31 ... 87 K3 ⓘ
Overlord Cl *CBLY* GU15 .... 173 M6 ⓘ
Owen Rd *BFOR* GU20 .... 176 A1
  NWBY RG14 .... 14 A8
Owl Cl *WWKG* RG41 .... 147 H1 ⓘ
Owlsmoor Rd *SHST* GU47 ..... 173 G6
Owston *EARL* RG6 .... 117 M4
Oxenhope *BRAK* RG12 .... 12 E9
Oxford Av *SL* SL1 .... 43 K3
Oxford Cl *ASHF* TW15 .... 128 F5 ⓘ
Oxford Rd *CALC* RG31 .... 86 F1
  KSCL RG20 .... 80 F5
  MLW SL7 .... 18 F4
  NWBY RG14 .... 14 D1
  NWBY RG14 .... 136 C1
  READ RG1 .... 8 C6
  SHST GU47 .... 173 H4
  TLHT RG30 .... 87 L6
  WDSR SL4 .... 6 F6
  WWKG RG41 .... 10 C5
Oxford Rd East *WDSR* SL4 ...... 7 H7
Oxford St *CAV/SC* RG4 .... 88 D4
  HUNG RG17 .... 49 L4
  HUNG RG17 .... 104 B7 ⓘ
  MARL SN8 .... 102 A2
  NWBY RG14 .... 14 D2

P

Pacific Cl *EBED/NFELT* TW14 .. 101 J7
Pack And Prime La *HEN* RG9 .. 37 M4
Packet Boat La *UX/CGN* UB8 .. 47 L7
Packman Dr *WAR/TWY* RG10 .. 65 G8 ⓘ
Padbury Cl *EBED/NFELT* TW14 .. 101 G7
Paddick Cl *CAV/SC* RG4 .... 90 B3
Paddick Dr *EARL* RG6 .... 118 A5
Paddock Cl *CBLY* GU15 .... 174 D8
Paddock Hts *WAR/TWY* RG10 .. 91 H2
Paddock Rd *CAV/SC* RG4 .... 9 L2
  NWBY RG14 .... 14 E2
The Paddocks *MARL* SN8 ..... 102 A2
Paddocks Wy *CHERT* KT16 ... 155 L5
The Paddock *BRAK* RG12 ...... 13 K7
  CWTH RG45 .... 148 D8
  DTCH/LGLY SL3 .... 71 L8
  MDHD SL6 .... 41 M4
  NWBY RG14 .... 15 K5

Padstow Cl *DTCH/LGLY* SL3 ... 72 B3 ⓘ
Padstow Gdns *WHIT* RG2 ...... 116 E5
Padstow Wk
  EBED/NFELT TW14 .... 101 J8
Padworth La *THLE* RG7 .... 141 H3
Padworth Rd *THLE* RG7 .... 142 B6
  EBED/NFELT TW14 .... 101 G5
Page's Cft *EWKG* RG40 .... 11 K7
Pages Orch *CAV/SC* RG4 .... 62 B1
Paget Cl *CBLY* GU15 .... 174 E7
  MLW SL7 .... 19 J2
Paget Dr *MDHD* SL6 .... 67 K2
Paget Rd *DTCH/LGLY* SL3 ...... 72 C4
The Pagoda *MDHD* SL6 .... 42 E5
Paice Gn *EWKG* RG40 .... 11 J3
Paices HI *THLE* RG7 .... 164 D2
Pakenham Rd *BRAK* RG12 .... 150 A4
Palace Cl *SL* SL1 .... 70 C1 ⓘ
Paley St *MDHD* SL6 .... 67 L8
Palmera Av *CALC* RG31 ...... 114 F2 ⓘ
Palmer Cl *EWKG* RG40 .... 148 D6
  KSCL RG20 .... 54 A7
Palmer Park Av *EARL* RG6 .... 89 J8
Palmer School Rd *EWKG* RG40 .. 11 H5
Palmers Cl *MDHD* SL6 .... 67 K3
Palmer's La *THLE* RG7 .... 142 D4
Palmer's Moor La *IVER* SLO ... 47 K5
Palmerston Av *DTCH/LGLY* SL3 .. 71 L3
Palmerstone Rd *EARL* RG6 .... 89 K7
Pamber Heath Rd *TADY* RG26 .. 165 G6
Pamber Rd *THLE* RG7 .... 165 K5
Pangbourne HI *GOR/PANG* RG8 .. 85 M1
Pangbourne Rd *GOR/PANG* RG8 .. 84 F2
Pangbourne St *TLHT* RG30 .... 87 L6
Pankhurst Dr *BRAK* RG12 .... 150 A2
Pannells Cl *CHERT* KT16 ...... 155 J5 ⓘ
Pan's Gdns *CBLY* GU15 .... 182 C2
Pantile Rw *DTCH/LGLY* SL3 ... 72 D4
Pantings La *KSCL* RG20 .... 159 J8
Paprika Cl *EARL* RG6 .... 117 J5
The Parade *BNEND* SL8 .... 20 D2
  SUN TW16 .... 129 J5
  TADY RG26 .... 164 E5 ⓘ
  WODY RG5 .... 90 C6
Paradise Rd *HEN* RG9 .... 37 M5
Paradise Wy *THLE* RG7 .... 111 M7
Park Av *CBLY* GU15 .... 181 M7
  EGH TW20 .... 126 F5
  EWKG RG40 .... 10 F6
  NTHA RG18 .... 138 A2
  SHPTN TW17 .... 129 H8
  STA TW18 .... 127 J4
  STWL/WRAY TW19 .... 98 A4
Park Cl *CAV/SC* RG4 .... 36 D8
Park Cnr *WDSR* SL4 .... 96 B2
Parkcorner La *WHIT* RG2 ..... 118 C5
Park Crs *ASC* SL5 .... 152 C2
  TLHT RG30 .... 87 K8
Park Dr *ASC* SL5 .... 152 C3
Park End *NWBY* RG14 .... 14 F2
Parker's La *BNFD* RG42 ...... 122 E1
Parkfield Av *FELT* TW13 ...... 129 K1 ⓘ
Parkfield Crs *FELT* TW13 ..... 129 K1
Parkfield Rd *FELT* TW13 ...... 129 K1
Parkfields *YTLY* GU46 .... 180 A1
Parkgate *SL* SL1 .... 43 M5 ⓘ
Parkhill Cl *BLKW* GU17 .... 181 G2
Parkhill Dr *CALC* RG31 .... 87 G4 ⓘ
Parkhill Rd *BLKW* GU17 ...... 181 G2
Parkhouse La *TLHT* RG30 ..... 88 A8 ⓘ
Parkland Av *DTCH/LGLY* SL3 .. 72 A5
Parkland Dr *BRAK* RG12 ...... 122 B6
Parkland Gv *ASHF* TW15 ..... 128 D2
Park La *BNFD* RG42 .... 12 A1
  CALC RG31 .... 86 F7
  CBLY GU15 .... 181 M1 ⓘ
  DTCH/LGLY SL3 .... 71 L3
  DTCH/LGLY SL3 .... 98 D2
  EWKG RG40 .... 70 D3
  GOR/PANG RG8 .... 35 H8
  KSCL RG20 .... 134 E4
  NTHA RG18 .... 138 A1
  THLE RG7 .... 166 F4
  THLE RG7 .... 167 L4
  WAR/TWY RG10 .... 90 E3
Park Ms *STWL/WRAY* TW19 ... 100 C6
Park Rd *ASHF* TW15 .... 128 E3
  BRAK RG12 .... 13 L3
  CBLY GU15 .... 181 M3
  EGH TW20 .... 126 D2
  EWKG RG40 .... 10 E6
  HEN RG9 .... 38 B5
  SHST GU47 .... 172 F7
  SLN SL2 .... 45 G3
  STWL/WRAY TW19 .... 99 L5
  SUN TW16 .... 129 L5
Parkside *HEN* RG9 .... 37 M4
  MDHD SL6 .... 2 D1
Parkside Rd *ASC* SL5 .... 152 D3
  NTHA RG18 .... 138 A1
  TLHT RG30 .... 88 A8
Parkside Wk *SL* SL1 .... 71 K3
Park Sowbury *KSCL* RG20 ..... 80 D6 ⓘ
Parkstone Dr *CBLY* GU15 ..... 181 M2
Park St *BAGS* GU19 .... 175 H3
  CBLY GU15 .... 173 M8
  DTCH/LGLY SL3 .... 73 G3
  HUNG RG17 .... 132 B1
  MDHD SL6 .... 3 H5
  NWBY RG14 .... 14 E2
  SL SL1 .... 71 J3
  SL SL1 .... 7 K7
The Park *HUNG* RG17 .... 49 K3
Park Vw *BAGS* GU19 .... 175 G3
  MDHD SL6 .... 3 G4
Parkview Cha *SL* SL1 .... 44 B7
Park View Rd North
  WAR/TWY RG10 .... 64 D8
Park View Dr South
  WAR/TWY RG10 .... 90 D1
Park Wk *GOR/PANG* RG8 ...... 87 G1 ⓘ
Park Wall La *GOR/PANG* RG8 .. 58 E6
Park Wy *EBED/NFELT* TW14 .. 101 L6
  HUNG RG17 .... 132 A2
  NWBY RG14 .... 14 E2
Parkway *CBLY* GU15 .... 181 M3

  CWTH RG45 .... 172 D1
  MLW SL7 .... 19 J4
Parkway Dr *CAV/SC* RG4 ...... 90 A3
The Parkway *IVER* SLO 46 F2
Parkwood Gv *SUN* TW16 ..... 129 K8 ⓘ
Parlaunt Rd *DTCH/LGLY* SL3 .. 72 E4
  IVER SLO 73 G3
Parliamentary Rd
  CHOB/PIR GU24 .... 183 K8
Parliament La *SL* SL1 .... 43 J1
Parnham Av *LTWR* GU18 ...... 176 A6 ⓘ
Parry Gn North
  DTCH/LGLY SL3 .... 72 C4 ⓘ
Parry Gn South
  DTCH/LGLY SL3 .... 72 D4 ⓘ
Parsley Cl *EARL* RG6 .... 117 J5
Parsonage Gdns *MLW* SL7 .... 19 H5 ⓘ
Parsonage La *HUNG* RG17 .... 49 K4
  HUNG RG17 .... 103 M8
  WDSR SL4 .... 6 D7
Parsonage Pl *HUNG* RG17 .... 49 K3 ⓘ
Parsonage Rd *EGH* TW20 .... 126 A3
Parsonage Wy *FRIM* GU16 ... 182 B5
Parsons Cl *NWBY* RG14 .... 14 A5
  WHIT RG2 .... 146 D7
Parsons Fld *SHST* GU47 .... 172 E6
Parson's Wood La *SLN* SL2 ... 45 G1
Parthia Cl *READ* RG1 .... 8 F8
Part La *THLE* RG7 .... 168 F3
Partridge Cl *FRIM* GU16 ...... 182 B5
Partridge Dr *CALC* RG31 .... 86 E5
Partridge Md *MDHD* SL6 ...... 42 C4 ⓘ
Paschal Rd *CBLY* GU15 .... 174 C6
Pasture Cl *EARL* RG6 .... 117 L6
Patches Fld *MLW* SL7 .... 19 H1
Paterson Cl *FRIM* GU16 .... 182 F3 ⓘ
Pates Manor Dr
  EBED/NFELT TW14 .... 101 G6
Patricia Cl *SL* SL1 .... 44 B8
Patrick Gdns *BNFD* RG42 .... 122 B5
Patrick Rd *READ* RG1 .... 9 G1
Patrington Cl *UX/CGN* UB8 .... 47 M4 ⓘ
Patriot Pl *READ* RG1 .... 9 K6
Patten Ash Dr *EWKG* RG40 ... 11 L4
Pattinson Rd *WHIT* RG2 .... 117 G8 ⓘ
Paul's Fld *HTWY* RG27 .... 171 H6
Pavenham Ct *EARL* RG6 .... 117 K6
Pavilion Gdns *STA* TW18 ...... 127 L5
The Pavilions End
  CBLY GU15 .... 182 A3 ⓘ
Pavy Cl *STHA* RG19 .... 138 C4
Paxton Av *SL* SL1 .... 70 F3
Payley Dr *EWKG* RG40 .... 11 M4
Paynes Cl *STHA* RG19 .... 162 B6
Paynesdown Rd *STHA* RG19 .. 137 L3
Peace La *MDHD* SL6 .... 20 B8
Peace Rd *DTCH/LGLY* SL3 ..... 46 D4
Peachey Dr *STHA* RG19 .... 138 C4
Peach St *EWKG* RG40 .... 11 H6
Peach Tree Cl *FARN* GU14 .... 181 K7
Peacock Av *EBED/NFELT* TW14 .. 101 G3
Peacock La *BRAK* RG12 .... 149 G1
Peacock Rd *MLW* SL7 .... 19 K3
Pear Av *SHPTN* TW17 .... 129 H8 ⓘ
Pearce Dr *MDHD* SL6 .... 20 C7
Pearce Rd *MDHD* SL6 .... 42 C5
Pearce's Orch *HEN* RG9 .... 38 A3
Pearl Gdns *SL* SL1 .... 70 E1
Pearson Rd *CAV/SC* RG4 .... 90 A3
Pearson Wy *WODY* RG5 ...... 118 B1
Peartree Cl *SL* SL1 .... 70 C1
Pear Tree La *NWBY* RG14 .... 136 F1
Pear Tree Rd *ASHF* TW15 ..... 128 F3
Peascod St *WDSR* SL4 .... 7 J7
Pease HI *THLE* RG7 .... 111 J6
Peasemore HI *KSCL* RG20 ..... 53 K5
Peatmore Dr *CHOB/PIR* GU24 .. 183 M8
Pebble HI *HUNG* RG17 .... 133 L7
Peddlars Gv *YTLY* GU46 .... 172 B8
Peel Av *FRIM* GU16 .... 182 D7
Peel Cl *CAV/SC* RG4 .... 89 G4
  WDSR SL4 .... 96 C2
Peel Ct *SL* SL1 .... 44 E6
Pegasus Cl *STHA* RG19 .... 137 K2
Pegasus Ct *CALC* RG31 .... 86 F7 ⓘ
Pegasus Rd *FARN* GU14 ...... 181 J7
Peggotty Pl *SHST* GU47 .... 173 H4 ⓘ
Peg's Gn *TLHT* RG30 .... 87 L7 ⓘ
Peg's Green Cl *TLHT* RG30 ... 87 L8 ⓘ
Peket Cl *STA* TW18 .... 127 H6
Pelican La *NWBY* RG14 .... 14 E2
Pelican Rd *TADY* RG26 .... 165 H4
Pelling HI *WDSR* SL4 .... 97 L6
Pell St *READ* RG1 .... 9 G9
Pemberton Gdns *CALC* RG31 .. 115 G2
Pemberton Rd *SLN* SL2 .... 44 B5
Pembroke *BRAK* RG12 .... 149 J4
Pembroke Broadway
  CBLY GU15 .... 181 M1
Pembroke Cl *ASC* SL5 .... 152 A2 ⓘ
  THLE RG7 .... 142 F3
Pembroke Pl *CAV/SC* RG4 ..... 88 F3
Pembroke Rd *NWBY* RG14 .... 14 D3
Pendals Cl *NTHA* RG18 .... 82 C1
Pendennis Av *CAV/SC* RG4 .... 63 H8
Pendine Pl *BRAK* RG12 .... 149 L2 ⓘ
Pendlebury *BRAK* RG12 ...... 149 K4
Pendragon Wy *CBLY* GU15 ... 183 G2
Pendred Rd *WHIT* RG2 .... 116 F8
Pendry's La *BNFD* RG42 .... 93 K5
Penfurzen La *BNFD* RG42 ..... 94 A6
Peninsular Cl
  EBED/NFELT TW14 .... 101 G5
Penling Cl *MDHD* SL6 .... 20 B8
The Pennards *SUN* TW16 .... 129 M8 ⓘ
Penn Cl *CAV/SC* RG4 .... 62 D8
Pennfields *WAR/TWY* RG10 ... 65 H8
Pennine Cl *CALC* RG31 .... 86 E3 ⓘ
Pennine Rd *SLN* SL2 .... 44 D6
Pennine Wy *FARN* GU14 ...... 181 G7
  WAR/TWY RG10 .... 90 E2
Penn Meadow *SLN* SL2 .... 45 J2
Penn Rd *DTCH/LGLY* SL3 ...... 72 A8
  NWBY RG14 .... 136 A1
  SLN SL2 .... 45 G5
Pennylets Gn *SLN* SL2 .... 45 J1
Pennypiece *GOR/PANG* RG8 .. 32 F7

Pennypot La *CHOB/PIR* GU24 ...... 176 E8
Pennyroyal Ct *READ* RG1 .... 8 E9
Penroath Av *TLHT* RG30 .... 87 M8
Penrose Av *WODY* RG5 .... 90 B8
Penrose Cl *NWBY* RG14 .... 136 C1
Penrose Ct *EGH* TW20 .... 125 M4
Pensford Cl *CWTH* RG45 .... 148 E7
Penshurst Ri *FRIM* GU16 .... 182 C6
Penshurst Rd *MDHD* SL6 .... 2 C8
Pentelow Gdns
  EBED/NFELT TW14 .... 101 K5
Pentland Cl *TLHT* RG30 .... 115 J1 🔲
Pentland Rd *SLN* SL2 .... 44 D6
The Pentlands *HUNG* RG17 .... 133 M4
Penton Av *STA* TW18 .... 127 J5
Penton Hall Dr *STA* TW18 .... 127 K6
Penton Hook Rd *STA* TW18 .... 127 K6
Penton Rd *STA* TW18 .... 127 J5
Penwood Ct *MDHD* SL6 .... 41 L7
Penwood Gdns *EWKG* RG40 .... 149 G3
Penwood Hts *KSCL* RG20 .... 159 K6
Penwood La *MLW* SL7 .... 18 F5 🔲
Penwood Rd *KSCL* RG20 .... 159 M3
Penyston Rd *MDHD* SL6 .... 2 B5
Penzance Sp *SLN* SL2 .... 44 E5
Peppard Hl *HEN* RG9 .... 36 C6
Peppard La *HEN* RG9 .... 38 A7
Peppard Rd *CAV/SC* RG4 .... 62 D1
  CAV/SC RG4 .... 88 C2
  CAV/SC RG4 .... 88 F1
Pepper La *EARL* RG6 .... 117 H2
Pepys Cl *DTCH/LGLY* SL3 .... 72 E6
Perch Cl *MLW* SL7 .... 18 F6
Percival Rd *FELT* TW13 .... 101 J8
Percy Av *ASHF* TW15 .... 128 D3
Percy Bryant Rd *SUN* TW16 ...... 129 H5 🔲
Peregrine Cl *BRAK* RG12 .... 149 L2 🔲
Peregrine Rd *SUN* TW16 .... 129 H7
Periam Cl *HEN* RG9 .... 37 M6
Perkins Wy *WWKG* RG41 .... 10 C7
Perrin Cl *ASHF* TW15 .... 128 C3 🔲
Perring Av *FARN* GU14 .... 181 H6
Perrycroft *WDSR* SL4 .... 96 C2
Perryfields Wy *SL* SL1 .... 43 M5 🔲
Perryhill Dr *SHST* GU47 .... 172 C5
Perryman Wy *SL* SL2 .... 44 C4
Perry Oak Dr *HTHAIR* TW6 .... 100 A1
Perry Oaks Brd *WDR/YW* UB7 ... 99 L1
Perry Wy *BRAK* RG12 .... 122 B7 🔲
  LTWR GU18 .... 175 J7
Perseverance Hl *HEN* RG9 .... 63 K1
Perth Av *SL* SL1 .... 44 E7
Perth Cl *WODY* RG5 .... 90 D5
Peterhead Ms *DTCH/LGLY* SL3 .. 72 D5
Peterhouse Cl *SHST* GU47 .... 173 J4
Petersfield Av *SLN* SL2 .... 5 J6
  STA TW18 .... 127 M3
Petersfield Rd *STA* TW18 .... 127 M3
Peters La *MDHD* SL6 .... 68 E6
Petrel Cl *WWKG* RG41 .... 147 H1 🔲
Petworth Av *CALC* RG31 .... 115 J3 🔲
Petworth Cl *FRIM* GU16 .... 182 C6 🔲
Pevensey Av *CAV/SC* RG4 .... 89 H1
Pevensey Rd *SLN* SL2 .... 44 D6
Pevensey Wy *FRIM* GU16 .... 182 C6
Pewsey V *BRAK* RG12 .... 150 C2
Pheasant Cl *WWKG* RG41 .... 118 F5
Pheasants Cft *MDHD* SL6 .... 67 K2
Philip Rd *STA* TW18 .... 128 A4
Phillimore Rd *CAV/SC* RG4 .... 62 F6
Phillips Cl *WODY* RG5 .... 90 E5
Philpot La *CHOB/PIR* GU24 ...... 177 M7
Phipps Cl *MDHD* SL6 .... 67 K4
Phipps Rd *SL* SL1 .... 44 A6
Phoebe Ct *READ* RG1 .... 8 F9
Phoenix Cl *WWKG* RG41 .... 119 H3 🔲
  BRAK RG12 .... 149 K2
Phyllis Court Dr *HEN* RG9 .... 38 B3
Pickering *BRAK* RG12 .... 12 F9
  BRAK RG12 .... 149 K2
Picket Post Cl *BRAK* RG12 .... 122 D8 🔲
Picketts La *GOR/PANG* RG8 .... 85 H2
Pickford Dr *DTCH/LGLY* SL3 .... 72 B1
Pickwell Cl *EARL* RG6 .... 117 M5
Picton Cl *CBLY* GU15 .... 174 F7
Picton Wy *CAV/SC* RG4 .... 88 E2
Piercefield *CALC* RG31 .... 114 E2
Pierce's Hl *CALC* RG31 .... 86 F5
Pier Rd *EBED/NFELT* TW14 ...... 101 J1 🔲
Pierson Rd *WDSR* SL4 .... 96 A1
Pigeonhouse La *WDSR* SL4 .... 123 H1
Pigeons Farm Rd *STHA* RG19 .. 137 G7
Piggott's Rd *CAV/SC* RG4 .... 9 K2
Piggott Rd *EWKG* RG40 .... 11 K1
Pike Cl *MLW* SL7 .... 18 F6
Pikeshaw Wy *CALC* RG31 .... 86 F4 🔲
Pike St *NWBY* RG14 .... 15 H1
Pimento Dr *EARL* RG6 .... 117 J5
Pimpernel Pl *NTHA* RG18 .... 138 C2 🔲
Pincents La *CALC* RG31 .... 114 D2
  THLE RG7 .... 114 D1
Pinchcut *THLE* RG7 .... 142 D3
Pinchington La *NWBY* RG14 .... 136 D7 🔲
Pindar Pl *NWBY* RG14 .... 137 H1 🔲
Pine Av *CBLY* GU15 .... 182 A2
Pine Cl *CBLY* GU15 .... 173 H7
  MDHD SL6 .... 41 L7
Pinecote Dr *ASC* SL5 .... 152 C4
Pinecroft *MLW* SL7 .... 18 F5
Pine Croft Rd *WWKG* RG41 ...... 147 K4
Pine Dr *BLKW* GU17 .... 181 H3
  EWKG RG40 .... 147 K7
  THLE RG7 .... 142 C8
Pinefields Cl *CWTH* RG45 .... 172 E1 🔲
Pine Gv *BFOR* GU20 .... 176 A2
  WAR/TWY RG10 .... 91 G1
Pinehill Rd *SHST* GU47 .... 172 E6
Pinehill Rd *CWTH* RG45 .... 172 E1
Pinehurst *ASC* SL5 .... 152 A2 🔲
  TADY RG26 .... 164 E7
Pinel Cl *VW* GU25 .... 153 B1 🔲
Pine Mount Rd *CBLY* GU15 ...... 182 A2
Pine Rdg *NWBY* RG14 .... 136 F1
Pine Ridge Rd *THLE* RG7 .... 142 D4
The Pines *CBLY* GU15 .... 174 C7
  SUN TW16 .... 129 K8
  WAR/TWY RG10 .... 65 H7

Pinetree Ct *CAV/SC* RG4 .... 88 D1 🔲
Pine Wy *EGH* TW20 .... 125 L4
Pine Wd *SLN* TW16 .... 129 K6
Pinewood Av *CWTH* RG45 .... 148 F8
Pinewood Cl *IVER* SL0 .... 46 F1
  SHST GU47 .... 172 C6
  TADY RG26 .... 164 A5
Pinewood Dr *KSCL* RG20 .... 160 D4
  STA TW18 .... 127 K3 🔲
Pinewood Gdns *BAGS* GU19 .... 174 F3
Pinewood Gn *IVER* SL0 .... 46 F1
Pinewood Ms
  STWL/WRAY TW19 .... 100 A5 🔲
Pinewood Pk *FARN* GU14 .... 180 F7
Pinewood Rd *FELT* TW13 .... 129 L1
  IVER SL0 .... 46 E2
  VW GU25 .... 125 K8
Pingewood Cl *TLHT* RG30 .... 115 K5 🔲
Pingewood Rd North
  TLHT RG30 .... 115 K4
Pingewood Rd South
  TLHT RG30 .... 115 L7
Pinkcoat Cl *FELT* TW13 .... 129 L1 🔲
Pink La *SL* SL1 .... 43 L3
Pinkneys Dr *MDHD* SL6 .... 41 J6
Pinkneys Rd *MDHD* SL6 .... 41 K6
Pinks La *TADY* RG26 .... 164 B5
Pipers Cl *SL* SL1 .... 43 M4
Piper's End *VW* GU25 .... 126 A8
Pipers La *STHA* RG19 .... 138 C5
Pipers Wy *STHA* RG19 .... 138 D4
Pipit Cl *STHA* RG19 .... 137 L3
Pippins Ct *ASHF* TW15 .... 128 E4
The Pippins *DTCH/LGLY* SL3 ...... 72 C1
Pipsons Cl *YTLY* GU46 .... 172 A8
Pitch Pl *BNFD* RG42 .... 121 G5 🔲
Pitcroft Av *EARL* RG6 .... 89 K8
Pitfield La *THLE* RG7 .... 166 F2
Pitford Rd *WODY* RG5 .... 90 C6
Pitts Cl *BNFD* RG42 .... 120 F4 🔲
Pitt's La *EARL* RG6 .... 89 L7
Pitts Rd *SL* SL1 .... 4 A6
Plackett Wy *SL* SL1 .... 70 A1
Plaines Cl *SL* SL1 .... 70 C1 🔲
The Planes *CHERT* KT16 .... 155 M4
Plane Tree Crs *FELT* TW13 .... 129 L1
Plantagenet Pk *BNFD* RG42 ..... 122 C6 🔲
Plantation Cl *NTHA* RG18 .... 109 J1
Plantation Rd *TADY* RG26 .... 164 B4
Platt La *HUNG* RG17 .... 48 F8
Players Gn *WODY* RG5 .... 118 B1 🔲
Play Platt *THLE* RG7 .... 114 A2
Pleasant Hl *TADY* RG26 .... 164 E6
Ploughlands *BNFD* RG42 .... 12 C2
Plough La *EWKG* RG40 .... 120 C7
  HEN RG9 .... 64 B5
  SL SL2 .... 45 L2
Ploughlees La *SL* SL1 .... 4 F5
Plough Rd *YTLY* GU46 .... 172 B7
Plover Cl *STA* TW18 .... 127 J1 🔲
Plowden Wy *HEN* RG9 .... 64 B5
Plumpton Rd *NWBY* RG14 .... 15 J8
Plumtrees *EARL* RG6 .... 117 L4
Plymouth Av *WODY* RG5 .... 117 M1
Plymouth Rd *SLN* SL2 .... 44 B7
Plympton Cl *EARL* RG6 .... 118 B3
Pocket Cl *BRAK* RG12 .... 121 C7 🔲
Pococks La *WDSR* SL4 .... 71 H5
Poffley Pl *STHA* RG19 .... 138 D3 🔲
Pointers Cl *KSCL* RG20 .... 80 E4 🔲
The Points *MDHD* SL6 .... 67 L3
Polden Cl *FARN* GU14 .... 181 H7
Polehampton Cl *WAR/TWY* RG10 .. 91 G2
Pollard Cl *WDSR* SL4 .... 97 L4
Pollard Gv *CBLY* GU15 .... 182 F2 🔲
Pollardrow Av *BNFD* RG42 .... 12 C3
Pollards Wy *CALC* RG31 .... 114 F2
Polsted Rd *CALC* RG31 .... 87 G5
Polyanthus Wy *CWTH* RG45 .... 148 E6
Pond Cl *NWBY* RG14 .... 136 A7
  WANT OX12 .... 27 H5
Pond Cft *YTLY* GU46 .... 172 B8
Pond End Rd *CAV/SC* RG4 .... 36 D8
Pond Head La *WODY* RG5 .... 118 A2
Pond La *CAV/SC* RG4 .... 61 J8
  NTHA RG18 .... 81 M7
Pond Moor Rd *BRAK* RG12 ...... 149 L2
Pond Rd *EGH* TW20 .... 126 F4
Poole Cl *TLHT* RG30 .... 87 J7
Pooley Cl *EGH* TW20 .... 126 E3
Pooley Green Rd *EGH* TW20 .... 126 E3
Pool La *SL* SL1 .... 4 E5
  WAR/TWY RG10 .... 92 D1
Poolmans Rd *WDSR* SL4 .... 96 A2
Popes Cl *DTCH/LGLY* SL3 .... 72 F7
Popes La *MDHD* SL6 .... 19 M7
Popeswood Rd *BNFD* RG42 ...... 121 G6
Popham Cl *BRAK* RG12 .... 150 C2 🔲
Poplar Av *BFOR* GU20 .... 151 K8
  TLHT RG30 .... 115 J1 🔲
Poplar Cl *DTCH/LGLY* SL3 .... 73 H8
  TADY RG26 .... 164 A6
Poplar Gdns *WHIT* RG2 .... 117 H5
Poplar La *WAR/TWY* RG10 .... 91 J5
  WWKG RG41 .... 119 G3
Poplar Pl *NWBY* RG14 .... 136 D1
Poplar Rd *ASHF* TW15 .... 128 F3
Poplars Gv *MDHD* SL6 .... 42 E4
The Poplars *ASC* SL5 .... 151 K2
Poplar Wy *FELT* TW13 .... 129 L1
Poppy Dr *NTHA* RG18 .... 138 C2
Poppyhills Rd *CBLY* GU15 .... 174 C6
Poppy Pl *EWKG* RG40 .... 10 F5
Poppy Wy *CALC* RG31 .... 114 F1
Porchester *ASC* SL5 .... 151 K1
Porchester Rd *NWBY* RG14 ..... 14 A8
Porchfield Cl *EARL* RG6 .... 117 K5
Porlock Cl *STHA* RG19 .... 138 A4 🔲
Porlock Pl *CALC* RG31 .... 114 F2 🔲
Port Down *HUNG* RG17 .... 132 B1
Porter Cl *EARL* RG6 .... 117 M6 🔲
Porter End *NWBY* RG14 .... 15 H9
Portesbery Rd *CBLY* GU15 .... 174 A8
Portesbery Hill Dr *CBLY* GU15 .. 174 A7
Portia Gv *BNFD* RG42 .... 122 B6
Portiswood Cl *TADY* RG26 .... 165 C6 🔲
Portland Cl *SL* SL1 .... 44 A5

Portland Crs *ASHF* TW15 .... 129 G2
Portland Gdns *MLW* SL7 .... 19 G5
  TLHT RG30 .... 86 F7
Portland Rd *ASHF* TW15 .... 128 B1
Portlock Rd *MDHD* SL6 .... 2 A5
Portman Cl *BNFD* RG42 .... 12 E3
Portman Rd *TLHT* RG30 .... 87 L5
Portmeirion Gdns *TLHT* RG30 .. 87 J5 🔲
Portnall Dr *VW* GU25 .... 153 H3
Portnall Ri *VW* GU25 .... 153 J2
Portnall Rd *VW* GU25 .... 153 J2
Portrush Cl *WODY* RG5 .... 90 A8
Portsmouth Rd *CBLY* GU15 ..... 174 D8
  FRIM GU16 .... 182 B3
Portway *TADY* RG26 .... 164 A5
Portway Cl *READ* RG1 .... 8 B9
Post Horn Pl *CALC* RG31 .... 115 J2 🔲
Posting House Ms *NWBY* RG14 ... 14 B1
Post Meadow *IVER* SL0 .... 47 G4
Post Office La *DTCH/LGLY* SL3 ... 46 A7
  TLHT RG30 .... 142 F1
Post Office Rd *HUNG* RG17 ...... 157 H1
Potkiln La *GOR/PANG* RG8 .... 34 B8
Potley Hill Rd *YTLY* GU46 .... 180 C1
The Potteries *FARN* GU14 .... 181 G8
Potters Cross *IVER* SL0 .... 47 H4
Pottery La *HUNG* RG17 .... 157 C1
Pottery Rd *TLHT* RG30 .... 87 H5
  TLHT RG30 .... 87 J5
Poulcott *STWL/WRAY* TW19 ..... 98 B5 🔲
Pound Crs *MLW* SL7 .... 18 F5
Poundfield La *MDHD* SL6 .... 20 C7
Poundfield Wy *WAR/TWY* RG10 .. 91 J3
Pound La *BFOR* GU20 .... 175 M2
  CAV/SC RG4 .... 90 A5
  KSCL RG20 .... 160 B8
  MLW SL7 .... 18 F5
  MLW SL7 .... 19 M2
  NWBY RG14 .... 136 A2
  STHA RG19 .... 137 K3
  WAR/TWY RG10 .... 119 L1
Pound Rd *CHERT* KT16 .... 155 L4
Pound St *NWBY* RG14 .... 14 D6
The Pound *MDHD* SL6 .... 20 C7
Powis Cl *MDHD* SL6 .... 67 L2
Powney Rd *MDHD* SL6 .... 2 B5
Poyle Gdns *BRAK* RG12 .... 13 L2
Poyle La *SL* SL1 .... 43 L2
Poyle Rd *DTCH/LGLY* SL3 .... 99 H1
Poynings *IVER* SL0 .... 73 J4
Prairie Cl *ADL/WDHM* KT15 ..... 155 L7
Prairie Rd *ADL/WDHM* KT15 .... 155 L7
The Precincts *SL* SL1 .... 43 L5
Prentice Cl *FARN* GU14 .... 181 L6 🔲
Prescott *BRAK* RG12 .... 149 J4
Prescott Rd *DTCH/LGLY* SL3 .... 99 H1
Preston Pl *NWBY* RG14 .... 137 G2 🔲
Preston Rd *SLN* SL2 .... 45 M8
  WHIT RG2 .... 116 F1
Prestwood *SLN* SL2 .... 5 J3
Pretoria Rd *CHERT* KT16 .... 155 J5
Price Gdns *BNFD* RG42 .... 121 L4 🔲
Prides Crossing *ASC* SL5 .... 123 K5
Priest Av *EWKG* RG40 .... 148 C1
Priest Hl *CAV/SC* RG4 .... 88 D3
  EGH TW20 .... 97 M8
Priest La *CHOB/PIR* GU24 .... 183 M2
Priestwood Av *BNFD* RG42 .... 12 C2
Priestwood Court Rd
  BNFD RG42 .... 12 D2
Primrose Cl *GOR/PANG* RG8 ..... 86 F1 🔲
Primrose La *MDHD* SL6 .... 68 D8
  WWKG RG41 .... 118 F3
Primrose Lea *MLW* SL7 .... 19 G4 🔲
Primrose Wk *BRAK* RG12 .... 149 M2
Primrose Wy *SHST* GU47 .... 172 E5
Prince Albert Dr *ASC* SL5 .... 151 G1
Prince Andrew Cl *MDHD* SL6 ...... 3 L1
Prince Andrew Rd *MDHD* SL6 ...... 3 L1
Prince Andrew Wy *ASC* SL5 ..... 123 G7
Prince Charles Crs *FARN* GU14 .. 181 L6
Prince Consort Cottages
  WDSR SL4 .... 7 J9
Prince Consort Dr *ASC* SL5 ...... 151 G1
Prince Consort's Dr *WDSR* SL4 .. 96 C6
Prince Dr *SHST* GU47 .... 172 D5
Prince Hold Rd *STHA* RG19 ...... 137 K3
Prince of Wales Av *TLHT* RG30 .. 88 A7
Princes Cl *BAGS* GU19 .... 175 H5
  WDSR SL4 .... 70 C5
Prince's La *KSCL* RG20 .... 53 M8
  KSCL RG20 .... 54 A8
Princes Rd *ASHF* TW15 .... 128 C3
  BNEND SL8 .... 20 F3
  EGH TW20 .... 126 C4
  FELT TW13 .... 101 L7
Princess Av *WDSR* SL4 .... 96 E2
Princess Marina Dr *EWKG* RG40 . 146 D5
  WHIT RG2 .... 146 C6
Princess Mary's Rd
  ADL/WDHM KT15 .... 155 M8
Princess St *MDHD* SL6 .... 3 G6
Prince's St *READ* RG1 .... 9 K7
  SL SL1 .... 5 L8
Princess Wy *CBLY* GU15 .... 181 M1
Prince William Dr *CALC* RG31 .. 86 F5
Prior Cft Cl *CBLY* GU15 .... 182 D2
Prior End *CBLY* GU15 .... 182 D1
Prior Rd *CBLY* GU15 .... 182 D1
Priors Cl *FARN* GU14 .... 181 L6
  MDHD SL6 .... 68 E4
  SL SL1 .... 71 K3
Prior's Ct *READ* RG1 .... 9 G8
Priors Court Rd *NTHA* RG18 ...... 80 F6
Prior's La *BLKW* GU17 .... 180 D1
Priors Rd *TADY* RG26 .... 164 D5
  WDSR SL4 .... 96 A2
Priors Wk *MDHD* SL6 .... 68 E4
Priors Wd *CWTH* RG45 .... 172 A2
Priory Av *CAV/SC* RG4 .... 88 D4
  HUNG RG17 .... 132 A2
Priory Cl *ASC* SL5 .... 152 D4
  HUNG RG17 .... 132 A2
  SUN TW16 .... 129 L5
Priory Ct *WWKG* RG41 .... 118 F5
Priory Gdns *ASHF* TW15 .... 129 G3
Priory Gn *STA* TW18 .... 127 L3

Priory La *BRAK* RG12 .... 121 M5
Priory Ms *STA* TW18 .... 127 L3 🔲
Priory Pl *HUNG* RG17 .... 132 A1
  NWBY RG14 .... 136 E3
Priory Rd *ASC* SL5 .... 152 D4
  HUNG RG17 .... 132 A1
  NWBY RG14 .... 14 E8
  SL SL1 .... 43 M6
The Priory *WWKG* RG41 .... 118 F5
Priory Wk *BRAK* RG12 .... 150 C1 🔲🔲
Pritchard Cl *STHA* RG19 .... 137 G7 🔲
Privet Cl *EARL* RG6 .... 117 L5
Proctors Cl *EBED/NFELT* TW14 . 101 K7
Proctors Rd *EWKG* RG40 .... 120 C8
Promenade Rd *READ* RG1 .... 8 E1
Prospect Av *FARN* GU14 .... 181 L8
Prospect La *EGH* TW20 .... 125 K3
Prospect Pl *MDHD* SL6 .... 40 C3
  NWBY RG14 .... 14 E7
  STA TW18 .... 127 J3
Prospect Rd *HUNG* RG17 .... 132 A1
  MLW SL7 .... 18 F4
Prospect St *CAV/SC* RG4 .... 88 D4
  READ RG1 .... 8 C7
Providence Pl *MDHD* SL6 .... 3 H4
  EGH TW20 .... 126 A5
Prune Hl *EGH* TW20 .... 126 C5
Prunus Cl *CHOB/PIR* GU24 ...... 176 B8
Pudding Hl *WAR/TWY* RG10 ...... 40 A8
Pudding La *KSCL* RG20 .... 53 H5
Pudseys Cl *MDHD* SL6 .... 19 L8
Puffers Wy *NWBY* RG14 .... 14 A5
Pulborough Av *HSLWW* TW4 .... 101 M3
Pullmans Pl *STA* TW18 .... 127 K3 🔲
Pump La *ASC* SL5 .... 124 B6
  THLE RG7 .... 143 M4
Pump La South *MLW* SL7 .... 19 K1
Purbrook Cl *BRAK* RG12 .... 150 B3
Purbrook Rd *TADY* RG26 .... 164 D6
Purcell Rd *CWTH* RG45 .... 148 E7
Purfield Dr *WAR/TWY* RG10 ...... 65 H4
Purley La *GOR/PANG* RG8 .... 86 F1
Purley Ri *GOR/PANG* RG8 .... 86 C1
Purley Village *GOR/PANG* RG8 .. 86 F1
Purley Wy *FRIM* GU16 .... 182 B6
  GOR/PANG RG8 .... 86 B1
Pursers Farm *THLE* RG7 .... 144 E3 🔲
Purslane *EWKG* RG40 .... 11 J8
Pursell Cl *MDHD* SL6 .... 67 K3
Purton Cl *SLN* SL2 .... 44 F1
Purton La *SLN* SL2 .... 44 F1
Pyegrove Cha *BRAK* RG12 .... 150 B4 🔲
Pyrcroft Rd *CHERT* KT16 .... 155 H4
  CHERT KT16 .... 155 J4

Q

Quadrant Ct *BRAK* RG12 .... 122 B8 🔲
Qualitas *BRAK* RG12 .... 149 J5
Quantock Av *CAV/SC* RG4 .... 89 G1
Quantock Cl *DTCH/LGLY* SL3 .... 72 D5
  WAR/TWY RG10 .... 90 E2 🔲
The Quantocks *STHA* RG19 ..... 138 A4
Quarrington Cl *STHA* RG19 ...... 138 B4
Quarry Bank *LTWR* GU18 .... 175 J6
Quarrydale Dr *MLW* SL7 .... 19 J4 🔲
Quarry La *HEN* RG9 .... 64 D2
  YTLY GU46 .... 180 B1
Quarry Wood Rd *MLW* SL7 .... 19 H6
Quartz Cl *WWKG* RG41 .... 119 G7
Quaves Rd *DTCH/LGLY* SL3 ...... 99 G1
Quebec Gdns *BLKW* GU17 .... 181 G2 🔲
Queen Anne's Cl *WDSR* SL4 .... 124 E1
Queen Anne's Ga *CAV/SC* RG4 .. 88 F3
Queen Anne's Ride *WDSR* SL4 .. 96 F3
Queen Cl *HEN* RG9 .... 38 B5
Queen Elizabeth Br *CBLY* GU15 . 174 A5
Queen Elizabeth's Wk *WDSR* SL4 . 7 M8
  WDSR SL4 .... 97 J1
Queen Mary Av *CBLY* GU15 ..... 181 K1
Queen Mary Rd *SHPTN* TW17 .. 128 F7 🔲
Queens Acre *WDSR* SL4 .... 97 G3
Queensbury Av *FELT* TW13 ..... 129 M2
Queensbury Pl *BLKW* GU17 .... 180 F3
Queen's Cl *WDSR* SL4 .... 97 K4
Queen's Cottages *READ* RG1 ...... 9 H2
The Queen's Dr *EARL* RG6 .... 117 C2
Queenshill Ldg *ASC* SL5 .... 123 L8
Queens Hill Ri *ASC* SL5 .... 123 M8
Queensmead *DTCH/LGLY* SL3 .. 71 L8 🔲
Queensmere Rd *SL* SL1 .... 5 H8
Queens Park Gdns
  FELT TW13 .... 129 J1 🔲
Queens Pine *BRAK* RG12 .... 150 B3
Queen's Pl *ASC* SL5 .... 123 K8
Queens Ride *CWTH* RG45 .... 148 D7
Queen's Rd *ASC* SL5 .... 152 A2
  CAV/SC RG4 .... 9 H2
  CBLY GU15 .... 181 L2
  DTCH/LGLY SL3 .... 71 L8
  EGH TW20 .... 126 C4
  FELT TW13 .... 101 L7
  MLW SL7 .... 18 F4
  NWBY RG14 .... 15 G6
  READ RG1 .... 9 G6
  SL SL1 .... 5 G5
  UX/CGN UB8 .... 47 M4
  WDSR SL4 .... 7 G9
  WDSR SL4 .... 70 B5
Queen St *CAV/SC* RG4 .... 88 D3
  CHERT KT16 .... 155 K5
  HEN RG9 .... 38 B5
  MDHD SL6 .... 3 H6
Queens Wk *ASHF* TW15 .... 128 A2
Queens Wy *FELT* TW13 .... 129 M2
  HUNG RG17 .... 133 L4
Queensway *CAV/SC* RG4 .... 63 G8
  FRIM GU16 .... 182 D7
  MDHD SL6 .... 42 B4
  SUN TW16 .... 129 L7
Queen Victoria St *READ* RG1 ...... 9 G6
Queen Victoria's Wk *WDSR* SL4 . 7 M6
Quelm La *BNFD* RG42 .... 121 L1

Quentin Rd *WODY* RG5 .... 90 A8
Quentin Wy *VW* GU25 .... 153 L1
Quiet Cl *ADL/WDHM* KT15 .... 155 K8
Quinbrookes *SLN* SL2 .... 45 M7
Quince Cl *ASC* SL5 .... 152 A1 🔲
Quincy Rd *EGH* TW20 .... 126 D3 🔲
Quintilis *BRAK* RG12 .... 149 J5
Quoitings Dr *MLW* SL7 .... 18 F4

R

Raccoon Wy *HSLWW* TW4 .... 101 M1
Rachaels Lake Vw
  BNFD RG42 .... 122 B5 🔲
Rackstraw Rd *SHST* GU47 .... 173 G5
Radbourne Rd *CALC* RG31 ...... 115 G2
Radcliffe Cl *FRIM* GU16 .... 182 C7
Radcliffe Wy *BNFD* RG42 .... 12 A3
Radcot Av *DTCH/LGLY* SL3 .... 72 E3
Radcot Cl *MDHD* SL6 .... 42 B3 🔲
  WODY RG5 .... 90 B5
Radical Ride *EWKG* RG40 .... 147 J7
Radley Bottom *HUNG* RG17 .... 105 H7
Radley Cl *EBED/NFELT* TW14 .. 101 J7 🔲
Radnor Cl *HEN* RG9 .... 38 B4
Radnor Rd *BRAK* RG12 .... 122 C8
  EARL RG6 .... 117 M3
Radnor Wy *DTCH/LGLY* SL3 ..... 72 B4
Radstock La *EARL* RG6 .... 117 K4
Radstock Rd *READ* RG1 .... 89 J7
Raeburn Wy *SHST* GU47 .... 173 G8
Ragdale *THLE* RG7 .... 142 D3
Ragglesswood Cl *EARL* RG6 .... 117 M3 🔲
Raghill *THLE* RG7 .... 141 G8
Raglan Cl *FRIM* GU16 .... 182 C6
Raglan Gdns *CAV/SC* RG4 .... 88 F2
Ragley Ms *CAV/SC* RG4 .... 63 G8 🔲
Ragstone Rd *SL* SL1 .... 71 G3
Railside *THLE* RG7 .... 140 C4
Railton Cl *WHIT* RG2 .... 117 G7 🔲
Railway Ap *CHERT* KT16 .... 155 J4 🔲
Railway Rd *NWBY* RG14 .... 15 G5
Railway Ter *FELT* TW13 .... 101 K7
  SLN SL2 .... 5 G7
  STA TW18 .... 127 G3
Rainbow Pk *WWKG* RG41 .... 119 J3 🔲
Rainsborough Cha *MDHD* SL6 .. 67 L3 🔲
Rainworth Cl *EARL* RG6 .... 117 K6 🔲
Raleigh Cl *SL* SL1 .... 70 D1 🔲
  WODY RG5 .... 118 B1
Raleigh Ct *STA* TW18 .... 127 K2
Raleigh Rd *FELT* TW13 .... 101 J8
Raleigh Wy *CBLY* GU15 .... 182 C3
  FELT TW13 .... 129 M3
Ralphs Ride *BRAK* RG12 .... 122 B8
Ram Aly *STHA* RG19 .... 162 F6
Rambler Cl *MDHD* SL6 .... 43 L7 🔲
Rambler La *DTCH/LGLY* SL3 ..... 71 M3
Ramptons La *THLE* RG7 .... 141 L8
Rampton's Meadow
  TADY RG26 .... 165 G7
Ramsay Cl *CBLY* GU15 .... 174 E6 🔲
Ramsay Rd *BFOR* GU20 .... 176 B1
Ramsbury Cl *BRAK* RG12 .... 149 H3 🔲
Ramsbury Dr *EARL* RG6 .... 117 K2
  HUNG RG17 .... 132 B1
Ramsdell Cl *TADY* RG26 .... 164 E7
Ramsey Cl *EARL* RG6 .... 118 B4
Ramsey Ct *SLN* SL2 .... 44 A5 🔲
Ramslade Rd *BRAK* RG12 .... 13 J6
  BRAK RG12 .... 149 M2
Rances La *EWKG* RG40 .... 11 L7
Randall Cl *DTCH/LGLY* SL3 .... 72 C5
Randall Md *BNFD* RG42 .... 120 E4 🔲
Randolph Rd *DTCH/LGLY* SL3 .. 72 B3
  READ RG1 .... 8 E2
Ranelagh Crs *ASC* SL5 .... 122 F6
Ranelagh Dr *BRAK* RG12 .... 13 K6
Range Ride *CBLY* GU15 .... 173 J7
Range Rd *EWKG* RG40 .... 147 G7
Range Vw *SHST* GU47 .... 173 H6
Rangewood Av *CALC* RG31 ..... 115 J3
Rapley Cl *CBLY* GU15 .... 174 C6
Rapley Gn *BRAK* RG12 .... 149 M3
Ratby Cl *EARL* RG6 .... 117 M4
Ratcliffe Rd *FARN* GU14 .... 181 J6
Raven Cl *YTLY* GU46 .... 171 L8 🔲
Ravendale Rd *SUN* TW16 .... 129 J3
Ravenglass Cl *EARL* RG6 .... 117 M4
Ravensbourne Av
  STWL/WRAY TW19 .... 100 B7
Ravensbourne Dr *WODY* RG5 ... 90 B6
Ravenscourt *SUN* TW16 .... 129 J6
Ravenscroft *HEN* RG9 .... 38 A4
Ravensdale Ms *STA* TW18 .... 127 L4 🔲
Ravensdale Rd *ASC* SL5 .... 151 K2
Ravens Fld *DTCH/LGLY* SL3 ...... 72 A2
Ravenshoe Cl *BNEND* SL8 .... 20 D3 🔲
Ravenstone Rd *CBLY* GU15 ..... 183 G1
Ravenswood Dr *CBLY* GU15 .... 182 D1
Ravensworth Rd *SLN* SL2 .... 44 D4 🔲
  THLE RG7 .... 142 B8
Rawlinson Rd *CBLY* GU15 .... 173 J8
Ray Dr *MDHD* SL6 .... 3 L2
Ray Lea Cl *MDHD* SL6 .... 3 L2
Ray Lea Rd *MDHD* SL6 .... 3 L2
Ray Mead Ct *MDHD* SL6 .... 42 F5 🔲
Ray Meadow *MDHD* SL6 .... 3 L2
Ray Mead Rd *MDHD* SL6 .... 42 F6
Ray Mill Rd East *MDHD* SL6 .... 3 L1
Ray Mill Rd West *MDHD* SL6 ...... 3 H2
Raymond Cl *DTCH/LGLY* SL3 .... 73 H8
Raymond Rd *DTCH/LGLY* SL3 .. 72 D4
  MDHD SL6 .... 2 D4
Rayners *DTCH/LGLY* SL3 .... 72 F7
Ray Park Av *MDHD* SL6 .... 3 M1
Ray Park La *MDHD* SL6 .... 3 L3
Ray Park Rd *MDHD* SL6 .... 3 L3
Rays Rd *WDSR* SL4 .... 3 L4
Ray St *MDHD* SL6 .... 3 L4
Reade's La *CAV/SC* RG4 .... 61 M1
Reading Rd *BLKW* GU17 .... 180 D1
  CAV/SC RG4 .... 61 J2
  EWKG RG40 .... 170 C2

GOR/PANG RG8 .... 32 D8
GOR/PANG RG8 .... 33 C8
GOR/PANG RG8 .... 34 C5
GOR/PANG RG8 .... 57 K4
GOR/PANG RG8 .... 59 L8
HEN RG9 .... 38 B6
HTWY RG27 .... 171 G6
HTWY RG27 .... 171 J7
THLE RG7 .... 142 C6
THLE RG7 .... 165 J1
TLHT RG30 .... 142 F2
WHIT RG2 .... 145 M2
WODY RG5 .... 90 A6
WWKG RG41 .... 119 C5
Recreation Cl BRAK RG12 .... 13 J8
Recreation La THLE RG7 .... 144 E4
Recreation Rd BNEND SL8 .... 20 E3
THLE RG7 .... 142 D4
TLHT RG30 .... 87 H6
WAR/TWY RG10 .... 65 H4
Rectory Cl BRAK RG12 .... 13 J8
EWKG RG40 .... 11 C5
NWBY RG14 .... 14 C7
SHPTN TW17 .... 128 D8
SHST GU47 .... 172 C6 🔢
SLN SL2 .... 44 F4
TADY RG26 .... 164 F8
WDSR SL4 .... 6 D7
Rectory La BFOR GU20 .... 175 M3
Rectory Rd CAV/SC RG4 .... 88 C4
EWKG RG40 .... 11 H5
GOR/PANG RG8 .... 31 M7
HEST TW5 .... 101 L1
MDHD SL6 .... 43 C5
THLE RG7 .... 141 J7
Redberry Cl CAV/SC RG4 .... 89 G1
Red Cottage Dr CALC RG31 .... 114 F2 🔢
Red Cottage Ms DTCH/LGLY SL3 .... 71 M3
Red Ct SL SL1 .... 4 E7
Redcrest Gdns CBLY GU15 .... 182 C1
Red Cross Rd GOR/PANG RG8 .... 32 F8 🔢
Reddington Dr DTCH/LGLY SL3 .... 72 C4
Redditch BRAK RG12 .... 150 A4
Redfern Cl UX/CGN UB8 .... 47 M2 🔢
Redford Cl FELT TW13 .... 101 J8
Redford Rd WDSR SL4 .... 70 A8
Redford Wy UX/CGN UB8 .... 47 M1
Redgauntlet EWKG RG40 .... 147 H8 🔢
Redgrave Pl MLW SL7 .... 19 J3
Redhatch Dr EARL RG6 .... 117 J4
Red Hl HEN RG9 .... 63 J1
Red House La EARL RG6 .... 117 L6
Red House Dr CAV/SC RG4 .... 62 C1
Redlake La EWKG RG40 .... 148 C3 🔢
Redlands Pl WWKG RG41 .... 147 J4
Redlands Rd READ RG1 .... 117 C1 🔢
Red La GOR/PANG RG8 .... 34 B5
THLE RG7 .... 165 L1
WGFD OX10 .... 33 M2
Redlane Rd KSCL RG20 .... 54 C2
Redleaves Av ASHF TW15 .... 128 E4
Red Lion La CHOB/PIR GU24 .... 177 H4
Red Lion Rd CHOB/PIR GU24 .... 177 H4
Redmayne CBLY GU15 .... 182 F2 🔢
Redriff Cl MDHD SL6 .... 2 D7
Red Rd LTWR GU18 .... 175 K7
Red Rose BNFD RG42 .... 120 F3
Redruth Gdns WHIT RG2 .... 116 E5
Redshots Cl MLW SL7 .... 19 H2
Redvers Rd BRAK RG12 .... 149 L2
Redwood EGH TW20 .... 127 H7
SL SL1 .... 43 K3
Redwood Av WODY RG5 .... 118 D1
Redwood Dr ASC SL5 .... 152 E3
CBLY GU15 .... 183 G2
Redwood Gdns SL SL1 .... 4 C4
The Redwoods WDSR SL4 .... 97 G2
Redwood Wy CALC RG31 .... 86 E5
Reed Cl IVER SL0 .... 47 H7
Reeds Av EARL RG6 .... 117 J3
Reedsfield Cl ASHF TW15 .... 128 E1 🔢
Reedsfield Rd ASHF TW15 .... 128 E2 🔢
Reed's Hl BRAK RG12 .... 149 L2
Reeve Rd MDHD SL6 .... 68 E6
Reeves Wy WWKG RG41 .... 147 K2
Reform Rd MDHD SL6 .... 3 L5
Regal Ct MDHD SL6 .... 68 E4 🔢
Regent Cl EARL RG6 .... 117 M5
HUNG RG17 .... 131 M1
Regent St BAGS GU19 .... 175 J4 🔢
MDHD SL6 .... 3 G5 🔢
READ RG1 .... 8 E4
Regents Pl SHST GU47 .... 172 F6
Regents Wk ASC SL5 .... 151 M3
Regent Wy FRIM GU16 .... 182 C5
Regis Cl WHIT RG2 .... 117 G7
Regnum Dr NWBY RG14 .... 136 E1
Reid Av MDHD SL6 .... 2 E9
Rembrandt Cl WWKG RG41 .... 119 C8 🔢
Rembrandt Wy READ RG1 .... 116 B1
Remembrance Rd NWBY RG14 .... 14 A6
Remenham Church La HEN RG9 .... 38 D2
Remenham La HEN RG9 .... 38 C4
Renault Rd WODY RG5 .... 90 D8
Rennie Cl ASHF TW15 .... 128 A1
Repton Cl MDHD SL6 .... 67 M3
Repton Rd EARL RG6 .... 117 M3
Restwold Cl TLHT RG30 .... 115 M2 🔢
Retford Cl WODY RG5 .... 90 C5
The Retreat EGH TW20 .... 126 A4
MDHD SL6 .... 69 C7
Reuben's Crs TADY RG26 .... 164 E6
Revelstoke Av FARN GU14 .... 181 L8
Revesby Cl CHOB/PIR GU24 .... 176 A8
MDHD SL6 .... 68 A3 🔢
Rex Av ASHF TW15 .... 128 D4
Reynards Av TADY RG26 .... 164 E6
WWKG RG41 .... 118 F4
Reynolds Gn SHST GU47 .... 173 G8 🔢
Rhigos CAV/SC RG4 .... 62 C8
Rhine Cl CAV/SC RG4 .... 89 G4
Rhodes Cl EARL RG6 .... 118 B3
EGH TW20 .... 126 F3 🔢
Rhododendron Cl ASC SL5 .... 123 H5
Rhododendron Ride EGH TW20.. 125 J3

Rhododendron Rd FRIM GU16.. 182 E6
Rhododendron Wk ASC SL5 .... 123 H5
Ribble Pl FARN GU14 .... 181 H8
Ribbleton Cl EARL RG6 .... 118 B3 🔢
Ribstone Rd MDHD SL6 .... 67 L3
Ricardo Rd WDSR SL4 .... 97 C1
Richards Wy SL SL1 .... 70 D1
Richborough Cl EARL RG6 .... 117 L4 🔢
Richfield Av READ RG1 .... 8 B2
Richfield Pl READ RG1 .... 8 C2
Richings Wy IVER SL0 .... 73 J3
Richmond Av
EBED/NFELT TW14 .... 101 H5
Richmond Cl FRIM GU16 .... 182 C5
Richmond Crs SL SL1 .... 5 J8
STA TW18 .... 127 J3 🔢
Richmond Ri WWKG RG41 .... 119 H7 🔢
Richmond Rd CAV/SC RG4.. 88 B2
SHST GU47 .... 173 H6
STA TW18 .... 127 J3
TLHT RG30 .... 87 M6
Richmondwood ASC SL5 .... 152 C5
Rickman Cl BRAK RG12 .... 149 M3 🔢
WHIT RG2 .... 146 B5
WODY RG5 .... 118 A1
Rickman Crs ADL/WDHM KT15.. 155 L7
Riddings La STHA RG19 .... 162 F4
Rider's La THLE RG7 .... 143 K2
Rideway Cl CBLY GU15 .... 181 L2
Ridgebank SL SL1 .... 44 C8 🔢
Ridge Hall Cl CAV/SC RG4.. 88 B3
Ridgemead Rd EGH TW20 .... 125 L1
Ridgemount Cl CALC RG31 .... 86 E4 🔢
Ridge Mount Rd ASC SL5 .... 152 D5
The Ridge GOR/PANG RG8.. 59 J6
NTHA RG18 .... 109 M5
Ridgeway GOR/PANG RG8 .... 32 D1
Ridge Wy IVER SL0 .... 47 H8
VW GU25 .... 154 B2
WAR/TWY RG10 .... 65 G4
Ridgeway Cl LTWR GU18 .... 175 K6
NTHA RG18 .... 81 L7
The Ridgeway BRAK RG12 .... 13 J7
CAV/SC RG4.. 88 D3
LTWR GU18 .... 175 L5
MLW SL7 .... 19 H2
WANT OX12 .... 26 B1
WODY RG5 .... 118 C1
Ridgewood Dr FRIM GU16 .... 183 C5
Riding Court Rd DTCH/LGLY SL3.. 72 B6
The Ridings CAV/SC RG4 .... 62 F6
FRIM GU16 .... 182 E3
IVER SL0 .... 73 J4
MDHD SL6 .... 41 J7
SUN TW16 .... 129 K6
Riding Wy WWKG RG41 .... 119 G8 🔢
Ridlington Cl EARL RG6 .... 118 C5
Righton Cl WAR/TWY RG10 .... 90 E3 🔢
Riley Rd MLW SL7 .... 19 G4
TLHT RG30 .... 87 J6
Rimes's La TADY RG26 .... 164 C8
Ringmead BRAK RG12 .... 149 H2
The Ring BRAK RG12 .... 12 E5
BRAK RG12 .... 13 H5
Ringwood BRAK RG12 .... 149 J4
Ringwood Cl ASC SL5 .... 151 L1 🔢
Ringwood Rd BLKW SL17 .... 172 F8 🔢
FARN GU14 .... 181 M7
TLHT RG30 .... 87 J5
Ripley Av EGH TW20 .... 126 B4
Ripley Cl DTCH/LGLY SL3 .... 72 B4 🔢
Ripley Rd TLHT RG30 .... 87 K5
Ripon Cl CBLY GU15 .... 183 G3
Ripon Rd BLKW GU17 .... 180 C5
Ripplesmere BRAK RG12 .... 150 A2
Ripplesmore Cl SHST GU47 .... 172 E6
Ripston Rd ASHF TW15 .... 129 C3
Risborough Rd MDHD SL6 .... 2 F2
Rise Hag Hl MDHD SL6 .... 43 K7
Riseley Rd MDHD SL6 .... 2 C5
Rise Rd ASC SL5 .... 152 B3
The Rise CAV/SC RG4 .... 88 C2
CWTH RG45 .... 172 C1
EWKG RG40 .... 170 D4
NTHA RG18 .... 109 M6
WWKG RG41 .... 10 C3
Rissington Cl CALC RG31 .... 87 H3
Rivacres GOR/PANG RG8 .... 60 B3
Riverdene Dr WWKG RG41 .... 118 C3
Riverfield Rd STA TW18 .... 127 J4
River Gdns EBED/NFELT TW14.. 101 L4
GOR/PANG RG8 .... 87 G1
MDHD SL6 .... 69 G2
Rivermead Rd CBLY GU15 .... 181 L4
WODY RG5 .... 118 C1
Riversdale BNEND SL8 .... 20 E5
Riversdale Ct READ RG1 .... 89 H6 🔢
Riversdell Cl CHERT KT16 .... 155 J4
Riverside STWL/WRAY TW19 .... 97 M6
Riverside Av LTWR GU18 .... 175 M6
Riverside Cl STA TW18 .... 123 H3
STA TW18 .... 127 H3
Riverside Dr STA TW18 .... 127 J6
Riverside Pl STWL/WRAY TW19.. 100 A5
Riverside Rd STA TW18 .... 127 J5
STWL/WRAY TW19 .... 100 A4
Riverside Wk WDSR SL4 .... 7 K5
Riverview Wy CBLY GU15 .... 181 K3
UX/CGN UB8 .... 47 L2
River St WDSR SL4 .... 7 J5
Riverview Rd GOR/PANG RG8.. 59 M8
Riverway HUNG RG17 .... 77 K3
STA TW18 .... 127 L6
Riverwood Av MLW SL7.. 19 K5
Riverwoods Dr MLW SL7.. 19 K5
Rixman Cl MDHD SL6 .... 2 C9
Rixon Cl DTCH/LGLY SL3 .... 46 B7
Roakes Av ADL/WDHM KT15.. 155 L6
Roberts Cl STWL/WRAY TW19.. 99 M5
Robertsfield STHA RG19 .... 137 J3

Roberts Gv WWKG RG41 .... 147 J3
Robertson Cl NWBY RG14 .... 136 E6 🔢
Roberts Rd CBLY GU15 .... 173 K8
Roberts Wy EGH TW20 .... 125 M5
Ross Rd MDHD SL6 .... 2 D9
READ RG1 .... 8 D3
Rostrevor Gdns IVER SL0 .... 47 G3
Rother Cl SHST GU47 .... 172 F6
Rotherfield Av WWKG RG41 .... 10 C3
Rotherfield Cl THLE RG7 .... 114 C2 🔢
Rotherfield Rd HEN RG9 .... 38 A7
Rotherwick Wy CAV/SC RG4 .... 88 D2
Rother Rd FARN GU14 .... 181 H8
Rotherwick Rd TADY RG26 .... 164 F7
Rothwell Gdns WODY RG5 .... 90 C5
Rotten Row Hl THLE RG7 .... 112 C5
Roughgrove Copse BNFD RG42.. 120 E4
Rounce La CHOB/PIR GU24 .... 176 A8
Roundabouts La WWKG RG41 .... 119 G6
Round Cl YTLY GU46 .... 180 C1
Round End NWBY RG14 .... 160 A1
Roundfield THLE RG7 .... 110 E8 🔢
Roundhead Rd THLE RG7 .... 114 A3
Roundshead Dr BNFD RG42 .... 13 M1
Roundway CBLY GU15 .... 174 F8
EGH TW20 .... 126 F3
Roundway Cl CBLY GU15 .... 174 F8
Routh La TLHT RG30 .... 87 H8
Rowallan Cl CAV/SC RG4 .... 63 G8
Rowan Av EGH TW20 .... 126 F5
Rowan Cl CAV/SC RG4 .... 62 C2
CBLY GU15 .... 174 C6
WWKG RG41 .... 10 A8
Rowan Dr CWTH RG45 .... 148 F7
NWBY RG14 .... 136 D1
WODY RG5 .... 90 B6
Rowan Gdns IVER SL0 .... 46 F3 🔢
Rowan Rd TADY RG26 .... 164 F7
Rowans Cl FARN GU14 .... 181 H5
The Rowans SUN TW16 .... 129 J3
Rowan Wy SL SL1 .... 44 E6 🔢
TLHT RG30 .... 142 E2
Rowcroft Pl WHIT RG2 .... 146 C7
Rowdell Dr WHIT RG2 .... 117 C5
Rowe Ct TLHT RG30 .... 87 L6
Rowland Rd WDSR SL4 .... 96 A2
Rowland's Cl THLE RG7 .... 165 M1
Rowland Wy ASHF TW15 .... 129 C5 🔢
EARL RG6 .... 117 J4
Row La CAV/SC RG4 .... 63 H6
Rowley La DTCH/LGLY SL3 .... 46 B3
Rowley Rd WHIT RG2 .... 116 E2
Roxburgh Cl CBLY GU15 .... 182 F2
Roxwell Cl SL SL1 .... 70 B1 🔢
Royal Av CALC RG31 .... 114 C2
Royal Oak Dr CWTH RG45 .... 148 E6
Royal Wy WHIT RG2 .... 116 C6
Roy Cl NTHA RG18 .... 81 J8 🔢
Roycroft La EWKG RG40 .... 147 H6
Royston Cl TLHT RG30 .... 87 J7
Royston Wy SL SL1 .... 44 A6
Rubus Cl CHOB/PIR GU24 .... 176 B8
Ruby Cl SL SL1 .... 70 D2
WWKG RG41 .... 119 H7 🔢
Rudd Hall Ri CBLY GU15 .... 182 A3
Ruddlesway WDSR SL4 .... 70 A8
Rudland Cl STHA RG19 .... 138 A4
Rudsworth Cl DTCH/LGLY SL3.. 73 G8 🔢
Rufus Isaacs Rd CAV/SC RG4.. 88 E4
Rugby Cl SHST GU47 .... 173 H5 🔢
Ruggles-brise Rd ASHF TW15.. 128 A3
Rugosa Rd CHOB/PIR GU24 .... 176 B8
Runnemede Rd EGH TW20 .... 126 C3
Runnymede Ct EGH TW20 .... 126 D2 🔢
Rupert Cl HEN RG9 .... 38 B3
Rupert Rd NWBY RG14 .... 136 C6
Rupert St READ RG1 .... 9 M7
Ruscombe Gdns DTCH/LGLY SL3.. 71 K7
Ruscombe La WAR/TWY RG10.. 91 H1
Ruscombe Pk WAR/TWY RG10.. 91 H1
Ruscombe Wy
EBED/NFELT TW14 .... 101 J6 🔢
Rushall Cl EARL RG6 .... 117 H7
Rusham Park Av EGH TW20 .... 126 C4
Rusham Rd EGH TW20 .... 126 C4
Rushbrook Rd WODY RG5 .... 89 M7
Rushbrook Wy WODY RG5 .... 90 A7
Rushden Dr WHIT RG2 .... 117 H5
Rushes Md UX/CGN UB8 .... 47 M2 🔢
The Rushes MDHD SL6 .... 3 M1
MLW SL7 .... 18 F6
Rushey Wy EARL RG6 .... 117 J6
Rushington Av MDHD SL6 .... 3 H8
Rushmere Pl EGH TW20 .... 126 B3
Rushmoor Gdns CALC RG31 .... 114 E2
Ruskin Av EBED/NFELT TW14.. 101 J6
Ruskin Ct CWTH RG45 .... 172 C2 🔢
Ruskin Rd STA TW18 .... 127 J4
Ruskin Wy WWKG RG41 .... 119 G8
Russell Cl BRAK RG12 .... 150 A5
Russell Ct BLKW GU17 .... 181 G1 🔢
MDHD SL6 .... 3 G4
Russell Dr STWL/WRAY TW19.. 100 A5
Russell Rd CAV/SC RG4 .... 62 A7
NWBY RG14 .... 14 B5
Russell St READ RG1 .... 8 D7
WDSR SL4 .... 7 H7
Russell Wy WWKG RG41 .... 118 E5
Russet Av SUN TW16 .... 129 H8
Russet Cl CAV/SC RG4 .... 62 B1
STWL/WRAY TW19 .... 99 J5
Russet Gdns CBLY GU15 .... 182 A3
Russet Gld CAV/SC RG4 .... 62 F7
THLE RG7 .... 142 E4
Russet Rd MDHD SL6 .... 67 M3
Russley Gn EWKG RG40 .... 147 K5
Rustington Cl EARL RG6 .... 117 L5 🔢
Ruston Wy ASC SL5 .... 123 H7
Rutherford Cl WDSR SL4 .... 6 B6
Rutherwyk Rd CHERT KT16 .... 155 H4
Rutland Av SL SL1 .... 4 B1
Rutland Cl STHA RG19 .... 138 C4
Rutland Pl MDHD SL6 .... 2 B6
Rutland Rd MDHD SL6 .... 2 B6
TLHT RG30 .... 88 A7 🔢
Ruxbury Rd CHERT KT16 .... 155 G3
Ryan Mt SHST GU47 .... 172 D6

Ryans Mt MLW SL7 .... 18 F4
Rycroft WDSR SL4 .... 96 C2
Rydal Av TLHT RG30 .... 87 J4
Rydal Cl CBLY GU15 .... 183 G1
Rydal Dr STA RG19 .... 137 K3
Rydal Pl LTWR GU18 .... 175 L6
Rydal Wy EGH TW20 .... 126 C5
The Ryde STA TW18 .... 127 L6
Rydings WDSR SL4 .... 96 C2
Rye Cl BRAK RG12 .... 13 L1
FARN GU14 .... 181 H8
MDHD SL6 .... 67 K2
Rye Ct SL SL1 .... 71 K3 🔢
Ryecroft Cl WAR/TWY RG10 .... 65 H4
WODY RG5 .... 90 B5
Ryecroft Gdns BLKW GU17 .... 181 H2 🔢
Rye Gv CHOB/PIR GU24 .... 176 B5
Ryehurst La BNFD RG42 .... 121 J1
Ryeish La THLE RG7 .... 144 F3
Ryemead La WDSR SL4 .... 122 F1
Ryhill Wy EARL RG6 .... 117 H6
Ryland Cl FELT TW13 .... 129 J2
Rylstone Cl MDHD SL6 .... 67 M3
Rylstone Rd TLHT RG30 .... 88 A6 🔢
Ryvers End DTCH/LGLY SL3 .... 72 C3
Ryvers Rd DTCH/LGLY SL3 .... 72 C3

S

Sable Cl HSLWW TW4 .... 101 M2
Sackville St READ RG1 .... 8 E5
Saddleback Rd CBLY GU15 .... 174 B6
Saddlebrook Pk SUN TW16 .... 129 H5 🔢
Saddlewood CBLY GU15 .... 181 M2
Sadler's Ct WWKG RG41 .... 119 C5 🔢
Sadlers End WWKG RG41 .... 118 E7
Sadler's La WWKG RG41 .... 119 G6
Sadlers Rd HUNG RG17 .... 132 C8
The Sadlers CALC RG31 .... 86 E5
Saffron Cl DTCH/LGLY SL3 .... 71 L8
EARL RG6 .... 117 M2
NWBY RG14 .... 14 D3
Saffron Rd BRAK RG12 .... 13 G9
Sage Cl EARL RG6 .... 117 K5 🔢
Sagecroft Rd NTHA RG18 .... 137 M1
Sage Rd CALC RG31 .... 86 F3 🔢
Sage Wk BNFD RG42 .... 13 M1
St Adrian's Cl MDHD SL6 .... 67 L2 🔢
St Alban's St WDSR SL4 .... 7 K6
St Andrews BRAK RG12 .... 149 H3
St Andrews Av WDSR SL4.. 6 B9
St Andrews Cl CWTH RG45 .... 148 F7
STWL/WRAY TW19 .... 98 B5
WDSR SL4 .... 97 K5
St Andrew's Crs WDSR SL4.. 6 A9
St Andrew's Rd CAV/SC RG4.. 88 C2
HEN RG9 .... 38 A6
St Andrew's Wy FRIM GU16 .... 182 C7
SL SL1 .... 44 A8
St Anne's Av STWL/WRAY TW19.. 100 A6
St Anne's Cl HEN RG9 .... 38 A5
St Annes Gld BAGS GU19 .... 175 G3
St Anne's Rd CAV/SC RG4 .... 88 D4
St Ann's Cl CHERT KT16 .... 155 J2
St Ann's Hill Rd CHERT KT16 .... 154 F3
St Ann's Rd CHERT KT16 .... 155 H3
CHERT KT16 .... 155 J3
CHERT KT16 .... 155 J3
St Anthonys Cl BNFD RG42 .... 12 F2
St Anthony's Wy
EBED/NFELT TW14.. 101 J3
St Barnabas Rd CAV/SC RG4 .... 62 D8
WHIT RG2 .... 117 J5
St Bartholomews Rd EARL RG6.. 89 J7
St Bernards Rd DTCH/LGLY SL3.. 71 M3
St Birinus Rd CALC RG31 .... 114 F1 🔢
St Catherine's Cl WWKG RG41.. 118 D5
St Catherines Cl FELT TW13 .... 101 K7 🔢
St Catherine's Hl THLE RG7 .... 166 B1
St Catherines Rd FRIM GU16 .... 182 D5
St Chad's Rd MDHD SL6 .... 67 L2
St Christophers Gdns ASC SL5 .... 123 G6
St Clements Cl EARL RG6 .... 117 M5 🔢
St-Cloud Wy MDHD SL6 .... 3 H4
St Columba's Cl MDHD SL6 .... 67 L2 🔢
St Cross Rd FRIM GU16 .... 182 D7
St Cuthbert's Cl EGH TW20 .... 126 A4
St David's Cl CAV/SC RG4 .... 88 C1
FARN GU14 .... 181 J6
IVER SL0 .... 47 G2
MDHD SL6 .... 67 K2
St David's Dr EGH TW20 .... 125 M5
St David's Rd NWBY RG14 .... 14 D5
St Donats Pl NWBY RG14 .... 14 F6
St Dunstan's Rd FELT TW13 .... 129 J1
HEST TW5 .... 101 M1 🔢
HSLWW TW4 .... 101 L1 🔢
St Edward's Rd EARL RG6 .... 89 K8
St Elizabeth Cl WHIT RG2 .... 116 E7 🔢
St Elmo Crs SLN SL2 .... 45 C5
St George's Av NWBY RG14 .... 14 B6
St George's Cl WDSR SL4 .... 70 B8
St George's Crs SL SL1 .... 44 A8
St George's La ASC SL5 .... 123 L8
St Georges Rd
ADL/WDHM KT15 .... 155 M8
CBLY GU15 .... 173 K8
TLHT RG30 .... 87 L6
St Giles Cl READ RG1 .... 9 G5
St Giles Ct READ RG1 .... 9 G4
St Helens Crs SHST GU47 .... 172 E6 🔢
St Helier Cl WWKG RG41 .... 147 L3
St Hilda's Av ASHF TW15 .... 128 B3
St Ives Cl THLE RG7 .... 143 H3
St Ives Rd MDHD SL6 .... 3 J5
St James Cl GOR/PANG RG8.. 59 M8
WAR/TWY RG10 .... 91 H1
St James Pl SL SL1 .... 43 M7 🔢
St James Rd EWKG RG40 .... 147 H6
St James Wk IVER SL0 .... 73 J2
St John's Cl UX/CGN UB8 .... 47 L2 🔢
WODY RG5 .... 90 C6
St Johns Ct EGH TW20 .... 126 D3 🔢
St Johns Dr WDSR SL4 .... 6 B8
St John's Hl READ RG1 .... 9 K6
St John's Rd ASC SL5 .... 123 J5

CAV/SC RG4.............................. 9 J1
CAV/SC RG4.............................. 88 F4
NWBY RG14 .... 14 E7
READ RG1 .... 9 K7
SHST GU47 .... 172 E7
SLN SL2 .... 5 J5
SLN SL2 .... 5 K6
STHA RG19 .... 137 M3
THLE RG7 .... 166 D1
UX/CGN UB8 .... 47 L2 ⓔ
WDSR SL4 .... 6 D8
St John's St READ RG1............. 9 K6
St John's Wy ADL/WDHM KT15... 155 K6
St Jude's CI EGH TW20 .... 125 M3
St Jude's Rd EGH TW20 .... 125 M2
St Katherine's Rd HEN RG9....... 38 A7
St Laurence CI UX/CGN UB8 ..... 47 M6
St Laurence Wy SL SL1 .... 71 K3
St Lawrence Sq HUNG RG17 .. 131 M1 ⓔ
St Leonard's Av ASHF TW15 ... 128 E3
St Leonard's HI WDSR SL4 .... 96 A3
St Leonard's Rd WDSR SL4 .... 7 H9
WDSR SL4 .... 96 A5
WDSR SL4 .... 96 E2
St Leonards Wk IVER SL0 .... 73 J3
St Luke's Rd MDHD SL6 .... 3 C4
St Lukes Wy CAV/SC RG4 .... 88 C2
St Margarets Av ASHF TW15 ... 128 E3
St Margaret's CI IVER SL0 .... 47 G3
St Margaret's Rd MDHD SL6 ..... 41 K7
St Marks CI STHA RG19........... 137 M3
St Mark's Crs MDHD SL6 .... 41 L7
St Mark's PI WDSR SL4 .... 7 H8
St Mark's Rd BNFD RG42 .... 120 F5
HEN RG9 .... 38 A6
MDHD SL6 .... 2 A4
WDSR SL4 .... 7 C8
St Martin's CI WDR/YW UB7 .... 73 M3
St Martin's Ct ASHF TW15 ..... 127 M3
St Mary's Av GOR/PANG RG8 .... 86 F1
STWL/WRAY TW19 .... 100 A6
St Mary's Butts READ RG1 .... 8 F6
St Mary's CI HEN RG9 .... 37 K6
MDHD SL6 .... 3 J4
SHST GU47 .... 172 E7
St Mary's Crs STWL/WRAY TW19.. 100 A6
St Mary's Dr EBED/NFELT TW14 .. 100 F6
St Mary's Gdns BAGS GU19 ... 175 H3 ⓔ
St Mary's HI ASC SL5 .... 151 M3
St Marys La WDSR SL4 .... 123 L1
St Mary's Rd ASC SL5 .... 151 L4
CBLY GU15 .... 173 M8 ⓔ
DTCH/LGLY SL3 .... 72 E2
NWBY RG14 .... 14 E7
THLE RG7 .... 166 D1
WWKG RG41 .... 118 F5
St Mary's Wy THLE RG7 .... 142 F3 ⓔ
St Michael's CI HUNG RG17 ..... 49 K4
WAR/TWY RG10 .... 65 H8
St Michaels La THLE RG7 .... 142 A1
St Michaels Rd ASHF TW15 .... 128 D3
CBLY GU15 .... 181 L1 ⓔ
FARN GU14 .... 181 L8
NWBY RG14 .... 14 C6
SHST GU47 .... 172 C6
TLHT RG30 .... 87 H7 ⓔ
St Nazaire CI EGH TW20 .... 126 F3 ⓔ
St Neot's Rd HTWY RG27 .... 170 C7
St Nicholas' Rd NWBY RG14 ..... 14 D5
St Olave's Rd STA TW18............ 127 J1
St Patrick's Av WAR/TWY RG10 .. 90 D1
St Patrick's Ct MDHD SL6 ...... 67 L2 ⓔ
St Pauls Av SLN SL2 .... 5 J5
St Paul's Ct ADL/WDHM KT15 .. 155 K8
ASHF TW15 .... 128 F3 ⓔ
St Paul's Ct READ RG1 .... 8 E9
St Paul's Ga WWKG RG41 .... 10 D4
St Paul's Rd STA TW18 .... 127 G3
St Peter's Av CAV/SC RG4 .... 88 B2
St Peter's CI SL SL1 .... 43 L5
STA TW18 .... 127 J4 ⓔ
WDSR SL4 .... 97 K4
St Peter's Gdns YTLY GU46 .... 172 A8
St Peter's HI CAV/SC RG4 .... 88 C3
St Peter's Rd EARL RG6 .... 89 K8
MDHD SL6 .... 42 A4
St Peter St MLW SL7 .... 19 H5
St Peter's Wy CHERT KT16 ..... 155 H8
FRIM GU16 .... 182 C7
St Pinnock Av STA TW18 .... 127 K6
St Richards Rd NWBY RG14.... 136 E1
St Ronans Rd TLHT RG30 .... 87 L6
St Saviour's Rd READ RG1 .... 116 C1
St Sebastian's CI EWKG RG40 .. 148 B6
St Stephens CI READ RG1 .... 8 F1
St Theresa's Rd
EBED/NFELT TW14 .... 101 J3
St Thomas Wk DTCH/LGLY SL3 .. 73 G7 ⓔ
Salamanca CWTH RG45 .... 172 B1 ⓔ
Salcombe Dr EARL RG6 .... 117 L2
Salcombe Rd ASHF TW15 .... 128 B2
NWBY RG14 .... 14 A7
WHIT RG2 .... 117 G3
Saleby CI EARL RG6 .... 118 B4
Salford CI WHIT RG2 .... 116 F7
Salisbury Av SLN SL2 .... 44 F5
Salisbury CI WWKG RG41 .... 147 K4
Salisbury Rd BLKW GU17 .... 180 F1 ⓔ
FELT TW13 .... 101 M7
HSLWW TW4 .... 101 M2
HUNG RG17 .... 131 M4
TLHT RG30 .... 8 A4
UX/CGN UB8 .... 47 L3
Salix CI SUN TW16 .... 129 L5 ⓔ
Salmon CI THLE RG7 .... 144 E4
Salmond Rd WHIT RG2 .... 116 F8
Salters CI MDHD SL6 .... 3 K4
Saltersgate CI EARL RG6 .... 118 A4 ⓔ
Salters' Rd MDHD SL6 .... 3 K4
Salt Hill Av SL SL1 .... 4 B6
Salt Hill Dr SL SL1 .... 4 C7
SL SL1 .... 4 C7
Salt Hill Wy SL SL1 .... 4 B6
Salwey CI BRAK RG12 .... 149 L3 ⓔ
Samarkand CI CBLY GU15 .... 182 E2 ⓔ
Samian PI BNFD RG42 .... 12 A1

Sampage CI WHIT RG2 .... 116 F8
Sampson Pk BNFD RG42 .... 121 G6
Sampsons Gn SLN SL2 .... 44 C4
Sanctuary CI TLHT RG30 .... 87 H6
Sanctuary Rd
STWL/WRAY TW19 .... 100 D5
Sandalwood Av CHERT KT16 ... 155 G7
Sandalwood Rd FELT TW13 .... 129 L1
Sandcroft Rd CAV/SC RG4 .... 62 B8
Sandell's Av ASHF TW15 .... 128 F2
Sanden CI HUNG RG17 .... 131 M1
Sandford CI GOR/PANG RG8 ..... 34 C5 ⓔ
Sandford Down BRAK RG12 .... 150 C2 ⓔ
Sandford La WODY RG5 .... 90 C5
Sandford Rd TADY RG26 .... 164 D6
Sandgate Av TLHT RG30 .... 87 J4 ⓔ
Sand Hi FARN GU14 .... 181 L7
Sandhills WAR/TWY RG10 .... 66 A3
Sandhills Ct VW GU25 .... 154 B2
Sandhills La VW GU25 .... 154 B2
Sandhurst La BLKW GU17 .... 172 E8
Sandhurst Rd CWTH RG45 ...... 172 E3
EWKG RG40 .... 147 L6
YTLY GU46 .... 172 B8
Sandisplatt Rd MDHD SL6 .... 41 K8
Sandleford CI WHIT RG2 .... 116 F8 ⓔ
Sandleford Ri NWBY RG14 ..... 136 D7
Sandlers End SLN SL2 .... 44 E5
Sandown Av CALC RG31 .... 114 E2
Sandown Ct BLKW GU17 .... 181 G1
Sandown Dr FRIM GU16 .... 182 A4
Sandown Rd SL SL1 .... 44 C6 ⓔ
Sandown Wy NWBY RG14 .... 15 J3
Sandpit Hall Rd
CHOB/PIR GU24 .... 177 K7
Sandpit La CAV/SC RG4 .... 63 H5
THLE RG7 .... 169 L1
Sandringham Ct SL SL1 .... 44 A7
Sandringham Dr ASHF TW15 ... 128 A2
Sandringham Rd MDHD SL6 ..... 42 B4
Sandringham Wy CALC RG31 .. 114 E2 ⓔ
FRIM GU16 .... 182 C6
Sands Farm Dr SL SL1 .... 43 M5
Sandstone CI WWKG RG41 ..... 118 F5
Sandy CI NTHA RG18 .... 109 J2
Sandycombe Rd
EBED/NFELT TW14 .... 101 M3
Sandy Dr EBED/NFELT TW14 .. 101 H7
Sandygate CI MLW SL7 .... 19 G3
Sandygate Rd MLW SL7 .... 19 G3
Sandy La ASC SL5 .... 122 F6
ASC SL5 .... 152 D2
BNFD RG42 .... 13 J3
BRAK RG12 .... 13 J2
CBLY GU15 .... 174 B8
CHOB/PIR GU24 .... 177 H4
FARN GU14 .... 180 F8
NTHA RG18 .... 109 J2
SHST GU47 .... 172 C5
TADY RG26 .... 165 G6
VW GU25 .... 154 B2
WWKG RG41 .... 146 F2
WWKG RG41 .... 147 G2
Sandy Md MDHD SL6 .... 68 F5
Sapphire CI WWKG RG41 .... 119 G7
Sargood CI STHA RG19 .... 138 B1 ⓔ
Sarisbury CI TADY RG26 .... 164 D6
Sarsby Dr STWL/WRAY TW19 ... 98 D3
Sarum BRAK RG12 .... 149 H5
Sarum Crs EWKG RG40 .... 11 J3
Sarum Rd TADY RG26 .... 164 D5
Sarum Wy HUNG RG17 .... 132 A2
Saturn CI WWKG RG41 .... 119 H8 ⓔ
Saturn Cft BNFD RG42 .... 12 E4
Satwell CI HEN RG9 .... 36 D3
Saunton Gdns FARN GU14 ..... 181 K8 ⓔ
Savernake CI TLHT RG30 .... 87 J7 ⓔ
Savernake Wy BRAK RG12 ..... 150 C4 ⓔ
Saville Crs ASHF TW15 .... 129 G4 ⓔ
Saville Gdns CBLY GU15 .... 182 E1
Savill Wy MLW SL7 .... 19 J4
Savory Wk BNFD RG42 .... 120 F4
Savoy Ct MDHD SL6 .... 42 C5
Savoy Gv BLKW GU17 .... 181 G3
Sawmill Rd NTHA RG18 .... 109 K2
Sawpit Rd WAR/TWY RG10 ...... 91 H7
Sawtry CI EARL RG6 .... 118 B4 ⓔ
Sawyers CI MDHD SL6 .... 67 J4 ⓔ
Sawyers Ley THLE RG7 .... 143 G6
Saxby CI THLE RG7 .... 142 E3
Saxonbury Av SUN TW16 .... 129 L8
Saxon CI DTCH/LGLY SL3 .... 72 C2
Saxon Ct STHA RG19 .... 137 K3 ⓔ
Saxon Dr BNFD RG42 .... 122 C6
Saxon Gdns MDHD SL6 .... 43 G6
Saxon Rd ASHF TW15 .... 129 G4
Saxons Acre KSCL RG20 .... 53 G3
Saxon Wy WDR/YW UB7 .... 73 M6
Saxton CI EARL RG6 .... 97 L5
Sayers CI FRIM GU16 .... 182 B7
NWBY RG14 .... 136 E6
Scafell CI CALC RG31 .... 86 E4
Scafell Rd SL SL1 .... 44 C6
Scania Wk BNFD RG42 .... 122 E4 ⓔ
Scarborough Wy SL SL1 .... 70 E2
Scarlet Oaks CBLY GU15 .... 182 B3
Scarletts La WAR/TWY RG10 .... 65 L6
Scholard's La MARL SN8 .... 102 A2
Scholars CI CAV/SC RG4 .... 88 C3 ⓔ
HUNG RG17 .... 77 K3 ⓔ
School HI CWTH RG45 .... 173 G2
WAR/TWY RG10 .... 65 G5
School La ADL/WDHM KT15 .... 155 K8
BAGS GU19 .... 175 G4
BFOR GU20 .... 176 A2
CAV/SC RG4 .... 88 E1
EGH TW20 .... 126 D3
HUNG RG17 .... 51 G8
KSCL RG20 .... 107 G2
MARL SN8 .... 130 C5
MDHD SL6 .... 19 L7
MDHD SL6 .... 20 D7

MDHD SL6 .... 42 B5
MDHD SL6 .... 66 E2
MLW SL7 .... 17 L8
MLW SL7 .... 19 M1
READ RG1 .... 8 F1
SLN SL2 .... 45 L1
THLE RG7 .... 142 C4
THLE RG7 .... 165 L5
THLE RG7 .... 169 H3
WAR/TWY RG10 .... 65 G3
YTLY GU46 .... 171 L8
School Ter READ RG1 .... 9 M5
Schroder Ct EGH TW20 .... 125 L3
Scotland HI SHST GU47 .... 172 D6
Scots CI STWL/WRAY TW19 .... 100 A7
Scots Dr WWKG RG41 .... 119 H6
Scottalls La NTHA RG18 .... 82 C1
Scott CI CAV/SC RG4 .... 88 D1
WODY RG5 .... 90 D7
Scotts Av SUN TW16 .... 129 H5
Scott's Ct FARN GU14 .... 181 L7
Scott's Grove CI
CHOB/PIR GU24 .... 177 G8
Scotts Wy SUN TW16 .... 129 H5
Scott Ter BNFD RG42 .... 122 B6
Scours La TLHT RG30 .... 87 L5
Scratchface La NTHA RG18 ...... 84 A7
Scrivens Md STHA RG19 .... 138 C3
Scylla Crs HTHAIR TW6 .... 100 E6
Scylla Rd HTHAIR TW6 .... 100 E5
Seacourt Rd DTCH/LGLY SL3 ..... 72 E4
Seaford Gdns WODY RG5 .... 90 B8
Seaford Rd EWKG RG40 .... 11 J6
Sealand Rd HTHAIR TW6 .... 100 D5
Searing Wy TADY RG26 .... 164 D5
Searles Farm La TLHT RG30 ... 115 L5
Seaton Dr ASHF TW15 .... 100 B8
Seaton Gdns WHIT RG2 .... 116 F4
Seaton Rd CBLY GU15 .... 181 L1
Second Av THLE RG7 .... 164 F4
Second Crs SL SL1 .... 4 B1
Second St THLE RG7 .... 161 J2
Seddon HI BNFD RG42 .... 121 L4 ⓔ
Sedgefield CI CAV/SC RG4 .... 36 C8
Sedgefield Rd NWBY RG14 .... 15 J9
Sedge Gv NTHA RG18 .... 138 B2
Sedgemoor FARN GU14 .... 181 L7
Sedgewell Rd CAV/SC RG4 .... 62 C1
Seebys Oak SHST GU47 .... 173 H8 ⓔ
Sefton CI CHOB/PIR GU24 ...... 176 C8
SLN SL2 .... 45 J2
Sefton Paddock SLN SL2 .... 45 K1
Sefton Wy UX/CGN UB8 .... 47 M7
Segsbury Gv BRAK RG12 .... 150 B1
Selborne Gdns TLHT RG30 .... 87 K5
Selby Rd ASHF TW15 .... 128 F4
Selcourt CI WODY RG5 .... 90 A6
Sellafield Wy EARL RG6 .... 117 M4
Sellwood Av WODY RG5 .... 90 C6
Selsey Wy EARL RG6 .... 117 L6
Selva Ct READ RG1 .... 9 J9
Selwood CI STWL/WRAY TW19 .. 99 M5 ⓔ
Selwood Gdns
STWL/WRAY TW19 .... 99 M5
Selwyn CI WDSR SL4 .... 96 A1
Selwyn Dr YTLY GU46 .... 171 L8
Sen CI BNFD RG42 .... 121 M4 ⓔ
Send Rd CAV/SC RG4 .... 9 K2
Setley Wy BRAK RG12 .... 122 C8
Seton Dr CALC RG31 .... 115 J1 ⓔ
Sevenoaks Dr THLE RG7 .... 144 D3
Sevenoaks Rd EARL RG6 .... 117 L3
Seventh St THLE RG7 .... 161 J1
Severn CI NTHA RG18 .... 137 L1
SHST GU47 .... 172 F6
Severn Crs DTCH/LGLY SL3 .... 72 E5
Severn Rd FARN GU14 .... 181 H8
Severn Wy TLHT RG30 .... 87 J8
Sewell Av WWKG RG41 .... 10 C1
Seymour Av WHIT RG2 .... 145 H1
Seymour CI MDHD SL6 .... 67 L3
Seymour Court La MLW SL7 ..... 18 E1
Seymour Court Rd MLW SL7 ..... 18 F1
Seymour Dr CBLY GU15 .... 174 E6
Seymour Gdns FELT TW13 ..... 129 L2
Seymour Park Rd MLW SL7 .... 19 G3
Seymour Pln MLW SL7 .... 18 F1
Seymour Rd SL SL1 .... 4 C8
Seymour Wy SUN TW16 .... 129 H4
Shackleton Rd SL SL1 .... 5 G5
Shackleton Wy WODY RG5 .... 90 D7
Shaftesbury Av
EBED/NFELT TW14 .... 101 K5
Shaftesbury CI BRAK RG12 ..... 150 A2
Shaftesbury Crs STA TW18 ..... 128 A5
Shaftesbury Mt BLKW GU17 ... 180 F3
Shaftesbury Rd TLHT RG30 ...... 87 L6
Shaggy Calf La SLN SL2 .... 5 H4

MDHD SL6 .... 42 B5
MDHD SL6 .... 66 E2
MLW SL7 .... 17 L8
MLW SL7 .... 19 M1
SLN SL2 .... 45 L1
THLE RG7 .... 142 C4
School Rd ASC SL5 .... 152 A2
ASHF TW15 .... 128 E4
BFOR GU20 .... 151 K8
CALC RG31 .... 87 G6
EWKG RG40 .... 11 J6
KSCL RG20 .... 56 B2
KSCL RG20 .... 80 C5
THLE RG7 .... 141 J5
THLE RG7 .... 169 H2
TLHT RG30 .... 114 F8
WAR/TWY RG10 .... 91 J7
WHIT RG2 .... 146 C4
Shaw Pk CWTH RG45 .... 172 E3
Shaw Rd NWBY RG14 .... 15 C1
READ RG1 .... 8 D9
The Shaw MDHD SL6 .... 42 B1
Sheehy Wy SLN SL2 .... 5 M4
Sheepcote La MDHD SL6 .... 93 M2
SL SL1 .... 21 J5
Sheepcote Rd WDSR SL4 .... 70 D5
WDSR SL4 .... 96 B1
Sheepdrove Rd HUNG RG17 ..... 49 M3
HUNG RG17 .... 50 B1
Sheep Fair Wy HUNG RG17 ..... 49 L4
Sheephouse Rd MDHD SL6 ...... 42 E4
Sheephouse Wy KSCL RG20 ..... 52 D8
Sheep Leaze La KSCL RG20 ...... 54 A4
Sheep Wk CAV/SC RG4 .... 88 E2
Sheepwash La KSCL RG20 ...... 160 D4
Sheepways La CAV/SC RG4 .... 61 L6
Sheerlands Rd EWKG RG40 .... 146 B8
Sheet St WDSR SL4 .... 7 K7
Sheet Street Rd WDSR SL4 ...... 96 C8
Sheffield Rd EBED/NFELT TW14 .. 100 F5
SL SL1 .... 4 B2
Sheffield Wy HTHAIR TW6 ...... 101 G4 ⓔ
Shefford Crs EWKG RG40 .... 11 J2
Shelley Av BRAK RG12 .... 122 B7
Shelley CI MDHD SL6 .... 67 K1
MLW SL7 .... 18 A7 ⓔ
WODY RG5 .... 118 B2 ⓔ
Shelley Crs CBLY GU15 .... 181 M1
Shelley Rd MLW SL7 .... 19 J3
NTHA RG18 .... 137 M2
Shelly Ri FARN GU14 .... 181 J8
Shelson Av FELT TW13 .... 129 J1
Shenstone CI EWKG RG40 ...... 147 K4
Shenstone Dr SL SL1 .... 44 A5 ⓔ
Shenstone Pk ASC SL5 .... 152 B1
Shenstone Rd WHIT RG2 .... 116 E2
Shepherds Av EARL RG6 .... 89 L6
Shepherds CI MDHD SL6 .... 40 C3
UX/CGN UB8 .... 47 M5 ⓔ
Shepherds HI BRAK RG12 .... 13 K2
EARL RG6 .... 89 M6 ⓔ
KSCL RG20 .... 56 B3
Shepherd's House La
EARL RG6 .... 89 K6 ⓔ
Shepherds La BFOR GU20 ...... 176 D1
BNFD RG42 .... 13 G1
CAV/SC RG4 .... 62 A8
MDHD SL6 .... 40 A2
Shepherds Mt KSCL RG20 .... 56 B3
Shepherds Ri KSCL RG20 .... 56 B2
Shepherds Wk FARN GU14 .... 181 H7
Shepherds Wy CWTH RG45 .... 172 B2
Shepley Dr ASC SL5 .... 153 G3
TLHT RG30 .... 115 M2
Shepley End ASC SL5 .... 152 F2
Sheraton CI BLKW GU17 .... 181 H1
Sheraton Dr CALC RG31 .... 86 E5
Sherborne CI DTCH/LGLY SL3 ... 73 H3
Sherborne Rd
EBED/NFELT TW14 .... 101 G6 ⓔ
VW GU25 .... 153 G2
WDSR SL4 .... 96 C3
WODY RG5 .... 90 C6
Sherborne Dr MDHD SL6 .... 67 M3
Sherfield CI WHIT RG2 .... 117 G3
Sherfield Dr WHIT RG2 .... 117 G2
Shergold Wy MDHD SL6 .... 20 C8
Sheridan Av CAV/SC RG4 .... 88 C2
Sheridan Crs TADY RG26 .... 164 B5
Sheridan Rd FRIM GU16 .... 182 A6
Sheridan Wy WWKG RG41 ..... 147 H1
Sherlock Lea HTWY RG27 .... 171 H7
Sherman Rd READ RG1 .... 9 G8
Sherrardmead NWBY RG14 .... 136 E1 ⓔ
Sherring CI BNFD RG42 .... 121 M5
Sherringham Av FELT TW13 ... 129 K1 ⓔ
Sherwin CI FARN GU14 .... 181 L6
Sherwood CI BRAK RG12 .... 122 D7 ⓔ
DTCH/LGLY SL3 .... 73 B3
Sherwood Dr MDHD SL6 .... 41 K8 ⓔ
Sherwood Gdns HEN RG9 .... 37 M6
Sherwood Ri GOR/PANG RG8 ... 86 E2
Sherwood Rd WWKG RG41 .... 118 F4
Sherwood St TLHT RG30 .... 87 M6
Shield Rd ASHF TW15 .... 128 F2
Shifford Crs MDHD SL6 .... 42 B4
Shildon CI CBLY GU15 .... 183 G3
Shilling CI TLHT RG30 .... 87 L8 ⓔ
Shinfield Ri WHIT RG2 .... 117 H2
Shinfield Rd WHIT RG2 .... 117 H2
WHIT RG2 .... 117 H8
Ship Aly FARN GU14 .... 181 M8
Shiplake Bottom HEN RG9 .... 36 B7
Ship La FARN GU14 .... 181 M8
Shipley CI WODY RG5 .... 90 D5
Shipton CI CALC RG31 .... 86 F3
Shire CI BAGS GU19 .... 175 K4
Shire's Head CI TLHT RG30 ...... 88 A8 ⓔ
The Shires WWKG RG41 .... 147 H2
Shires Wy YTLY GU46 .... 172 A6
Shirley Av WDSR SL4 .... 6 B7
WHIT RG2 .... 116 F7
Shirley Rd MDHD SL6 .... 2 A9
Shirvell's HI GOR/PANG RG8 ..... 34 A7
Shooters Wy WHIT RG2 .... 116 C6
Shop La KSCL RG20 .... 79 J2
NWBY RG14 .... 108 C8
Shoppenhanger's Rd MDHD SL6 ... 67 L3
MDHD SL6 .... 67 L3
MDHD SL6 .... 68 B2
Shore CI EBED/NFELT TW14 ... 101 K6
Shoreham Ri SLN SL2 .... 44 F3
Shorland Oaks BNFD RG42 ..... 121 M4 ⓔ
Shortfern SLN SL2 .... 45 M7 ⓔ
Shortheath La THLE RG7 .... 142 A3
Shortlands HI WGFD OX10 .... 31 M2
Short La STWL/WRAY TW19 .... 100 C4
Short St CAV/SC RG4 .... 88 E7
GOR/PANG RG8 .... 86 A1 ⓔ
READ RG1 .... 9 H9
The Short GOR/PANG RG8 .... 87 G1
Shortwood Av STA TW18 .... 127 L1
Shrewsbury Rd
EBED/NFELT TW14 .... 100 F5

HTHAIR TW6 .... 100 F5
Shrivenham CI SHST GU47 ..... 173 G6 ⓔ
Shropshire Gdns BNFD RG42 .. 122 C5 ⓔ
Shrubbs HI CHOB/PIR GU24 ... 176 F4
Shrubbs Hill La ASC SL5 .... 152 F5
Shrubland Dr TLHT RG30 .... 115 K2
Shrublands Dr LTWR GU18 .... 175 L6
Shute End EWKG RG40 .... 10 F5
Shyshack La TADY RG26 .... 164 B5
Sibley Park Rd EARL RG6 .... 117 K5
Sibson EARL RG6 .... 117 M4
Sidbury CI ASC SL5 .... 152 D2
Sidestrand Rd NWBY RG14 .... 136 A6
The Sidings STA TW18 .... 127 L2
Sidlaws Rd FARN GU14........... 180 F8
Sidmouth Grange CI EARL RG6 .. 89 L7
Sidmouth Grange Rd EARL RG6 .. 89 L7
Sidmouth St READ RG1 .... 9 J6
Sidney Rd STA TW18 .... 127 K2
WDSR SL4 .... 95 M2
Silbury CI CALC RG31 .... 114 E2 ⓔ
Silchester Rd TADY RG26 .... 164 E5
TLHT RG30 .... 115 M2
Silco Dr MDHD SL6 .... 2 F7
Silver Birches WWKG RG41 .... 146 F3 ⓔ
Silver CI MDHD SL6 .... 67 K1
Silverdale Dr SUN TW16 .... 129 L7
Silverdale Rd EARL RG6 .... 117 L3
TADY RG26 .... 164 D5
WAR/TWY RG10 .... 65 G5
Silver Dr FRIM GU16 .... 182 F3
Silver Fox Crs WODY RG5 .... 90 A8
Silver HI SHST GU47 .... 173 H6
Silverlands CI CHERT KT16 ..... 155 G7 ⓔ
Silver La THLE RG7 .... 141 K6
Silver St READ RG1 .... 9 HR
Silverthorne Dr CAV/SC RG4 ..... 62 A8
Silvertrees Dr MDHD SL6 .... 67 K1
Silverwood Dr CBLY GU15 ...... 174 D7 ⓔ
Silwood BRAK RG12 .... 149 H5
Silwood CI ASC SL5 .... 124 A7
Silwood Rd ASC SL5 .... 152 C1
Simkins CI BNFD RG42 .... 122 E4 ⓔ
Simmonds St BNFD RG42 .... 8 F7
Simmons CI DTCH/LGLY SL3 ..... 72 D4 ⓔ
Simmons Fld NTHA RG18 .... 108 D8
Simmons Flds WAR/TWY RG10 .. 90 E3
Simmons PI STA TW18 .... 127 H3 ⓔ
Simmons Rd HEN RG9 .... 38 A3
Simms Farm La THLE RG7 ...... 166 C2
Simons CI CALC RG31 .... 86 F2 ⓔ
Simon's La WWKG RG41 .... 119 C6
Simons Wk EGH TW20 .... 125 M5 ⓔ
Simplemarsh Rd
ADL/WDHM KT15 .... 155 K8
Simpson CI MDHD SL6 .... 3 L3
Sindle CI WWKG RG41 .... 118 E4
Sindlesham Rd WHIT RG2 ...... 146 B3
Sine CI FARN GU14 .... 181 L6
Singers La HEN RG9 .... 38 B6
Sinhurst Rd CBLY GU15 .... 181 L2
Sirius CI WWKG RG41 .... 10 A5
Six Acre La HUNG RG17 .... 131 J8
Sixth St STHA RG19 .... 161 J1
Skarries Vw CAV/SC RG4 .... 62 A6
Skeffling CI EARL RG6 .... 118 B4 ⓔ
Skelmerdale Wy EARL RG6 ..... 118 B3
Skelton Flds BNFD RG42 .... 121 M5 ⓔ
Skerritt Wy GOR/PANG RG8 ..... 87 G2
Skilman Dr STHA RG19 .... 138 C3
Skilton Rd CALC RG31 .... 86 F3
Skimpedhill La BRAK RG12 .... 13 G4
Skinner's Green La KSCL RG20 .. 135 J3
Skippons CI NWBY RG14 .... 135 M8
Skye CI CALC RG31 .... 115 H2 ⓔ
Skyes Dr STA TW18 .... 127 L3
Skyllings NWBY RG14.............. 15 J2
Slaidburn Gn BRAK RG12 .... 150 B4
Slanting HI NTHA RG18 .... 109 L1
Slattery Rd FELT TW13 .... 101 M7
Slim Rd CBLY GU15 .... 173 L7
The Slopes CAV/SC RG4 .... 89 G4
Slough Rd DTCH/LGLY SL3 .... 71 K5
DTCH/LGLY SL3........................ 71 L7
IVER SL0 .... 47 C4 ⓔ
IVER SL0 .... 47 J3
IVER SL0 .... 7 K1
WDSR SL4 .... 71 G5
Smallmead Rd WHIT RG2 .... 116 A5
Smallridge KSCL RG20 .... 159 M2
Smewins Rd MDHD SL6 .... 67 G8
Smitham Bridge Rd
HUNG RG17 .... 131 M1
Smith CI CAV/SC RG4 .... 62 C1
Smithfield CI MDHD SL6 .... 67 J3 ⓔ
Smithfield Rd MDHD SL6 .... 67 K3
Smith's HI WANT OX12 .... 25 H1
Smith's La WDSR SL4 .... 96 B1
Smith Sq BRAK RG12 .... 13 L4
Smithy's Gn BFOR GU20 .... 176 A2 ⓔ
Snake La KSCL RG20 .... 107 K8
Snape Sp SL SL1 .... 4 E2
Snowball HI MDHD SL6 .... 67 L5
Snowberry CI WWKG RG41 ...... 10 B7
Snowden Dr CALC RG31 .... 86 D8 ⓔ
Snowdon CI STHA RG19 .... 138 A4 ⓔ
Snowdon Rd FARN GU14 .... 181 H7 ⓔ
Snowdon Rd West HTHAIR TW6 .. 100 F5
Snowdrop Copse NTHA RG18 .. 138 C2 ⓔ
Snowdrop Gv WWKG RG41 ..... 118 F3
Snows Paddock BFOR GU20 ... 151 L7
Snows Ride BFOR GU20 .... 151 L8
Soane End CAV/SC RG4 .... 62 D8
Soham CI EARL RG6 .... 117 M6 ⓔ
Soho Crs FLKWH HP10 .... 21 G2
Soke Rd THLE RG7 .... 165 H2
Soldiers Ri EWKG RG40 .... 148 A7
Somerford CI MDHD SL6 .... 3 M3
Somersby Crs MDHD SL6 .... 68 A3
Somerset CI HUNG RG17 .... 131 M1 ⓔ
WWKG RG41 .... 119 C8 ⓔ
Somerset Gv BNFD RG42 .... 122 C5
Somerset Wy IVER SL0 .... 73 J2
Somerstown Ct READ RG1 .... 8 C7
Somerton Gdns EARL RG6 ...... 117 K4
Somerton Gv STHA RG19 .... 137 M4

Somerville Cl *WWKG* RG41 .... 147 G2 🔟
Somerville Crs *YTLY* GU46 .... 172 B8
Somerville Rd *WDSR* SL4 .... 7 G1
Sonninge Cl *SHST* GU47 .... 173 G6 🔟
Sonning La *CAV/SC* RG4 .... 90 A4
Sonning Mdw *CAV/SC* RG4 .... 89 M5
Sopwith Rd *WODY* RG5 .... 90 D7 🔟
Sorrel Cl *EWKG* RG40 .... 11 L2
NWBY RG14 .... 137 G1
THLE RG7 .... 142 E3 🔟
Sorrel Dr *LTWR* GU18 .... 175 J7
Sospel Ct *SLN* SL2 .... 44 F3
Southampton Cl *BLKW* GU17 .... 172 F8 🔟
Southampton St *READ* RG1 .... 9 C8
South Av *EGH* TW20 .... 126 F4
HEN RG9 .... 38 B6
Southbank Gdns *HUNG* RG17 .... 49 M4
Southbourne Dr *BNEND* SL8 .... 20 D3
Southbury La *WAR/TWY* RG10 .... 91 J1
South Cl *EWKG* RG40 .... 11 H8
MLW SL7 .... 18 A7
SL SL1 .... 44 B8
Southcote Av *FELT* TW13 .... 101 K8
Southcote Dr *CBLY* GU15 .... 182 D1 🔟
Southcote Farm La *TLHT* RG30 .... 116 A1
Southcote La *TLHT* RG30 .... 115 K2
TLHT RG30 .... 116 A1
Southcote Rd *TLHT* RG30 .... 88 A8
Southcroft *EGH* TW20 .... 125 L3
SLN SL2 .... 44 E5 🔟
Southdown Rd *CAV/SC* RG4 .... 88 C1
STHA RG19 .... 137 J2 🔟
TADY RG26 .... 164 D5
South Dr *CAV/SC* RG4 .... 89 M5
CHOB/PIR GU24 .... 183 M8
EARL RG6 .... 117 J4
EWKG RG40 .... 11 H8
THLE RG7 .... 114 A7
VW GU25 .... 153 K4
Southend *NTHA* RG18 .... 109 M8
South End Rd *THLE* RG7 .... 112 E4
Southern Av *EBED/NFELT* TW14 .... 101 K7
Southerndene Cl *CALC* RG31 .... 87 G4 🔟
Southern Hl *READ* RG1 .... 117 C1
Southern Perimeter Rd
HTHAIR TW6 .... 99 M4
HTHAIR TW6 .... 100 E5
HTHAIR TW6 .... 100 F4
Southern Rd *CBLY* GU15 .... 173 M8
South Farm La *BAGS* GU19 .... 175 K4
Southfield Gdns *SL* SL1 .... 43 L6
Southfields Av *ASHF* TW15 .... 128 C4
South Gate Av *FELT* TW13 .... 129 J2 🔟
Southglade *WHIT* RG2 .... 117 G6 🔟
South Gn *SL* SL1 .... 4 F5
South Gv *CHERT* KT16 .... 155 J3
South Hill Rd *BRAK* RG12 .... 149 L3
South Lake Crs *WODY* RG5 .... 118 B1
Southlands Cl *EWKG* RG40 .... 11 K8
Southlands Rd *EWKG* RG40 .... 11 K9
Southlea Rd *WDSR* SL4 .... 97 K2
South Lynn Crs *BRAK* RG12 .... 149 L2
South Meadow *CWTH* RG45 .... 173 C3
South Meadow La *WDSR* SL4 .... 7 G3
South Pl *MLW* SL7 .... 19 H5
South Rd *CWTH* RG45 .... 173 H3
EGH TW20 .... 125 M4
EWKG RG40 .... 149 H5
HEN RG9 .... 35 L5
MDHD SL6 .... 2 F6
South Stoke Rd *WGFD* OX10 .... 33 K3
South St *READ* RG1 .... 9 H7
READ RG1 .... 88 A4
STA TW18 .... 127 J3
South Vw *HUNG* RG17 .... 132 A1
South View Av *CAV/SC* RG4 .... 88 E4
Southview Cl *WAR/TWY* RG10 .... 65 H8 🔟
South View Pk *CAV/SC* RG4 .... 88 F4
Southview Rd *MLW* SL7 .... 19 H2
Southville Cl *EBED/NFELT* TW14 .... 101 H6
Southville Crs
EBED/NFELT TW14 .... 101 H7
Southville Rd
EBED/NFELT TW14 .... 101 H7
Southwark Cl *YTLY* GU46 .... 171 M8
Southway *CBLY* GU15 .... 181 L2
Southwell Park Rd *CBLY* GU15 .... 181 L1
Southwick *BAGS* GU19 .... 175 H5
Southwick Ct *BRAK* RG12 .... 150 B3
Southwold *BRAK* RG12 .... 149 H5
Southwold Cl *EARL* RG6 .... 118 A4
Southwold Sp *DTCH/LGLY* SL3 .... 72 F2
Southwood *EWKG* RG40 .... 11 K9
Southwood Gdns *MDHD* SL6 .... 42 B1
THLE RG7 .... 142 D3
Southwood Rd *FARN* GU14 .... 180 B5
MDHD SL6 .... 42 B1
Sovereign Dr *CBLY* GU15 .... 174 E7
Sovereign Wy *CALC* RG31 .... 114 F1 🔟
Space Waye *EBED/NFELT* TW14 .... 101 K4
Spackman Cl *STHA* RG19 .... 138 A4
Spackmans Wy *WDSR* SL4 .... 70 F3
Spade Oak Meadow *BNEND* SL8 .... 20 B2
Sparrowbill *KSCL* RG20 .... 53 H4
Sparrow Cl *WWKG* RG41 .... 147 H1 🔟
Sparrow Farm Dr
EBED/NFELT TW14 .... 101 M6
Sparrow Rw *CHOB/PIR* GU24 .... 176 J5 🔟
Sparvells *HTWY* RG27 .... 171 H6 🔟
Speedbird Wy *WDR/YW* UB7 .... 73 L7
Speedwell Wy *NTHA* RG18 .... 138 C2
Speen Hill Cl *NWBY* RG14 .... 14 A2
Speen La *NWBY* RG14 .... 14 B2
Speen Lodge Ct *NWBY* RG14 .... 14 A1
Speen Pl *NWBY* RG14 .... 14 A1
Spelthorne Gv *SUN* TW16 .... 129 J5
Spelthorne La *ASHF* TW15 .... 128 C5
Spencer Cl *FRIM* GU16 .... 182 B8
TADY RG26 .... 165 H5 🔟
UX/CGN UB8 .... 47 M4
WWKG RG41 .... 119 G8 🔟
Spencer Gdns *EGH* TW20 .... 126 A3
Spencer Rd *BNFD* RG42 .... 12 D3
DTCH/LGLY SL3 .... 72 C3
NWBY RG14 .... 136 A8
WHIT RG2 .... 116 E7
Spencers Cl *MDHD* SL6 .... 2 B3

Spencers La *MDHD* SL6 .... 20 B8
Spencers Rd *MDHD* SL6 .... 2 B3
Sperling La *MDHD* SL6 .... 42 C5
Spey Rd *TLHT* RG30 .... 87 K6
Spiers Cl *TADY* RG26 .... 165 G6
Spinfield La *MLW* SL7 .... 18 E5
Spinfield La West *MLW* SL7 .... 18 F5
Spinfield Mt *MLW* SL7 .... 18 E5
Spinfield Pk *MLW* SL7 .... 18 F5
Spinis *BRAK* RG12 .... 149 H5
Spinner Gn *BRAK* RG12 .... 149 K2
Spinners Wk *MLW* SL7 .... 19 G5 🔟
WDSR SL4 .... 7 H7
Spinney *SL* SL1 .... 70 E1
Spinney Cl *CAV/SC* RG4 .... 62 E7 🔟
Spinney Dr *EBED/NFELT* TW14 .... 100 F6
Spinney La *WDSR* SL4 .... 95 L7
The Spinney *ASC* SL5 .... 152 B2
CBLY GU15 .... 174 F8
EWKG RG40 .... 147 J6
SUN TW16 .... 129 K6
YTLY GU46 .... 171 M7
Spinningwheel La *BNFD* RG42 .... 93 G5
Spitfire Wy *WODY* RG5 .... 90 D7
Spittal St *MLW* SL7 .... 19 G4
The Splash *BNFD* RG42 .... 121 L4
Spode Cl *TLHT* RG30 .... 87 H6
Spout La *STWL/WRAY* TW19 .... 99 K4
Spout La North
STWL/WRAY TW19 .... 99 L3
Spray La *KSCL* RG20 .... 52 F5
Spray Rd *MARL* SL6 .... 156 B3 🔟
Spriggs Cl *STHA* RG19 .... 138 A4
Springate Fld *DTCH/LGLY* SL3 .... 72 B2
Spring Cl *GOR/PANG* RG8 .... 85 C1
MDHD SL6 .... 42 C4
Springcross Av *BLKW* GU17 .... 181 G2 🔟
Springdale *EARL* RG6 .... 117 L4
EWKG RG40 .... 147 H6
Springfield *LTWR* GU18 .... 175 M6
Springfield Cl *WDSR* SL4 .... 6 F9
Springfield End
GOR/PANG RG8 .... 32 F6 🔟
Springfield Gv *SUN* TW16 .... 129 K6 🔟
Springfield La *NWBY* RG14 .... 136 D6
Springfield Pk *MDHD* SL6 .... 68 F5
WAR/TWY RG10 .... 91 H2
Springfield Rd *ASHF* TW15 .... 128 C3
BRAK RG12 .... 120 F7
CBLY GU15 .... 182 D1
DTCH/LGLY SL3 .... 72 E7
TADY RG26 .... 165 H5
WDSR SL4 .... 6 F9
Springfields Cl *CHERT* KT16 .... 155 L5
Spring Gdns *ASC* SL5 .... 151 L1 🔟
CBLY GU15 .... 182 D1
FARN GU14 .... 181 K7 🔟
MLW SL7 .... 19 G3
THLE RG7 .... 144 E5
BNEND SL8 .... 20 D2
Spring Gv *READ* RG1 .... 9 H9
Spring Hl *MDHD* SL6 .... 68 B3
Springhill Rd *GOR/PANG* RG8 .... 32 F6
Spring La *CAV/SC* RG4 .... 63 L8
KSCL RG20 .... 160 C8
MDHD SL6 .... 19 L8
NTHA RG18 .... 109 M6
SL SL1 .... 70 C1
SLN SL2 .... 44 E1
THLE RG7 .... 140 F8
THLE RG7 .... 142 D7
THLE RG7 .... 168 D3
Spring Meadow *BRAK* RG12 .... 13 M2
Spring Mdw *HUNG* RG17 .... 77 L2
Spring Ri *EGH* TW20 .... 126 B4
Spring Rd *FELT* TW13 .... 129 J1
The Springs *THLE* RG7 .... 167 G6
Spring Wk *WAR/TWY* RG10 .... 65 G5 🔟
Springwood La *HEN* RG9 .... 36 C6
Spring Wood La *THLE* RG7 .... 142 D4
Spring Woods *SHST* GU47 .... 172 F5
VW GU25 .... 153 L1
Spruce Dr *LTWR* GU18 .... 175 K7
Spruce Rd *WODY* RG5 .... 90 D8
Spurcroft Rd *STHA* RG19 .... 138 A4
Spur Rd *EBED/NFELT* TW14 .... 101 L4
The Spur *SL* SL1 .... 44 A6
WAR/TWY RG10 .... 65 H3 🔟
The Square *THLE* RG7 .... 144 E4
WDR/YW UB7 .... 73 L8 🔟
Squires Wk *ASHF* TW15 .... 129 C5 🔟
Squirrel Cl *HSLWW* TW4 .... 101 M2
SHST GU47 .... 172 E6
Squirrel Dr *WDSR* SL4 .... 95 L7
Squirrels Drey *CWTH* RG45 .... 172 C1 🔟
Squirrels Wy *EARL* RG6 .... 117 L4
Stable Cl *THLE* RG7 .... 142 D3
Stable Ct *NWBY* RG14 .... 136 E1
Stable Cft *BAGS* GU19 .... 175 G4
Stables Ct *MLW* SL7 .... 18 E5
Stables Wy *YTLY* GU46 .... 172 A7
Staddlestone Cl *CALC* RG31 .... 86 F4 🔟
Stadium Wy *TLHT* RG30 .... 87 L5
Staff College Rd *CBLY* GU15 .... 173 L8
Stafferton Wy *MDHD* SL6 .... 3 J7
Stafford Av *SLN* SL2 .... 44 F5
Stafford Cl *MDHD* SL6 .... 43 L7 🔟
WODY RG5 .... 90 C7
Staffordshire Cl *TLHT* RG30 .... 87 J5 🔟
Staffordshire Cft *BNFD* RG42 .... 122 C4 🔟
Stag Hl *HUNG* RG17 .... 75 L5
HUNG RG17 .... 103 K5
Stainash Crs *STA* TW18 .... 127 L3
Staines By-pass
STWL/WRAY TW19 .... 127 H1
Staines La *CHERT* KT16 .... 155 K3 🔟
Staines Lane Ct *CHERT* KT16 .... 155 J2 🔟
Staines Rd *STWL/WRAY* TW19 .... 155 H5
CHERT KT16 .... 155 K1
Staines Rd East *SUN* TW16 .... 129 M6
Staines Rd West *ASHF* TW15 .... 128 F5
Stainford Cl *ASHF* TW15 .... 129 G3

Stamford Av *FRIM* GU16 .... 182 C5 🔟
Stamford Rd *MDHD* SL6 .... 2 B7
Stanbrook Cl *THLE* RG7 .... 112 D5
Stanfield *TADY* RG26 .... 164 E6
Stanham Rd *TLHT* RG30 .... 87 J6 🔟
Stanhope Heath
STWL/WRAY TW19 .... 99 M5 🔟
Stanhope Rd *CBLY* GU15 .... 181 J2
SL SL1 .... 44 A7
WHIT RG2 .... 117 C3
Stanhope Wy
STWL/WRAY TW19 .... 99 M5 🔟
Stanlake La *WAR/TWY* RG10 .... 91 J2
Stanley Cl *MLW* SL7 .... 19 J3 🔟
Stanley Cottages *SLN* SL2 .... 5 C6
Stanley Gn West
DTCH/LGLY SL3 .... 72 C4 🔟
Stanley Gv *READ* RG1 .... 8 B5
Stanley Rd *ASHF* TW15 .... 128 C3
EWKG RG40 .... 11 L6
NWBY RG14 .... 15 C6
Stanley St *READ* RG1 .... 8 C5
Stanmore Cl *ASC* SL5 .... 151 K1 🔟
Stanmore Gdns *THLE* RG7 .... 166 C1
Stanmore Rd *KSCL* RG20 .... 29 H7
KSCL RG20 .... 54 E4
Stansfield Rd *HSLWW* TW4 .... 101 L1
Stanshawe Rd *READ* RG1 .... 8 E1
Stanton Cl *EARL* RG6 .... 117 M2
Stanton Wy *DTCH/LGLY* SL3 .... 72 B4
Stanwell Cl
STWL/WRAY TW19 .... 100 A5 🔟
Stanwell Gdns
STWL/WRAY TW19 .... 100 A5
Stanwell Moor Rd
STWL/WRAY TW19 .... 99 L8
WDR/YW UB7 .... 73 L8
Stanwell New Rd *STA* TW18 .... 127 L2
Stanwell Rd *ASHF* TW15 .... 128 B3
ASHF TW15 .... 128 B3
DTCH/LGLY SL3 .... 98 E2
EBED/NFELT TW14 .... 100 E6
Stapleford Rd *TLHT* RG30 .... 115 M2 🔟
Staple Hl *CHOB/PIR* GU24 .... 177 C2
Staplehurst *BRAK* RG12 .... 149 H4
Stapleton Cl *MLW* SL7 .... 19 J2
NWBY RG14 .... 135 M8
Star La *KSCL* RG20 .... 159 J8
WAR/TWY RG10 .... 39 M8
Starling Cl *WWKG* RG41 .... 10 A7
Starlings Dr *CALC* RG31 .... 86 E8
Starmead Dr *EWKG* RG40 .... 11 K8
Star Post Rd *CBLY* GU15 .... 174 B6
Starting Gates *NWBY* RG14 .... 15 J8
Startins La *MDHD* SL6 .... 19 M6
Starwood Ct *DTCH/LGLY* SL3 .... 71 M3 🔟
Statham Ct *BNFD* RG42 .... 12 A3
Station Ap *ASHF* TW15 .... 128 C2 🔟
MDHD SL6 .... 3 C6
MLW SL7 .... 19 H4
READ RG1 .... 8 F4
STA TW18 .... 127 K2 🔟
SUN TW16 .... 129 K6
VW GU25 .... 154 A1
Station Crs *ASHF* TW15 .... 128 A2
Station Estate Rd
EBED/NFELT TW14 .... 101 L7
Station Hl *ASC* SL5 .... 123 K8
MDHD SL6 .... 20 C7
READ RG1 .... 8 F4
Station Pde *VW* GU25 .... 154 A1
Station Ri *MLW* SL7 .... 19 H4
Station Rd *ADL/WDHM* KT15 .... 155 M8
ASC SL5 .... 152 D3
ASHF TW15 .... 128 C2
BAGS GU19 .... 175 H2
BNEND SL8 .... 20 D3
BRAK RG12 .... 13 H5
CHERT KT16 .... 155 J5
CHOB/PIR GU24 .... 177 J7
DTCH/LGLY SL3 .... 72 D2
EARL RG6 .... 117 M2
EGH TW20 .... 126 D3
EWKG RG40 .... 10 E6
FRIM GU16 .... 181 M5
GOR/PANG RG8 .... 32 F8
HEN RG9 .... 38 B5
HEN RG9 .... 64 D2
HUNG RG17 .... 49 L4
HUNG RG17 .... 50 F8
HUNG RG17 .... 77 K3
HUNG RG17 .... 105 K6
KSCL RG20 .... 159 K3
MDHD SL6 .... 20 C7
MDHD SL6 .... 43 J7
MLW SL7 .... 19 H5
NWBY RG14 .... 14 E6
NWBY RG14 .... 136 A1
READ RG1 .... 8 F5
SL SL1 .... 44 B7
STHA RG19 .... 138 B3
STWL/WRAY TW19 .... 98 C5
SUN TW16 .... 129 K5 🔟
THLE RG7 .... 139 M4
THLE RG7 .... 167 H1
UX/CGN UB8 .... 47 M5 🔟
WAR/TWY RG10 .... 64 F5
WAR/TWY RG10 .... 91 G2
Staunton Rd *SLN* SL2 .... 45 G6
Staveley Rd *ASHF* TW15 .... 129 G4 🔟
Staverton Cl *EWKG* RG40 .... 120 C8 🔟
Staverton Rd *WHIT* RG2 .... 116 F3
Stayne End *VW* GU25 .... 153 K1
Steam Farm La
EBED/NFELT TW14 .... 101 J3 🔟
Steep Hl *CHOB/PIR* GU24 .... 176 F3
Steeple Wk *EARL* RG6 .... 117 J6
Steerforth Copse *SHST* GU47 .... 173 H4 🔟
Steggles Cl *WODY* RG5 .... 90 A6
Stephanie Chase Ct *EWKG* RG40 .... 11 J4
Stephen Cl *EGH* TW20 .... 126 F4
WAR/TWY RG10 .... 91 J3
Stephen's Cl *THLE* RG7 .... 142 C8
Stephens Firs *THLE* RG7 .... 142 C8
Stephenson Cl *NTHA* RG18 .... 137 M2
Stephenson Ct *SL* SL1 .... 5 H9 🔟

Stephenson Dr *WDSR* SL4 .... 6 E6
Stephenson Rd *WHIT* RG2 .... 146 D7
Stephens Rd *TADY* RG26 .... 164 F6
THLE RG7 .... 142 C8
Sterling Av *SHPTN* TW17 .... 129 H8
Sterling Wy *TLHT* RG30 .... 87 K5
Stevens Hl *YTLY* GU46 .... 180 B1
Stevens La *HEN* RG9 .... 36 A5
Stevenson Dr *BNFD* RG42 .... 120 F3
Stewart Av *SHPTN* TW17 .... 128 D8
SL SL1 .... 5 G1
Stewart Cl *MDHD* SL6 .... 69 G8
Steyning Wy *HSLWW* TW4 .... 101 M3
Stile Pth *SUN* TW16 .... 129 K8 🔟
Stile Rd *DTCH/LGLY* SL3 .... 72 A4
Stilton Cl *EARL* RG6 .... 118 B4 🔟
Stilwell Cl *YTLY* GU46 .... 172 B8
Stirling Cl *CAV/SC* RG4 .... 63 G8 🔟
FRIM GU16 .... 182 B4 🔟
UX/CGN UB8 .... 47 M4 🔟
WDSR SL4 .... 96 A1
Stirling Gv *MDHD* SL6 .... 41 L6 🔟
Stirling Rd *SL* SL1 .... 44 D6
Stirling Wy *NTHA* RG18 .... 137 M2
Stirrup Pightle *NWBY* RG14 .... 136 E7 🔟
Stockbridge Wy *YTLY* GU46 .... 180 A2
Stockbury Cl *EARL* RG6 .... 117 L5
Stockdales Rd *WDSR* SL4 .... 70 C4 🔟
Stockton Rd *WHIT* RG2 .... 116 F5
Stockwells *MDHD* SL6 .... 43 G5
Stockwood Rd *CBLY* GU15 .... 182 C1
Stoke Court Dr *SLN* SL2 .... 45 H2
Stokeford Cl *BRAK* RG12 .... 150 C2 🔟
Stoke Gdns *SL* SL1 .... 4 F5
Stoke Gn *SLN* SL2 .... 45 K5
Stoke Park Av *SLN* SL2 .... 44 F4
Stoke Poges La *SL* SL1 .... 4 E6
Stoke Rd *SLN* SL2 .... 45 K6
Stoke Row Rd *HEN* RG9 .... 36 B6
Stokesay *SLN* SL2 .... 5 H4
Stokes La *STHA* RG19 .... 163 M5 🔟
Stokes Vw *GOR/PANG* RG8 .... 85 M1
Stompits Rd *MDHD* SL6 .... 68 E6
Stomp Rd *SL* SL1 .... 43 L6
Stonea Cl *EARL* RG6 .... 117 M6 🔟
Stonebridge Fld *WDSR* SL4 .... 70 E5
Stone Copse *NTHA* RG18 .... 109 H7
Stone Crs *EBED/NFELT* TW14 .... 101 J6
Stonecroft Av *IVER* SL0 .... 47 H7
Stonefield Pk *MDHD* SL6 .... 2 B4
Stonegate *CBLY* GU15 .... 174 F8
Stoneham Cl *TLHT* RG30 .... 87 K8
Stonehaven Dr *WODY* RG5 .... 90 D8
Stonehill Rd *LTWR* GU18 .... 175 K5
Stone House La *MDHD* SL6 .... 19 M5
Stonehouse Ri *FRIM* GU16 .... 182 B5
Stoneleigh Ct *FRIM* GU16 .... 182 C5
Stone St *TLHT* RG30 .... 87 L5
Stoney Cl *YTLY* GU46 .... 180 A2
Stoneyfield *THLE* RG7 .... 112 D8
Stoneyland Ct *EGH* TW20 .... 126 C3 🔟
Stoneylands Rd *EGH* TW20 .... 126 C3
Stoney La *NWBY* RG14 .... 109 C8
SLN SL2 .... 44 D2
STHA RG19 .... 138 B3
Stoney Meade *SL* SL1 .... 70 E1 🔟
Stoney Rd *BNFD* RG42 .... 12 E3
Stoney Ware *MLW* SL7 .... 19 G6
Stoney Ware Cl *MLW* SL7 .... 19 G6
Stony La *HUNG* RG17 .... 75 M3
Stornaway Rd *DTCH/LGLY* SL3 .... 72 F4
Stour Cl *TLHT* RG30 .... 87 K6 🔟
WDSR SL4 .... 70 E3
Stovell Rd *WDSR* SL4 .... 6 E5
Stowe Rd *SL* SL1 .... 44 B8
Stow Rd *HEN* RG9 .... 38 C6
St Patrick's Br *WAR/TWY* RG10 .... 64 C8
Strachey Cl *GOR/PANG* RG8 .... 85 M3
Straight La *HUNG* RG17 .... 50 C8
The Straight Mile
WAR/TWY RG10 .... 92 A6
Straight Rd *WDSR* SL4 .... 97 L5
Strande La *MDHD* SL6 .... 42 C1
Strande View Wk *MDHD* SL6 .... 42 C1
Strand Wy *EARL* RG6 .... 117 L5
Stranraer Gdns *SL* SL1 .... 4 F7
Stratfield *BRAK* RG12 .... 149 H5
Stratfield Av *TADY* RG26 .... 164 E7
Stratfield Rd *SL* SL1 .... 5 J8
Stratford Cl *SLN* SL2 .... 44 A5
Stratford Dr *FLKWH* HP10 .... 21 G2
Stratford Gdns *MDHD* SL6 .... 67 M2
Stratford Wy *CALC* RG31 .... 86 D8
Stratheden Pl *READ* RG1 .... 8 D5
Strathmore Dr *WAR/TWY* RG10 .... 90 D2
Strathy Cl *TLHT* RG30 .... 87 L6
Stratton Gdns *WHIT* RG2 .... 116 F5
Stratton Rd *SUN* TW16 .... 129 J7
Stratton Wk *NWBY* RG14 .... 181 K7 🔟
Strawberry Hl *BNFD* RG42 .... 122 B4
NWBY RG14 .... 14 D2
Streamside *SL* SL1 .... 70 C1 🔟
Streatley Rd *GOR/PANG* RG8 .... 32 B8
Streets Heath *CHOB/PIR* GU24 .... 176 C6
The Street *GOR/PANG* RG8 .... 32 E2
THLE RG7 .... 113 L1
THLE RG7 .... 140 D7
THLE RG7 .... 142 E8
THLE RG7 .... 166 E1
WAR/TWY RG10 .... 66 C8
WGFD OX10 .... 32 D1
Stretton Cl *THLE* RG7 .... 112 D5
Strodes College La
EGH TW20 .... 126 C3 🔟
Strode St *EGH* TW20 .... 126 D2
Stroma Ct *SL* SL1 .... 44 A8 🔟
Strood La *ASC* SL5 .... 123 M4
Stroud Cl *WDSR* SL4 .... 96 A2
Stroude Rd *EGH* TW20 .... 126 D4
VW GU25 .... 126 D8
VW GU25 .... 154 B1
Stroud Farm Rd *MDHD* SL6 .... 68 B6
Strouds Meadow *NTHA* RG18 .... 109 M7
The Strouds *THLE* RG7 .... 112 C8
Stuart Cl *WAR/TWY* RG10 .... 91 H3
Stuart Cl *CAV/SC* RG4 .... 88 E1
WDSR SL4 .... 6 A8
Stuart Rd *NWBY* RG14 .... 135 M8

Stuart Wy *STA* TW18 .... 127 L4
VW GU25 .... 153 K1
WDSR SL4 .... 6 A8
WDSR SL4 .... 96 B1
Stubbles La *MDHD* SL6 .... 19 K8
Stubbs Folly *SHST* GU47 .... 173 G7
Studios Rd *SHPTN* TW17 .... 128 C8
Studland Cl *WHIT* RG2 .... 116 F7 🔟
Sturbridge Cl *EARL* RG6 .... 117 M5 🔟
Sturges Rd *EWKG* RG40 .... 11 H7
Sturt Gn *MDHD* SL6 .... 68 B6
Styventon Pl *CHERT* KT16 .... 155 J4 🔟
Suck's La *GOR/PANG* RG8 .... 84 A4
Suffolk Cl *BAGS* GU19 .... 175 H4 🔟
SL SL1 .... 44 A7
WWKG RG41 .... 119 G8 🔟
Suffolk Combe *BNFD* RG42 .... 122 C5 🔟
Suffolk Rd *MDHD* SL6 .... 2 D9
MDHD SL6 .... 68 A2
TLHT RG30 .... 87 M7 🔟
Sulham La *GOR/PANG* RG8 .... 86 B2
Sulhamstead Hl *THLE* RG7 .... 113 M8
Sulhamstead Rd *THLE* RG7 .... 142 A2
Sullivan Rd *CBLY* GU15 .... 181 K1
Sumburgh Wy *SL* SL1 .... 4 E1
Summerfield Cl *WWKG* RG41 .... 119 J5
Summerfield Ri *GOR/PANG* RG8 .... 33 G7
Summer Gdns *CBLY* GU15 .... 182 F1
Summerlea *SL* SL1 .... 70 E1 🔟
Summerleaze Rd *MDHD* SL6 .... 42 D5
Summers Rd *SL* SL1 .... 43 M4
Summer Trees *SUN* TW16 .... 129 L6 🔟
Summit Cl *EWKG* RG40 .... 147 J8
Sunbury Court Rd *SUN* TW16 .... 129 M7
Sunbury Rd *FELT* TW13 .... 129 J1
WDSR SL4 .... 7 J3
Sunbury Wy *FELT* TW13 .... 129 M3
Sun Cl *WDSR* SL4 .... 7 J3
Sunderland Cl *WODY* RG5 .... 90 E6
Sunderland Pl *NTHA* RG18 .... 137 M2 🔟
Sunderland Rd *MDHD* SL6 .... 41 L6
Sundew Cl *EWKG* RG40 .... 11 L3
LTWR GU18 .... 176 A6
Sundial Cl *TLHT* RG30 .... 87 K8 🔟
Sundon Crs *VW* GU25 .... 153 L2
Sundown Rd *ASHF* TW15 .... 128 F3 🔟
Sun Gdns *THLE* RG7 .... 142 D5
Sun La *MDHD* SL6 .... 3 G4
THLE RG7 .... 168 G4
Sunley Cl *NWBY* RG14 .... 136 A8
Sunmead Rd *SUN* TW16 .... 129 K8
Sunna Gdns *SUN* TW16 .... 129 L7
Sunning Av *ASC* SL5 .... 152 B4
Sunninghill Cl *ASC* SL5 .... 152 A1
Sunninghill Rd *ASC* SL5 .... 124 A3
ASC SL5 .... 152 A2
BFOR GU20 .... 151 K7
Sunnybank *ASC* SL5 .... 151 K1 🔟
MLW SL7 .... 18 F2
Sunnybank Rd *FARN* GU14 .... 181 G8
Sun Ray Est *SHST* GU47 .... 172 C6
Sun St *READ* RG1 .... 9 M6
Surbiton Rd *CBLY* GU15 .... 174 D5
Surley Rw *CAV/SC* RG4 .... 88 D1
Surly Hall Wk *WDSR* SL4 .... 6 A7
Surrey Av *CBLY* GU15 .... 181 K2
SLN SL2 .... 44 F6
Surrey Ct *BNFD* RG42 .... 122 C5 🔟
Surridge Ct *BAGS* GU19 .... 175 H4 🔟
Sussex Gdns *WODY* RG5 .... 90 B7
Sussex La *THLE* RG7 .... 144 F5
Sussex Pl *DTCH/LGLY* SL3 .... 5 M9
SL SL1 .... 5 K9
Sutcliffe Av *EARL* RG6 .... 118 A3
Sutherland Av *SUN* TW16 .... 129 J7
Sutherland Cha *ASC* SL5 .... 123 H7
Sutherland Gdns *SUN* TW16 .... 129 J7 🔟
Sutherland Gv *CALC* RG31 .... 115 H2
Sutherlands *NWBY* RG14 .... 136 B7 🔟
Sutherlands Av *READ* RG1 .... 116 F1
Sutton Av *DTCH/LGLY* SL3 .... 71 M2
Sutton Cl *MDHD* SL6 .... 20 E8
Sutton La *DTCH/LGLY* SL3 .... 72 E6
Sutton Pl *DTCH/LGLY* SL3 .... 72 E6
Sutton Rd *CBLY* GU15 .... 174 D5
MDHD SL6 .... 20 E8
NWBY RG14 .... 136 A1
Suttons Park Av *EARL* RG6 .... 89 J6
READ RG1 .... 89 H6
Swabey Rd *DTCH/LGLY* SL3 .... 72 D4
Swains Cl *TADY* RG26 .... 164 E6
Swains Rd *TADY* RG26 .... 164 E6
Swainstone Rd *WHIT* RG2 .... 116 E1
Swaledale *BRAK* RG12 .... 149 K2
Swale Rd *FARN* GU14 .... 181 G8
Swallow Cl *CALC* RG31 .... 86 F8 🔟
STA TW18 .... 127 J2
YTLY GU46 .... 171 L8
Swallowdale *IVER* SL0 .... 47 G4
Swallowfield *EGH* TW20 .... 125 L4 🔟
Swallowfield Rd *THLE* RG7 .... 145 K8
Swallowfield Dr *WHIT* RG2 .... 116 E8
Swallow Field Gdns
THLE RG7 .... 114 B2 🔟
Swallow St *IVER* SL0 .... 47 G4
Swallow Wy *WWKG* RG41 .... 147 H1
Swancote Gn *BRAK* RG12 .... 149 L2 🔟
Swan Dr *THLE* RG7 .... 140 E3
Swangate *HUNG* RG17 .... 104 A7 🔟
Swan La *SHST* GU47 .... 172 E8
Swanmore Ct *EARL* RG6 .... 118 B5
Swan Pl *READ* RG1 .... 8 F7
Swan Rd *IVER* SL0 .... 47 J7
Swan's Cl *MARL* SN8 .... 102 A2
Swans Ct *WAR/TWY* RG10 .... 91 H3 🔟
Swansea Rd *HTHAIR* TW6 .... 100 F5
READ RG1 .... 8 F1
Swansea Ter *CALC* RG31 .... 87 G5
Swanston Fld *GOR/PANG* RG8 .... 60 A7
Swedish Houses *TADY* RG26 .... 164 F7 🔟
Sweeps Ditch Cl *STA* TW18 .... 127 K6
Sweeps La *EGH* TW20 .... 126 C3
Sweetbriar *CWTH* RG45 .... 148 D7 🔟
Sweet Briar Dr *CALC* RG31 .... 114 F2 🔟
Sweetzer's Piece *THLE* RG7 .... 142 B8
Swepstone Cl *EARL* RG6 .... 117 M4
Swift Cl *WWKG* RG41 .... 147 H1 🔟

Swift La *BAGS* GU19 .... 175 J3
Swinbrook Cl *CALC* RG31 .... 87 G3
Swindon Rd *HTHAIR* TW6 ...... 100 F5
Swinley Rd *ASC* SL5 .... 150 F1
Swiss Cottage Cl *CALC* RG31 ..... 86 F6
Switchback Cl *MDHD* SL6 .... 42 A4
Switchback Rd North *MDHD* SL6.. 42 B3
Switchback Rd South
 MDHD SL6........................ 42 A5
Swithin Cha *BNFD* RG42 .... 122 B5
Sycamore Cl *BNEND* SL8 .... 20 E3
 FELT TW13 .... 129 K1
 FRIM GU16 .... 182 B5
 SHST GU47 .... 172 E7
 TLHT RG30 .... 142 E1
 WODY RG5 .... 117 M1
Sycamore Dr *FRIM* GU16 .... 182 B4
 MLW SL7 .... 19 G1
 WAR/TWY RG10 .... 91 G1
Sycamore Ri *BRAK* RG12 .... 13 M6
 NWBY RG14 .... 108 F8
Sycamore Rd *WHIT* RG2 .... 117 H4
The Sycamores *BLKW* GU17 .... 180 C1
Sycamore Wk *DTCH/LGLY* SL3 .. 46 B7
 EGH TW20 .... 125 L4
The Sydings *NWBY* RG14 .... 136 A1
Sydney Cl *CWTH* RG45 .... 148 F3
Sydney Crs *ASHF* TW15 .... 128 C4
Sydney Gv *SL* SL1 .... 4 B2
Sydney Rd *EBED/NFELT* TW14 .. 101 K7
Syke Cluan *IVER* SL0 .... 73 H2
Syke Ings *IVER* SL0 .... 73 H3
Sykes Rd *SL* SL1 .... 44 F2
Sylvan Rdg *SHST* GU47 .... 172 D5
Sylvanus *BRAK* RG12 .... 149 J4
Sylverns Ct *BNFD* RG42 .... 122 A5
Sylvester Cl *NWBY* RG14 .... 136 B1
 WAR/TWY RG10 .... 119 G3
Sylvester Rd *MDHD* SL6 .... 42 B4
Symondson Ms *BNFD* RG42 .... 120 F2
Sympson Rd *TADY* RG26 .... 165 G5

T

Tachbrook Rd
 EBED/NFELT TW14 .... 101 J6
 UX/CGN UB8 .... 47 M3
Tadham Pl *STHA* RG19 .... 137 M4
Tadley Common Rd *TADY* RG26 .. 164 F5
Taff Wy *TLHT* RG30 .... 87 K7
Tag La *WAR/TWY* RG10 .... 65 K5
Talbot Av *DTCH/LGLY* SL3 ...... 72 C3
Talbot Cl *NWBY* RG14 .... 136 B1
Talbot Ct *READ* RG1 .... 8 E7
Talbot Pl *BAGS* GU19 .... 175 H3
 DTCH/LGLY SL3................. 71 M8
Talbot Rd *ASHF* TW15 .... 128 A3
Talbots Dr *MDHD* SL6 .... 41 K8
Talbot Wy *CALC* RG31 .... 86 F3
Talfourd Av *EARL* RG6 .... 117 K1
Talisman Cl *CWTH* RG45 .... 172 A1
Tallis La *TLHT* RG30 .... 116 A2
Tall Trees *DTCH/LGLY* SL3....... 73 H8
Tamar Gdns *WHIT* RG2 .... 116 F3
Tamarisk Av *WHIT* RG2 .... 117 H5
Tamarisk Ct *NTHA* RG18 .... 138 C2
Tamarisk Ri *EWKG* RG40 .... 11 G3
Tamarisk Wy *SL* SL1 .... 70 D1
Tamar Wy *DTCH/LGLY* SL3 ...... 72 E5
 WWKG RG41 .... 10 A4
 WWKG RG41 .... 119 H8
Tamian Wy *HSLWW* TW4 .... 101 M3
Tamworth *BRAK* RG12 .... 150 A4
Tamworth Cl *EARL* RG6 .... 117 M5
Tangier La *WDSR* SL4 .... 7 J3
Tanglewood *EWKG* RG40 .... 147 K7
Tanglewood Cl *CHERT* KT16 .... 153 L7
Tanglewood Ride
 CHOB/PIR GU24 .... 176 B7
Tanglewood Wy *FELT* TW13 .... 129 L1
Tangley Dr *WWKG* RG41 .... 147 L2
Tanhouse La *WWKG* RG41 .... 10 D7
Tankard La *MARL* SN8 .... 102 A2
Tank Rd *CBLY* GU15............. 181 J1
Tanners Cl *THLE* RG7 .... 142 C5
Tanners La *CAV/SC* RG4 .... 62 C6
Tape La *WAR/TWY* RG10 .... 91 J6
Taplow Common Rd *SL* SL1 ..... 21 J8
Taplow Rd *BNFD* RG42 .... 120 F2
Tarbat Ct *SHST* GU47 .... 173 G6
Tarbay La *WDSR* SL4 .... 95 L1
Target Cl *EBED/NFELT* TW14 .... 101 H5
Target Hl *BNFD* RG42 .... 122 A5
Targett Ct *WWKG* RG41 .... 118 E4
Tarlton Ct *TLHT* RG30 .... 87 H8
Tarmac Wy *WDR/YW* UB7 .... 73 L7
Tarnbrook Wy *BRAK* RG12....... 150 B4
Tarn La *NWBY* RG14 .... 14 C9
Tarragon Cl *BNFD* RG42 .... 13 M1
 EARL RG6 .... 117 J5
Tarragon Wy *THLE* RG7 .... 142 E3
Tarrant Gn *BNFD* RG42 .... 121 M5
Tarrant's Hl *HUNG* RG17 .... 132 A1
Tatchbrook Cl *MDHD* SL6 .... 3 J2
Tattersall Cl *EWKG* RG40 .... 11 M7
Tavistock Cl *MDHD* SL6 .... 41 K7
 STA TW18 .... 128 A3
Tavistock Gdns *FARN* GU14 .... 181 L7
Tavistock Rd *WHIT* RG2 .... 116 E3
Tawfield *BRAK* RG12 .... 149 H4
Tawny Cl *FELT* TW13 .... 129 K1
Tay Cl *FARN* GU14 .... 181 H8
Taylors Cl *MLW* SL7 .... 19 J4
Taylors Ct *FELT* TW13 .... 101 K8
 MDHD SL6 .... 41 L6
Tay Rd *TLHT* RG30 .... 87 K6
Tazewell Ct *READ* RG1 .... 8 C9
Tealgate *HUNG* RG17 .... 104 A7
Tebbit Cl *BRAK* RG12 .... 13 L5
Tees Cl *FARN* GU14 .... 181 H8
Teesdale Rd *SL* SL1 .... 44 C6
Tekels Av *CBLY* GU15 .... 182 A2
Tekels Wy *CBLY* GU15 .... 182 C3
Telford Crs *WODY* RG5 .... 90 C5

Telford Dr *SL* SL1 .... 70 D2
Telston Cl *BNEND* SL8 .... 20 D1
Tempest Rd *EGH* TW20 .... 126 F4
Templar Cl *SHST* GU47 .... 172 D6
Templecroft *ASHF* TW15 .... 129 G4
Templedene Av *STA* TW18 ..... 127 L5
Temple Gdns *STA* TW18 .... 127 J6
Temple La *MLW* SL7 .... 40 F1
Temple Ms *WODY* RG5 .... 90 C7
Temple Mill Island *MLW* SL7 ... 40 F1
Temple Pk *MDHD* SL6 .... 40 C3
Temple Pl *READ* RG1 .... 8 F8
Temple Rd *WDSR* SL4 .... 7 H8
Templeton Gdns *WHIT* RG2 .... 116 F5
Temple Wy *BNFD* RG42 .... 12 A1
Ten Acre La *EGH* TW20 .... 126 F7
Tenby Av *CAV/SC* RG4 .... 89 C1
Tenby Dr *ASC* SL5 .... 152 A2
Tenby Rd *FRIM* GU16 .... 182 D6
Tennyson Cl
 EBED/NFELT TW14 .... 101 K5
Tennyson Rd *ASHF* TW15 ...... 128 B3
 NTHA RG18 .... 137 M2
 WODY RG5 .... 118 B2
Tennyson Wy *SLN* SL2 .... 44 B5
Teresa V *BNFD* RG42 .... 122 B4
Tern Cl *TLHT* RG30 .... 87 K7
Terrace Rd North *BNFD* RG42 .. 120 F3
Terrace Rd South *BNFD* RG42 .. 120 F4
The Terrace *ASC* SL5 .... 152 A2
 CBLY GU15 .... 181 J1
 CWTH RG45 .... 173 G1
 EWKG RG40 .... 10 F5
Tessa Rd *READ* RG1 .... 8 C2
Test Cl *TLHT* RG30 .... 87 K6
Test Wy *MARL* SN8 .... 178 D2
Testwood Rd *WDSR* SL4 .... 70 A8
Teviot Rd *TLHT* RG30 .... 87 H7
The Thakerays *STHA* RG19 .... 138 A4
Thames Av *CHERT* KT16 .... 127 K8
 GOR/PANG RG8 .... 60 A8
 READ RG1 .... 8 F2
 WDSR SL4 .... 7 J5
Thames Cl *BNEND* SL8 .... 20 D2
 CHERT KT16 .... 155 L4
Thames Ct *READ* RG1 .... 8 B3
Thames Crs *MDHD* SL6 .... 42 E5
Thames Dr *WAR/TWY* RG10.... 64 C8
Thamesfield Gdns *MLW* SL7 .... 19 H5
Thamesgate *STA* TW18 .... 127 L7
Thames Md *WDSR* SL4 .... 70 B8
Thames Pth *EGH* TW20 .... 98 B8
 GOR/PANG RG8 .... 32 F6
 GOR/PANG RG8 .... 86 F1
 HEN RG9 .... 39 K3
 MDHD SL6 .... 68 F2
 READ RG1 .... 88 B4
 STA TW18 .... 127 H1
 STA TW18 .... 127 J5
 WOT/HER KT12 .... 129 M8
Thames Reach *GOR/PANG* RG8 .. 87 G2
Thames Rd *DTCH/LGLY* SL3 .... 72 E4
 GOR/PANG RG8 .... 32 E8
 NTHA RG18 .... 137 L1
Thames Side *HEN* RG9 .... 38 B4
 STA TW18 .... 155 M2
 WDSR SL4 .... 7 K5
Thames Side Prom *READ* RG1 .. 8 D1
Thames St *CAV/SC* RG4 .... 90 A2
 STA TW18 .... 127 J3
 SUN TW16 .... 129 L8
 WDSR SL4 .... 7 K5
Thanington Wy *EARL* RG6...... 117 L4
Thatchers Dr *MDHD* SL6 .... 67 K1
Theal Cl *SHST* GU47 .... 173 G6
Theale Rd *TLHT* RG30 .... 114 E8
Theobald Dr *CALC* RG31 .... 87 G2
Theobalds Wy *FRIM* GU16....... 182 F3
Thetford Ms *CAV/SC* RG4 .... 63 G8
Thetford Rd *ASHF* TW15 .... 128 B2
Thibet Rd *SHST* GU47 .... 172 F6
Thicket Gv *MDHD* SL6 .... 41 J7
Thicket Rd *TLHT* RG30 .... 87 H6
Thickthorne La *STA* TW18 ..... 127 M5
Third Av *MLW* SL7 .... 19 J4
Third Crs *SL* SL1 .... 4 B1
Third St *STHA* RG19 .... 161 J1
Thirkleby Cl *SL* SL1 .... 4 A6
Thirlmere Av *SL* SL1 .... 43 M6
 TLHT RG30 .... 87 J5
Thirlmere Cl *EGH* TW20 .... 126 E5
Thirtover *NTHA* RG18 .... 109 L5
Thistledown *CALC* RG31 .... 86 F5
Thistleton Wy *EARL* RG6 .... 118 B4
Thomas Dr *BNFD* RG42 .... 122 B5
Thomas La *EWKG* RG40 .... 147 H6
Thomas Rd *FLKWH* HP10 .... 21 G2
Thompkins La *SLN* SL2 .... 44 C1
Thompson Cl *DTCH/LGLY* SL3 .. 72 D4
 NTHA RG18 .... 81 J8
Thompson Dr *STHA* RG19 ..... 138 B4
Thompson's La *CHOB/PIR* GU24.. 177 G4
Thomson Wk *CALC* RG31 ...... 115 H2
Thorburn Cha *SHST* GU47 ..... 173 H8
Thornbank Cl
 STWL/WRAY TW19 .... 99 K4
Thornbers Wy *WAR/TWY* RG10.. 90 E1
Thornbridge Rd *IVER* SL0 .... 46 F2
 WHIT RG2 .... 116 E6
Thornbury Cl *CWTH* RG45 ...... 172 E1
Thorncroft *EWKG* RG40 .... 125 M5
Thorndike *SLN* SL2 .... 44 D6
Thorndown La *BFOR* GU20 .... 176 A3
Thorn Dr *DTCH/LGLY* SL3 ...... 46 B7
Thorne Cl *ASHF* TW15 .... 128 F5
 CWTH RG45 .... 148 D7
 WWKG RG41 .... 119 G4
Thorney Cl *EARL* RG6 .... 118 B4
Thorney La North *IVER* SL0 .... 47 J7
Thorney La South *IVER* SL0 .... 73 J1
Thorney Mill Rd *IVER* SL0 ...... 73 L3
Thornfield *STHA* RG19 .... 162 A3
Thornfield Gn *BLKW* GU17...... 181 J3
Thornford Rd *STHA* RG19 ...... 162 A4
Thornhill *BRAK* RG12 .... 150 B1

Thorn La *READ* RG1 .... 9 G6
Thorn St *READ* RG1 .... 8 E6
Thornton Ms *TLHT* RG30 .... 87 M6
Thorp Cl *BNFD* RG42 .... 120 F3
Thorpe By-pass *EGH* TW20 ... 126 E8
Thorpe Lea Rd *EGH* TW20 .... 126 E7
 EGH TW20 .... 126 E7
Thorpe Rd *CHERT* KT16 .... 155 G4
 EGH TW20 .... 127 G4
Thorpeside Cl *EGH* TW20 ..... 127 H7
Thrale Ms *TLHT* RG30 .... 87 L6
Three Acre Rd *NWBY* RG14 ... 136 C6
Three Castles Pth *ASC* SL5 ... 122 F8
 ASC SL5 .... 124 B5
 HTWY RG27 .... 171 K7
 WDSR SL4 .... 7 L9
 WDSR SL4 .... 97 G4
Three Firs Wy *THLE* RG7 ...... 142 B5
Three Gables La *GOR/PANG* RG8 .. 32 D7
Threshfield *BRAK* RG12 .... 149 K2
Thrift La *MDHD* SL6 .... 68 A5
Thrush Cl *TLHT* RG30 .... 87 K7
Thurlby Wy *MDHD* SL6 .... 68 A3
Thurlestone Gdns *WHIT* RG2 .. 116 F4
Thurnscoe Cl *EARL* RG6 .... 117 J6
Thurso Cl *TLHT* RG30 .... 87 K6
Thurston Rd *SL* SL1 .... 4 D2
Thyme Cl *EARL* RG6 .... 117 J5
Tichborne Cl *BLKW* GU17 ...... 181 G1
Tichbourne Cl *FRIM* GU16 ..... 182 C3
Tickenor Dr *EWKG* RG40 .... 147 J7
Tickhill Cl *EARL* RG6 .... 117 J7
Tickleback Rw *BNFD* RG42 ..... 93 L8
Tidmarsh La *GOR/PANG* RG8.... 85 K4
Tidmarsh Rd *GOR/PANG* RG8 .. 85 M2
Tidmarsh St *TLHT* RG30 .... 87 L6
Tidmore La *GOR/PANG* RG8.... 34 C5
Tidwells Lea *BNFD* RG42 ...... 122 B6
Tiffany Cl *WWKG* RG41 .... 119 G8
Tiger Cl *WODY* RG5 .... 90 E7
Tigerseye Cl *WWKG* RG41 ..... 119 C7
Tilbury Cl *CAV/SC* RG4 .... 88 C3
Tilbury Wk *DTCH/LGLY* SL3.... 72 E3
Tile Barn Cl *FARN* GU14 .... 181 K8
Tilecotes Cl *MLW* SL7 .... 19 G4
Tilehurst La *BNFD* RG42 .... 120 F3
 BNFD RG42 .... 121 G3
Tilehurst Rd *READ* RG1 .... 8 B7
 TLHT RG30 .... 87 L8
 TLHT RG30 .... 87 M7
Tilling Cl *CALC* RG31 .... 86 E4
Tilney Wy *EARL* RG6 .... 117 J6
Tilstone Av *WDSR* SL4 .... 70 B5
Tilstone Cl *WDSR* SL4 .... 70 B4
Timberley Pl *CWTH* RG45 ...... 172 B2
Timbers Wk *MDHD* SL6 .... 67 L1
Timline Gn *BRAK* RG12 .... 122 C7
Timsway *STA* TW18 .... 127 J3
Tindal Cl *YTLY* GU46 .... 172 A8
Tinkers La *WDSR* SL4 .... 96 A1
Tinsey Cl *EGH* TW20 .... 126 E3
Tinsley Cl *EARL* RG6 .... 117 J6
Tintagel Dr *FRIM* GU16 .... 182 C5
Tintagel Rd *EWKG* RG40 .... 147 K6
Tintern Cl *SL* SL1 .... 70 F3
Tintern Crs *READ* RG1 .... 116 C1
Tinwell Cl *EARL* RG6 .... 118 B4
Tippett Ri *WHIT* RG2 .... 116 E1
Tippings La *WODY* RG5 .... 90 D5
Tippits Md *BNFD* RG42 .... 121 G7
Tiptree Cl *EARL* RG6 .... 117 J6
Titchfield Cl *TADY* RG26 .... 164 F7
Titcombe Wy *HUNG* RG17 ..... 133 K4
Tite Hl *EGH* TW20 .... 126 A3
Tithe Barn Dr *MDHD* SL6 .... 69 H5
Tithebarn Gv *CALC* RG31 ...... 115 J2
Tithe Cl *MDHD* SL6 .... 68 F5
 VW GU25 .... 154 A3
Tithe Ct *DTCH/LGLY* SL3 .... 72 D4
Tithe La *STWL/WRAY* TW19 .... 98 C5
Titlarks Hill Rd *ASC* SL5 .... 152 E5
Tiverton Cl *WODY* RG5 .... 90 B5
Toad La *BLKW* GU17 .... 181 H2
Tocker Gdns *BNFD* RG42 .... 121 L4
Tockley Rd *SL* SL1 .... 43 L4
Tofrek Ter *TLHT* RG30 .... 87 M7
Tokers Green La *CAV/SC* RG4 .. 62 A7
Toll Gdns *BRAK* RG12 .... 122 B8
Tollgate *MDHD* SL6 .... 41 K8
Tolpuddle Wy *YTLY* GU46...... 180 C1
Tomlin Cl *STHA* RG19 .... 138 B4
Tomlin Rd *SLN* SL2 .... 44 B5
Tomlins Av *FRIM* GU16 .... 182 C4
Tomlins Cl *TADY* RG26 .... 164 E7
Tomlinscote Wy *FRIM* GU16.... 182 D4
Tomlinson Dr *EWKG* RG40 ..... 147 K8
Topaz Cl *SL* SL1 .... 70 E1
 WWKG RG41 .... 119 H7
Top Common *BRAK* RG12 ...... 13 L1
Tope Rd *WHIT* RG2 .... 146 C6
Torcross Gv *CALC* RG31 .... 114 C2
Torin Ct *EGH* TW20 .... 125 M3
Torquay Sp *SLN* SL2 .... 44 E4
Torridge Rd *DTCH/LGLY* SL3 .. 72 E6
Torrington Rd *WHIT* RG2 ...... 116 F4
Toseland Wy *EARL* RG6 .... 118 B3
Totale Ri *BNFD* RG42 .... 121 L4
Totland Cl *FARN* GU14 .... 181 K8
Totnes Rd *WHIT* RG2 .... 116 F4
Totterdown *THLE* RG7 .... 142 C5
Toutley Cl *WWKG* RG41 .... 119 H5
Toutley Rd *WWKG* RG41 .... 119 K5
Tower Cl *CAV/SC* RG4 .... 62 F7
Tower Hl *KSCL* RG20 .... 52 D6
Towers Dr *CWTH* RG45 .... 172 C2
Town Farm Wy
 STWL/WRAY TW19 .... 100 A6
Townfield *MARL* SN8 .... 102 A2
Town La *FLKWH* HP10 .... 21 G2
 STWL/WRAY TW19 .... 100 A6
Town Quay *STA* TW18 .... 127 M8
Townsend Cl *BRAK* RG12 ...... 150 B2
Townsend Rd *ASHF* TW15 ..... 128 B3
 GOR/PANG RG8 .... 32 D7
 GOR/PANG RG8 .... 57 H3

Townside Pl *CBLY* GU15 .... 174 A8
Town Tree Rd *ASHF* TW15 .... 128 C3
Trafalgar Cl *WWKG* RG41 ...... 119 H8
Trafalgar Ct *TLHT* RG30 .... 88 A8
Trafalgar Wy *CBLY* GU15 ...... 181 J2
Trafford Rd *FRIM* GU16 .... 182 A6
 READ RG1 .... 8 B3
Travellers Wy *HEST* TW5 ...... 101 M1
Travic Rd *SLN* SL2 .... 44 C4
Travis Ct *SLN* SL2 .... 44 E4
Travis La *SHST* GU47 .... 172 F7
 SHST GU47 .... 173 G7
Tredegar Rd *CAV/SC* RG4 ...... 88 C1
Tree Cl *TLHT* RG30 .... 87 G6
Treesmill Dr *MDHD* SL6 .... 67 L3
Trees Rd *BNEND* SL8 .... 20 D3
Treeton Cl *EARL* RG6 .... 117 J6
Tree Tops Av *CBLY* GU15 ...... 174 D6
Trefoil Cl *EWKG* RG40 .... 11 M3
Trefoil Dro *EWKG* RG40 .... 138 C2
Treforgan *CAV/SC* RG4 .... 88 C1
 DTCH/LGLY SL3 .... 72 A3
Trelawney Av *DTCH/LGLY* SL3.. 72 C4
Trelawney Dr *CALC* RG31 ...... 86 E5
Trelleck Rd *READ* RG1 .... 116 C1
Tremayne Wk *CBLY* GU15 ..... 182 F2
Trenchard Rd *MDHD* SL6 .... 68 E6
Trenches La *DTCH/LGLY* SL3 .. 72 D1
Trent Cl *FARN* GU14 .... 181 H8
 WWKG RG41 .... 119 H7
Trent Crs *NTHA* RG18 .... 137 L1
Trenton Cl *FRIM* GU16 .... 182 D4
Trent Rd *DTCH/LGLY* SL3 ...... 72 E6
Tresham Crs *YTLY* GU46 .... 171 K8
Trevelyan *BRAK* RG12 .... 149 H4
Trevithick Cl *EBED/NFELT* TW14 .. 101 J7
Trewarden Av *IVER* SL0 .... 47 G3
The Triangle *NWBY* RG14 ...... 136 E7
Trindledown *BNFD* RG42 ...... 121 K5
Tring Cl *CALC* RG31 .... 86 F3
Trinity *SHST* GU47 .... 173 H4
Trinity Av *MLW* SL7 .... 19 G3
Trinity Cl *STWL/WRAY* TW19 .. 99 M5
Trinity Ct *THLE* RG7 .... 114 A3
Trinity Crs *ASC* SL5 .... 152 D2
Trinity Pl *READ* RG1 .... 8 D6
 WDSR SL4 .... 7 H8
Trinity Rd *MLW* SL7 .... 19 G4
Triumph Cl *WODY* RG5 .... 118 C1
Trotsworth Av *VW* GU25 ...... 154 A1
Trotters La *CHOB/PIR* GU24 ... 177 L7
Trotwood Cl *SHST* GU47 .... 173 H4
Troutbeck Cl *SLN* SL2 .... 5 J5
 WAR/TWY RG10 .... 65 G8
Trout Cl *EARL* RG6 .... 89 K6
 MLW SL7 .... 18 F6
Trout La *WDR/YW* UB7 .... 47 M8
Trout Wk *NWBY* RG14 .... 136 E1
Trowe's La *THLE* RG7 .... 168 A2
 THLE RG7 .... 169 G1
Trumball Rd *BNFD* RG42 ...... 121 K5
Trumper Wy *SL* SL1 .... 70 C1
Trumps Green Av *VW* GU25 ... 154 A3
Trumps Green Cl *VW* GU25 .... 154 B2
Trumpsgreen Rd *VW* GU25 .... 154 B2
Trumps Mill La *VW* GU25 ...... 154 C3
Truro Cl *MDHD* SL6 .... 41 K7
Truss Hill Rd *ASC* SL5 .... 151 M2
Trust Cnr *HEN* RG9 .... 38 B6
Trusthorpe Cl *EARL* RG6 .... 118 B4
Trys Hill Longcross Rd
 CHERT KT16 .... 154 B7
Tubbs Farm Cl *HUNG* RG17 .... 49 L4
Tubb's La *KSCL* RG20 .... 159 J8
Tubwell Rd *SLN* SL2 .... 45 L2
Tudor Av *KSCL* RG20 .... 80 F2
Tudor Cl *ASHF* TW15 .... 128 B2
 EWKG RG40 .... 148 C1
Tudor Ct *MDHD* SL6 .... 42 F4
Tudor Dr *YTLY* GU46 .... 180 A1
Tudor Gdns *SL* SL1 .... 43 M6
Tudor La *WDSR* SL4 .... 97 M6
Tudor Rd *ASHF* TW15 .... 129 G4
 NWBY RG14 .... 14 F7
 READ RG1 .... 8 E4
Tudor Wy *WDSR* SL4 .... 70 B8
Tunnel Link Rd *HTHAIR* TW6 .. 100 D4
Tunnel Rd West *HTHAIR* TW6 .. 100 D1
Tuns La *HEN* RG9 .... 38 B4
 SL SL1 .... 4 B7
 SL SL1 .... 70 F3
Tunworth Ms *TADY* RG26 ...... 164 F6
Tupsley Rd *READ* RG1 .... 116 C1
Turbary Gdns *TADY* RG26 ..... 164 E5
Turf Hill Rd *CBLY* GU15 .... 174 C6
Turfhouse La *CHOB/PIR* GU24 .. 177 H4
Turk's La *THLE* RG7 .... 166 C2
Turmeric Cl *EARL* RG6 .... 117 J5
Turnberry *BRAK* RG12 .... 149 H3
Turnbridge Cl *EARL* RG6 ...... 117 L6
Turner Pl *SHST* GU47 .... 173 G8
Turner Rd *DTCH/LGLY* SL3 .... 71 M2
Turners Cl *STA* TW18 .... 127 L3
Turners Dr *STHA* RG19 .... 138 B3
The Turnery *STHA* RG19....... 137 M3
Turnfields *STHA* RG19 .... 138 A3
Turnoak Pk *WDSR* SL4 .... 96 B3
Turnpike Rd *BNFD* RG42 ...... 121 G7
 NTHA RG18 .... 137 H2
 NWBY RG14 .... 15 M1
Turnstone Cl *WWKG* RG41 .... 118 C3
Turnstone End *YTLY* GU46 .... 171 L8
Turnville Cl *LTWR* GU18 .... 175 K5
Turpin Rd *EBED/NFELT* TW14 .. 101 J5
Turpins Gn *MDHD* SL6 .... 67 K1
Turton Wy *SL* SL1 .... 71 G3
Tuscan Cl *TLHT* RG30 .... 87 H6
Tuxford Ms *TLHT* RG30 .... 87 L7
Tweed Cl *FARN* GU14 .... 181 H8
Tweed Ct *DTCH/LGLY* SL3 ..... 72 E6
Twinches La *SL* SL1 .... 44 C5
Twin Oaks *CAV/SC* RG4 .... 62 E8
Twinwoods *KSCL* RG20 .... 78 D2
Two Rivers Wy *NWBY* RG14 ... 15 M3
Two Tree Hl *HEN* RG9 .... 37 L6
Twycross Rd *EWKG* RG40 ...... 11 M4
Twyford Rd *BNFD* RG42 .... 92 F6

Twynersh Av *CHERT* KT16 ..... 155 J3
Twynham Rd *MDHD* SL6 .... 41 L7
Tyberton Pl *READ* RG1 .... 116 C1
Tydehams *NWBY* RG14 .... 136 B7
Tyle Pl *WDSR* SL4 .... 97 K4
Tyler Cl *CAV/SC* RG4 .... 88 B1
Tyler Gdns *ADL/WDHM* KT15 .. 155 M8
Tyle Rd *TLHT* RG30 .... 87 G6
Tyler's La *THLE* RG7 .... 110 E4
Tylers Pl *TLHT* RG30 .... 87 J6
Tylorstown *CAV/SC* RG4 .... 62 C8
Tynan Cl *EBED/NFELT* TW14 .. 101 K7
Tyne Cl *FARN* GU14 .... 181 H8
Tyne Wy *NTHA* RG18 .... 137 L1
Tyrell Gdns *WDSR* SL4 .... 96 C3
Tytherton *BRAK* RG12 .... 13 K5

U

Uffcott Cl *EARL* RG6 .... 117 J6
Uffington Cl *CALC* RG31 .... 86 F6
Uffington Dr *BRAK* RG12 ...... 150 B1
Ullswater *BRAK* RG12 .... 149 H4
Ullswater Cl *LTWR* GU18 ...... 175 L5
 STHA RG19 .... 137 K3
Ullswater Dr *CALC* RG31 ...... 87 G3
Ullswater Rd *LTWR* GU18 ..... 175 L5
Ulster Cl *CAV/SC* RG4 .... 89 G1
Umberville Wy *SLN* SL2 .... 44 C5
Underhill Cl *MDHD* SL6 .... 2 E6
Underwood *BRAK* RG12........ 149 H3
Underwood Rd *TLHT* RG30 .... 115 J2
Union Cl *SHST* GU47 .... 173 H4
Union Rd *FRIM* GU16 .... 183 G6
 THLE RG7 .... 112 F3
Union St *CHOB/PIR* GU24 ..... 183 K8
 MARL SN8 .... 102 A2
Unity Cl *CAV/SC* RG4 .... 62 E8
Unwin Av *EBED/NFELT* TW14 .. 101 G4
Upavon Dr *READ* RG1 .... 116 B1
Upavon Gdns *BRAK* RG12 ..... 150 C2
Upcroft *WDSR* SL4 .... 96 C2
Updown Hl *BFOR* GU20 .... 176 A2
Upland Rd *CBLY* GU15 .... 174 D6
Uplands *HUNG* RG17 .... 131 M1
Uplands Cl *SHST* GU47 .... 172 E6
Uplands Rd *CAV/SC* RG4 ...... 88 B1
Upper Bray Rd *MDHD* SL6.... 68 F4
Upper Broadmoor Rd
 CWTH RG45 .... 172 F1
 CWTH RG45 .... 173 G1
Upper Charles St *CBLY* GU15 .. 173 M8
Upper Chobham Rd *CBLY* GU15.. 182 E2
 FRIM GU16 .... 182 D3
Upper College Ride *CBLY* GU15 .. 174 B6
Upper Crown St *READ* RG1.... 9 H8
Upper Eddington *HUNG* RG17 .. 104 B6
Upper End *KSCL* RG20 .... 52 D6
Upper Gordon Rd *CBLY* GU15 .. 182 A1
Upper Halliford Rd
 SHPTN TW17 .... 129 H7
Upper Lambourn Rd
 HUNG RG17 .... 49 K3
Upper Lees Rd *SLN* SL2 .... 44 D4
Upper Meadow Rd
 WHIT RG2 .... 117 G4
Upper Park Rd *CBLY* GU15 .... 182 A1
Upper Red Cross Rd
 GOR/PANG RG8 .... 32 F7
Upper Redlands Rd *READ* RG1 .. 117 G1
Upper Verran Rd *CBLY* GU15.. 182 A3
Upper Village Rd *ASC* SL5 .... 151 M2
Upper Wk *VW* GU25 .... 154 B1
Upper Warren Av *CAV/SC* RG4 .. 87 K3
Upper Woodcote Rd
 CAV/SC RG4.................... 88 A1
Uppingham Dr *WODY* RG5 .... 90 C5
Uppingham Gdns *CAV/SC* RG4 .. 63 G8
Upshire Gdns *BRAK* RG12 ..... 150 C1
Upton Cl *HEN* RG9 .... 38 B5
Upton Court Rd *DTCH/LGLY* SL3.. 71 K3
Upton Pk *SL* SL1 .... 71 H3
Upton Rd *DTCH/LGLY* SL3 ..... 71 K3
 TLHT RG30 .... 87 K7
Urquhart Rd *STHA* RG19 ...... 138 A3
Usk Rd *TLHT* RG30 .... 87 J8
Uxbridge Rd *DTCH/LGLY* SL3.. 46 B6
 SL SL1 .... 5 L8
 SLN SL2 .... 45 M8
Uxmore Rd *GOR/PANG* RG8 ... 35 H2

V

Vachel Rd *READ* RG1 .... 8 E5
Vale Crs *TLHT* RG30 .... 87 H5
Vale Gv *SL* SL1 .... 71 H3
Valentia Rd *TLHT* RG30 .... 88 A6
Valentine Cl *WHIT* RG2 .... 117 H5
Valentine Crs *CAV/SC* RG4 ..... 88 F2
Vale Rd *CBLY* GU15 .... 181 K2
 WDSR SL4 .... 6 B6
The Vale *EBED/NFELT* TW14 .. 101 L5
 SUN TW16 .... 129 K4
Vale Vw *WAR/TWY* RG10 ...... 90 E2
Vale View Dr *THLE* RG7 .... 168 A1
Valley Cl *CAV/SC* RG4 .... 88 D2
 GOR/PANG RG8 .... 32 F8
Valley Crs *WWKG* RG41 .... 10 C2
Valley End *CALC* RG31 .... 45 M5
Valley End Rd *CHOB/PIR* GU24 .. 176 C2
Valley Rd *FRIM* GU16 .... 182 E6
 HEN RG9 .... 37 L6
 NWBY RG14 .... 14 A9
 THLE RG7 .... 142 D3
Valley Vw *SHST* GU47 .... 172 D7
Valley Wy *TADY* RG26 .... 165 H5
Valon Rd *WHIT* RG2 .... 146 B5
Valpy St *READ* RG1 .... 9 G5
Valroy Cl *CBLY* GU15 .... 174 A8
Vandyke *BRAK* RG12 .... 149 H3
Vanlore Wy *CALC* RG31 .... 114 F1

Vanners La KSCL RG20 159 G1
Vansittart Rd MLW SL7 19 H7
WDSR SL4 6 F6
Vastern Rd READ RG1 8 F3
Vaughan Wy SLN SL2 44 B5
Vauxhall Dr WODY RG5 90 C8
Vegal Crs EGH TW20 125 M3
Venetia Cl CAV/SC RG4 62 F7
Venning Rd WHIT RG2 146 C6
Ventnor Rd CALC RG31 87 G5
Verbena Cl WWKG RG41 118 D3
Vereker Dr SUN TW16 129 K8
Verey Cl WAR/TWY RG10 91 J3
Vermont Rd SLN SL2 44 B5
Vermont Woods EWKG RG40 147 H7
Verney Cl MLW SL7 19 G4
Verney Ms TLHT RG30 87 M7
Verney Rd DTCH/LGLY SL3 72 D4
Vernon Crs WHIT RG2 116 E7
Vernon Dr ASC SL5 123 G7
Vernon Rd FELT TW13 101 J8
Verona Cl UX/CGN UB8 47 M7
Verran Rd CBLY GU15 182 A3
Vibia Cl STWL/WRAY TW19 100 A6
Viburnum Ct
CHOB/PIR GU24 176 B8
Vicarage Av EGH TW20 126 E4
Vicarage Cl EWKG RG40 147 J8
MDHD SL6 20 D7
Vicarage Ct EGH TW20 126 E4
Vicarage Crs EGH TW20 126 E3
Vicarage Dr MDHD SL6 68 F2
Vicarage Gdns ASC SL5 151 K2
MDHD SL6 67 J6
Vicarage La NTHA RG18 109 M6
STA TW18 127 L8
STWL/WRAY TW19 98 B7
YTLY GU46 171 M7
Vicarage Rd BFOR GU20 174 F3
BLKW GU17 181 H2
CHOB/PIR GU24 177 G6
EGH TW20 126 E3
HEN RG9 38 B6
MDHD SL6 3 G3
STA TW18 127 G1
STA TW18 127 H2
SUN TW16 129 J3
WHIT RG2 116 F1
YTLY GU46 171 M7
Vicarage Wy DTCH/LGLY SL3 73 G7
Vicarage Wood Wy
CALC RG31 86 E5
Victor Cl MDHD SL6 41 L6
Victoria Av CBLY GU15 181 K1
Victoria Cl BAGS GU19 175 H5
Victoria Crs IVER SL0 47 K8
Victoria Dr BLKW GU17 180 F2
Victoria Gdns NWBY RG14 14 F2
Victoria Rd ASC SL5 151 L2
CALC RG31 87 G6
CAV/SC RG4 88 D3
FELT TW13 101 L7
MLW SL7 19 H4
SHST GU47 173 H5
SLN SL2 5 M7
STA TW18 127 H1
THLE RG7 142 C8
WAR/TWY RG10 65 H4
WDSR SL4 70 C5
Victoria St EGH TW20 125 M4
READ RG1 9 L7
SL SL1 5 H9
WDSR SL4 7 J7
Victor Pl THLE RG7 139 M4
Victor Rd STHA RG19 138 B3
WDSR SL4 96 F2
Victor Wy WODY RG5 90 D7
Victory Park Rd
ADL/WDHM KT15 155 M8
Victory Rd CHERT KT16 155 K5
Viking BRAK RG12 149 H2
Village Cl WHIT RG2 116 E8
Village Rd EGH TW20 126 F8
WDSR SL4 69 L3
The Village EWKG RG40 171 H3
Village Wy ASHF TW15 128 C2
YTLY GU46 172 A7
Villiers Md WWKG RG41 10 C5
Villiers Rd SLN SL2 45 G6
Villiers Wy NWBY RG14 135 M8
Vincent Cl CHERT KT16 155 H4
WODY RG5 90 C8
Vincent Dr SHPTN TW17 129 H8
Vincent Ri BRAK RG12 122 B8
Vincent Rd CHERT KT16 155 H4
NTHA RG18 138 B2
Vine Cl STWL/WRAY TW19 99 K4
Vine Crs TLHT RG30 115 K2
The Vines WWKG RG41 146 F3
Vine Tree Cl TADY RG26 165 G7
Vineyard Dr BNEND SL8 20 C1
Vineyard Rd FELT TW13 129 K1
Viola Av EBED/NFELT TW14 101 M5
STWL/WRAY TW19 100 B7
Viola Cft BNFD RG42 122 C6
Violet Gv NTHA RG18 138 B1
Violet La TADY RG26 163 M8
Virginia Av VW GU25 153 M2
Virginia Cl STA TW18 127 M8
Virginia Dr VW GU25 153 M2
Virginia Wy TLHT RG30 115 L1
Viscount Rd STWL/WRAY TW19 100 A6
Viscount Wy HTHAIR TW6 101 H3
WODY RG5 90 C7
Vivien Cl MDHD SL6 20 C8
Voller Dr CALC RG31 86 F8
Vulcan Cl WODY RG5 90 E5
Vulcan Wy SHST GU47 172 D7

W

Waborne Rd BNEND SL8 20 E2
Wade Dr SL SL1 70 D1
Wadham SHST GU47 173 J5
Wagbullock Ri BRAK RG12 149 M3
Waggoners Hollow
BAGS GU19 175 H4
Wagner Cl MDHD SL6 67 J3
Wagtail Cl WAR/TWY RG10 91 H2
Waingels Rd WODY RG5 90 D4
Wakeford Cl TADY RG26 165 H5
Wakelins End MDHD SL6 20 B7
Wakeman Rd BNEND SL8 20 D3
Wakemans GOR/PANG RG8 85 G2
Walbury BRAK RG12 150 B1
Waldeck Rd MDHD SL6 3 K5
Waldeck St WHIT RG2 116 E1
Walden Av WHIT RG2 145 M3
Waldens Cl BNEND SL8 20 D3
Waldorf Hts BLKW GU17 181 G2
Waldron Hl BRAK RG12 122 C6
Walford Rd UX/CGN UB8 47 M3
Walgrove Gdns MDHD SL6 67 H8
Walker Cl EBED/NFELT TW14 101 J6
GOR/PANG RG8 34 B5
Walker Rd MDHD SL6 68 D2
Walker's La HUNG RG17 49 L3
Walkers Pl TLHT RG30 87 M7
Walker's Rdg CBLY GU15 182 B1
Wallace Cl MLW SL7 19 J2
WODY RG5 118 A1
Wallace Wk ADL/WDHM KT15 155 M8
DTCH/LGLY SL3 71 J5
Wallcroft Cl BNFD RG42 12 B1
The Walled Gdn WAR/TWY RG10 65 G4
Waller Ct CAV/SC RG4 88 E4
Waller Dr NWBY RG14 137 H1
Wallingford Cl BRAK RG12 150 B1
Wallingford Rd GOR/PANG RG8 32 F3
KSCL RG20 56 B1
UX/CGN UB8 47 L3
Wallington Rd CBLY GU15 174 D5
Wallingtons Rd HUNG RG17 133 J4
Wall La THLE RG7 165 M4
Wallner Wy EWKG RG40 11 K7
Walmer Cl CWTH RG45 172 F1
FRIM GU16 182 C7
TLHT RG30 87 K8
Walmer Rd WODY RG5 90 C5
Walnut Cl CAV/SC RG4 62 B1
WWKG RG41 10 A7
YTLY GU46 180 A2
Walnut Tree Cl BNEND SL8 20 E4
WAR/TWY RG10 65 H8
Walnut Tree Ct
GOR/PANG RG8 32 F8
Walnut Tree Rd SHPTN TW17 128 F8
Walnut Wy BNEND SL8 20 E4
TLHT RG30 87 G6
Walpole Rd SL SL1 44 A7
WDSR SL4 97 L6
Walronds Cl MARL SN8 48 B6
Walrus Cl WODY RG5 90 E7
Walsham Rd EBED/NFELT TW14 101 L6
Walsh Av BNFD RG42 122 B5
Walter Rd WWKG RG41 119 H6
Walters Cl NTHA RG18 109 M6
Waltham Cl MDHD SL6 67 J4
SHST GU47 173 G5
Waltham Rd MDHD SL6 67 H6
WAR/TWY RG10 91 G2
WAR/TWY RG10 91 L1
Walton Av HEN RG9 38 B6
Walton Cl WODY RG5 89 M7
Walton Dr ASC SL5 123 J6
Walton Gdns FELT TW13 129 J2
Walton La SLN SL2 44 C3
Walton Wy NWBY RG14 15 J1
Wandhope Wy CALC RG31 86 F4
Wandsdyke Cl FRIM GU16 182 C6
Wansdyke Rd MARL SN8 130 B7
Wansey Gdns NWBY RG14 137 G1
Wanstraw Gv BRAK RG12 150 B4
Wantage Cl BRAK RG12 150 B2
Wantage Rd GOR/PANG RG8 32 C5
HUNG RG17 49 M3
HUNG RG17 77 L2
SHST GU47 173 G6
TLHT RG30 87 M7
Wapshott Rd STA TW18 127 H4
Waram Cl HUNG RG17 104 B7
Warbler Cl CALC RG31 86 E8
Warborough Av CALC RG31 86 E7
Warbreck Dr CALC RG31 86 E3
Warbrook La HTWY RG27 170 D6
Ward Cl EWKG RG40 11 J2
IVER SL0 47 J8
Ward Gdns SL SL1 44 B8
Wardle Av CALC RG31 87 G5
Wardle Cl BAGS GU19 175 H3
Wards Pl EGH TW20 126 F4
Wards Stone Pk BRAK RG12 150 B4
Wareham Rd BRAK RG12 150 C2
Warehouse Rd STHA RG19 161 J1
Warfield Rd EBED/NFELT TW14 101 H6
Warfield St BNFD RG42 121 M3
BNFD RG42 122 A3
Wargrave Hl WAR/TWY RG10 65 G4
Wargrave Rd HEN RG9 38 D6
WAR/TWY RG10 65 G8
Wargrove Dr SHST GU47 173 G6
Waring Cl EARL RG6 117 M6
The Warings THLE RG7 112 D7
Warley Ri CALC RG31 86 E2
Warner Cl SL SL1 70 B1
Warners Hl MDHD SL6 19 M7
Warnford Rd TLHT RG30 87 J7
Warnham La KSCL RG20 55 L4
Warnsham Cl EARL RG6 117 L5
Warren Cl DTCH/LGLY SL3 72 B3
SHST GU47 172 D6
THLE RG7 142 D4
Warren Down BNFD RG42 12 B2
Warren Fld IVER SL0 46 F3
Warren House Rd EWKG RG40 11 H2
Warren La EWKG RG40 171 G1
Warren Ri FRIM GU16 182 B3
Warren Rd ASHF TW15 129 H5
NWBY RG14 136 A8
WODY RG5 90 A5
Warren Rw ASC SL5 123 G7
Warren Row Rd WAR/TWY RG10 39 J7
WAR/TWY RG10 66 B2
The Warren CAV/SC RG4 87 M3
CAV/SC RG4 88 C4
READ RG1 88 C4
TADY RG26 164 D6
Warrington Av SL SL1 4 B2
Warrington Sp WDSR SL4 97 L6
Warwick BRAK RG12 150 B4
Warwick Av EGH TW20 126 F6
SLN SL2 44 F5
STA TW18 127 M4
Warwick Cl CBLY GU15 182 E3
MDHD SL6 67 L2
Warwick Dr NWBY RG14 15 H8
Warwick Pl UX/CGN UB8 47 M1
Warwick Rd ASHF TW15 128 B3
HSLWW TW4 101 L2
WHIT RG2 116 F2
Wasdale Cl SHST GU47 173 G4
Wash Hl FLKWH HP10 21 H3
Wash Hill Lea FLKWH HP10 21 G2
Washington Dr SL SL1 44 A8
WDSR SL4 96 B2
Washington Gdns EWKG RG40 147 K6
Washington Rd CAV/SC RG4 88 E4
Wash Water KSCL RG20 159 K3
Wasing La THLE RG7 140 A8
Watchetts Dr CBLY GU15 181 M4
Watchetts Lake Cl
CBLY GU15 182 A3
Watchetts Rd CBLY GU15 181 L3
Watchmoor Rd CBLY GU15 181 K2
Waterbeach Cl SL SL1 4 D2
Waterbeach Rd SL SL1 4 D2
Waterfall Cl VW GU25 125 J8
Waterford Wy EWKG RG40 11 G6
Waterham Rd BRAK RG12 149 L3
Waterhouse Md SHST GU47 173 G7
Water La FARN GU14 181 K7
STHA RG19 136 F7
Waterloo Cl CBLY GU15 174 E7
EBED/NFELT TW14 101 J7
Waterloo Crs EWKG RG40 11 L9
Waterloo Ri WHIT RG2 116 E2
Waterloo Rd CWTH RG45 172 D2
EWKG RG40 11 L8
EWKG RG40 148 C1
UX/CGN UB8 47 M2
WHIT RG2 116 E1
Waterman Ct SL SL1 70 B1
Waterman Pl READ RG1 8 E2
Waterman's Rd HEN RG9 38 B6
Watermans Wy WAR/TWY RG10 64 F5
Watermead EBED/NFELT TW14 101 H7
Waterperry La CHOB/PIR GU24 177 J5
Water Rd TLHT RG30 87 L7
Waters Dr STA TW18 127 J2
Watersfield Cl EARL RG6 117 L5
Waterside UX/CGN UB8 47 M6
Waterside Dr DTCH/LGLY SL3 72 C2
GOR/PANG RG8 87 G1
THLE RG7 114 C3
Waterside Gdns READ RG1 8 F7
Water Splash La ASC SL5 124 B6
Watersplash La BNFD RG42 121 L4
Water St NTHA RG18 56 C8
Watery La CHOB/PIR GU24 177 G5
KSCL RG20 158 C1
Watlington St READ RG1 9 J6
Watmore La WWKG RG41 119 G3
Wavell Cl WHIT RG2 117 J5
Wavell Gdns SLN SL2 44 C4
Wavell Rd MDHD SL6 41 L8
Wavendene Av EGH TW20 126 F5
Waverley BRAK RG12 149 H2
Waverley Cl CBLY GU15 182 C2
Waverley Dr CBLY GU15 182 B1
CHERT KT16 155 G7
VW GU25 153 K1
Waverley Rd BAGS GU19 175 H3
SL SL1 4 A1
TLHT RG30 87 L7
The Waverleys NTHA RG18 138 A2
Waverley Wy EWKG RG40 147 H5
Waybrook Crs READ RG1 89 J8
Wayfarer's Wk KSCL RG20 157 L7
Wayland Cl BRAK RG12 150 C1
Waylands STWL/WRAY TW19 98 B5
THLE RG7 112 F2
Waylen St READ RG1 8 D6
Wayman Rd FARN GU14 181 H6
Ways End CBLY GU15 182 B2
Wayside Gn GOR/PANG RG8 34 A5
GOR/PANG RG8 34 B6
GOR/PANG RG8 34 B6
Wayside Ms MDHD SL6 3 H2
Wealden Wy TLHT RG30 87 H6
Weald Ri TLHT RG30 87 J4
Weavers Wy WAR/TWY RG10 91 G2
Webb Cl BAGS GU19 175 H5
BNFD RG42 12 B1
DTCH/LGLY SL3 72 A4
Webb Ct EWKG RG40 11 M2
Webbs Acre STHA RG19 138 C4
Webbs La THLE RG7 112 F6
Webster Cl MDHD SL6 67 K1
Wedderburn Cl WWKG RG41 119 G4
Wedgewood Wy TLHT RG30 87 J5
Weekes Dr SL SL1 70 E2
Weighbridge Rw READ RG1 8 D3
Weir Cl CALC RG31 115 J2
Weir Pl STA TW18 127 H6
Weir Rd CHERT KT16 155 L4
Welbeck BRAK RG12 149 H2
Welbeck Rd MDHD SL6 2 C8
Welby Cl MDHD SL6 67 K2
Welby Crs WWKG RG41 118 E5
Weldale St READ RG1 8 D5
Welden SLN SL2 45 M7
Welford Rd KSCL RG20 106 A2
WODY RG5 90 D6
Welland Cl CALC RG31 86 F5
DTCH/LGLY SL3 72 D6
Wellbank MDHD SL6 43 H5
Wellburn Cl SHST GU47 172 E7
Well Cl CBLY GU15 181 L2
Wellcroft Rd SL SL1 70 E1
Weller Dr CBLY GU15 181 M3
EWKG RG40 146 D8
Weller's La BNFD RG42 121 M1
Wellesley Av IVER SL0 73 J3
Wellesley Cl BAGS GU19 174 F3
Wellesley Dr CWTH RG45 172 B1
Wellesley Rd SL SL1 5 J8
Welley Av STWL/WRAY TW19 98 B3
Welley Rd STWL/WRAY TW19 98 B4
Wellfield Cl CALC RG31 86 F7
Wellhill Rd WANT OX12 51 M1
Well House La HTWY RG27 169 L3
Wellhouse La NTHA RG18 82 A8
Wellhouse Rd MDHD SL6 42 B4
Wellington Av VW GU25 153 L3
WHIT RG2 117 G2
Wellington Cl NWBY RG14 136 F1
SHST GU47 172 F6
Wellington Crs TADY RG26 164 A5
Wellington Dr BRAK RG12 150 A2
Wellington Gdns THLE RG7 112 C5
Wellingtonia Av EWKG RG40 171 L2
Wellington Rd ASHF TW15 128 B3
CWTH RG45 172 F2
EBED/NFELT TW14 101 H4
EWKG RG40 10 E7
MDHD SL6 2 C4
SHST GU47 172 E6
UX/CGN UB8 47 M2
Wellington St SL SL1 4 E7
Wellington Ter SHST GU47 172 F6
Well Meadow NWBY RG14 136 E1
Wells Cl WDSR SL4 6 D5
Wells La ASC SL5 123 L8
ASC SL5 151 L1
Well St KSCL RG20 160 D8
Well Vw HEN RG9 35 J2
Welsh La THLE RG7 168 D4
Welshman's Rd THLE RG7 165 L1
Welwick Cl EARL RG6 118 B4
Welwyn Av
EBED/NFELT TW14 101 J5
Wendan Rd NWBY RG14 14 D9
Wendover Dr FRIM GU16 182 F3
Wendover Pl STA TW18 127 G3
Wendover Rd BNEND SL8 20 D2
SL SL1 43 L6
STA TW18 127 G3
Wendover Wy TLHT RG30 87 G7
Wenlock Edge WAR/TWY RG10 90 E2
Wenlock Wy STHA RG19 138 A4
Wensley Cl WAR/TWY RG10 91 G1
Wensleydale Dr CBLY GU15 183 G1
Wensley Rd READ RG1 116 B2
READ RG1 116 C1
Wentworth Av ASC SL5 122 F7
SLN SL2 44 D4
WHIT RG2 117 G6
Wentworth Cl ASHF TW15 128 E2
CWTH RG45 148 C8
YTLY GU46 180 A1
Wentworth Ct NWBY RG14 15 G7
Wentworth Crs MDHD SL6 2 A7
Wentworth Dr VW GU25 153 J1
Wentworth Wy ASC SL5 123 J2
Wescott Rd EWKG RG40 11 J6
Wescott Wy UX/CGN UB8 47 M3
Wesley Dr EGH TW20 126 D4
Wessex Cl HUNG RG17 131 M1
Wessex Gdns WAR/TWY RG10 91 H3
Wessex Rd BNEND SL8 20 E4
HTHAIR TW6 99 M3
Wessex Wy MDHD SL6 67 L2
Westacott Wy MDHD SL6 67 G2
Westborough Ct MDHD SL6 2 B7
Westborough Rd MDHD SL6 2 B6
Westbourne Rd FELT TW13 129 J1
SHST GU47 173 H7
STA TW18 127 L5
Westbourne Ter TLHT RG30 87 M7
Westbrook MDHD SL6 69 H5
Westbrook Cl HUNG RG17 131 M1
Westbrook Gdns BRAK RG12 13 K3
Westbrook Rd STA TW18 127 J3
TLHT RG30 87 M5
Westbury Cl CWTH RG45 148 E8
Westbury La GOR/PANG RG8 60 D8
West Chiltern GOR/PANG RG8 34 B6
West Cl ASHF TW15 128 B2
Westcombe Cl BRAK RG12 150 A4
Westcote Rd TLHT RG30 88 A8
Westcotts Gn BNFD RG42 122 A5
West Ct CAV/SC RG4 90 B4
West Crs WDSR SL4 6 B7
Westcroft SLN SL2 44 E5
West Dean MDHD SL6 3 H2
Westdene Crescent CAV/SC RG4 88 B2
West Dr ASC SL5 153 G2
CALC RG31 115 H1
CAV/SC RG4 90 A5
VW GU25 153 G3
West End La BNFD RG42 121 L3
SLN SL2 45 H2
West End Rd THLE RG7 166 B1
Westerdale STHA RG19 137 M3
Westerdale Dr FRIM GU16 182 E3
Western Av CHERT KT16 127 K8
EGH TW20 126 E8
HEN RG9 38 B6
NWBY RG14 14 C1
NWBY RG14 14 E1
WODY RG5 90 A6
Western Dr FLKWH HP10 21 H1
Western Elms Av TLHT RG30 8 A7
Western End NWBY RG14 14 A6
Western Oaks CALC RG31 87 H4
Western Perimeter Rd
STWL/WRAY TW19 99 L3
Western Rd BNFD RG42 12 B3
BRAK RG12 12 C4
HEN RG9 38 B6
READ RG1 8 A8
West Field Cl TADY RG26 165 G6
Westfield Crs HEN RG9 64 E3
NTHA RG18 137 L2
Westfield Rd CBLY GU15 181 L4
MDHD SL6 41 L8
NTHA RG18 137 K1
SLN SL2 44 E5
WWKG RG41 118 E4
Westfields KSCL RG20 56 A2
Westfield Wy NWBY RG14 14 A6
West Fryerne YTLY GU46 172 A7
Westgate Crs SL SL1 44 C8
Westgate Rd NWBY RG14 14 A6
West Gn YTLY GU46 171 L7
Westhatch La BNFD RG42 121 M2
West Hl READ RG1 9 G9
Westhorpe Rd MLW SL7 19 J3
Westland NTHA RG18 137 L2
Westland Cl
STWL/WRAY TW19 100 B5
Westlands Av SL SL1 43 M7
WHIT RG2 117 H5
Westlands Cl SL SL1 43 M7
Westlands Rd NWBY RG14 14 F9
West La HEN RG9 38 A4
Westleigh Dr CAV/SC RG4 62 D2
Westley Ml BNFD RG42 93 H6
Westlyn Rd TADY RG26 165 H5
Westmacott Dr
EBED/NFELT TW14 101 J6
West Md MDHD SL6 42 C4
Westmead WDSR SL4 96 E2
Westmead Dr NWBY RG14 136 C6
West Mills NWBY RG14 14 D4
Westminster Cl
EBED/NFELT TW14 101 K7
Westminster Wy EARL RG6 117 M5
Westmorland Cl WWKG RG41 119 G8
Westmorland Dr BNFD RG42 122 C4
CBLY GU15 182 E3
Westmorland Rd MDHD SL6 2 D5
Weston Av ADL/WDHM KT15 155 K8
Westonbirt Dr CAV/SC RG4 88 B3
Weston Gv BAGS GU19 175 J4
Weston Rd SL SL1 44 C6
Weston's KSCL RG20 55 G6
West Point WDSR SL4 70 A1
West Rdg BNEND SL8 20 E2
Westridge Av GOR/PANG RG8 86 F1
West Rd CBLY GU15 182 A1
EBED/NFELT TW14 101 G6
EWKG RG40 148 F4
FARN GU14 181 K6
HEN RG9 35 L4
MDHD SL6 2 F5
West St HEN RG9 38 A4
MDHD SL6 3 G5
MLW SL7 18 F5
NWBY RG14 14 D3
READ RG1 8 E5
TADY RG26 164 F6
TADY RG26 165 G6
West Vw EBED/NFELT TW14 100 F7
KSCL RG20 53 M7
Westview Dr WAR/TWY RG10 65 G8
Westward Rd WWKG RG41 10 A3
Westway GOR/PANG RG8 32 F6
Westwick Gdns HEST TW5 101 L1
Westwood Gln CALC RG31 86 F6
Westwood Gn MDHD SL6 20 C8
Westwood Rd BFOR GU20 152 B6
BFOR GU20 176 A1
CALC RG31 87 G5
MLW SL7 18 F5
NWBY RG14 15 H9
Westwood Rw CALC RG31 86 F4
Wetherby Cl CAV/SC RG4 62 F8
Wethered Pk MLW SL7 19 G5
Wethered Rd MLW SL7 19 G4
SL SL1 43 L7
Wetton Pl EGH TW20 126 C3
Wexham Park La DTCH/LGLY SL3 45 M5
Wexham Rd SL SL1 5 K9
SLN SL2 5 L2
Wexham St SLN SL2 45 L4
Wexham Woods DTCH/LGLY SL3 45 M6
Wey Av CHERT KT16 127 K8
Weybridge Md YTLY GU46 172 B7
Wey Cl CBLY GU15 181 L1
Weycrofts BNFD RG42 12 D1
Weyhill Cl TADY RG26 164 E7
Weymead Cl CHERT KT16 155 M5
Whaley Rd EWKG RG40 11 K2
Wharfe La HEN RG9 38 B4
Wharfenden Wy FRIM GU16 182 C8
Wharf La BNEND SL8 20 D3
Wharf Rd FRIM GU16 182 C8
NWBY RG14 14 F4
STWL/WRAY TW19 97 M6
Wharfside THLE RG7 140 F3
Wharf St NWBY RG14 14 E4
Wharf Wy FRIM GU16 182 C8
Whatley Gn BRAK RG12 149 L3
Whatmore Cl
STWL/WRAY TW19 99 K5
Wheatash Rd ADL/WDHM KT15 155 L6
The Wheatbutts WDSR SL4 70 C4
Wheatfield Cl MDHD SL6 67 K2
Wheatfields Rd WHIT RG2 145 H1
Wheatlands Cl CALC RG31 115 H2
Wheatlands La NWBY RG14 135 L8
Wheatlands Rd DTCH/LGLY SL3 71 L3
Wheatley BRAK RG12 149 H2
Wheatley Cl WHIT RG2 117 H5
Wheatsheaf La STA TW18 127 J5
Wheble Dr WODY RG5 90 A6
Wheeler Cl THLE RG7 142 E3
Wheeler Ct CALC RG31 87 H5
Wheelers Green Wy STHA RG19 138 B4
Wheelton Cl EARL RG6 118 B3
Whins Cl CBLY GU15 181 L2
Whins Dr CBLY GU15 181 L2
Whinshill Ct ASC SL5 152 D5
Whistler Gv SHST GU47 173 G8
Whistlers La THLE RG7 165 L5
Whistley Cl BRAK RG12 122 B8
Whitby Gn CAV/SC RG4 63 G8
Whitby Rd SL SL1 4 B4
Whitchurch Cl MDHD SL6 42 B3
Whitebeam Cl WWKG RG41 147 G3
White Bridge Cl
EBED/NFELT TW14 101 J5
Whitebrook Pk MDHD SL6 42 F2
White City CWTH RG45 173 G1
White Cl NTHA RG18 81 J8
SL SL1 4 C6

Whitedown Rd *TADY* RG26 .... **164** C6
White Farm La *MARL* SN8 .... **178** A1
Whiteford Rd *SLN* SL2 .... **4** F1
Whitegates La *EARL* RG6 .... **89** K7
Whitehall Dr *WHIT* RG2 .... **146** B6
Whitehall Farm La *VW* GU25 .... **126** B8
Whitehall La *EGH* TW20 .... **126** C6
  GOR/PANG RG8 .... **35** G3
  STWL/WRAY TW19 ...... **98** D5
Whiteham Cl *THLE* RG7 .... **114** B2 ▣
White Hart Rd *WDSR* SL4 .... **71** G3
White Hart Rw *CHERT* KT16 .... **155** K4 ▣
White Hl *BFOR* GU20 .... **151** L8
  GOR/PANG RG8 .... **58** A8
  HEN RG9 .... **38** D4
  HEN RG9 .... **63** K1
Whitehill Cl *CBLY* GU15 .... **174** A7
  MARL SN8 .... **102** A2 ▣
Whitehill Pl *VW* GU25 .... **154** B2
Whitehills Gn *GOR/PANG* RG8 .. **32** F8
White Horse La *EWKG* RG40 .... **170** F1
White Horse Rd *WDSR* SL4 ...... **96** A1
White House Gdns
  YTLY GU46 .... **171** M7 ▣
Whitehouse Rd *GOR/PANG* RG8.. **34** B6
Whitehouse Wy *WHIT* RG2 ...... **47** G4 ▣
Whiteknights Rd *EARL* RG6 ...... **117** K1
Whitelands Dr *ASC* SL5 .... **123** C6
Whitelands Rd *NTHA* RG18 ...... **137** M2
Whiteley *WDSR* SL4 .... **70** B7
White Lilies Island *WDSR* SL4 .. **6** E4
White Lion Wy *YTLY* GU46 ...... **172** A7
Whitelocks Piece *HUNG* RG17 .. **103** K4
White Lodge La *CALC* RG31 ...... **86** E3
Whitemoor La *GOR/PANG* RG8.. **84** B1
Whitenights Rd *READ* RG1 ...... **117** J1
White Paddock *MDHD* SL6 ...... **67** K4
White Rd *CBLY* GU15 .... **173** J8
White's Hl *THLE* RG7 .... **142** B2
  THLE RG7 .... **142** D2
Whitestone Cl *EARL* RG6 .... **118** B3 ▣
Whitewalls Cl *KSCL* RG20 .... **56** A1
Whitewell Cl *WHIT* RG2 .... **146** B4 ▣
Whitley Cl *STWL/WRAY* TW19 .. **100** B5
Whitley Park La *WHIT* RG2 ...... **117** C2
Whitley Rd *YTLY* GU46 .... **180** A2
Whitley St *READ* RG1 .... **116** E1
Whitley Wood La *WHIT* RG2 .... **116** E6
Whitley Wood Rd *WHIT* RG2 .... **117** H5 ▣
Whitmoor Rd *BAGS* GU19 .... **175** H4
Whitmore Cl *SHST* GU47 .... **173** C6
Whitmore La *ASC* SL5 .... **152** D2
Whitstone Gdns *WHIT* RG2 ...... **116** F5
Whittaker Rd *SLN* SL2 .... **44** B5
Whittenham Cl *SLN* SL2 .... **5** J7
Whittle Cl *EWKG* RG40 .... **147** H7
  SHST GU47 .... **172** D5 ▣
Whittle Crs *FARN* GU14 .... **181** J1
Whittle Pkwy *SL* SL1 .... **44** A7
Whitton Cl *EARL* RG6 .... **118** A4
Whittonditch Rd *MARL* SN8 .... **102** B2
Whitton Rd *BRAK* RG12 .... **122** C8
Whitworth Rd *WHIT* RG2 .... **146** D7
Whurley Wy *MDHD* SL6 .... **42** B4
Whynstones Rd *ASC* SL5 .... **151** K4
Whyteladyes La *MDHD* SL6 .... **20** B8
Wickers Cl *WHIT* RG2 .... **145** J2 ▣
The Wickets *ASHF* TW15 .... **128** B2
  MDHD SL6. .... **2** A5
Wickford Wy *EARL* RG6 .... **117** H6 ▣
Wickham Cl *TADY* RG26 .... **164** C6
Wickham La *EGH* TW20 .... **126** D5
Wickham Rd *CBLY* GU15 .... **174** B6
  EARL RG6 .... **117** H6
Wickham V *BRAK* RG12 .... **149** H3 ▣
Wick Hill La *EWKG* RG40 .... **147** K8
  EWKG RG40 .... **171** K1
Wick La *EGH* TW20 .... **125** J4
Wick Rd *EGH* TW20 .... **125** L5
Wick's Gn *BNFD* RG42. .... **120** E3
Wicks La *WAR/TWY* RG10 ...... **92** B4
Widbrook Rd *MDHD* SL6 .... **42** E3
Widecroft Rd *IVER* SL0. .... **47** H7
Widmore La *CAV/SC* RG4 .... **58** D8
Wield Ct *EARL* RG6 .... **118** B5 ▣
Wiggett Gv *BRAK* RG42 .... **120** F4
Wigmore La *THLE* RG7 .... **113** M4
  TLHT RG30 .... **87** L5 ▣
Wigmore Rd *TLHT* RG30 .... **164** C5
Wilberforce Ms *MDHD* SL6 ...... **3** G4
Wilberforce Wy *BRAK* RG12 .... **150** A2 ▣
Wilcox Gdns *SHPTN* TW17 ...... **128** C8 ▣
Wild Briar *EWKG* RG40 .... **147** J7
Wild Cl *EARL* RG6 .... **117** H6 ▣
Wildcroft Dr *EWKG* RG40 .... **147** K5
Wilder Av *GOR/PANG* RG8 ...... **86** B1 ▣
Wilderness Ct *EARL* RG6 .... **117** K3
Wilderness Rd *EARL* RG6 .... **117** J3
  FRIM GU16 .... **182** B4
Wilders Cl *BNFD* RG42 .... **12** E1
  FRIM GU16 .... **182** A3
Wildgreen North
  DTCH/LGLY SL3 .... **72** D4 ▣
Wildgreen South
  DTCH/LGLY SL3 .... **72** D4 ▣
Wildridings Rd *BRAK* RG12 ...... **12** F6
Wilford Rd *DTCH/LGLY* SL3 .... **72** B4
Wilfred Wy *STHA* RG19 .... **138** C3
Willant Cl *MDHD* SL6 .... **67** J4
Willats Cl *CHERT* KT16 .... **155** J3 ▣
William Cl *STHA* RG19 .... **138** A4
William Ellis Cl *WDSR* SL4 ...... **97** K4
William Sim Wd *BNFD* RG42 .... **122** E4
William St *READ* RG1 .... **8** C5
  SL SL1 .... **5** G7
  WDSR SL4 .... **7** J7
Willington Cl *CBLY* GU15 .... **173** L8 ▣
Willis Cl *MARL* SN8 .... **130** A8
  NTHA RG18 .... **109** L3

Willoners *SLN* SL2 .... **44** D5 ▣
Willoughby Rd *BRAK* RG12 ...... **12** C7
  DTCH/LGLY SL3. .... **72** E3
Willow Bank *MLW* SL7 .... **19** G1 ▣
Willowbrook *WDSR* SL4. .... **71** G4
Willowbrook Rd
  STWL/WRAY TW19 ...... **100** B7
Willow Cl *DTCH/LGLY* SL3 ...... **72** F7 ▣
  NWBY RG14 .... **14** D8
  TLHT RG30. .... **142** E1
Willow Ct *FRIM* GU16 .... **182** A5
Willow Crs *FARN* GU14 .... **181** L7
Willowdale *EWKG* RG40 .... **147** J6 ▣
Willow Dr *BRAK* RG12. .... **13** K3
  MDHD SL6. .... **68** E4
Willowford *WGFD* OX10 .... **32** C1
Willow Gdns *CALC* RG31 .... **86** E4 ▣
  WHIT RG2 .... **117** G5
Willow Gn *CHOB/PIR* GU24 .... **176** D8
Willowherb Cl *EWKG* RG40 ...... **11** L4
Willow La *BLKW* GU17 .... **181** G2
  HEN RG9 .... **64** F2
Willowmead *STA* TW18 .... **127** L6 ▣
Willowmead Cl *MLW* SL7 .... **19** J3 ▣
  NWBY RG14 .... **159** M1
Willowmead Gdns *MLW* SL7 .... **19** J3 ▣
Willowmead Rd *MLW* SL7 ...... **19** J3 ▣
Willowmead Sq *MLW* SL7 ...... **19** J3 ▣
Willow Pk *SLN* SL2 .... **45** K1
Willow Pl *WDSR* SL4. .... **7** G2
Willow Rd *DTCH/LGLY* SL3 ...... **99** H1
  KSCL RG20 .... **161** J4
  TADY RG26 .... **164** E6
Willows End *SHST* GU47 .... **172** E6 ▣
Willowside *WODY* RG5 .... **90** B5
Willows Rd *BNEND* SL8 .... **20** E3
The Willows *LTWR* GU18 .... **175** M6
  READ RG1 .... **8** F1
Willow St *READ* RG1 .... **8** E7
Willow Tree Gld *CALC* RG31 .... **114** F2 ▣
Willow Wk *EGH* TW20. .... **125** M3
Willow Wy *SHST* GU47 .... **172** C5
Willson Rd *EGH* TW20 .... **125** L3
Wilmington Cl *WODY* RG5 ...... **90** B6
Wilmot Cl *BNFD* RG42 .... **120** F4 ▣
Wilmot Rd *SL* SL1 .... **43** L4
Wilmot Wy *CBLY* GU15 .... **182** C3
Wilsford Cl *WHIT* RG2 .... **117** H7
Wilson Av *HEN* RG9 .... **38** B6
Wilson Cl *KSCL* RG20 .... **56** B2
Wilson Ct *WWKG* RG41 .... **118** E5 ▣
Wilson Rd *TLHT* RG30 .... **87** M7
Wilstrode Av *BNFD* RG42 .... **121** J5
Wilton Crs *WDSR* SL4 .... **96** A3
Wilton Rd *CBLY* GU15 .... **181** L3
  TLHT RG30. .... **87** M6
Wiltshire Av *CWTH* RG45 ...... **148** E8
  SL SL1 .... **44** F5
Wiltshire Dr *EWKG* RG40 .... **11** J4
Wiltshire Gv *BNFD* RG42 .... **122** C4
Wiltshire Rd *EWKG* RG40 .... **11** H2
  MLW SL7 .... **19** J1
Wilwood Rd *BNFD* RG42 .... **119** G2
Wilwyne Cl *CAV/SC* RG4 .... **88** F3
Wimbledon Cl *CBLY* GU15 ...... **174** C5
Wimbledon Rd *CBLY* GU15 ...... **174** C5
Wimblington Dr *EARL* RG6 ...... **117** L6
Wimborne Gdns *TLHT* RG30 .... **87** K5 ▣
Wimbushes *EWKG* RG40 .... **147** G8
Winbury Ct *MDHD* SL6. .... **2** F5
Wincanton Rd *WHIT* RG2 ...... **116** F6
Winch Cl *BNFD* RG42 .... **120** F3 ▣
Winchcombe Rd *NWBY* RG14 .. **14** F1
  WAR/TWY RG10 .... **91** H3
Winchester Cl *DTCH/LGLY* SL3 .. **73** H8
Winchester Dr *MDHD* SL6 ...... **67** L3
Winchester Rd *WHIT* RG2 ...... **116** E2
Winchester Wy *BLKW* GU17 .... **172** F8 ▣
Winchgrove Rd *BNFD* RG42 .... **12** F1
Wincroft Rd *CAV/SC* RG4 ...... **88** B1
Windermere Cl
  EBED/NFELT TW14 .... **101** J7 ▣
  EGH TW20 .... **126** E5 ▣
  STWL/WRAY TW19 .... **100** A7 ▣
  WWKG RG41 .... **118** F3 ▣
Windermere Rd *LTWR* GU18 .... **175** L5
  WHIT RG2 .... **117** G3
Windermere Wy *SL* SL1 .... **43** M6
  STHA RG19 .... **137** K3
Winding Wood Dr *CBLY* GU15.. **182** E2
Windle Cl *BFOR* GU20 .... **176** A2
Windlesham Ct *BFOR* GU20...... **151** M8
Windlesham Rd *BNFD* RG42 .... **12** D2
  CHOB/PIR GU24 .... **176** B6
  CHOB/PIR GU24 .... **176** D3
Windmill Av *WWKG* RG41 ...... **119** H6
Windmill Cl *SUN* TW16 .... **129** H5
  WDSR SL4 .... **6** E8
Windmill Cnr *THLE* RG7 .... **142** D8
Windmill Fld *BFOR* GU20 ...... **176** A2
Windmill La *THLE* RG7 .... **139** K1
Windmill Rd *BNFD* RG42 .... **12** D2
  MDHD SL6. .... **20** B8
  SL SL1 .... **4** C7
  SUN TW16 .... **129** H6
  THLE RG7 .... **142** D8
Windmill Rd West *SUN* TW16 .. **129** H6 ▣
Windmill Shott *EGH* TW20 ...... **126** C4 ▣
Windrush Av *DTCH/LGLY* SL3 .. **72** E3
Windrush Hts *SHST* GU47 ...... **172** E6 ▣
Windrush Wy *MDHD* SL6. .... **3** H3
  TLHT RG30 .... **87** L7 ▣
Windsor Br *WDSR* SL4 .... **7** J5
Windsor Court Rd
  CHOB/PIR GU24 .... **177** H4
Windsor Dr *ASHF* TW15 .... **128** A2
Windsor Hl *FLKWH* HP10 .... **21** H1
Windsor La *SL* SL1. .... **43** M5

Windsor Ride *ASC* SL5 .... **150** E2
  BFOR GU20. .... **150** B5
  CBLY GU15 .... **173** K6
  EWKG RG40. .... **147** K7
Windsor Ri *NWBY* RG14 .... **15** J9
Windsor Rd *ASC* SL5 .... **123** L5
  CHOB/PIR GU24 .... **177** H4
  DTCH/LGLY SL3. .... **71** K7
  EGH TW20 .... **126** C1
  HSLWW TW4. .... **101** L1
  MDHD SL6 .... **68** E4
  SL SL1 .... **5** G9
  SL SL1 .... **71** H3
  STWL/WRAY TW19 .... **98** B5
  SUN TW16 .... **129** K5
  WDSR SL4 .... **97** M6
Windsor St *CHERT* KT16 .... **155** K3
  UX/CGN UB8. .... **47** M2
Windsor Wy *CALC* RG31 .... **114** E2 ▣▣
  FRIM GU16 .... **182** C6
Wingate Rd *WODY* RG5 .... **90** B8
Wing Cl *MLW* SL7 .... **18** F5
Wingfield Gdns *FRIM* GU16 .... **183** G5
Wingrove Rd *TLHT* RG30 .... **87** M8
Winkfield La *WDSR* SL4 .... **94** E8
Winkfield Rd *ASC* SL5 .... **123** K6
  WDSR SL4 .... **95** M6
Winkfield St *WDSR* SL4 .... **94** F8
Winkworth La *THLE* RG7 .... **164** F4
Winnersh Ga *WWKG* RG41 ...... **119** G4
Winnersh Gv *WWKG* RG41 ...... **118** F5
Winscombe *BRAK* RG12 .... **149** H2
Winser Dr *TLHT* RG30 .... **116** A2
Winston Av *TADY* RG26 .... **165** G7
Winston Cl *FRIM* GU16 .... **182** C8
  THLE RG7 .... **145** G4
Winston Wy *STHA* RG19 .... **137** J2
Winterberry Wy *CAV/SC* RG4 .. **62** B8
Winterbourne Rd *KSCL* RG20 .. **107** H2
Winter Hl *MDHD* SL6 .... **19** L5
Winter Hill Rd *MDHD* SL6 ...... **19** K8
Winterton Dr *NWBY* RG14 ...... **136** A1
Winton Crs *YTLY* GU46 .... **180** A1
Winton Rd *WHIT* RG2 .... **117** G6
Wintringham Wy
  GOR/PANG RG8 .... **87** G1
Winvale *SL* SL1 .... **71** H3
Winwood *SLN* SL2 .... **45** M7
Wise's Firs *THLE* RG7 .... **142** A3
Wishmoor Cl *CBLY* GU15 .... **174** B6
Wishmoor Rd *CBLY* GU15 ...... **174** B6
Wispington Cl *EARL* RG6 .... **118** A4
Wisteria Cl *WWKG* RG41 .... **10** B8
Wiston Ter *READ* RG1. .... **9** G3
Witcham Cl *EARL* RG6 .... **118** A6 ▣
Withey Cl *WDSR* SL4 .... **70** B8
Witheygate Av *STA* TW18 ...... **127** L4
Withybed La *HUNG* RG17 .... **133** H4
Withybed Wy *NTHA* RG18 ...... **138** B1
Withy Cl *CALC* RG31 .... **114** F1
  LTWR GU18 .... **175** M5
Withy Cft *DTCH/LGLY* SL3 ...... **46** B7
The Withys *NTHA* RG18 .... **83** H5
Wittenham Av *CALC* RG31 ...... **86** E6
Wittenham Cl
  GOR/PANG RG8 .... **34** C6 ▣
Wittenham Rd *BRAK* RG12 ...... **122** C6
Woburn Cl *CAV/SC* RG4 .... **88** B2
  FRIM GU16 .... **182** D5
Woburn Hl *ADL/WDHM* KT15 .. **155** M6
Wokefield Rw *THLE* RG7 .... **143** C6
Wokingham Rd *BNFD* RG42 .... **12** A2
  BNFD RG42 .... **13** C3
  CWTH RG45 .... **172** B3
  EARL RG6 .... **89** H7
  WAR/TWY RG10 .... **91** J6
Wolf La *WDSR* SL4. .... **96** A2
Wolseley St *READ* RG1 .... **8** E9
Wolsey Rd *ASHF* TW15 .... **128** B2
  READ RG1 .... **8** F1
  SUN TW16 .... **129** J5
Wolsingham Wy *STHA* RG19 .... **138** A1 ▣
Wondesford Dl *BNFD* RG42...... **120** F2
Wooburn Common Rd
  FLKWH HP10. .... **21** L4
Wooburn Gra *FLKWH* HP10 ...... **21** L2
Wooburn Ms *FLKWH* HP10 ...... **21** H1 ▣
Woodberry Cl *SUN* TW16. ...... **129** K4
Woodbine Cl *EARL* RG6 .... **117** M5 ▣
  SHST GU47 .... **172** E7
Woodbine La *KSCL* RG20 ...... **160** C5
Woodbourne Cl *YTLY* GU46 .... **172** A8 ▣
Woodbridge Dr *CBLY* GU15 .... **174** A1
Woodbridge Rd *BLKW* GU17 .... **180** L1
  CALC RG31 .... **86** E8 ▣
Woodbury *HUNG* RG17 .... **49** M4
Woodby Dr *ASC* SL5 .... **152** C4
Wood Cl *WDSR* SL4. .... **96** F3
Woodcock Cl *THLE* RG7 .... **144** D2
Woodcock Dr *CHOB/PIR* GU24 .. **176** F3
Woodcock La *CHOB/PIR* GU24 .. **176** E3
Woodcote *MDHD* SL6. .... **2** D6
Woodcote Pl *ASC* SL5 .... **123** J6
Woodcote Rd *CAV/SC* RG4 ...... **88** B2
  GOR/PANG RG8 .... **33** G2
Woodcote Wy *CAV/SC* RG4 .... **88** A1
Wood End *CWTH* RG45. .... **172** C2
Woodend Dr *ASC* SL5 .... **151** L2
Woodend Rd *FRIM* GU16 .... **182** F7
Woodenhill Rd *BRAK* RG12 .... **149** H4
Woodfield Dr *MDHD* SL6 .... **41** K8 ▣
Woodfield Rd *HSLWW* TW4 .... **101** L1
Woodfield Wy *THLE* RG7 .... **114** B2 ▣
Woodford Cl *CAV/SC* RG4 ...... **88** D2
Woodford Gn *BRAK* RG12 ...... **150** C1
Woodford Wy *SLN* SL2 .... **22** C8
Wood Gn *GOR/PANG* RG8 ...... **34** B6 ▣
Wood Green Cl *TLHT* RG30 ...... **8** A7

Woodhall La *BFOR* GU20 .... **152** B6
Woodhaw *EGH* TW20 .... **126** E2
Woodhouse La *STHA* RG19 ...... **163** H3
Woodhouse St *BNFD* RG42 ...... **12** A2
Woodhurst La *WWKG* RG41 .... **119** J5 ▣
Woodies Cl *BNFD* RG42 .... **120** F5
Woodland Av *SL* SL1. .... **4** C4
  WDSR SL4 .... **96** C3
  WWKG RG41 .... **119** H6
Woodland Cl *MLW* SL7 .... **19** C2
Woodland Crs *BNFD* RG42....... **13** J1
Woodland Dr *TLHT* RG30 ...... **87** C7
Woodlands *CWTH* RG45 .... **172** E5
  KSCL RG20 .... **159** K7
  YTLY GU46 .... **180** A3
Woodlands Av *THLE* RG7 .... **142** D3
  WODY RG5. .... **90** A7
Woodlands Cl *ASC* SL5 .... **151** J3
  FARN GU14 .... **181** H5
  NTHA RG18 .... **109** C1
Woodlands Ct *SHST* GU47 ...... **173** J5
Woodlands Dr *SUN* TW16 ...... **129** M7
Woodlands Gv *CAV/SC* RG4 .... **89** C2
Woodlands La *CHOB/PIR* GU24 .. **176** C3
Woodlands Pde *ASHF* TW15 .... **128** F4 ▣
Woodlands Park Av *MDHD* SL6 .. **67** K4
Woodlands Park Rd *MDHD* SL6.. **67** K4
Woodlands Ride *ASC* SL5 ...... **151** J3
Woodlands Rd *CAV/SC* RG4. .... **36** B8
  CBLY GU15 .... **181** L1
  FARN GU14 .... **181** L8
  HEN RG9 .... **38** B8
  TADY RG26 .... **164** A5
  VW GU25. .... **153** H1
Woodlands Rd East *VW* GU25... **153** M1
Woodlands Rd West *VW* GU25.. **125** M8
The Woodlands *WWKG* RG41 .. **147** G2
Woodlands Wk *FARN* GU14...... **181** H5
Woodland Wy *MLW* SL7. .... **19** H2
Wood La *CAV/SC* RG4 .... **61** M3
  CAV/SC RG4 .... **62** C1
  GOR/PANG RG8 .... **34** A6
  IVER SL0 .... **46** F5
  SL SL1 .... **70** C3
  THLE RG7 .... **168** B1
  WHIT RG2 .... **146** C4
Wood Lane Cl *CAV/SC* RG4 ...... **62** C1
Woodley Gn *WODY* RG5. .... **90** C6
Woodman Cl *WHIT* RG2 .... **116** FB ▣
Woodmancott Cl *BRAK* RG12 .. **150** C2
Woodman's La *THLE* RG7 ...... **142** C3
Woodmere *BRAK* RG12 .... **150** B1
Woodmere Cl *EARL* RG6 .... **117** L4 ▣
Wood Moor *EWKG* RG40 ...... **171** J4
Woodmoor End *MDHD* SL6 .... **20** E7 ▣
Woodpecker Cl *WAR/TWY* RG10.. **91** H3
Wood Rdg *NWBY* RG14 .... **136** B7
Woodridge Cl *BRAK* RG12 ...... **13** J7
Wood Rd *CBLY* GU15 .... **181** L5
Woodrow Dr *EWKG* RG40 ...... **11** M5
Woodsend Cl *EARL* RG6 .... **117** H6
Woodshore Cl *VW* GU25 .... **153** L3
Woodside *BLKW* GU17 .... **180** F3
  CBLY GU15 .... **173** J7
  NTHA RG18 .... **109** M5
  NWBY RG14 .... **136** A7
Woodside Cl *EWKG* RG40 ...... **147** H6 ▣
  THLE RG7 .... **142** B3
  THLE RG7 .... **142** D8 ▣
Woodside Dr *NTHA* RG18........ **81** L8
Woodside La *ASC* SL5 .... **123** M3
  CAV/SC RG4 .... **61** M1
  WDSR SL4 .... **123** M2
Woodside Rd *ASC* SL5 .... **123** L3
Woodside Wy *VW* GU25 .... **125** L8
  WHIT RG2 .... **117** G7
Woods Rd *CAV/SC* RG4. .... **89** G2
Woodstock Av *DTCH/LGLY* SL3 .. **72** A4
Woodstock Cl *MDHD* SL6 ...... **42** C5 ▣
Woodstocks *FARN* GU14 .... **181** M8
Woodstock St *READ* RG1 ...... **9** M6
Woodthorpe Rd *ASHF* TW15.... **128** A3
Woodvicw Rd *GOR/PANG* RG8 .. **86** A1 ▣
Woodward Cl *WWKG* RG41 .... **119** G4
Woodway *CBLY* GU15 .... **181** L1 ▣
Woodwaye *WODY* RG5 .... **90** A7
Woodyer Cl *WODY* RG5 .... **118** B1
Woolacombe Dr *EARL* RG6 ...... **117** H4
Woolford Cl *BNFD* RG42 .... **122** C5
Woolhampton Hl *THLE* RG7 .... **139** M4
Woolhampton Wy *BRAK* RG12 .. **150** A2
Woolton Lodge Gdns
  KSCL RG20 .... **159** J4 ▣
Woosehill *WWKG* RG41........... **10** A5
  WWKG RG41 .... **119** H8
Woosehill La *WWKG* RG41 ...... **10** B6
Wootton Cl *CALC* RG31 .... **86** F6 ▣
Wootton Rd *HEN* RG9 .... **37** M6
Wootton Wy *MDHD* SL6 .... **42** F1
Worcester Cl *FARN* GU14 ...... **181** L7 ▣
  MDHD SL6. .... **67** M3
  TLHT RG30. .... **115** K1
Worcester Dr *ASHF* TW15 ...... **128** E3 ▣
Worcester Gdns *SL* SL1 .... **4** D9
Worcester Rd *UX/CGN* UB8...... **47** M6
Worcestershire Lea
  BNFD RG42 .... **122** C5 ▣
Wordsworth *BRAK* RG12 .... **149** J2
Wordsworth Rd *NTHA* RG18 .... **137** M2 ▣
  SLN SL2. .... **44** A5
Worlds End Hl *BRAK* RG12 ...... **150** C5
Wormersley Rd *STHA* RG19 .... **137** G7
Worple Av *STA* TW18 .... **127** L4
Worple Rd *STA* TW18 .... **127** L4
The Worple *STWL/WRAY* TW19 .. **98** C5 ▣
Worrall Wy *EARL* RG6 .... **117** J6
Worsley Pl *THLE* RG7 .... **114** B3
Worsley Rd *FRIM* GU16 .... **182** C7

Worster Rd *MDHD* SL6 .... **20** B8
Worton Dr *WHIT* RG2 .... **116** D6
Wrabness Wy *STA* TW18 .... **127** L6
Wraysbury Rd
  STWL/WRAY TW19 ...... **126** F1
Wren Cl *THLE* RG7 .... **142** E3 ▣
  WWKG RG41 .... **147** H1
  YTLY GU46 .... **171** L8 ▣
Wrenfield Dr *CAV/SC* RG4 ...... **88** C1
Wren's Av *ASHF* TW15 .... **128** F3
Wrensfield *MLW* SL7. .... **18** F5
Wrenswood Cl *WHIT* RG2 ...... **116** E8
Wren Wy *FARN* GU14 .... **181** J7
Wright *WDSR* SL4. .... **95** M2
Wroxham *BRAK* RG12 .... **149** J2
Wroxham Rd *WODY* RG5 .... **90** A6
Wurford Dr *STHA* RG19 .... **138** C3
Wyatt Rd *STA* TW18 .... **127** K3
  WDSR SL4 .... **96** A2
Wychcotes *READ* RG1 .... **88** C4
Wychelm Rd *LTWR* GU18 .... **175** M6
  WHIT RG2 .... **145** H1
Wychwood Av *BRAK* RG12 ...... **150** C1
Wychwood Cl *EARL* RG6 .... **117** J4
  SUN TW16 .... **129** K4
Wychwood Pl *CBLY* GU15 ...... **174** E5
Wycombe Rd *MLW* SL7 .... **19** H1
Wye Cl *ASHF* TW15 .... **128** E2
  TLHT RG30. .... **87** J8
Wyfold La *CAV/SC* RG4. .... **35** K7
  HEN RG9 .... **36** B6
Wykeham Rd *EARL* RG6 .... **89** K8
Wylam *BRAK* RG12 .... **149** J2
Wylands Rd *DTCH/LGLY* SL3 .... **72** D5
Wyld Court Hl *NTHA* RG18 ...... **82** E1
Wymers Cl *SL* SL1 .... **43** L3
Wymers Wood Rd *SL* SL1 ...... **43** K2
Wyncote Cl *WHIT* RG2 .... **117** J5
Wyndale Cl *HEN* RG9 .... **38** B5
Wyndham Cl *YTLY* GU46 .... **172** A7
Wyndham Crs *SL* SL1. .... **43** L3
  WODY RG5. .... **90** A5
Wyndham Rd *NWBY* RG14 ...... **137** G1
Wynford Cl *TLHT* RG30 .... **115** M2 ▣
Wynnstay Gdns *MLW* SL7 ...... **19** H1
Wynsham Wy *BFOR* GU20 ...... **175** L1
Wyre Ct *CALC* RG31. .... **86** F3
Wyresdale *BRAK* RG12 .... **150** C4 ▣
Wythemede *BNFD* RG42 .... **120** E4 ▣
Wyvern Cl *BRAK* RG12 .... **12** F8
Wyvern Wy *UX/CGN* UB8. ...... **47** L1

Y

Yale Cl *SHST* GU47 .... **173** J4
Yardley *BRAK* RG12. .... **149** J2
Yard Md *EGH* TW20 .... **126** D1
Yarmouth Rd *SL* SL1. .... **4** A3
Yarnold Cl *EWKG* RG40 .... **120** C7 ▣
Yarnton Cl *CAV/SC* RG4 .... **62** F8
Yateley Rd *YTLY* GU46 .... **172** C7
Yates Copse *NTHA* RG18 .... **137** H1
Yattendon La *NTHA* RG18 ...... **83** K5
Yattendon Rd *NTHA* RG18 ...... **81** M7
Yaverland Dr *BAGS* GU19........ **175** G4
Yelverton Rd *WHIT* RG2 .... **116** F3
Ye Meads *MDHD* SL6. .... **69** J1
Yeomans *HTWY* RG27. .... **171** H7
Yeomans La *KSCL* RG20 .... **160** D5
Yeomans Wy *KSCL* RG20 .... **160** D5
Yeoveney Cl *STWL/WRAY* TW19 .. **99** G8
Yeovil Rd *SHST* GU47 .... **173** H5
  SL SL1 .... **44** B6
Yew Cl *WWKG* RG41 .... **10** A7
Yew Ga *NWBY* RG14 .... **108** C8
Yewhurst Cl *WAR/TWY* RG10 .. **64** F3
Yew La *READ* RG1 .... **116** C2
Yew Tree Cl *MDHD* SL6. .... **2** F3
Yew Tree Ct *GOR/PANG* RG8 .. **32** F8 ▣
Yew Tree Ri *CALC* RG31 .... **114** F1
Yew Tree Rd *SL* SL1. .... **71** K3
Yewtrees *EGH* TW20. .... **126** F8
Yew Tree Stables *KSCL* RG20 .. **56** B2
Yew Tree Wk *FRIM* GU16 ...... **182** B5
Yield Hall La *READ* RG1 .... **9** G6
Yield Hall Pl *READ* RG1. .... **9** G6
Yockley Cl *CBLY* GU15 .... **183** G2
Yoreham Cl *EARL* RG6 .... **118** B5 ▣
York Av *SL* SL1 .... **4** C3
  WDSR SL4 .... **6** F9
York Cl *NWBY* RG14 .... **15** G6
York Pl *CBLY* GU15 .... **174** A7
York Rd *BNFD* RG42 .... **121** G3
  CBLY GU15 .... **174** A7
  HEN RG9 .... **38** A4
  HUNG RG17 .... **132** A2
  MDHD SL6. .... **3** H6
  MLW SL7 .... **19** G4
  NWBY RG14 .... **15** G6
  READ RG1 .... **8** F9
  WDSR SL4 .... **6** F9
Yorkshire Pl *BNFD* RG42 .... **122** B5 ▣▣
Yorktown Rd *SHST* GU47........ **172** F7
York Wy *SHST* GU47 .... **172** D6
Youlden Cl *CBLY* GU15 .... **182** D1
Youlden Dr *CBLY* GU15........... **182** D1
Young Crs *STHA* RG19 .... **15** M9

Z

Zinnia Cl *WWKG* RG41 .... **119** G7 ▣
Zinzan St *READ* RG1 .... **8** D6

The Abbey School
  READ RG1 .... 9 J9
A B C Cinema
  STA TW18 .... 127 H3
Acre Business Park
  WHIT RG2 .... 116 E6
Addington School
  WODY RG5 .... 90 C8
AFC Newbury Football Ground
  NWBY RG14 .... 15 G3
Aldermaston C of E School
  THLE RG7 .... 140 C7
Alexander Barracks
  CHOB/PIR GU24 .... 183 L8
Alexander First School
  WDSR SL4 .... 95 M1
Alfred Sutton Primary School
  EARL RG6 .... 89 J8
All Saints Infants School
  READ RG1 .... 8 B7
All Saints Junior School
  MDHD SL6 .... 2 B7
Altwood C of E School
  MDHD SL6 .... 67 L1
Alwyn County Infant School
  MDHD SL6 .... 2 A2
Ambulance Station
  READ RG1 .... 8 D5
Animal Care College
  ASC SL5 .... 123 K8
Arborfield C of E School
  WHIT RG2 .... 146 C3
Arbour Vale School
  SLN SL2 .... 5 J3
Arcade Gallery
  GOR/PANG RG8 .... 32 E8
Arena Leisure Centre
  CBLY GU15 .... 173 L8
The Argyle Clinic
  READ RG1 .... 8 B6
The Ark School
  THLE RG7 .... 141 J5
Arlington Business Park
  BRAK RG12 .... 13 J4
Army Training Regiment
  CHOB/PIR GU24 .... 183 M8
Art Gallery
  HEN RG9 .... 38 B4
The Art Gallery
  READ RG1 .... 8 F7
Arthur Hill Memorial
  Swimming Baths
  READ RG1 .... 9 M7
Arts Centre
  WDSR SL4 .... 7 H8
Ascot Heath Junior School
  ASC SL5 .... 123 H5
Ashford Clinic
  ASHF TW15 .... 128 B1
Ashford C of E School
  ASHF TW15 .... 128 E4
Ashford High School
  ASHF TW15 .... 128 B1
Ashford Hill Primary School
  STHA RG19 .... 163 H5
Ashford Hospital A & E
  STWL/WRAY TW19 .... 100 B8
The Ashford & St Peters
  Hospitals NHS Trust
  CHERT KT16 .... 155 G7
Ashford Sports Club
  ASHF TW15 .... 128 A2
Ashford Sports Club
  STWL/WRAY TW19 .... 100 C7
Ashmead School
  WHIT RG2 .... 116 F5
Auction Market
  READ RG1 .... 8 D4
Avenue Medical Centre
  SLN SL2 .... 44 D4
The Avenue School
  WHIT RG2 .... 116 F2
Aysgarth Medical Centre
  IVER SL0 .... 47 G3
Badgemore CP School
  HEN RG9 .... 37 M4
Bank Gallery
  CHOB/PIR GU24 .... 177 H6
Basildon House
  GOR/PANG RG8 .... 59 H5
Basildon School
  GOR/PANG RG8 .... 58 D8
Battle Farm Trading Estate
  TLHT RG30 .... 88 A5
Battle Primary School
  TLHT RG30 .... 87 M7
Baylis Court School for Girls
  SL SL1 .... 4 C1
Bearwood College
  WWKG RG41 .... 118 E7
Bearwood Primary School
  WWKG RG41 .... 118 E6
Beauclerc County
  Infant School
  SUN TW16 .... 129 M8
Beavers Primary School
  HSLWW TW4 .... 101 M2
Bedfont Health Clinic
  EBED/NFELT TW14 .... 101 H6
Bedfont Junior & Infant School
  EBED/NFELT TW14 .... 101 H5
Beechwood County
  Junior & Infant School
  WODY RG5 .... 90 B7
Beechwood Secondary School
  SLN SL2 .... 44 E4
Beedon Primary School
  KSCL RG20 .... 55 G6
The Bell Surgery
  HEN RG9 .... 38 A4
Benham Park
  KSCL RG20 .... 135 K2
Berkshire Business Centre
  STHA RG19 .... 138 D4
Berkshire College
  of Art & Design
  MDHD SL6 .... 2 D4

Berkshire County Council
  NWBY RG14 .... 14 E7
Berkshire County Council
  NWBY RG14 .... 14 B8
Berkshire County Council
  NWBY RG14 .... 14 D3
Berkshire County Council
  READ RG1 .... 9 H4
Berkshire County Council
  SL SL1 .... 4 F9
The Berkshire Golf Club
  ASC SL5 .... 150 F1
The Bharani Medical Centre
  SL SL1 .... 44 A7
Bilton Industrial Estate
  BRAK RG12 .... 12 A9
Binfield Primary School
  BNFD RG42 .... 120 F4
Binfield Surgery
  BNFD RG42 .... 120 F3
Birch Copse Primary School
  CALC RG31 .... 86 F6
Birch Hill Medical Centre
  BRAK RG12 .... 149 L4
Birch Hill Primary School
  BRAK RG12 .... 149 M5
Bisham Abbey National
  Sports Centre
  MLW SL7 .... 19 G7
Bisham Primary School
  MLW SL7 .... 19 G7
Bishopsgate School
  EGH TW20 .... 125 K1
Bishopswood Co Junior School
  TADY RG26 .... 164 E6
Bishop Wand C of E School
  SUN TW16 .... 129 J7
Bishopwood Co Infant School
  TADY RG26 .... 164 E7
Blackburn Trading Estate
  STWL/WRAY TW19 .... 100 C5
Blackdown Primary School
  FRIM GU16 .... 183 H6
Blackwater & Hawley
  Leisure Centre
  BLKW GU17 .... 181 G3
Blackwater Industrial Estate
  BLKW GU17 .... 181 H2
Blakes Lock Museum
  READ RG1 .... 9 L5
Blands Infant School
  THLE RG7 .... 142 C4
Blue Mountain Golf Club
  & Conference Centre
  BNFD RG42 .... 121 G4
Boathouse Surgery
  GOR/PANG RG8 .... 32 E8
Bohun Gallery
  HEN RG9 .... 38 B5
Borocourt Hospital
  CAV/SC RG4 .... 35 K4
Boundary House Surgery
  BRAK RG12 .... 13 K5
Bourne End Business Centre
  BNEND SL8 .... 20 E3
Bournewood Community
  & Mental NHS Trust
  EGH TW20 .... 126 D3
Boyn Hill C of E Infants School
  MDHD SL6 .... 2 A4
Boyn Valley Industrial Estate
  MDHD SL6 .... 2 F7
Bracknell Business Centre
  BRAK RG12 .... 12 D5
Bracknell College
  BRAK RG12 .... 13 J2
Bracknell College
  BRAK RG12 .... 13 K5
Bracknell Forest
  Borough Council
  BRAK RG12 .... 13 G5
Bracknell Forest
  Borough Council
  BRAK RG12 .... 13 J4
Bracknell Rugby Football Club
  BRAK RG12 .... 122 B7
Bracknell Sports Centre
  BRAK RG12 .... 149 M2
Bracknell Town Council
  BRAK RG12 .... 13 H4
Bracknell Town Football Club
  BRAK RG12 .... 13 K5
Bradfield C of E
  Primary School
  THLE RG7 .... 112 E4
Bradfield College
  THLE RG7 .... 84 F8
Brakenhale School
  BRAK RG12 .... 13 H9
Braywood C of E First School
  WDSR SL4 .... 95 H1
Brickfields Industrial Park
  BRAK RG12 .... 12 E5
Brick Kiln Industrial Estate
  TADY RG26 .... 164 E5
Brightwalton C of E
  Primary School
  KSCL RG20 .... 53 G3
The Brigidine School
  WDSR SL4 .... 97 G2
Brimpton School
  THLE RG7 .... 139 J8
Bristow County First School
  CBLY GU15 .... 181 L4
Britannia Industrial Estate
  DTCH/LGLY SL3 .... 99 H1
Britwell Health Clinic
  SLN SL2 .... 44 D4
Broadmoor County
  Primary School
  CWTH RG45 .... 173 G2
Broadmoor Hospital
  CWTH RG45 .... 173 G2
Brockhurst
  Preparatory School
  NTHA RG18 .... 110 C2
Brook Business Centre
  IVER SL0 .... 47 K3

Brookfields School
  CALC RG31 .... 86 F3
Brookside Business Centre
  THLE RG7 .... 145 G8
The Brookside Group Practice
  EARL RG6 .... 118 A3
Buckinghamshire
  County Council
  DTCH/LGLY SL3 .... 72 D1
Buckland County
  Junior & Infant School
  STA TW18 .... 127 M5
Bucklebury C of E
  Primary School
  THLE RG7 .... 110 F8
Building Design School
  WHIT RG2 .... 145 J2
The Bulmershe School
  EARL RG6 .... 89 M7
Burchetts Green Primary School
  MDHD SL6 .... 40 E7
Burdwood Surgery
  STHA RG19 .... 138 B4
Burford County
  Combined School
  MLW SL7 .... 18 F1
Burghclere CP School
  KSCL RG20 .... 160 D8
Burghfield Aqua Sports Club
  TLHT RG30 .... 115 K5
Burghfield Health Centre
  THLE RG7 .... 142 E3
Burma Hills Surgery
  EWKG RG40 .... 11 J3
Burnham Beeches Golf Club
  SL SL1 .... 44 A2
Burnham Copse Junior School
  TADY RG26 .... 164 D5
Burnham Football Club
  SL SL1 .... 43 L3
Burnham Grammar School
  SL SL1 .... 44 A5
Burnham Health Centre
  SL SL1 .... 43 L4
Burnham Upper School
  SL SL1 .... 43 L5
Bus Depot
  READ RG1 .... 8 D4
The Business Centre
  THLE RG7 .... 139 J8
The Business Centre
  WWKG RG41 .... 10 E9
Calcot Junior and Infant School
  CALC RG31 .... 114 E2
Calleva Roman Antiquity
  and Museum
  THLE RG7 .... 165 L5
Camberley County
  Infant School
  CBLY GU15 .... 181 L1
Camberley Cricket Club
  CBLY GU15 .... 182 A3
Camberley Health Centre
  CBLY GU15 .... 181 L3
Camberley Heath Golf Club
  CBLY GU15 .... 182 D2
Camberley Magistrates Court
  CBLY GU15 .... 174 E2
Camberley Rugby
  Football Club
  CBLY GU15 .... 181 M3
Camberley Town
  Football Club
  CBLY GU15 .... 181 L3
Cardinal Road School
  FELT TW13 .... 101 L7
Carlyle Business Centre
  CHERT KT16 .... 155 K4
Carwarden House School
  CBLY GU15 .... 182 D3
Castle Hill Clinic
  READ RG1 .... 8 C8
Castle Hill Clinic
  READ RG1 .... 8 C7
Castle Industrial Park
  NWBY RG14 .... 136 F1
Castle Royle Golf Club
  WAR/TWY RG10 .... 66 A4
Castle School
  NWBY RG14 .... 108 C8
Castleview School
  DTCH/LGLY SL3 .... 72 A4
Caversham Park Primary School
  CAV/SC RG4 .... 63 H8
Caversham Primary School
  CAV/SC RG4 .... 88 D3
Cedar Park School
  WAR/TWY RG10 .... 90 F1
Cedars School
  THLE RG7 .... 140 D7
Centenary Business Park
  HEN RG9 .... 38 C5
Central Swimming Pool
  READ RG1 .... 8 C5
Century Galleries
  HEN RG9 .... 38 B4
Century Gallery
  DTCH/LGLY SL3 .... 71 L7
Chalfont Surgery
  EARL RG6 .... 117 K5
Chapel Hill Surgery
  CALC RG31 .... 86 F6
Chapel Row Surgery
  THLE RG7 .... 111 M6
Charles Kingsley School
  HTWY RG27 .... 170 F6
Charters Comprehensive
  School
  ASC SL5 .... 152 A4
Chatham Street Surgery
  READ RG1 .... 8 D6
Cheapside C of E School
  ASC SL5 .... 124 B6
Checkendon C of E
  Aided Primary School
  GOR/PANG RG8 .... 34 F3

Chennestone County
  Middle School
  SUN TW16 .... 129 L7
Chertsey Business Centre
  CHERT KT16 .... 155 K4
Chertsey Museum
  CHERT KT16 .... 155 K4
Chertsey Recreation Centre
  CHERT KT16 .... 155 J5
Chertsey Town Football Club
  CHERT KT16 .... 155 J3
Chieveley County
  Primary School
  KSCL RG20 .... 80 D6
Chiltern Edge
  Secondary School
  CAV/SC RG4 .... 62 B2
Chiltern House Surgery
  SLN SL2 .... 45 K2
Chilton Foliat C of E
  Aided School
  HUNG RG17 .... 103 J4
Chobham Football Club
  CHOB/PIR GU24 .... 177 J6
Chobham Parish Council
  CHOB/PIR GU24 .... 177 H6
Chobham St Lawrence C of E
  First & Middle School
  CHOB/PIR GU24 .... 177 H6
Christchurch C of E
  Infant School
  VW GU25 .... 125 K8
Christchurch Primary School
  WHIT RG2 .... 116 E1
Christ the King RC First School
  STWL/WRAY TW19 .... 100 A5
Christ the King School
  WHIT RG2 .... 116 F6
Church Hill House Hospital
  BRAK RG12 .... 149 K2
Churchmead School
  DTCH/LGLY SL3 .... 71 L7
Church of England School
  THLE RG7 .... 140 A2
Cippenham County
  First School
  SL SL1 .... 44 A8
Cippenham Medical Centre
  SL SL1 .... 70 E1
Cippenham Middle School
  SL SL1 .... 44 A8
Civil Service College
  ASC SL5 .... 152 C2
Claires Court School
  MDHD SL6 .... 3 M1
Clarendon County
  Primary School
  ASHF TW15 .... 128 C1
Claycots Middle School
  SLN SL2 .... 44 D5
Claytons Combined School
  BNEND SL8 .... 20 C1
The Clere Secondary School
  KSCL RG20 .... 160 D7
Clewborough House
  Preparatory School
  CBLY GU15 .... 174 D8
Clockhouse Industrial Estate
  EBED/NFELT TW14 .... 100 E7
Club House
  BAGS GU19 .... 150 A5
Coley Park School
  READ RG1 .... 116 B1
Coley Park Surgery
  READ RG1 .... 116 B1
Coley Primary School
  READ RG1 .... 8 E8
Coliseum Business Centre
  CBLY GU15 .... 181 K3
Colleton CP School
  WAR/TWY RG10 .... 91 H3
Collingwood College
  CBLY GU15 .... 174 D6
Colnbrook C of E
  Combined School
  DTCH/LGLY SL3 .... 72 F7
Colnbrook Sports Club
  DTCH/LGLY SL3 .... 73 J8
Coin Industrial Estate
  DTCH/LGLY SL3 .... 73 J8
Combermere Barracks
  WDSR SL4 .... 96 E2
Compton C of E
  Primary School
  KSCL RG20 .... 56 B2
Connaught County
  Junior School
  BAGS GU19 .... 175 H4
Contemporary Fine Art Gallery
  WDSR SL4 .... 7 J4
Cookham Dean School
  MDHD SL6 .... 19 L7
Cookham Reach Sailing Club
  MDHD SL6 .... 20 D6
Coombe Infants School
  WHIT RG2 .... 146 B3
Cordwalles County
  Middle School
  CBLY GU15 .... 174 C6
Council Offices
  LTWR GU18 .... 175 K5
Country Gardens Estate
  BFOR GU20 .... 151 M6
Court House Junior School
  MDHD SL6 .... 41 L6
Cove County Infant School
  FARN GU14 .... 181 H8
Cove Manor County
  Junior & Infant School
  FARN GU14 .... 181 J8
Cowarth Park School
  CHOB/PIR GU24 .... 152 E8
Cowley Business Park
  UX/CGN UB8 .... 47 M4
Cowley Mill Industrial Estate
  IVER SL0 .... 47 K3
Cowley Mill Trading Estate
  IVER SL0 .... 47 K3

The Coworth Gallery
  ASC SL5 .... 152 C2
Cox Green School
  MDHD SL6 .... 67 K2
Cranbourne School
  ASC SL5 .... 123 K2
Cranford House School
  WGFD OX10 .... 32 C1
Cranford Infant School
  HSLWW TW4 .... 101 K1
Cranford School
  HSLWW TW4 .... 101 L1
Crawley Ridge First School
  CBLY GU15 .... 174 C8
Crazies Hill Primary School
  WAR/TWY RG10 .... 39 J8
The Cricket Club
  SLN SL2 .... 44 F4
The Cricket Club
  SLN SL2 .... 45 K5
Crosby House Surgery
  SL SL1 .... 4 F4
Crosfields School
  WHIT RG2 .... 117 H6
Crown Wood CP School
  BRAK RG12 .... 150 A3
Crowthorne Business Centre
  CWTH RG45 .... 148 F7
Crowthorne C of E
  Primary School
  CWTH RG45 .... 172 E1
Curridge CP School
  NTHA RG18 .... 109 G2
Curtain Gallery
  WWKG RG41 .... 118 F5
Danesfield County
  Combined School
  MLW SL7 .... 18 B7
Datchet C of E School
  DTCH/LGLY SL3 .... 71 L7
Datchet Sports Club
  DTCH/LGLY SL3 .... 71 L7
David Lloyd Sports Centre
  EARL RG6 .... 89 K5
Dedworth Clinic
  WDSR SL4 .... 70 B8
Dedworth County
  Middle School
  WDSR SL4 .... 70 B8
Dedworth Green County
  First School
  WDSR SL4 .... 96 B1
Delwood Hospital
  TLHT RG30 .... 87 H8
Dene House Hospital
  WDSR SL4 .... 96 F2
Desborough School
  MDHD SL6 .... 2 F8
The Doctors House Surgery
  MLW SL7 .... 19 H4
The Dolphin School
  WAR/TWY RG10 .... 91 K4
Donnington Castle
  NWBY RG14 .... 108 B7
Dorney County
  Combined School
  MDHD SL6 .... 69 J2
Dorney Court
  WDSR SL4 .... 69 L3
Douai School
  THLE RG7 .... 140 A1
Downe House School
  NTHA RG18 .... 109 K3
Downlands Sports Centre
  KSCL RG20 .... 56 A2
The Downs School
  KSCL RG20 .... 56 A2
Downs Way School
  CALC RG31 .... 86 F3
Dropmore County First School
  SL SL1 .... 21 M5
Dr Shafiq Surgery
  SL SL1 .... 44 C8
Dryleas Sports Ground
  HEN RG9 .... 38 A3
Duffield Road CP School
  WODY RG5 .... 90 C5
Dunston Park School
  NTHA RG18 .... 138 A2
Eagle House School
  SHST GU47 .... 172 D4
East Berkshire College
  DTCH/LGLY SL3 .... 72 D2
East Berkshire College
  MDHD SL6 .... 2 D6
East Berkshire College
  WDSR SL4 .... 7 H8
East Berkshire Golf Club
  CWTH RG45 .... 172 B1
East Berkshire
  Health Authority
  SL SL1 .... 5 G9
Eastern Business Centre
  BRAK RG12 .... 13 M5
Eastfield House Surgery
  NWBY RG14 .... 14 E6
Easthampstead Park School
  EWKG RG40 .... 149 G3
Ebony Health Centre
  WAR/TWY RG10 .... 91 G1
Echelford Primary School
  ASHF TW15 .... 128 E3
Edgebarrow School
  CWTH RG45 .... 172 E3
Edgebarrow Sports Centre
  CWTH RG45 .... 172 F3
Edward Pauling School
  FELT TW13 .... 101 H8
Egham Cricket Club
  EGH TW20 .... 126 E3
Egham Sports Centre
  EGH TW20 .... 126 E4
Egham Town Football Club
  EGH TW20 .... 126 F4
Elizabeth Barracks
  CHOB/PIR GU24 .... 183 K8

Ellington County
  Junior & Infant School
  MDHD SL6 .... **3** G1
Elstree School
  THLE RG7 .... **140** A2
Emmbrook County
  Junior & Infant School
  WWKG RG41 .... **119** J5
The Emmbrook School
  WWKG RG41 .... **10** B1
Emmer Green Clinic
  CAV/SC RG4 .... **88** E1
Emmer Green CP School
  CAV/SC RG4 .... **62** E8
Emmer Green Surgery
  CAV/SC RG4 .... **62** D8
Enborne C of E School
  KSCL RG20 .... **135** H8
Enborne Lodge
  NWBY RG14 .... **159** L1
Englefield Estate Yard
  THLE RG7 .... **113** L1
Englefield Green School
  EGH TW20 .... **125** M3
Englefield School
  THLE RG7 .... **113** L2
English Martyrs RC
  Primary School
  TLHT RG30 .... **87** K7
E P Collier School
  READ RG1 .... **8** E3
Eton College
  WDSR SL4 .... **7** J1
Eton Porny C of E
  Combined School
  WDSR SL4 .... **7** J3
Eton Town Council
  WDSR SL4 .... **7** J4
Eton Wick C of E
  Combined School
  WDSR SL4 .... **70** D5
Eton Wick Football
  & Social Club
  WDSR SL4 .... **70** C5
Eversley Cricket Club
  HTWY RG27 .... **171** J6
Fairacres Industrial Estate
  WDSR SL4 .... **95** M1
Fairholme Junior
  & Infant School
  EBED/NFELT TW14 .... **101** G7
Fairview Trading Estate
  HEN RG9 .... **38** C6
Falkland CP School
  NWBY RG14 .... **136** A8
Family Planning Clinic
  READ RG1 .... **9** K8
Farley Hill Primary School
  THLE RG7 .... **169** M1
Farmhouse Gallery
  KSCL RG20 .... **159** L7
Farnborough Grange
  County Junior School
  FARN GU14 .... **181** J6
Farnborough Rugby
  Football Club
  FARN GU14 .... **181** K8
Farnborough Town
  Football Club
  FARN GU14 .... **181** K6
Farnham Road Surgery
  SLN SL2 .... **44** E5
Farnham Royal
  Combined School
  SLN SL2 .... **44** F4
Feltham Hill Junior School
  FELT TW13 .... **129** J1
Feltham & Hounslow
  Boro Football Club
  EBED/NFELT TW14 .... **101** K6
The Feltham School
  FELT TW13 .... **101** M8
Feltham Superbowl
  FELT TW13 .... **101** L8
Fernhill Comprehensive School
  FARN GU14 .... **181** J5
Fernhill Primary School
  FARN GU14 .... **181** J5
Finchampstead C of E
  Primary School
  EWKG RG40 .... **171** H3
Finchampstead Sports Club
  EWKG RG40 .... **171** H3
Fireplace Gallery
  EWKG RG40 .... **11** H6
Firestation
  READ RG1 .... **8** E3
Fir Tree CP School
  NTHA RG18 .... **137** H2
Five Ways Business Centre
  FELT TW13 .... **129** L1
Food Gallery
  READ RG1 .... **9** M6
Football Club
  HEN RG9 .... **38** C6
Forbury Retail Park
  READ RG1 .... **9** J5
Fordbridge Medical Centre
  ASHF TW15 .... **128** C2
Fordwater Trading Estate
  ADL/WDHM KT15 .... **155** M5
The Forest
  Comprehensive School
  WWKG RG41 .... **118** E4
Forest End Medical Centre
  BRAK RG12 .... **149** L3
Foxborough School
  DTCH/LGLY SL3 .... **72** D5
Foxes Piece School
  MLW SL7 .... **19** H3
Foxhill Primary School
  BRAK RG12 .... **149** L2
Foxley P N E U School
  WAR/TWY RG10 .... **92** D5
France Hill School
  CBLY GU15 .... **181** M4
Francis Bailey School
  STHA RG19 .... **138** B3

Freehold Industrial Centre
  HSLWW TW4 .... **101** M4
Freemantles School
  CHERT KT16 .... **155** H4
Friar's Walk Shopping Centre
  READ RG1 .... **8** F5
Frimley C of E First
  & Middle School
  FRIM GU16 .... **182** B7
Frimley Green Medical Centre
  FRIM GU16 .... **182** C8
Frimley Park Hospital
  FRIM GU16 .... **182** A4
Frogmore Community School
  BLKW GU17 .... **180** C1
Frogmore County
  Infant School
  BLKW GU17 .... **180** E2
Frogmore Ho
  WDSR SL4 .... **71** K8
Frogmore Junior School
  BLKW GU17 .... **180** E1
Furze Platt
  Comprehensive School
  MDHD SL6 .... **42** A4
Furze Platt Junior
  & Infant School
  MDHD SL6 .... **41** M5
Gaflac Sports Ground Pavilion
  SUN TW16 .... **129** K6
The Gallery
  CAV/SC RG4 .... **89** L1
The Gallery
  MLW SL7 .... **19** G4
The Gallery
  SHST GU47 .... **172** F6
Garlands County Junior School
  THLE RG7 .... **142** D3
The Garth Hill School
  BRAK RG12 .... **13** J2
Genevieve the Gallery
  EGH TW20 .... **125** M3
George Palmer Junior School
  WHIT RG2 .... **116** F2
Gillotts School
  HEN RG9 .... **37** L7
Gladstone Industrial Estate
  MDHD SL6 .... **2** F2
Godolphin County First School
  SL SL1 .... **4** B2
Godolphin County
  Middle School
  SL SL1 .... **4** C2
Golf Course
  STHA RG19 .... **137** J7
Goring C of E Primary School
  GOR/PANG RG8 .... **32** F7
Goring & Streatley Golf Club
  GOR/PANG RG8 .... **32** B7
Gorse Ride Junior School
  EWKG RG40 .... **147** H7
Grazeley School
  THLE RG7 .... **144** B4
Great Bedwyn C of E
  Controlled School
  MARL SN8 .... **130** B7
Great Hollands County
  Infant School
  BRAK RG12 .... **149** H2
Great Hollands County
  Junior School
  BRAK RG12 .... **149** H2
Great Hollands Health Centre
  BRAK RG12 .... **149** J3
Great Hollands
  Recreation Centre
  BRAK RG12 .... **149** H5
Great Marlow School
  MLW SL7 .... **19** J2
Green Business Centre
  EGH TW20 .... **126** F2
Green Croft School
  FARN GU14 .... **182** A8
Greenham Road Retail Park
  NWBY RG14 .... **14** F6
Green Meadows Surgery
  ASC SL5 .... **123** J4
Green Road Surgery
  EARL RG6 .... **89** J8
Gresham Way Industrial Estate
  TLHT RG30 .... **87** K4
Greys Gallery
  HEN RG9 .... **38** B5
Grimsbury Castle
  NTHA RG18 .... **109** M1
Grove County Primary School
  FRIM GU16 .... **182** B4
Grovelands Surgery
  TLHT RG30 .... **87** L6
Grove Park Industrial Estate
  MDHD SL6 .... **67** H6
Grove Village Medical Centre
  EBED/NFELT TW14 .... **101** H7
Guillemont County
  Junior School
  FARN GU14 .... **180** F7
Gun Street Gallery
  READ RG1 .... **9** G6
Hall Grove School
  BAGS GU19 .... **175** K1
Hammond Middle School
  LTWR GU18 .... **175** K5
Hampstead Norreys
  Primary School
  NTHA RG18 .... **82** C1
Harleyford Golf Club
  MLW SL7 .... **18** C8
Harmans Water Infant
  & Junior School
  BRAK RG12 .... **150** B2
The Hart Surgery
  HEN RG9 .... **38** A4
Hatch Ride Primary School
  CWTH RG45 .... **148** E7
Hatton Medical Practice
  EBED/NFELT TW14 .... **101** H5
Hawkedale Gm School
  SUN TW16 .... **129** J8

Hawkedon Primary School
  EARL RG6 .... **118** B4
Hawley CP School
  BLKW GU17 .... **181** H3
Hawley Lane Industrial Estate
  FARN GU14 .... **181** L6
Hawley Place School
  BLKW GU17 .... **181** G5
Hawthornden Surgery
  BNEND SL8 .... **20** D3
Hawthorns Primary School
  WWKG RG41 .... **119** H7
Headmaster Bradfield College
  THLE RG7 .... **84** F8
The Health Centre
  WHIT RG2 .... **117** H3
Heathermount School
  ASC SL5 .... **152** A3
Heather Ridge County
  Infants School
  CBLY GU15 .... **183** C3
Heatherside Surgery
  CBLY GU15 .... **182** F2
Heatherwood Hospital
  ASC SL5 .... **123** H8
Heathfield School
  ASC SL5 .... **122** F7
Heath Hill Surgery
  CWTH RG45 .... **172** C2
Heathrow Airport
  WDR/YW UB7 .... **73** M8
Heathrow International
  Trading Estate
  HSLWW TW4 .... **101** L2
Hedsor School
  BNEND SL8 .... **21** G4
Hemdean House School
  CAV/SC RG4 .... **88** D3
Hengrove CP School
  ASHF TW15 .... **128** C2
The Henley College
  HEN RG9 .... **37** M5
Henley District Indoor
  Sports Centre
  HEN RG9 .... **37** L7
Henley Golf Club
  HEN RG9 .... **38** A8
Henley Town Football Club
  HEN RG9 .... **38** C6
Hermitage Primary School
  NTHA RG18 .... **81** L6
Hernes Estate
  HEN RG9 .... **37** J6
Heron Industrial Estate
  THLE RG7 .... **144** D6
Herries School
  MDHD SL6 .... **19** L6
Herschel Grammar School
  SL SL1 .... **4** B3
The Herschel Medical Centre
  SL SL1 .... **5** H9
The Herschel Medical Centre
  SL SL1 .... **71** J3
The Hexagon
  READ RG1 .... **8** E6
Highdown School
  CAV/SC RG4 .... **88** D1
Highfield School
  MDHD SL6 .... **2** F5
Highwood Primary School
  EARL RG6 .... **89** M8
The Hill Primary School
  CAV/SC RG4 .... **88** F1
Hillside Primary School
  EARL RG6 .... **117** J6
Hilltop First School
  WDSR SL4 .... **96** B2
Hindu Temple
  SL SL1 .... **4** A8
HM Prison
  READ RG1 .... **9** J5
HM Young Offender Institution
  FELT TW13 .... **129** G1
Hollyspring Junior
  & Infants School
  BRAK RG12 .... **122** B7
Hollywood Bowl
  BRAK RG12 .... **13** G4
Holme Grange School
  EWKG RG40 .... **148** C3
Holmers First School
  WDSR SL4 .... **70** A8
Holmwood Health Centre
  TADY RG26 .... **164** D5
The Holt School
  WWKG RG41 .... **10** E3
Holy Family RC School
  DTCH/LGLY SL3 .... **72** C5
Holyport C E Primary School
  MDHD SL6 .... **68** E6
Holyport Manor School
  MDHD SL6 .... **68** D8
Holy Trinity Middle School
  MLW SL7 .... **19** G3
Holy Trinity Primary School
  MDHD SL6 .... **20** D7
Holy Trinity School
  CHOB/PIR GU24 .... **176** D7
Home Farm School
  THLE RG7 .... **140** A3
Horris Hill Preparatory School
  KSCL RG20 .... **160** B3
Horton Trading Estate
  DTCH/LGLY SL3 .... **98** C2
The Hospital
  CBLY GU15 .... **173** K6
Hounslow & Spelthorne
  Community & Mental Health
  NHS Trust
  STA TW18 .... **127** K3
H R H Princess
  Christians Hospital
  WDSR SL4 .... **7** G7
H & S Community & NHS Trust
  STWL/WRAY TW19 .... **100** B8
Humphries Industrial Estate
  BRAK RG12 .... **13** J9

Hungerford Community
  Health Clinic
  HUNG RG17 .... **103** M8
Hungerford CP School
  HUNG RG17 .... **132** A1
Hungerford Gallery
  HUNG RG17 .... **132** A1
Hungerford Leisure Centre
  HUNG RG17 .... **132** A3
Hungerford Town
  Football Club
  HUNG RG17 .... **132** A2
Huntercombe Manor Hospital
  WDSR SL4 .... **43** M8
The Hurst Community School
  TADY RG26 .... **164** A5
Hurst Lodge School
  ASC SL5 .... **151** L5
The Hythe School
  STA TW18 .... **127** G3
Ibis Sports Club
  CAV/SC RG4 .... **87** L4
Imperial College of Science
  Technology & Medicine
  ASC SL5 .... **124** C8
Industrial Health Clinic
  UX/CGN UB8 .... **47** L4
Inhurst House School
  STHA RG19 .... **163** M5
Inkpen Primary School
  HUNG RG17 .... **133** G8
Iver Doctors Surgery
  IVER SL0 .... **47** H7
Iver Golf & Leisure Centre
  IVER SL0 .... **72** E1
Iver Heath First School
  IVER SL0 .... **47** G4
Iver Heath Health Centre
  IVER SL0 .... **47** G3
Iver Heath Middle School
  IVER SL0 .... **47** G3
Iver Village Infant School
  IVER SL0 .... **47** J7
Iver Village Junior School
  IVER SL0 .... **47** H7
Ivyleaf WM School
  MDHD SL6 .... **3** J4
James Elliman School
  SL SL1 .... **4** F4
John O'gaunt School
  HUNG RG17 .... **132** A3
John Rankin County
  Infants School
  NWBY RG14 .... **136** A6
John Rankin Junior
  NWBY RG14 .... **136** A6
The Junior School
  GOR/PANG RG8 .... **85** J1
Katesgrove Primary School
  READ RG1 .... **8** F8
Keep Hatch County
  Junior School
  EWKG RG40 .... **11** K3
Kendrick Girls School
  READ RG1 .... **9** H7
Kennet Secondary School
  STHA RG19 .... **138** B3
Kennet Surgery
  READ RG1 .... **89** H7
Kennet Valley Primary School
  TLHT RG30 .... **115** J2
Kenton Theatre
  HEN RG9 .... **38** B4
Kenyngton Manor CP School
  SUN TW16 .... **129** K4
Kidmore End Primary School
  CAV/SC RG4 .... **62** A3
King Edward Vii Hospital
  WDSR SL4 .... **96** F2
Kings Corner Surgery
  ASC SL5 .... **152** B2
Kings Court Primary School
  WDSR SL4 .... **97** K6
Kingscroft School
  STA TW18 .... **127** K4
Kings Grove Industrial Estate
  MDHD SL6 .... **2** F6
Kintbury St Marys C of E
  Primary School
  HUNG RG17 .... **133** K4
Knowle Park County School
  STA TW18 .... **127** K3
Knowl Hill Church
  of England Primary School
  WAR/TWY RG10 .... **66** C2
Laffords Industrial Estate
  THLE RG7 .... **114** D4
Lakeside Business Park
  SHST GU47 .... **172** D7
Lakeside Country Club
  FRIM GU16 .... **182** D8
Lakeside County
  Primary School
  FRIM GU16 .... **182** C5
Lakeside Industrial Estate
  DTCH/LGLY SL3 .... **73** K6
Lakeside Industrial Estate
  DTCH/LGLY SL3 .... **73** H7
Laleham C of E Primary School
  STA TW18 .... **127** M7
Lambourn C of E
  Primary School
  HUNG RG17 .... **49** L5
Lambourne Golf Club
  SL SL1 .... **21** L8
The Lambourn Sports Club
  HUNG RG17 .... **49** L4
The Lambourn Surgery
  HUNG RG17 .... **49** L5
Lambrook Haileybury School
  BNFD RG42 .... **122** D3
Lambs Farm Business Park
  THLE RG7 .... **144** D6
Lambs Lane CP School
  THLE RG7 .... **144** D6
Lambwood Industrial Estate
  THLE RG7 .... **143** M5

Langley Business Centre
  DTCH/LGLY SL3 .... **72** D2
Langley Grammar School
  DTCH/LGLY SL3 .... **72** C4
Langley Health Centre
  DTCH/LGLY SL3 .... **72** D5
Langley Manor School
  DTCH/LGLY SL3 .... **72** B1
Langleywood Secondary School
  DTCH/LGLY SL3 .... **72** B3
Langtree Secondary School
  GOR/PANG RG8 .... **34** C6
Lavender Golf Club
  ASC SL5 .... **122** F8
Lazards Sports Club
  SUN TW16 .... **129** L6
Lea County First School
  SLN SL2 .... **5** L5
Lea County Middle School
  SLN SL2 .... **5** K5
Leighton Park School
  WHIT RG2 .... **117** H3
Leisure Centre
  WDSR SL4 .... **6** F5
Lent Rise County
  Combined School
  SL SL1 .... **43** L6
The Licensed Victuallers School
  ASC SL5 .... **122** F7
Lightwater First School
  LTWR GU18 .... **175** K5
The Lilley Clinic
  HUNG RG17 .... **131** L8
Linden Medical Centre
  MDIID SL6 .... **2** C1
Littledown School
  SL SL1 .... **5** G6
Little Marlow C of E School
  MLW SL7 .... **20** A1
Littleton C of E Infant School
  SHPTN TW17 .... **128** D8
Littlewick Green
  Montessori School
  MDHD SL6 .... **66** F6
Loddon County Infants School
  EARL RG6 .... **118** A3
Loddon County Junior School
  EARL RG6 .... **118** A3
The Loddon Vale Practice
  WODY RG5 .... **90** D7
Loddon Valley Leisure Centre
  EARL RG6 .... **117** K5
London Irish Rugby
  Football Club
  SUN TW16 .... **129** K6
Long Barn Lane Surgery
  WHIT RG2 .... **116** E3
Long Close School
  DTCH/LGLY SL3 .... **71** K4
Longford School
  EBED/NFELT TW14 .... **101** J6
Long Lane Primary School
  GOR/PANG RG8 .... **86** E2
Longshot Industrial Estate
  BRAK RG12 .... **12** A5
Lorraine County First School
  CBLY GU15 .... **174** D6
Luckley Oakfield School
  WWKG RG41 .... **147** L3
Ludgrove Preparatory School
  EWKG RG40 .... **148** A3
Lynch Hill Combined School
  SLN SL2 .... **22** C4
Lyndhurst School
  CBLY GU15 .... **181** L1
Lyne & Longcross C of E School
  CHERT KT16 .... **154** E6
Lyons Industrial Estate
  WDR/YW UB7 .... **47** M7
Magna Carta Secondary School
  EGH TW20 .... **127** G4
The Magnet Leisure Centre
  MDHD SL6 .... **3** H8
Magnolia House Surgery
  ASC SL5 .... **152** C2
Maiden Erlegh School
  EARL RG6 .... **117** L2
Maidenhead Clinic
  MDHD SL6 .... **3** H5
Maidenhead College for Girls
  MDHD SL6 .... **2** E4
Maidenhead Golf Club
  MDHD SL6 .... **3** G7
Maidenhead Rowing Club
  MDHD SL6 .... **42** F7
Maidenhead Rugby Club
  MDHD SL6 .... **3** J9
Maidenhead Sailing Club
  MDHD SL6 .... **42** D4
Maidenhead Superbowl
  MDHD SL6 .... **3** H3
Maidenhead Synagogue
  MDHD SL6 .... **2** E6
Maidenhead United
  Football Club
  MDHD SL6 .... **3** J6
Manor County School
  TLHT RG30 .... **115** K2
Manorcroft School
  EGH TW20 .... **126** D4
Manor Park Medical Centre
  SLN SL2 .... **4** E1
Mansbridge House School
  EARL RG6 .... **89** J8
Mapledurhamhouse
  CAV/SC RG4 .... **61** H8
Maple Grove Business Centre
  HSLWW TW4 .... **101** M3
Maple Industrial Estate
  FELT TW13 .... **101** K8
Marish County Middle School
  DTCH/LGLY SL3 .... **72** C3
Marist Senior School
  ASC SL5 .... **152** A1
The Marjory Kinnon School
  EBED/NFELT TW14 .... **101** H4
Marlow Community Hospital
  MLW SL7 .... **19** H4

Marlow Football Club
MLW SL7 .... **19** H3
Marlow Rowing Club
MLW SL7 .... **19** H6
Marlow Rugby Club
MLW SL7 .... **19** K5
Marlow Sports Club
Pavilion Ground
MLW SL7 .... **19** G5
Mary Hare Grammar School
NWBY RG14 .... **108** C3
Matthew Arnold County
Secondary School
STA TW18 .... **127** M4
Mayfield County Junior
& Infant School
FARN GU14 .... **181** K8
Mckay Trading Estate
DTCH/LGLY SL3 .... **99** H1
Meadowcroft County
First School
CHERT KT16 .... **155** T3
Meadow Vale CP School
BNFD RG42 .... **12** D2
Meadowview Squash Club
HUNG RG17 .... **104** B7
Meadway Comprehensive
School
TLHT RG30 .... **87** J7
Meadway Sports Centre
TLHT RG30 .... **87** J8
Medical Health Centre
MDHD SL6 .... **20** B7
Melrose Surgery
READ RG1 .... **9** K7
Membury Airfield
Industrial Estate
HUNG RG17 .... **75** G2
Membury Business Park
HUNG RG17 .... **75** H2
Micklands CP School
CAV/SC RG4 .... **89** G2
The Micro Centre
WHIT RG2 .... **116** D3
Midas Industrial Estate
UX/CGN UB8 .... **47** L3
Middlegreen Trading Estate
DTCH/LGLY SL3 .... **72** B2
The Mill at Sonning
CAV/SC RG4 .... **89** M2
Mill Ride Golf Club
ASC SL5 .... **123** G6
Milman Road Health Centre
WHIT RG2 .... **116** E1
Montem County
Middle School
SL SL1 .... **70** E2
Montem Sports Centre
SL SL1 .... **4** C8
Montessori School
MDHD SL6 .... **20** C7
Moorlands Primary School
TLHT RG30 .... **87** H7
Morland Surgery
TADY RG26 .... **164** C7
Mortimer Surgery
THLE RG7 .... **142** C8
Mosque
MDHD SL6 .... **3** J3
Mulberry Business Park
WWKG RG41 .... **147** K2
Museum
EWKG RG40 .... **146** D6
The Museum
of Berkshire Aviation
WODY RG5 .... **90** E8
The Natural Health Centre
NWBY RG14 .... **136** A8
Newbold College
BNFD RG42 .... **121** G5
Newbold School
BNFD RG42 .... **121** G5
Newbury Business Park
NWBY RG14 .... **15** J2
Newbury College of Further
Education
NWBY RG14 .... **14** C1
Newbury District Council
NWBY RG14 .... **15** G6
Newbury District Hospital
NWBY RG14 .... **14** D7
Newbury District Museum
& Tourist Information Centre
NWBY RG14 .... **14** C7
Newbury Retail Park
NWBY RG14 .... **136** A6
Newbury Rugby Football Club
NWBY RG14 .... **136** C4
Newbury Town Council
NWBY RG14 .... **14** C4
The New College
WDSR SL4 .... **7** J4
New Greenham Park
Leisure Centre
STHA RG19 .... **161** K2
Newlands School
MDHD SL6 .... **41** K7
New Scotland Hill CP School
SHST GU47 .... **172** D4
Newtown Junior
& Infant School
READ RG1 .... **9** M5
Nimrod Industrial Estate
WHIT RG2 .... **116** D1
Northcroft Surgery
NWBY RG14 .... **14** D4
Northfield Farm
Industrial Estate
HUNG RG17 .... **51** L8
North Maidenhead Cricket Club
MDHD SL6 .... **42** D4
The Norton Practice
READ RG1 .... **9** J7
Novello Theatre
ASC SL5 .... **152** A2
Oak Farm Community School
FARN GU14 .... **181** K8

Oakfield First School
WDSR SL4 .... **6** E9
Oaklands Business Centre
WWKG RG41 .... **147** K3
Oaklands County Junior
& Infant School
CWTH RG45 .... **148** D8
Odeon Cinema
UX/CGN UB8 .... **47** M1
Old Art Gallery
EWKG RG40 .... **148** C4
Old Bank Gallery
DTCH/LGLY SL3 .... **71** L7
Oldfield County Primary School
MDHD SL6 .... **3** M7
Old Kiln Industrial Estate
MDHD SL6 .... **41** K3
Oracle Shopping Centre
READ RG1 .... **9** G6
The Oratory Preparatory School
GOR/PANG RG8 .... **60** A2
The Oratory School
GOR/PANG RG8 .... **34** D6
The Orchard Surgery
BNEND SL8 .... **20** E3
Oriental Rug Gallery
WDSR SL4 .... **7** J3
Our Lady of Peace R C
Middle School
SL SL1 .... **43** M6
Our Lady of the Rosary School
STA TW18 .... **127** K4
Our Ladys Preparatory School
CWTH RG45 .... **172** D1
Owlsmoor Primary School
SHST GU47 .... **173** H5
Oxford Rd Surgery
READ RG1 .... **8** E6
Oxford Road Primary School
READ RG1 .... **8** B6
Paddock Road Industrial Estate
CAV/SC RG4 .... **9** L2
Paddock Road Industrial Estate
CAV/SC RG4 .... **9** L1
Padworth College
THLE RG7 .... **141** H5
Palmer C of E Junior School
EWKG RG40 .... **11** J3
Pangbourne College
GOR/PANG RG8 .... **85** J3
Pangbourne Infants School
GOR/PANG RG8 .... **86** B1
Pangbourne Medical Centre
GOR/PANG RG8 .... **59** M8
Papplewick School
ASC SL5 .... **123** J6
Park House School
NWBY RG14 .... **136** B8
Park Lane Primary School
CALC RG31 .... **86** F6
Parks Golf Courses
& Sports Grounds
STA TW18 .... **127** L1
Parkside Business Park
WODY RG5 .... **90** B6
Parlaunt Park County
Combined School
DTCH/LGLY SL3 .... **72** E3
Parsons Down Infant School
STHA RG19 .... **137** L3
Parsons Down Junior School
STHA RG19 .... **137** K3
Pearl Galleries of Windsor
WDSR SL4 .... **7** K6
Pearl Galleries of Windsor
WDSR SL4 .... **7** H7
Peppard C of E School
HEN RG9 .... **36** D6
Perborough Castle
KSCL RG20 .... **56** B6
Perth Trading Estate
SL SL1 .... **44** E6
Phoenix Business Park
BRAK RG12 .... **120** F7
Phoenix Plaza Bowling Alley
EWKG RG40 .... **10** F7
Physiotherapy Surgery
GOR/PANG RG8 .... **60** A8
The Piggott C of E School
WAR/TWY RG10 .... **64** F6
Pineridge County First School
CBLY GU15 .... **174** D5
The Pines Junior
& Infant School
BRAK RG12 .... **149** K4
Pinewood Infants School
FARN GU14 .... **181** G7
Pinewood Leisure Centre
EWKG RG40 .... **148** E6
Pipers Industrial Estate
STHA RG19 .... **138** C5
Pippins School
DTCH/LGLY SL3 .... **73** H8
Pirbright Camp
CHOB/PIR GU24 .... **183** L7
P M S Health Centre
READ RG1 .... **9** J9
Polehampton County
Infant School
WAR/TWY RG10 .... **91** G1
Polehampton Junior School
WAR/TWY RG10 .... **65** G8
Polygon Business Centre
DTCH/LGLY SL3 .... **99** J1
Portesbery School
CBLY GU15 .... **174** A8
Portland Business Centre
DTCH/LGLY SL3 .... **71** L8
Portland Business Centre
DTCH/LGLY SL3 .... **71** L7
Potley Hill County
Primary School
BLKW GU17 .... **180** D1
Presentation College
READ RG1 .... **8** A1
Princess Margaret Hospital
WDSR SL4 .... **7** J9

Princess Margaret Royal
Free C of E School
WDSR SL4 .... **96** F3
Princess Marina College
EWKG RG40 .... **146** C6
Prior Heath School
CBLY GU15 .... **182** D1
Priors Court School
NTHA RG18 .... **81** G6
Priory School
SL SL1 .... **44** A6
Progress Business Centre
SL SL1 .... **44** A7
Progress Theatre
WHIT RG2 .... **116** F1
Prospect Foot Clinic
CAV/SC RG4 .... **88** D3
Prospect School
TLHT RG30 .... **115** K1
Purley C of E School
GOR/PANG RG8 .... **86** F1
Pyrcroft Grange
Primary School
CHERT KT16 .... **155** H4
Queen Anne First School
WDSR SL4 .... **97** G2
Queen Annes School
CAV/SC RG4 .... **88** E3
Queens Schools
WDSR SL4 .... **7** J2
Raceview Business Centre
NWBY RG14 .... **15** H5
Rachor House Surgery
ASC SL5 .... **123** L8
Radstock CP School
EARL RG6 .... **117** L4
Randolph Medical Centre
DTCH/LGLY SL3 .... **71** L7
Ranelagh School
BRAK RG12 .... **13** J6
Ranikhet Primary School
TLHT RG30 .... **87** K6
Reading Adult College
TLHT RG30 .... **87** M6
Reading Adult
& Community College
READ RG1 .... **8** F1
Reading Blue Coat School
CAV/SC RG4 .... **89** M3
Reading Borough Council
READ RG1 .... **8** E7
Reading Business Centre
READ RG1 .... **9** H7
Reading Clinic
READ RG1 .... **9** K7
Reading College
READ RG1 .... **9** M6
Reading College of Technology
READ RG1 .... **89** J8
Reading County Court
READ RG1 .... **9** H5
Reading Girls School
WHIT RG2 .... **116** F3
Reading Leisure Centre
WHIT RG2 .... **116** F5
Reading Retail Park
TLHT RG30 .... **87** L5
Reading School
READ RG1 .... **9** L8
Reading Superbowl
CALC RG31 .... **114** D2
Reading University
READ RG1 .... **117** G1
Redlands Primary School
READ RG1 .... **117** H1
Redroofs Theatre School
MDHD SL6 .... **2** C5
Red Shute Hill Industrial Estate
NTHA RG18 .... **109** K1
Regal Gallery
EGH TW20 .... **126** C3
Register Office
READ RG1 .... **8** D8
Retail Park
NWBY RG14 .... **15** K3
Retail Park
READ RG1 .... **9** K5
R H M Medical Centre
WDSR SL4 .... **7** A4
Richings Park Sports Club
IVER SL0 .... **73** J3
Ridge House School
NTHA RG18 .... **110** A6
Ridgeway School
NTHA RG18 .... **67** H1
River Gardens Business Centre
EBED/NFELT TW14 .... **101** L3
Rivermead CP School
WODY RG5 .... **90** C8
Rivermead Leisure Centre
READ RG1 .... **8** C1
Riverpark Industrial Estate
NWBY RG14 .... **15** J3
The River & Rowing Museum at
Henley
HEN RG9 .... **38** C5
Robert Cort Industrial Estate
WHIT RG2 .... **116** E1
Robert Piggott
C of E Infant School
WAR/TWY RG10 .... **65** H5
Robert Piggott
C of E Junior School
WAR/TWY RG10 .... **65** G5
Rosedale Clinic
READ RG1 .... **117** G1
Rose Industrial Estate
MLW SL7 .... **19** G1
Rosemead Surgery
MDHD SL6 .... **3** M4
Ross Road Medical Centre
MDHD SL6 .... **68** B2
The Rowing Club
MDHD SL6 .... **42** F7
Royal Ascot Golf Club
ASC SL5 .... **123** L7

Royal Berkshire
& Battle Hospital
TLHT RG30 .... **88** A6
Royal Berkshire Hospital
READ RG1 .... **9** L9
Royal Berkshire Hospital
READ RG1 .... **9** K8
Royal Borough of Windsor &
Maidenhead District Council
WDSR SL4 .... **7** K8
Royal Holloway College
EGH TW20 .... **126** A6
Royal Holloway College
EGH TW20 .... **126** A2
Royal Holloway University
of London
EGH TW20 .... **126** A4
Royal Holloway University
of London
EGH TW20 .... **126** B5
Royal Logistocs
Corps Museum
FRIM GU16 .... **183** G6
The Rugby Club
CHOB/PIR GU24 .... **177** H5
Runnymede Borough Council
CHERT KT16 .... **155** L5
Runnymede Borough Council
CHERT KT16 .... **155** K4
Runnymede Hospital
CHERT KT16 .... **155** J5
Runnymede Medical Practice
WDSR SL4 .... **97** K6
Rupert House School
HEN RG9 .... **38** B3
Russell Street Surgery
READ RG1 .... **8** D7
Ryeish Green
Comprehensive School
THLE RG7 .... **144** B7
Ryvers County First
& Middle School
DTCH/LGLY SL3 .... **72** A3
Sacred Heart RC School
HEN RG9 .... **38** A5
St Andrews C of E
Primary School
KSCL RG20 .... **52** E7
St Andrews School
GOR/PANG RG8 .... **84** F5
St Annes House Surgery
MDHD SL6 .... **20** C7
St Annes Primary School
CHERT KT16 .... **155** K5
St Annes Primary School
STWL/WRAY TW19 .... **100** B6
St Annes RC Primary School
CAV/SC RG4 .... **88** E4
St Anns Heath County
Junior School
VW GU25 .... **154** C2
St Anthonys RC
Combined School
SLN SL2 .... **44** F5
St Anthonys RC First School
SLN SL2 .... **44** F4
St Bartholomews
NWBY RG14 .... **14** B7
St Bartholomews School
NWBY RG14 .... **14** B8
St Cassian's College
HUNG RG17 .... **133** G6
St Catherines School
CBLY GU15 .... **181** M2
St Crispins Secondary School
EWKG RG40 .... **11** K6
St Crispins Sports Centre
EWKG RG40 .... **11** L6
St Cuthberts RC
Primary School
EGH TW20 .... **125** M5
St Davids Group Practise
FELT TW13 .... **101** K3
St Davids Health Centre
STWL/WRAY TW19 .... **100** A6
St Davids School
ASHF TW15 .... **128** C1
St Dominic Savio RC
Primary School
WODY RG5 .... **90** A4
St Edmund Campion
RC Primary School
MDHD SL6 .... **41** J8
St Edwards RC First School
WDSR SL4 .... **6** D6
St Edwards Royal Free
Ecumenical Middle School
WDSR SL4 .... **6** C6
St Edwards School
TLHT RG30 .... **8** A7
St Edwards School
TLHT RG30 .... **88** A7
St Ethelberts RC First
& Middle School
SLN SL2 .... **5** K3
St Finians School
NTHA RG18 .... **110** A6
St Francis RC School
ASC SL5 .... **151** K3
St Gabriels School
KSCL RG20 .... **136** E8
St Georges Industrial Estate
CBLY GU15 .... **181** L3
St Georges School
ASC SL5 .... **151** L1
St Georges School
WDSR SL4 .... **7** K5
St Ignatius RC Primary School
SUN TW16 .... **129** K6
St Johns C of E School
READ RG1 .... **9** K7
St Johns School
NWBY RG14 .... **14** D9
St Johns School
THLE RG7 .... **166** D1
St Josephs Convent School
READ RG1 .... **117** H1

St Josephs RC Primary School
BRAK RG12 .... **13** L5
St Josephs RC Primary School
NWBY RG14 .... **15** H1
St Josephs RC Secondary School
SLN SL2 .... **5** J3
St Judes C of E School
EGH TW20 .... **125** M4
St Lawrence Business Centre
FELT TW13 .... **101** L8
St Lawrence Catholic School
FELT TW13 .... **101** L7
St Lawrence C of E
Junior School
UX/CGN UB8 .... **47** M6
St Lukes Primary School
MDHD SL6 .... **3** H2
St Margaret Clitherow
Primary School
BRAK RG12 .... **149** J4
St Marks C of E School
NTHA RG18 .... **109** M5
St Marks Hospital
MDHD SL6 .... **2** A4
St Martins East Woodhay C of E
Primary School
KSCL RG20 .... **158** D7
St Martins RC Primary School
CAV/SC RG4 .... **63** H8
St Marys All Saints
C of E Primary School
READ RG1 .... **116** B1
St Marys C of E Junior School
NTHA RG18 .... **138** A2
St Marys C of E Primary School
BNFD RG42 .... **122** E3
St Marys Preparatory School
HEN RG9 .... **38** B6
St Marys Primary School
TLHT RG30 .... **114** F8
St Marys RC Primary School
MDHD SL6 .... **42** B4
St Marys School
ASC SL5 .... **151** L4
St Marys School
THLE RG7 .... **167** G1
St Marys School
UX/CGN UB8 .... **47** M2
St Michaels C of E
Primary School
SHST GU47 .... **172** B6
St Michaels C of E School
BRAK RG12 .... **149** K2
St Michaels Primary School
TLHT RG30 .... **87** K8
St Michaels RC School
ASHF TW15 .... **128** D3
St Michaels School
KSCL RG20 .... **160** C8
St Neots Preparatory School
HTWY RG27 .... **170** B6
St Nicholas C of E
Combined School
MDHD SL6 .... **43** G5
St Nicholas C of E
Primary School
MARL SN8 .... **48** B5
St Nicholas C of E
Primary School
WAR/TWY RG10 .... **91** J6
St Nicholas C of E School
NWBY RG14 .... **14** D6
St Pauls Catholic School
SUN TW16 .... **129** K6
St Pauls C of E
Combined School
FLKWH HP10 .... **21** G2
St Pauls C of E Junior School
WWKG RG41 .... **10** C5
St Pauls Middle School
ADL/WDHM KT15 .... **155** K8
St Pauls RC Primary School
CALC RG31 .... **86** F7
St Peter C of E School
EARL RG6 .... **117** L1
St Peters C of E
Combined School
SL SL1 .... **43** L4
St Peters C of E School
WDSR SL4 .... **97** J5
St Peters GM C of E School
YTLY GU46 .... **172** A8
St Peters RC Combined School
MLW SL7 .... **18** F3
St Sebastians Primary School
EWKG RG40 .... **148** B6
St Teresa RC Primary School
EWKG RG40 .... **11** J7
St Thomas Infant School
KSCL RG20 .... **159** H6
Salesian College
CHERT KT16 .... **155** K5
Salesian School
CHERT KT16 .... **155** H6
Sampson Business Park
CBLY GU15 .... **181** L3
Sandhurst College
Town County Junior School
SHST GU47 .... **173** H6
Sandhurst School
SHST GU47 .... **173** G6
Sandhurst Sports Club
SHST GU47 .... **172** F7
Sandhurst Surgery
SHST GU47 .... **172** E7
Sandleford Hospital
NWBY RG14 .... **136** D6
Sandmartins Golf Club
EWKG RG40 .... **147** L5
Sandygate C of E First School
MLW SL7 .... **19** G3
Sandy Lane County
Infant School
BNFD RG42 .... **13** J1
Sandy Lane Junior School
BNFD RG42 .... **13** J1
Shaw-cum-donnington School
NWBY RG14 .... **108** D8

Sheeji Medical Centre
  SL SL1 .... 4 D4
Shefford C of E Primary School
  HUNG RG17 .... 77 L2
Shinfield C of E Junior School
  WHIT RG2 .... 145 J2
Shinfield Infant School
  WHIT RG2 .... 145 H2
Shiplake C of E Primary School
  HEN RG9 .... 64 B4
Shiplake College
  HEN RG9 .... 64 C5
Shopping Centre
  WDSR SL4 .... 7 H6
Shortwood County
  Infant School
  STA TW18 .... 127 L1
Showcase Cinemas Reading
  WODY RG5 .... 118 C2
Shute End Medical Practice
  WWKG RG41 .... 10 E5
Sikh Temple
  SL SL1 .... 4 D5
Silchester House School
  MDHD SL6 .... 43 D1
Silchester Primary School
  THLE RG7 .... 165 L1
Sindlesham School
  WWKG RG41 .... 118 C7
Sir William Borlase's
  Grammar School
  MLW SL7 .... 18 F4
Sir William Perkins School
  CHERT KT16 .... 155 J5
The Sixth Form College
  FARN GU14 .... 181 L7
Skimped Hill Health Centre
  BRAK RG12 .... 13 H4
Sky Business Park
  EGH TW20 .... 126 F7
Slough Borough Council
  SL SL1 .... 4 C6
Slough Borough Council
  SL SL1 .... 5 J9
Slough Borough Council
  SLN SL2 .... 5 L4
Slough Community
  Mental Health Centre
  DTCH/LGLY SL3 .... 72 D4
Slough & Eton C of E School
  SL SL1 .... 71 G3
Slough Grammar School
  DTCH/LGLY SL3 .... 71 L3
Slough Museum
  SL SL1 .... 5 J9
Slough Rugby Club
  DTCH/LGLY SL3 .... 71 L5
Slough Sports Club
  SL SL1 .... 71 H3
Slough Town Football Club
  SLN SL2 .... 5 K1
Slough Trading Estate
  SL SL1 .... 44 D6
Sonning Church
  of England Primary School
  CAV/SC RG4 .... 90 A3
Sonning Common CP School
  CAV/SC RG4 .... 62 C1
Sonning Common Health Centre
  CAV/SC RG4 .... 62 C1
South Bucks District Council
  SL SL1 .... 4 E9
Southcote Clinic
  TLHT RG30 .... 115 L2
Southcote CP School
  TLHT RG30 .... 115 M2
Southfields Special School
  EWKG RG40 .... 11 J8
Southlake County Junior School
  WODY RG5 .... 118 A1
Southlake Primary School
  WODY RG5 .... 118 B1
South Meadow Surgery
  WDSR SL4 .... 7 J3
South Stoke Primary School
  GOR/PANG RG8 .... 32 C4
21 South Street Arts Centrel
  READ RG1 .... 9 H7
Southville Junior School
  EBED/NFELT TW14 .... 101 J7
Sparrow Farm Infant School
  EBED/NFELT TW14 .... 101 M6
Sparrow Farm Junior School
  EBED/NFELT TW14 .... 101 M6
Speenhamland CP School
  NWBY RG14 .... 14 D1
Spelthorne Borough Council
  STA TW18 .... 127 K3
Spelthorne Borough Council
  STA TW18 .... 127 K1
Spelthorne Clinic
  ASHF TW15 .... 129 H4
Spelthorne College
  ASHF TW15 .... 128 C2
Spelthorne Council for Voluntary
  Services
  STA TW18 .... 127 K2
Spelthorne County School
  ASHF TW15 .... 129 G4
Spelthorne Leisure Centre
  STA TW18 .... 127 K3
Spelthorne Museum
  STA TW18 .... 127 H3
Spelthorne Sports Club
  ASHF TW15 .... 129 G5

Spinfield County
  Combined School
  MLW SL7 .... 18 E4
Sports Ground
  WDSR SL4 .... 6 F8
Springfield Primary School
  CALC RG31 .... 86 E7
Springfield Primary School
  SUN TW16 .... 129 J6
Spurcroft Primary School
  STHA RG19 .... 138 A4
Stadium Industrial Estate
  TLHT RG30 .... 87 L5
Staff College
  CBLY GU15 .... 173 M7
Staines County Court
  STA TW18 .... 127 K3
Staines & District Synagogue
  STA TW18 .... 127 J3
Staines Preparatory School
  STA TW18 .... 127 K3
Staines Rugby Football Club
  FELT TW13 .... 129 K2
Staines Town Football Club
  STA TW18 .... 127 K5
Staines Youth Sports Centre
  STA TW18 .... 127 K2
Stanley Spencer Gallery
  MDHD SL6 .... 20 E7
Station Industrial Estate
  WWKG RG41 .... 10 E5
Station Road Surgery
  FRIM GU16 .... 182 A6
Stepgates Primary School
  CHERT KT16 .... 155 L4
Sterling Industrial Estate
  NWBY RG14 .... 15 G5
Stockcross School
  KSCL RG20 .... 107 H8
Stoke Poges City First School
  SLN SL2 .... 45 L2
Stoke Poges County
  Middle School
  SLN SL2 .... 45 J1
Stratfield Saye
  THLE RG7 .... 168 A7
Streatley School
  GOR/PANG RG8 .... 32 C8
Strodes College
  EGH TW20 .... 126 C3
Studholme Medical Centre
  ASHF TW15 .... 128 C2
Summit Business Park
  SUN TW16 .... 129 K5
Sunbury Business Centre
  SUN TW16 .... 129 H6
Sunbury Health Centre
  SUN TW16 .... 129 K7
Sunbury Leisure Centre
  SUN TW16 .... 129 J6
Sunbury Manor School
  SUN TW16 .... 129 J6
Sunningdale Golf Coursel
  ASC SL5 .... 152 D6
Sunningdale School
  ASC SL5 .... 152 B3
Surrey County Council
  ADL/WDHM KT15 .... 155 M6
The Sussex Place Surgery
  SL SL1 .... 5 K9
Suttons Business Park
  EARL RG6 .... 89 J6
Suttons Business Park
  READ RG1 .... 89 H6
Swallowfield
  Medical Practice
  THLE RG7 .... 144 F7
Swallowfield Park
  THLE RG7 .... 145 H6
Swan Wharf Business Centre
  UX/CGN UB8 .... 47 L3
Swinley CP School
  ASC SL5 .... 151 K2
Swinley Forest Golf Club
  ASC SL5 .... 151 J4
The Symonds Medical Centre
  MDHD SL6 .... 2 C5
Tadley CP School
  TADY RG26 .... 164 F8
Tadley Police Station
  TADY RG26 .... 164 E5
Taplow Health Centre
  MDHD SL6 .... 43 L7
Tavistock Industrial Estate
  WAR/TWY RG10 .... 91 J1
Teikyo School
  DTCH/LGLY SL3 .... 46 A1
Temple
  READ RG1 .... 8 F7
Temple Golf Club
  MDHD SL6 .... 40 E4
The Temple
  GOR/PANG RG8 .... 32 F6
Templewood Surgery
  IVER SL0 .... 46 F3
Tennis Lawn Club
  WDSR SL4 .... 95 L2
Thames Gallery
  HEN RG9 .... 38 B4
Thameside School
  READ RG1 .... 9 G1
Thames Industrial Estate
  MLW SL7 .... 19 J4
Thames Valley Business Park
  EARL RG6 .... 89 L5

The Thames Valley
  Nuffield Hospital
  DTCH/LGLY SL3 .... 45 M2
Thames Valley University
  SL SL1 .... 5 G7
Thatcham Bowling Club
  NTHA RG18 .... 138 A2
Thatcham Health Centre
  NTHA RG18 .... 137 M2
Thatcham Town Council
  NTHA RG18 .... 137 M2
Thatcham Town Football Club
  STHA RG19 .... 138 C6
Theale C of E Primary School
  THLE RG7 .... 114 A3
Theale Green School
  THLE RG7 .... 114 A3
Theale Medical Centre
  THLE RG7 .... 114 A3
Theatre & Arts Centre
  WHIT RG2 .... 117 G7
Theatre Royal
  WDSR SL4 .... 7 K5
Thorngrove School
  KSCL RG20 .... 159 H7
Thorpe C of E Infant School
  EGH TW20 .... 126 F8
Thorpe Cricket Club
  EGH TW20 .... 154 C1
Thorpe Lea Primary School
  EGH TW20 .... 127 G4
Three Way Surgery
  SLN SL2 .... 45 J2
Tilehurst Medical Centre
  TLHT RG30 .... 87 H6
Tilehurst Parish Council
  CALC RG31 .... 114 E1
Tilehurst Village Surgery
  CALC RG31 .... 87 G6
Tomlinscote School
  FRIM GU16 .... 182 C4
Tomo Industrial Estate
  UX/CGN UB8 .... 47 M7
Toutley Industrial Estate
  EWKG RG40 .... 119 K4
Toutley Industrial Estate
  EWKG RG40 .... 119 J4
Town Farm County
  Primary School
  STWL/WRAY TW19 .... 100 A6
Townlands Hospital
  HEN RG9 .... 37 M4
Trevelyan Middle School
  WDSR SL4 .... 6 D8
Trident Industrial Estate
  DTCH/LGLY SL3 .... 99 H2
Trinity Primary School
  HEN RG9 .... 38 B5
Trinity St Stephen First School
  WDSR SL4 .... 6 F6
Trinity School
  NWBY RG14 .... 136 E1
Trumps Green County
  First School
  VW GU25 .... 154 A3
Two Rivers Retail Park
  STA TW18 .... 127 H2
Twyford Business Park
  WAR/TWY RG10 .... 91 G2
Twyford Health Centre
  WAR/TWY RG10 .... 91 H1
U C I Cinema
  BRAK RG12 .... 13 G4
Ufton Nervet Parochial
  Primary School
  THLE RG7 .... 141 M2
University Health Centre
  WHIT RG2 .... 117 G2
University of Reading
  EARL RG6 .... 89 L8
University of Reading
  EARL RG6 .... 117 J1
University of Reading
  EARL RG6 .... 117 J2
University of Reading
  READ RG1 .... 9 J8
University of Reading
  READ RG1 .... 117 G1
University of Reading
  READ RG1 .... 117 H1
University of Reading
  READ RG1 .... 117 G2
Upcroft Primary School
  TLHT RG30 .... 87 J6
Uplands CP School
  SHST GU47 .... 172 E6
Upton House School
  WDSR SL4 .... 7 H9
Uxbridge County Court
  UX/CGN UB8 .... 47 M1
Valley End C of E Infant School
  CHOB/PIR GU24 .... 176 D2
Valley End Cricket Club
  CHOB/PIR GU24 .... 176 D3
Valley Road Primary School
  HEN RG9 .... 37 M6
Van Alloys Industrial Estate
  HEN RG9 .... 35 J2
Victoria Barracks
  WDSR SL4 .... 7 J7
Victoria Junior School
  FELT TW13 .... 101 L7
The Village Medical Centre
  SL SL1 .... 70 A1

Village Shopping Centre
  SL SL1 .... 5 C8
Virgin Cinemas
  SL SL1 .... 5 H8
Viscount Industrial Estate
  DTCH/LGLY SL3 .... 99 H2
Waingels Copse School
  WODY RG5 .... 90 D4
Wallbrook Business Centre
  HSLWW TW4 .... 101 L2
Walter County Infant School
  WWKG RG41 .... 10 D5
Waltham St Lawrence School
  WAR/TWY RG10 .... 92 C3
Warfield C of E Controlled
  Primary School
  BNFD RG42 .... 122 B5
Watchetts County
  Middle School
  CBLY GU15 .... 181 M4
Watermans Business Park
  STA TW18 .... 127 J2
Watermill Theatre
  STHA RG19 .... 161 J1
Watermill Theatre
  & Restaurant
  KSCL RG20 .... 107 L7
Waverley School
  EWKG RG40 .... 147 J5
Welfare Clinic
  TLHT RG30 .... 87 G6
Welford & Wickham C of E
  Primary School
  KSCL RG20 .... 106 A2
Wellington Business Park
  CWTH RG45 .... 172 B2
Wellington College
  CWTH RG45 .... 172 D3
Wellington Industrial Estate
  THLE RG7 .... 144 D5
Wellington Sports Centre
  CWTH RG45 .... 172 C2
Wescott County Infants School
  EWKG RG40 .... 11 H6
Wessex County Junior School
  MDHD SL6 .... 67 L3
Wessex Downs Golf Club
  THLE RG7 .... 140 B2
Westacott Business Centre
  MDHD SL6 .... 67 H3
West Berks Golf Club
  KSCL RG20 .... 78 C1
West Berkshire Council
  NWBY RG14 .... 14 D5
West Berkshire District Council
  NWBY RG14 .... 14 D3
West Berkshire District Council
  NWBY RG14 .... 14 E5
West Berkshire District Council
  NWBY RG14 .... 14 E4
West Berkshire District Council
  NWBY RG14 .... 15 G2
West Berkshire District Council
  THLE RG7 .... 114 B3
West Drayton Cricket Club
  WDR/YW UB7 .... 73 M4
Westende County Junior School
  EWKG RG40 .... 11 K6
Western Elms Surgery
  TLHT RG30 .... 8 A4
Western House City First School
  SL SL1 .... 44 C7
Westgate Retail Park
  SL SL1 .... 44 D8
Westgate School
  SL SL1 .... 70 D1
The West Street Practice
  HEN RG9 .... 38 A4
West Suuex County Council
  CBLY GU15 .... 181 L1
Westwood Farm County Junior
  School
  CALC RG31 .... 86 F3
Westwood Road Health Centre
  CALC RG31 .... 87 G5
Wexham Court County
  First School
  SLN SL2 .... 45 M4
Wexham School
  SLN SL2 .... 45 L6
Wharf Business Centre
  BNEND SL8 .... 20 D3
Whitchurch Primary School
  GOR/PANG RG8 .... 60 B7
White County Infants School
  EWKG RG40 .... 11 K4
White Hall Primary School
  UX/CGN UB8 .... 47 M2
White Hart Industrial Estate
  BLKW GU17 .... 181 H1
White House School
  WWKG RG41 .... 147 K3
Whiteknights CP School
  EARL RG6 .... 117 J5
Whitelands Park CP School
  NTHA RG18 .... 137 M1
White Waltham C of E School
  MDHD SL6 .... 67 G6
White Waltham Cricket Club
  MDHD SL6 .... 67 G7
Whitley Park School
  WHIT RG2 .... 116 E4
Whitley Villa Surgery
  READ RG1 .... 116 F1

Whitley Wood Surgery
  WHIT RG2 .... 116 E7
Whittle Business Centre
  SL SL1 .... 44 A7
Wilderness Medical Centre
  MDHD SL6 .... 3 H4
Wildridings CP School
  BRAK RG12 .... 12 G9
William Penn County
  Middle School
  SLN SL2 .... 45 G5
Willink Leisure Centre
  THLE RG7 .... 142 C4
Willink School
  THLE RG7 .... 142 C4
Wilson Junior & Infant School
  TLHT RG30 .... 87 M7
Winchcombe CP Infant School
  NWBY RG14 .... 136 D1
Winchcombe Junior School
  NWBY RG14 .... 14 E1
Windlesham Golf Club
  BAGS GU19 .... 175 J2
Windsor Boys School
  WDSR SL4 .... 6 F6
Windsor Business Centre
  WDSR SL4 .... 7 G5
Windsor Castle
  WDSR SL4 .... 7 L5
Windsor & Eton Cricket Club
  WDSR SL4 .... 7 L3
Windsor & Eton Football Club
  WDSR SL4 .... 96 E3
Windsor Girls School
  WDSR SL4 .... 96 D2
Windsor Rugby Football Club
  WDSR SL4 .... 7 L3
Windsor Victoria Cricket Club
  WDSR SL4 .... 7 L2
Winnersh CP School
  WWKG RG41 .... 119 G3
Winsbury School
  MDHD SL6 .... 68 D2
Winterbourne House Clinic
  READ RG1 .... 8 A6
Wishmore Cross School
  CHOB/PIR GU24 .... 177 H5
Wokingham Child
  Guidance Clinic
  EWKG RG40 .... 10 E6
Wokingham Cricket Club
  EWKG RG40 .... 10 E7
Wokingham District Council
  EWKG RG40 .... 10 F7
Wokingham District Council
  EWKG RG40 .... 10 F6
Wokingham Hospital
  WWKG RG41 .... 10 D6
Wokingham Theatre
  EWKG RG40 .... 10 E2
Wokingham Town Council
  EWKG RG40 .... 11 G6
Woodcote CP School
  GOR/PANG RG8 .... 34 B5
Woodcote House School
  BFOR GU20 .... 175 L1
Woodlands Business Park
  MDHD SL6 .... 67 K4
Woodlands Park CP School
  MDHD SL6 .... 67 K5
Woodley Centre Surgery
  WODY RG5 .... 90 B7
Woodley C of E Primary School
  WODY RG5 .... 90 E6
Woodley Park Estate 59-69
  WODY RG5 .... 90 A6
Woodley Town Council
  WODY RG5 .... 90 B6
Woodside Business Park
  WHIT RG2 .... 116 E7
Woolton Hill County
  Junior School
  KSCL RG20 .... 159 H7
Woosehill Surgery
  WWKG RG41 .... 10 A4
Wraysbury Combined School
  STWL/WRAY TW19 .... 98 B5
Wraysbury Medical Centre
  STWL/WRAY TW19 .... 98 C5
Wrexham Park Hospital
  SLN SL2 .... 45 M5
Wycombe District Council
  MLW SL7 .... 19 G5
The Wye Valley School
  BNEND SL8 .... 20 E2
Yateley County Infant School
  YTLY GU46 .... 172 A8
Yateley Health Centre
  YTLY GU46 .... 172 A8
Yateley Manor
  Preparatory School
  YTLY GU46 .... 172 A7
Yattendon C of E
  Primary School
  NTHA RG18 .... 83 H4
Youngs Industrial Estate
  THLE RG7 .... 164 C2

Page 19

H5
1 The Causeway
2 Fishermans Retreat
3 Parsonage Gdns

J3
1 Beechingstoke
2 Stanley Cl
3 Willowmead Cl
4 Willowmead Gdns
5 Willowmead Rd
6 Willowmead Sq

K3
1 Kiln Croft Cl

Page 34

C6
1 Abbots Cl
2 Baldons Cl
3 Beckley Cl
4 Beeson Cl
5 Bensgrove Cl
6 Birchen Cl
7 The Close
8 Cuddesdon Cl
9 Hagbourne Cl
10 Sandford Cl
11 Wittenham Cl

Page 42

B7
1 Alston Gdns
2 Castle Hl
3 Castle Ms
4 Elm Gv
5 Killarney Dr
6 Monycrower Dr
7 Winbury Ct

C5
1 Donnington Gdns
2 Green Cl
3 North Dean
4 Northfield Rd
5 North Gn
6 North Town Mead
7 Woodstock Cl

C7
1 Albert St
2 Brock La
3 High Town Rd
4 Kidwells Park Dr
5 Old Post Office La
6 Park Vw
7 Providence Pl
8 Queens La
9 Russell Ct
10 White Hart Rd
11 Wilberforce Ms

D8
1 Forlease Rd

E2
1 Oakhurst

E5
1 Camperdown
2 White Rock

E6
1 Auckland Cl
2 Brampton Ct
3 Somerford Cl

E7
1 Crown Sq
2 Medallion Pl

E8
1 Cheviot Cl

F3
1 Lovett Gdns

F5
1 Boulters Gdns
2 Longworth Dr
3 Ray Mead Ct

F6
1 Lockbridge Ct

F7
1 Ellington Gdns

Page 44

A6
1 Hurst Rd

D7
1 Bradford Rd
2 Durham Av
3 Eastbourne Rd
4 Falmouth Rd
5 Glasgow Av
6 Gresham Rd

D8
1 Corfe Gdns
2 Dunster Gdns
3 Fotheringay Gdns

E6
1 Faraday Cl
2 Rowan Wy

F3
1 Home Meadow

F5
1 Ardrossan Cl
2 Broad Oak
3 Broad Oak Ct

Page 67

L3
1 Gatward Av
2 Milverton Cl
3 Rainsborough Cha

M3
1 Ashbourne Gv
2 Bramley Cl
3 Laxton Gn
4 Merton Cl

Page 70

B1
1 Biddles Cl
2 Chapels Cl
3 Duchess St
4 Molyns Ms
5 Nicholas Gdns
6 Roxwell Cl
7 Waterman Ct

Page 71

H2
1 Edwards Ct
2 Emerald Ct
3 Hilperton Rd
4 Moorstown Ct

J2
1 Buckingham Gdns
2 Hencroft St North
3 New Sq
4 Stephenson Ct

K3
1 Eastfield Cl
2 Hornbeam Gdns
3 Mountbatten Cl
4 Rye Ct

Page 86

E3
1 Addiscombe Cha
2 Longleat Dr
3 Lucey Cl
4 Lytham End
5 Rosemead Av

E5
1 Meadowside
2 Vicarage Wood Wy

F2
1 Brierley Pl
2 Duncan Gdns
3 Goodliffe Gdns
4 Huckleberry Cl
5 Huscarle Wy
6 The Hydes
7 Simons Cl

F4
1 Bowfell Cl
2 Marling Cl
3 Old Farm Crs
4 Pikeshaw Wy
5 Staddlestone Cl

F5
1 Bracken Cl
2 Cromer Cl
3 Fern Gln
4 Hazelwood Cl
5 Thistledown

F7
1 Ayrton Senna Rd
2 Pegasus Cl
3 Welfield Cl

F8
1 Boundary Cl
2 Manor Park Cl
3 Swallow Cl

Page 87

G3
1 Barbrook Cl
2 The Beeches
3 Larkswood Cl
4 Nevis Rd

G5
1 Andover Cl
2 Armour Wk
3 Newbery Cl
4 Ventnor Rd

G6
1 Alford Cl
2 Dunstall Cl
3 Green Acre Mt
4 Lambourne Cl
5 Old Elm Dr
6 Tree Cl
7 Tyle Rd

H5
1 Brendon Cl
2 Dudley Ms
3 Hirstwood
4 Hornsea Cl
5 Larissa Cl

J4
1 Sandgate Av

J6
1 Atherton Cl
2 Delft Cl
3 Minton Cl
4 Stanham Rd
5 Tylers Pl

J8
1 Cheddington Cl

K8
1 Sundial Cl
2 Walmer Cl

L7
1 Appleby End
2 Longridge Cl
3 Peg's Gn
4 Tuxford Ms
5 Windrush Wy

L8
1 Peg's Green Cl
2 Shilling Cl

M5
1 Bridgewater Cl
2 Broughton Cl
3 Westbrook Rd

M6
1 August End
2 Bridgewater Cl
3 Ledbury Cl
4 Little John's La
5 Thornton Ms

M7
1 Aberford Cl
2 Suffolk Rd
3 Walkers Pl

M8
1 Amethyst La
2 Inglewood Cl
3 Jenkins Cl
4 Liebenrood Rd

Page 88

D1
1 Pinetree Ct

D7
1 Maltings Pl
2 Rose Wk
3 Swan Pl
4 Talbot Ct
5 Waterside Gdns

E4
1 Waller Ct

E7
1 Bourne-stevens Cl
2 Earley Pl
3 Highbridge Whf
4 Letcombe St
5 Thorn La
6 Yield Hall La
7 Yield Hall Pl

E8
1 Chesterman St
2 Prior's Ct

F3
1 Banbury Gdns

F4
1 Eccles Cl
2 Elmleigh Cl
3 Gosbrook Rd

F7
1 Bembridge Pl
2 Blakes Cottages

Page 100

A7
1 Buttercup Sq
2 Windermere Cl

B8
1 Maple Gdns

Page 101

J5
1 Turpin Rd
2 Welwyn Av

J7
1 Allcot Cl
2 Ambleside Dr
3 Andover Cl
4 Appleby Gdns
5 Buttermere Cl
6 Churchill Cl
7 Ennerdale Cl
8 Crasmere Cl
9 Invicta Cl
10 Kendal Cl
11 Missenden Cl
12 Nelson Cl
13 New Elms Cl
14 Pope Cl
15 Radley Cl
16 Windermere Cl

K8
1 Bowsley Ct
2 Ivory Ct
3 Ordnance Cl
4 Taylors Ct

M1
1 Aston Gn
2 Badger Cl
3 Ermine Cl
4 Musquash Wy
5 St Dunstan's Rd

M5
1 Byward Av

M6
1 Chichester Wy

M8
1 Lafone Av

Page 114

B2
1 Chestnut Cl
2 Ellerton Cl
3 Kathleen Sanders Ct
4 North Wk
5 The Orchard
6 Swallow Field Gdns
7 Whiteham Cl
8 Woodfield Wy

B3
1 Bamford Pl
2 Caistor Cl
3 Camden Pl
4 Charlville Dr
5 Clamis Wy
6 Hatfield Cl
7 Lennox Cl
8 Marlborough Wy
9 Sandringham Wy
10 Silbury Cl
11 Windsor Wy

F2
1 Ashmere Cl
2 Cranbourne Av
3 Derrick Cl
4 Fernhurst Rd
5 Hawley Cl
6 Latimer Dr
7 Palmera Av
8 Porlock Pl
9 Red Cottage Dr
10 Sweet Briar Dr
11 Willow Tree Cld

Page 115

G2
1 Barclay Rd
2 Calbourne Dr
3 Calshot Pl
4 Coliston Cl
5 Fairlop Cl
6 Flodden Dr
7 Hanbury Dr
8 Kemble Ct
9 Kemerton Cl
10 Kilburn Cl
11 Kirkstall Ct
12 Ledbury Dr

J1
1 Greenwood Rd
2 Horncastle Dr
3 Pentland Cl
4 Poplar Av
5 Seton Dr

J3
1 Burbidge Cl
2 Petworth Av

Page 116

F6
1 Denbury Gdns
2 Cratton Rd
3 Lulworth Rd
4 Moreleigh Cl
5 Rossington Pl

Page 117

J6
1 Beauchief Cl
2 Beighton Cl
3 Chippenham Cl
4 Dove Cl
5 Coldthorpe Gdns
6 Thurnscoe Cl
7 Tilney Wy
8 Tiptree Cl
9 Treeton Cl
10 Uffcott Cl
11 Wickford Wy

K5
1 Larkes-meade
2 Mcnair Cl
3 Robinson Cl
4 Sage Cl

K6
1 Anston Cl
2 Chalfont Wy
3 Colmworth Cl
4 Fakenham Cl
5 Farnsfield Cl
6 Felthorpe Cl
7 Heacham Cl
8 Rainworth Cl

L5
1 Berstead Cl
2 Rustington Cl
3 Sharpethorpe Cl
4 Watersfield Cl

M5
1 Bourn Cl
2 Elford Cl
3 Fordham Wy
4 Martins St
5 St Clements Cl
6 Sturbridge Cl
7 Tamworth Cl
8 Woodbine Cl

M6
1 Bassett Cl
2 Bottisham Cl
3 Ebborn Sq
4 Gregory Cl
5 Harlton Cl
6 Irvine Wy
7 Ledran Cl
8 Littington Cl
9 Manea Cl
10 Porter Cl
11 Soham Cl
12 Stonea Cl
13 Waring Cl
14 Wild Cl

Page 118

A6
1 Witcham Cl

B4
1 Barholm Cl
2 Barkwith Cl
3 Burniston Cl
4 Dunholme Cl
5 Flamborough Cl
6 Forndon Cl
7 Hengrave Cl
8 Marfleet Cl
9 Sawtry Cl
10 Skeffling Cl
11 Stilton Cl
12 Welwick Cl

Page 119

C7
1 Amethyst Cl
2 Camellia Wy
3 Cornflower Cl
4 Crocus Wy
5 Freesia Cl
6 Jasmine Cl
7 Tigerseye Cl
8 Zinnia Cl

C8
1 Cornwall Cl
2 Cumberland Wy
3 Rembrandt Cl
4 Riding Wy
5 Somerset Cl
6 Spencer Cl
7 Suffolk Cl
8 Westmorland Cl

H7
1 Agate Cl
2 Diamond Wy
3 Emerald Cl
4 The Green
5 Opal Wy
6 Richmond Ri
7 Ruby Cl

H8
1 Agincourt Cl
2 Bedfordshire Wy
3 Blenheim Cl
4 Cambridgeshire Cl
5 Crecy Cl
6 Derwent Cl
7 Dieppe Cl
8 Dunkirk Cl
9 Fleet Cl
10 Jutland Cl
11 Kesteven Wy
12 Lalande Cl
13 Mercury Av
14 Minden Cl
15 Mons Cl
16 Neptune Cl
17 Phoenix Cl
18 Saturn Cl
19 Trafalgar Cl

J8
1 Old Forest Rd

L8
1 Alderman Willey Cl
2 Bell House Gdns
3 Bird Ms
4 The Terrace

Page 121

G7
1 Blomfield Dl
2 Cloves Farm Wd
3 Jacob Cl
4 Pocket Cl

H6
1 Simmonds Cl
2 Warren Down

K6
1 Appletree Pl
2 Portman Cl
3 Priestwood Court Rd
4 Windlebrook Gn

L4
1 Price Gdns
2 Seddon Cl
3 Tocker Gdns
4 Totale Ri

M4
1 Cooke Ri
2 Hemmyng Cnr
3 Sen Cl
4 Shorland Oaks

M6
1 Edmonds Ct

Page 122

A5
1 Big Barn Gv
2 Broadrick Heath
3 Chives Pl
4 Corn Cft
5 Sage Wk
6 Sylverns Ct

A7
1 Drayton Cl
2 Farnham Cl
3 Forest Gn
4 Kenton Cl
5 Tebbit Cl

B5
1 All Saints Ri
2 Augustine Wk
3 Barley Mead
4 Bartholomew Pl
5 Benedict Gn
6 Bernadine Cl
7 Burnthouse Gdns
8 Caesars Ga
9 Cleopatra Pl
10 Cressida Cha
11 Jig's La South
12 Ormathwaites Cnr
13 Rachaels Lake Vw
14 Shakespeare Wy
15 Swithin Cha
16 Thomas Dr
17 Yorkshire Pl

C4
1 Devon Cha
2 Hampshire Ri
3 Lancashire Hl
4 Staffordshire Cft

C5
1 Juliet Gdns
2 Julius Hl
3 Northumberland Av
4 Shakespeare Wy
5 Shropshire Gdns
6 Suffolk Combe
7 Surrey Ct
8 Worcestershire Lea

D7
1 Milman Cl
2 Sherwood Cl

Page 126

C4
1 Windmill Shott

F3
1 Charta Rd
2 Jutland Rd
3 Mons Wk
4 Rhodes Cl
5 St Nazaire Cl

F4
1 Junction Ter
2 The Paddock

F5
1 Plumpton Rd

Page 127

G4
1 Knights Cl
2 Malet Cl

J3
1 Augur Cl
2 The Cygnets
3 Elmsleigh Rd
4 Eton Ct
5 Richmond Crs
6 Thames St
7 Westbrook Rd

K3
1 Broadacre
2 Chiltern Cl
3 Cotswold Cl
4 Pinewood Dr
5 Pullmans Pl

L7
1 Beech Tree La
2 Thamesgate

M4
1 Matthew Arnold Cl

M5
1 Thickthorne La

M8
1 Blacksmith's La
2 Cedar Cl
3 Town Quay
4 Virginia Cl

Page 128

C8
1 Goddard Cl
2 Wilcox Gdns

F5
1 Ashdene Cl
2 Cornerside
3 Oxford Cl
4 Thorne Cl

F7
1 Crosswell Cl
2 Harrow Wy
3 Lodge Wk
4 Queen Mary Rd

Page 129

G4
1 Alexandra Ct
2 Cheyne Rd
3 Saville Crs
4 Staveley Rd
5 Templecroft

G5
1 Alexandra Cl
2 Rowland Wy
3 Squires Wk

H5
1 Percy Bryant Rd
2 Saddlebrook Pk

H8
1 Allington Av
2 Bramley Av
3 Coxs Av
4 Keswick Av
5 Pear Av

J5
1 Dale Rd

K1
1 Charleston Cl
2 Chervil Cl
3 Parkfield Av
4 Sherringham Av

K6
1 Benwell Cl
2 Springfield Gv

K7
1 Heathlands Cl

K8
1 Parkwood Gv
2 Stile Pth

L1
1 Chestnut Wy
2 Elmgate Av
3 Pinkcoat Cl
4 Tanglewood Wy

L2
1 Huntsman Cl

L5
1 Barnard Cl
2 Salix Cl

L6
1 The Chase
2 Laburnum Crs
3 Summer Trees

M2
1 Blakewood Cl

M7
1 Ilex Cl

M8
1 The Pennards

Page 136

A2
1 Caunter Rd

B2
1 Posting House Ms
2 Speen Hill Cl
3 Speen La
4 Speen Lodge Cl
5 Speen Pl

C2
1 Herewood Cl
2 Jesmond Dene
3 Linden Cl
4 Old Bath Rd

D7
1 Pinchington La

E1
1 Coachman's Cl
2 Glebefields
3 Sherrardmead

E2
1 Leslie Southern Ct
2 Newport Cl
3 Newport Rd

E3
1 Connaught Rd
2 Denmark Rd

E4
1 Adey's Cl

E5
1 Fontwell Rd
2 Wentworth Ct

E6
1 Coppice Cl
2 Robertson Cl

F2
1 The Halters
2 Horseshoe End
3 Stirrup Pightle

F1
1 Fieldridge
2 Mountbatten Cl
3 Wellington Cl

F2
1 Collins Cl

F4
1 Chaucer Wy
2 Flamingo Cl
3 Owl Cl
4 Petrel Cl
5 Sparrow Cl
6 Swift Cl

Page 147

H1
1 Chaucer Wy
2 Flamingo Cl
3 Owl Cl
4 Petrel Cl
5 Sparrow Cl
6 Swift Cl

H7
1 Chivers Dr
2 Columbia Cl
3 Copse Wy
4 Heather Cl

J1
1 Apple Cl
2 Eagle Cl
3 Evergreen Wy
4 Hazel Cl
5 Holly Orch
6 Peregrine Cl
7 Plover Cl
8 Snowberry Cl
9 Walnut Cl
10 Wisteria Cl

J7
1 Challenor Cl

K7
1 Finchampstead Rd
2 Ingle Gln

Page 150

B4
1 Burn Moor Cha
2 Cabin Moss
3 Higher Alham
4 Kilmington Cl
5 Mallowdale Rd
6 Pyegrove Cha
7 Wanstraw Gv
8 Wards Stone Pk

C1
1 Bloxworth Cl
2 Buckhurst Hl
3 Charlbury Cl
4 Fawler Mead
5 Finstock Gn
6 High Beech
7 Holton Heath
8 Membury Wk
9 Morden Cl
10 Priory Wk

C2
1 Burbage Gn
2 East Stratton Cl
3 Froxfield Down
4 Lytchet Minster Cl
5 Popham Cl
6 Sandford Down
7 Stokeford Cl

C3
1 Horndean Rd
2 Northbrook Copse
3 Nothington Cl

Page 155

J7
1 Inglewood
2 Jersey Cl

K4
1 Beomonds Rw
2 Blacksmiths La
3 Chertsey Wk
4 Foundry Ct
5 Galsworthy Rd
6 Gogmore La
7 Guildford St
8 White Hart Rw

M8
1 Cabbell Pl
2 Cedar Ct
3 Crockford Cl
4 Garfield Rd
5 Tyler Gdns

Page 172

B6
1 Montgomery Cl
2 St Helens Crs
3 Uplands Cl
4 Willows End
5 Windrush Heights

F8
1 Ringwood Rd
2 Romsey Cl
3 Selborne Cl
4 Southampton Cl
5 Winchester Wy

Page 173

G5
1 Cherry Tree Cl
2 Faversham Rd
3 Hailsham Cl
4 Helksham Cl
5 Horner Cl
6 Hornbeam Cl
7 Magnolia Cl
8 Okingham Cl
9 Waltham Cl

G7
1 Balintore Ct
2 Burghead Cl
3 Castlecraig Ct
4 Findhorn Cl
5 Fortrose Cl
6 Hopeman Cl
7 Waterhouse Mead

J7
1 Church Rd

Page 181

G2
1 Harlech Rd
2 Jays Nest Cl
3 Quebec Gdns
4 Springcross Av

J5
1 Cypress
2 Fernhill Wk
3 Recreation Cl

K7
1 Appledore Ms
2 Belstone Ms
3 Grace Bennett Cl
4 Heddon Wk
5 Instow Gdns
6 Lydford Cl
7 Spring Gdns
8 Stratton Wk

L1
1 Hatfield Cl
2 Heatherley Cl
3 Hollyfields Cl
4 Montague Cl
5 St Michaels Rd
6 Woodway

L3
1 Dorcas Ct

M2
1 Birchfields

Page 182

B4
1 Lanark Cl
2 Montrose Cl
3 Nairn Cl
4 Stirling Cl

C1
1 Crawley Wood Cl